MARIJUANA ALERT

PEGGY MANN

McGRAW-HILL BOOK COMPANY

New York • St. Louis • San Francisco • Bogotá • Guatemala • Hamburg • Lisbon
Madrid • Mexico • Montreal • Panama • Paris • San Juan
São Paulo • Tokyo • Toronto

For my editor
Joanne Dolinar
who helped to make this book
one that we both hope
will help

Copyright © 1985 by Peggy Mann

1 2 3 4 5 6 7 8 9 D O C D O C 8 7 6 5 4

ISBN 0-07-039907-7 {H.C.}
ISBN 0-07-039906-9 {PBK.}

Library of Congress Cataloging in Publication Data

Mann, Peggy.
Marijuana alert.
Includes index.
1. Marijuana. 2. Youth—United States—Drug use—
Prevention. 3. Drugs—Physiological effect. I. Title.
HV5822.M3M258 1984   362.2'9   84-4398
ISBN 0-07-039907-7 (h.c.)
ISBN 0-07-039906-9 (pbk.)

Book design by A. Christopher Simon

Author's Note

My deepest appreciation goes first to Dan O'Keefe, *Reader's Digest*'s brilliant senior staff editor, who, in 1978, awakened my interest in the damaging effects of marijuana when he suggested I research the subject of pot's effects on driving. My article, "Marijuana and Driving: The Sobering Truth," which appeared in the May 1979 issue, was the first article on this subject in a major magazine—and my first "pot piece."

With Dan's encouragement, I then researched and wrote "Marijuana Alert: Brain and Sex Damage," followed by "Marijuana Alert II: More of the Grim Story" (on the lungs and the heart), and "Marijuana Alert III: The Devastation of Personality." These articles appeared in the *Reader's Digest* in December 1979, November 1980, and December 1981, and, according to Reprint Editor Cynthia Stone, "made reprint history for the *Digest.*" Individually and in a booklet, "Marijuana Update," over seven million copies were sold by the *Digest;* more orders on a single subject than the magazine had ever received in so short a space of time.

In addition to these orders, the *Digest* not only donated copies of each piece (sent by the National Association of Secondary School Principals to some thirty-five thousand high schools), but, for the first time, the magazine permitted—indeed, encouraged—schools to copy the articles free of charge for distribution to students, teachers, and parents.

There are other editors whom I would like to thank: Harry Rosenfeld, then assistant managing editor of the *Washington Post,* who assigned me to cover the International Marijuana Conference in Reims, France, in July 1978; and Alexander Horne, then editor of the "Outlook" section, who edited "The Case Against Marijuana." (This full-page article in the "Outlook" section of the *Post* was subsequently used by many newspaper-members of the *Washington Post* syndicate—the first long piece these papers had run on the dangers of marijuana.) My thanks also to Myrna Blyth, then articles editor of *Family Circle;* to Amy Levin, then articles editor of *Ladies' Home Journal;* to Allan Priaulx, then articles editor of the King Features newspaper syndicate; to Cory Servass, editor and publisher of *Saturday Evening Post,* and to other editors who published my articles on marijuana, on kids and drugs, and on alcohol/marijuana and driving.

I want to express my deep appreciation to Kathryn de Koster for her conscientious and skillful copyediting of the manuscript.

I would also like to thank all the scientists whose research is discussed in this book. Without exception, these busy and dedicated men and women took the time and trouble to make sure that I fully understood their work so that I could write about it accurately.

Finally, I would like to thank the scientists and other experts in various areas who read chapters of this book, giving me their suggestions and corrections, as well as those who read sections that concerned their own work. I am very grateful to the people who either read an entire chapter for accuracy, or who read and approved the section of the chapter concerning their own work. They are all acknowledged on pages 501 through 507.

Contents

CONTENTS

Foreword

Marijuana Alert is a true story about a drug that is taking America captive.

This book is important because for the first time it tells the whole story about marijuana and puts it in the proper perspective.

It has three parts: The Crisis, The Health Hazards, and What Is Being Done about the Marijuana Epidemic. It's an eye-opener and one that needs to be read now. We can't wait. America has the highest incidence of drug use—more than any other developed nation—in the world. And the use of marijuana by our young people is one of our country's greatest problems. There is a crying need for correct information about marijuana and I thank Peggy Mann for writing this book.

The author sounds the alarm loud and clear about the physical and psychological effects of this drug and sets the record straight: Marijuana *is* harmful! And she offers many wonderful ideas in Part Three about what is being done by parent groups, in some areas of the workplace, in some schools, and in the armed forces. Many of these are pilot projects that can be adapted by anyone in the community.

Peggy Mann has been writing about the harmful effects of marijuana since 1978. In fact, she has written more articles on this subject for the general public than any other writer. There were 6.5 million orders for reprints of her four articles about marijuana in *Reader's Digest*—more than that magazine has ever received in such a short time on any one subject.

I am delighted to have the opportunity to write the Foreword for her book because we have a lot in common. We are both determined to alert as many people as we can to this terrible problem. After all, the cure starts with awareness.

Never in my life have I felt so compelled to do something about an issue as I do about this one. Drugs are a plague that is ruining the minds and bodies of our children. And this book clearly underscores the harmful effects marijuana is having on young adults as well.

My primary purpose in this battle against drugs is to draw attention to the problem, to make people aware and get them involved. That's why I am traveling around the country to visit as many drug rehabilitation centers and prevention programs as possible and talk with as many young people as I can.

The things I have seen and heard in the last few years are enough to make the strongest hearts break. The victims are getting younger all the time. When I visited a third grade class in Atlanta, I asked how many students had ever been offered marijuana. I was shocked when almost every little hand—of boys dressed in Cub Scout uniforms and girls in jumpers—went up. As I have traveled throughout the country, this scene has repeated itself over and over again.

We are, however, making some progress. The latest National Survey on Drug Abuse shows a decrease in the number of daily marijuana users. One of the reasons for this drop is that kids are becoming much more informed about the harmful effects of marijuana. So information does clearly have an impact on youth.

Yet we have a long way to go. All of us must recognize our responsibility to let the children and adults of this nation know the facts about the very dangerous health hazards of marijuana use.

The wall of denial has surrounded the issue of drug use too long. This book denies nothing and it will help break down this wall that parents, school administrators and so many others have erected.

NANCY REAGAN

PART ONE

THE CRISIS

Chapter 1

The Briefing

Never before had any president of the United States called a White House briefing of this kind. Never before in anyone's memory had so many top-ranking heads of federal agencies met with a president on any subject. For the first time there was a full complement of the agency directors and administrators most responsible for dealing with the varied areas of drug abuse and prevention in this nation. In addition to the eighteen federal agency heads, the vice president was there; the first lady was there; the counselor to the president was there, as well as other assorted VIPs, including a Coast Guard admiral, a navy admiral, the commissioner of the Internal Revenue Service, and the assistant secretary of state.

They met first in the Roosevelt Room, where agency heads discussed the drastic national problem of drugs in the armed forces and the destructive effects of drugs on the health of young people in our country, the most drug-pervaded of any developed nation in the world today.

They then moved out to the Rose Garden, where more VIPs were waiting on chairs set out on the grassy area framed by flowering magnolia and crab apple trees. The White House press corps was on a raised platform to the president's right. And, through them, President Reagan addressed the American public—or thought he did.

"Drugs," he said, "already reach deeply into our social structure, so we must mobilize all our forces to stop the flow into this country, to let kids know the truth, to erase the false glamor that surrounds them, and to brand drugs such as marijuana exactly for what they are—dangerous and particularly to school-age youth."

He spoke about the new federal strategy: a massive coordinated effort

3

of a type that had never before been attempted. It would also involve "as many elements of this society as possible—state and local officials, volunteer groups, parents, teachers, students, independent agencies and law enforcement officials."

At this point the wife of one of the VIPs overheard a reporter remark: "I'll be glad when he stops the BS and I can get out and smoke a joint."

The president concluded, "We're rejecting the helpless attitude that drug use is so rampant that we're defenseless to do anything about it. We're taking down the surrender flag that has flown over so many drug efforts; we're running up a battle flag. We can fight the drug problem, and we can win. And that is exactly what we intend to do."

He then introduced Dr. Carlton Turner who, said the president, "will henceforth be the person responsible for overseeing all domestic and international drug functions. He will head the new campaign against drug abuse." And he signed an executive order naming Turner director of the White House Drug Policy Office.

At that point Dr. Turner and the press and TV camera crews adjourned to the White House Briefing Room where the new drug policy director answered questions about the program, in which nine federal departments and twenty-six federal agencies would cooperate and coordinate their efforts. It would involve five basic areas: international initiatives, law enforcement initiatives, research and development, treatment, and education and prevention.

Reporters questioned him about these areas. Then someone asked, "Dr. Turner, do you agree with the president that marijuana is a real threat?"

"I agree with the president wholeheartedly," said Turner.

Dr. Carlton Turner was, perhaps, the most qualified individual in the United States to answer that particular question. He had published over a hundred scientific papers on cannabis and its constituents. (Cannabis is the plant from which marijuana, hashish, and hash oil are processed.) For a decade he had served as director of the government-sponsored Marijuana Research Project at the University of Mississippi. It is at the Research Project's "pot farm" that cannabis is grown for all marijuana researchers in the United States and for many researchers in other countries, and that "street pot," hashish, and hash oil are analyzed on a regular basis to ascertain the average potency of the drug being used in this country. Turner was, therefore, familiar not only with the varieties that are grown in the United States or smuggled into this country, but also with over two hundred different strains of the plant from other countries. He was well aware of the drug's steady increase in potency over the years.

The Marijuana Research Project has the world's most complete collection of published scientific papers on cannabis. Dr. Turner had not only read nearly six thousand of them, but he and his staff had summarized each of them for the two fat published volumes of *Marijuana: An Annotated Bibliography*. And as Turner had frequently pointed out, "Not one of these published research papers gives marijuana a clean bill of health."

However, at the White House press briefing, since time was short and the reporters seemed more interested in smuggling initiatives and other aspects of the five-pronged program, Turner spoke but briefly about marijuana, mentioning only the psychological damage done to young users. "Over sixty thousand young people below age eighteen," said Turner, "are in treatment because of marijuana. And it requires an average of eleven and a half months to get them off the drug."

These figures came from the federal government's reporting network, which showed that, for the past five years, marijuana had consistently accounted for the second largest number of admissions into federally funded drug treatment facilities; half of these patients had started using pot at age thirteen or younger.

These figures covered only the federally funded drug treatment facilities, not the thousands of people in privately funded treatment programs and the many thousands more being seen by private psychiatrists and psychologists.

At noon the briefing was over. The press left, presumably to write the story. And Dr. Turner walked back through the corridor past the now-empty Rose Garden to his office on the second floor of the Old Executive Office Building adjacent to the White House.

That night, in New York City, I listened to NBC news—local and network—from 5:00 till 7:30 P.M., and again at 11:00 P.M. NBC had, of course, covered the briefing. Yet there was not a mention of it on any of the NBC news reports. Was this because it had been such a news-heavy day that the story got bumped? As it happened, on that day, June 24, 1982, there had not been much other news of note. For example, NBC ran a segment about three sets of twins who had graduated that day from the same kindergarten class.

The next morning I turned to the *New York Times*, which journalism schools refer to as "the newspaper of record." There was a long front-page story headlined DEMAND FOR WATER IN ARIZONA CAUSING DEEP GROUND CRACKS—a subject certainly of great fascination to New York City dwellers.

5

But there was nothing on the front page about the White House briefing. I looked carefully through the paper. Not a paragraph, not a sentence, on the subject.

That afternoon, I put in a call to Dr. Carlton Turner's office. Turner works hard and he works late. He returned the call at 10:30 that night. I then learned that the *New York Times* and NBC had not been alone in their nonreporting of this pivotal event.

"It shocked us," Turner said, "the scale at which the story was downplayed."

I later received clippings on the briefing from the White House press office. In none of the major papers had the story rated front-page coverage. The *Washington Post* gave it four columns, headlined PRESIDENT FORMS DRUG ABUSE TASK FORCE: HITS "FALSE GLAMOR" OF MARIJUANA. But few other papers gave it so much as a back-page four inches. A handful of papers used an AP or UPI photo with a two-sentence caption. Two days later the *New York Times* ran a 2½-inch story on page 24.

Over 2000 daily papers had access to the story, for an accurate report on the briefing had been sent out on the AP wire to its thirteen hundred daily newspaper subscribers, and an equally accurate story had been sent on the UPI wire service to its more than one thousand daily newspaper subscribers. But few of the papers used the story in any form at all.

AP also had over fifty-eight hundred TV and radio newsroom subscribers, and UPI thirty-six hundred; but during the following weeks it became evident that NBC's noncoverage of the briefing had been typical of radio and TV news response throughout the nation.

During those weeks I happened to be doing initial interviews with top "parent group" leaders for the final chapter in this book, which concerns the nationwide and ever-growing movement of over four thousand groups who organized around a single seemingly simple, but actually horrendously complex, concept: drug-free youth. Parent group leaders were among those who would have been vitally interested in what amounted to a promise to the people, with no ifs, ands, or buts, that this country was, at last, going to fight drug abuse on all fronts at once.

Presidential statements are not traditionally dynamic. But this one would have provided an immediate catalyst, a sense of direction and support for the pioneering parent groups. In fact, for years these groups had pressured first the Carter administration and then the Reagan administration for just such a firm presidential stand and comprehensive strategy against drug abuse.

But none of the parent group leaders I interviewed in various parts of the country had read about the White House briefing or had seen any reports of it on radio or television. Patricia Barton, then director of Florida Informed Parents, a network of over seventy parent groups, put it this way: "I always get clippings and phone calls when there's any news about drug abuse in the local papers or on radio and TV. I didn't get a single clipping or call about the White House briefing. Incredibly, no one had heard about it. And I mean *no one!*"

Had the nonattention given to this major story been an inexplicable nation-wide oversight on the part of media?

If so, seven weeks later, they had a second chance at an equally important story. This, in fact, was an event for which parents, teachers, school guidance counselors, drug treatment professionals, physicians, and countless others had long been waiting. On August 12, 1982, Dr. C. Everett Koop, surgeon general of the United States, issued a strong warning about the health hazards of marijuana.

As surgeon general, I urge other physicians and professionals to advise parents and patients about the harmful effects of using marijuana and to urge discontinuation of its use.

The health consequences of marijuana use have been the subject of scientific and public debate for almost 20 years. Based on scientific evidence published to date, the Public Health Service has concluded that marijuana has a broad range of psychological and biological effects, many of which are dangerous and harmful to health.

Marijuana use is a major public health problem in the United States. In the past 20 years, there has been a 30-fold increase in the drug's use among youth. More than a quarter of the American population has used the drug. The age at which people first use marijuana has been getting consistently lower and is now most often in the junior high school years. Daily use of marijuana is greater than that of alcohol among this age group. More high school seniors smoke marijuana than smoke cigarettes. The current use (during previous 30 days) of marijuana is 32 percent; 29 percent smoke tobacco.

The surgeon general then enumerated many of the biological and psycho-logical health hazards of marijuana, concluding:

In recent national surveys up to 40 percent of heavy users report that they observe some or all of these symptoms in themselves.

The Public Health Service review of the health consequences of marijuana supports the major conclusion of the National Academy of Sciences' Institute of Medicine: "What we know about the effects of marijuana on human health justifies serious national concern."

7

When the U.S. surgeon general issued warnings about tobacco smoking, this had always been front-page news. How was the marijuana story handled?

On August 13, the next day, the *New York Times* gave it two inches on the bottom of page 45, the next-to-last page of the paper. And, according to John Keller, then Dr. Turner's press representative, "The *Times* gave the story more play than any other daily newspaper we've seen. I got my job around the time the surgeon general's marijuana statement was issued. I expected to receive a mass of front-page clippings on the subject. We got nothing but that small item in the *New York Times.*"

The surgeon general story, which was specifically on marijuana, received, if possible, even less media attention than the presidential briefing on drug abuse had. Dr. William Pollin, director of the federal National Institute on Drug Abuse (NIDA), used one word to sum up the media coverage on the surgeon general's marijuana statement: "Miserable!"

Perhaps newspaper, TV, and radio news editors throughout the nation assumed that this was a subject in which the American public had not one iota of interest. Yet during the past decade, these same media outlets had been using stories on local, state, and national polls that clearly evidenced the public's intense interest in the problem of drug abuse in general, and marijuana in particular. For example, a 1980 national Roper poll had shown that 71 percent of the American public considered marijuana a major problem. This intense concern with the subject dated back at least to the late 1970s. In a 1978 Gallup poll, more than three out of four parents had said they "were willing to pay additional taxes for courses for parents on how to deal with their children's problems. These courses would be offered as a regular part of the public school system." The parents were then asked, "If such courses were given, which subject would interest you MOST?" Among the sixteen subjects given "for those parents whose eldest child is thirteen to twenty," the number-one choice was "what to do about drugs, smoking and use of alcohol." For "parents whose eldest child was twelve years or younger," of the sixteen subjects listed, *their* number-one choice: "What to do about drugs, smoking and use of alcohol."

In a nationwide Gallup youth survey taken in May 1977, 27 percent of teenagers from thirteen to eighteen said they "considered the use and abuse of drugs the biggest problem facing their generation." This was the number-one problem named by the highest percentage of teens. In those years particularly, the term "drug use" was commonly seen as synonymous with "pot use."

In addition to local, state, and national polls that showed unequivocally that marijuana use was a subject of increasing concern to the American public, there were other public opinion indicators. For example, the second of this writer's series of four articles on the health hazards of marijuana, which appeared in *Reader's Digest* between 1979 and 1982, received more orders for reprints in less time than any article the magazine had published since the reprint department was started in 1935—over 3.5 million orders; by the end of 1982, 6.5 million reprints of the four articles had been ordered.

On February 12, 1982, the Gannett Broadcasting Group first aired its hour-long news documentary "Epidemic! Why Your Kid Is on Drugs" on KARK-TV in Little Rock, Arkansas. After the filmed documentary, there was a live hour-long phone-in, during which experts answered questions from viewers about youth drug abuse. Forty thousand phone calls were logged. Collin Siedor, producer of "Epidemic!" said, "KARK was completely blown away. They had never before received so many phone calls on any issue."

Three months later, the program was aired over KTRK-TV in Houston. This time there was a live ninety-minute phone-in session. During that time the phone company's mechanical counter clocked 150,000 calls. Forty minutes into the program the phone company urgently requested that the program moderator announce on the air that no one else should call the TV station, because the city's entire telephone exchange was completely tied up. No one in Houston could get a phone call through to anyone!

In May 1982, WQED-TV, a public television station in Pittsburgh, aired a nine-night series on youth drug and alcohol abuse, called *The Chemical People*. One purpose was to stimulate the formation of task forces that would be ongoing and would do something about the problem after the series went off the air. In addition to the many thousands who watched at home, over twelve thousand people attended ninety-eight town meetings in twelve counties in western Pennsylvania to watch the program. In addition, local telephone lines were overloaded as people phoned in for information and help. Some calls came from grade-school youngsters asking for help for themselves; some came from children asking how they could get their parents to stop smoking pot. The series resulted in the formation of over one hundred task forces in fifteen counties.

Within a year this task-force concept had gone nationwide. On November 2 and 9, 1983, three hundred PBS stations presented a special two-hour version of *The Chemical People* to many millions of viewers, including those who had gathered at *almost eleven thousand town meetings* throughout the country to form task forces concerning the problem of youth drug abuse—an event unprecedented in our nation's communications history.

Obviously, the public's interest in the subject was intense, and had been so for years. Why then, in general, was media's coverage of the subject—notably the health hazards of marijuana—so lax?

In 1978, Dr. Robert DuPont, then director of NIDA, called the "global silence" on marijuana health hazards "a kind of conspiracy."

> It seems to me that the smart people and the powerful people in the world are literally turning in the other direction and saying nothing . . . about what the policy implications should be or anything else.
>
> It's as if we've all joined a conspiracy of silence on the subject. I think it's very scary.

As founding director of NIDA, Dr. DuPont had years of experience with media's turnoff on the subject of the physical and psychological health hazards of marijuana. NIDA funded most of the U.S. research in this area—and the United States was doing more marijuana research than any other nation. Almost every year the agency released, with a major national press conference, a comprehensive summary of the new findings in a volume called *Marijuana and Health.* The volume itself was distributed widely to the wire services, the radio and television networks, and all major national newspapers and magazines. But, as Dr. DuPont noted:

> Each year's *Marijuana and Health* report was more devastating in its indictment of marijuana than the year before, yet each year the media continued to treat this as a controversial, relatively minor news story—if, indeed, they treated it at all. At the same time that this was happening, a national consensus about the negative health effects of tobacco was becoming almost universal and a drumfire of public warnings was emanating from the media. The contrast between the treatment accorded these two types of smoke was stunning to me. The reason for the difference was not because the types of studies were different, *or* because the findings were different. Indeed, virtually all the tobacco health hazards were showing up in the marijuana research findings, the chief difference being that marijuana was clearly a more pervasively dangerous substance than tobacco because of the intoxication, plus the long-term harmful residual effects in certain organs of the body that were not affected by tobacco smoking. Furthermore, in the lungs, which were affected by *both* types of smoke, research studies showed that marijuana smoking was even more deleterious than tobacco smoking.
>
> Yet we continued to get media coverage that tended to confirm the well-established national belief that pot was, if not harmless, then almost harmless, and certainly nowhere near as dangerous as tobacco or alcohol. Imagine media reaction to any other sort of plague that, in the course of a decade, involved fifty-five million Americans—and then you realize the extent of the under-reporting of the health aspects of the marijuana story.

Media: The Marijuana "Treatment"

Until 1979—and in many cases after that date—media, with few exceptions, treated the marijuana health hazard in one of six ways:

1. *Misrepresentation of the facts.* Strangely, marijuana was the only illicit or illicitly used drug accorded this treatment. All other drugs consistently received the accurate and responsible coverage for which the American media are justifiably known. But experts trying to reach the public with information on the health hazards of marijuana became inured to the inaccuracy of the reporting on this one subject. Misrepresentation ranged from trivializing serious findings to direct falsification of facts.

One of the most serious examples of this occurred on May 25, 1978, when Dr. DuPont addressed parents, teachers, and drug-abuse professionals at a conference run by PRIDE (Parent Resources Institute on Drug Education) at Georgia State University in Atlanta. He detailed new findings on the health hazards—and some that were not so new but that had not been reported by the media. He concluded: "We are extremely concerned about the increased use of marijuana by adolescents." In another context he defined "occasional use" as "smoking once a month, or less."

The following day, Saturday, the *Atlanta Journal-Constitution* ran a page-two story headlined DRUG AGENCY DIRECTOR SAYS POT HARMLESS.

> The director of the federal agency responsible for a $260 million drug treatment and prevention program said in Atlanta Friday he believed occasional marijuana smoking is physically and psychologically harmless. Dr. Robert DuPont, since 1973 director of the National Institute on Drug Abuse, defined "occasional" smoking as "anything less than once a day."

The story was exactly the opposite of what Dr. DuPont had said. It was promptly picked up by AP, UPI, and many thousands of their subscribers, by newspapers and radio and TV stations in the United States, Canada, and 108 countries overseas.

Furious and dismayed, DuPont phoned the editor, demanded a correction, and asked him to review the videotape of his speech. The editor sent the young reporter who had written the story to do just that. The next day the paper ran a brief back-page story headlined FOR THE RECORD. It included this sentence: "Even occasional use of marijuana by people under the age of 16 to 18 is very serious." UPI picked up the correction, but it was largely ignored by papers and news programs that had used the original story.

2. *One-sidedness.* If, for example, there was a conference at which a number of researchers presented new aspects of the health hazard story and one presented information on possible medical uses of THC (the most psychoactive chemical in marijuana), the "good news" was invariably headlined and featured. Furthermore, although THC was helpful in treatment of nausea and vomiting for cancer chemotherapy patients, the story would usually refer to marijuana itself as the beneficial element. The health hazard aspects were almost invariably relegated to a few back-page paragraphs.

3. *Spiking.* An accurate story might be written—but not used. For example, in April 1976, a press conference was called on the publication of a five-hundred-page volume, *Marijuana: Chemistry, Biochemistry and Cellular Effects,* comprising forty-two research papers, all of which contained significant new findings about the harmful biological effects of marijuana. One of the editors of the volume, world-famed pharmacologist Dr. William Paton, flew from Oxford, England, to address the science editors of the major U.S. journals and newspapers, as well as radio and TV reporters who had been invited. But only one showed up: Brian Sullivan of AP. Undaunted, Paton and the book's co-editor, Dr. Gabriel Nahas, proceeded as though they had a full house and Sullivan wrote an accurate story, which went out on the AP wire. But, according to the newspaper clipping service retained by the publisher, the story was not used by a single major newspaper in the United States.

4. *The "balanced" approach.* The marijuana health hazard story is written to be read by the uninitiated as if it were a balanced piece of reporting. In fact, however, it is filled with subtle pro-pot propaganda, half-truths, distortions, and ridicule. The typical pot-smokers' put-down buzzwords are frequently used: "Reefer madness" . . . "pushing panic buttons" . . . "sowing misinformation," and so on. Scientific information on health hazards is presented but then shrugged off with a sentence stating that not enough is known as yet to come to any conclusions. (This despite the fact that far more research has been done on cannabis than on any other illegal drug.)

5. *The legalization plug.* This is either stated or implied in the frequently featured story on U.S. or "homegrown" marijuana and the impossible-seeming difficulties and expense involved in trying to eradicate what is often inaccurately referred to as "our largest cash crop" (or second or third largest). Estimates of the value of this "crop" are invariably greatly inflated. In June

1983, Dr. William Pollin, Director of NIDA, had this to say on the subject:

> *Time, Newsweek,* and network news shows have featured recent accounts of domestic cultivation of marijuana as a huge and growing cash crop— the nation's third largest, it is claimed. Based on this supposedly "uncontrolled" acceleration of domestic marijuana cultivation, the following argument is made: "Since we are unable to control its growth and supply, let's be realistic and legalize marijuana, tax it and thereby help deal with the national debt. Legalization won't cause any increase in its use—thus there is everything to gain and nothing to lose." This is an inaccurate, misleading, and dangerous position. Though marijuana may indeed be an important cash crop in one or two isolated counties in California, there is no part of the country, according to the Drug Enforcement Administration, in which it even approaches the dimensions described by these widely circulated stories. An increasing number of states, with technical assistance from appropriate federal agencies, are increasing their campaigns against domestic marijuana cultivation. It would be tragic if at the very time we are making real progress in fighting drug abuse, misinformed nihilism about domestic cultivation were to be used as the rationale for making this dangerous drug more available.

6. *Blackout.* In conferences or scientific reports where only damaging findings are presented, the story is not covered at all. One of the most serious examples of this occured in 1974 when Dr. Gabriel Nahas, a pioneer marijuana researcher, and David Martin, senior analyst for the Senate Subcommitee on Internal Security, organized U.S. Senate hearings on the health hazards of marijuana, *hearings of a more ambitious scope than had ever been held about any drug—or, indeed, about any U.S. epidemic.* From a list of over one hundred scientists who had done new research on various aspects of marijuana's harmful effects, they selected twenty-one, who came to Washington from England, Switzerland, Norway, Egypt, Jamaica, Canada, and from all over the United States, to testify. There was, purposely, no testimony on the possible medical uses of THC; therefore, the media would not have the opportunity to headline this aspect. Many of the scientists whose work is mentioned in Part Two of this book testified. The Senate hearings lasted for six days, and all the testimony was later published by the Government Printing Office in a 524-page volume, which was sent to the most important media outlets in the country. Result: Aside from a few conservative columnists and an accurate story in *U.S. News and World Report,* the six days of Senate hearings remained unheard by the nation at large. Columnist John Chamberlain, one of the very few who did cover it, asked his readers: "How many

stories have you seen devoted to the remarkable marijuana investigation conducted by the U.S. Senate? . . . Information that might have a great effect on the nation's life is left to moulder."

Although reports on the hazards of this drug have continued to emerge from the scientific community at a growing rate, enough was known at the time of the U.S. Senate hearings in 1974 to alert the public to the grave dangers of the swelling epidemic—had the public been given the information.

Newspapers and news magazines faced with the proposition that they have failed to report this story fairly and responsibly can usually produce some clippings on the problems inherent in pot use. However, the fact that the six listed methods of "coverage" prevailed would seem proved by the myth of harmlessness that surrounded this drug for so long. Indeed, today there are still many millions of Americans who believe pot to be a benign drug, a pleasurable, natural substance, far less harmful than tobacco cigarettes or alcohol.

The "conspiracy of silence," as DuPont termed it, has come from many sources, not media alone. Other sources, which will be discussed further on in this book, have helped maintain the vast chasm between the public and the research scientists who are continually coming out with new and extremely sobering findings. The chasm unfortunately has not remained empty. Instead, the public has been continually bombarded with *mis*information, which came not primarily from the media, but from other sources which will be discussed later in this book. In addition, "do-drug" messages have been mainlined into our lives from sources including the commercialized drug culture, segments of the rock music industry, some TV comics, and certain feature films.

As a result of all this, the use of marijuana was widely regarded for years as a recreational pastime—as one of the Beatles put it, "a harmless giggle." Millions of youngsters adopted it as a symbol of peace, liberty, and a new era of easy ridin' through Elysian fields to the accompaniment of rock music that blatantly extolled the joys of getting high. Some felt too that sharing a joint broke down barriers of race and snobbery. Marijuana was an integral part of their way of life. No one had told them that it was harmful both to their bodies and to their minds. Consequently, an entire generation of our young people grew up believing, as one teenager put it: "Pot's as normal as blue jeans."

As this generation entered the workforce and the armed forces, a large proportion retained their pot-smoking habits.

How has marijuana affected our young people, our schools, the armed forces, the workplace?

What are the physical and psychological health hazards of this drug?

What is being done and what can be done about the use of marijuana, which now pervades our nation?

This book hopes to supplant the many question marks with accurate, up-to-date, helpful information concerning the drug variously known as pot, reefer, weed, grass, dope—marijuana.

It is a three-part book. Part One: The Crisis concerns the marijuana epidemic raging in our nation today. Beginning with an overview of the situation, we then move to an in-depth look at marijuana's impact in three vital areas of our society: the workplace, the armed forces, and the schools.

Part Two: The Health Hazards deals, it can well be said, with the tip of the iceberg. When reading these chapters, three points should be kept in mind:

1. The studies discussed are only a selection of those this author happened to feel were important and interesting. An entire book could be written describing different studies by different researchers that are equally sobering. As Dr. Carlton Turner put it after reading and summarizing virtually all the scientific papers published on cannabis, from 1964 through 1980, "There is no other drug used or abused by man that has the staying power and broad cellular actions on the body that cannabis does."

2. You will note that some of the studies listed in the references for Part Two were done as early as the mid-seventies. This is of interest for two reasons. The first we have already noted: Sufficient scientific information was available a decade ago to have helped stem the marijuana epidemic— if the public had known of the scientists' finding. Second: The marijuana of the mid-seventies was far less potent than that being smoked today. Street pot then had an average THC potency of 0.5 percent. Today, it averages 3 or 4 percent, with "homegrown" varieties double that of "average street pot." Yet, even the "weak pot" of the mid-seventies produced some deleterious effects. Since most effects have been shown to be dose- and potency-related, this potency factor should be kept in mind when reviewing the early studies.

3. Even the latest research done in the marijuana area uses pot with a THC potency of about 2 percent. The reason for this is explained in Chapter 6: What *Is* Marijuana? If you are shocked or dismayed at the clear evidence of the damage done by marijuana as shown in the scientists' studies, keep

in mind the fact that the pot potency they use even now would be regarded as weak by today's street standards.

Part Three has a more cheerful title, and theme: *What Is Being Done About It?* Fortunately, and finally, steps are being taken—giant steps on some fronts, such as in the armed forces, and the remarkable statewide effort called Texans' War on Drugs. There is also a history-making national movement, Parents for Drug-Free Youth. But as we will see in Part Three, in most areas of our society the problem is not being addressed; the steps that are being taken, while helpful and hopeful, must be regarded merely as pilot projects showing what can be done, clearly illustrating that if there is a will, there *is* a way. Seeing the way and taking it are poles apart. Perhaps Part Three of this book can help bring the two a little closer together.

Chapter 2

The Situation

Most experts in the field agree that although drug use is prevalent and rising in both developed and developing nations, no other country matches the broad spectrum of drug use in the United States today. And marijuana is far and away our most pervasive illegal drug.

This is true despite the fact that demand for marijuana and current usage has begun to decrease.

National pot-smoking statistics bring both statements into focus.

There are two ongoing national surveys on drug abuse, supported by the National Institute on Drug Abuse (NIDA). The National Survey on Drug Abuse (frequently referred to as the National Household Survey, because only people living in households, not those in dormitories, military bases, jails, hospitals, and so on, are surveyed) represents all states except Alaska and Hawaii. It is a random survey of three age groups: youth (twelve to seventeen), young adults (eighteen to twenty-five), and older adults (twenty-six and up). It has been conducted almost every two years since 1972 by the Social Research Group of George Washington University and the Response Analysis Corporation of Princeton, New Jersey.

The National High School Senior Survey has been conducted every year since 1975 by researchers from the University of Michigan. It also includes every state except Alaska and Hawaii. Although its target is specifically twelfth-graders, questions are asked concerning beginning age of pot use and, in one instance, a follow-up survey was done on the seniors of the class of 1975 who smoked pot daily. Consequently, this survey throws light on age groups other than seventeen- and eighteen-year-old high-school seniors.

17

(It should be noted that the survey does not include those millions of young people who dropped out before the twelfth grade, nor those who were absent from school on the day the survey was taken. Since chronic pot use often results in truancy and is a prime cause of school dropouts, the Michigan researchers point out that their findings must be regarded as an under-representation of drug use among seventeen- and eighteen-year-olds.)

Let us look at both these national surveys. (The figures from the 1982 National Household Survey, published in 1983, and from the 1983 National High School Senior Survey, published in 1984, were the latest available at press time.)

The National Household Survey on Drug Abuse

The *overall statistics* are these: In 1982

- 20,000,000 Americans were current users of marijuana, defined as having used the drug within the past month;
- 31,400,000 had used marijuana within the past year;
- 56,300,000 had "ever used" the drug (includes current use).

Let us now break these figures into age categories:

Current use—within the past month

• *Youth* (twelve to seventeen years old): 12 percent, or 2.7 million children in the United States, are regular pot-smokers. The researchers broke down the youth category still further: 23 percent of those sixteen to seventeen years old were current pot-smokers, as were 8 percent of the fourteen- and fifteen-year-olds, and 2 percent of the twelve- and thirteen-year-olds.

• *Young adults* (eighteen to twenty-five years old): 27.4 percent. Among the eighteen- to twenty-one-year-olds this was 28 percent; among the twenty-two- to twenty-five-year-olds, 27 percent.

• *Older Americans* (twenty-six and over): 6.6 percent were current users. Note, however, this overall figure was dramatically watered down by those age fifty and over. The age-related aspect becomes clear in this breakdown: Of the twenty-six- to twenty-nine-year-olds, 19 percent had used pot within the past month; ages thirty to thirty-four, the figure dropped to 15 percent;

ages thirty-five to forty-nine, it was 8 percent; and in the fifty-and-older group it was less than 0.5 percent.

Daily Use

The National Household Survey defines daily use as "use on 20 or more days in a month." Furthermore, daily use is defined in two different ways: current daily use and daily use now and/or at some prior period.

- *Youth* (twelve to seventeen): Current daily use, 2 percent; at some point in their lives, 6 percent.
- *Young adults* (eighteen to twenty-five): Current daily use, 7 percent; daily use at some point in their lives, 21 percent.
- *Older adults* (twenty-six and older): Current daily use, 1 percent; daily use at some point in their lives, 4 percent.

In this survey, 1982 was the first year that showed a drop in use for both youth and young adults. Prior to that, there had been a significant increase each year since 1971. Despite the drop, we must remember that *over one in every four young Americans is a current pot-smoker,* defined as smoking from once a month to more than one joint a day.

National High School Senior Survey

- Forty-two percent of the senior class smoked pot during the year, and stayed stoned at least "an average of three hours" each time they smoked; over one-third "usually stay high three to six hours."

- Of those who smoked pot at all during the year, one in eight were daily users, averaging 3.5 joints a day; 14 percent of daily users smoked 7 or more joints a day. *Of those who had ever used marijuana at any time in their lives, one in ten were daily users at the time of the survey, and one in three had been daily users for a month or more at some point in their lives.*

Furthermore, each year the survey shows that half of those who use marijuana at all are also users of one or more additional illegal drugs and/ or of prescription drugs used illegally. (Alcohol is not considered an illegal drug in this context, even though it is illegal in many states for twelfth-graders, and even though 27 percent of the daily pot-smokers were also daily drinkers.) On the other hand, *of the seniors who do not use marijuana at all, there are virtually no regular users of any other illegal drug.* Thus, pot use not only plays a devastating role in and of itself, but it has been shown statistically to be related to the polydrug use of millions of American teenagers and young adults.

What About Pre-teens?

From January 7 to 21, 1983, *The Weekly Reader* did a nationwide study of "Children's Attitudes and Perceptions about Drugs and Alcohol." Questionnaires were distributed to 3.7 million students in all fifty states. Over 500,000 students answered the questionnaire. The researchers tabulated a random sampling per grade, representing 101,000 students. Unlike other national surveys, this one included grades four through twelve.

In this survey students reported on what they believed to be happening in their peer group, not on their own drug or alcohol use. However, since 39 percent of fourth-graders reported that "using drugs is a big problem among kids their age," and 30 percent said that "the main reason kids start to use marijuana is to fit in," the fact that they *think* drug use in the fourth grade is so common is, in itself, an obvious cause for concern. Furthermore, one out of four fourth-graders felt "some" to "a lot" of pressure to try beer, wine, liquor, or marijuana.

By the fifth grade, 40 percent of the students think "the main reason kids use marijuana in their age group is to fit in with the other kids." Almost half feel this by the sixth grade, while only 16 to 17 percent say the reason is "to feel older" or "to have a good time." Indeed, about a quarter of the fifth- and sixth-graders report that "kids push each other to try marijuana."

Thus in 1983, even grade-school children were reflecting the concerns shown in the 1977 Gallup youth poll mentioned earlier, wherein the highest percentage of youngsters aged thirteen to eighteen named use and abuse of drugs as "the number-one problem facing their generation" (27 percent). Note: the term "drugs" did not include alcohol, which rated 7 percent. Since, aside from alcohol, the number-one drug of youngsters in that age group is marijuana, it was obviously pot they were worrying about. And they still are worrying. Over half (51 percent) of the ninth- to twelfth-graders in *The Weekly Reader* survey reported that "using drugs was a big problem" among kids their age.

The Survey of Mayors

As we will note in the next two chapters, numerous surveys, small and large, have been done relating to adult drug use in the workplace and in the armed forces. But besides the three surveys mentioned above, the only recent national survey was carried out by the Elks in 1982 and 1983. One in every four mayors in the United States was visited by a member of the Elks service organization and presented with a questionnaire in which the mayor himself or herself was asked to "rate the seriousness of ten community problems which can be addressed by volunteers." Drug abuse was rated first by seven out of every ten mayors. Furthermore, in answer to the question regarding "the ten problems currently receiving the least amount of volunteer support," drug abuse again rated number one. (As we will see in later chapters, the term "drug abuse" invariably includes marijuana, and illegal drug use almost invariably starts with marijuana.)

Obviously the public was concerned.

However, as we have seen in Chapter 1, there was a vast chasm between the scientists on one shore publishing an increasingly indicting body of work on the biological and psychological effects of marijuana, and the public on the other shore, who were, in the main, unaware of the scientists' findings. Unfortunately, the chasm did not remain empty. It was filled instead with a continual flow of misinformation, misinterpretations and, in some cases, outright falsehoods concerning the scientists' findings.

There was also a morass of confusion concerning the legal aspects of pot smoking. This emanated from countless sources. But it focused around a concept engendered by a nationwide organization named NORML—National Organization for the Reform of Marijuana Laws. The concept was called decriminalization; and it was the forerunner of another NORML concept: legalization.

Decriminalization, Legalization, and NORML

Decriminalization is a legal term that applies only to marijuana. Indeed, it is a term made up *for* the marijuana situation by leaders of the organization with a purposefully contrived acronym—NORML. Founded in 1971, the organization attracted not only a fervent following of pot-smokers, but also a number of highly respected organizations that, at the time, favored the concept of decriminalization of marijuana.

Decriminalization—in the minds of many—did not mean that marijuana use would become legal, merely that possession of small amounts of marijuana for personal use would not be treated as a criminal offense with a possible jail sentence. It would, instead, be legally categorized as a civil offense, the penalty being a small fine and no criminal record. This seemed perfectly reasonable to many people. And if there had been no other agendas, and if NORML had reported fully on the marijuana health-hazard story as it unfolded from the scientific community, the organization might have served a useful function, as far as meaningful laws were concerned.

However, from statements made by NORML board members, it seems that the term "decrim" was a first step toward NORML's true goal—the legalization of marijuana. For example, at NORML's 1978 annual conference, Keith Stroup, then executive director of the organization, said, "It's time we finally took the honest step to declare to the world: We want legal marijuana."

In January 1979, in the "official policy" adopted by NORML's board of directors, executive committee, advisory board, and regional and state coordinators, NORML *redefined* its concept of decriminalization. It now included "the *removal* of all criminal and *civil penalties* for the private possession of marijuana for personal use." (Emphasis added.) (Civil penalties include such regulatory measures as tickets and fines for traffic violations.) Other clauses from the NORML policy statement:

> The right of possession should include other acts incidental to such possession, *including cultivation* and *transportation* for personal use, and the casual, non-profit transfers of small amounts of marijuana. . . . It must be recognized that where personal use and possession of marijuana are no longer serious crimes, it is both inconsistent and *irrational to provide lengthy prison terms for those who distribute marijuana for profit.* (Emphasis added.)

The statement concludes: "Specifically, NORML supports the eventual legalization of marijuana."

Thus, even while NORML was running its well-orchestrated and well-financed campaign for decriminalization of marijuana, the organization was officially on record as being in favor of legalization.

Decriminalization laws were passed in eleven states, the first being Oregon in 1973, the last, Nebraska, in 1978.

When decrim was passed in Oregon, Major H. D. Watson was head of the state police narcotics division. "Within a matter of months," he recalls, "we saw a drastic change in people's attitudes about the use of marijuana. Many even thought it was legal and that they could smoke it on the street."

In California, one simple statistic indicates the immediate increase in problems that arose after decriminalization in 1976: In the first six months following decrim, arrests for driving under the influence of drugs increased 46.2 percent in the case of adults, and 71.4 percent in the case of juveniles, when compared to the same six months of the previous year.

NORML and other pro-pot forces continually quoted statistics such as these: "450,000 marijuana arrests were made last year." Invariably, the figure was followed up with a statement like this: "The trauma of an arrest and a child's being thrown into jail is far more harmful than the drug itself." Some pot proponents go much further, claiming this is the only really harmful thing about the drug.

What is *not* made clear is the fact that for simple possession, arrests are *not* followed by jail sentences. Indeed, according to Norman Darwick, executive director of the International Chiefs of Police, "Since 1976, most of those charged with 'simple possession' of an ounce or less of marijuana have really been arrested for some other violation of the law. Then, because marijuana was found on them, they were also charged with possession of marijuana."

For a time, when Dr. Robert DuPont was director of NIDÁ, he favored decriminalization. But he is just one of a number of leading experts who have completely changed their minds on the issue. In June 1979 he said:

I have learned that it is impossible to be pro-decrim and anti-pot because no matter how you try to explain it to them, young people interpret decrim as meaning that pot must be okay because the government has legally sanctioned it. Furthermore, while we do continue to arrest people for possession of marijuana each year, virtually none of those people go to jail for even one day. We therefore have *de facto* decriminalization in every state in the union.

In June 1984 DuPont pointed out:

Throughout this period a majority of Americans—young and old alike— have favored maintaining tough anti-pot laws. The brief romance with decriminalization was trendy in the early 70's, but never caught on with the American public. For example, in a March 1981 national Roper survey, when asked "How important to society do you feel it is that the laws related to the use of marijuana be enforced?" 58 percent answered that "Strict enforcement of the law is very important"; 20 percent said, "Fairly important"; 14 percent "Not very important"; 7 percent "Not at all important", and 2 percent "Don't know".

Since the National High School Senior Survey began in 1975, a consistent finding among seniors—the *least* anti-pot segment of our society—has been that a majority never favored legalization. For example, in the 1983 survey, 37 percent felt that marijuana use should be a crime, while only 19 percent felt that using pot should be legal.

Such statistics remained "in place," despite the fact that NORML's decrim and/or pro-legalization stance reverberated widely, and was echoed back to the public under all manner of unlikely auspices. Two examples:

• Prestigious insurance companies put out booklets on drug abuse which not only trivialized the health hazards of marijuana, but which inserted the legal question of marijuana use, and plugged decriminalization in publications which otherwise were concerned exclusively with matters of health.

• Decrim and legalization messages crept into junior high, high school, and college textbooks. For example, a popular high school text has this as number two among twelve comma-less sentences in which the student is asked to "enter commas where needed": "Marijuana should be legalized for all studies show it to be less harmful than alcohol."

At its 1982 annual conference, NORML introduced another route toward legalization. It sounded sensible to many people: Forget decrim, forget legalization, let's talk about regulation and taxation of marijuana. Some of the funds can then be earmarked for drug prevention, drug treatment, and . . . and wiping out the national debt. An intriguing argument indeed—until we look at the alcohol model, where few if any designated funds from taxing alcohol have been authorized for treatment or prevention. An intriguing argument—until we look at the statistics engendered by our two legal drugs, alcohol and tobacco, statistics that show their toll in health care, sickness, and death, costs to our society that far outswell any monies derived from taxation of liquor and tobacco. As Part Two of this book shows, it seems clear that legalizing marijuana, with its concurrent burgeoning increase in use, would bring a disastrous increase not only in medical damage and monetary costs, but in psychological and psychiatric damage and costs as well. Legalization of marijuana is thus not the answer. It is the opposite of the answer.

NORML has many activities, ranging from seminars for lawyers (instructing "how best to defend drug dealers and smugglers") to "The Initiative" (attempting to collect enough signatures to introduce legalization of marijuana on the ballot). But perhaps the activity that has been the most detrimental to the general public is NORML's reporting of the marijuana health-hazard story.

It is of course difficult to make a case for legalizing pot if the drug is proven dangerous for people's health. NORML has consistently minimized the scientific findings of the marijuana researchers in publications such as its *Marijuana and Health Newsletter*.

At least, however, people knew where NORML "was coming from." This was not true of:

The Do It Now Foundation

With the possible exception of NIDA, Do It Now is the nation's largest supplier of drug education materials, with over eighty different drug- and alcohol-related books, posters, pamphlets, booklets, films, comic books, and so on. It describes itself as "a diversified publishing operation which markets low-cost drug, alcohol and health information to organizations around the world who have need of our materials." And through aggressive merchandising techniques, Do It Now became the major source of drug-abuse materials to many publicly funded single-state agencies. (Each state has its own drug-abuse and prevention agency located in the state capital. Such agencies have different names, but they are known collectively as SSAs or single-state agencies. A list of them, with their addresses, is found in the Appendix.) According to Do It Now, "About 20,000 organizations—libraries, drug and alcohol groups, schools, mental health programs use Do It Now publications each year."

All information distributed by the SSAs is paid for with state and federal tax dollars and much of the Do It Now material is then sent out free, for example to drug rehabilitation centers, schools, libraries. (Sometimes there is a slight charge.) In many, if not most, states, when students, as well as parents, teachers, school guidance counselors, and other concerned adults, request material on drug abuse from their SSA, they are sent Do It Now literature. Often this is all they receive.

A new executive editor took over Do It Now in May 1981, and he dissociates himself from the "old literature." Since then, it has been updated, although in a number of instances it still does not convey the serious potential consequences to health from using marijuana.

Furthermore, some of the old literature is still circulating. Some still surfaces on SSA shelves, in public libraries, and at drug-abuse prevention conferences. Here are a few examples of the type of information which was disseminated by Do It Now since that organization was founded in the mid-seventies.

A Do It Now booklet originally published in 1976, "Chemical Use/Abuse: Its Effect on the Female Reproductive System and Pregnancy," made this remarkable statement:

> As yet, no study has proven any reason for alarm among marijuana-smoking women. There is no substantiated evidence that marijuana harms either the mother or the fetus/child . . . unless the mother is an 80-joint-a-day smoker, which would be a little unlikely even among the heaviest marijuana smokers. (Average heavy smoker five per day.)

"Drug Abuse: A Realistic Primer for Parents," a Do It Now bestseller booklet that has gone through many editions, informs parents that:

> Marijuana is the key to effective communication between parent and child. . . . Parents who take a hard-line "killer weed" stance stand to lose communication with their kids for the following reasons: Marijuana, to date, has not been proven physically harmful, even in remote ways (i.e.—lung cancer from smoking too many joints). . . . Kids who have tried marijuana know that it is not physically harmful, so if you argue that it is, you are widening the gap. Street information, in this case only, is as accurate as any other source.

In a Do It Now pamphlet, "Drug I.Q. Test," out of twenty-five multiple-choice questions, the sole question on marijuana was "For certain types of people, which of the following drugs can be the most physically dangerous? (a) aspirin, (b) marijuana, (c) green tea." The answer was "(a) aspirin."

Do It Now's "Drugs: A Primer for Young People," does not even have a category about marijuana.

Why have state agencies as well as countless numbers of drug rehabilitation centers, libraries, and schools annually paid substantial sums for Do It Now material? There are four main reasons.

First, and perhaps most important, the material was given invaluable credibility by the fact that from 1976 to 1981 Do It Now received dual recommendations from NIDA (as well as in other government publications), in both its "Recommended Reading" list and its "Recommended Resources" list. (NORML was also recommended "for general marijuana information and decriminalization information.") The NIDA suggested reading list specifically included the above-mentioned Do It Now booklet, "Drug Abuse: A Realistic Primer for Parents," as well as Do It Now's *Conscientious Guide to Drug Abuse* (6th revised edition) which states: "Unless further scientific research proves otherwise, which seems doubtful at this point, the greatest current danger of marijuana use is arrest and incarceration of the user."

No organization, book, or pamphlet giving full, up-to-date information about the health hazards of marijuana was mentioned in these NIDA lists prepared for children, teachers, and parents, and distributed through state agencies, departments of education, and other networks.

Indeed, the NIDA publications themselves, while containing accurate information on alcohol, cigarettes, and other drugs, had what may best be termed "waffling" information on marijuana.

In 1980, NIDA's director, Dr. William Pollin, established a task force within NIDA to review its publications. Virtually all the material concerning marijuana was subsequently rewritten and all nongovernmental organizations and publications were dropped from NIDA's recommended lists. Furthermore, in July 1981 Pollin sent a letter to all state agencies concerned with drug-abuse education and prevention, informing them of NIDA's new editions and stating that "the old editions contain outdated and often misleading information, especially on marijuana. . . . I urge you to discard the older publications; and we will be glad to provide you our most recent materials listed below."

However, over two million copies of the old NIDA literature had been distributed. It did not simply disappear. These booklets recommending NORML, Do It Now, and Drug Abuse Council publications can still be found in some state drug-abuse agencies and in many schools across the country.

The second reason the Do It Now material achieved such popularity is that the material is inexpensive. What parents, following NIDA's "recommended reading" lead and concerned about their youngster's pot smoking, wouldn't put fifty cents in the mail for "Drugs: A Primer for Young People"? This twenty-six-page booklet contains information on a wide range of drugs, legal and illegal, ranging from heroin to paint sniffing. But the *only* mention of marijuana is these three confusing sentences: "Another thing dealers will try to sell you is synthetic marijuana. (In five years of testing street drugs no one has ever been able to find one real dose of THC. THC is even harder and more expensive to make than mescaline or psilocybin.)"

A third reason for Do It Now's success is the fact that its material on alcohol, vitamins, and tobacco has always been excellent. When marijuana was discussed in these publications, it usually followed the section filled with grim hard-hitting facts about tobacco smoking; the inconclusive remarks on marijuana may have given the implied message that pot was "the safer smoke."

And the fourth reason is this: For years, the inexpensive, easy-to-read, well-marketed Do It Now material had little competition, aside from NIDA publications, which, as we have seen, were no great help in the marijuana area until 1981.

Since Do It Now material was so widely distributed by state drug-abuse prevention agencies, school guidance counselors, and other "authorities," its influence undoubtedly had a great impact on an unsuspecting public.

The Drug Abuse Council

Perhaps the organization that achieved the greatest impact of all in further-ing the concept of marijuana as a "recreational pastime" was the Drug Abuse Council (DAC). Nor did the council's underlying philosophies "stop" with marijuana. One of DAC's cornerstone concepts was to teach people, including young people, "the responsible use of drugs."

Most people who had heard of it at all vaguely assumed that the Drug Abuse Council was some sort of government agency. It was not, although during the eight years of its existence its influence was felt in many government agencies, and its message was accepted and passed on by many top-ranking government officials.

The Drug Abuse Council was founded with the best intentions. In 1971 a nationwide Ford Foundation survey revealed that the number-one concern of Americans was drug abuse. Consequently, the following year Ford estab-lished the Drug Abuse Council. The Ford, Carnegie, Commonwealth, and Kaiser foundations, the United Methodist Church, the Equitable Life Assur-ance Society, the city of Phoenix, and other prominent foundations and institu-tions—including the U.S. State Department—allocated a total of ten million dollars to establish a private, nonprofit, tax-exempt think tank. According to the *New York Times,* the Drug Abuse Council was to "study drug abuse in a thorough, objective fashion untainted by government policies and private fervors."

By virtue of DAC's solid foundation support and of the presence on its board of respected leaders in the fields of education, law, medicine, the social sciences, government, and philanthropy, its "teachings" were held in highest esteem by drug-abuse professionals in and out of government. As noted by Sue Rusche at the Columbia University Symposium on Drug Abuse in the Modern World,

> The concepts of "harmless pot" and "responsible use" permeated federal drug-abuse agencies; publicly funded state, regional and county drug prevention and treatment centers; drug education programs developed by school guidance counselors; and private non-profit drug abuse crisis centers, many of them funded by federal grants. And from there they filtered down throughout society. These messages also found their way into the drug prevention literature of many respected institutions and university drug education courses.

The Drug Abuse Council, from the outset, made no secret of its stance. Indeed, in 1970, as a first step in the formation of the organization, the Ford Foundation asked Patricia M. Wald, now a United States circuit judge in the District of Columbia, and Peter B. Hutt, a Washington lawyer, to undertake a survey concerning the depth of drug abuse in our nation and to suggest what private foundations might contribute to the understanding of the problem. In their report, published in 1972, Wald and Hutt said:

> It is of fundamental importance that man has and will inevitably continue to have potentially dangerous drugs at his disposal . . . which he may either use properly or abuse. . . . Therefore, the fundamental objective of a modern drug-abuse program must be to help the public learn to understand these drugs and how to cope with their use in the context of everyday life. An approach emphasizing suppression of all drugs or repression of all drug users will only contribute to national problems.

Throughout the influential lifetime of the Drug Abuse Council, the premise was put forth that "psychoactive substances have been available for use since the beginning of recorded time and will predictably remain so. . . . This certainty of drug availability should be at the forefront of our thinking." Indeed, these words comprise the first statement set forth in the council's "Final Report to the Nation" in 1980. But the statement is misleading, since in the early 1960s, *less than 5 percent of the entire U.S. population had had any experience with marijuana or other illicit drugs.*

When, after eight years, the DAC's ten million dollars dwindled toward its end, the council concluded its work by preparing its final report, a 291-page volume called *The Facts About Drug Abuse,* published by the Free

Press/Macmillan. The book was enthusiastically reviewed by much of the media. The AP review, for example, termed it the work of "a blue ribbon panel of experts." It ignored the escalation of illicit drug use by adolescents, and advocated the "responsible use of drugs." For example, the book says: "By adhering to an unrealistic goal of total abstinence from the use of illicit drugs, opportunities to encourage responsible drug-using behavior are missed."

The council distinguished between illicit drug "use" and "misuse" and concluded: "The price of an effective strategy for eliminating drug misuse would be perceived by many Americans as too high in terms of the invasion of privacy and the abrogation of individual freedoms."

Regarding the policy outlawing cocaine use: "A society that puts such great emphasis on due process of law ought to be prepared to modify that law in response to the weight of evidence, putting aside irrational fears and emotions."

After citing several studies that "postulate the existence of from two to four million unaddicted [heroin] users," the council discussed a number of heroin policy options, including *removal of criminal penalties for personal possession;* prescription of heroin by private physicians; *regulation of heroin as an over-the-counter drug;* and development of a "pure food and drug" model for distribution of the drug. (Emphasis added.)

From 1972 to 1978 the DAC, operating with two million dollars a year, funded grants, contracts, internal projects, and fellowships. It also published handbooks, monographs, special studies, public policy series, and reports on trends, issues, and special studies. In all these activities, it reemphasized and embellished the concepts with which it had started, as Wald and Hutt had put it way back in 1970: "An approach emphasizing suppression of all drugs . . . will only contribute to national problems."

After publication of its well-publicized book, the DAC went out of business. Though little known by the general public, the council, probably more than any other single entity, shaped our nation's drug policy for years, and its influence lives on primarily through the education it imparted for years to drug-abuse professionals and through its book, *The Facts About Drug Abuse.*

As a result of the combined effects of media's past failure to report the marijuana health hazard story adequately, plus the marijuana *mis*information generated by NORML, Do It Now, the Drug Abuse Council, and others, marijuana is still regarded by millions of Americans—pot-smokers and non–

pot-smokers alike—as a relatively benign drug, certainly far less harmful than alcohol and/or tobacco.

For a more realistic assessment of the pervasive effects this drug has on the health and well-being of our society, let us turn to four internationally recognized experts on the subject of drug abuse in general, and marijuana in particular.

Four Experts Sum Up the Situation

Dr. Robert DuPont served for five years as founding director of the federal National Institute on Drug Abuse (NIDA). He also was chairman of the Drug and Alcohol Dependency Section of the World Psychiatric Association until 1979, and since 1980 has been president of the American Council on Drug Education. As a psychiatrist in private practice, he specializes in the treatment of drug-users, and among professionals he is recognized as one of the most experienced in the physical, psychological, and social ramifications of marijuana in our society.

DuPont sums up the present crisis in these words:

During the sixties and seventies there was a tumultuous change in values in the United States, particularly for young people. The emphasis was on the present tense and not the future, and also on the individual's personal pleasure and not on responsibilities to others in his or her life, or in society. This was something new and entirely out of character in terms of the previous history of our country. *The leading edge of this cultural change was marijuana use.*

Marijuana smoke promised this generation a harmless high; it seemed to be a way to have personal pleasure now, without paying a price later. We are now seeing not only the awful consequences of this shift in values for the individuals involved and for our society, but the dire reality of the marijuana epidemic. Many people caught up in this shift of values refused to look at the negative health effects of marijuana smoking, but with more than twenty million pot-smokers these effects can no longer be ignored—even by the pot apologists. The people who have covered up the evidence of marijuana's negative physical, psychological, and cultural effects will make the apologists for the cigarette industry look like sincere humanitarians. Their message that marijuana use is okay, which appeared so trendy in the 1970s, looks deadly in the 1980s.

In my personal experience, the most tragic result of our marijuana epidemic—visible wherever you look in our country today—is the fact that millions of young people are living as shadows of themselves, empty shells of what they could have been and would have been without pot.

There is a slowly growing awareness among some Americans, even young people, that the consequences of this tragic national search for a safe chemical high are already horrendous. I find it chilling, however, that young people accept the loss of 20 percent or more of their peer group to drugs and alcohol as the natural order of things. Instead of being angry about it and saying, "We've got to get organized and stop this!" kids tend to shrug it off and say, "Well, that's the way it is!"

If Americans of all ages do not create an active commitment to eliminating marijuana from the lives of our youth, this epidemic will pervade not only youth but all segments of our society—as has occurred with alcohol—vastly escalating the current damage being done by marijuana.

When Dr. DuPont left the directorship of NIDA in 1979, his successor was Dr. William Pollin, who had been director of NIDA's Division of Research since 1974. Pollin points out that marijuana is of particular concern for several major reasons:

It is used by four times as many people as any other illicit drug. Its use begins very often at a young and particularly vulnerable age—in junior high school, or even younger. It is the gateway drug par excellence, containing over four hundred different components. And the effects of many of these chemicals are only now beginning to be studied.

Peter Bensinger comes at the problem from another perspective. For five and a half years Bensinger was head of the Drug Enforcement Administration (DEA), and thus the principal law enforcement official with responsibility for illegal drugs in the United States. He served under presidents Ford, Carter, and, for seven months, under Reagan.

In 1981 Bensinger became president of one of the nation's principal consulting firms to private industry on the subject of drug abuse in the workplace. He therefore has a unique dual perspective on the matter of marijuana, and has this to say about it:

Marijuana is far and away the country's biggest drug problem. The statistics are overwhelming. Furthermore, there is not a state in the country where marijuana is not grown illegally. And I'm not talking about growing pot in windowboxes. In 1980, the DEA made a thorough countrywide survey and we found hundreds of acres of marijuana growing in every state. We found high-potency sinsemilla in well over a dozen states. And we found large trafficking organizations built and developed on the basis of marijuana, in as many as eighteen states. . . .

I do not want to dignify marijuana by comparing it to legitimate businesses, but it ranks only slightly lower in profits than AT&T and Exxon.

In Florida, for example, Colombian and Cuban drug trafficking organizations literally took over banks. In Miami alone a total of four banks were owned by U.S., Cuban, and Colombian traffickers, and they were laundering money in daily amounts that were regularly in excess of half a million dollars, and frequently in excess of a million dollars per banking day. In 1980, the Atlanta Federal Reserve Bank, which is in charge of the Florida area, reported an increase of over two billion dollars in circulating cash for that year, which law enforcement believes was principally fueled by illegal marijuana and cocaine traffic.

The illegal cash profits of the pot industry are threatening legitimate industries in the United States and abroad: several agricultural markets and timber-growing areas in California, for example; the fishing industry in Colombia; coffee and fruit products in Hawaii; coffee and sugar cane plantations in Jamaica. The damage of the illegal money flow is not only found in disrupted land values on the Florida coast, for example, but in offshore banking havens in the Caribbean. In Colombia, the U.S. dollar buys less on the black market than it does at the official rate of exchange because there is such a large amount of unauthorized U.S. currency. And, of course, violence goes hand-in-hand with the drug traffic, as the homicide rate in Miami clearly shows (the highest per capita in the country).

Another destructive area concerning the economics of marijuana is that it generates illegal business enterprises, which attract a wide spectrum of supposedly "respectable" Americans: Hollywood stars, sports stars, bank presidents, airline pilots, and public officials—to mention just a few categories. These are not white-collar criminals who deserve lenient treatment, but, rather, the reverse. They are infiltrating and corrupting legitimate businesses and government while compromising health and safety in schools and colleges, on the highways, in the workplace, and in our armed forces. And all for their personal illegal pot profits. . . .

The many millions of people who now use marijuana in the United States do so because they haven't been discouraged from using it. This is what we now must do. We must cut both the supply and the demand. There needs to be enforcement of the laws that we have, a dedicated and concerted international effort to reduce availability, and a massive educational program to provide users, parents, teachers, and communities with accurate facts about the health hazards concerning this drug.

Some action is finally being taken on many fronts. But the front lines are still pitifully underfinanced and overextended. We must wake up to the full realities of what the marijuana epidemic has been doing to our country. We have not yet reached the point of no return. But time is running out.

Dr. Carlton Turner, who in 1983 was appointed special assistant to the president for drug abuse policy, put it this way:

The inescapable fact is that unless our current pot-smoking habits are reversed sharply, marijuana will have . . . destructive long-term effects that no laboratory experiments can anticipate. These effects are already clearly stamped in our workplace, in our armed forces, in our schools, on our highways. Furthermore, our escalating increase in such social ills as venereal disease and unwanted pregnancies are all patterns found in disproportionate numbers among chronic pot-users in our society. Chronic use is highest in the fifteen- to twenty-four-year-old age bracket. Within the past decade in America the death rate of *all* other age brackets has decreased. But—for the first time—the death rate among fifteen- to twenty-four-year-olds has *increased.* The primary contributor to the death-rate increase among our young people is alcohol and drug abuse. And our primary illegal drug is marijuana.

We must realize that there will be no free ride for marijuana users. Unless we come to grips with this problem, they may take our nation with them on their downhill course, one which we never traveled before.

Let us now take a closer look at the specific impact marijuana is having in three key areas of our national life: the workplace, the armed forces, and schools and colleges.

Chapter 3

Crisis in the Workplace

Not only is the United States the most drug-pervaded of any developed country in the world today, but drug use in the United States workplace may well be our nation's most serious under-recognized problem.

Marijuana came into the workplace picture in the early 1970s. By now pot has served as the open sesame to a whole cornucopia of illicit drugs and legal drugs illicitly used during working hours.

The Scope of the Problem

Dr. Joseph Pursch, corporate medical director of Comp Care (Comprehensive Care Corporation), the nation's largest provider of alcoholism and drug treatment programs, sums up succinctly: "Drugs in the workplace are the number-one public health problem in this society today." In April 1983, Comp Care conducted a survey of all its units in thirty-eight states. Whereas a decade ago, almost all their patients were involved with alcohol and no other drug, today over one in three patients has multiple addictions, using two or more drugs, or alcohol and other drugs. Alcohol, of course, potentiates ("fires up") the impairing effects of virtually all illicitly used drugs.

Many experts point out, regarding drug use in the workplace, that only the tip of the tremendous iceberg is showing. As Dr. Pursch puts it: "In surveys like ours, the only time you see the workers with problems is when they reach the surface, and by then they're pretty well gone."

A September 1980 *Newsweek* article, "Drugs on the Job," pointed out that: "Numbers are difficult to verify, but one thing is clear: a veritable pharmacy of illicit drugs is bought and sold in practically every industry."

Clearly, illicit drug use of all varieties abounds in the U.S. workplace. However, as Dr. William Mayer, then head of the Alcohol, Drug Abuse, and Mental Health Administration, reported to the U.S. Senate in July 1982:

> According to a recent survey on drugs in the workplace conducted for our agency by the Research Triangle Institute, marijuana appears to be the primary substance of use: 90 percent of current drug users [in the workplace] indicated use of marijuana, and 37 percent of all current drug users reported use of marijuana exclusively. Use of amphetamines was cited by 34 percent and use of barbiturates was cited by 21 percent of the respondents, although nearly all respondents reporting use of these drugs also report use of marijuana. Use of heroin was cited by 5 percent of the respondents. All heroin users also reported use of other drugs, usually including marijuana.

We will concentrate on marijuana, with the underlying understanding that not only is use of marijuana often accompanied by use of other illicit drugs, but the worker who is "only" a pot-smoker today may well switch to another drug tomorrow, often using it in conjunction with pot.

How much are these pot-smoking workers smoking? No large-scale survey has ever specifically addressed this question. However, as noted, the 1982 National Household Survey showed that over one in four Americans aged eighteen to twenty-five is a current pot-smoker. Furthermore, the follow-up survey to the 1975 High School Senior Survey showed that four years after graduation, of those who had been daily pot-users, half remained daily users, smoking an average of three and a half joints a day. Had the other half given up pot smoking? Hardly. Seventy percent of them still used marijuana on a regular basis. Most of those daily pot-smokers who did not go on to college would have entered the workforce in 1975 and 1976. Those who made it to and through college would have entered the workforce around 1979. Half of them were presumably still getting stoned every day.

Since illegal drug use in the workplace differs in many ways from alcohol abuse, it is strange that most surveys lump alcohol and drugs together under the term "substance abuse." Most such surveys show that of the approximately one hundred million employees in the United States, *one in every ten* has a substance-abuse problem: alcohol and/or drugs. And, as noted, very frequently it *is* a matter of alcohol *and/or* drugs. However, because we are looking at marijuana rather than alcohol abuse, let us turn to comprehensive surveys that differentiated between drug and alcohol abuse.

In 1974 the Conference Board, a business research organization, published a report indicating that drug abuse had become a problem in almost one-third (31 percent) of the eight hundred large companies surveyed. Drug abuse was found to be most prevalent in companies located in, or employing most of their workforce in, cities with populations of one hundred thousand or more.

Another important early survey, called "Drug Use in Industry," was commissioned by the National Institute on Drug Abuse (NIDA). In 1973–74, 197 companies were carefully selected to represent small, medium, and large companies in small, medium, and large cities, as well as suburban and rural areas, in each of the four census areas of the United States (west, north central, south, and northeast). Almost forty-five hundred employees were questioned in depth. An average of 38 percent said drug use occurred on the job. According to the report:

> All respondents who indicated the existence of a drug problem were asked to estimate the extent of use for various substances. Marijuana was perceived most frequently as being a problem. Sixty-eight percent of the respondent subgroup cited marijuana use as a problem. Further, one-sixth of these respondents classified marijuana use as a "great" problem. The frequency with which marijuana was identified varied with company size, from 59 percent of respondents in small companies to 77 percent of those in large companies.

In 1982, Dr. Lee Croft, director of Croft Consultants, a drug education and counseling firm in Phoenix, Arizona, surveyed Employee Assistance Programs (EAPs) in twenty large companies including Grumman Aerospace, Firestone, General Motors, Kimberly-Clark, and Gillette. Given the commonly accepted figure that 1 in 10 United States employees are substance abusers (alcohol and/or drugs), Croft found that about 40 percent of the substance-abuse referrals were drug-abusers. As a very conservative estimate, said Croft, this would mean that some four million workers in the United States are abusing drugs to the extent that they have sought or have been referred for treatment.

Although drug use in the workplace in the early 1970s was, in the main, confined to cities, the demographics have changed in recent years. In August 1981 the Health Insurance Association of America reported that drug use in small-town America was fast approaching big-city levels. But it is in the metropolitan centers that pot use in the workplace flourishes most openly, particularly among white-collar workers. As long ago as August 25, 1978, the *Wall Street Journal* reported:

Marijuana is now found at the Friday afternoon brainstorming sessions of a New York publishing house. In the cabs of long-haul trucks. In the office of a president of a cosmetics firm. Even, it is alleged, among executives of major American banks. . . .

"There's always a location at work where people can blow pot," says Fred Kotzen, executive director of a counseling firm that works the drug field. "Somebody has an office that's off the beaten path, or there's the parking lot, or sometimes a jogging area on the roof of the building."

Editors of newspapers, including this paper, are aware that some of their employees indulge. "Marijuana always comes out at parties among press people in this town," says a Pittsburgh public relations man.

By 1980 the business magazine *Forbes* was reporting:

They've created a new exchange in the Wall Street area that's reminiscent of the old Curb Exchange (now the Amex) in that it operates out on the street, and of the Commodities Exchanges in that it trades in agricultural products; mostly marijuana, with cocaine and "uppers" available on special order.

On August 18, 1983, an ex–drug-user on the New York Stock Exchange called into a *Phil Donahue* show on Drugs in the Workplace, as he put it, to "report on the rampant use of drugs in the New York Stock Exchange." He said: "I have seen brokers so high before ten o'clock in the morning when the opening bell rings that there's no way in the world they can make a straight trade."

Police crackdowns have put a crimp in the blatant open-air pot smoking and drug dealing in the downtown Wall Street area. However, at lunchtime in Manhattan's midtown office area, the picturesque plazas are gathering places for pot-smoking employees. On warm days the smell of marijuana blends with the pungent odor of hot dogs from the vendors' stands. According to Inspector Dennis Ryan, commanding officer of the New York police narcotics division, "The lunchtime pot-smokers we've arrested range from mailroom boys to executive vice presidents. From the blue-jeans set to the Brooks Brothers suits, they're all out there smoking openly, even in the wintertime."

Much has been written about drug use in Hollywood. An executive at one of the larger studios no doubt has justification for his claim: "Just because it's the film business, it becomes big news. I mean, if someone in the textile business is found using drugs, who cares?" But what *about* the textile business? According to an October 1980 article in the magazine *Textile World,* "Does Marijuana Loom as Problem for Textiles?" one industry old-timer says: "Around here, we call it the 'new dope wagon.' In the olden days the cart that came around with soft drinks and candy bars was called the 'dope wagon.' This new dope wagon is carting people off into the clouds. I've seen people higher than a kite around here from smoking marijuana."

Today there is barely a workplace category without its quotient of drug-users. Robert Doyle, alcohol and drug program coordinator at Bethlehem Steel's Sparrows Point plant in Maryland, calls marijuana "the most commonly used drug on the job. . . . It used to be that pot was for soft lights at parties. The kids smoked it with Boone's Farm wine and listened to music and relaxed. Now they're using it in a dirty old hot stinking steel mill. I think that shows a big change."

Serious as the alcohol problem in the workplace has always been and still is, drug use may be even more devastating because it is less visible; also, it affects the workplace in ways alcohol does not. Peter Bensinger puts it this way:

> The alcohol abuser generally will not show up on the job drunk. He'll be late or will call in sick, for fear of losing his job. Supervisors can recognize symptoms of alcohol intoxication: the breath smell, the tipsiness, the attitude, the gait. However, most supervisors are not familiar with the look and behavior of illicit-drug-users. Furthermore, the drug-user is often confident that he can mask his intoxication. Therefore, he's far more likely to go to work while under the influence of drugs, and to use on the job. After all, it's a lot easier to hide a few joints than a bottle of bourbon or a six-pack.

Not only do drug-involved employees "use" on the job, they frequently sell drugs in the workplace. Otto Jones, founder and director of Human Affairs, Inc., which has treated some eight hundred thousand drug-abusing workers since 1971, says:

> In most places, dealing during work hours is done with an attempt at secrecy—in the washrooms or locker rooms, or in the vending-machine area, where more than soda and chocolate bars are sold. But in heavy-metal industries such as steel plants, with a lot of dimly lit areas, employees often deal while they're working.
> Furthermore, whereas alcoholics almost invariably support their drinking with their paychecks, chronic drug-users often cannot do so. This encourages on-site loan sharking. The "friendly shark" willingly finances a baggie of grass, a hit of acid (LSD), or a gram of cocaine until next payday—for fifty cents on the dollar.

"Another growing problem is on-site theft, since the drug-user often resorts to stealing from the company to help support his habit. Jones points

39

out that "people who are otherwise quite law-abiding often consider the cost of their drug habit an emergency need justifying theft, and they ignore their normal scruples."

Drug-Induced Theft in the Workplace

Workplace theft to pay for drugs is a relatively new problem; the business of providing security services to industry has grown as drug use in the workplace has increased. According to David R. Dearborn, assistant vice president of Pinkerton's, one of the largest firms supplying security services to corporations and industry:

> Even when we undertake assignments totally unrelated to drugs, once we're into the investigation we inevitably run into drug activities among the employees. Employees often steal company goods to pay for their drugs. This rarely happens in the case of the alcohol-abuser, who supports his or her habit from the paycheck. Drug-users often need "supplements." Wherever there is a young workforce, we almost inevitably find pot use on the job.

Marijuana alone can put a chronic user into debt. But, as noted, many pot-smokers are also "into" other drugs—including cocaine, which is more expensive than its weight in gold dust. Once confined to the executive suite, "snow" has drifted down to the assembly line, where use is steadily increasing. A 1983 survey done for *Time* magazine showed that 14 percent of blue-collar workers had tried cocaine, compared to 9 percent of professionals.

All of this results in workplace theft that ranges from small items—the assembly-line employee who carries out maintenance tools in his lunchbox or the executive who smuggles computer chips in his credit-card case—to large items hauled off in trucks. Mark Lipman of the security firm Guardsmark, Inc., points out: "It takes one minute or less for a forklift to pick up a pallet of merchandise—which may have arrived only seconds before— and to put it into the vendor's empty truck and out she goes." Other easy ways out: "Employees . . . mail packages of company merchandise to themselves—usually using the company's mail meter to take care of the postage. The garbage disposal also makes a handy stash for stolen goods—until employees on the way out for the evening can conveniently cart off the goods."

In the "good old days" three decades ago, when employers "only" had alcohol abuse to worry about, theft did not play a major role in the cost-factor picture. Today, estimates on losses incurred by drug-induced theft are in the billions. They *must* be estimates, since so much of the theft is undetected and therefore obviously unreported. But one dollar factor is certain: Theft losses, like productivity losses, show up in the increased price tag on U.S.–made goods and services.

Harm to Workers' Health

Health, of course, is the single most serious component of the drugs-in-the-workplace problem—although it is largely unrecognized by employers, supervisors, and the drug-using employees.

"Many adult drug-users," says Dr. Robert DuPont, "accept the notion that children are harmed by marijuana use, while denying that they themselves are extremely vulnerable to physical health damage of the same sort from the same drug." DuPont also notes the psychological symptoms characteristic of the adult chronic pot-user. "These include irritability, impulsiveness, unreliability, and ultimately social isolation. There is also a whole range of family disruptions caused by drug use, which have reverberations on work performance."

According to a 1979 thirteen-plant survey of some three thousand drug-abusing General Motors workers, before treatment drug-dependent employees visited the medical department fifteen times as often as non–drug-users for nonoccupational complaints, and they lost twenty-five more days per year on disability leave. They also experienced twice as many occupational injuries as non–drug-dependent employees.

Injuries caused by accidents are of course the most immediate health danger posed by the drug-user. Says DuPont, "The principal causes of death and injury in occupational health are motor-vehicle accidents and other accidents with machinery, and most of these are related to drugs and alcohol. The worker who is high is a threat to himself and to everyone around him."

William H. Taft, Jr., president of the Manufacturers' Association of Southern Connecticut, points out:

Marijuana slows reactions and, therefore, can cause an accident. So industry has a very practical concern here. A worker who is hurt, who has lost fingers, lost toes, who has broken bones and worse than that, is a very valuable human being who is no longer able to participate in production. Also, in a very practical vein, the employer pays workers' compensation insurance, and every time we have another one of these industrial accidents, great or small, the workers' compensation premiums go up. So for these reasons, industry has not only a humanitarian, but also a very practical stake in this problem.

41

Ira Lipman of Guardsmark raises another point:

Not only are drug-abusers a potential source of dangerous industrial accidents to themselves and others, but if abuse of any illegal drug can be shown to be a contributing factor to an industrial accident or injury, especially one involving an innocent victim, a question can be raised about management's potential liability.

Despite the obvious health hazards caused by drugs in the workplace, Comp Care's Dr. Pursch points out: "Alcoholism and drug abuse are the nation's most *untreated* treatable diseases."

Only 12 percent of all firms provide Employee Assistance Programs (EAPs) for drug- and alcohol-abusers. This is, to be sure, an improvement. In 1972 there were fewer than three hundred EAPs in the nation. Now there are over fifty-five hundred and, although all began as alcohol-only programs, about 70 percent now handle drug abuse as well. However, very few EAPs do "in-house" treatment; almost all refer employees to local community treatment facilities.

Treatment centers and clinics handling drug- and alcohol-abuse problems have also proliferated. They have become a $450-million business, a new growth industry with listings on the stock exchange. Even so, they do not begin to meet the need. The medical director of a large Manhattan-based corporation puts it this way:

It's hard enough to get the drug-abuser to the point where he or she agrees to go for treatment. But when the treatment facilities tell you there is no opening for a month, this gives the drug-abuser the excuse to continue using. It's very, very discouraging because you don't have enough treatment centers—and there is a continual influx of the drugs, of all types.

This largely unrecognized threat to the health and productivity of the American worker also reaches out to engulf workers who are not drug-involved. In factories, drug-caused injuries have increased, not only for users but also for co-workers. In addition, many workplaces have been invaded by an insidious drug-culture atmosphere with by-products of lowered morale, antagonisms, continual peer pressure to draw nonusers into the do-drug workplace world, and a pervasive fear generated by the secrecy, the illegality, and the unpredictable, often dangerous, actions on the part of drug-users. At an Iowa meat plant, for example, drug-high workers started throwing hunks of meat at each other "for fun," and ended up flailing about with meat cleavers to see how close they could come without cutting flesh.

Decline in Productivity

American products used to be prized around the world for their fine workmanship. No longer. By 1981 public opinion polls were consistently showing that Americans believe that products produced in this country are generally of low quality, and that many foreign-made products have the reputation of "being better."

What percentage of America's productivity decline can be attributed to the fact that the American worker—who until 1965 used to be more productive than workers in any other country—is now either likely to be on drugs; or is under continual peer pressure to begin drug use?

No hard figures are available to answer this question. But medical directors of large U.S. companies have strong feelings on the subject. According to Ed Johnson, manager of all Firestone Tire and Rubber EAPs worldwide: "The drug-user functions at about 65 percent of his or her capacity."

Lee Croft mentions another area of productivity concern:

Not only are drugs insidiously reducing the physical productivity and mental creativity of millions of working citizens, but college placement personnel are finding that drug use restricts the eligibility of thousands of graduates for a host of high-responsibility occupations in which security clearances and polygraph-backed questionnaires justifiably discriminate against the drug-user. This massive loss of personal potential is just one of the tragic aspects of drug abuse in the workplace. Many of the best young brains of our nation are keeping themselves ineligible for a host of high-responsibility positions by dint of their drug use.

Referring to another effect of pot use on production, Pinkerton's David Dearborn noted:

Employees under the influence of marijuana may be extremely difficult to supervise. Pot-high factory employees, for example, are often irritable, hostile to authority; they sometimes intimidate "second-line supervision." This phenomenon is found frequently in the second and third shifts where the employees are often younger and working under less supervision.

A dichotomy often develops between the older workers and the younger pot-users. The nonuser not only resents the "druggy" employees, but resents management for allowing such conditions to exist, even flourish. And management often prefers to "play ostrich," chiefly because it does not know how to deal with the situation.

All of these factors, and others, have an impact on the profit picture of the business or industry. This in turn is reflected in cost to the consumer.

The Cost of the Problem

Business is generally measured in terms of profits. In most industries, bottom-line profits are dependent on the productivity of individual workers. Recently government and industry alike have been pointing at decreasing productivity as a prime cause of U.S. economic ills. One of the chief contributors to the productivity decline is drug abuse in general and marijuana use in particular.

In 1981 the Research Triangle Institute published a survey directed by Dr. Alvin Cruze. Based on 1977 figures, it showed that drug abuse in the workplace costs our nation $2.8 billion annually in lost productivity alone (from absenteeism, slowdowns, and sick leave). This figure, which does not include alcohol, covers industry only, not the workplace in general.

In his testimony at the 1982 Senate hearings on drugs in the workplace, Dr. William Mayer, then head of the Alcohol, Drug Abuse and Mental Health Administration, summed up by saying that the impact of drug abuse in a work setting can be wide-ranging, affecting both the employee and the employer. These effects include "higher accident rates, loss of productivity, decreased quality of work products, increased health insurance premiums, increased workers' compensation claims, increased grievance submissions, increased thefts on the job, increased employee turnover and increased interpersonal and morale problems."

The Effects on All of Us

We have noted the increased consumer price tag. But the effects on all of us also encompass two other areas; one may be termed inconvenience, the other, potential danger.

Indeed, aside from its effect on driving, which we discuss at length in Chapter 14, pot use in the workplace has great potential for affecting any of us, at any time—whether or not we have ever so much as sniffed the musky sweet smell of marijuana.

As noted, for example, by Dr. Robert G. Wiencek, general director of occupational safety and health of General Motors' 140 plants in North America: "The automobile assembly line goes at a certain rate per minute. The pot-high worker whose time, speed, and spatial relationship sense is off may miss putting a certain bolt in a hole. True, firms have random inspection. But what about missing links that get through?"

Multiply this "oversight" by that of the stoned bank teller, the stoned pharmacist, the stoned telephone repair person, and the innumerable others in plants and offices whose work touches your life in some way. Then multiply this countrywide and we begin to get some conception of the impairing effects this drug may be having on the products and services on which we depend in our daily lives.

Inevitably, chronic pot-smokers are eliminating themselves from being able to handle a job that calls for precision timing and precision thinking. Those who do hold such jobs and who continue pot smoking may, in some instances, run the risk of eliminating many of the rest of us. This is especially evident in the transportation industry. Anyone who ever takes an airplane may be particularly interested in the May 27, 1983, *Wall Street Journal* front-page story headlined SKY HIGH: AIR-TRAFFIC CONTROLLERS' ABUSE OF DRUGS ALARMS MANY IN THE PROFESSION. The story pointed out that "there is disturbing evidence that many . . . air traffic controllers have been users of mind-altering drugs, including marijuana, hashish and cocaine, and that many still are—though FAA officials and controllers alike have tried to keep the problem quiet."

Nor should air traffic controllers be our only concern when we are airborne. For example, an AP story dated May 21, 1983, noted: "The Federal Aviation Administration said Friday it is investigating a year-old marijuana case against one of two Eastern Airlines mechanics whose mistakes almost forced a jumbo jet to ditch in the Atlantic." The mechanic pleaded no contest to a misdemeanor charge of marijuana possession.

Nor do most trucking companies inform their drivers about the hazards of driving high. People with CB radios can do their own private surveys on the extent of drugs in the trucking industry. Typical dialog: "Hey, this is an eighteen-wheeler. Anyone got some good grass? I'm all out." . . . "Yeah, man, I can help you out. Meet me at the next truck stop."

No truckers' conversation is heard about "booze"; it's "speed" and grass. Some are under the same misapprehension as "four-wheel" pot-smokers—that marijuana helps their driving. This is of special concern, since not only are truckers on the road for longer stretches of time than other drivers, but trucks are getting larger, and truckers pose a greater hazard than ever with their mammoth vehicles.

Two fields that one might assume would be reasonably drug-free are law and medicine. However, a survey reported on in the *Journal of the American Medical Association* revealed that 73 percent of law students had broken the law by smoking pot. As for medical students, the same journal reported:

Investigators at the Stanford Medical School Department of Psychiatry distributed 1,708 questionnaires to medical students at four schools in different parts of the country. A total of 1,063 questionnaires were returned with the response rate varying from 57 percent to 65 percent at each school.

The questionnaires showed more than 500 medical students had some experience with marijuana. In two schools, more than two-thirds of the respondents had smoked pot, and many had smoked marijuana for several years. According to Dr. Samuel G. Benson, "These figures are higher than those reported for most other groups. Only University of California law students and Vietnam soldiers have equivalent usage."

In a *Medical Economics* piece entitled "Why Some of Your Colleagues Are Going to Pot," a Philadelphia surgeon complained of residents coming in stoned to early surgery after what had apparently been long-run pot parties. Furthermore, if med students have followed the pattern of other young Americans as shown in state and local surveys, their pot use has escalated since 1971 and 1972, when the *JAMA* and *Medical Economics* articles appeared.

As for lawyers, the *National Law Journal* recognized the problem in a lead story in its August 8, 1983, issue. The banner read DRUGS CRISIS FOR THE BAR? USERS AND DEALERS ABOUND IN THE LEGAL PROFESSION.

The one workplace area we might all expect would be kept drug-free is that of nuclear plants. But sobering evidence to the contrary keeps surfacing. In July 1979, the discovery of two marijuana cigarettes in the control room of an underground missile silo forty miles from Tucson, Arizona, led to the suspension of the launching crew and guards assigned to the site. In January 1980, eight construction workers at the Seabrook, New Hampshire, nuclear power plant were arrested for selling marijuana, hashish, cocaine, and barbiturates on the site of the $2.6 billion atomic power facility.

In July 1980, a security guard at the Beaver Valley Nuclear Power Station in Shippingsport, Pennsylvania, was discovered by a supervisor dividing an ounce of marijuana. He'd bought it from a fellow worker and was planning to split it with a third plant guard. Thirty marijuana plants were found "growing wild" near a guard post at the plant, and investigators came up with the names of thirty-five guards who allegedly smoked marijuana on and off duty.

A *Newsweek* cover story recorded that in August 1983 a spokesman for the Nuclear Regulatory Commission in San Francisco said that within the past five years the number of nuclear plant workers arrested or fired because of drug abuse or trafficking had risen dramatically. According to the article,

"This spokesman said: 'Most of the cases involve employees selling marijuana in the parking lot, people carrying cocaine into a plant, or security smoking marijuana on patrol. You name it,' he said. 'We see it!' "

To Sum Up

Accidents, injuries, lost productivity, quality deterioration, absenteeism, health deterioration and increased sick leave, higher insurance rates and worker compensation claims, increased turnover, more grievance submissions, more management time spent on drug-abusing employees, and lowered morale among nonusing workers as well as drug-users: these are the results of drug abuse in the U.S. workplace.

Senator Gordon Humphrey, former chairman of the U.S. Senate Subcommittee on Alcoholism and Drug Abuse, reminds us:

The costs to our society in both financial and social terms are devastating. The studies and surveys on the subject give us astoundingly high figures on the cost of drug abuse to the U.S. economy. But none of the surveys can compute the pain, suffering, and family disruption that can never be assigned a monetary value.

Dr. Carlton Turner sums up the situation with this sobering thought:

If our country does not wake up and address the disastrous and wide-ranging effects of drug abuse in the workplace, the United States is doomed to become a second-rate power.

Chapter 4

Crisis in
the Armed Forces

During the Vietnam War Americans were well aware of the fact that a drug problem of crisis proportions existed among our troops. Hundreds of thousands of U.S. soldiers were stationed in close proximity to the so-called Golden Triangle—Pakistan, Afghanistan, and Burma—where dangerously pure and expensive heroin was processed for export.

However, from 1974 through 1977, many of these soldiers became Vietnam vets; others were reassigned to units in West Germany, Italy, and elsewhere in the world. The draft had been replaced by an all-volunteer army. The military began to shift its drug-abuse treatment and prevention resources into race relations, recruiting, training, and other such "peacetime" areas. And the public was generally lulled by the feeling that the drug crisis in the military had "gone away."

It had not.

Lured, in part, by the GI dollars of some four hundred thousand soldiers and dependents stationed in West Germany, heroin traffickers transported the drug from the Golden Triangle to Amsterdam. From there it was often smuggled by car into West Germany. Hashish from the Middle East flooded the country, hash that was eight to ten times stronger than the marijuana then available in the states.

Most of the new recruits in the all-volunteer army were young men and women who came from a world in which drug abuse was an accepted way of coping with problems. Marijuana was regarded as a natural part of partying, and for many it had become an integral part of life. Naturally, when they found hashish that was eminently available, less expensive, and more potent than the pot they smoked in the States, they were not about to bypass the bargain.

48

Unfortunately, in the general staff-cutting in the peacetime military, drug-abuse counselors and other professionals in the field were fired—just when renewed need for attention to drug abuse in our armed forces was ominously rising.

The top brass in the military had long recognized the problem. They drew up plans, programs, policies—all of which sounded good on paper. But nothing very much seemed to be happening.

Then, in September 1976, the U.S. House of Representatives reconstituted the Select Committee on Narcotics Abuse and Control. The word "narcotics" was something of a misnomer, for the concerns went far beyond the orbit of narcotic drugs. Indeed, one of the committee's most active members, Congressman Billy Lee Evans of Georgia, was also one of the first U.S. congressmen to speak out eloquently and often about the health hazards of marijuana.

The committee was directed by Congress "to conduct a continuing, comprehensive study and review of the problems of narcotics abuse and control." It therefore established a series of task forces to look into drug abuse in schools, in the prisons, among minority groups, and so on.

One of the task forces, chaired by Congressman Glenn English, was mandated to look into the matter of drug abuse in the military. As English recalled:

> I was named chairman in 1977. . . . In one of the first briefings I received from Department of Defense I was told that the drug-abuse problem in the military was a problem that was related to Vietnam and since we had left Vietnam and had gone to the all-volunteer force that it was no longer a problem. In fact, I was told that roughly 10 percent of our military personnel might from time to time experiment with marijuana cigarettes and that, furthermore, certainly far less than 1 percent would ever have anything to do with hard drugs. As we began our investigation in 1977 we soon discovered that that was not correct, that the enlisted man had a far different story. It was then that we first devised the questionnaire, which was only intended to give us a ballpark figure, an indication as to what was really happening within the military services.

The questionnaire English referred to was handed out to over twenty-four hundred enlisted men and officers in military installations in the United States. It was a "perceptions" survey, not a "personal use" survey.

The results were eye-opening. Only 17 percent of the officers surveyed said drug abuse was "a small problem" in their unit; 61 percent said it was "a moderate problem," while 21 percent said it was "a great problem." Marijuana was far and away the most widely used illegal drug, and 91 percent of the officers and enlisted men said it was "very easy" to purchase marijuana.

Question 6 of the survey was "Do you see any of the following *as a result of drug abuse on this installation?*"

- Additional difficulty senior or junior NCO has in providing leadership in his unit (64 percent answered yes)
- Personnel not caring about their jobs (72 percent said yes)
- Disciplinary problems (88 percent said yes)
- Lack of unit pride (50 percent said yes)
- Additional use of alcohol as additional result of drug use (46 percent said yes)

Question 7 asked: "Given the amount of drug abuse as you perceive it in this installation, do you think that today the men and women could go into combat and perform to the best of their abilities?" Over one in three (34 percent) said no.

Congressman English further pointed out:

One of the reasons that we started this survey was that when we first began our investigation we talked mainly to senior officers, and it is very seldom that one would admit that on his installation even 10 percent of the enlisted personnel would ever smoke a marijuana cigarette. But once we started talking to the enlisted personnel themselves, we began to pick up large amounts of use, first of marijuana, then of other drugs. That was rather startling to the committee all the way through. . . . Further- more, this completely different perception of the problem was age-re- lated—the younger the officer and enlisted man was, the more drug use he said took place.

Joseph Addabbo of New York was just one of the congressmen who were shocked by the results of this initial survey. Addabbo was chairman of the appropriations subcommittee on defense. Said he:

Sitting on Defense Appropriations, we hear every year [from the military] how much they need for drug abuse, but the problem never goes away. They are always "doing something," but we find they are always doing what they did last year. If we match their testimony to the testimony of the previous year it is always the same, year for year. What we are doing, and what we are accomplishing are different things.

Addabbo's comments were based on the fact that from May to July of 1978 the Select Committee on Narcotics Abuse and Control had held hearings about drug abuse in the military, during which high-ranking officers in the army, navy, marines, and air force had expressed their deep concern about the subject. Furthermore, in July 1978, the Department of Defense (DOD) had come out with a twelve-point program to improve efforts in the area of drug-abuse prevention, detection, identification, and treatment.

What priority was marijuana/hashish to have in the DOD's twelve-point program?

All survey data had clearly shown that cannabis was by far the most prevalent drug of abuse in the armed forces. However, so far as this particular drug was concerned, the DOD found itself in a double catch-22, neither of its own making.

First there was the perception among enlisted men and officers alike that marijuana and hashish were harmless drugs. In his testimony before the committee on May 25, 1978, Gen. William Henry Fitts expressed the generally held opinion that "many of today's young soldiers would not include hashish or marijuana in the category of drug abuse."

It was further pointed out at these hearings that

in addition to its relatively low cost and ready availability, its use is further encouraged by the move, particularly in the United States, to decriminalize marijuana. The decriminalization movement has tended to create a more permissive attitude in our society that has been misinterpreted by military personnel who are governed by the Uniform Code of Military Justice (UCMJ), and not civilian law.

According to the UCMJ, as noted by Dr. John Johns, DOD's deputy assistant secretary of defense for health promotion, "any use of illicit drugs is classified as abuse in the military regardless of the behavioral consequences. On the other hand," said Johns,

laws which are not widely supported by peer pressure are difficult to enforce. If cannabis does not impair duty performance, many youth argue, it is a personal affair. Unfortunately many of the . . . users do not appreciate that their behavior is impaired. This is especially true of marijuana users, who tend to view the "high" as the only effect of that drug. Since the "high" lasts only a short while, they do not consider it bad if not used on duty. Ignored is the strong evidence that impairment persists, often in very subtle but dangerous ways.

The second catch-22 was the fact that if, for example, a soldier was proved to be a pot-smoker, and refused or did not respond to treatment, the only punishment was an honorable discharge with full veteran's benefits. If, as seemed likely from the National High School Senior Surveys, over half the young enlisted soldiers were pot-smokers, ranging from occasionally to daily, and if the only deterrence law then available were put into practice,

51

our armed forces would shortly be decimated. As Johns put it, "Commanders and NCOs tell me they are so frustrated with the honorable discharge punishment that they say, 'Hell, as long as a man is doing his job, I turn my head.' That is not acceptable. But I can understand the frustration."

The Task Force on Drug Abuse in the Military well recognized the "catches." Nevertheless, it also recognized that if it were to be of any meaningful help in the situation, the first essential was to find out what the situation *was.* It had made a start with the drug-abuse survey on U.S. installations. Now it must go abroad where, according to all reports, not only was hashish use rife among U.S. soldiers, but other drugs were also widely used from Mandrax (similar to U.S. Quaalude), which could be bought over the counter in Germany, to heroin.

On November 10, 1978, the task force landed in Europe. It consisted of five members of the House of Representatives: Chairman English, Cardiss Collins of Illinois, Georgia's Billy Lee Evans, Ben Gilman of New York, and John Jenrette of South Carolina. There were also a dozen staff members, plus Dr. John Johns from DOD who, from the start, had not been bent on covering up, but on finding out.

The task force broke into four separate study groups and visited U.S. military installations in thirteen German locations. James E. McDonald, special assistant to Congressman English, recalled:

> On each base we split into further small groups, each accompanied by a commanding officer. We'd decided to survey drug use among E-1s to E-4s only, since, presumably, this would be the population at greatest risk. [*E* stands for enlisted man; E-1s are the lowest on the military totem pole. In the army E-1 is a private, E-4 is a corporal.] We'd pick soldiers at random as we met them and we'd request that they report at a certain time to a previously selected location: the chapel, a movie theater, a classroom. The commanding officer with us would assure them, "It's fine. Go ahead."

When the soldiers met they were greeted by one of the task force members. Then all the officers and non-coms were asked to leave the room and for the first time the soldiers were told the purpose of this gathering: that there was concern at home about drug use in the military and the congressional task force had come to investigate the problem. Questionnaires would be given out. But the soldiers were assured that no names would be asked for, nor would the questionnaires they filled out be given to any officers on the base.

Assured of total anonymity, the soldiers filled out a five-page questionnaire that asked about their personal use of drugs as well as their perceptions about use in their units.

The questionnaires were put into large, sealed cardboard boxes, which, said McDonald, "we carried with us all around Germany." Since no computers were available to the task force in Europe, they would have to wait until they returned to the States to tabulate the responses. However, they had not come all this way merely to hand out questionnaires. The study groups spent five days going through army camps and personally interviewing hundreds of men and women from the highest ranking officers to privates, from every region of the United States and from almost every state in the union. They also interviewed civilians, professionals in the army's Community Drug and Alcohol Assistance Centers (CDAACs). The U.S. Army in Europe operated eighty CDAACs in various communities, plus five extended-care facilities for those judged physically addicted.

Perhaps the most striking overall view of the situation resulted from the task force's tours of the installations. Congressman Evans put it like this:

When I was in the service, I remember the barracks areas as active places. Something was always going on. But in almost all of the barracks we saw on this tour there was no card-playing, volleyball, no physical activity at all.

What we saw in the barracks was either men lying on their bunks listening to records with earphones, or asleep—though whether they were asleep or stoned we had no way of knowing. The impression I got was everybody was tuning out. There were very few units where the soldiers were active off duty. And these were units actively engaged in physical training for field missions, tank and artillery training, and so forth.

All the areas had differing rules concerning drugs. But in many cases, even if there were firm rules from on top, such as "You'll be busted for possession," there was a great break in communications between the high-ranking officers who laid down these rules and the non-coms in direct contact with the men, who enforced the rules in varying degrees.

On November 20 and 22, the task force held hearings in Stuttgart, hearings unlike those ever held on the subject in Washington—for the task force had invited enlisted men to testify. Testimony also came, of course, from commanding officers—from General Blanchard, commander in chief of the U.S. Army in Europe, on down. And there was testimony from some of the CDAAC drug-abuse treatment professionals. But the most telling testimony came from the E-1s through E-4s. They made it clear that not only was drug abuse in general a problem among enlisted men, but that hashish use had become virtually endemic. Many of the reasons for the soaring use, which the task force had uncovered during the past week, were now put into the printed record.

One obvious reason was demographics. As had been pointed out in all the National Household Surveys, marijuana use in the United States is heaviest in the eighteen- to twenty-four-year-old population, and this age bracket forms the vast bulk of our armed forces personnel. Furthermore, according to Lloyd Johnston, chief investigator for the National High School Senior Surveys, daily pot use among the non–college-bound was double the rate of those planning to continue their schooling (13 percent vs. 7 percent), and almost double the rate among males as females (again, 13 percent vs. 7 percent).

All of these characteristics fit military personnel more closely than any other segment of our society. As noted by Maj. Larry H. Ingraham:

> The majority of first-term soldiers are young high school grads or near graduates of lower- and lower-middle-class backgrounds, working at their first real job. They are basically hometown-oriented boys who would ordinarily never have considered taking a job far away from their family and roots, where they had neither friends and relatives.
>
> In Germany, they are five thousand miles from home and all it means to them. They're separated from the boys and girls who grew up with them and whose interests they shared and whose backgrounds were similar. Here in Germany, they know nothing about the people and cannot speak the language.

The matter of language barrier proved a significant element in the drug-abuse picture, since it served to close soldiers off from an environment where they might have found interesting alternatives to drug abuse. Their paychecks also isolated the U.S. soldiers, for at that time the dollar was notably weak compared to the German mark. Such sources of entertainment as tours, movies, and dances seemed prohibitively expensive to enlisted men. As Sgt. Daniel M. Wynne of Company A, 317th Engineering Battalion, explained:

> A lot of the young troops are really scared to go out . . . because they can't afford it. There are a lot of bars and facilities that flat won't let the average GI come in. . . . You kind of have to look at it from their standpoint. . . . They are in there for the money, and the poor soldier, he just don't have it no more.

The task force members had noted that proprietors of some clubs, bars, and other establishments refused to serve American soldiers and even posted "off limits" signs on their doors and windows. There were, however, places that did cater to the young GI; in fact they were frequented almost exclusively by U.S. enlisted men and German prostitutes. In many of these night spots, drugs were readily available.

A further reason for GIs' turning to "recreational drugs" was the fact that the physical facilities on most of the bases offered little in the way of recreation. Most of the bases were, in fact, German army barracks built over forty years ago. One camp, for example, had only one gymnasium for fourteen thousand soldiers. Another had one swimming pool for ten thousand soldiers.

A further factor in drug use, particularly hashish use, was peer pressure. As the task force's final report put it:

> With hashish use estimated as high as 90 percent in some units, a non-user is under great pressure to conform with the status quo. This peer pressure, coupled with the generally accepted belief that marijuana/hashish is socially acceptable, is often enough to convince the non-user to become involved.

Congressman Glenn English made a point relating this peer pressure to the inadequate facilities: "In Germany we've got three guys bunking where two should be. If two are users, eventually you may have a third."

The lack of a "sense of mission" contributed to the soldiers' vulnerability. As noted in the final report:

> During training exercises the soldier, particularly in a frontline combat unit, is busy and has a minimum of free time. However, training exercises are only periodical events, and much time is spent between exercises with very little to do, and the familiar symptoms of boredom and frustration begin to surface. Even during training, there is often a failure of the enlisted man to understand the importance of his mission. It is difficult for the young soldier to understand why he is helping to defend a country that appears so properous, refuses to accept him socially in many instances, and whose currency erodes the value of his currency. These factors cause him to question his self image and self esteem and often, as a result of the ensuing despair, the young soldier turns to drugs.

Social isolation . . . boredom . . . loneliness . . . peer pressure . . . low self-esteem, and, in more severe cases, depression: all classic conditions leading to drug abuse.

But there were two all-important additional factors in Germany: the easy availability and the low cost of drugs. Indeed, the only "bargain" most soldiers identified was drugs, particularly hashish and heroin, which were not only far less expensive but far more potent than their counterparts back home.

"It's a buyer's market," Congressman Evans reported.

There are some eight hundred thousand visitors through Germany every year, many of them from Afghanistan and Pakistan who come to Germany to work. They body-carry one or two kilos of hashish or heroin with them each trip, and they keep going back and forth. The hashish is generally six to ten times stronger than "quality marijuana" in the States. And for twenty dollars you can be stoned all weekend. Heroin in Frankfurt costs one-twentieth what it does in New York City, and it's ten times stronger than that available in the States.

So far as drug-abuse treatment went, Congressman English noted, "Many times this consists of only an hour or two of counseling a week, often by someone who's had no more than ninety days' training." The report noted:

> Soldiers are referred to CDAAC in a sort of dumping ground fashion.
> . . . Commanding officers indicated to committee members that they
> often were reluctant to refer a soldier to the CDAAC program because
> of their lack of confidence in the program. . . . Many junior enlisted
> personnel told committee members that they considered assignment to
> a CDAAC program punitive. They also expressed a lack of confidence
> in the ability of CDAAC personnel to assist them, stating that having
> a 20-year-old drug counselor tell them how to straighten out their lives
> was not their idea of effective counseling.

Furthermore, treatment was often used by soldiers as a means of escaping punishment for drug abuse. As Sgt. James Henderson, Company C, 547th Engineering Battalion, explained:

> A lot of the men may feel . . . "I am getting some heat from up above,
> my officers know I'm going out and smoking hash. . . . Well, I know
> how I'll get out of it. I'll go in and drop it on the CO's desk and say I
> got a problem, send me to CDAAC, help me." They know they can't
> be prosecuted, no legal action can be taken against them. They go through
> the program, they feel they can pull the wool over the eyes of the counselors
> and then the heat is off them, and they can go right back doing the
> same thing.

Some GIs also used the treatment program to obtain an honorable discharge, as mentioned earlier. As the report put it:

> Far more damaging to the credibility of the CDAAC program, however,
> is the young soldier who deliberately abuses drugs in order to obtain
> an honorable discharge from the Armed Forces under Chapter IX. . . .
> We were told by commanding officers, drug abuse counselors, and junior
> enlisted persons that there is widespread abuse of the Chapter IX discharge

by soldiers who simply want to leave the Army prior to the expiration of their term of service. In many instances, the young soldier deliberately abuses narcotics in order to be referred to the CDAAC for treatment. He continues to abuse narcotics, knowing that the recourse of the Army will be to provide him with an honorable discharge with full veteran's benefits.

The report summed up:

The CDAAC program has clearly benefitted large numbers of drug abusers, returning many to full and honorable duty. But it is imperative that in order to receive the credibility necessary to operate effectively, substantial changes are going to have to be made in many areas.

It was obvious to the task force members that "substantial changes" would have to be made in countless areas affecting both the daily life and the combat readiness of the U.S. Army in Germany.

General Blanchard agreed. Not only had he testified at the Stuttgart hearings, but he had listened to most of the others who testified. At the conclusion of the hearings he requested a meeting with the congressional task force. Congressman Evans later reported: "He was shocked at the extent of drug use we had documented. He agreed that there was a drug-abuse problem of great concern within the U.S. Army in Europe, which would require immediate action to contain."

Blanchard was concerned not only about the drug problem, but also about the image of the U.S. armed forces. As head of the U.S. Army in Europe, he understandably was conscious of the impact that news of our "drug-ridden army" might have on our enemies, as well as on potential members of the all-volunteer army. "It would distress me," he said, "and I think be a disservice to our soldiers if a picture were painted that we've got a command of druggies and losers over here."

These were valid concerns, and there seemed only one way to address them: First, explore the situation; second, define the problem, facing it squarely; third, do everything possible to rectify it.

At Blanchard's meeting with the task force, many ideas were aired. For example, although the task force had found army officers eminently cooperative throughout their visit, it was evident that base commanders viewed drug use in their units as proof of poor command. This led to the same denial of the problem so evident in other areas of our society: parents, schools, the workplace. There was no incentive for a young commander to find drug abusers in his or her unit.

English suggested that the army should encourage officers to address the problem actively and effectively by providing special recognition on the records of those who demonstrated a determination to do so.

Some other ideas suggested by the task force concerned small slivers of the overall problem. For example, the task force had seen that soldiers charged with dealing in illegal drugs remained in the barracks, continuing their "trade" while the case was pending, which might be a matter of several months. The task force recommended a simple policy change: Individuals charged with drug trafficking or multiple use/possession offenses should be placed in special housing pending disposition of the case. This did not mean "incarceration," just keeping those suspected of being hard-core drug-users and/or dealers from influencing the recreational off-duty time of other soldiers.

Other suggestions involved major changes. For example, as noted in the final report, "one point of unanimous agreement from the highest levels of command to the lowest enlisted personnel and the committee is that the four-year tour of duty was in itself a cause of drug abuse."

By the end of their conference, the task force and the general had "reached an agreement on eight major observations." Number 8 was "A shortened tour of duty for the first term unaccompanied (unmarried) soldier will help in resolving the drug problem." The statement concluded: "The command has recognized that the general environment in which soldiers live and work must be improved and has asked the help of Congress in support of these efforts."

The task force returned home the day before Thanksgiving, 1978. The following Monday the cardboard boxes filled with questionnaires were opened, and the responses of the 626 soldiers who had filled them out were fed into a computer.

The results were startling, even to the task force members who had expected "the worst."

Before issuing them to the media, Chairman English was careful to point out that the figures related only to the army E-1s to E-4s in West Germany, the youngest and most at-risk of the army population. Their age range was seventeen to twenty-five. No non-coms or officers had been surveyed. He also pointed out that "because of budget considerations they had not been able to administer a survey that would comply fully with accepted scientific sampling procedure." The task force did not maintain, therefore, that this was "a definitive and unchallengeable picture. . . . Nevertheless it was sufficiently valid to identify the general scope of the problem."

58

Although all categories of drugs were covered, cannabis was clearly the drug of choice; its use was now virtually pandemic among the low-ranking E's: 16 percent of the soldiers used hash daily; 26 percent used it several times a week, and 58 percent used it once a month or more. In some units use was as high as 80 percent. Furthermore, 91.8 percent said that hashish was "easy to obtain."

The comparison to other drugs was clear in the figures of "monthly or more frequent use of the following drugs" (all figures are percentages): cannabis, 58.2; cocaine, 9.4; heroin, 10.3; amphetamines, 12.7; barbiturates (including over-the-counter Mandrax), 16.9; PCP, 3.5; other drugs (LSD, peyote, etc.), 7.3; beer, wine, or hard liquor, 81.4 percent.

One survey question read "In my unit, smoking marijuana/hashish is no different than going out for beer." Sixty-one percent marked "Agree."

Question 6 was "How many of the men/women in your unit use each of the following?" In the "almost all (more than 81 percent)" category, marijuana or hashish rated 30.6. (The next highest figure in this "almost all" category was for "uppers," 4.6 percent.)

In answer to question 7, "Do soldiers in your unit frequently use beer, wine or hard liquor with the drugs mentioned in question six?" 86.6 percent said "yes." As we will see in Chapter 10, the impairing effects of alcohol plus pot or hashish are additive in respect to driving, handling machinery, time/speed sense, and other skills essential in military units. Thus, "booze and hash" mean double trouble, and in some respects the combination is synergistic: One plus one equals three or four on the impairment scale.

The real significance of the alcohol-plus-drugs factor became clear in the figure produced by the answers to question 11. It was this figure that was most startling to the task force members, for good reason. In assessing both drug-usage patterns and their effects on combat readiness, the army— and other services as well—had consistently maintained that most if not all drug abuse occurred off-duty. But in the task force's survey, *52.3 percent said they had used marijuana or hashish on duty,* and 53.3 percent had used alcohol on duty. (The overlapping factor was not examined in the survey.)

What is more, 51 percent of those surveyed said that drugs were being used as much on-duty as they were during off-duty hours.

To question 9, "Given the amount of drugs that men/women in your unit use, do you think they could go into combat?" 50.1 percent said "No."

What help was being given to the drug-abusing soldier? To the question "How would you rate the Army's drug abuse treatment program?" 33.3 percent answered "Fair"; 48.6 percent, "Poor."

Congressman Glenn English commented: "Our whole concept of defense is to rely heavily on technology as opposed to large numbers of people. However, if half the people who use or maintain our military hardware are stoned or drug-impaired on duty, then these billion-dollar weapon systems become just so much scrap metal."

One result of the task force survey was that the Department of Defense, which had long been planning to do a comprehensive worldwide survey on drug abuse in the U.S. armed forces, hurried the process along. The DOD survey was conducted in 1980. This *was* a survey that complied fully with accepted scientific sampling procedure. It focused on "nonmedical use" of nine types of drugs and three types of alcoholic beverages (beer, wine, and hard liquor). Questionnaires were given out at eighty installations worldwide, to 19,582 active duty personnel—E's, W's (warrant officers), and O's (officers)—in each of the four services. The last two digits of the individual's Social Security account number were used as the device for random selection of those given the questionnaire. The sites were also randomly selected.

The survey broke down respondents into various pay grades, the lowest category being E-1 through E-5, the highest 0–4 through 0–6.

Some members of the military top brass had discounted the results of the task force's survey, saying that it was not a true random sampling and the numbers surveyed were too small to be significant. They could not, however, discount the results of this huge DOD worldwide survey done by professionals who used impeccable survey techniques in every respect.

Some of the findings were not unexpected. For example: Drug use among the E-1 to E-5 group soared far beyond that of other groups. Indeed, as pay rose, use dropped.

The percentage figures by pay-grade group in the population using each drug read as follows:

	E-1—E-5	E-6—E-9	W-1—W-4	O-1—O-3	O-4—O-6
Any drug use within past 30 days	38	5	3	4	1

As the researchers noted, "The figures for marijuana or hashish use are much the same as those for 'any drug use,' indicating that nearly all users of nonmedical drugs used at least marijuana or hashish. None of the other eight drugs approaches marijuana or hashish in popularity." This becomes clear in the following percentages:

FREQUENCY OF USING DRUG NONMEDICALLY AT LEAST ONCE A WEEK DURING THE PAST 30 DAYS

	Army	Navy	Marine Corps	Air Force
Marijuana/hashish	23	24	29	10
Amphetamines or other uppers (the second most commonly used drug)	3	5	4	1

(*Note:* In this chart all respondents, E-1 through O-6, are lumped together; thus there is an obvious "dilution" of the figures when compared with the task force survey, which dealt only with E-1s through E-4s. It should also be noted that the DOD survey did not look into the matter of "daily use." One may wonder why not, especially since the researchers later compared their figures to those of the National High School Senior Surveys, which did ask about daily use.)

The researchers then looked at the percentage of E-1s to E-5s using each drug in each service, within the past thirty days.

	Army	Navy	Marine Corps	Air Force
Marijuana/hashish	40	47	47	20

Perhaps the most sobering section of the entire survey was the one titled "Work Impairment Because of Drug Use." The researchers noted: "The type of work impairment most frequently reported by junior enlisted personnel was 'high while working' (19 percent); *nearly one-half of the E-1—E-5 respondents reported experiencing this on 40 or more days during the preceding 12 months*" (emphasis added).

E-1s to E-5s were also asked if they had been high on two or more days in a row. Their responses, in percentages:

Army	Navy	Marine Corps	Air Force
16	22	24	6

This figure bore out the statement Congressman Evans had made after touring the barracks and interviewing soldiers in West Germany: "Looks to me like a lot of our soldiers are stoned all weekend long."

After the DOD worldwide survey appeared, the House Select Committee on Narcotics Abuse and Control held another hearing in 1980 to find out what the services had been doing about drug abuse, how far they had gone in implementing previous committee recommendations as well as the "twelve-point program" of major new policy initiatives presented before the Select Committee by former Deputy Secretary of Defense Charles Duncan on July 27, 1978. Various VIPs spoke at this hearing, including Dr. John Johns, the only representative of the DOD who had accompanied the task force on the 1978 trip to West Germany.

In commenting on the task force's survey as compared to the DOD survey, Johns said: "I believe the results of the two surveys, when demographic variables are controlled, are not far apart." By demographics he was primarily referring to two factors. First, the task force had obtained responses only from E-1s through E-4s, whereas the DOD survey of this group had covered E-1s through E-5s. "Any time you get higher pay levels, you're going to get less usage," said Johns. Second, the task force had primarily interviewed combat troops. But the DOD survey was designed to control for as many variables as possible; one of the variables was different types of units. The worldwide survey, therefore, included units with a higher educational level, such as signal units and communications units, as well as units with a large number of women—who were far less drug-abusing than the men. This, of course, also tended to have a leveling-off effect on overall usage figures.

After the overview hearings the committee published a report on the subject. The first sentence of the summary read: "With minor fluctuations in certain high-risk regions, the nature of the drug abuse problem in the military appears relatively unchanged from that revealed in previous committee reports."

Despite this gloomy conclusion, it was true that the 1980 DOD drug-use figures among the lower echelon of enlisted men were lower than those brought back by the task force in 1978. Could this have been accounted for by the factors Dr. Johns had mentioned? Or had there been some improvement since 1978? And might any such improvement point to future productive roads to take?

Perhaps one way to find answers to these vital questions would be for the congressional task force to repeat its 1978 survey in 1981. Go to the same thirteen military installations. Use the same methods. Hand out the same questionnaire. And see if there were differences in the drug-abuse response levels.

It seemed a worthwhile project, so much so that it was decided to increase the scope of the operation to include selected naval units of our Mediterranean fleet and the personnel at a major air force base in Wiesbaden. Furthermore, non-coms and officers would be included in the survey.

Though the survey scope was larger, the task force was even more restricted by budget considerations than in 1978. The group now consisted of two congressmen (Chairman Glenn English and Benjamin Gilman of New York) plus five staff members, including James McDonald, special assistant to English.

McDonald pointed out that, although this survey, like its predecessor, "was not a statistically predetermined random sample in the sense of being preselected by social security number, it was random 'opportunity sampling.' " Using the USS *Forrestal* as an example, he described "opportunity sampling."

The three ships visited were anchored in Naples harbor. The task force went out on a motor launch, climbed the catwalk ladder to the deck, then went down to the briefing room for the ship's officers. "An aircraft carrier," said McDonald, "is like a city in itself. There were some four thousand men on the *Forrestal.* We told the officers that we wanted to cover the whole ship: engine room, flight deck, kitchen, maintenance shops, hangar area—the works. Each of us was to be accompanied by an officer. I went into the boiler room with a navy pilot. I told the officer in charge who we were and got his permission to approach the men. I chose them completely at random and asked if they'd come with me for a survey to be taken in the officer's briefing room. To my knowledge, no one who was asked by any of our team refused to come. We gave out four hundred surveys. Thus, we got ten percent of all the people on the ship. I have no doubt in my mind that we had a very good random representation."

The task force conducted its surveys from June 26 to July 7. This time they returned home with 1,906 questionnaires in cardboard boxes. The results were presented to the select committee on September 10, 1981.

In most categories of monthly or more frequent use, there was a significant drop between the 1978 and the 1981 figures. This was particularly notable as far as heroin use was concerned. In the 1978 survey this had been 10.3 percent; in 1981 it was 4 percent. Monthly or more frequent cocaine use had declined from 9.4 in 1978 to 6.2 in 1981, although cocaine use was rising in the States. Even alcohol use had declined from 81.3 percent to 73.4 percent.

But monthly or more frequent marijuana/hashish use remained stubbornly high: 52.6 percent in 1981, compared to 58.2 percent in 1978. And the daily use figures remained exactly the same: 16 percent.

As for the services looked at for the first time by the task force—daily marijuana/hashish use in the air force was 3.53 percent; in the marines it was 11.9 percent; and *in the navy, daily use was 24.4 percent.* One in every four sailors surveyed on the USS *Forrestal,* the USS *Ponce,* and the USS *Guadalcanal* used pot or hashish every day!

Even more startling was the fact that 60.2 percent of the navy's E-1 to E-4 sailors on the *Forrestal* admitted "using drugs/alcohol at least once during the month preceding the administering of the Select Committee's Survey," and *over half (52.4 percent) had used marijuana/hashish on duty.*

Furthermore, in the army, navy, and marines, on-duty marijuana/hashish use far outranked on-duty alcohol use. In the navy, on-duty cannabis use for all personnel was 41.9 percent, whereas on-duty alcohol use was 20.9 percent.

McDonald commented: "Since the *Forrestal* had been out at sea on patrol for over two months just before the survey, they must have had a pretty hefty supply of hash on board with them."

(It later became clear that drugs had also been sent through the mail. For example, at that time military law did not permit examining the mail. However, after two ship's commanders let it be known that this law might shortly be changed, half the mail on the two ships was marked by the addressees "return to sender" and returned unopened.)

The army's figure for those who had used cannabis on duty within the past month was 42.7 percent. (Note: The 1978 survey, with its figure of 52.3 percent, merely asked whether the soldier had "ever used" the drug on duty; therefore the two figures cannot be compared.)

This time the task force also surveyed non-commissioned officers E-5 and above about their marijuana/hashish and alcohol use on duty in the month preceding the survey. The results for the navy—marijuana/hashish: 13 percent; alcohol: 17 percent. But in the army, cannabis use (25.5 percent) outranked alcohol use (24.6 percent). Since alcohol included beer, this was a surprising statistic.

Another telling set of statistics: A far higher percentage of lower-echelon E's than upper E's believed that "almost all" in their units used cannabis. For example, when the E-1s to E-4s were asked "how many of the men and women in your unit use marijuana/hashish?" 27.9 in the army, 2.7 percent in the air force, 18.9 in the marines, and 27 percent in the navy checked the "almost all" category. However, in grades E-5 and above, the percentages were far lower: army, 17.9; air force, 0; marines, 9; and navy, 12.4.

All pay grades were combined to answer the strategic question concerning on-duty use. In the army and the navy, over one-third said drugs were used as frequently on duty as off duty (army 36.4, navy 38.9 percent).

In regard to the matter of combat readiness, E-1s to E-4s were asked: "Given the amount of drugs that men/women in your unit use, do you think they could go into combat and perform to the best of their abilities?" The response was "no" for 43 percent of the army; 41.3 percent, air force; 45.2 percent, marines; and 38.5 percent, navy.

Aside from the air force, the E-5s and above were even less sanguine on this subject: 53.3 percent of the army, 27.3 percent of the air force, 60 percent of the marines, and 51.9 percent of the navy said: "No."

Clearly the problem was not going away.

Brig. Gen. William C. Louisell, deputy assistant secretary of defense for drug and alcohol abuse prevention, commented: "Congress, in speaking through the Narcotics Select Committee, damned well said to the Department of Defense: 'We the people are concerned about the drug and alcohol problem in the Armed Forces of the United States.' I think we were properly chagrined. You can't ignore that."

The top brass were obviously shaken by the results of the surveys—particularly their own worldwide survey. But a single dramatic tragedy made the DOD realize that an entire shakeup of their drug-abuse policies *and practices* was essential if such vital concepts as combat readiness and armed forces prestige were to be retrieved.

On the night of May 26, 1981, a navy jet, while trying to land on the aircraft carrier USS *Nimitz,* crashed into fueled and armed F-14s on deck. Tanks exploded. Planes were ripped asunder. Ammunition and a missile ignited. Sailors fought the raging flames till dawn. By that time fourteen were dead and forty-four seriously injured. Twenty aircraft were damaged at a cost of over one hundred million dollars.

It was determined in the ensuing autopsies that six of the dead crewmen had cannabinoids in their blood and urine. Although these six men were in no way responsible for the crash, the fact made headlines around the nation and brought to life the implications of such statistics as the survey finding that 60 percent of the sailors on the USS *Forrestal* had been stoned while on duty.

It was obvious that, for many reasons, the U.S. armed forces had to cope with inducements to use drugs that were not faced by the schools, parents, the workplace, or any other segment of our society. Furthermore, the armed forces population is a huge and diffuse one: over 4.5 million people on 1,300 military installations including 920 in the United States, 27 in the U.S. territories, and 334 in 21 countries overseas.

Yet, in 1981, for the first time, the four services went all out in their war against drug abuse. What they accomplished is described in Chapter 19. It is an inspiring story. And, as we shall see, many aspects of what the armed forces accomplished can serve as pilot projects for the rest of our society.

Chapter 5

Crisis in the Schools

JUNIOR HIGH AND HIGH SCHOOL USE

Only one national survey on drug abuse by youth has been done every year since 1975: the National High School Senior Survey. Consequently, its annual findings are watched with keen interest by those concerned with the subject, including the media. And, when marijuana shows a gradual drop, as it has during the past few years, this is naturally highlighted in headlines—which gives many millions of parents, teachers, and others who are "in denial" the comfortable feeling that the pot problem is going away and they can relax and forget about it. The term "in denial" is used by professionals, parent-group leaders, and others who *are* deeply aware of the seriousness and scope of the drug epidemic. It is these men and women who keep in mind the fact that despite the much-heralded drop in drug use, American young people still rank as the most drug-pervaded in the developed world.

Survey statistics are faceless, anonymous. It is important to remember that each individual digit that goes to make up the overall percentage in each category is somebody's vulnerable child.

NIDA's director, Dr. William Pollin, puts it this way:

We still have a problem which is tragically severe. Though "only" 5.5 percent of our high school seniors are currently using marijuana daily, the same 1983 class reported that of those who had ever been daily users, more than a quarter *had used daily for two years or more, and had started daily use when they were in elementary or junior high school.* There are essentially as many high school seniors who are current smokers of pot as there are current smokers of cigarettes. While drug use levels remain at this unacceptably high level, they always have the potential to once again resume their upward surge.

In 1983, the National High School Senior Survey showed that the percentage of twelfth graders who had used marijuana during the year dropped from 44 percent in 1982 to 42 percent in 1983. This included everything from use once a year to more than one joint daily. The average user stayed stoned three hours each time he or she lit up a joint. But over one-third "usually stayed stoned three to six hours."

The "current-use" (within the past month) figures dropped from 28.5 percent in 1982 to 27 percent in 1983.

The "daily-use" figures dropped from 6.3 percent in 1982 to 5.5 percent in 1983, or 1 in 18 seniors. The average number of joints smoked by the daily users was 3½ a day, and 14 percent of them smoked 7 or more joints a day.

Dr. Carlton Turner noted that 1 in 18 high-school seniors smoking pot daily equaled about 160,000 twelfth-graders. Furthermore, as Turner pointed out before the House Select Committee on Narcotics Abuse and Control, "While we appreciate the value of the survey of high school seniors, often these data do not present the total picture. Twenty-five percent of students across the nation do not graduate from high school. School drop-outs are probably the highest drug-using group. Therefore, the High School Senior Survey only reports drug use information about the survivors—those young people who have stayed in school."

State surveys—such as the Maryland Survey on Drug Abuse which has been done almost every other year since 1972—consistently show that drug use among tenth-graders is even higher than among seniors, presumably— as Dr. Turner noted—because the truly dedicated drug-users drop out after the tenth grade.

The only other national drug abuse survey is the National Survey on Drug Abuse, generally referred to as the National Household Survey, since only people who live in households are randomly surveyed. It has been done approximately every two years since 1971. Like the National High School Senior Survey, it represents all states except Hawaii and Alaska.

The National Household Survey presents detailed questionnaires to three distinct age categories: Twelve to seventeen years old (termed youth), eighteen to twenty-five (young adult), and twenty-six and older (adult). In the age twelve to seventeen category, the 1982 survey showed that:

• Six percent have been daily users at some period, and 2 percent were daily users at the time of the survey.

• Eleven and one-half percent were current pot-smokers ("current" is defined by the researchers as use in the month prior to the survey; use may range from once a month to more than once a day.) About half the current users smoked pot on one to four days a month; the other half used it on from five days a month to daily (defined as twenty or more days a month).

• Thus, over one in nine of our junior-high and high-school-aged youngsters are current pot-smokers.

• Of all sixteen- and seventeen-year-olds surveyed, 23 percent had used pot during the past month; 8 percent of the fourteen- to fifteen-year-olds surveyed were current pot-smokers; and 2 percent of the twelve- to thirteen-year-olds surveyed were current pot-smokers. (This may be compared to the figure for the over-fifties: less than one half of one percent of those surveyed were current pot-smokers.)

• Although in the other two age categories (eighteen to twenty-five and twenty-six and older) there is a substantial difference in current pot use between males and females, with use by males more than double that of females, in the youth group, there is little difference: 10 percent of the females and 13 percent of the males are current users.

Three interesting sets of statistics consistently emerge from both the National Drug Abuse Survey and the National High School Senior Survey:

1. Of those who have "ever used" marijuana, *one in three become daily users at some point in their lives;* and one in ten or more (depending on the year of the survey) was a daily user at the time the survey was made. This fact should be noted by youngsters who shrug, "One joint's not going to hurt me." True, but that "one joint" makes the next one harder to resist. Parents who say, "All kids experiment with pot—it's part of growing up," should not only be aware of the above statistic, but of this one:

2. Of those who never use marijuana, at least half the class in the High School Senior Surveys, virtually *none* are regular users of any other illegal drug (including alcohol). However:

3. Of those who do smoke pot at some point during the year, about half use one or more additional illicit drugs—and/or legal drugs used illegally.

What other drugs are the pot-smokers using—often in combination with marijuana and alcohol, both of which potentiate ("fire up") the mind-altering effects of whatever else has been swallowed, injected, or snorted? Stimulants, depressants, hallucinogens, tranquilizers, and to a small degree, narcotics.

Kids know them by an intriguing variety of names, including the following: Ludes (Quaaludes); speed, crystal (methamphetamines); tueys, Christmas trees, bennies, co-pilots, black beauties, dexies (amphetamines); reds, rainbows, blockbusters, blues, goof balls, yellow jackets (barbiturates); tranks, downs (tranquilizers). In addition, some junior and senior high school and college students go in for an ominous alphabet of drugs: LSD, PCP, MDA. PCP, often known by the enticing title "angel dust," has a more somber alphabetical appellation, which seems to add to its allure: DOA—Dead on Arrival.

Cocaine use has also increased among high-school and college-age students. But, because of its prohibitive prices, the new coke vogue among youngsters is to use the drug not to get high but to enable them to "nurse" a fifth or two of distilled spirits for an entire night. Thus the effects of the alcohol, which would otherwise put them to sleep or even render them comatose, are warded off by small snorts of cocaine. But coke is a relatively short-acting drug compared to alcohol. Thus partying youngsters may get behind the wheel to drive home, feeling alert. The cocaine effects wear off; the alcohol effects take over, and they may fall asleep while driving.

Heroin? In the 1983 National High School Senior Survey, less than .1 percent of the seniors reported daily use. However, the investigators noted in the report that: "Heroin is the drug most likely to be under-reported in surveys, so this prevalence figure may well be understated."

Marijuana is thus important not only because of its intrinsic physical and psychological health hazards, but also because it is the gateway drug that provides an "open sesame" to all the dangerous drugs in the cornucopia offered to American youngsters. As Dr. Carlton Turner put it:

> The number and amount of abusable drugs available today and the pervasiveness of drug abuse among broad segments of society is staggering. We have approximately 23 million youngsters between the ages of 12 and 17 in this country. . . . The use of drugs by American youngsters between 12 and 17 creates over 100,000 acute, drug-related visits to federally funded drug treatment facilities each year. Of these 100,000 young people, 60,000 require treatment for problems related to marijuana. In comparison, less than 1,000 youngsters under 18 seek treatment for heroin use each year.

No section of our nation is immune to this school-drug epidemic, which rages from overcrowded city ghetto schools to one-room schoolhouses in small rural villages. It has pervaded public schools, private schools, parochial schools, and boarding schools.

Countless school administrators and principals still claim: "Not here! *We* have no problem." But investigation almost inevitably proves that such is not the case—unless the school authorities have recognized the problem, have taken a firm stand against drug use, and have implemented their policy with fairness and firmness. Some schools have done this (see Chapter 18). Unfortunately, they are still the rare exceptions to the rule.

A 1981 *Washington Post*/ABC News poll showed striking differences between the public's and school principals' perceptions of school problems and drug use. Three hundred three school principals were asked about major school problems. Twelve percent said that drug use in school was a major problem and 13 percent found alcohol use in school a major problem. However, 1,501 adults (referred to in the findings as "the public") perceived the problem differently. Sixty-six percent of "the public" thought drug use in school was a major problem; 49 percent cited alcohol use in school as a major problem.

Dr. Scott Thomson is executive director of the National Association of Secondary School Principals (NASSP), which represents thirty-four thousand high-school principals from some 80 percent of the public and private schools in the United States and Canada. In April 1984, Dr. Thomson made this statement:

> Pot poses the most serious single challenge faced by our high schools today. It constitutes the greatest barrier to student motivation and rigorous study that exists.
>
> Most principals became discouraged during the 1970s and many gave up the fight against marijuana. The mass media carried numerous articles saying that it was a benign substance, which meant that the kids would just ignore the principal. The kids believed the psychologists and the newspaper reporters—not the principals. The principals don't have that much credibility in a special area like this.
>
> Marijuana demotivates students, makes them lackadaisical. Pot-smokers also drop out of student activities and athletics, and this harms their social and physical development.
>
> Marijuana really does penalize the potential of students to develop in all areas, in leadership and academic growth. It's a terrible thing.

Elementary School Drug Use

It has been clearly shown by studies and surveys that the younger the pot-user starts, the heavier and more persistent the use will be. According to the 1982 National High School Senior Survey, over one in three seniors (35 percent) reported that his or her initial experience with marijuana occurred prior to age fifteen, primarily in the seventh, eighth, and ninth grades, between the ages of twelve and fourteen. No national survey of drug *use* has looked below the age of twelve, although as previously noted, in 1982, the *Weekly Reader* did a national survey of half a million youngsters—including fourth-, fifth-, and sixth-graders—concerning their *perceptions* of drug use in their class. One in four fourth-graders reported that children in their age-group feel "some" to "a lot" of peer pressure to try alcohol and marijuana. Thirty-nine percent reported that using drugs was "a big problem among kids their age." And about 20 percent of fourth-graders saw "no risk" in smoking one marijuana cigarette a day.

Local surveys have looked at actual grade-school *use*. For example, a 1979 two-county survey in rural Maine showed that in the fourth grade, 6 percent had tried marijuana at least once and 1 percent had used it "many times." ("And," said Mel Tremper of Maine's Office of Alcohol and Drug Abuse Prevention, "as drug use goes, we in Maine are kind of behind the times.")

Another type of survey has been taken every school year since 1978 by Dr. Ingrid Lantner of Willoughby, Ohio, one of the first pediatricians in the United States to fully recognize the physical and psychological problems caused by marijuana among young users, and to do something about it above and beyond her own practice. She speaks on the subject in classrooms, at school assemblies and, in the evening, to parent groups. After her talk, she asks for written questions. She invariably receives one or two indicating that parents give pot to their young children. Two typical questions from youngsters:

I am ten. My parents let me smok pot sins I was six. Will my eggs be damiged?

My brother smoked M.J. since age seven but not every day. Will he have his growth effected? He is now 11. He gets the M.J. from my mother.

Another question Dr. Lantner often receives from fifth- and sixth-graders is "What should I do if someone physically forces me to smoke pot?"

"School principals tell me," says Lantner, "that after a ballgame, a group of older students often come around to sell pot, and they're very aggressive with the little ones, insisting they buy and smoke on the spot. This happens in nice, upper-middle-class areas in the suburbs of Cleveland."

Corporal Ed Moses is drug information officer for the state of Missouri and works full-time traveling the state to talk to kids. He reports:

Youngsters often tell me they feel the pressure to turn on as early as the fifth and sixth grades. Also, every year the marijuana is getting stronger, and more easily available in larger quantities.

I think the most disturbing thing I've found is many parents' attitude that marijuana is so harmless that it's okay to reward young children with "a toke" to get them high. This is becoming more and more common among young parents who are heavy users.

However, the chief source of supply for the grade-schoolers is older siblings—who often feel they are doing their smaller brothers and sisters a favor by getting them high. There is also another motive. If the younger child gets involved, he or she won't "narc" (tell Mom and Dad).

Drug Use in Colleges

Although the NIDA-sponsored National Household Surveys have consistently shown that one in every three to four of our young people aged eighteen to twenty-four is a current pot-smoker, surprisingly few large-scale professional surveys of drug use in colleges and universities have been conducted. One of the few was a comprehensive statewide survey of drug use among college students sponsored by the New York State Division of Substance Abuse Services and released in March 1981.

According to National Household Survey and National High School Senior Survey investigators, as well as professionals at NIDA, to their knowledge there has been no statewide survey of drug use in colleges since that date. The National Household Survey does have a "full-time college student" category; however, the very definition of the "Household Survey" eliminates all students who live in dorms. Only two categories of college students are questioned: those who live at home and those who live with friends. As investigator Dr. Judith Miller points out: "It should be remembered that those living with their parents are less drug abusing than those living with friends." This fact would tend to water down the overall use findings of the "full-time college students" as shown in the National Household Survey. When the "at home" students' use is combined with the "living with friends" students, the "ever use" figures were 64 percent in 1979 and 62 percent in 1982. The "current-use" figures showed a drop from 37 percent in 1979 to 26 percent in 1982.

Let us now take an in-depth look at the major survey which *does* include drug use by college students who live in dorms as well as in off-campus housing: The New York State Survey of Drug Use Among College Students.

A stratified random sample of twenty-two colleges participated. Over 7,700 full-time undergraduate students completed a ten-page questionnaire that maintained the anonymity and confidentiality of the respondents. The sample was projected to reflect drug use among the 500,000 full-time undergraduate students enrolled in the state's two hundred public and private four-year and two-year colleges.

The major findings were that drug use is widespread among college students in New York State. *Two out of every three full-time undergraduate students* enrolled in colleges in New York State *had recently taken an illegal drug or used a legal drug nonmedically.* ("Recently" was defined as use in the six months prior to the survey.) Marijuana was the prime drug of abuse— recently used by over half (59 percent) of the students.

When severity of drug use was considered, 180,000 students (36 percent) were regular users (defined as users of at least three drugs in the last six months and/or users of cannabis at least ten times in the past month). These included the 19 percent (95,000 students) who were substantial or extensive users of illicit drugs or legal drugs used nonmedically (defined as users of at least seven drugs in the last six months and/or users of a non-cannabis drug at least four times in the past month).

The study showed that the drugs most frequently used in the past six months were:

* Marijuana—used by 59 percent or 291,000 students (23 percent reported being high on marijuana or hashish while in class);
* Hashish—used by 28 percent or 138,000 students;
* Stimulants—used by 21 percent or 103,000 students;
* Cocaine—used by 20 percent or 101,000 students.

The figures showed, too, that more college students smoked marijuana than smoked cigarettes, and that white students were more likely to use drugs than Hispanics or blacks.

Also, *most students who used drugs at high levels also used alcohol. Among substantial and extensive drug users, 45 percent consumed more than one ounce of alcohol per day. Of those who never used drugs, only four percent drank at these levels.* (An ounce of alcohol is the equivalent of one shot of whiskey, one four-ounce glass of wine, or one twelve-ounce can of beer.)

Students' concern about drug use was also measured in the survey. *More than one in every five students admitted having problems as a result of using drugs.* Twenty percent indicated that one or more of their friends had a "drug problem," and 14 percent said that drug use was a "major" problem on the college campus. *Approximately 40 percent of the students said they were extremely or very interested in counseling for drug-abuse problems.* But the students who were most involved in using drugs and/or alcohol were least interested in such services. The survey noted that "special efforts may be required to reach the almost three in ten students who might benefit from counseling or treatment services aimed at coping with problems related to their drug and/or alcohol abuse."

In countless college courses ranging from sociology to law to drug education, students were taught that marijuana was a virtually harmless drug. For example, in a course at New York's Hunter College entitled "Altered States of Consciousness," one of the questions on the 1978 midterm examination was: "One of the following drugs is thought to be harmless: heroin, cocaine, marijuana, LSD." The "correct answer" was marijuana.

In 1983, in a course on psychoactive drugs given at Ithaca College in New York State, School of Health, Physical Education and Recreation, one of the four textbooks was *Chocolate to Morphine,* by Dr. Andrew Weil and Winifred Rosen, which has as its underlying thesis that there are no dangerous drugs, only people who do not use drugs in a responsible fashion. Other required reading included an article in The *New York Times Magazine* (November 19, 1972) by Edward Brecher, "Overdose Explanation Is a Myth," which claims that overdose deaths are due to impurities in drugs, not to the drugs themselves. (It is well known that opiates—heroin, morphine, opium, codeine—with or without impurities, can, for example, produce respiratory arrest leading to death.)

It is interesting to note that although New York's survey called for "special efforts" to reach the almost three in ten college students who might benefit from counseling or treatment services for drug and/or alcohol abuse, very little has been done in colleges in that state—or in any other—to fulfill that obvious need as far as drugs are concerned.

There is a national alcohol-awareness program named BACCHUS (Boost Alcohol Consciousness Concerning the Health of University Students), with chapters on more than ninety college campuses in over thirty-five states. However, the BACCHUS program, like most college programs of this type, puts its emphasis almost exclusively on alcohol, regarding drugs as a different domain. The attitude of most of those concerned with alcohol treatment and prevention is "Let us work on alcohol abuse first—since that is our most prevalant problem. *Then* we can turn to drug abuse." However, as we have seen in the New York State Survey, the National High School Senior Survey, the National Household Survey, and others, most chronic drug users are also heavy drinkers. Therefore, since alcohol is a drug, the more realistic approach would seem to be to treat alcohol and drug abuse in the same programs. Unfortunately, many professionals scorn this concept. Both the "alcohol people" and the "drug-abuse people" seem to regard such an idea as infringement on their private turf.

It should also be noted that, despite the plethora of hard scientific data now available on the physical and psychological health hazards of marijuana, at the time this book went to press there was only one college or university in the nation offering a full-credit course on the health hazards of marijuana—a course given by Lee Croft at Arizona State University in Tempe, Arizona.

Could the School Epidemic Have Been Halted?

Although large-scale, professional drug-use surveys in our colleges and universities have been notable for their near-absence, the opposite has been true of high-school and junior-high surveys. Not only has the twelve-to-seventeen school-age group been well surveyed and reported upon, but many of these reports and studies were amply funded and well executed. Furthermore, reports made in the early 1970s gave us ample warning of exactly what would happen—but, tragically, they were filed away and forgotten, their warnings unheeded. One of the most important of these reports was called "Drugs in Our Schools," done by the House of Representatives Select Committee on Crime and circulated to every member of the U.S. Congress. It was particularly notable for three reasons:

1. It was perhaps the most comprehensive single study ever done on drug use in our high schools.

Prior to making the report to Congress, the committee visited New York, Miami, Chicago, San Francisco, Kansas City, and Los Angeles. They interviewed over two thousand witnesses, and came up with *ten thousand pages of transcribed testimony,* from

responsible individuals who represented every major occupation or group concerned with drug abuse among our nation's youth. From the school systems we heard from presidents of school boards, superintendents of schools, principals, teachers, counselors, nurses, PTA officials and students. From the criminal justice system we heard from judges, prosecutors, defense counsel, probation officials, police officers and undercover policemen and women. From the scientific and medical professions, we heard testimony of medical examiners, doctors, professors and other experts who have specialized knowledge of drug-abuse treatment and rehabilitative methods.

In addition to the testimony, the committee staff "collected, evaluated, and analyzed a large number of treatises, surveys, and other reports relating to this subject published by a broad spectrum of public and private institutions concerned with youthful drug abuse. These documents and exhibits totaled approximately 16,000 pages of printed material."

2. The report was based largely on research done in 1972. The National Household Survey, started in 1971, showed that among youth of junior high and high-school age, pot use *was far lower* in 1972 than it was in 1982—the year of the much-heralded "drop" in use.

The National Household Survey decade span of comparisons concerning marijuana use among the twelve-to-seventeen age group appears on page 78.

3. "Drugs in Our Schools" clearly predicted what would happen—unless attention was paid and dramatic steps were taken to rectify the situation. Presumably, if the situation threatening our youth had concerned any *other* type of epidemic, effective steps would have been taken at once. But in the case of drug abuse, being forewarned did not mean being forearmed. As we will see later in this chapter, not only national surveys but also state and city surveys taken *since* that report to Congress all show that the drug situation became even more disastrous than it was when the report was published. The following excerpts from the fifty-seven-page report to Congress, "Drugs in Our Schools," clearly illustrate that the situation in the early seventies was dire indeed.

An extremely deadly epidemic is presently raging in our schools. . . . The chances are substantial that when a parent sends his child to high school each day he is sending him into a drug-filled environment, where drugs are usually bought and sold—an atmosphere where there is considerable pressure from other students to use drugs. Drug abuse in our schools has become so extensive and pervasive that it is only the uniquely gifted and self-possessed child who is capable of avoiding involvement with some form of drug abuse.

Sales of all sorts of drugs regularly and persistently take place in the cafeterias, hallways, washrooms, playgrounds, and parking lots of

1972	(12- to 17-year-olds)	1982

Ever used

14 percent   26.7 percent

(Note: "Ever used" might seem a meaningless figure were it not for the fact that according to the National Household Survey, about one in three who ever tried the drug eventually used on a daily basis at some point in their lives. This coincides almost exactly with National High School Senior Survey figures.)

Use in Past Year

This question was not asked   20.6 percent
in 1972. In 1974, the figure
was 18.5 percent.

Use in Past Month

7 percent   11.5 percent

Daily Use
(20 or more days a month)

This question was not asked until 1979—   2.1 percent
when pot use peaked at 3.6 percent.

Ever used
(age breakdown)

12–13: 4 percent   12–13: 8 percent
14–15: 10 percent   14–15: 24 percent
16–17: 29 percent   16–17: 46 percent

Use in past month
(age breakdown)

12–13: 1 percent   12–13: 2 percent
14–15: 6 percent   14–15: 8 percent
16–17: 16 percent   16–17: 23 percent

our schools. The ease with which students can purchase drugs in a high school is truly astounding. With little or no effort a teenager can obtain amphetamines, barbiturates, LSD, and marijuana. With some additional effort, cocaine and heroin are generally available in most schools. . . .

The vast majority of the individuals who are selling drugs in our schools are students. The drug pusher is a friend to the teenage drug user—often looked up to and even admired. In Kansas City, the state police had recently arrested a youngster for selling drugs. The student drove to high school in a new Mustang, was captain of the school football team, and dated the prettiest girl on campus. Perhaps the best description of drug pushing in high school was given to the Committee by a high school student: "Let me dispute the term 'pusher.' Nobody has to push drugs in school. If a guy has some drugs, all he has to do is sit in one place and people will come to him. He is not out trying to induce people to buy drugs.". . .

Most of the youngsters who were selling drugs were doing so to support their own habit. More often the drug habit was getting worse.

Why Were Students Taking Drugs? Twelve answers were provided; yet, the most prevalent were "because their friends do" and "to escape reality." The first answer certainly substantiates testimony given before our Committee during hearings in six cities across the country and their answer corroborates the "infectious disease" theory of drug abuse. The second answer, "to escape reality," relates—we think—to drug advertising . . . which encourages our young people to think in escapist terms.

By "drug advertising," the committee meant the advertising done by pharmaceutical companies. The blatant do-illegal-drugs advertising found in *High Times* and elsewhere had not then surfaced beyond the underground "hippie press." (*High Times* was not published until 1975.)

There was another type of survey that kept cropping up. Newspaper reporters in various cities and counties did series about drug use in local schools. Although their statistics cannot be regarded as "hard data" and they claimed no expertise in survey techniques, their reports served to bring flesh-and-blood reality to the figures published by the professional researchers. Reporter Kay Black and photographer Jim Reid of the *Memphis* (Tennessee) *Press-Scimitar* did such a series on high-school kids' use of marijuana in Memphis, and were asked to testify at 1980 congressional hearings on "Drug Use and Abuse in the Memphis–Shelby County School System," held by the House Select Committee on Narcotics Abuse and Control. As Congressman Billy Lee Evans pointed out: "The only other hearing of this type was held in the city of New York. Memphis is a little more in line with the average American city."

Black and Reid described the scope of their investigations:

We visited four schools, and we told the children we did not want to know their names. We interviewed about 100 students, all of whom estimated that 50 to 75 percent of the students in their school were using marijuana. . . . They said they didn't smoke more than two or three joints a day, which they considered minimum. Most of the students said that. . . . They also said no one bothered about it; they wouldn't be arrested or anything like that. . . . In fact, at one school during the time we were out there in the morning, a law enforcement car came by. We said, "You all out here to arrest the kids smoking marijuana?" They said, No, they would have to arrest the whole city.

I think the shocking thing to us was that the kids used it so freely in front of us.

Regarding principals' perceptions, Black and Reid testified:

We went to one school where the principal said, "Possibly we have one, maybe two percent of our students involved." There were two young men standing there. She said, "Here are two good students on our campus, let's ask them." One said, "You want the real figures?" She said, "Of course." He told her fifty percent were actively using marijuana. She was amazed. Another principal estimated three, four, or five percent at the most. We had just left a whole street of [his] youngsters involved in marijuana smoking . . . but he seemed unaware of this problem, which was half a block from his school. One of the teachers in the Germantown area said she and other teachers had complained to the principal about pushers who would sell marijuana over the fence during the recess period to the junior high and high school students. The principal told the teachers to leave it alone. He didn't seem to want to get into the whole problem. . . . Most of the kids said, "If there is any action taken, there is a two- or three-day suspension and it is a nice holiday." They like the holiday.

As for the parents, Black and Reid reported that after their four-part series was published:

Parents involved in these particular schools called us and were highly indignant. They said, "You have done a discredit to that particular school and to the faculty and to the good students in that school." They seemed more concerned about the bad image that they said we had created than they were concerned about the fact that so many students were on marijuana.

Those 1980 Congressional hearings lasted two days. Perhaps the most telling of the testimonies came from the schoolkids themselves. For example, one said that about 60 to 65 percent of tenth-graders were smoking pot on a *daily* basis. Just as the national surveys are generally regarded as underestimations, student perceptions of drug use may be overestimations. But the significant factor is that if kids *think* daily use is in the 60- to 65-percent category, this (a) makes it harder to say no to the constant peer pressure to do drugs, and (b) makes anything less than daily use seem "like nothing."

Through the years, further dire warnings about the effects on schoolchildren of drugs in general, and marijuana in particular, have been sounded by experts who spoke before the U.S. Congress and elsewhere. For example, at a hearing before the Senate Subcommittee on Alcoholism and Drug Abuse, on October 21, 1981, Dr. Mel J. Riddle, coordinator of substance abuse prevention for the Fairfax County (Virginia) public schools, had this to say:

> Probably the worst effect of marijuana use is on the school climate and the general school environment. First of all, it contributes to the formation of an alienated subculture in the school that wants to have nothing to do with anything that goes on in the school, but does want to have something to do with talking about, finding, purchasing, distributing and using drugs, particularly marijuana.
>
> That alienated subculture often engages in a variety of negative behaviors. So, we try to treat the negative behaviors, and we are only treating the symptoms of the problem, when the real problem is drug use. Anytime a school activity is held you must account for the fact that there may be some drug use, and plan to control or prevent it.
>
> Drug use also contributes to low staff morale. Teachers, administrators and counselors attempt to deal with the problems and they experience the same kind of guilt and frustration and anxiety that parents experience who have children that are abusing substances. So, in that sense, drug use is not only an individual disease and a family disease, but it is also a school disease, because everyone in that school feels those emotions and experiences the emotional pain.
>
> We find teachers becoming increasingly frustrated and ready to give up in terms of trying to deal with these problems because no matter what we do, we find that the problems persist—unexplainable continuation of inappropriate behavior. It is difficult for us to comprehend a rational person continuing to misbehave in the way some of these students do, so it is very frustrating to deal with that.
>
> Finally, we begin to lower our expectations, both about academic performance on the part of students and about their behavior. Students also lower their expectations about how they should behave. They begin to gauge and compare their behavior to the worst behavior in the school.

The Do-Drug Messages

These come from two sources, and no youngster is immune. The first is the widely recognized peer pressure to do drugs which kids meet from their contemporaries. The other comes in many guises, which range from subtle to blatant. But all of these emanate from the adult world, and in many cases money is the sole motive. The most notable case in point is drug paraphernalia, with many specialty items aimed directly at the teen and preteen market.

In some states, items intended to promote the use and/or enhance the pleasurable aspects of drugs such as marijuana and cocaine are perfectly legal, a do-drug message that comes to kids loud and clear. In these states, drug paraphernalia may be purchased by teenagers not only in headshops, but also in numerous record shops, boutiques, smoke shops, card shops, and novelty shops in posh suburban shopping malls. Furthermore, in some areas, full-fledged headshops can be found only a few blocks away from the local high school.

In many states, the manufacture and sale of drug paraphernalia has been banned (see the Appendix), but paraphernalia and other drug-related items can still be legally purchased (via credit cards) through such drug-promoting publications as *High Times*—which started in a Greenwich Village cellar in 1974, billing itself as "the only magazine dedicated to getting high," and now claims a pass-on circulation of four million readers, many of whom are high-school students.

According to Harry Myers, the Drug Enforcement Administration's "paraphernalia expert" and associate chief counsel of the DEA:

As of April 1984, 38 states had officially outlawed drug paraphernalia. But 12 states have done nothing to stop the sale of these objects. A teenager might not be able to buy drug paraphernalia in his own locality. But if he can borrow a car he can cross into a neighboring state to buy bongs. Large mail order shops with elaborate catalogues have sprung up in the 12 states which do not have drug paraphernalia bans. They sell millions of dollars worth of paraphernalia to anyone anywhere who wants to shop by mail. Advertisements for drug paraphernalia still appear in national drug-oriented magazines. Furthermore, even states with paraphernalia laws may not be enforcing them.

These are some of the "kiddie paraphernalia" items available to youngsters in shops, or via mail order: red plastic space guns, transformed into "power hitters" that blast marijuana smoke deep into the lungs; "Catch-a-Buzz" flying discs (an unauthorized version of Whamo's Frisbee), which double as pot-smoking devices; schoolroom pens that transform into pot pipes; kiddie belt buckles for hiding your "stash" (of marijuana); and marijuana rolling papers in cherry, banana, peanut butter, and strawberry flavors.

There are also practice pot-smoking kits, such as Polynesian Kava Kava Root with rolling papers included; and "Practice Grass" (alfalfa), which comes with *McGrassey's Reader,* a twenty-page easy-read primer that teaches children how to roll a joint, "what to wear to your first practice grass party," "basic pot vocabulary," and "Phrase Practice"—for example, "I just made a buy of a lid of clean grass for my stash." "When a joint becomes a roach,

I'm gone." "Some heads never come down." "One hit and I was wiped out." "I love to put a good high on, eat lots of munchies, and mellow out." "(Suggestion: Practice with a tape recorder and/or in front of a mirror. *Note:* Don't misplace the tape.)"

For more advanced readers, there's *The Whole Drug Manufacturers Catalogue.* The table of contents for Part One lists sections on synthesis of drugs including "LSD (Three Methods), DMT, TMA, PCP (Angel Dust), STP, MDA (Two Methods), THC (Three Methods) and Heroin (Two Methods)." Part Two is described as "Kitchen Chemistry and Bathtub Dope: home production methods to produce drugs from non-prescription items and household chemicals in your kitchen without prior chemical knowledge." Included are sections on "How to Make Marijuana Stronger (Three Methods)," "How to Produce Hashish from Marijuana," and "How to Grow Three Ounces of Marijuana Per Week Indoors in a 4 ft. × 4 ft. area." This ninety-one-page book costs twelve dollars.

There are also games such as "Pot Luck," which bills itself as "a game for dopes." Indeed, the ad claims, it's "More than a game. . . . It's a way of life! Wow . . . now you can buy, sell, and deal dope right in your own living room . . . win by being the wealthiest dealer around the board. . . . Fill in the coupon and get the ultimate legal high yet."

There's also Dealer McDope Dealing Game. ("Indulge your greatest fantasies with this simulation of real-drug dealing.") An ad reads: "Bring the million dollar deal into your living room without fear of the feds."

And there are countless posters with "do-drug" messages, as well as clothing and accessories, ranging from T-shirts with such slogans as "Thank You for Pot Smoking: American Cannabis Society" and "A Day without Dope is a Day without Sunshine" to cocaine spoon earrings—which can, in fact, sometimes be found for sale in elegant department stores.

Other pervasive and persuasive do-drug messages come to kids loud and clear through rock lyrics, particularly those of the sixties and seventies. Although drug-related lyrics have taken a back seat in the eighties, kids still buy and listen to records made in the sixties and seventies which they regard as cool—songs such as "Fire It Up," and "Mary Jane" (a street name for marijuana); "Smokin' "; "A Gallon of Gas" (which talks about "scoring coke" and getting grade A grass).

Besides the musical message in the lyrics, performers at rock concerts sometimes put into words a clear "come on" to the audience to do drugs during the show. Cpl. Ed Moses, drug information officer for Missouri, visits many rock concerts as part of his "route." In April 1984, Moses said:

The amount of pressure to use drugs at concerts is phenomenal. For example, in one typical concert in Kirksville, Missouri, the lead performer of a nationally known group told the audience: "If we went on one big high together—a group high—what a feeling it would be." Everybody cheered and lit up. It looked like fireflies on a June evening.

Parents drive by the stadium and make jokes about the cloud of pot smoke that rises from it. They have no idea what's going on inside. They should, for example, visit the first-aid area and see the OD's [overdose victims] being carried in.

"These drug-rock concerts," Moses sums up, "are not a safe place to be."

Movies also make their do-drug mark. When images are seen on the wide screen, their impact is magnified. One can look long and hard for a feature film that has had a solid anti-marijuana impact. On the other hand, movies giving a clear "smoke pot" message abound.

Many youth-oriented movies (particularly those rated PG) present a casual, accepting view of pot smoking by teenagers. In these films, for example, joints are passed around at parties, on the beach, and so on.

Up in Smoke, starring Cheech and Chong, was the first major studio movie dependent on an "in" audience of pot-smokers who recognized the dope jokes. During its first run in movie houses, TV commercials for *Up in Smoke* were sometimes aired during the 3:00 to 5:00 P.M. "kiddie hours," along with the film's well-known promo slogan: "Don't come straight to this movie" (i.e., come stoned). *Variety* reported that *Up In Smoke* scored high with young audiences. Cheech and Chong's financial success led to follow-up films by this duo, who are now strongly identified with marijuana, as well as a slew of other so-called "dope movies" or "dope operas."

But certainly the most harmful of all are the fine feature films that incorporate a pot-smoking scene or casual references to marijuana as though pot were a natural part of life. *Nine to Five,* for example, showed the three secretaries enjoying their first joints—a scene that could easily have hit the cutting-room floor without disturbing the intent or flow of the film.

Jane Fonda says: "Would you two show a little spunk?" They do, and light up. Later, after a delightful session of giggles and camaraderie, Fonda is told, "It's called Maui Wowie," and she exclaims: "Well, I love it!" making the entire experience seem not only harmless but totally pleasurable. How many young, or not so young, movie aficionados followed their heroine's footsteps by trying a joint, after seeing this film?

Other major films in which pot smoking is introduced as a normal ingredient of life include *Private Benjamin, Animal House,* Steven Spielberg's *Polter-*

geist (where parents light up), Woody Allen's memorable *Annie Hall,* where Diane Keaton claims she can't enjoy sex unless she first smokes a joint, *10, The Big Chill,* and *Terms of Endearment.*

All these films have extended life via frequent replays on cable and network television. It is worthy of note that although network censors forbid pot smoking and coke snorting on shows made for TV, they have no control over such scenes in films shown on cable or pay TV—one reason *Up in Smoke* has become a cable staple.

Although television has made a few noteworthy contributions in the area of informing the public about the health hazards of marijuana, the do-drug contributions, particularly of TV comics, have had massive impact in getting out the message that drugs are cool.

In the clothing, jewelry, and cosmetics area, do-drug messages come through loud and clear in mainstream merchandising. For example, until 1980, Sears Roebuck, J. C. Penney, and Montgomery Ward catalogs featured "waterpipes" (bongs) for potsmoking.

Eyedrops used to get rid of the telltale pot-redness are advertised in teen magazines. The ads tell kids to use the drops after "partying"—which is virtually synonymous with "booze and pot." In other words, the adult world *expects* teenagers to smoke pot at parties. Jewelry counters in the country's most elegant department stores sell such items as expensive roach clips, and gold-plated razor blades and tiny spoons to cut and snort cocaine. Cosmetics counters sell the lavishly packaged, merchandised, and heavily advertised perfume called "Opium" (note that heroin is a derivative of opium).

With the continual peer pressure to do drugs, reinforced by the adult merchandisers' messages, it cannot be surprising that so many of our young people regard pot use as a normal part of growing up.

Another important factor in the school picture is this: Many professionals concerned with education still give no consideration to the impact drug abuse is having on our children.

For example, two major reports were published in the spring of 1983 on the dire state of education in the United States, but neither mentioned drug abuse as a possible contributing cause. And although all manner of solutions were proposed, few, if any, mentioned dealing with the drug-abuse problem.

One report, for example, "A Nation at Risk," was issued by a blue-ribbon group, the National Commission on Excellence in Education. Concluding that our school system is a nationwide educational catastrophe, the commission noted that "if an unfriendly foreign power had attempted to impose on America the mediocre education performance that exists today, we might have viewed it as an act of war." In nineteen international comparisons of student achievement, Americans rated *last* seven times, and failed to place first or second in any comparison.

Obviously, there are many causes for this "educational catastrophe." But the correlation between the statistics and the symptoms of chronic marijuana use would seem at least to demand consideration of student drug use as one of the causes. For example, one of the classic symptoms of chronic marijuana use by youngsters is the so-called "dropout syndrome." This starts with dropping out of academic courses in favor of "snap courses," and sometimes ends with dropping out of school. The commission's study notes that since the late 1960s, the proportion of school time spent in academic subjects such as English, social studies, math, and foreign languages fell from about 70 percent to 62 percent. On the other hand, during that same period, time spent in courses such as personal service, driver training, chorus, consumer education, and personal guidance rose from 8 percent to 13 percent.

As for literally dropping out, as one educator put it: "I suppose the single most alarming statistic is the dropout rate, which has remained fairly constant over the last several years. In New York City, for example, the dropout rate is 45 percent." But despite all the comment on soaring absenteeism and dropout rates, virtually nothing was said about drug abuse as a cause.

This is particularly puzzling in view of the fact that numerous local, state, and national surveys on the subject were available to the National Commission on Excellence in Education. For example, a 1982 Ohio statewide survey showed that approximately 44 percent of students in grades seven through twelve used marijuana regularly, ranging from a few times a month to almost every day. Eleven percent of the boys had started before age ten, compared to 2 percent of the girls. However, sex differences vanished by age fifteen; three-fourths of all marijuana users in the survey had started on the drug by this age. The survey further pointed out that "almost one in five—or 185,000 students in Ohio—have experienced severe negative consequences of drug use." *One of the most obvious long-term effects was "performing poorly at school."*

Another common symptom of chronic pot use among youngsters is a flatness, a lack of caring about anything except where, when, and how to get high. Members of the National Commission noted the flatness and apathy that pervade our nation's classrooms, but again drug abuse was not mentioned as a possible cause.

What *was* mentioned? Television. Higher divorce rates. Growth of the suburbs, and "the radicalism of the 1960s, which helped undermine both the educational tradition and serious efforts at reform."

The second report, "A Study of Schooling," sponsored by the independent Institute for the Development of Educational Activities, was the result of eight years of classroom research by forty-three researchers in thirteen communities who conducted more than twenty-seven thousand interviews. John Goodlad, former dean of the Graduate School of Education at UCLA, who directed the project, described the atmosphere in most classes as "emotionally flat."

The report was called "one of the most extensive on-the-scene investigations ever undertaken," and became the basis of a book by Dr. Goodlad, *A Place Called School.* Neither the report nor the book mention drug-abuse prevention as one of the possible solutions. Instead, according to the book, "Suggestions for significant improvement begin with the premise that our schools must be redesigned piece by piece." For example, "Public schools should be broken down into 'single houses' of perhaps 100 students to reduce anonymity," a process involving "some internal reconstruction."

Presumably, it would cost communities far less to incorporate into health and science classes accurate up-to-date information on the health hazards of marijuana and other drugs than it would to finance "internal reconstruction" for schools. As is clearly shown in Chapter 17, "Schools: Pilot Projects That Work," eliminating drug abuse in schools dramatically reduces many of the problems discussed in the two extensive reports, "A Nation at Risk" and "A Study of Schooling."

Furthermore, examination of the National High School Senior Survey figures gives clear indication of the fact that bringing to students, parents, and teachers accurate information on the health hazards of drugs in general and marijuana in particular does effectively raise perception of harm, which correlates with a decrease in use.

During 1975 to 1978, there was very little information in the nation's media about the harmful effects of marijuana. Indeed, media in the main passed on the message that pot was a benign and pleasurable recreational pastime.

From 1975 to 1978, daily use of marijuana by high school seniors increased at a precipitous rate, until it reached the staggering figure of 10.7 percent. Furthermore, from 1975 to 1978 there was a "decline in the harmfulness perceived to be associated with all levels of marijuana use." For example, in 1975, when the annual survey was done for the first time, 43 percent of seniors felt that "people risk harming themselves physically or in other ways if they smoke marijuana regularly." However, by 1978, only 35 percent felt people risked harming themselves by regular use.

Then, in July 1978, there appeared the first extensive article on the health hazards of marijuana. This was a full-page story in the Outlook section of the *Washington Post.* It was widely syndicated in other major newspapers throughout the country. Also, on December 10 of that year, NBC did an hour-long documentary, "Reading, Writing and Reefer," on marijuana's deleterious effects on preteens and teenagers. This was rebroadcast as an afternoon program for young viewers in 1979.

In 1979, not only did the increase in daily use come to a halt, but there was a rise in the proportion of seniors perceiving "regular marijuana use as involving great risk." This jumped from 35 percent in 1978 to 42 percent in 1979.

From 1979 on, two further media avenues had an impact on the myth of harmlessness encasing marijuana. One was the *Reader's Digest,* which ran five articles on the subject, and later reproduced them as a booklet, "Marijuana Update"; the other was the mass-market women's magazines: *Good Housekeeping, Family Circle, Ladies' Home Journal, McCall's,* and *Woman's Day.*

The first *Digest* article, "Marijuana Alert: Brain and Sex Damage," was a two-part piece that ran in the December 1979 issue. Cynthia Stone, director of the reprint department, wrote that "these articles made reprint history for the *Digest.* In the 43 years the *Digest* has offered reprints, no other article has sold so many copies in so short a time. Within eleven months, over three million copies were sold to individuals, schools, colleges, churches, courts, scout groups, PTAs, businesses, etc. Comments come in by the hundreds, and they all say essentially the same thing: We recognize the symptoms you talk about, and why haven't we been told of the harmful effects of marijuana before now?"

Also, in the spring of 1981, King Features Syndicate commissioned a five-part series on the health hazards of marijuana, which ran in major newspapers throughout the United States.

During those years, when a substantial amount of information on marijuana's health hazards began appearing in these mass-market publications as well as in such important television programs as "Epidemic!" and "The Chemical People," there was a 50 percent jump in the proportion of seniors perceiving regular marijuana use as involving great risk. This rose from 42 percent in 1979 to 54 percent in 1980, to 58 percent in 1981, to 60 percent in 1982, and 63 percent in 1983.

Again, the rise in perception of risk correlated with a decrease in daily use. In 1980, there was a drop of 1.2 percent; in 1981, a further drop of 2.1 percent. And, as noted, by 1983, the daily use figure was 5.5 percent—down by almost half since 1979. There was also a drop in those who had used the drug at all during the year, from 50.2 percent in 1978 down to 42 percent in 1983.

Said Dr. Patrick O'Malley, one of three researchers in the ongoing National High School Senior Survey: "We asked the kids who don't smoke pot, or who quit, why—and 67 percent said they were concerned about possible physical and psychological damage."

Dr. Jerald Bachman, another of the three researchers, put it this way: "Kids and their parents had begun to read reports in the media that let them know for the first time that marijuana was not at all the harmless drug they had believed it to be."

The clear fact is that *the single most essential ingredient in reducing marijuana use is knowledge on the part of youngsters and adults concerning the biological and psychological hazards involved.*

Therefore, let us now look at findings from marijuana researchers concerning the effects of the drug on the lungs; on sex and reproduction, and on the offspring of women who smoke pot during pregnancy; effects on the brain; on the immune system; and psychological effects. These subjects and more are dealt with in depth in Part Two: The Health Hazards.

PART TWO

THE HEALTH HAZARDS

Chapter 6

What Is Marijuana?

Before we look at what marijuana does, it is important to understand what marijuana is; for what it is—chemically—affects what it does, not only physically but also to a large degree psychologically as well.

Marijuana, sinsemilla, hashish, and hashish oil are all prepared from the plant *cannabis sativa* (*cannabis* for short). In other parts of the world cannabis has other names, often related to the form in which it is ingested or smoked. For example, *charas,* primarily from Kashmir and Afghanistan, is the resin from the flowering tops of cultivated female plants. *Ganja* in Jamaica and central India is often pressed into fat or round cakes, which are "cut" with tobacco and then smoked. *Bhang* comes from the older leaves of wild plants in some Indian provinces. Hashish is made by crushing and boiling leaves and stems in water to produce a water-insoluble resin that, when it cools, becomes a semi-solid mass, a piece of which can be broken off, chewed, mixed with food, or put in the bowl of a pipe and smoked. There's *kif* in northern Africa, *dagga* in South Africa, and so on. Hashish oil or hash oil is prepared by extracting the drug ingredients from the cannabis plant with organic solvents such as alcohol or petroleum products such as gasoline. The resultant oil looks like a dark, gooey syrup. Hash oil is the most potent of all cannabis products, often having a THC potency of 20 to 30 percent or more. Sometimes used to "juice up a joint," it is so powerful that the user can inject a few drops into a tobacco cigarette and walk around "looking legal" while getting stoned.

And there's marijuana, processed from the leaves and flowering tops of the cannabis plant. A U.N. treaty, the 1961 Single Convention on Narcotic Drugs, officially defines marijuana as "the flowering or fruiting tops of the cannabis plant (excluding the seeds and leaves not accompanied by the tops) from which the resin has not been extracted." (Resin comprises all the water-insoluble components.)

Incidentally, over 130 countries are parties to this treaty, including the United States and virtually every other developed country in the world. These nations are obligated to carry out the international treaty stipulations, one of which forbids any of the signees from legalizing cannabis. The treaty further states that "all parties are obligated to limit exclusively to medical and scientific purposes the production, manufacture, export, import, distribution of, trade in, use and possession of cannabis. . . . This does not apply to cultivation exclusively for industrial purposes, such as rope, but such parties must adopt such measures as may be necessary to prevent misuse of and any illicit traffic of the cannabis plant."

Cannabis is divided into three types, based on biological action. The fiber type is used primarily for the manufacture of hemp rope and paper. Some headshops display posters of a stoned-looking George Washington smoking a joint, with the message that old George, the father of our country, grew grass. Many colonists did. But it was the fiber type of cannabis, used for making rope, which has very low concentrations of mind-altering chemicals.

The second type of cannabis, intermediate, produces neither good fiber nor, in its unrefined state, potent pot. This type, which grows well in such countries as Lebanon, Morocco, Afghanistan, and Pakistan, is used to produce hashish.

Marijuana as we know it and its most potent version, sinsemilla, are processed from the third type of cannabis, the drug type. The mix of leaves, small stems, and flowering tops of the plant is dried; it is then usually rolled into a joint and smoked, although it may be boiled and served as tea, or cooked into foods such as brownies and eaten. (The mind-altering chemicals are activated by heat.)

There are 421 known chemicals in cannabis. The most important of these are a special group found only in the cannabis plant and the drugs made from it. They take their name from the family tree (or weed): the cannabinoids. The chief mind-altering cannabinoid is delta-9-tetrahydrocannabinol, which scientists often refer to as delta-9 and others call simply THC.

Since the early seventies, cannabis growers have responded to the demand for more and more potent pot by selectively harvesting the plant to increase the THC potency. For example, the very small leaves contain more potent chemicals than the larger ones, so growers often pick off the large leaves. Improved cultivation procedures have also enabled growers to get more bulk in the plants so that they produce more material.

However, few growers have been as dedicated as the illegal U.S. "agriculturalists" who produce sinsemilla. In the case of the drug-type cannabis, the female plant is more potent than the male, particularly when unfertilized. Therefore, these growers go to great lengths to keep their plants virginal. (*Sinsemilla* is Spanish for "seedless.") The male plants are harvested and removed before they can pollinate the females; often the female plants are covered so they will not be contaminated by any stray airborne male spores. Sinsemilla may have a potency of 8 to 10 percent THC or higher, as compared to the marijuana now smuggled in from Colombia, Jamaica, and so on, which averages 3 to 4 percent THC.

At one time the hashish used in the United States and Europe far outdistanced pot in potency, but now, thanks to the enthusiasm for the high-potency U.S.-grown products and to the increased THC potency in much of the "imported" pot, marijuana often outranks street hash in its mind-altering effects.

Mind-altering potencies differ widely in the various varieties of the drug. The cannabinoids are always present, but the level of each cannabinoid can vary from harvest to harvest in different areas of the world. Cannabis is an annual, herbaceous plant. Pot-smokers often refer to marijuana fondly as "a simple, natural weed," the implication being that anything simple and natural must be harmless. Some also refer to "God-grown marijuana plants," contrasting cannabis to "manmade liquor" and detailing the societal ills occasioned by alcohol to "prove" the safety and superiority of pot. They overlook the fact that many God-grown plants (such as the deadly poisonous hemlock) are far from harmless.

As for the "simple, natural weed" argument—yes, marijuana is natural; yes, it is a weed. But it is far from simple. Indeed, it is the most chemically complex of all commonly used illegal drugs. Most of the others are a single chemical. If they are cut or adulterated, one or two other chemicals may be added. But when "the weed" is smoked, its 421 chemicals are combusted into over 2,000. And when these 2,000 are metabolized, or broken down in the body, hundreds *more* chemicals are produced. For example, the single chemical delta-9-THC breaks down into over 35 known metabolites. It is impossible for researchers to decipher everything that *all* the chemicals in marijuana may be doing in and to the body. Since the effects are so complex, some researchers concentrate on just one cannabinoid rather than dealing with all the chemicals at once.

For a further insight into the problems faced by researchers: The 421 known chemicals come from 18 different chemical classes. For example, there are 50 different types of waxy hydrocarbons, which help make the tar in pot smoke. There are 103 different terpines, most of which, like the tars, are very irritating to the lungs. There are 12 fatty acids, 11 steroids, 20 nitrogen compounds. There are toxic agents, including carbon monoxide, ammonia, acetone, and benzene. There are also the cancer-inducing benzathracene and benzopyrene, which occur in pot smoke in amounts 50 to 100 percent greater than in tobacco smoke.

Does cannabis contain anything "healthy"?

Yes, vitamins.

How many? One. An infinitesimal amount of vitamin K (a vitamin normally made in the lower colon by intestinal bacteria and involved in blood clotting).

Of the 61 known cannabinoids, only 5 have been studied to any extent. What the other 56 or so may be doing in and to the body we do not yet know.

Of the 5 major cannabinoids, delta-9-tetrahydrocannabinol is the most *psychoactive,* or mind-altering. (The more scientific term is *psychotomimetic,* which means "mimicking psychosis.") A major metabolite of delta-9-THC is also potent in the mind-altering realm, and has therefore been studied as a bonafide cannabinoid; it has a name even longer than that of its progenitor— 11-hydroxy-delta-9-tetrahydrocannabinol. Also in the psychoactive class is the congener (close cousin) called delta-8-tetrahydrocannabinol, but "delta-8" is present in relatively small amounts, and apparently is sometimes not present at all. There are nine other known cannabinoids in the THC class, but to date these remain virtually unstudied. In this book, when the term THC is used, it will refer to the most famous of the cannabinoids: delta-9.

THC potency refers to the mind-altering potential of the individual sample of marijuana; 1 percent THC is sufficiently potent to induce a "high." (The percentage is reported by dry weight. For example, 2 percent THC means that there would be 2 pounds of pure delta-9-THC in 100 pounds of marijuana. A one-gram joint has twenty mg. THC.)

It should be noted that virtually all the marijuana research done in the United States since 1971 has used about 2 percent THC marijuana. By 1984, average street pot was 3 or 4 percent THC. Since most effects are dose and potency related, presumably most of the deleterious results shown by the studies would be even worse with pot of the potency used by Americans today.

Scientists who have studied several of the nonpsychoactive cannabinoids that are present in significant amounts—notably cannabinol (CBN) and cannabichromene (CBC)—have found that in some respects the nonpsychoactive cannabinoids are even more damaging to certain body systems than the psychoactive ones. As Dr. Carlton Turner put it:

> All cannabinoids have biological activity and can potentiate and/or antagonize [increase] the pharmacological actions of delta-9-THC or any other cannabinoid.
> By biologically active we mean that each cannabinoid will alter some normal function of a living organism. These alterations may not be visible since they occur at the cellular level, but they can be documented in research laboratories.
> As the ratios of cannabinoids in individual marijuana samples vary, so will the biological effects. In fact, it is impossible to produce two batches of cannabis that are identical, even though the delta-9-THC content may be the same. In order to understand marijuana and its effects on the health of our society, one must study systems of the body and understand that marijuana is a unique crude drug which acts at the cellular level. Biological effects are myriad. Indeed, cannabinoids and other components from marijuana smoke affect every system of the body. *There is no other drug used or abused by man that has the staying power and broad cellular actions on the body that cannabis does.* (Emphasis added.)

Psychoactive or not, all the cannabinoids studied thus far have one thing in common, and *this is their single most important factor.* It accounts for the subtle, pervasive, wide-ranging physical impairments caused by cannabis, and may account for psychological effects as well. This is the *fat-solubility* factor.

Alcohol, for example (like most other drugs), is water soluble. An ounce of ethyl alcohol (the amount in one shot-glass of whiskey, a 4-ounce glass of wine, or a twelve-ounce can of beer) is metabolized by the human body and—since our bodies have a water-based disposal system using blood and urine—it can be excreted within an hour or two.

The cannabinoids, however, are quite a different kettle of chemicals. Not only fat soluble, they are lipophilic: fat loving. When a joint is smoked, the cannabinoids enter the bloodstream via the tiny alveoli that line the lungs. Blood is, as the saying goes, thicker than water. Among the blood-thickeners are corpuscles and natural chemicals called *lipoproteins.* The fat-loving cannabinoids latch on to the fatty surfaces of corpuscles and bind to lipoproteins, both of which are carried throughout the body. But not *out* of the body—for there are far more attractive (fattier) spots to seep into: fatty organs such as the gonads (testes and ovaries) and the brain—which is one-third fat. (As one scientist put it, "We're all fatheads from that point of view.")

The body has three prime types of fat depots attractive to the cannabinoids:

- the aforementioned fatty organs, including the adrenals, the liver, and other major organs, which act as fat-storage depots;
- the protective cushions of fat that surround many major organs, such as the heart and kidneys;
- the surface and internal membranes of every cell in the body; these contain several types of fat, such as phospholipids and cholesterol.

The fat-loving cannabinoids not only seek out and seep into these fat depots, but they "hang out" there. Only very slowly do they leak back into the bloodstream, to be metabolized by the liver and broken down sufficiently so they can finally leave the body, primarily in the feces but also via urine. During their emergence and excretion they exert new actions on body functions.

Radioactive marking tests have traced the course of cannabinoids in the body. According to the most comprehensive comparative study ever done on the subject, a person who has been smoking marijuana regularly for six to twelve months will usually show cannabis in his or her urine for three to four weeks after all pot smoking has been stopped. This 1982 study headed by Dr. Charles Dackis was done in a hospital setting, under conditions of extremely well supervised abstinence. Dr. Dackis points out, "Even if you smoke only one joint every three weeks or so, the cannabinoids can collect in the body. The pot-smoker may come down from his "high" a half hour to an hour after smoking a joint. But the chronic user is never drug-free." One researcher put it this way: "When the high is gone, the pot is not."

Another substance once commonly used by humans has a fat-solubility factor commensurate with that of the cannabinoids: DDT. Despite its usefulness, DDT was banned because it collects in the body—even though it has a relatively low order of toxicity for man. Marijuana, of course, is an intoxicant. Putting the accent on *toxic* gives some idea of what the fat-soluble cannabinoids are up to as they collect, for example, in the brain, in the reproductive organs, and in the cells of the immune system. (The damage that marijuana does to lungs is in part related to the fat-solubility factor, but more importantly to the broad spectrum of chemicals in the combusted "weed," and to the so-called "particulate matter.")

The marijuana used by almost all the "pot researchers" in the United States, most of the researchers in Canada, and many in other countries comes from the same five-and-a-half acres. This is the U.S. government's "pot plantation" on the outskirts of the University of Mississippi.

The "pot plantation" is part of the Marijuana Research Project at RIPS—the Research Institute of Pharmaceutical Sciences—at the university, funded by the National Institute on Drug Abuse (NIDA). Supplying "NIDA marijuana" to the scientists is just one of the important marijuana programs conducted at RIPS, "the marijuana research capital of the world." Dr. Carlton Turner was director of the multifaceted program for a decade, until he became senior policy advisor to the president on drug abuse policy in July 1981, and director of the Drug Abuse Policy Office in the White House in June 1982.

Until 1971, when "standardized NIDA marijuana" was made available to scientists, many researchers used street pot of unknown potency for their studies. In 1971, when street pot was officially analyzed for the first time at RIPS, THC potency averaged a low one-half of one percent. This is one reason that some research studies done in the late sixties and early seventies gave marijuana fairly good grades as an illicit drug. Little wonder that pot aficionados quote the early studies to back up their claims that marijuana barely rates as a drug at all; that it is, instead, a mere "recreational pastime." In the early days of marijuana research, scientists had not yet developed the special techniques required for study of this very complex drug. Despite all this, it is apparent in many of the early studies that even the mildest of marijuanas—the .5-percent varieties—did yield, at the least, distinct warning signals and, in some cases, conclusive evidence of danger.

The pot plantation in Mississippi has grown some 228 different varieties of cannabis, using seeds from sixty-one countries. Each section of the five-and-a-half acres has a small wooden sign, which notes each plant group's family history. For example, a stand of fifteen-foot-high plants is labeled "ME-A/5 C-79," which means that these are fifth-generation Mexican plants from the original seed, the offspring of seeds from the fourth generation produced on campus in the year 1979. (The pot plantation *is* geographically considered on campus, since the land is owned by the University of Mississippi, but it is definitely off limits. It is surrounded by a ten-foot-high cyclone fence, topped with barbed wire. There are three wooden watchtowers, manned by armed guards. At night it is ablaze with spotlights. And in case anyone should claim to have entered the area accidentally, road signs proclaim in large capital letters: ALL UNAUTHORIZED PERSONS IN THIS AREA WILL BE ARRESTED AND PROSECUTED.)

Most of the marijuana prepared for the researchers is of the Mexican variety, for the experts at RIPS have had most experience with this type. The TLC (Tender Loving Care) accorded the THC outdoes even the pampering accorded the illegal "homegrown" varieties by the most profit-oriented U.S. growers.

The extreme care is necessary because the cannabinoids are jumpy, jittery, and keep changing in strength. They not only change while they're in the growing weed, but they vary in strength in different types of plant (male or female), and in different parts of the same plant. Cannabinoids also vary according to the age of the plant, the length of time it has been stored, where it's stored, and the storage temperature. All of which means that the pot-smoker who dreams of being able to go down to the grocery store and slip some coins into the marijuana machine for a pack of "Acapulco Gold" or "Maui Wowie" neatly labeled as to THC content is indulging in a fantasy. Those who favor legalizing marijuana often believe that legal pot would mean standardized brands—just as tobacco cigarettes are standardized, with each cigarette in each package exactly the same size and chemical content—including the same THC content. Even the most ardent pot advocate is likely to agree that there would have to be a legal limit on THC potency, if legalization of marijuana were ever to come to pass.

However, the bald fact is that marijuana—unlike tobacco cigarettes—could never be standardized for mass distribution. The cannabinoids are too ever-changing to be harnessed into specified standards. As Dr. Turner puts it:

> Just as no two individuals have the same fingerprints, no two samples of crude marijuana, drawn from different batches, will have the same chemical composition. They are, therefore, two different drugs. The differential factor is so critical that marijuana obtained from a single cannabis plant at 8 A.M. will be different from marijuana obtained from that plant at 10 A.M. and so forth. And this differential remains true even if the delta-9-THC content remains the same from batch to batch, because other cannabinoids (and there are 60 others) will not be present in the same concentrations. Many cannabinoids, such as CBD, CBC, and CBN, alter the effects of delta-9-THC, and some (delta-8-THC, delta-9-THCV and CBN) even have mind-altering properties of their own.

Turner further points out that many other factors affecting biochemical potency could not be standardized; these include, for example, the plant's moisture content and pH (acidity), and the soil in which it was grown.

There are many non-pot-smokers who favor legalizing marijuana for the perfectly sound-sounding reason that "then we could tax it, and use the money for drug education and so forth"—money that otherwise goes to pushers, drug traffickers, criminals. Furthermore, as they see it, the drug sold would then be pure, clean, a "reliable product."

However, the characteristics of cannabis almost ensure that even if pot were legalized, there would always be illegal marijuana—because of the development of *tolerance*.

After a while, the chronic user becomes tolerant to the effects of the drug. For example, a joint of 2 percent THC potency may no longer produce a high. The user must therefore smoke more and/or more potent joints. Tolerance accounts for the fact that illegal growers continually aim to produce an ever more potent product. (The more potent, the higher price they can charge.) Consequently, even if the THC potency of "legal pot" *could* be standardized at, say, 2 percent (which itself is nearly impossible), many chronic users would eventually search out the illegal, more potent product. Since the aim is to get high, there would be no reason to pay for a product that "did nothing" for them.

The main reason, however, for not legalizing marijuana lies not in what the drug does *for* the user, but in what it does *to* the user—which will be examined in subsequent chapters.

If marijuana is so variable, how can "NIDA marijuana" grown for the researchers be standardized? The answer is that at RIPS and at the Research Triangle Institute in North Carolina, where the "government grass" is processed into "NIDA joints," a great deal of money, time, manpower, and special machinery is used to assure that researchers can be provided with material carefully labeled as to THC potency, as well as to amounts of three or four—sometimes up to ten—other cannabinoids. And, yes, a standardized joint can be produced for the scientist. But "cost of production" leads to a high price for each marijuana cigarette.

Furthermore, when scientists receive the marijuana, or the individual cannabinoids with which some prefer to work in order to differentiate individual biological activities, the product must be stored in a freezer; otherwise the cannabinoids will eventually decompose into other compounds.

Since the THC potency of the NIDA joints is usually 2 percent, and since average street pot is more potent than this, one might ask why the NIDA marijuana does not match what is actually being used by millions of Americans. The answer will be made obvious in the subsequent chapters on the damage done by 2 percent THC. Human males are used in many of the studies, and the government could not take responsibility for what might happen to a subject given a THC dose higher than 2 percent, since most of the animal and human studies show that the impairing results are dose related. (This refers both to the number of joints smoked and to the potency of those joints. The higher the potency, the worse the effects.)

Bear in mind, too, as Dr. Turner has pointed out, that "the long-term effects of marijuana cannot be assessed by any study using a short-term research protocol (such as the 90-day protocol often employed in marijuana research)." The long-term user may get some idea from a short-term study of what may be happening to his or her lungs, reproductive system, immune system, brain cells, and so on. But the cumulative effects of cannabinoids continuously consumed and stored in body cells and vital organs for years might not show up after only a three-month study.

Another important function of RIPS is to keep tabs on the potency of street pot. It has the best equipment available for separating the chemicals in marijuana. One machine used for isolating cannabinoids is the same type as that sent to Mars to test the soil for evidence of life.

RIPS also has a network of "reporters" throughout the United States who send in samples of street pot, sinsemilla, hashish, and hash oil. This network includes doctors, school guidance counselors, and professionals at drug-abuse treatment centers, as well as DEA (Drug Enforcement Administration) agents and police who send in confiscated samples. All samples are analyzed in the RIPS lab, and an average is taken for each variety of the product.

Much original research is done at RIPS on substances ranging from poison ivy to heroin, but most of its effort is devoted to marijuana. During the decade in which he was director of the multifaceted program at RIPS, Dr. Carlton Turner and his associates published over a hundred scientific papers on cannabis—probably more than any other research group in the world.

RIPS also has the world's largest collection of published scientific papers on cannabis, over seventy-five hundred published in professional journals around the world from 1965 to the present. Most are written in English; by researchers in the U.S., Canada, England, Israel, Scandinavia, India, and Holland, but RIPS also receives papers written in French, Spanish, Swedish, Japanese, and so on, which are then translated into English.

Before he left RIPS in 1981 for his position at the White House, Dr. Turner had read virtually all of these research papers; he and his associates summarized over fifty-seven hundred of them for their definitive two-volume work, *Marijuana: An Annotated Bibliography*. (One of the co-editors was Dr. Coy Waller, who founded the marijuana research center at RIPS in 1968.) The 560 pages of Volume One contain summaries of 3,045 papers on cannabis from international scientific journals published from 1964 through 1974; the 620 pages of Volume Two contain summaries of 2,699 papers published from 1975 to 1979. Over 100 more have been published since 1980 and they too are in the RIPS computerized collection. And as Turner points out, "I have never read a scientific publication that exonerates cannabis from [causing] some health effects."

A staggering amount of research has been done proving that cannabis is harmful in a wide spectrum of ways, with impairing effects on the lungs, the heart, the sex organs, the reproductive system, the brain, the immune system, as well as on the babies born to animals and humans exposed to pot smoke or THC. Studies show that the damage done by this drug reaches from the molecular matter that is the cornerstone of life to the highest levels of human life—the mind and the personality.

Chapter 7

Effects on the Lungs
and the Heart

Aside from those who prefer to ingest their pot via brownies or other edibles, or to boil it in their tea—a distinct minority—most, of course, get their high through smoke. Since the lungs are usually the first port of entry into the body, it is here that the drug is most concentrated. The lungs also offer the smoke easy access to the blood; thus the cardiovascular system is the next "target system" to be affected. We will therefore look at these two systems first.

Dr. Robert Petersen, former editor of NIDA's *Marijuana and Health Reports,* had this to say about marijuana and the lungs:

> We're talking about unfiltered material that's inhaled as deeply as possible, held in as long as possible, and smoked to the dregs. We must never forget it took half a century before we could firmly document the frightening link between cigarette smoking and lung cancer, and other diseases. Marijuana has been used by substantial numbers of Americans for little more than a decade. However, since most of the ingredients in tobacco cigarettes and joints are so similar, it would be prudent, to say the least, to look at the relationship between the two.

Let us then "be prudent" and begin our look at marijuana's effects on the lungs by comparing the constituents in the joint to those in the tobacco cigarette.

All comparative studies done in this area show that, aside from the fact that tobacco contains nicotine and marijuana contains cannabinoids, the two types of smoke have in common many of the same compounds that four decades of tobacco research have shown to cause most of the deleterious effects. (Incidentally, nicotine—though it has important and destructive pharmacologic effects—probably, in itself, leads to little irritation of the respiratory tract, because of its rapid transfer to the blood. On the other hand, some of the cannabinoids *are* respiratory irritants, because of the time they remain in lung tissue.)

The first comparative study was started in 1971. Its findings are especially interesting, for it gave tobacco four "head starts" on pot. It was done by Dr. Dietrich Hoffman of the American Health Foundation in Valhalla, New York.

Today, 90 percent of tobacco cigarettes are filtered, but back in the early seventies, many people were still smoking unfiltered high-tar cigarettes, so that is what Dr. Hoffman used for his study. Since NIDA marijuana was not yet available when Hoffman began his study, the National Cancer Institute supplied him with a blend of confiscated street pot—analyzed to be certain that nothing but marijuana was in the sample. As noted, marijuana today is five- to twenty-fold more THC-potent than it was in 1971. Hoffman's joints averaged only .6 percent THC—thus giving the unfiltered tobacco cigarette its first head start in the comparative study over the marijuana being smoked today.

A corps of medical students went out to observe hundreds of thousands of tobacco-smokers in the United States and Canada, in order to ascertain the length of the "average puff." It was put at two seconds. Although the average pot-smoker draws the smoke deeper into his lungs and holds it in longer than the tobacco-smoker, in order to make the study statistically comparative, the researchers tested the joints on the same elaborate smoking machine set at standard two-second puffs—giving tobacco a second head start over pot.

Also, both types of cigarette were of the same length, both used the same type and amounts of paper, and both were "professionally rolled." "But," Dr. Hoffman pointed out, "hand-rolled joints are often fatter and heavier than tobacco cigarettes, and therefore produce a greater quantity of harmful constituents in the smoke." Thus, the tobacco cigarettes had three "advantages" over the joints.

A fourth "advantage" was this: Most tobacco-smokers stub out their cigarettes without smoking the final half-inch—for it is in the butt that all the most harmful elements are concentrated. On the other hand, the pot-smoker regards this stub—or "roach" (short for "cockroach")—as the best part of the joint. He or she often uses a "roach clip" to hold the stub so the concentration of cannabinoids can be inhaled without burning the fingers. It is, of course, in the roach that the potential toxic and cancer-causing chemicals are collected in their most concentrated form. Pot pipes also enable the user to smoke every last shred of "the weed" with no wasted butt.

When reviewing the results of Hoffman's 1971 study, it is important to bear this in mind: In the *amount* of each cigarette smoked, as well as in length of puff and cigarette weight, the joint was treated exactly like the tobacco cigarette—even though in "real-life smoking" these three factors are all more harmful in joint-smoking. Also, Hoffman used far weaker pot and far stronger tobacco than is used today.

Despite all that, the study showed that "the amounts of ammonia, hydrogen, cyanide, acrolein, acetonitrile, benzene and toluene, and the volatile carcinogenic N-nitrosamines dimethyl and methylethyl are not significantly different between the two types of smoke." Furthermore, the study found "significantly higher amounts of PAH in marijuana smoke." (PAH—polynuclear aromatic hydrocarbons—is the generic term used to describe a group of compounds isolated from coal tars and other combustion products, many of which have been proven carcinogenic.) Specifically, the study found "significantly higher amounts of . . . the weak carcinogen, benzanthracene, and the strong carcinogen, benzopyrene, in the marijuana smoke."

Part of the study involved painting tar condensate from both types of smoke onto the shaved backs of mice. "Mouse back" cells are remarkably similar to human lung cells; they are both squamous epithelial cells. Two hundred mice were given this "treatment" three times a week for eighteen months (about two-thirds the lifetime of a mouse). Both the tobacco-tar mice and the pot-tar mice developed skin tumors, beginning after seventeen weeks of application.

A further pulmonary concern has surfaced since Hoffman did his landmark study. An entire branch of the billion-dollar drug-paraphernalia industry now aids the pot-smoker in his or her aim of inhaling as deeply as possible and losing none of the precious smoke. Bongs (water pipes) in all shapes and sizes are the chief staple of this industry. In many college dorms today, bongs are displayed openly on bookshelves or tabletops, an accepted part of the collegian's accoutrements. Pot-smokers use them in the belief that drawing the smoke through water or ice lessens the harshness. The bong, however, concentrates all the smoke inside a chamber so none is diffused into the air. One bong manufacturer advertises: "The only thing wasted is you." Electric bongs are bestsellers—including pot pipes that plug into the cigarette lighter of your car. An ad exhorts: "Hit the high road!"

Also popular are "power hitters"—designed to blast marijuana smoke into the delicate alveoli in the deepest recesses of the lungs. Some power hitters are designed for their kiddie appeal—red plastic "space guns," for example. One brand advertises "a big hit for tiny hands" (a "hit" is a deep drag of pot smoke). There are also expensive "isomerization machines," which, the ads claim, are "guaranteed to increase the potency of marijuana up to 800 percent!" Such items, still legal in some states, obviously increase the harmful effects of the marijuana cigarette manyfold.

In addition, as noted, the typical cigarette-smoker inhales for a mere two-second puff, while the typical pot-smoker aims to hold the smoke in as long and as deeply as possible so the THC-laden particles can be deposited on the walls of the many thousands of smaller air passages and millions of tiny fragile air sacs adjacent to the capillaries—where the THC is then absorbed into the blood. Indeed, some pot-smokers do such a thorough job of inhaling that virtually no smoke can be seen when they exhale.

Writing in the British medical journal *The Lancet,* Dr. Robert Petersen points out the importance of considering inhalation patterns:

> It is generally conceded that the much more serious health consequences of cigarette versus pipe and cigar smoking are the result of the difference in inhalation which typically accompanies these varying modes of tobacco use. If variation of inhalation patterns is of similar importance with respect to cannabis use—a not unreasonable assumption—health implications, especially for the lung, would also be expected to vary with inhalation. One characteristic of the newer American and European use of marijuana and hashish is the habit of deep inhalation.

Dr. Forest S. Tennant, Jr., a pioneer pot researcher, notes in this regard: "Traditional users of cannabis in Jamaica, Greece, and Costa Rica, do not inhale cannabis smoke as deeply and retain it in their lungs as do American users."

One obvious difference between marijuana and tobacco use is that the tobacco-smoker tends to smoke more per day than the pot-smoker, but the difference in inhalation patterns may often make up for this. Instead of the two-second puff typical of cigarette-smokers, most pot-smokers, according to Hoffman, keep the smoke in their lungs from ten seconds to a minute, which can be equivalent to smoking increased numbers of cigarettes. Furthermore, the National High School Senior Surveys show that 14 percent of daily pot-smokers use seven or more joints a day. It may be, therefore, that the lungs of some pot-smokers are exposed to as much smoke as those of a regular cigarette-smoker.

Gerri Silverman, PTA Drug Awareness Chairman of Milburn/Short Hills, New Jersey, has a handy way of summing up the comparative health hazards of cigarette- and pot-smoking. She asks one of the students to hold high in the air a 4½-pound, 2¾-inch-thick paperbound volume—*Smoking and Health: A Report of the Surgeon General* (1979). She tells her class:

> This twelve-hundred-page book has summaries of over thirty thousand scientific papers on all the ways cigarette smoking can harm you. Marijuana and tobacco smoke both have many of the same harmful ingredients—except pot also has THC, which does other kinds of damage. Now what does this tell you about *marijuana* and health?

As the then–Surgeon General, Dr. Julius B. Richmond, said in that report:

> From the total body of experimental evidence accumulated to date, it appears that daily use of marijuana leads to damage similar to that from heavy cigarette smoking. Although, thus far, there is no direct evidence that smoking marijuana is correlated with lung cancer, it must be remembered that it takes a lung cancer twenty to thirty years to grow. Therefore, there is very good reason for concern about the possibility of pulmonary cancer resulting from extended use of marijuana over ten or twenty years.

Dr. Stephen Szara, chief of the biomedical branch of the National Institute on Drug Abuse, has been involved in almost all the marijuana clinical studies (on human beings) NIDA has funded. (NIDA funds the vast majority of the marijuana studies done in the United States.) Dr. Szara noted:

> Our basic marijuana studies have been modeled after tobacco studies. However, the *key* papers that were involved in the surgeon general's decision to label cigarette packages "dangerous to health" were long-term epidemiological studies involving several thousand subjects—how many smokers died, compared to deaths in matched control groups. This kind of evidence is not yet available for today's marijuana smokers. But from the evidence we already have, we can say the following: Tobacco smoking has been irrefutably proved to aggravate virtually every existing health problem, as well as harming the healthy person. *It is, furthermore, the largest preventable cause of death in America. We have no reason whatever to believe that marijuana smoking is any less harmful.*

According to the two-volume *Marijuana: An Annotated Bibliography,* over a hundred research studies have directly examined marijuana's effects on the lungs. As Dr. Carlton Turner points out, "Obviously, no single paper can give a complete picture. Only by critical review and analysis of *all* these papers can the effects of marijuana on the lungs be understood, at least as far as present scientific knowledge allows." Yet the lung studies described in this chapter should give ample evidence of what marijuana is doing to the lungs of the user, from the weekend smoker to the daily "toker." There is also striking evidence of subclinical effects, pot-caused lung impairment that does not "show"—yet, but that is clearly evident when the user is examined via sophisticated laboratory equipment.

Marijuana smoke affects the entire pulmonary "tree," from the sinus cavities around the nose down to the deepest recesses of the lung. We will examine studies done on human cells in the test tube, studies done on animals, studies done on humans, and two large survey-studies done in India, where cannabis has been used among low-income males for centuries.

Research on any human health problem usually starts in the test tube. It progresses to the use of laboratory animals as experimental models, and then advances to human subjects. However, some types of research are better done in test tubes and on animals than on humans. For example, animals are used for studies exploring the effects of marijuana smoke on the deepest recesses of the lungs. An autopsy of a human known to be a heavy pot-smoker might show lung damage, but this might also be accounted for by cigarette smoking, pneumonia, and so on. Animal research is "pure" in that the treated subjects and the controls differ in only one factor: that which the experimenters induce. Furthermore, animals can be "sacrificed"—as scientists so delicately put it—in numbers that allow significant analysis and assessment.

Cell and Animal Studies

Let us look first at the marijuana lung-cell studies done *in vitro* (in the test tube) by Dr. Cecile Leuchtenberger (who had over thirty years' experience in cancer research and headed the department of cytochemistry at the Swiss Institute for Experimental Cancer Research in Lausanne), and her husband, Dr. Rudolf Leuchtenberger, an experimental pathologist. They exposed over five thousand human adult and fetal lung-cell cultures to comparable quantities of tobacco smoke and marijuana smoke. Result: "Fresh smoke from marijuana cigarettes is harmful to lung cells in that it contributes to the development of pre-malignant and malignant lesions. The smoke from the tobacco cigarettes had much less effect." Cecile Leuchtenberger pointed out, "We did not see actual cancer, but we used relatively short-term inhalation and short-term exposure." In longer-exposure studies involving hamster lung cultures—which survive for up to two years, as opposed to human lung cells, which survive less than six months—exposure to either tobacco or marijuana smoke led to the accelerated development of malignancy within three to six months of exposure. Marijuana smoke was more effective than tobacco in producing these changes.

Now let's move up the scale—to rats.

Dr. Harris Rosenkrantz, director of biochemical pharmacology of the EG&G Mason Research Institute in Worcester, Massachusetts, is one of the pot-research pioneers; he has published over fifty significant papers on marijuana. He works chiefly with rodents, and he has also worked out a formula for "human equivalency doses" of pot smoke for laboratory animals.

Rosenkrantz became interested in marijuana research in 1971. But when reviewing the studies done up to that time, he noted tremendous differences in results from the same type of study. Scientists criticized each other's work, partly because no one knew how much marijuana smoke animals or humans were being exposed to, or how potent that smoke was. Furthermore, no one knew how the amount of smoke given to animals was related to the amount people were smoking. Rosenkrantz decided there was no use doing *any* animal work in the marijuana area *unless the work was relevant to what humans were smoking.*

"It was like fitting together the pieces in a jigsaw puzzle," he recalls. "First I had to get the pieces. One was: How much *are* humans smoking?" After reading papers and surveys and interviewing people, he decided to tie his figures to the human equivalent of one joint a day—at 2 percent THC.

Rosenkrantz had to determine the rate at which each species of laboratory animal absorbed THC according to the way the drug was administered— by smoke inhalation, intravenously or by other routes of injection with emulsifiers, or orally in solubilizers. He found that oral doses of THC have about one-third as much effect on the body as THC in smoked marijuana. Injected THC is about twice as active as oral THC, but THC given intravenously is as active as that in smoked marijuana. Injection and the intravenous route give direct access to blood. Smoked marijuana would presumably have far more harmful effects on the lungs than administration by any other route.

Other pieces of the puzzle included the body weight of the animal compared to the body weight of the human, and the body surface area of the animal compared to the human's. Still another was the inhalation pattern (how many puffs and how deeply inhaled over a period of time, lung volume, and respiration rate).

Finally the pieces of the puzzle were fitted together and the scientist "activated" his formula: Three "NIDA joints" of 2-percent THC were put into a smoking apparatus and lit. Rosenkrantz pressed a button that automatically began a standardized smoking-pattern sequence: The joints were puffed (air was forced through the cigarettes) for two seconds; the pot smoke entered a "smoking chamber" about one-third of a quart in volume. Eight to ten rats were placed head first—exposing mouth and nose only—into this chamber and, for thirty seconds, the rats inhaled the pot smoke. Then the pot smoke was forced out of the chamber by a thirty-second burst of fresh air. This process was repeated four times. This, said Rosenkrantz, was the equivalent of a human adult smoking one entire joint at 2 percent THC. Increasing the number of puffing cycles could simulate a human's smoking three to six joints. But a rat was never exposed to more than sixteen puffs at a time, so there would be no adverse effects from the carbon monoxide that is generated during combustion. If an experiment called for a larger dose, there would be a three-hour wait before the next "puffing session."

Once Rosenkrantz had worked out his careful formula for rats, he used the same formula to devise "human equivalency ratios" for other laboratory animals—rabbits, hamsters, mice, monkeys, and so on.

"The next step," said Rosenkrantz, "was to test the accuracy of the formula. We tried to do this by seeing how long it took a mouse or a rabbit or a rat to *act* stoned." The formula seemed to work, but he could not really be *sure* until one day in 1975, when he learned from NIDA that a British researcher, Dr. Richard Marks, and another researcher, Dr. Stanley Gross of UCLA, had each worked out a different method for determining exactly how much THC was in the blood of a human. Now Rosenkrantz's formulas could be double-checked for accuracy; if their methods worked on animal blood, and if the ratio of THC in an animal's blood to treatment dose was the same as the ratio of THC in a human's blood to treatment dose, the formula would hold up.

Rosenkrantz immediately sent frozen blood samples of his pot-exposed rats to both researchers, along with his dose formulas. And the formulas checked out almost exactly. In 1976, Rosenkrantz's human equivalency pot formulas were published in the proceedings of the International Marijuana Conference held in Helsinki, Finland, and they have been used ever since by scientists doing marijuana research on animals.

In one of his most significant rat-lung studies, Dr. Rosenkrantz exposed the rodents to varying amounts of pot smoke to equal the human-equivalency dose of one to six joints a day. Then they were sacrificed in groups, at various stages, ranging from two months to a year. The rats autopsied after two months showed no lung damage. But after three months, rather startling changes began to show up, including extensive lung inflammation and blockage of the deepest air passageways with tissue debris; the damage grew more serious as the smoke exposure went on. "This," said Rosenkrantz, "is a serious condition, which can lead to complete lung failure. Not only in the rat, but in the human being."

The scientist and his co-workers also found potentially pre-cancerous lesions in the lung tissue of the rats. Furthermore, the normal arrangement of lung cells was in marked disarray. Said Rosenkrantz,

> These cells cannot function. They die. And they become part of the debris clogging up the tiny alveolar sacs in the small airways. The more clogging there is, the more trouble oxygen has getting from the lungs into the bloodstream. Also, carbon dioxide, the main toxic waste product, has trouble getting out. Of course, what we're talking about here, in rats or in man, is interference with the most fundamental process of life—breathing!

To test the reversibility of the symptoms, the smoke exposure of all the rats was stopped after twelve months, then half the group was sacrificed and their lung tissue examined. The rest went without pot smoke for another thirty days. Then they were sacrificed and *their* lung tissue was studied.

Result: There was virtually no difference between the lung tissue of the two groups. Said Rosenkrantz: "Even after one month of no smoke exposure, the lungs were still in terrible condition. One month in a rat's life is about two years in a human life."

In another study, Rosenkrantz exposed rats to puffs of standardized marijuana *or* tobacco smoke. He found that lungs were damaged by the pot smoke faster and more severely than by the same amount of tobacco smoke.

Another Rosenkrantz study concerned the lung's immune system. When lung tissue is irritated by foreign matter, cells called *macrophages* mobilize to attack the invader. Macrophages are the most important cells in the lung's defense against infection and injury by toxic substances. They fight by devouring the enemy. Said Rosenkrantz:

> When we see lung tissue dark with an army of macrophages, we know that signals have gone out. Something is very wrong. In our macrophage study, after 180 days—six to ten years of daily smoking in a human life—some of the small airway passages were blocked solid with macrophages.

Our control rats were handled in the same way as the "pot rats"—except they were not exposed to pot smoke. When we looked at slices of their lungs under the microscope, we saw the normal number of macrophages; just a few clumps of them "standing guard." But when we looked at lung tissue from the same area of the pot-exposed rats, we found so many macrophages that it was impossible to count them. They had clumped together in groups. An average of fifty clumps instead of the normal two to twelve macrophage clumps. The number of clumps increased as the marijuana dose increased.

Furthermore, pot produced a very "laid back" army. The macrophages couldn't fight back efficiently as they normally would have done, if the invader was bacteria or some other so-to-speak usual foreign substance. In fact, some of the small airways were blocked so solid with macrophage clumps that this part of the "army" couldn't fight back at all. They were immobilized.

Other researchers using Rosenkrantz's human equivalency formulas came up with more sobering pot-pulmonary findings. In February 1980, Dr. Gary Huber, then director of Harvard University's Smoking and Health Research Program, published a rat study that showed that marijuana activates—by some 200 percent—enzymes that potentially contribute to the "eating" or digesting of the lung itself.

And in the spring of 1980, Dr. Freddy Homburger, director of the Bio-Research Institute in Cambridge, Massachusetts, who has published numerous scientific papers on tobacco smoke inhalation in animals, completed an inhalation study in which he and his associate, Dr. Peter Bernfeld, exposed one group of hamsters to tobacco smoke and another group to marijuana smoke. Said Homburger:

Though we know the human pot smoker holds the smoke in the lungs deeper and longer, we nevertheless used the tobacco inhalation pattern for both sets of subjects. They both got 28 seconds of smoke exposure, followed by 33 seconds of fresh air. Neither set liked the smoke. They fought it, tried to escape, held their breath—until they had to breathe. The tobacco-smoked hamsters continued to fight. But the pot-smoked hamsters soon got stoned.

The smoking was kept up for a few hours—until the animals died. The hamsters exposed to marijuana smoke *died in half the time* it took to kill the hamsters exposed to cigarette smoke. Dr. Homburger noted, "Presumably, if the marijuana deep-inhalation pattern had been used instead, the results would be even more dramatic."

Over seventy-five lung studies have been done, exposing mice, rats, hamsters, rabbits, monkeys, even mongrel dogs to pot smoke or pure THC, many using human equivalency doses. For example, one researcher working with mongrel dogs exposed some to pot smoke, some to tobacco smoke for thirty months. Both types of smoke produced inflammation of the smaller airways and the squamous epithelium cells in the trachea, but the pot smoke produced more marked changes.

The various animal studies have looked at different functions and different sections of the pulmonary tree—from the cavities behind the nose and mouth down to the deepest and most fragile air sacs in the lung itself. Not only did each study show pot smoke to be damaging to the animal lung, but in most of the studies it produced changes similar to the type of lung damage we see in man.

Studies on Humans

Many pot-smokers say, "I've been smoking dope every day for a year (or two . . . or three). It hasn't hurt me one bit. I feel great!"

That may well have been the thought of the 102 healthy young men who were selected as subjects in Dr. Donald P. Tashkin's studies on the subclinical pulmonary effects of pot smoking. (Subclinical effects do not show up in routine physical examinations.) Dr. Tashkin is director of the Pulmonary Function Laboratory at UCLA Hospital and, since 1969, he has been a member of the faculty of the department of medicine in the division of pulmonary medicine at UCLA.

In 1976 Tashkin did his first study on young male pot-smokers who not only said they were perfectly healthy, but had to pass a series of medical tests to prove it. Furthermore, each had to fill out a thirteen-page questionnaire, which gave Dr. Tashkin information on where they were born, what jobs they had held, whether or not they smoked tobacco cigarettes or "did" drugs besides pot, and so forth. Those who had grown up in a smoggy locale or who had ever worked in an environment that might have affected their lung function were eliminated. The scientist wanted no other variables that might have affected the pulmonary functioning of his pot-smoking subjects.

Tashkin finally selected twenty-eight men who had smoked at least four joints a week for the past six months. They were all in splendid health and did not use other drugs; twenty-four of them had either never smoked tobacco cigarettes or had not smoked them within the past six months.

The men were confined to a hospital ward, and for eleven days were given no marijuana. This was a "washout period," to get rid of collected cannabinoids in the pulmonary system. Then they were given all the NIDA marijuana they wanted. They averaged five joints a day, for forty-seven to fifty-nine days. Sophisticated lung-function tests were made at frequent intervals.

Results: All the subjects had "significant lung function impairment in several areas. These impairments were similar to those found by other researchers studying people who had smoked tobacco moderately to heavily for many years." Some of the symptoms, such as "decrease of mid-expiratory flow rate" and "impairment of airway conductance," were decidedly dose related; they had grown progressively worse as smoking days increased.

The twenty-eight young men were stunned when they were shown the results of the tests, for all of them had felt just as healthy after the "smoke-in" as they had before they became research subjects.

The study went on for another potless month. All symptoms disappeared in a week to a month—proof positive that these subclinical symptoms had been caused by marijuana and nothing else.

Tashkin pointed out to the twenty-eight young men that if they kept on smoking, one day the symptoms *would* show. He later wrote: "These changes suggest a potential for the development of chronic bronchitis and pulmonary emphysema in chronic heavy marijuana smokers." (Emphysema can be a progressive lung disease leading to death. The person may feel fine in the early stages; later stages have been described as "drowning for air.")

Then Tashkin and a co-researcher, Barry Calvarese, did a larger study, this time using "controls." Their subjects were seventy-four healthy young pot-smokers selected by the same strict criteria as for the earlier study— except that this time all the subjects had smoked an average of 2.2 joints a day for an average of five years. None had any symptoms that "showed" (e.g., a "pot cough") or that would be revealed in traditional medical examinations.

Then, with the aid of a computer that "searched" some twelve thousand people in the Los Angeles area, each of the seventy-four subjects was matched with a young man of the same age, weight, height, tobacco-smoking history, general good health, and so on.

All subjects and controls answered a detailed questionnaire with questions related to cough, phlegm production, shortness of breath, and other respiratory symptoms. There was no difference between the responses of the subjects and the controls.

115

All the young men, subjects and controls, were given a series of tests using highly sophisticated equipment able to detect lung impairments that would not show up in a standard physical checkup. For example, one machine, called the Body Plethysmograph, measured airflow resistance (the relative ease or difficulty of moving air in or out of the lungs). The subject or control stepped into a glass booth, put a clip on his nose and a rubber mouthpiece in his mouth, and panted for a few seconds; stopped; then panted again. The hose leading from the mouthpiece was attached to pressure sensors, which passed into an electronic recorder. Electronic readings appeared on a TV screen. The camera photographed the readings, and they were recorded on a roll of paper. This turned the term "airflow resistance" into a visually measurable reality.

A separate control group consisted of fifty young men who did not smoke pot, but who *had* smoked sixteen or more tobacco cigarettes a day for over four years. The pot-smokers who did not smoke tobacco had significantly more airflow resistance than the controls who smoked only tobacco. Tashkin put it this way: "Smoking one joint a day causes significantly more airflow resistance than smoking sixteen tobacco cigarettes a day."

There was also a group of pot-smokers and controls who did not smoke tobacco cigarettes. When no tobacco was involved in either case, the pot-smokers had 25 percent more airflow resistance than did the controls.

Tashkin concluded that the factors accounting for the increased airflow resistance include irritation and inflammation in the larger airways and mucus secretion and clogging—this despite the fact that when they filled out the detailed respiratory questionnaire, the seventy-four pot-smokers had not been aware of any of these symptoms.

Then, to test reversibility of the impairment in lung function, the pot-smokers were asked to give up their grass completely for two weeks. Results: The Body Plethysmograph showed that, in most cases, the airflow resistance had returned to normal.

How long does the pot-smoker have before such subclinical impairments cease to be reversible—as was the case with Dr. Rosenkrantz's rats? Thus far, no one has attempted to look at this question so it remains unanswered.

Another researcher looked at the effects of cannabis, and cannabis plus tobacco, on the human lung itself. It is a landmark study, one unlikely ever to be repeated. It was conducted in 1971 by Dr. Forest S. Tennant, Jr., who now directs Community Health Projects, Inc., the largest drug-abuse rehabilitation and research program west of the Mississippi River, with facilities at over twenty sites in four California counties. Of the more than one hundred papers Tennant has published in scientific journals on drug abuse, he considers this 1971 study one of his most important. The paper was not published until 1980. The results of the study were so startling to him that he had the work reviewed by ten noted pathologists before writing it up for publication.

The impetus for Tennant's study came when he was a twenty-seven-year-old battalion surgeon stationed in Wurzburg, West Germany, in 1968. He remembers:

> We kept seeing all these soldiers who came in complaining of identical-sounding symptoms. Coughs, sore throats, sinusitis, chest pains. But these were only part of the picture. Lots of acne. Nausea. Depression. Fatigue. Apathy. What we now call the "amotivational" syndrome. Also, paranoid-type symptoms. "My captain's out to get me." That sort of thing. And the soldiers kept coming in by the dozens. All the same symptoms. They sounded like a broken record.
>
> I happen to believe that the patient will often tell you what's caused the symptoms, if you just ask. And when I asked, a number of them said, "Well, Doc, I guess it's all the hash I've been smoking."

Tennant told them to stop the hash smoking and see if the symptoms went away. Some did stop, and their symptoms did go away in six to eight weeks—even for those who continued to smoke tobacco cigarettes. But those who kept puffing hash showed no improvement, despite all the medication they were given.

This seemed to Tennant pretty clear evidence that hash lay behind the symptoms. He gave anonymous questionnaire surveys to 492 hash-smoking soldiers and found that 290 of them experienced one or more of the following "undesired side-effects: bronchitis, 6.1 percent; sore throat, 24.8 percent; running nose, 8.7 percent; diarrhea, 4.7 percent; headache, 14.2 percent; emotional problems, 8.5 percent. In addition, 69 of the soldiers said they had to visit a physician at least one time for an ailment caused by hashish."

Tennant later commented that such "clinical reports are extremely important to the cannabis body of knowledge because they deal with the realities of health care and treatment."

In 1971 Tennant was made a major and put in charge of the United States Army's drug program in West Germany. He continued to keep "hash records" on over a thousand soldiers—whose symptoms disappeared when hash-smoking was stopped. "But," he said, "I kept wondering what was actually going on in the lungs of these men. There was only one way to find out. Take a lung sliver from each subject and examine it under the microscope."

It was not difficult to enlist thirty hash-smoking soldiers. They were concerned enough about their bothersome symptoms to agree to have lung biopsies. But how to enlist the necessary "controls"—nonsmoking soldiers, as well as "tobacco only" smokers? What lure could persuade them to undergo surgery and hospitalization so that a small section of the lung could be extracted, examined, and photomicrographed? The bonus of a long furlough proved to be the answer.

All the soldiers in the study appeared to be healthy young men. The average age of the "tobacco onlys" was twenty-seven; they had smoked an average of 1½ packs a day for an average of eleven years. The average age of the hash-smokers was twenty. They had used the drug daily for only eight months to a year. This group was subdivided into "hash without cigarettes" and "hash plus cigarettes" (averaging a pack a day for five years).

Though Tennant did not realize it then, his study was done in the right place at the right time. As he said:

Today, kids—and adults too—are "doing" a bunch of drugs, in addition to pot. But back in 1968 and the early 1970s when I did my studies, hash was cheap and easily available to the United States soldiers in West Germany, and they didn't do other drugs—which made them perfect human subjects for studying the effects of cannabis on the lungs.

Also, in those days, the amount and potency of the hash the soldiers were smoking seemed to us enormous compared to the very mild pot being smoked then in the States. *But* the amount they smoked every day, and the potency of the stuff they smoked, in fact was very relevant to the amounts and the THC potency of the pot being smoked in the States today by many thousands of American teenagers and adults.

The hashish the soldiers were smoking had a THC potency of 5 to 10 percent. They were using 25 to 150 grams of hash a month—today's equivalent of one to five marijuana cigarettes a day. Tennant put all the soldiers in the hospital, operated on them, took a small slice of their lung tissue, and made slides.

Results: None of the nonsmokers had any symptoms. One third of the "cigarettes only" soldiers had a chronic cough, atypical cells, and a precancerous condition identified as squamous metaplasia. These soldiers, however, had none of the other symptoms listed.

Squamous metaplasia was potentially the most dangerous symptom. And the lung biopsies of *91 percent* of the "hash plus cigarettes" and 14 percent of the "hash only" soldiers showed these precancerous cells.

Among the Other Symptoms:	Hashish Plus Cigarettes	Hash Only
Chronic cough	95%	85%
Rales (abnormal sounds in the lungs or air passages)	87%	71%
Excess sputum production	52%	29%
Hemoptysis (coughing up blood)	61%	0%
Erytheuma (inflammation of the lungs)	57%	0%
Dyspnea (shortness of breath)	61%	51%
Atypical cells (the step before squamous metaplasia)	100%	29%

This was the startling result of Dr. Tennant's landmark study, published in February 1980. But he summed up the conclusions of his years of cannabis-pulmonary studies in these words:

It seems clear that the lungs are simply not strong enough to withstand the assault of both tobacco and cannabis. The harmful effects are synergistic. One plus one equals far more than two. And most cannabis smokers do seem to use tobacco cigarettes as well.

A further worrying factor: Early emphysema and chronic bronchitis are normally not seen unless you've smoked a pack a day of tobacco cigarettes for twenty to twenty-five years. But among the many hundreds of soldiers I treated in West Germany, I sometimes saw those conditions in eighteen-, nineteen-, and twenty-year-old men.

Although the hash-smoking soldiers in Tennant's study had come to see him because they were worried about their symptoms, they thought of themselves as healthy. They were all on active duty. As far as they knew, they just had a cough. Some of them had been scared when they spit up blood, but when their TB tests came out negative, they hadn't thought much more about it.

However, when they saw the *pictures* of their lung cells, they were horrified (see page 120). All of them told Tennant they were giving up hash smoking. Most of them said they would also give up cigarettes. Since no further pulmonary records were kept of those soldiers, the effects of their having given up the drug, possibly reversing these symptoms, are not known.

Normal lining of the bronchial wall; note the smooth, outer lining, with the cells in a regular line. The other three pictures are from the same area of the lung of three different men who smoked hashish daily for from three to twelve months. They also smoked cigarettes, *but* all were young men, twenty or twenty-two years old. Said Tennant, "Lung conditions of the type seen in pictures 3 and 4 only occur when someone has smoked a pack of tobacco cigarettes every day for twenty to thirty years, or two packs a day for fifteen years."

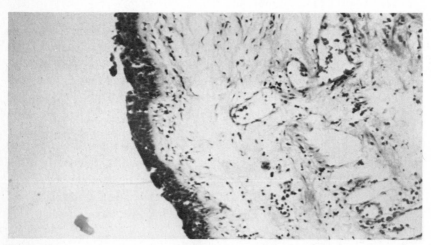

From a twenty-year-old hashish and cigarette smoker. Note the profusion of irregular dark cells. Says Tennant: "There are too many cells in the outer lining; they are too thick and inflamed. Also, the underlying tissue of the lung is starting to break down. There are very abnormal gaps in it. This is a typical picture of chronic bronchitis, which may be a lifelong condition, though it sometimes disappears when smoking stops. A pot cough can be a sign of this condition."

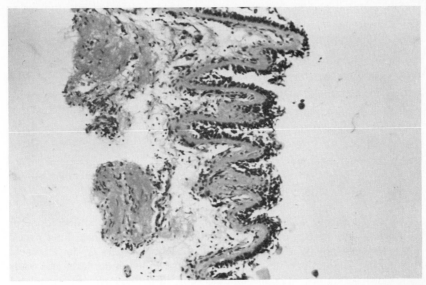

From a twenty-two-year-old soldier, a more severe stage. The dark cells have not only gotten thicker, but are irregular in shape. There is further disorganization underneath the dark cells in the bronchial wall lining. "This," says Tennant, "represents a permanent change of the tissue, which is probably not totally reversible even if smoking is stopped."

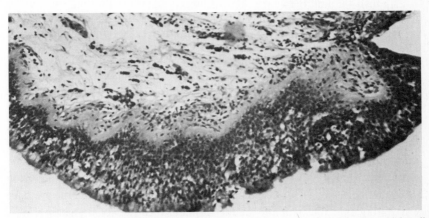

From a lung biopsy of a twenty-year-old hashish and cigarette smoker. The bronchial wall cells, which should be one layer thick, are now six to fifteen layers thick and are starting to grow into the lung, which cuts down on the ability to breathe. "These cells," says Tennant, "are so abnormal in size and shape that they would be considered precancerous: squamous metaplasia. Although not everyone who has this condition develops lung cancer, you never get lung cancer unless you first have areas of squamous metaplasia. This indicates why scientists have been very concerned about these biopsies. We assume that some of the millions of cannabis smokers will eventually develop lung cancer—unless they stop smoking."

121

Dr. Tennant had this to say about youngsters who start pot smoking in junior high, the fastest-growing group of marijuana users in the United States today: "If a child started daily marijuana smoking in junior high school, and if he continued as a daily pot *and* tobacco smoker, in my judgment, based on my studies, he or she would be at high risk of cancer of the lungs and/or emphysema at age twenty-five to thirty-five. The heavy tobacco-only smoker is at high risk from these diseases at ages forty-five to fifty-five."

If the precancerous cells that Tennant found in the soldiers' lungs could, one day, lead to lung cancer, the obvious question is: Why hasn't this finding shown up in countries like India, where they have been smoking cannabis for centuries? Tennant's answer:

No one has ever *looked!* There haven't even been any studies done on *tobacco* and lung cancer in those countries. Furthermore, lung cancer grows very slowly. It takes twenty-five to thirty years of daily tobacco smoking to produce a lung cancer. In the so-called underdeveloped countries, there's a low life expectancy compared to the developed countries. Therefore, it's very likely that many people die of other causes before lung cancer has time to manifest itself. Also, cancer may be misdiagnosed as TB, or some other ailment.

In this country, after all, it took half a century before we could firmly establish the link between lung cancer and cigarette smoking. And we've only been smoking pot here for a little over a decade. However, since the ingredients in tobacco cigarettes and joints are so similar, I can't see any good reason to assume that pot smoking won't cause a new wave of cancer deaths in another twenty years or less.

Although no studies have looked at possible cancer-cannabis connections in those countries where the drug has been used for centuries, two wide-scale studies done in India looked at other pulmonary effects of the drug. The first was done in Queen Victoria's day: *Report on Marijuana of the Indian Hemp Commission, 1893–1894.* It consisted of a survey in which 1,140 men were given seventy questions to answer. This was the conclusion about cannabis and the lungs: "Long continued smoking . . . and the presence of irritating substances in the smoke ultimately causes local irritation . . . resulting in the condition described as chronic bronchitis in *ganja* smokers." (*Ganja* is the name for one form of cannabis smoked in India.)

The second study was done by Dr. G. S. Chopra in 1973. Of 275 chronic users of a potent form of cannabis, *charas,* 48 percent had chronic bronchitis and 8.2 percent had emphysema. Dr. Chopra compared these figures with pulmonary symptoms from users of a mild form of cannabis, *bangh;* 6 percent of these had bronchitis and 2 percent had emphysema.

A widely publicized book, *Ganja in Jamaica: The Effects of Marijuana Use,* is often quoted by pot-smokers to "prove" that marijuana is harmless. The subjects were a nonrandomly selected group of "30 ganja smokers and 30 controls . . . all belonged to the lower income group and had completed four to five school years." Many marijuana researchers have seriously criticized the inadequate methodology of various aspects of the study. But even this report showed that twice as many smokers as nonsmokers had a lowered air-flow capacity. Also, the ability of the lungs to provide the blood with oxygen tended to be lower in the subjects than in the controls. The longer the person had smoked, the greater the decrement in lung function.

Far more telling, however, was the report on the effects of ganja in Jamaica made by Dr. John A. Hall to the U.S. Senate in 1974. Hall had been chairman of the department of medicine at Kingston Hospital in Jamaica since 1965 and had made a specific study of the effects of ganja on the population he saw in his hospital. He enumerated various physical effects, including the following: "An emphysema-bronchitis syndrome, common among Indian laborers of a past generation, who were well known for their ganga-smoking habits, is now a well-recognized present-day finding among black male laborers. . . . In the autopsy room in general, the barrel-shaped emphysematon's chest is a common finding in Rastafarian cultists." (Most Rastafarians use ganja heavily as part of their religious ritual.)

Thus far, no epidemiological studies concerning cannabis and the pulmonary system have been done in the United States or any other Western nation. The Institute of Medicine's 1982 *Marijuana and Health* report listed five "recommendations for research" in the pulmonary area, which they noted "would be informative." But they termed the following study "essential": "An epidemiological survey to determine over the next twenty to thirty years if there will be an increased incidence of primary lung, laryngeal, oropharyngeal, esophageal, nasal, or sinus cancer in chronic marijuana smokers."

In 1983 the American Cancer Society (ACS) embarked on a nine-million-dollar Cancer Prevention Study II, a questionnaire study of 1.2 million people. This will be a six- to eight-year study of people forty-five years old and over, conducted by eighty-five thousand volunteers. The questionnaire covers such environmental and lifestyle factors as diet, medical histories, occupational exposure, use of the pill, and, of course, tobacco-smoking habits. But ACS decided not to include any questions about marijuana in their massive survey. The chief reason given for this was "people of 45 years and over probably would not be pot smokers." Perhaps. However, when the eighty-five thousand volunteers enter homes (which the volunteers themselves select) with the questionnaire, what would prevent ACS from providing them with an additional questionnaire concerning tobacco and marijuana use to give to younger members of the household? It was ACS's invaluable first Cancer Prevention Study, also conducted by volunteers, that gave us the irrefutable information concerning tobacco's relation to cancer. Nine million dollars and eighty-five thousand volunteer workers are not easily come by these days for massive epidemiological studies. It seems far more than unfortunate that the American Cancer Society does not now expand its scope to include questions about our nation's "other smoke."

As for NIDA, although there has been talk since 1980 of doing a marijuana and health—or ill-health—study in conjunction with a large health-service organization, thus far such a project has not gotten onto the drawing board, much less off it. According to NIDA, the chief reason they cannot do a broad-scale survey of the type called for by the Institute of Medicine is lack of funding. A small sample study of mortality among drug-users has been funded, and NIDA hopes to cooperate with the National Center for Health Statistics in their large-scale national mortality "follow-back" survey— in which the survey-taker goes back to the living kin and asks questions about the death. But neither of these surveys answers the Institute of Medicine's call for an *essential* epidemiological survey specifically related to cannabis use and a possible increased incidence of cancer.

In May 1980, pediatrician Donald Ian Macdonald, then president of the Florida Pediatric Society, conducted his own small nonfunded cannabis survey at STRAIGHT, a drug rehabilitation center in St. Petersburg, Florida. Macdonald gave questionnaires to 104 youngsters, all from middle- and upper-income families. All had been heavy marijuana users before entering the program. In STRAIGHT the use of any medication is very closely monitored; the 104 youngsters in this survey received virtually no medication. They ranged in age from twelve to eighteen, and all had been drug-free from four months to a year when the survey was made. As soon as they entered the program, they stopped smoking pot and cigarettes.

Results:

• Seventy-five percent had coughs when they entered the program, most of which were productive of phlegm. At the time of the survey, three-quarters of these were still coughing, but most were coughing less, and producing less phlegm.

- Seventy-five percent had chest pains when they entered the program. All said the pains had disappeared in a month to three months after they stopped smoking.

- Prior to entering STRAIGHT, 40 percent had been taken to doctors with such symptoms as chest pains, chronic cough, sinus condition, sore throat, laryngitis, and fatigue. The doctors had done a variety of tests including ECGs, X rays, nasal smears, TB skin tests, sputum cultures, urine tests, and complete blood tests. Their diagnoses ranged from bronchitis to allergies. Two diagnosed "smoker's cough." Only eight physicians had asked about drugs. All eight youngsters had denied use, and all eight doctors had dropped the subject at once.

- Ninety-four percent of the youngsters said they felt better physically after they stopped smoking pot. In what way? Among the answers: All said they had more energy. Fifteen percent said they were no longer "clogged up." Eight percent said, "No more headaches." And one twelve-year-old wrote: "I just feel cleaner all through me."

- Aside from the coughs, all symptoms for which they had been taken to the doctor had disappeared.

This STRAIGHT survey also, inadvertently, had something to say about pediatricians' slowness to recognize cannabis-caused symptoms.

Pediatricians and family doctors who *are* aware of pulmonary symptoms connected with chronic pot smoking report the following commonly seen complaints:

- Sore throat (some heavy smokers call this "hash throat.") Examination of the pharynx and oral cavity usually reveals pharyngeal inflammation and swelling of the uvula (the hanging fleshy lobe in the middle of the back of the soft palate). Indeed, uvular edema (a watery swelling), which may persist for one to two days after smoking pot, may alert the physician to a suspected chronic pot-user.

- Increased nasal secretions.

- Irritation of the pharynx (the part of the alimentary canal between the mouth and the esophagus).

- Recurrent rhinopharyngitis (inflammation of the nose and pharynx).

- Thickening of mucous membranes in the paranasal sinuses (located next to or near the nasal cavities), with the sinus cavities at times being completely blocked.
- A chronic, persistent cough, which may or may not produce sputum or phlegm.
- Wheezing identical to that of the asthmatic.
- Unusual sounds (rhonchi and rales) heard in the chest when using a stethoscope.

These pulmonary symptoms are found in some, but not all, pot smokers. Dr. Tashkin's "healthy" young subjects had subclinical symptoms, not any of those listed above. However, according to Dr. Gary Huber, in some pot-smoking patients the symptoms "may be severe enough to disable the user and may even require hospitalization."

Donald Macdonald and pediatrician Ingrid Lantner of Willoughby, Ohio, were in the forefront of physicians who recognized that cannabis was the *sole* cause of numerous symptoms they were seeing in teenage patients.

Instead of sending parents a host of bills for various tests done on their teenager or, not infrequently, their preteen child, Dr. Lantner often tries another approach first. She prescribes no medication at all, merely advising the child to stop pot smoking for three weeks to see whether the symptom will disappear. When the youngster follows her suggestion, the symptoms often do disappear; the child feels so much better that he or she is sometimes able to withstand peer pressure and remain off the drug.

The youngsters who are most likely to try to "get off the pot" are those who come in complaining of chest pains. In such a case Dr. Lantner invariably asks: "How much pot do you smoke?"

And the invariable response is surprise. How does she *know?* Lantner notes:

This type of chest pain is extremely rare among teenagers—except in the case of chronic pot-smokers. It doesn't occur with heavy cigarette smokers. I don't prescribe any medicine. I tell the youngster to try an experiment: Give up marijuana for a month and see if the pains go away. They are usually very concerned about the pains, which they think may have something to do with their heart, and this scares some of them enough to get off the pot. When they do, the chest pains disappear within a month to three months.

Chest pain, a symptom common among teenage pot-smokers, may be caused by an effect on the lungs—or an effect on the heart. No studies have yet been done on this, and the causal relationship is not clear. But the symptom is clear—and frightening to those who experience it. According to noted cardiac specialist Dr. Wilbert S. Aronow, "There is no doubt that cardiovascular research should be done as soon as possible on the causes of marijuana-induced chest pain."

Marijuana and the Heart

When considering this matter, two important points should be kept in mind:

1. Since the first surgeon general's report in 1964, it has been clear that many more deaths were due to the coronary effects of tobacco smoking than to tobacco-caused lung cancer or other types of cancer, or to lung disease such as pulmonary emphysema. Indeed, *coronary heart disease is now known to be the biggest tobacco-cigarette–connected killer.*

2. Aside from the fact that marijuana contains cannabinoids and tobacco contains nicotine, most of the other substances and gases in each smoke are virtually the same, and are present in very similar amounts.

As every pot-smoker knows, "the weed" has an effect on the heart. It speeds the heartbeat. Studies done by Dr. Louis Vashon and Dr. Adam Sulkowski on pot-smokers aged eighteen to twenty-five showed their heart rate was significantly elevated (tachycardia) during all the hours of their high, in many cases rising from 70 beats a minute to 130 to 150 beats. The tachycardia generally is dose related, becomes evident within fifteen to thirty minutes after use, and persists for approximately two hours or more.

The question must be asked: What is happening to the hearts of the hundreds of thousands of daily pot-smoking teenagers who are stoned more than three hours every day? What is the result of this long-term daily over-stimulation of the heart? But this has not yet been answered, or even addressed, by research scientists.

According to Dr. Gary Huber, who worked on the problem of marijuana and health for a number of years while he was director of the Smoking and Health Research Program at Harvard University and who is now professor of medicine at the Medical College, University of Kentucky, "The long-term effects of chronic pot smoking on the heart have not yet been adequately addressed. This is a vitally important question which can be answered only through additional research."

In 1979 Dr. Gary Huber and another prominent cardiopulmonary specialist and researcher, Dr. Vijay K. Mahajan, reviewed the animal and human research done on marijuana in the area for a paper published in *Primary Cardiology*. Dr. Mahajan is chief of pulmonary medicine and director of medical education, St. Vincent's Hospital, Toledo, Ohio, and former Director of the Pulmonary Laboratory at Beth Israel Hospital in Boston.

Their chief conclusions were these: Both the heart and blood pressure are affected by marijuana. The elevation in blood pressure is dose related, but it is variable and less marked than the rapid heartbeat. It may be seen within 10 minutes of smoking marijuana, with blood pressure usually returning to baseline values within 90 minutes. (*Baseline* means the person's pressure before he or she started smoking.) Systolic blood pressure is a measure of the contraction force of the heart and the resistance offered by the blood vessels. Diastolic pressure essentially reflects the load—or the challenge—to the resting heart (between beats) in order to maintain the blood pressure. An increase in the diastolic pressure means that the heart, even at rest, is under an increased load. Marijuana is known to decrease the force with which the heart can pump the blood, and it decreases the amount of blood that can be pumped every minute. It also decreases the volume capacity of the heart. The effect of the drug on the functions of the heart is apparent in humans within 10 minutes of smoking and usually lasts for 60 to 120 minutes.

Dr. Mahajan pointed out:

The mechanisms by which marijuana and its derivatives affect the cardio-vascular system are not yet well understood. It is generally accepted that cannabinoids exert their influence by acting at various levels of the nervous system, which directly and indirectly influence the function of the heart and the blood vessels. The cannabinoids seem to act on the centers located in the lower part of the brain—the brain stem—which control the working of the heart and the blood vessels. Some of the effects of marijuana seem to resemble effects of barbiturates [downers] on the heart and blood vessels.

Dr. Huber adds, "Large doses of marijuana and/or high-potency marijuana may so dominate one center of the brain that this may indirectly and adversely affect the heart."

Mahajan summed up:

Marijuana smoke in usual doses has not been reported to cause major symptomatic cardiac distress in healthy persons. However, it is clear that the effects of smoking marijuana may become extremely important to individuals who already have heart disease, or in whom the heart function is already less than optimum. Further studies will be required before we adequately understand the relationship between THC and other individual cannabinoids, as well as smoked marijuana and its many other components, on the heart.

Dr. Huber notes that although some 460 chemicals in marijuana have thus far been identified, further analysis will probably reveal that, when burned, marijuana generates components that number in the thousands—as has been demonstrated with tobacco during the last ten years of research.

Huber also points out that a substance that has adverse effects on the less-than-healthy heart may also be expected to have adverse effects on the healthy heart after long-term exposure.

Dr. Wilbert S. Aronow, professor of medicine and director of cardiovascular research at Creighton University School of Medicine in Omaha, Nebraska, did two significant studies concerning the effects of pot smoking on "individuals with compromised heart function."

In one study he gave 1.9-percent THC joints to ten patients with angina pectoris, a common heart pain condition caused by a narrowing of the coronary arteries so that the heart receives insufficient oxygen. The average pre-pot heart rate of these patients was seventy beats a minute. After only ten puffs on the marijuana cigarette, the heart rate jumped to an average of one hundred beats a minute. Blood pressure also increased significantly.

Aronow pointed out:

By increasing either the heart rate *or* the blood pressure, you increase the amount of oxygen which is needed by the heart muscle. With ten puffs of pot, you increase both these oxygen needs at the same time. However, that's not all the ten puffs are doing. Marijuana also increases the amount of carbon monoxide in the blood. And this reduces the amount of oxygen delivered to the heart. So you increase the heart's demand for oxygen and, at the very same time, decrease the supply. Not a reassuring equation.

In his second study, Aronow compared the effects of pot smoking and cigarette smoking on people with angina pectoris. He showed that exercise time on a bicycle machine before chest pain set in was reduced 50 percent after only ten puffs of the marijuana cigarette. Ten puffs of a tobacco cigarette had one-half this effect.

Dr. Aronow summed up with this warning: "All existing studies clearly show that marijuana should never be used by anyone with coronary heart trouble. It might precipitate a heart attack, or cause sudden death."

Although, as noted, very little research has been done on the matter, it is generally assumed that marijuana does no harm to the healthy heart. But Dr. Aronow presents some startling food for thought on this matter:

How do you *know* if you have a healthy heart? Many people have subclinical heart disease—which means without any symptoms. Such individuals can be taking a great risk by smoking marijuana. Remember, *approximately one-quarter of the people who have coronary heart disease have had no prior recognized symptoms of heart disease.* Their first recognized symptom is—they're dead.

Chapter 8

Effects on Sex and
Reproduction: Female

Over two hundred studies have been done on animals and humans since 1975 regarding the effects of the crude drug marijuana, or one or more of the cannabinoids, on various aspects of sex and reproduction, and the effects on infants of pot-smoking mothers. As with the lung studies, none of the news is good.

The sex and reproductive system is one of the most complex of any in the body. And, since marijuana is such a complex drug, the difficulties of establishing which cannabinoid does what to which facet of the "network" have made this type of investigation a Chinese puzzle for researchers. They are solving it by homing in on a variety of specific aspects of the complex whole. The pieces are fitting together into an ominous picture.

Researchers have found that, unlike most other drugs, the impairing effects of *this* one come via two distinct and unrelated routes, either directly on the organs themselves, or through the brain. Perhaps the most important structure in the deep-set limbic area of the brain (site of sexual responsiveness, appetite, emotions, pleasure, and so on) is a small lump of tissue in the center of the brain, the hypothalamus. Connected to this is a still smaller lump, the pituitary gland. As tiny an amount as *a billionth of a gram of THC* affects the hypothalamus, which, in turn, affects the pituitary, which regulates endocrine function and hormones controlling the sex organs: the testes, ovaries, placenta, and other essential elements in the reproductive system.

There are not only two routes, but are three different levels to consider in the sex and reproductive systems. Marijuana appears to produce detrimental effects in each of them. Some effects are reversible; some may not be.

The first level is the so-called hypothalamic-pituitary axis. The second is the endocrine-regulated system. The third level is the sex organs themselves (the testicles and the ovaries) and the "accessory sex organs," the prostate gland and the seminal vesicles in the male and the uterus and vagina in females.

The first American researchers to study effects of marijuana on human female reproduction were Dr. Joan Bauman and Dr. Robert Kolodny of the Masters and Johnson Institute in St. Louis. The study was done in 1977, when street pot was far less potent than it is today. Their subjects were twenty-six women, aged eighteen to thirty, who had smoked pot for at least six months prior to the study, from three times a week to daily. The controls were women of "matched" ages, background, and so on, who had never smoked pot. All the women were "in general good health." None had used birth control pills or other drugs for eighteen months prior to the study, and none knew that the study had anything to do with marijuana—they were told it was a study on stress.

Results: The scientists found that 38.3 percent of the pot-smokers had defective menstrual cycles, compared to 12.5 percent of the non–pot-smokers. The cycles were defective in two ways. Either the women did not ovulate (no egg was released from the ovary), or the luteal phase—the time between ovulation and the end of the menstrual cycle—was shorter than normal. During the normal luteal phase, the ovary produces large amounts of hormones and the wall of the uterus is prepared to nourish a fertilized egg, if one should be available. "But," Dr. Bauman pointed out, "if the luteal phase is too short, the fertilized egg might not be able to implant itself in the uterine wall, or—if it does implant—it might not be properly nourished."

Bauman and Kolodny also found "statistically and consistently higher testosterone levels in the marijuana-using group." Testosterone, the male sex hormone, is found in a very low level in females. But an increased level in females can result in increased facial and body hair, and can also cause acne in teenage girls.

"We are particularly worried about what marijuana might be doing to pre-teens and teenaged girls," Dr. Bauman said.

Any of the effects found in the study could be even stronger before the body's endocrine-regulated systems have matured. For instance, THC inhibits gonadotropins—sex hormones originating in the pituitary. The levels of gonadotropins in the blood and levels of steroid sex hormones in the brain control the onset of sexual development. The critical period of secretion of these vital hormones is around age twelve and thirteen, but the process can start as early as age nine. The gonadotropins, called LH and FSH, stimulate the ovaries—an action which, in turn, stimulates the secretion of estrogens. And it is estrogen which causes a young girl to develop hips, breasts and pubic hair, as well as stimulating the development of the reproductive tract, including the uterus and the vagina. Brain estrogen may also play a role in sexual behavior. We know for a fact that THC inhibits the release of gonadotropins and thereby estrogens. We are, of course, forbidden by FDA regulations to administer marijuana to teenagers in the course of controlled experiments. However, we can at least state *potential* hazards. For example, pot smoking on a regular basis could slow normal breast development. And suppression of the gonadotropins before regular menstrual patterns are established could lead to fertility problems later in life.

Bauman and Kolodny also found a significantly lower prolactin level in the marijuana-using women. This is a pituitary hormone involved in milk production of a nursing mother; it is also thought to have other effects on the reproductive system.

Numerous animal studies have also shown that pot suppresses prolactin. For example, in one study done in 1978, Dr. Josel Szepsenwol found that all the babies born to a particular strain of mice starved to death because the mothers were milkless. The mothers had been given a tiny speck of THC once a week: a 20-microgram dose. (A microgram is one millionth of a gram). This, said Szepsenwol, was the "human equivalent" of one to two joints a week. Even this small dose was sufficient to cause a dramatic drop in prolactin levels.

Since the breasts are eminently fatty organs, and since the cannabinoids are lipophilic (fat-loving), it should not be surprising to find that THC has been detected in the milk of nursing mothers. Yet many physicians seem unaware of this vital point. Dr. Carlton Turner notes, for example, that he receives letters from obstetricians who ask about "the new findings" in this regard. As Turner reported at the 1980 U.S. Senate Hearings on Marijuana Use: "The startling and alarming fact that marijuana is stored in mammalian milk . . . has been known for over five years."

Although no studies have been done to trace THC in human babies of pot-smoking mothers, radioactively tagged THC has been found in suckling rats, mice, ewes, and monkeys following exposure to the cannabinoid through their mother's milk. For example, Canadian researchers Dr. P. L. McGeer and Dr. A. Jakubovic of the University of Vancouver injected mother rats with a relatively small dose of THC one day after the rats gave birth. The

THC and its metabolites were traced four to twenty-four hours later in the suckling babies. Said Jakubovic, "Not only is mother's milk—animal and human—very high in fat, and therefore a prime place for the deposit of and accumulation of cannabinoids—but milk is one of the routes through which the body excretes or gets rid of THC. We found cannabinoids in almost all organs that we looked at in the baby rat: the liver, kidney, spleen, heart and lungs." The scientists did the same experiments with a lactating lamb. The baby was not sacrificed, so the organs were not examined. "But," said Jakubovic, "it is clear that cannabinoids were there because they were excreted in the baby's urine and feces."

Dr. Carol Grace Smith is a reproductive pharmacologist at the School of Medicine of the Uniformed Services of the Health Sciences at Bethesda, Maryland. She has done a great deal of work on marijuana's effects on sex and reproduction. Her subjects are rhesus monkeys, and her investigations concentrate on the effects of marijuana extract (which contains all the chemicals in the marijuana plant in their same proportions) as well as individual cannabinoids.

Smith uses rhesus monkeys as subjects for two reasons. First, to accurately pinpoint effects of specific cannabinoids on specific sex hormones, it is essential to use animals. In human beings there are too many lifestyle and other variables that are difficult or impossible for the scientist to control.

Second, the reproductive system of the rhesus monkey is very similar to the human's. Under the microscope it is virtually impossible to tell rhesus sperm from human sperm. The male and female rhesus endocrine physiology also closely resembles that of humans. The female rhesus, for example, has a twenty-eight-day menstrual cycle. Human reproductive findings in many areas have been based on work with rhesus monkeys. Indeed, the blood Rh factor is "named" after the rhesus.

Dr. Smith started with infertility because she had been told by several physicians that a number of their pot-smoking patients had had trouble getting pregnant, but when they gave up the drug, pregnancy often occurred within a few months. Smith did further reading and found that today 15 to 20 percent of American couples are having infertility problems. Might this correlate in any way with the fact that in 1979, for example (according to the National Household Survey on Drug Abuse), 26 percent of women and 45 percent of men aged eighteen to twenty-four were current pot-smokers?

Smith first looked at marijuana's effect on the monkeys' menstrual cycles. Each of her subjects was given THC injections from day 1 (the first day of menstruation) to day 18 of one menstrual cycle only. Blood was drawn daily, not only to assure, via blood levels, that the ratio of THC in the monkey's blood was the same as that in a human after smoking one joint, but also to measure the sex steroid hormones, estrogen and progesterone, and the gonadotropins LH and FSH, which affect the menstrual cycle.

Result: None of the THC monkeys ovulated during that cycle; frequently, no egg was released during the following two, three, or even four cycles— even though the THC was given *only* during the first cycle.

The menstrual cycle in all of the monkeys was disturbed. The hormones were so inhibited that there was no ovulation and no normal menstruation; in some cases, this lasted for as long as 141 days after the administration of THC.

Pot-smokers looking for positive aspects of their drug-taking might conclude from this finding that "the weed" offers an enjoyable form of birth control. However, Smith warns that pot should not be used as a contraceptive. One reason is that the birth control pill, for example, contains the necessary estrogen and progesterone, whereas THC merely inhibits and does not replace.

A more important reason not to use pot for birth control was made clear in a study Dr. Smith concluded in 1982. THC was given to female monkeys on a Monday, Wednesday, Friday schedule to approximate the social use of marijuana more closely. Again, the menstrual cycles were immediately disrupted; again, the disruption lasted for four to five months while the drug was being given. However, *after* this period of time, the reproductive system became tolerant to the drug effect and apparently normal menstrual cycles were reestablished.

Some long-term, heavy pot-smokers claim that THC has no effect on their menstrual cycles. However, Smith points out that the monkey studies make it clear that regular users may have normal cycles merely because tolerance to the drug has developed. However, if pregnancy should occur during this period of tolerance, the fetus will not have any tolerance to the drug, and it *will* be affected, as shown by other studies on both animals and humans.

After seven years of studying the effects of marijuana on the female reproductive system, Dr. Smith sums up:

> *There is increasing evidence to indicate that the reproductive system may be more impaired by marijuana than any other system.* The reproductive system is unique because it has so many different types of control mechanisms. The impairment is a subtle, lifelong process. Only when we want to have a baby do we notice that the system has been damaged. It can

be heartbreaking if you lose your chance of being a parent because you've been smoking so much pot.

Clinical reports are beginning to bear out Smith's findings on THC and ovulation. For example, Dr. William Bates, a reproductive endocrinologist at the University of Mississippi Medical Center in Jackson says:

> The kinds of patients I see are women who do not menstruate and women who are having trouble conceiving. When we measure the pituitary hormones FSH [follicle-stimulating hormone] and LH [luteinizing hormone], which stimulate ovulation, we often find that the concentration of these hormones is abnormally low for a sexually mature woman. The three prime reasons we have found for this unusual condition are anorexia nervosa, strenuous jogging (forty miles a week), and marijuana use.
> When the marijuana users discontinue the drug, menstruation and ovulation resume spontaneously within six to eight weeks. If there is no other cause for infertility, then my experience with my patients is that pregnancy occurs quickly.

An interesting case in point is one of Bates's patients who consulted him at age nineteen because she had never menstruated. She also had incomplete breast development and incomplete pubic hair growth. She had been to several medical centers; the consistent finding was that her LH and FSH levels were abnormally low. But no one had asked about her pot use—until she came to Dr. Bates. When he asked, she told him readily. She had smoked two to three joints a day since age fourteen.

> What had happened was that after she'd started developing, the marijuana blocked the process from being completed. She had "turned off" her pituitary gland. Ultimately he succeeded in getting her to stop smoking pot. Within six months the LH and FSH levels returned to normal, her breasts started filling out, the pubic hair became normal, and, at age twenty-one, for the first time in her life, she started menstruating.

Dr. Ethel Sassenrath, working with rhesus monkeys at the primate center of the University of California Medical School at Davis, has done the only truly long-term study of pot's effects on the female reproductive system.

In 1972 Sassenrath began a study of the behavioral effects of chronic pot smoking. She worked with 48 monkeys; 38 were controls and 10 received the THC human equivalency dose of one joint a day. Instead of injecting the cannabinoid as Smith does, she "flavored" cookies with a single drop of alcohol containing 200 milligrams per milliliter of THC. (The alcohol evaporates quickly.)

Two of the THC mothers became pregnant. Their THC dose continued during pregnancy. One of the infants was born with hydrocephalus, a very rare condition among monkeys; he died at once. The other infant, named Milo, was extremely hyperactive compared to the babies born at the same time to control mothers. He played harder, slept less, and was more aggressive than his baby peers.

Sassenrath wondered whether Milo and the dead baby were merely an unhappy coincidence—or was it possible that long-term daily use of marijuana had affected the offspring? She decided to change the focus of her study and broaden its scope beyond behavior.

For three to five years the scientist gave her "breeders" their daily dose of THC-spiked cookies. "I even came in on Christmas," she said. The dose each monkey received was injected into the cookie with a syringe. This permitted Sassenrath to be sure of exactly how much THC each was getting every day, and made it possible to relate each dose to the individual monkey's size and weight. Each was given a dose sufficient to produce the same concentration of THC in its blood as a human would have smoking one joint a day.

As had occurred with Dr. Smith's monkeys, the menstrual cycles were upset for three to five months. And, as with Smith's monkeys, at the beginning, they seemed disconcerted by the "high." But after a few months tolerance set in, and they didn't appear to be intoxicated by the daily dose.

In newly drugged monkeys, after a short period of daily exposure to the drug, conception was delayed for three to five menstrual cycles, compared to the nondrugged monkeys who conceived normally (which means, in rhesus terms, at the first or second "encounter"). "Furthermore," said Sassenrath, "at the time of menstruation, the THC breeders showed a new phenomenon of prolonged vaginal bleeding—not followed by pregnancy. This suggested a drug-related interference with implantation of the embryo, or early resorption of the embryo." (Resorption means that the fertilized and implanted egg disappears rather than developing.) After two or three months, when the THC breeders became used to the drug, their menstrual cycles returned to normal. This did not mean, however, that their reproductive capacity returned to normal. Far from it.

Some of the monkeys were exposed to THC daily for three years; some up to five years. During this time there were over fifty pregnancies.

What were the reproductive implications?

"All of the THC pregnancies," said Dr. Sassenrath, "had characteristics which put them into the category of high-risk pregnancies."

The results can be summed up in one startling statistic. The "reproductive *loss"*—as scientists term it—*was 44 percent for the THC mothers, and 12 percent for the undrugged mothers.* Ten to 12 percent is a normal birth loss in a monkey colony, resulting from injury, infection, and other ordinary causes. In the case of the THC mothers, birth loss occurred from a wide spectrum of causes: early spontaneous abortion, *in utero* fetal death, stillbirth, and infant death just after birth. In addition, the pregnant THC mothers had a "significantly" lower body-weight gain than the control mothers, and the male offspring of the THC mothers had "slight but significantly" lower birth weight than the male babies of the undrugged mothers.

A quadrupling of the birth loss in "THC mothers" as compared to non-drugged mothers is sobering enough. But the most startling aspect of Dr. Sassenrath's pioneering study became clear when the pathologist examined the tissues and organs of the dead fetuses, stillborns, and "neonates" that had died within six months after birth.

To the naked eye there was no difference between the dead babies from undrugged mothers and the so-called "THC babies" who had been exposed to the drug only through their mother's exposure. The pathologist did double-blind studies. When he put the slides under the microscope, he did not know which slides came from which dead fetuses or baby monkeys, whether they were offspring of THC breeders or controls.

Result: There was a wide spectrum of subtle abnormalities among the THC babies. Few, if any, of these abnormalities were found in the control babies, or in any of the eighty rhesus babies from nondrugged mothers in the primate colony who had died during that same period of time.

Furthermore, *every THC baby had some subtle developmental abnormality in one or more systems (nervous, cardiovascular, or urinary) and/or some placental abnormality.* (The placenta, the tissue that connects the mother and baby, serves as a conduit, bringing nutrients to the fetus and carrying fetal wastes away.) In human studies, radioactively tagged THC has been shown to accumulate in and to cross through the placenta. Consequently, when the pot-smoking mother gets high so, presumably, does her developing baby.

The subtle abnormalities found in the THC fetuses and dead babies of Sassenrath's THC breeders included the following:

- *Internal hydrocephalus* (water on the brain).

- *Degenerative changes in cardiovascular structures,* including the heart muscle and umbilical vessels.

• *Acute renal tubular necrosis.* (*Renal* means "kidney." The *tubular* part of the kidney structure is where the necessary parts of the nutrients and so forth in the blood are recycled, leaving only the wastes. *Necrosis* is degeneration leading to death.)

• *Unilateral inguinal hernia.* (*Unilateral* means "one side." The *inguina* is the canal through which the testes descend. A *hernia* is an out-of-place loop, which can cause blockage.)

• *Major placental infarction* (dead tissue).

• *Depletion of hematopoiesis in lymphoid organs and the bone marrow.* (*Hemato* means "blood"; *poiesis* means "production." This is the system that forms the blood cells. Lymphoid organs—bone marrow, thymus, and lymph nodes—are the centers where the immune system's white blood cells, the T and B lymphocytes, develop and are stored, poised to combat infections. The bone marrow is where the formation of red, white, and platelet blood cells occurs.)

• *Hepatocellular degeneration.* (Change in the appearance of the liver cells, indicating that "an insult" has happened to these cells. The liver metabolizes most nutrients, makes and recycles blood proteins, and has other vital functions. It is said that "you really cannot be without your liver.")

• *Mild necrotizing meningeal phlebitis.* (Destructive inflammation of the brain. This might mean that the veins would be "leaky," letting toxic wastes back into the brain, which would eventually compromise the basic function of the neurons in the brain.)

• *Ectopic pancreatic tissue in the duodenal wall.* (*Ectopic* means "in a site other than the usual." The pancreas is a "diffuse organ" along the length of part of the small intestines; it makes and releases two hormones, insulin and glucogen, to control blood-sugar levels. It also makes digestive enzymes, which degrade proteins and carbohydrates to smaller, absorbable pieces. The duodenal wall is part of the small intestines.)

• *Mild acute nephrosis* (a harmful kidney condition).

Three surviving offspring of the THC-treated mothers were sacrificed at various ages after birth. One, aged twenty months, had "a zone of small undeveloped fetal-like glomeruli beneath the kidney capsule and a corresponding lack of tubular development. The number of undeveloped glomeruli were ten times more frequent than in any age-matched monkey from the rhesus colony at large." (Glomeruli filter out toxic wastes and excessive useful substances from the blood. The young monkey had an area underneath the kidney that had undeveloped glomeruli. This could mean that the kidney was not functioning "up to snuff.") The other two THC offspring had minimal lesions (inflamed areas) when sacrificed, but these were also seen in untreated monkeys.

THC also caused behavioral effects in both the mothers and the babies. After the initial "stoned" period, which lasted several months, the THC breeders displayed signs of increased irritability. They hit, bit, and chased other monkeys more frequently. Under conditions of high stress or tension, they could wound or even kill a cagemate.

Furthermore, when their babies were born, these mothers seemed disinterested in their babies. They did not cuddle them, groom them, or chase after and retrieve them as much as normal rhesus monkeys do. (See Figures 1 and 2, below.) Much of the time it seemed that the THC-mothers "couldn't care less."

Pictures from a behavioral study done by Dr. Ethel Sassenrath of the University of California Medical School at Davis. The mother monkey at left is an undrugged "control." The mother monkey at right was given the human equivalency THC dose of one joint a day for three years. Said Sassenrath, "The drugged mothers did not care for their babies in a normal way." (*Photos by Gail Goo*)

Perhaps this was one reason their babies behaved differently than the control babies of undrugged mothers. Or perhaps the drug has a direct effect on a baby's central nervous system (CNS), which includes the brain. Or maybe both played a role. In any case, *all* of the THC babies showed behavioral abnormalities, particularly when they were weaned from their mothers and put in cages with other young "weanlings" their age.

The THC babies had been exposed to the drug only through the placenta prior to birth, and only through their mother's milk after birth. But their behavioral differences lasted far beyond the nursing period—indeed, at least until they were a year old. (After that, the THC offspring rejoined the general monkey colony and were no longer observed separately.)

What were the behavioral differences? Said Sassenrath:

> The THC babies had similarities to the hyperactive child. Normally baby monkeys really enjoy playing. They wrestle around and chase each other and bat each other, in a friendly way. But the THC babies were often so persistent that it turned from playing to harassment. They would also scream longer and louder than the other babies. They'd "embrace" or cling to cagemates harder and longer. All of them had some types of exaggerated behavioral qualities. They also seemed to have higher levels of irritability. All in all, the THC babies were not very popular with the others, who tended to avoid them.

At the age of three months (two or three years old in human terms), the babies were given a visual attention test by Dr. Mari Golub, who specializes in detection of prenatal drug effects on behavior of offspring. Each baby was placed in a three-foot test box with an eye-level peep hole. Then a "slide show" was put on for the monkey: indoor and outdoor scenes, which it viewed through the hole. The average control baby looked at each slide for two seconds before turning away. But the THC babies stared at the slide for an average of thirty seconds. Said Sassenrath: "A monkey living in the wild has to be able to case its environment quickly. This type of delayed reaction to visual stimuli can be suggestive of central nervous system impairment."

The THC babies that lived showed no physical abnormalities. Although the male babies had been underweight at birth, they caught up in weight. The behavioral abnormalities were subtle—the sort of thing that could be overlooked if they were not being specifically studied.

The daily long-term dose of THC given to Sassenrath's rhesus monkeys affected the reproductive systems of the mothers, affected all of the offspring who died in a wide spectrum of subtle ways, and produced lasting effects on the behavior of all the surviving THC babies. It should be remembered that the breeder monkeys' blood THC level matched that of a human who smoked a joint a day. *However, the monkeys were exposed to only one cannabinoid.* The human pregnant mother who smokes pot during her pregnancy is exposing herself and her developing baby to all sixty-one cannabinoids, as well as to the other two thousand–plus chemicals in the marijuana smoke.

Psychologist Peter Fried of Carleton University in Ottawa, Canada, has done the only human study to date on pot-smoking pregnant women and the behavioral effects on their infants.

Fried first worked with animals and found that the younger the animal was when exposed to the drug, the longer the impairing effects lasted. When he next worked with "a very, very young animal"—the rat fetus—he found some startling effects, as noted later in this chapter. But when he "went to the literature" to see what was known about marijuana and human pregnancy, said Fried, "to my amazement there wasn't a single study that was directly related to looking at effects on the newborn when a woman smokes pot during pregnancy." So in 1980, Dr. Fried undertook such a study.

Women who visited their obstetricians in two hospitals, Ottawa Civic and Ottawa General, were informed by a notice or by nurses that volunteers were needed for a study being done on prenatal habits. About five hundred women volunteered. They were interviewed on a number of factors, including eating habits, smoking, alcohol, and marijuana use. None of the women knew that the focus of the study was to be marijuana.

Of the five hundred, sixty used pot and no other drugs. They were divided into three categories: irregular users (no more than a joint a week, or nonusers who were exposed to the pot smoke of others, usually their husbands); regular users, who smoked two to five joints a week; and heavy users, who smoked five or more joints a week. (This category included one woman who had been a heavy pot-smoker but who gave it up completely during pregnancy.) There were also non–pot-smoking controls. Most of the women were middle-class, and in all cases nutrition was good before and during pregnancy.

It is interesting to note that in collecting their subjects the researchers found that, before pregnancy, about 12 percent of the five hundred women had been regular pot-smokers. Upon learning they were pregnant, about half gave up the drug. *But* it was the light to moderate smokers who gave it up. Only one of the heavy smokers stopped or even cut down her use. Their attitude ranged from curious ("I just don't know if it has any effect on the baby or not") to certain ("If it makes me feel good, it shouldn't be bad for the baby").

The women who continued pot smoking during pregnancy were interviewed extensively on lifestyle subjects three times during their pregnancy. Their babies were examined at birth, at four days of age in the hospital, at the mother's home at nine days and at thirty days, and every six months thereafter for a period of several years.

Results: There were significant distinct dose-related behavioral effects. The more the mother smoked during pregnancy, the more marked were the abnormal effects. Babies of the irregular users showed very few to no behavioral abnormalities. But *100 percent of the babies born to heavy users showed abnormal behavioral effects.* (The baby born to the mother who *had* been a heavy pot-smoker but who abstained completely during pregnancy showed no such abnormal effects.)

Three of these abnormal effects suggested subtle alterations in the nervous system:

1. *Slow response to visual stimuli.* Babies born to the heavy users reacted abnormally to, as Fried put it, "a fairly modest light shining in their eyes. If a light is repeatedly shined into the eyes of a normal baby of four days of age (for a second every 10 seconds), the baby will close its eyes and will ignore the light. But the 'marijuana baby,' even with its eyes closed, continues to blink, squirm, and struggle. They don't habituate normally to this stimulus."

2. *Tremors.* "Every baby," says Fried, "exhibits tremors to some degree, but all of the babies of the heavy users exhibited tremors to a very marked degree; not only were the tremors qualitatively different from normal, but quantitatively different—they were exhibited more often." This type of exaggerated tremor was observed in the babies of 38 percent of the irregular users, 72 percent of the regular users, and 100 percent of heavy users.

3. *Exaggerated startles* (such as a response to a hand clap). These were observed in 14 percent of the babies of nonusing controls, 38 percent of the irregular users, 72 percent of the regular users, and 100 percent of the babies whose mothers smoked more than five joints a week.

A distinct high-pitched, shrill, cat-like cry (*cri de chat*) was noted in over a third of the babies of the heavy users. "This," said Fried, "may be a symptom of drug withdrawal. We hear the same kind of cry from infants born to mothers who are addicted to heroin."

When the babies were about one month old, the abnormal symptoms started to disappear. Some of the children have been followed up to three years of age and given motor, verbal, and cognitive development tests. "The babies all appear to be normal. However," says Dr. Fried, "these preliminary results have to be taken with a grain of salt. The tests might not be sensitive enough to detect subtle abnormalities, or abnormalities may only show up under particularly demanding situations."

A 1981 study done at UCLA Medical School by Drs. Sander Greenland, Klaus Staisch, and Stanley Gross, and nurse Nancy Brown looked particularly at the effects of pot smoking on pregnancy and the newborn. About 13 percent of the women used pot during pregnancy, and it was not easy to find pregnant women who only used marijuana. However, the researchers did find thirty-five women who fitted the criteria; to double-check that they used no other illegal drugs, all were given blood and urine radioimmunoassay (RIA) tests to validate their questionnaire responses. Subjects were further restricted to women with no medical problems, who were less than thirty weeks pregnant when they were entered in the study. Their ages ranged from 18 to 31; the average age was 23.7.

Then thirty-six controls were selected, each matched to one of the pot-smokers for age, race, number of previous pregnancies, and alcohol and cigarette-smoking habits. Most of the users smoked pot once a week or more during pregnancy, although during the last trimester weekly use dropped from 97 percent to 56 percent. Only subjects who used marijuana at least once a month during pregnancy were classified as "users." The nonuser controls did not use pot at all during pregnancy or for three months prior to conception.

Results: The marijuana users exhibited higher levels of anemia and poor weight gain; intrauterine growth retardation was suspected. However, the researchers reported, these differences were not "statistically significant." What *was* statistically significant was the fact that 31 percent of the users experienced prolonged, protracted, or arrested labor, compared to 19 percent of nonusers. Several of the users had abnormally short labor but the researchers felt that this was because they had used marijuana to help control the pain and thus delayed their arrival at the hospital.

The study also reported:

Users exhibited a higher proportion of abnormal fetal tests and manual removal of the placenta. Thus, overall, the course of labor appeared more hazardous for users than nonusers. Parallel with the more difficult course of labor among users, an unusually high proportion of the newborn infants in the user group exhibited meconium [fetal feces], 57 percent versus 25 percent among nonusers. Over half the newborns of pot smokers defecated immediately before or during labor.

Meconium is an infant response to stress. There also was a higher percentage of abnormal fetal heart rate among babies born to marijuana-smoking women than to control mothers.

The pot-smokers' babies were also more likely to be sedated, and in need of oxygen; 41 percent required resuscitation, versus 21 percent among nonusers. The researchers found THC in the umbilical-cord blood of several of the pot-smokers' babies that needed resuscitation.

Dr. Klaus Staisch, the obstetrician on the study, further pointed out that there were two complications of clinical significance for the management of labor which occurred in the majority of users and to a much lesser extent in the controls. The first was dysfunctional labor—the lack of regularity of contractions. This resulted in the need to stimulate labor with medication. Second was the necessity in many cases to perform an additional surgical procedure to remove placenta, normally expelled spontaneously at the end of the birth process. This requires additional general anesthesia.

As for the meconium situation, Dr. Staisch pointed out: "The presence of meconium is hazardous to the newborn. The meconium can get into the lungs when the baby takes its first breath and can cause respiratory depression. This requires expertise in resuscitation on the part of the obstetrician and/ or pediatrician at the time of birth. Since almost 60 percent of the potsmokers' babies in our study exhibited meconium, it is extremely important that a woman tell the obstetrician about her use of the drug so that the doctor can be prepared for the need for resuscitation, which may involve immediate use of special equipment such as a suction trap and a laryngoscope."

The largest study so far conducted concerning pregnant women and their babies was done by a group of doctors at Boston City Hospital. Published in 1982, it revealed three important new findings.

Before examining these findings, let us look at the impressive study design. From February 1977 to October 1979, 2,514 newborn babies at Boston City Hospital received a thorough physical examination from one of four pediatricians in the study. These pediatricians did not know the mothers and were unaware of their lifestyles or habits. Three-quarters of the babies were examined before they were three days old. The examination included "detailed neurologic, morphologic, and growth assessment."

The mothers of 1,690 of those babies were interviewed in depth, a thirty-to forty-minute structured interview (in English or Spanish) in the hospital; 328 of the English-speaking women were also interviewed at registration for prenatal care at the hospital's Women's Clinic. This permitted a "reliability check" with information given after delivery.

The study was "designed to test whether maternal alcohol consumption at various levels prior to and during pregnancy is associated with several aspects of adverse fetal development when possible confounding variables are controlled." But, as with all good studies, the purpose of the study was hidden from the interviewees. The questions they were asked ranged from what they ate on a typical day during pregnancy to illnesses they had had prior to and/or during pregnancy. One of the "possible confounding variables" was "frequency of marijuana use during pregnancy," ranging from "never" to "three or more times a week."

When the hundreds of thousands of data points were fed into computers, the most surprising overall finding was this: Although the study had been specifically designed to examine maternal *alcohol* consumption and its effects on the baby, what clearly emerged was the fact that pot smoking during pregnancy was as strongly or more strongly associated with adverse fetal outcome than alcohol (two or more drinks a day), or than tobacco cigarettes (a pack or more a day).

The fetal alcohol syndrome (FAS) has been thoroughly described in medical literature. The pure FAS occurs in about one in every fifteen hundred babies of mothers who drink during pregnancy. However, the Boston City Hospital study showed that more women who smoked pot during pregnancy delivered babies with "features compatible with the fetal alcohol syndrome" than did those who drank alcohol, but did not smoke pot. Furthermore, *women who smoked pot during pregnancy were five times more likely than non–pot-smokers to deliver infants with some features considered compatible with the fetal alcohol syndrome.* Said Dr. Ralph Hingson, coordinating analyst of the study, "This figure held true even after other maternal habits such as drinking and smoking were taken into consideration." Women who drank two or more drinks a day *and* smoked pot during pregnancy delivered a greater percentage of babies with features compatible with the fetal alcohol syndrome than those who drank but did not smoke marijuana.

The following symptoms were considered in making these assessments of the infants:

1. Small size, according to length of pregnancy.
2. Microcephaly (small head size).

3. Small eye openings.

4. Multiple dysmorphic features, including cardiac murmurs, epicanthic folds (folds of upper eyelid skin that come down over the eye opening), poorly developed philitrum (groove in the upper lip), limitation of joint movement, large hemangiomas (proliferation of blood vessels on the surface of the skin), broad low nasal bridge, and ear anomalies (such as abnormal shape or being low set).

Infants were classified as having features compatible with FAS if they were rated abnormal on at least two of the four criteria. One of the two had to be either "short palpebral fissures" (small eye openings) or multiple dysmorphic features. Any infant exhibiting three or more minor malformations or one or more major malformations was rated as having congenital abnormality, although not necessarily compatible with fetal alcohol syndrome.

Despite the fact that it is called the fetal *alcohol* syndrome, the study showed that the relationship between the presence of FAS symptoms and marijuana use existed among drinkers *and nondrinkers,* among cigarette smokers *and nonsmokers,* among mothers who smoked *and* drank, and mothers who neither smoked *nor* drank.

Hingson summed up, "It was quite consistent that regardless of which of these other habits women engaged in, women who smoked marijuana during pregnancy were more likely to have babies with symptoms compatible with fetal alcohol syndrome than those who did not."

The study also revealed another highly significant finding: The more often the pregnant women smoked marijuana during their pregnancy, the more likely they were to deliver low-birthweight babies. Women who smoked marijuana less than three times a week during pregnancy delivered infants who were an average of 95 grams smaller than babies of non–pot-smokers. Babies of women who used marijuana three or more times per week were an average of 139 grams smaller than those of mothers who never smoked pot. (In comparison, the babies of women who smoked one or more packs of cigarettes per day during pregnancy averaged 83 grams smaller than those who did not smoke cigarettes.)

Women who smoked marijuana *and* tobacco cigarettes usually delivered smaller babies than women who smoked tobacco cigarettes alone. (Tobacco smokers were defined as those who smoked one or more packs a day.) A higher percentage of women who smoked pot *and* drank delivered smaller babies than those who used alcohol alone (two or more drinks a day). A drink was defined as the ethyl alcohol content in 1.5 ounces of distilled spirits, or in one four-ounce glass of wine, or in one 12-ounce can of beer.

(Although not many people realize it, the alcohol content in each of these is about the same.)

As Dr. Hingson pointed out: "The size of the baby is a significant factor. Growth measures and other important elements in a child's development are often influenced by gestational age and size at birth."

The third important marijuana-related finding was this: The number of maternal illnesses—as reported in the mother's pre-pregnancy medical record—was related to length of gestation, infant size, and congenital abnormalities in the infant. Women who smoked pot prior to pregnancy had a higher proportion of pre-pregnancy illnesses than those who did not use the drug.

The investigators summed up: "Our findings that maternal marijuana use during pregnancy was associated with smaller infant size at birth and features considered compatible with the fetal alcohol syndrome underline the need for further exploration into teratogenicity in offspring of women using that substance during pregnancy." (Teratogenic means "producing behavioral, tissue, or skeletal abnormalities in the first trimester of pregnancy.")

While a good deal of publicity has been given to the hazards of smoking cigarettes and drinking alcohol during pregnancy, there has been very little on the hazards of pot smoking during pregnancy, as indicated by this substantial study, among others. Although this study specifically separated factors so that they could be individually identified and quantified, it also pointed out, as Hingson put it, that:

> what we are picking up is that there seems to be a whole lifestyle involved. For example, 44 percent of the women who drank two or more drinks a day also smoked a pack or more of cigarettes a day. And, coincidentally, 44 percent of the women who drank "two plus" drinks a day also smoked marijuana during the pregnancy. This was not necessarily the same 44 percent as those who also smoked cigarettes.
>
> Clearly, alcohol, tobacco cigarettes and marijuana each have a separate and independent adverse effect on the baby. When used together it appears that the adverse effects are additive. Furthermore, women who smoke marijuana also tend to smoke tobacco cigarettes and to drink alcohol. That cumulative association of the pregnant pot smoker's lifestyle should be of paramount concern.

What *causes* marijuana's effects on the developing baby, especially fetal growth retardation? One obvious place to look is the placenta, since it is the organ through which metabolic exchanges take place.

An artery leads from the mother's body through the placenta and umbilical cord to the developing baby, and a vein leads back through the placenta from the baby to the mother. The placenta performs nutritional, respirational, and excretory functions and also secretes special hormones for the fetus. It also helps protect the fetus by screening out some of the chemicals circulating in the mother's blood that might harm the baby.

All animal studies have shown that THC passes easily through the placenta to the developing baby. The fetal liver cannot metabolize cannabinoids, which therefore accumulate in the tissues of the baby. One study on hamsters showed that early in pregnancy, THC concentrations in the fetus were four times as high as in the maternal tissues.

Dr. Carol Smith points out that the "gross retardant effects on the fetus are thought to be accounted for in part by the fact that the placenta tries to detoxify the THC, and in the process of doing this, the normal nutrition and hormone-producing functions of the placenta are interfered with."

Although most marijuana placenta research has been done with rats and mice, Drs. Paige and Norma Besche of the Reproductive Research Laboratory, Baylor College of Medicine in Houston, Texas, have done a four-year study on the effects of marijuana and THC on rhesus-monkey *and* human placentas.

Since the FDA forbids giving marijuana to pregnant women, "pure" controlled human studies on the placenta are impossible. Consequently, the Besches obtained rhesus monkey placentas from Dr. Sassenrath's breeders, who had received no drug but THC for three to five years. The monkey placentas were deep-frozen immediately after the breeders gave birth, then air-expressed to Texas.

The human placentas for the Besches' study were taken only from women who did not smoke pot or "do" any drugs. Only women who gave birth by Caesarean section were used in this study so the placenta would not have gone through the contractions of labor with possible areas of tissue hemorrhaging, etc. Then various quantities of THC were added to different placenta tissue samples. All THC quantities were measured in amounts relevant to human doses.

Results: Both the monkey and human studies showed that the more THC in the placenta, the less estrogen was produced, and as Dr. Paige Besche pointed out, it is well known to clinicians that decreased estrogen results in decreased nutrition to the developing fetus. This, in turn, can cause low-birthweight babies.

"Placenta work" by the Besches and others also highlights the fact that THC acts on reproductive functions in a double-barreled manner, not only via the brain, but also directly since THC has been shown to collect in as well as to pass through the placenta.

There may well be other constituents in marijuana and effects on other organs besides the placenta that result in low-birthweight babies. But one thing is eminently clear. *In virtually all animal studies, exposure to pot smoke or THC has resulted in smaller litters and smaller babies.*

In this context it is interesting to note a story reported in The *New York Times,* December 28, 1980:

> One of the great ironies of American life is that the United States, despite the most advanced medical technology and facilities in the world, has one of the highest rates of infant mortality among industrialized nations. The key to this anomaly is birth weight. Low-weight infants are 40 times as likely to die within a month of birth as infants of normal weight, and American women bear an unusually high number of low-weight babies.

The Surgeon General of the United States reported in 1980 that, after remaining almost stable for many years, since 1965 the infant mortality rate has been increasing.

In 1965, marijuana use began its climb in the United States. By 1979, one out of every four American women aged eighteen to twenty-five was a current pot-smoker. Might this statistic be related to the figures on low-birthweight babies and high infant mortality? The question certainly bears scientific examination.

On July 18, 1983, a front-page story in The *New York Times* began:

> Physicians and statisticians who analyze patterns of births in the United States have concluded that the number of babies born with some physical and mental defect has doubled over the last 25 years. . . . The data was generated by the National Health Interview Survey, a Federal program mandated by Congress that since 1956 has conducted continuing interviews with residents of thousands of households around the country. . . . The researchers said they had found an increase in moderate physical or mental impairment, but no large increase in the number of children who are so deformed or retarded that they have to be institutionalized. . . . Many cases of learning impairment are not identified until a child starts school, or even until the third or fourth grade.
>
> One expert said: "The increases were all the more startling because the 1950s were a terrible time for children because of polio and other diseases. With new vaccines and improvements in medical care, one might expect real improvements, not the other way around.". . .
>
> Dr. John E. Marshall, director of the National Center for Health Services Research in Rockville, Md., . . . and other experts listed four possible causes for this doubling of defects. The first was cigarette smoking which is known to reduce the birth weight of babies, thus placing them at increased risk of having some mental or physical abnormality.

Marijuana smoking was not mentioned. But, as noted in the Boston City Hospital study, the more frequently a woman smoked marijuana during her pregnancy, the smaller her baby. And more women who smoked marijuana

149

and tobacco cigarettes delivered smaller babies than women who smoked tobacco cigarettes alone. Might marijuana play a causal role in the statistics concerning the *doubling* of the number of babies born "with moderate physical or mental impairment"? Only a minimal amount of research has yet been done in this area, compared to the massive amount of research done on birth anomalies and tobacco cigarettes.

Thus far no one has studied the day-to-day development of the children of pot-smoking human mothers. But Dr. Ethel Sassenrath studied the first year's day-to-day development of rhesus babies born to mothers who had been given a daily oral dose of the single cannabinoid THC for three to five years.

At the 1980 Senate Hearings on Health Consequences of Marijuana Use, at which Drs. Smith, Bauman, Sassenrath, and Rosenkrantz testified on pot's effects on the female reproductive system, Senator Charles Mathias ended this section of the hearings with a question: "You have all been very cautious, you have been very correct, you have been very conservative. But at this stage of your considerations, what message have you got for the young women of America, the families of this country?"

Dr. Sassenrath's "message" was this:

Marijuana has taken its place along with other substances that are detrimental during pregnancy. I would also say that the prognosis for a reduced functional potential in offspring is something that should be considered and needs a great deal of attention. It would not be a matter of the child's physical growth. It would not be observable immediately. But it is something that really needs much more study.

One area that could obviously cause reproductive problems is the accumulation of cannabinoids in the fatty ovaries. In animal studies, radioactively tagged THC has clearly been shown to collect there. By contrast to males, who have about three hundred thousand sperm in each ejaculate and whose testes are continually at work manufacturing more, females have a limited supply of eggs. A large limit, to be sure—each infant girl is born with germ cells that form a total of around four hundred thousand eggs. But what if some, or many, of these are pot-damaged by the girl who starts using the drug in her preteen or early teen years, and keeps on "toking"? How might this be affecting the supply of eggs in her ovaries?

The first and thus far the only marijuana researcher to explore this critical subject was Dr. Akira Morishima, director of pediatric endocrinology at Columbia University's College of Physicians and Surgeons. Morishima points out that throughout history, cannabis has been limited in use to grown adult males. Thus far, *only in the United States has pot use become prevalent among young girls.* In order to see what might be happening to the eggs of human teenagers, he did a study on a species in which "egg counting" is at least feasible, even though difficult. He gave 150 "teenaged mice" a daily injection of THC with the human equivalency dose of, for example, a teenage girl who is stoned three or four hours a day. The control group received the injecting fluid with no THC. All the mice were mated, and were sacrificed when their fertilized eggs had multiplied into two to four cells.

Result: The fertilized eggs of the control mice were normal. In the THC mice, almost 20 percent of the eggs had died or were about to die, or had divided abnormally (see picture on page 152). The implication for humans? "THC might affect fertility," said Dr. Morishima. "If the fertilized egg died in its early stages before a woman missed her first period, she would never even know she had been pregnant. If an unhealthy egg was fertilized, this would probably result in miscarriage."

Morishima adds, "There is no way to repair the damage of eggs which may already have been affected by THC and perhaps other toxic cannabinoids as well. The only way to assure against possible damage is not to use the drug."

Other mice findings are equally disturbing. If *any* of the following effects were found for a drug being reviewed by the Food and Drug Administration, it would, without a doubt, be immediately forbidden for human consumption.

Dr. Harris Rosenkrantz did rodent and rabbit studies primarily examining the pot-dose-related incidence of fetal deaths. In the case of the rats, experimental groups of fifteen to thirty pregnant animals were exposed to either a low, medium, or high dose of smoke from the automatic smoking machine, using four, eight, twelve, or sixteen puffs of the same puff volume, puff duration, and exposure interval. THC blood levels showed that this was the equivalent of a human who smoked from three to thirty joints a week. The control group of rats received sixteen puffs of pot smoke from marijuana from which the cannabinoids had been removed. To be certain any untoward effects were not caused by the smoke itself, another group of controls were placed in the inhalator for an equal amount of time, but were not exposed to any smoke.

A day or two before the expected delivery date, the fetuses were removed by Caesarean delivery. There was a normal number of dead babies in the control group: 1.6 percent. There were double that number, 2.5 to 3.6 percent of dead babies, in the marijuana-exposed groups. It might be assumed that

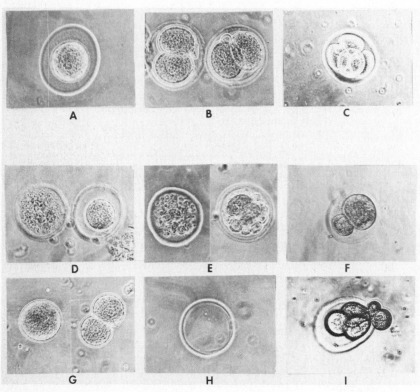

Females are born with their lifetime supply of eggs. Does THC, which is collected in the ovaries, harm them? Dr. Akira Morishima was the first scientist to explore this. He gave 150 mice the "mouse equivalency" dose of a teenage girl who is stoned three or four hours a day. The fertilized eggs of the control mice divided normally (Photos A, B, and C.). The six lower photos show abnormalities in eggs from the THC mice: 19.1 percent were abnormal—either dead or dying, or divided abnormally. "The chance of this occurring by chance alone," said Morishima, "would have been less than a one in a thousand. This is, therefore, a very significant finding."

the higher percentage of deaths came from the groups of animals exposed to the most puffs of pot smoke. But this was not the case. *The incidence of dead babies was not dose-related.*

The study was repeated with mice and with rabbits. In both cases there was also a non-dose-related doubling of fetal deaths. Yet, as was the case with Sassenrath's monkeys, all of the dead fetuses *looked* perfectly normal.

In order to try to pinpoint which cannabinoid caused the doubling of the death rate, Rosenkrantz did another study. When a group of rats and mice were in their sixth day of pregnancy, one of Rosenkrantz's co-workers performed a laporotomy (similar to a Caesarean incision) on each of the pregnant animals. He counted and located the exact position of each fetus. Then Rosenkrantz fed the "mothers-to-be" delta-9-THC. (Their THC blood levels were in the range of humans who smoked one to six joints a day.) Two or three days before normal delivery another colleague—who did not know the results of the laporotomy—performed a Caesarean section on each of the pregnant rats and mice. Result: A number of the fetuses had simply disappeared, and there was no residual tissue to be found. This is termed fetal resorption. Furthermore, all the fetuses that had not been resorbed were dead.

Then, in another study, Rosenkrantz gave pregnant mice somewhat higher THC doses—and the entire litter was resorbed. All the embryos simply disappeared. Said Rosenkrantz: "To my knowledge, it has not been reported for any other drug of abuse that a similar total resorption of all embryos ever took place."

Rosenkrantz pointed out:

> The extrapolation of these findings in animals to human female marijuana users is difficult, but a potential hazard to normal pregnancy must be considered for two reasons. First, because only two to three days' use in the first trimester, when the organs are forming, induced embryo toxicity. Second, a pot-using mother who wanted a baby might lose the pregnancy without even knowing she had aborted; in the early stages there would be no recognizable trace of fetal tissue.

Although the dead, nonresorbed babies in Rosenkrantz's marijuana-reproduction studies looked normal, this was not always the case with other researchers. For example, in 1978 the late Dr. Vincent de Paul Lynch, professor of pharmacology and director of the toxicology program at St. John's University in Jamaica, New York, published a study on pregnant mice exposed to pot smoke that contained the human equivalency dose of one joint a day during only four days of the pregnancy. The one hundred mother mice generally gave birth at night. When Dr. Lynch arrived in the morning he found that invariably they had, as he put it, "savaged most of their pups" (killed them). Since mice tend to do away with their abnormal offspring, Lynch wondered whether the THC had, in fact, produced birth anomalies. He repeated the pot-smoke exposure with another hundred pregnant mice, but this time he did Caesareans, delivering the babies before term. A significant number of the pups had two congenital defects: cleft palate and a condition called *micrognathia* (a shortening of the lower jaw), which, said Dr. Lynch, "forms quite an impediment for eating."

Lynch separated the female THC babies who had been exposed *only* through the few puffs of pot smoke given their pregnant mothers during the seventh to tenth days of gestation, the period called *organogenesis*. These babies received no direct marijuana exposure at all. When *those* females grew up and had babies, some of the pups were sacrificed and autopsied. A significant number had a kidney anomaly, which, said Dr. Lynch, "was quite unique. They had some sort of accumulation of kidney fluid, which would probably have caused a nephrosis [an inflammation] of the glomerulus, which in turn would ultimately result in kidney failure." The offspring that were not sacrificed were much slower to develop than the pups of the controls. For example, said Dr. Lynch, the normal baby is "haired" by the tenth day, but these babies were "naked" until the twelfth to fourteenth day. This is an appreciable time in a young mouse's life, since its entire life span is only about twenty-four months.

Dr. Lynch was not the only researcher to find carryover effects into future rodent generations. Prior to his work with human females, Dr. Peter Fried did a marijuana study using pregnant female rats as subjects. He exposed the subject groups to pot smoke for nine minutes a day, the control group to smoke with all the cannabinoids removed. Their babies (who were exposed to marijuana during gestation, nursing, or both) received no pot smoke directly at all, yet these babies were retarded in growth and development. When the females of this group grew up and had babies of their own, these offspring were also retarded in growth and development—even though the only family member to have been exposed to pot smoke was their *grandmother*.

In the grandchildren, Fried looked at fifteen different sets of reflexes that are considered "physiological milestones" for developing rats. "We know the animal ought to be able to do certain things at certain ages," said Fried. Among the milestones significantly delayed were the eye-opening reflexes and teething. The grandchildren also weighed less at birth when compared to normal newborn rats, although the difference was not as great as in the case of their mothers, who had been exposed to pot only through *their* mothers.

In another study, Fried gave pregnant female rats cannabis smoke throughout gestation. Their male and female offspring received a 2-milligram "THC shot" (a milligram is 1/1000th of a gram) two months prior to mating. *Their* male and female offspring, who received no direct exposure, took longer to mate. Only 18 percent became fertile, compared to 50 percent of the control rats that were exposed to smoke with the cannabinoids removed. Their reproductive organs were smaller than those of the controls. Furthermore, *their* offspring also weighed less and were slow in some aspects of physiological development. Exposure to cannabis smoke as a fetus plus THC as a young adult had a far greater two-generational effect on fertility than exposure *only* to the THC injection two months prior to mating.

Fried concluded:

> This would suggest that the effect of marijuana inhalation was genetic in nature rather than merely a hormone change in the females of the first generation of offspring. What must be emphasized about these latter results is that *they are caused by cannabis smoke administered two generations earlier.* One characteristic of humans who smoke marijuana regularly is that their age span coincides with their peak reproductive years; thus these results, although obtained with rodents, indicate a potential area of significance with respect to human cannabis usage.

As noted earlier, the Institute of Medicine has pointed out an "urgent need for more comprehensive endocrine and gynecologic investigations of women who use marijuana." But there is also an "urgent need" for the research findings that have already been published in scientific journals to reach pot-smoking pregnant women—and their physicians. As one pot-smoking woman put it: "My gynecologist said nothing conclusive has been proven. He said you were much better off than if you smoked tobacco."

Pediatrician Ingrid Lantner of Willoughby, Ohio, one of the first physicians in the United States to become aware of the effects of marijuana on her young patients, reports: "I tried very hard to get obstetricians in the Cleveland area to inform pregnant patients about the harm pot smoking can do to the fetus. I didn't get anywhere. So I wrote a letter to the chairman of the department of obstetrics and gynecology at a local hospital. He didn't answer."

Lantner also points out the harm that a pot-smoking mother can do to her child after birth. Some parents have become aware of the effects on the baby of passive inhalation. As one mother told Dr. Lantner, "I get high and my baby gets high. She sleeps for hours. I don't even have to feed her."

"Virtually none of the pot-smoking mothers I've met," said Lantner, "had been warned about marijuana by their obstetrician."

American physicians might take a cue from the Committee on Public Health of the Ontario Medical Association, a professional organization of physicians affiliated with the Canadian Medical Association. In July 1983 they sent this statement to each of their members—almost all of the doctors in the province:

> *The Committee on Public Health recommends that all physicians in Ontario be urged to actively question their patients on the use of cannabis as a part of their medical and surgical assessments.*

The committee noted that pregnant women are "the first priority of patients in particular health situations whom physicians should query and counsel about cannabis use":

> Cannabinoids from cannabis cross the placenta and become a potential teratogen. To date no strong trend to single defect has arisen, but subtle developmental defects are being observed now, especially of the central nervous system, along with evidence of decreased size and weight of infants at term.

The second and third priorities were "women who wish to become mothers" and "men who wish to become fathers." (This was followed by three more priorities: respiratory, epileptic, and cardiovascular patients.)

The Committee on Public Health is not the only important Ontario medical and research organization to take such a stand. In a booklet published in September 1981, "Cannabis, Health & the Law," the Addiction Research Foundation, an Ontario government foundation under the Ministry of Health, summed up:

> The risks to health are real. *Adverse consequences will occur for some people on the basis of even occasional use.* The consequences at high levels of use may severely damage health. . . . There is a possibility of genetic mutations affecting future generations. These consequences are very serious for society and therefore on the evidence available, *the Foundation advocates strongly that cannabis not be used. . . . It would make no sense from a public health perspective . . . to acquiesce to any use of cannabis.*

Chapter 9

Effects on
Sex and Reproduction:
Male

Pot-smokers often claim that the drug is an aphrodisiac. Pot may well produce a laid-back state in some users, allowing uptight lovers to become more relaxed; for some people, sexual sensations become heightened.

However, clinical evidence shows that any sexual pluses pot may have can eventually degenerate into minuses. The time span varies with the individual. Some smokers report that they can't reach an orgasm when they are stoned; others find that orgasm is accompanied by painful anal spasms, which may last for several hours. Still others report painfully overextended erections. And a not uncommon phenomenon of the chronic, heavy pot-smoker was expressed by one young man who said, shrugging: "I don't bother much with women anymore. Who needs all that hassle? I get all the satisfaction I need from my joint."

Dr. Ingrid Lantner has spoken about marijuana on numerous radio call-in shows. She reports:

> This call was typical of many: A young man asked, "If I stop using pot, do you think I will feel like a man again?" Other chronic pot-smokers say they are impotent, but are not bothered by the fact—since they no longer feel sexual desires. I have also had calls from men who say that it takes about a month after quitting their pot smoking completely before their sexual drive begins to return.

Reports from marriage and sex counselors indicate that these symptoms are typical of pot-smoking women as well as men, but the only scientific studies of the matter have thus far been limited to men. In fact, the only large-scale American study on marijuana and sexual performance ever done was conducted by Robert C. Kolodny of the Masters and Johnson Institute

157

in 1973—when pot was far less potent than it is today. Kolodny had in-depth interviews with five hundred men, aged eighteen to thirty, whose pot use ranged from sporadic to daily for six or seven years. Kolodny summed up: "The general trend was that with increasing use, there were lower rates of sexual activity and a lower frequency of orgasm."

In a study of 1,238 cannabis-using men done in India by Drs. G. S. Chopra and R. N. Chopra in 1939, 24 percent said cannabis had no effect on their sexual desire and performance; 20 percent reported initial stimulation, then later depression; 16 percent said it produced sexual stimulation; and 40 percent reported that it resulted in sexual depression.

In April 1984, Dr. John Hall, chairman of the department of medicine at Kingston Hospital, Jamaica, reported a high incidence of impotence among males who had smoked ganja for five or more years. "This finding," he said, "has been replicated by other colleagues in Jamaica."

Many U.S. marriage and sex counselors report that if their patients give up marijuana completely, interest in sex starts to return after a month or so, and often the condition of impotence is reversed.

Dr. Wylie Hembree of Columbia University College of Physicians and Surgeons did a study on pot's effects on sperm. He began his research in 1975 by placing ads in the *Village Voice* and the *Columbia Spectator,* asking for healthy young male pot-smokers who agreed to be hospitalized for three months. During the middle month, they would receive as much free pot as they could smoke. Hembree's phone rang for days.

He selected sixteen subjects, all of whom used only pot. (Their urine was screened for other drugs when they checked in.) An in-depth sexual history was taken of each, starting with their earliest memory of masturbation.

Hembree put the subjects in the hospital so he could do a controlled study. The first month they went potless. The following month they were allowed to smoke all the "government-issued joints" they wished (2 percent THC). They smoked five to twenty a day, averaging twelve joints daily. Then came another pot-free "washout month." Throughout their entire stay, sperm analyses were done twice weekly, and hormone profiles were done on each subject once a week.

Results: During the pot-smoking period there was a 40 percent decrease in the number of sperm in each ejaculation, and a 20 percent decrease in sperm motility (the ability of sperm to swim). "The others," said Hembree, "just lie there." There was also a slight increase in the percentage of abnormal forms of sperm in the semen.

What about the reversibility of sperm changes? Hembree put it this way: "Some improvement in the characteristics of ejaculated sperm was observed in the third month, following cessation of marijuana use, in a few of the subjects. Sperm remained abnormal in other subjects." However, he pointed out that it takes about three months to complete one generation of sperm development, and the subjects had been potless for only one month after their "smoke-in." Because multiple factors determine reversibility, further studies will be necessary, he said, "for as long as six months or one year, in a relatively large number of chronic marijuana users who have abnormal semen characteristics."

Dr. Hembree also noted that:

The lower the percent of normal sperm, the more likely it is that the man will be infertile, since most abnormally shaped sperm do not fertilize eggs. My concern is whether marijuana is altering the biosynthetic process of sperm production within the testes. If something in marijuana, which may be THC or other cannabinoids, is, in fact, altering the process of sperm production, then we are obligated to find out what the consequences of this alteration are upon fertility and the offspring. It could produce subtle abnormalities in the offspring. Whatever we're going to find in the human—it's going to be subtle.

Dr. Ricardo Asch is looking for the "mechanisms" that produce the THC/sperm results found in animals and humans. Asch is director of clinical research in the department of obstetrics and gynecology, University of Texas Health Science Center at San Antonio. His subjects include rats, rabbits, rhesus monkeys, and man. His findings include the following:

1. Asch showed that THC significantly inhibits sperm from taking in fructose. Since sperm cells in human and monkey ejaculate get their chemical energy from fructose in the seminal plasma, and the sperms' motility (mobility) comes from the metabolism of fructose, the result is that sperm either become less mobile, or they die.

2. Gonadotropins (brain hormones that control the function of the ovaries and the testes) in the pituitary are regulated by the secretion of the neuro-transmitters dopamine, serotonin, and epinephrin, and gonadotropin-releasing hormones in the hypothalamus. Asch and his co-researchers showed that THC alters the metabolism of the neurotransmitters, which disturbs the regu-latory signals given to the pituitary hormones—causing much of THC's anti-reproductive effects.

159

Clearly, therefore, THC has a two-pronged effect on sperm: an indirect effect via the neurotransmitters in the brain, and a direct effect on fructose utilization by the sperm themselves, since THC accumulates in both the testes and the semen. THC may also have an impairing effect on the developing sperm, although this has not yet been firmly established.

Teenagers and preteens are particularly vulnerable to the effects of marijuana because the secretion of gonadotropins, which control the *onset* of sexual development, starts between ages eight and twelve, and is completed around age eighteen. In the boy this produces, among other things, bodily changes, broader shoulders, narrow hips, muscles, beard, and pubic hair. The male sex hormone, testosterone, produced in the testes, plays an essential role. As Dr. Carol Smith points out, "The increase in testosterone is also responsible for the development of the prostate and the seminal vesicles, which make secretions that keep the sperm alive after ejaculation. Also affected is the growth of the penis itself, which becomes capable of the mature pattern of erection and ejaculation."

A few case reports in medical journals indicate that heavy marijuana use may retard the sexual development of teenage boys. But, of course, no one is allowed to do controlled marijuana studies on human teenagers. Consequently, when Smith decided to do the most rigidly controlled study possible on marijuana's effects on male sexuality, she worked with "teenaged" male rhesus monkeys. Not only are the sperm of the rhesus and the human virtually indistinguishable under the microscope, the entire sexual hormone system of the rhesus is a virtual carbon copy of the human male's.

Dr. Smith injected her monkeys with THC to produce the blood-level equivalent of a human smoking one to two joints, then examined the effects on the production of testosterone (the male sex hormone) and other hormones vital to normal sexual development and activity. She was interested in seeing the short-term effects—if any—of a *single dose* of THC on testosterone and other hormones vital to normal sexual development and activity.

Results: Said Dr. Smith, "One dose 'shuts down production' for as long as 24 hours. THC profoundly inhibits testosterone and other hormones which stimulate the sex organs, bringing them down to the level of a castrated animal." Besides marijuana, Smith has studied alcohol, certain narcotics, tranquilizers, and barbiturates for their possible effects on testosterone and other sex hormones. She summed up: "Of the drugs that we've studied, none has as potent an effect on these hormones as THC."

There is controversy among researchers as to whether, in fact, marijuana does affect the testosterone level in human males. Some found it did; some

160

found it didn't. Some short-term studies indicate the drop might depend on how long it was after smoking that the testosterone level was measured. In all studies of short-term exposure, testosterone levels have returned to normal when the subjects stopped smoking pot. There have been no testosterone-level studies on long-term chronic users.

Besides puberty, there is another time in a male animal or human's life when the testosterone level is normally extremely high—before birth. Another marijuana researcher, Dr. Susan Dalterio of the University of Texas Health Science Center at San Antonio, decided to measure exactly what happened to this sex hormone at these two critical times. Dalterio favors mice for reproductive studies since they are inexpensive, so large groups can be studied; also, one does not have to wait long for the next litter to be born (the gestation period is only twenty days). Every day for five days during the middle week of their pregnancy, she gave female mice a one-joint human equivalency dose of THC or CBN (cannabinol—a nonpsychoactive cannabinoid), dissolving it in a drop of sesame oil to facilitate ingestion. Then the mothers were sacrificed. About 15 percent of the pups of the THC mothers had died. But all whose mothers had received CBN lived. Then the scientist examined the amount of testosterone in the testes of the male fetuses—not an easy job. Said Dalterio: "Because the fetus was so tiny, so fatty, I had to extract testosterone out of the whole mouse 'mixture.' And then I measured it." She found that in both the THC mice and the CBN mice, there was a significant decrease in testosterone, which is essential for the development of a normal male. Said the scientist: "Without testosterone, made by its own testes before birth, any male mammal will look like a female—no matter what the genes say. Without enough testosterone at the fetal stage, it is unlikely that an animal will grow up to look like a normal male or to act like one."

In another study, Dalterio looked at the other time when there is a normal and essential surge of the testosterone level: at puberty. She injected one group of pubertal mice with one tiny drop of sesame oil "flavored" with THC, and others with a dose of CBN (both groups got the human equivalent of one to three joints). The testosterone level dropped sharply in THC-treated males. The testosterone levels of the CBN-treated mice did not fall after acute exposure, but was lower after repeated CBN exposure.

Other researchers have shown significant testosterone-level drops in other species of laboratory animals, looking at the levels in mature males.

Since dealers sometimes lace low-grade pot with PCP or "angel dust" (and then sell it for higher prices as "good stuff"), Dr. Jack Harclerode looked at the combined effects of these drugs on the testosterone level of rats. In all cases, THC plus PCP "significantly depressed" the testosterone level below the level produced by an equal amount of THC alone.

There have been many studies of the effects of THC on reproduction of a variety of male research animals. Virtually all show clearly that marijuana smoke, or THC or other individual cannabinoids such as CBN, markedly decrease sperm count and motility.

Studies have also shown deformed sperm in animals exposed to human equivalency doses of pot smoke. Dr. Arthur Zimmerman of the University of Toronto found that CBN created a five-fold increase in abnormal sperm in mice, while THC created a three-fold increase.

Work with animals has also shown that THC creates abnormalities, such as shrinkage of prostate and seminal vesicles and abnormal testicular function.

In Canada, Dr. Peter Fried had shown that when pregnant mice were exposed to THC, the impairing effects showed up in their grandchildren. In Texas, Dr. Susan Dalterio also examined generational carryover, examining the male offspring of pregnant mice exposed to THC. In one group, she gave one drop of THC-"flavored" sesame oil to each mother the day before she was due to give birth, and for the first six days of nursing. She gave another daily drop containing CBN to another batch of mice. The mouse doses were the human equivalent of one to three joints a day. The babies received their THC or CBN *only* through the mother's one-day prenatal exposure, and through the milk. At birth they looked the same as the control mice. At age twenty-one days (about eight to ten years in human terms) they all still weighed in normally. Then at thirty days (puberty), the scientist teamed up some of the males with normal pre-adolescent female mice. Each pair had its own plastic shoebox home.

"When you introduce a normal teenaged male mouse to a pre-adolescent female," said Dalterio, "the boys get all excited. But the THC and CBN male mice slunk off into the corner. They left the girls strictly alone. They were clearly under stress because when they were sacrificed it was clear that their adrenals were swollen—a sign of stress."

But that wasn't all. A number of THC male mice had not been sacrificed. When they reached adulthood most of them became grossly overweight. Whereas a normal adult mouse weighs about 40 grams, *they* weighed in at 55 grams. Said Dalterio:

They looked like mice we had castrated in other studies. Castrated mice get fat. What's more, they acted like castrated mice. Their sex behavior was definitely affected. Half the THC animals didn't mount at all. Most of the CBN's would start mounting. Then they'd give up in the middle and go away—very unusual behavior for a mouse. In fact, I never saw this before in any animal. Maybe their brain was giving messages that it wasn't that much fun after all.

A Dalterio study published in 1982 had even more startling generational results. This time she divided seventy-two male mice into four groups. One group served as controls. One group got a dose of THC, the next got CBN, and the third got CBD (which, like CBN, is nonpsychoactive). Each was given the human equivalency dose of the cannabinoid in one to three joints, administered in sesame oil. The controls got sesame oil only.

Each mouse received "his drug" three times a week for five weeks. After the first two weeks, they all got something else—a "straight" female mouse (no drugs). Each lived with his mate for a week and then was given a new one. This pairing continued up to two weeks after the cannabinoid treatment was stopped.

First result: The fertility in the THC, CBN, and CBD males was reduced by an average of 20 percent. Either their female mates did not conceive or, if they did, there was significant increase in prenatal or postnatal loss (the babies died before or soon after birth.)

"Since none of the female mice had been given any of the drug," said Dalterio, "this means that the cannabinoids cause so much damage to the sperm that it results in observable changes in their fertility and in damage to their offspring. Having a dead baby is, after all, pretty heavy damage."

Second result: "We took out some of the testes of the males, and looked at their chromosomes. And," said Dalterio, "they were abnormal. They didn't separate normally. They changed places when they shouldn't have. Or, they stuck together, forming rings. They're not supposed to form rings. They're supposed to go side by side." (See picture on page 164).

Third result: The male babies that lived were given no drugs directly. They had been exposed only through their fathers' sperm. When the sons grew up they were mated with normal female mice. Over 25 percent of these THC and CBN *sons* never produced a normal pregnancy. Either the males were infertile (the mate produced no offspring), or the mates had an abnormally high percentage of prenatal or postnatal deaths, or they produced abnormal offspring.

Dalterio also examined the testes in these male mice. The sons showed

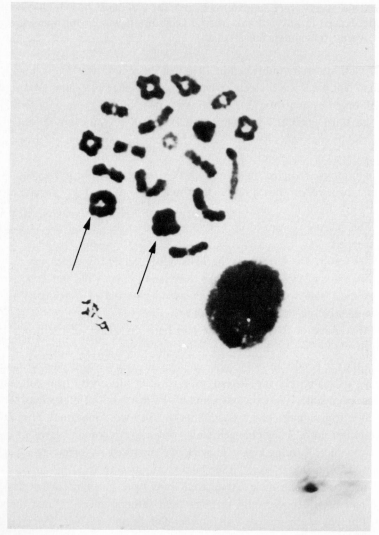

Chromosomes from testis of male mouse whose *only* exposure to cannabinoids was through their father. The arrows point to abnormal ring formations. Other slides showed other distinct abnormalities. The same types of chromosomal abnormalities showed up in their fathers—with the same frequencies. "This would indicate," said Dr. Susan Dalterio, who did this study, "that cannabinoid-caused chromosome abnormalities are transmitted from generation to generation."

chromosomal abnormalities, just as their fathers' had. The scientist then repeated the study using another group of mice, with the same results. But the second time around, something new was added: Two of the sons had offspring with severe brain defects. What kind of defect? One had no skull. "The brain was just sitting there," said Dalterio, "covered only by skin. One of these mice also had an open spine and the intestines were on the outside of the body."

> In the thousands of fetuses I've examined in the past ten years, mice exposed to alcohol and other drugs, I've never seen this severe a birth defect before. And here I found two in one week—*among mice who had been exposed to THC only through their grandfathers!* It certainly seems that cannabinoids are mutagenic—they can transmit abnormalities across generations.

When testifying about her work at U.S. Senate hearings in 1980, Dalterio pointed out that although it is difficult to extrapolate from results obtained in studies with laboratory animals to predict effects in man, nevertheless such studies are able to suggest implications for human exposure to marijuana during critical periods in development. As an example of the unexpected generational carryover of substances once deemed harmless, she mentioned that:

> diethylstilbestrol (DES) and other drugs used in the past in the medical management of pregnancy complications clearly demonstrate that the effects of prenatal exposure to some agents are not apparent until maturity. Thus, the fetus, both in the human and in the laboratory animal, is very vulnerable, much more so than the adult individual, to assault by a wide variety of chemical agents. These effects may be profound or subtle, obvious at birth or late-appearing, but nonetheless have an impact on the health and well-being of the affected individual.

Dalterio has been involved in marijuana research on mice since 1976. She noted that "the design of our studies was such that the results could probably be relevant to the heavy marijuana user. The implications for other user categories remain to be determined." Further,

> Many of us involved in the elucidation of marijuana's effects on the male reproductive system in rats, mice, or rhesus monkeys were inspired to do so by earlier reports that these parameters were being affected in young adult men who were heavy chronic users. . . . For example, there were reports, starting as early as 1974, suggesting that young adult men who use marijuana chronically had potency problems.
> Also, the possibility that marijuana use by pregnant women could affect the development of their sons should probably be seriously consid-

ered before a generation or two of children have been exposed in this way to this substance.

As is the case with most of the scientists mentioned in this book, Dalterio has done many more marijuana studies than those described here. And, as is the case with all of the scientists, all of her studies showed various harmful effects of this drug. At the Senate hearings on Health Consequences of Marijuana Use, Dalterio summed up her findings in these five categories:

1. Both psychoactive and nonpsychoactive components of marijuana affect male reproductive functions in mice.

2. In both adult and immature male mice, exposure to THC or CBN decreases levels of the male sex hormone testosterone, as well as pituitary hormones, which stimulate the testes.

3. These changes in hormone levels are accompanied by decreases in adult sexual activity in male mice.

4. Maternal exposure to THC or CBN results in long-term alterations in body regulation, pituitary-testicular function, and sexual behavior in their male offspring.

5. Ingestion of these cannabinoids by pregnant female mice can result in decreased testosterone levels in their male fetuses.

In most animal studies there has been one encouraging note: When exposure to pot smoke or cannabinoids was stopped, the system returned to normal. However, as Dr. Carol Smith pointed out, "We don't know whether the effects on chronic pot-smoking human teenagers might not produce permanent disruption of sexual development in males and females. This question has not yet been looked at by research scientists."

Another point to keep in mind: Scientists Fried, Dalterio, and Lynch found that exposure of the mother *or* father to a single cannabinoid (THC, CBD, or CBN) resulted in abnormalities in the offspring two generations later, showing that the cannabinoids effect a change that is not "merely" hormonal, but genetic in nature. As Dr. Fried puts it: "Since the age span of men and women who smoke marijuana regularly coincides with their peak reproductive years, we should take serious note of these generational findings. Although obtained with rodents, they indicate a potential area of significance with respect to human cannabis usage."

Effects on Long-Term Users

Only one scientist has taken a close look—indeed, an electron-microscopic look—at the sperm of long-term cannabis smokers. She is Dr. Marietta Issidorides, of Athens, Greece—one of Europe's most respected cell biologists.

People smoke hashish in the Middle East, not marijuana. But for years the Greek government has cracked down heavily on hash smokers. By 1980, less than 1 percent of Greek teenagers had ever used cannabis (compared to over 60 percent of American teenagers).

However, even the very real possibility of a jail term as a deterrent did not stop one group from their daily hash-pipe habit. This colony lives on the outskirts of the Greek port of Piraeus. They proved ideal subjects for cannabis studies since there were many among the group who had used hash daily for years, but used no other drugs. Furthermore, other members of this same colony had never used hashish or other drugs. Thus the group provided both subjects and controls for studies of possible effects of long-term cannabis use.

All subjects and controls were given an extensive medical examination. Anyone with any sign of incapacitating illness or disorder was disqualified. The scientist did not want to cloud her findings with the possibility that a disease or genetic inadequacy might have caused any untoward results.

The healthy hash-smoking subjects ranged in age from twenty-two to fifty-eight; their average age was forty. All had been daily hash-smokers for at least ten years (most had started around age sixteen). None had used other addictive drugs, apart from moderate use of alcohol and regular use of tobacco.

The controls were carefully "matched" with the subjects in age, place of upbringing and residence, socioeconomic level, and education (both groups averaged a third-grade education). They were also matched for tobacco and alcohol use; both subjects and controls used these substances only moderately. The controls had the same diet, the same lifestyle, and the same occupation as the subjects; most worked in the local slaughterhouse.

Ten users and ten controls provided freshly ejaculated spermatozoa. Dr. Issidorides then became the first scientist to see the sperm of long-term cannabis users under an electron microscope, which blows up an image one hundred thousand times. The cells are placed on a metal grid, which goes into the microscope. Instead of bright light—which is used in all other types of microscopes—electrons are beamed through the cells and form a highly magnified image on a saucer-sized fluorescent screen. At the press of a button, the image can be recorded on film. It is then possible to blow up the picture so that a single cell becomes the size of a door or half a wall. This obviously saves a lot of squinting—and allows the scientist to see subtle cell changes that are not noticeable under an ordinary microscope.

Results: "Our observations," said Issidorides, "revealed distinct differences between the sperm of users and controls." Among the findings: a significant decrease in sperm count and motility. Also, the majority of sperm of all of the hash-smoking subjects were abnormal in structure to some degree. These abnormalities came in three forms. And many of the sperm were abnormal in all three ways. (See picture on page 169.)

First was the deformed cap. It was not firm and presumably, therefore, could not penetrate and fertilize an egg normally. In some cases there was no cap at all. This was the most prevalent abnormality, and the majority of the sperm were like this.

The second most prevalent abnormality was diffuse or dispersed chromatin. "Well-packed chromatin in a normal sperm looks like well-packed crystal fibers," said Issidorides. "Loose-packed chromatin seen in the sperm of the hash-smokers was very fibrous. Chromatin contains the vital genetic material; the genes. If sperm like this did penetrate the egg, there would probably be a natural aborting because," said the scientist, "something is not right." There was also a striking decrease in essential argenine-rich proteins.

The third-most-prevalent abnormality was:

sperm so immature that in the normal healthy male they would never be seen in the ejaculate. They're not completed. But in the hash-smoker's sperm, some did emerge in the ejaculate, indicating that something in cannabis affects the sperm maturity process at many levels, releasing sperm that had no business being out of the testis. They probably couldn't fertilize an egg.

But most important of all the sperm findings was the fact that, for the first time, we had tangible proof of the reaction of cannabis on the chemical makeup of the sperm. This was evident in the striking decrease in certain proteins containing essential amino acids. Does cannabis alter the biosynthetic process of sperm production within the testis? That is certainly an important issue for further research.

How do these "hash findings" relate to the pot being smoked in the United States today? Since the subjects had smoked hash daily for an average of sixteen years, they "outrank" most U.S. daily users by a decade or so. The Greek subjects smoked hash with a 5- to 6-percent THC potency; average U.S. street pot is 3 to 4 percent THC. But the increasingly popular U.S.-grown sinsemilla far outranks the Greek hash in THC potency.

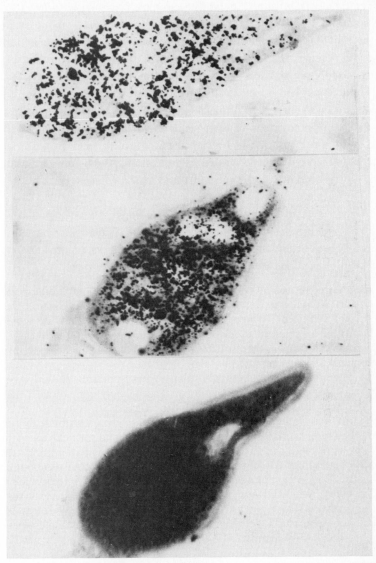

Dr. Issidorides looked at the sperm of long-term hash-smokers. The majority were abnormal in structure to some degree. Sperm at top is normal, from a non-hash-smoking control. Middle and bottom pictures show typical abnormalities. A deformed cap was seen in the majority of sperm. The cap was not firm and presumably could not penetrate and fertilize an egg normally. In some cases there was no cap at all. Also, the chromatin was diffuse or dispersed. Chromatin contains the vital genetic material, the genes. There was also a striking decrease in the essential arginine-rich proteins.

The Greek subjects smoked the hashish equivalent of six joints a day. The National High School Senior Surveys have consistently shown that daily users smoke an average of three-and-a-half joints a day; about 14 percent of the daily users smoke seven or more joints a day. Thus, in terms of dose and potency, the Issidorides findings may be applicable to tens of thousands of daily pot-smokers in the United States today.

The scientist had hoped to study the reversibility of the sperm-cell symptoms she saw in the group of hash-smokers. When the subjects were shown the enlarged photographs of their sickly-looking sperm cells, most of them reacted in shock and insisted that they would quit their hash-smoking at once. However, only one succeeded in giving it up. And before Dr. Issidorides could do reversibility studies on him—the man moved away.

Many dedicated users tend to dismiss findings on marijuana's effects on male and female reproduction with the comment: "Pot smokers have perfectly normal babies—everyone can see that!" However, as pointed out by Dr. William Pollin, director of NIDA:

> After three thousand years of alcohol consumption—including consumption by women—it was not until 1973 that doctors discovered the fetal alcohol syndrome, which results in abnormal babies. After more than forty years of cigarette-smoking among women, it was not until this decade that it was proved that smoking during pregnancy—and even prior to pregnancy—can damage the fetus.
>
> Therefore, pot-smokers who plan to have children should take heed of the present research in this area. I completely concur with the June 1983 recommendation of the Ontario, Canada, Committee on Public Health that "all physicians be urged to actively question their patients on the use of cannabis as a part of their medical and surgical assessments." I also agree with their listing of priorities "identifying patients in particular health situations whom physicians should query and counsel about cannabis use: first, pregnant women; second, women who wish to become mothers; third, men who wish to become fathers." From the clear signs we are receiving from research scientists, it is these three groups of pot-smokers who run a genuine risk of impairing the most defenseless and most vulnerable members of the human race: unborn and newly born babies.

170

Chapter 10

Effects on the Brain

People smoke marijuana for one reason only: its mind-altering qualities. They do not, however, expect the drug to alter the structure of their brain cells. Yet, if monkey findings can be extrapolated to humans, this is exactly what *is* happening.

The scientist who has done the most research on this subject is Dr. Robert Heath, who was chairman of the Department of Psychiatry and Neurology at Tulane Medical School for thirty-two years and chairman of the departments of psychiatry and neurology at New Orleans' huge Charity Hospital, Tulane University Hospital, Veterans' Hospital, and two large state hospitals. He has published 365 scientific papers about psychiatry and the brain.

Some of Heath's most important work in the late 1960s and early 1970s concerned the identification of the brain's neural network for pleasure and for painful emotions. In humans, Heath explains, electrical stimulation of certain interconnected deep brain sites induces profoundly pleasurable feelings, whereas stimulation of certain other well-demarcated sites induces profoundly negative feelings, including anxiety and anger.

While Dr. Heath the neurologist was mapping the mind, Dr. Heath the psychiatrist was seeing patients, and noticing that many had exactly the same pattern of psychological symptoms. When he asked about their drug taking, he found out they were regular pot-smokers who, for the most part, did not use other illicit drugs.

Their "carbon copy" symptoms included the amotivational (or dropout) syndrome, abnormal irritability and hostility, abrupt mood swings, and impaired short-term memory. Some of the patients had experienced panic reactions and paranoia. Another frequent symptom was depression, sometimes

171

even suicidal feelings, which, in a few instances, led to actual suicide attempts.

Heath discussed these symptoms with colleagues all over the country—who, it turned out, were seeing exactly the same thing among their pot-smoking patients. Furthermore, when the patients stopped their pot smoking completely, these specific symptoms almost invariably disappeared within three or four months—the exception being the impairment in recent (short-term) memory. Memory improved, but often not to what it had been prior to the heavy pot smoking.

Heath wondered whether the symptoms, though seemingly psychological, might in fact be physical, caused by actual brain-cell changes. He decided to do research in this area. He used rhesus monkeys, for the same reasons as Sassenrath, Smith, and others had used them in their reproductive studies, and because the limbic area—the so-called "old brain"—is so similar in humans and rhesus monkeys that under the microscope human and monkey brain cells are virtually indistinguishable. The limbic area is the center of pleasure, hostility, hunger (the "munchies"), and other emotional and physical signs and symptoms related to chronic pot use.

In one of his first marijuana/monkey studies, Heath implanted electrodes in the limbic area's septal region—a center for pleasure. Other electrodes went to the hippocampus, which is related to hostile, aggressive, inappropriate activities and anxiety; others into the amygdala, also a site of irritability, hostility, and fear. Small electrodes were deep-planted into ten different areas in the limbic system. Surface electrodes, the type attached to the scalp of humans for electroencephalogram (EEG) or brain-wave tests, were also used. Control monkeys got both the deep-brain and surface electrodes.

The implantation procedure itself caused brain-wave changes in both subjects and controls; therefore, Heath and his team waited for three weeks to begin exposing the subjects to pot smoke. By that time the EEGs of both subjects and controls had returned to normal.

To assure that it was not the marijuana *smoke* causing possible cell damage, the control monkeys received exactly the same amounts of pot smoke as the subjects, but from a special "brand" of "NIDA joints": "placebo" marijuana from which the delta-9-THC had been removed by a chemical process similar to decaffeinating coffee. (Only the THC was removed, not the other cannabinoids.)

Unlike their human counterparts, monkeys do not like pot smoke. When exposed to it, they hold their breath as long as possible, and then take short shallow breaths. Since Heath wanted to imitate the inhalation patterns of the typical pot-smoker, he and his co-workers, Drs. John and Austin Fitzjarrell, Stanley John, and Charles Fontana, developed an adaptation of an infant's respirator, which forced smoke through a face mask and into the monkey's lungs. It took about ten to fifteen minutes for each monkey to smoke a monkey-sized joint in this manner. A monkey-sized joint is one-quarter the size of a human joint.

The marijuana, which came from the "pot farm" in Mississippi, had a delta-9-THC potency of 2.5-percent. After exposure to marijuana, the blood levels of THC were checked to assure "human equivalency." It is important to bear this in mind for the following reason: There are many sources— ranging from NORML's "Marijuana and Health Newsletter" to *Hospital Physician*—which grossly exaggerate the amount of marijuana Heath gave to the monkeys. For example, Edward Brecher, then Advisory Board member of NORML, stated in an article in the May 1979 issue of *Hospital Physician* that the doses used by Heath were "the equivalent of 63 marijuana cigarettes a day for humans." Actually, in all of Dr. Heath's various rhesus monkey brain-cell studies, the largest dose any monkey received was smoke from three monkey-sized joints a day, five days a week, for six months.

Let us now look at the *results* of the EEG study.

The *scalp* electrodes of subjects and controls read "normal" in the EEG test. This was not surprising, since encephalographers doing traditional EEG tests on human pot-smokers generally get normal readings. However, the deep-planted electrodes showed distinct abnormalities in the monkeys with THC in their pot smoke. The controls, exposed to pot smoke without THC, had completely normal EEGs.

As with humans, some monkeys had more resistance to the drug's harmful effects than others. However, *in all cases, the most abnormal electrical reactions came from the areas of the brain directly related to the most common symptoms evidenced by chronic pot users.*

Some of the monkeys—the "heavy smokers"—got the human equivalency dose of three joints a day, five days a week, for six months, with a rest period of at least one hour between "smokes." Others, so-called "weekend smokers," got their dose on two consecutive days each week.

Results: In both of these groups of monkeys, persistent (lasting after the high) brain-wave abnormalities showed up two-and-a-half to three months after the monkeys were first exposed to the marijuana smoke. Abnormalities were more profound in the heavy-smoking monkeys. Beginning with the first exposure, however, there were marked changes—spiking—in brain-wave recordings, most pronounced in recordings from the septal region, a pleasure center. (Spiking means that the brain waves change from normal frequency

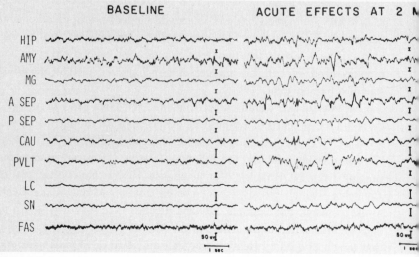

EEGs (brain waves) from deep-brain sites. Baseline picture shows normal brain waves, before exposure to pot smoke. The second set shows acute effects during the high after two months' exposure to smoke of one "monkey-sized" joint a day, five days a week. Third picture shows brain waves after such exposure for six months. Then all pot exposure was stopped for eight months. Last picture shows *persisting abnormalities* in different brain areas. Many relate to "pot personality" symptoms; for example, stimulating the hippocampus causes irritability or rage. HIP is hippocampus; AMY is medial amygdala; SEP is septal region; CAU is caudate nucleus; PVLT is posterior ventrolateral thalamus; LC is locus cereus; SN is substantia nigra; FAS is fastigial nucleus of the cerebellum. (Note: This picture illustrates some, but not all, of the brain areas affected.

and shape to intermittent sharp waves, or spikes, and slower frequencies.) After the smoking sessions, the recordings gradually returned to baseline (normal) within an hour.

The abnormal brain waves were associated with behavioral changes. The monkeys appeared "stoned": Their pupils were dilated and they stared out sleepily. Like the brain waves, behavior gradually returned to baseline so it was impossible to distinguish between the control monkeys and those that had received THC.

However, after three months of exposure to pot smoke, spiking from the pleasure center and other sites in the limbic system did *not* return to normal when the high was over. Nor did the behavior of the monkeys completely return to normal. As recorded by video cameras, the subjects appeared more apathetic and disinterested than the control monkeys. Heath wondered whether the pleasure-center cells, initially charged up by THC, had become damaged, possibly explaining the amotivational syndrome observed in human smokers of marijuana.

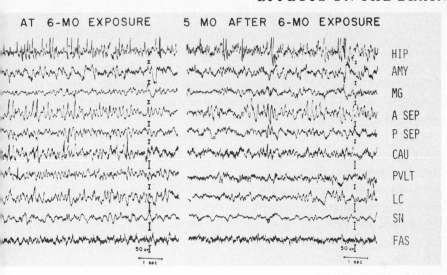

After six months of exposure to marijuana smoke, all the smoking was stopped completely for eight months—to test the *reversibility factor*. (In human terms, eight months is almost two years.) Then EEG recordings were taken again. In the case of the heavy-smoking monkeys, there was some improvement in some areas. However, in other areas the disturbances remained almost as severe as they had been immediately after six months of exposure to pot smoke with THC. The EEGs of the control monkeys exposed to pot smoke without THC remained normal throughout. (See EEG pictures on page 174 and above.)

The monkeys were then sacrificed—not only the marijuana *with* THC-smoking monkeys and the non–THC-smoking controls, but two other groups as well. In the event that the implantation of electrodes might have caused cell damage that did not show up on the EEG taken prior to the "smoke-in," another group of monkeys—with no electrodes—had been exposed to the same doses of pot smoke with THC as the subject monkeys. Furthermore, in the event that the smoke itself might have caused some untoward effects, still another group received no electrodes and no smoke; they received their THC intravenously at the same dose levels as the monkeys exposed to the pot smoke with THC.

Then Dr. Fitzjarrell and Dr. John Harper, specialists in cell biology, made brain-cell slides, and Heath and his team spent a year carefully examining and photographing many thousands of brain cells. Their findings were far more extensive and distinct than anticipated.

Monkeys that had received THC intravenously showed exactly the same

175

brain-cell abnormalities as those that received it through pot smoke. Therefore, it was obviously the delta-9-THC and not the smoke that caused the damage. The monkeys that had received pot smoke with THC but had not been implanted with electrodes had exactly the same structural cell damage as the monkeys with electrodes. Therefore, it was the pot smoke and not the electrodes that caused the cell damage.

Similar changes were seen in the brains of the "weekend smokers" and the heavy-smoking monkeys, but they were more pronounced in the latter: distinctly dose-related. For example, the rough endoplasmic reticulum (RER) manufactures proteins necessary for the cell to function, and some researchers think it has something to do with memory. *In the control monkeys,* the RER strands were neatly lined up in the cell interior. *The weekend smokers'* RER was just beginning to fall out of line. But in the *heavy-smoking monkeys,* as Dr. Fitzjarrell put it, "There was RER chaos. "

The "weekenders" also had an increase in inclusion bodies—dark, swollen, fused fatty lipofusion granules, associated with old age. In the heavy-smoking monkeys there was a dramatic increase in these "old age granules." Yet all of the monkey subjects were young—Heath had purposely selected teenage-equivalent monkeys for his study. In normal young animals, inclusion bodies are found in less than one half of one percent of all brain-cell nuclei. They are found to a greater extent in very old animals—but even then not to the extent found in the young, heavy-smoking monkeys. In the controls (with THC removed from the pot smoke), inclusion bodies were found in only one nucleus on two sites. But in some brain regions of the heavy-smoking monkeys, the inclusion bodies were present in as many as 30 percent of the nuclei. (See picture on page 179.) Dr. Fitzjarrell, an electronmicroscopist for thirty years who had looked at hundreds of thousands of monkey and human brain cells, had never before seen these old age symptoms in the brain cells of young animals.

Other abnormalities occurred in the synaptic vesicles (SVs) and in the synaptic cleft (space between nerve connections). The vesicles (small sacs) hold the all-important chemical activators of the brain—neurotransmitters, the chemical message-carriers. Every cell has a long skinny fiber, or axon. The SVs are housed in boutons ("buttons") at the end of the axons. Electrical impulses shoot down the axons, giving a message to the SVs, which then "dump" their chemical activators. These in turn flow across the long thin gaps, or clefts, that separate every nerve cell in the body from other cells. Once on the other side, the neurotransmitters are picked up by dendrites (non-axon fibers, or message receivers). This type of activity in millions of brain cells is what is necessary for our thinking, feeling, and doing.

In the limbic-area brain cells of the heavy-smoking monkeys, the SVs were abnormally clumped together, which interferes with the function of neurotransmitters. Furthermore, the synaptic clefts in these cells were significantly wider than normal and were filled with abnormal deposits of material, which may further slow down the transmission of messages. (See picture on page 180.) In humans, this condition has been reported with some types of early brain damage, with exposure to carbon tetracholoride and other toxic chemicals, with some viral diseases, and with some types of cancer cells; it is also seen in people who are senile.

Heath pointed out that the widening of the synaptic cleft and the abnormal opaque deposits occur in association with the physiological changes shown by the EEG recordings; he speculated that these changes could cause the typical clinical symptoms seen in chronic human pot-smokers, such as impairment of short-term memory, apathy and lack of motivation, and episodic inappropriate emotional flareups.

The brain cell picture on page 180, showing the synaptic cleft and synaptic vesicle abnormalities, was an average sample; in some cells this condition was more pronounced, and in some, less. But almost all of the thousands of cells the scientists looked at from the limbic area showed this type of damage to some degree.

The scientists looked at cells in forty-two different brain sites. This included sites in the cerebrum, which, in humans, is the center of creativity and higher thought processes. There was some cell damage in all of the forty-two sites. But the most dramatic damage was seen in the limbic area of the brains of all of the heavy-smoking monkeys.

Furthermore, the most damaged sites were those directly related to specific symptoms typical of the chronic pot-smoker. For example, when examining the "pleasure center cells" magnified 125,000 times in the photomicrographs, Dr. Heath found his hypothesis borne out. At the beginning THC—being a foreign agent—had merely irritated the cells, charging them up. In humans, that is when the enjoyable, giggly, euphoric mood of the high is felt full force. After continued exposure, however, the pleasure center cells became damaged. That is the point at which tolerance begins to set in. The human user feels he or she must use more and/or more potent pot to achieve the enjoyable high. Presently the flattened look and demeanor, the unmotivated way of life takes over. Also, presumably, not only does it take more of the drug to achieve a drug effect, but more intense stimulation is required to achieve any effect from outside sources.

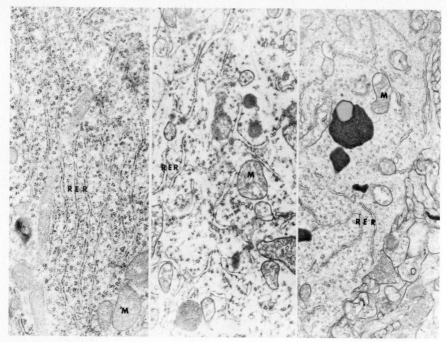

Normal brain cell   *"Weekend smoker"*   *"Heavy smoker"*

Even weekend smoking can begin to impair brain cells. In brain cell, *left,* from a control monkey, note normal lineup of RER (rough endoplasmic reticulum) strands, which manufacture proteins essential for brain cells to function. *Middle* picture from "weekend smoker" (two monkey-sized joints a day, two days a week, for six months) shows strands beginning to fall out of line. In third picture, *right,* from "heavy smoker," there is "RER choas." To transmit messages, the brain requires both electrical and chemical stimulation. The RER is, in fact, a "chemical factory" producing all of the chemicals necessary for message transmission. If the factory is "disorganized" the RER cannot produce the chemicals correctly.

Particular cell damage was seen in the hippocampus, the amygdala, and the cingulate gyrus sections of the limbic area, which are correlated with such negative emotions as irritability and hostility. These areas are also centers of fear. (Symptoms of paranoia are common among heavy pot-smokers.) In addition, damage to the hippocampus is thought to impinge on the pot-smoker's short-term memory.

The paraventricular thalamus and other THC-impaired sites are related to the typical pot symptoms of apathy and flatness.

Brain-cell impairment, which also appears in the hypothalamus, can cause either lack of appetite or compulsive bouts of eating (the "munchies"). And,

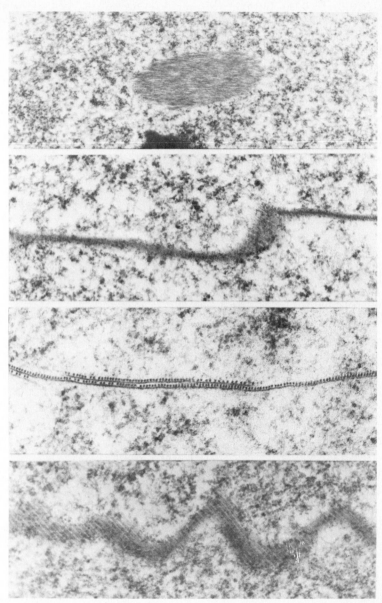

Various types of intranucleus inclusion bodies, a classic brain-cell indication of old age, were found in profusion in young ("teenage") monkeys. In controls, inclusion bodies were practically nonexistent, found in one half of one percent of nuclei. However, in some brain regions of "heavy-smoking monkeys" exposed to THC in pot smoke—or to THC given by injection—inclusion bodies were found in 30 percent of nuclei. Indeed, these "old age granules" were found to a greater extent in these young monkeys than in normal old monkeys, or humans.

as we have seen, the hypothalamus also controls the pituitary, which in turn controls the body's changes from childhood to adolescence, as well as the sex urge and reproductive functions.

Still another type of THC-damage was done to the brain cells. Every neuron (nerve cell) has suppression regulators, for one of the vital functions of nerve cells in the brain is deciding which messages *not* to pass on. If this were not done, a person would be in a state of impossible confusion, since the cell may receive ten thousand messages at the same time. This impairing of the suppressors is the reason that the stoned pot-smoker often becomes overpoweringly interested in one segment of a whole—the cap on the toothpaste tube, for example.

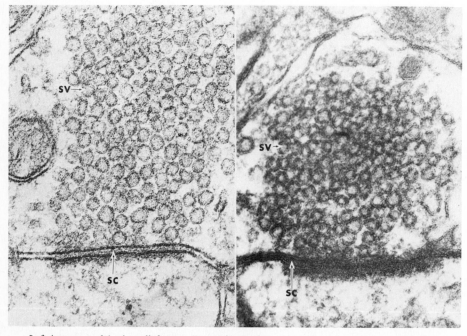

Left is a normal brain cell from a "control" monkey, exposed to the same amount of pot smoke as the subjects—*but with the THC removed. Right* is a typical impaired brain cell from "heavy-smoker" monkey, exposed to pot smoke with THC. The round sacs are synaptic vesicles (SVs), which hold the chemical activators of the brain (neurotransmitters). When they "get the message," SVs pop open and the neurotransmitters flow across the space or synaptic cleft (SC). They are picked up by receivers (dendrites) from another neuron. This is the basis of all brain activity. In pot-impaired cells, SVs are abnormally clumped together, and the synaptic cleft is wider and clogged with abnormal deposits. Both abnormalities presumably slow passage of messages from one brain cell to the next.

This might seem harmless enough when the activity is no more demanding than brushing one's teeth. But if the impairment of the suppression regulators results in this singleminded focusing-in on a single element while driving a car or operating a high-powered machine, for example, the result can be disaster.

Heath points out that the impairment of the suppressors accounts in part for what the pot-smoker regards as "mind expansion." In the stoned state, such ordinarily unnoticed details as the taste of an orange, the flame of a candle, or the shape of a pillow may become totally engrossing. This is the same type of response babies have to their surroundings. But by the time a child is a year old, the suppression regulators start developing, and they continue to develop as the child progresses. Consequently, the mind-expansion extolled by the pot smoker is in fact a reversion to a baby's way of seeing the world. This, coupled with Heath's findings of increased inclusion bodies and other cellular-damage symptoms normally seen in old age, indicates that the heavy, chronic pot-smoker may reflect inappropriate cellular traits of infancy and old age at the same time.

The medulla oblongata in the brain stem also appears to be affected by THC. This is the center of nausea control as well as other regulations. THC apparently "turns off" this "vomit center." For cancer patients suffering from nausea and vomiting after chemotherapy or radiation treatments, THC can serve a useful purpose. However, in other cases, effects can range from unpleasant to dangerous. For example, many teenagers have learned that when they drink to get drunk and smoke pot at the same time, they don't "upchuck." But vomiting is, of course, nature's way of purging the body of toxic substances. As a result of this vomit suppression by pot-smoking drinkers, for the first time we are seeing youngsters OD'ing, and sometimes dying, from alcohol.

Heath has done a variety of studies on marijuana (or THC) and the brain. All have shown similar results. In a paper on his work published in *Biological Psychiatry* in January 1980, Heath summed up: "The findings indicate that exposure to delta-9-THC at doses commensurate with those used by human marijuana smokers can produce permanent alterations in brain function and structure of monkeys."

In relating his monkey findings to humans, Heath expressed concern that so many of our young people are potentially damaging their brains by pot smoking, which is a threat, he said, not only to their future as individuals, but to the future of our nation.

No other researcher has ever tried to duplicate Heath's brain cell studies with rhesus monkeys. These monkeys cost over fifteen hundred dollars each, and few scientists want to use hard-to-come-by funding to repeat exactly the same study that another research team has already done. However, some researchers have done similar THC/brain-cell studies using rats and mice. And they found the same types of damage.

For example, Drs. Toshi Hattori, Patrick L. McGeer, and Alexander Jakubovic of the Division of Neurological Sciences, Department of Psychiatry, University of British Columbia, Vancouver, Canada, gave human equivalency doses of THC—and of the nonpsychoactive or only mildly psychoactive cannabinoids cannabinol, cannabidiol, and cannabigerol—to rats of various ages, ranging from infant to elderly. The researchers not only found types of structural brain-cell changes in rats similar to the changes Heath had found in monkeys, but they also found biochemical changes, such as significantly decreased protein and nucleic acids, the building blocks for the normal function of each living cell. For instance, normally over 30 percent of the nuclear membrane is covered by attached ribosomes. The cannabinoids significantly decreased the area covered by the ribosomes—in some cases by about 50 percent. This bears out Dr. Heath's finding about the disruption of RER because ribosomes are an essential part of RER.

Jakubovic pointed out that if this decrease in ribosome coverage happened to a human being, it would slow down the brain-cell functions. Furthermore, "Since sexual functioning depends on new protein synthesis and memory is also thought to do so, it might be anticipated that these could be processes particularly affected by cannabis derivatives."

In another study McGeer and Jakubovic found that the younger the experimental animal (in this case, the rat), the more severe was the biochemical damage done by delta-9-THC. "This," said Dr. Jakubovic, "indicates the possibility of a greater vulnerability of the brain cells of young human users to the damaging effects of various cannabinoids."

Jakubovic further pointed out:

> Our studies showed that THC affects the protein and nucleic acids in the brain cells—key molecules in each cell. Perhaps the reason that the young brains of the infant and the "teenage" rats were more affected than the brains of the "grandparent" rats is that the older metabolism is slower, therefore the damage is less. The developing animal requires a greater rate of synthesis to grow, whereas the adult animal needs a slower synthetic rate appropriate for cell replacement only.

Other researchers have found other brain-impairing effects of THC and its metabolites. For example, five different researchers working with animals and humans have shown that microscopic doses of cannabinoids, particularly THC, cause a reduction in acetylcholine turnover in the hippocampus, resulting from reduced activity of the acetylcholine neurons. According to the Institute of Medicine's *Marijuana and Health,* "the exact nature of this action is not known, but it may be related to memory deficits produced."

Acetylcholine is one of four main neurotransmitters found throughout the brain. Neurotransmitters are the chemicals that are necessary for a chemical-electric transmission of messages from one nerve cell to the next.

Heath notes further pot damage which users may do to the brain's natural pleasure chemicals. These chemicals are able to give "a natural high," a raised consciousness, a euphoria, such as the "high" joggers often experience, or music lovers at a concert. "But," says Heath,

> the sad fact is that not only do pot-smokers get their high from a toxic chemical, which first irritates and then damages the cells in the pleasure center, but THC also seems to suppress the "natural high substances," so that chronic pot-smokers may actually be injuring their abilities to get a natural high. This may be one reason they feel that they can't get a heightened awareness from music, a sunset, and so forth *unless* they are stoned.
>
> Also, because of tolerance which develops to the effects of the drug, chronic pot smokers not only need more stimulation from marijuana to achieve an effect from the drug, they also need more and more pot, and/ or more potent pot, to achieve stimulation from other sources. It's quite possible that the heavy pot-smoker may eventually damage so many of the pleasure-center cells that he or she becomes unable to experience natural pleasure that is not drug-induced.

Heath further points out that "pleasure-inducing drugs have been categorized as 'hard' or 'soft,' with marijuana falling into the soft category, in contrast, for example, with the opiates, which are classified as hard drugs. In view of recent data, this distinction has become invalid and misleading."

The "hard/soft drug" label came in large measure from the fact that, for example, stopping the intake of narcotics such as opium and heroin results in severe withdrawal symptoms. Heath explains:

> This is because the chemical configuration of the opiates is such that they can substitute or bind to endogenous molecules in the brain, which normally regulate the pleasure-pain circuits. Stopping intake of these drugs results in severe withdrawal symptoms while the brain scrambles to replen-

ish its own supply of the molecule to regulate pleasure-pain. . . . The delta-9-THC molecule does not act by substitution for a normal body chemical; rather, it acts more like a foreign body in the brain. It is not readily broken down and therefore accumulates in the brain. Recent data indicates its accumulation results in altered brain function and pathological changes in structure. Sudden discontinuance produces only mild withdrawal symptoms. This is understandable since it is broken down very slowly—after a single dose 50 percent is still present in the brain after two weeks.

These comments were made at the 1980 Senate hearings on Health Consequences of Marijuana Use. In answer to a senator's question concerning reversibility, Heath said:

We are doing studies, and we have some data on that. We have a device with which we can take little biopsies from the significant regions of the brain after the monkeys have stopped being exposed to pot smoke for a prolonged period. We have done that. A great deal of it is reversed. Some seems to be irreversible. It is no different from any other assault on the nervous system. I am sure some of your friends have had strokes. There is usually a period of recovery. But in most instances they do not get back altogether to where they were before they had it. Any assault on the nervous system acts that way.

It is perhaps not surprising that the brain should be the site of so much cell damage: Cannabinoids accumulate in fatty cells, and the three-pound human brain is one-third fat. Each nerve-cell axon in the brain is covered with a protective fatty myelin sheath. Therefore, in the brain of the chronic pot-smoker, millions of these all-important axons are continually surrounded by THC.

When other types of body cells are severely damaged or die, they are replaced by new cells of the same type. But brain cells are different. When they die they are not replaced. There are, of course, billions of brain cells, so that new pathways can be formed to take over the functions of cells that have died. However, if enough damage has been done over a long enough period of time, that takeover may not be completely successful.

A difficult and potentially dangerous human brain study was published in 1971 by the late Dr. A. M. G. Campbell of the Royal United Hospital, Bristol, England. His subjects were ten chronic pot-smokers, aged eighteen to twenty-six. They had used the drug on a regular basis for three to eleven years. All ten evidenced personality changes, loss of short-term memory, and other typical symptoms of the "pot personality." Campbell and his team performed air encephalography, a type of X-ray, on the ten men. The fluid of the inner cavity of the brain was withdrawn and replaced by air. Then the cerebral structures were measured by a process called roentgenographic examination of the brain.

Result: Campbell found that a loss of brain substance had resulted in atrophy of the brain, comparable to that which occurs in people seventy to ninety years old. Furthermore, Campbell found that his subjects who had used marijuana for eleven years showed more atrophy than those who had used it for three years. He concluded that "regular use of cannabis produces cerebral atrophy in young adults."

This study had many critics who pointed out that all of the subjects had used LSD, many of them over twenty times, and eight of the ten had used amphetamines. Furthermore, one had a history of convulsions, and four had suffered head injuries. Campbell countered that although his subjects had used other drugs, and two had used alcohol heavily, pot was the predominant drug. Furthermore, LSD and amphetamines had not been shown in rodent studies to cause brain atrophy, whereas rodent and squirrel-monkey studies had shown that cannabis *could* cause brain atrophy. Alcohol could have contributed to the brain atrophy of two of his subjects, but even heavy drinking had not been shown to cause brain atrophy in young users.

The Campbell study and the clouds and controversy surrounding it made it very clear why rhesus monkeys are preferred for the "pure" studies necessary for brain and reproductive research.

In 1983 Dr. John P. McGahan, a diagnostic radiologist at the University of California School of Medicine, announced his brain-scan findings on rhesus monkeys. He did high-resolution computerized tomography (CT scans) of the brains of the monkeys to whom Sassenrath had given daily THC doses of the human equivalent of one joint a day for three to five years. The monkeys had been drug-free for a year when Dr. McGahan looked at the size of their brains. He found brain atrophy, compared to the short-term THC-treated monkeys and the control monkeys who had never received any drugs. The atrophic changes were in the frontal region of the brain, in the caudate nucleus area. (Note the marked disturbances in this area, marked CAU, in the brain-wave photographs on page 174.) The caudate nucleus is an elongated area which lies next to the septal region in the so-called "old brain" studied by Heath and Fitzjarrell. The caudate nucleus helps regulate the neurotransmitter content of the cerebral cortex—the so-called "new brain." The caudate nucleus itself is rich in the neurotransmitter dopamine, which is involved in brain arousal and in the smooth coordination of muscles and movement.

Dr. McGahan concluded: "While our study of twelve rhesus monkeys was small, it was well-controlled, and correlates with Campbell's work in humans."

The work of animal researchers concentrates on the brainstem, the first part of the brain to develop in evolution, and on the limbic system. The brainstem is sometimes called "the reptilian brain" because it is found in everything from lizards to man. It is through the brainstem that all messages come and go between brain and body—for example, the heartbeat rate, which is increased during a high.

The limbic system looks like two ram's horns, curving around the brainstem. It was the second part of the brain to develop in evolution, and is sometimes called "the old mammalian brain" because it is found in all mammals.

Then there's the cerebrum, a large puffy mass around and above the limbic system. It looks like tightly packed spaghetti. The cerebrum has billions of brain-cell connections to both the limbic system and the brainstem. The limbic system has its own cell connections to the brainstem, connections that help keep a human alert and emotionally balanced.

Of course it is what goes on in the cerebrum that truly separates humans from other mammals. Dr. Robert C. Gilkeson of Cleveland, Ohio, is studying marijuana's effects on the cerebrum. Gilkeson is a specialist in adolescent psychiatry and, for a decade, had done neurophysiologic research and EEGs on learning disabilities and on dyslexic youngsters.

He became interested in the area of marijuana/brain-wave research in 1976 when a tall, good-looking teenager came into his office. Stephen (not his real name) told Gilkeson, "I used to dig school and, if anything, I was into too many things at once. But everything I used to like has become a drag. Even chicks. I've dropped out of extracurricular activities and sports. My marks have dropped from A's and B's to C's and D's with a bunch of incompletes and withdrawals. I can't seem to stay with anything anymore. I feel bummed out all the time now!"

As Gilkeson put it:

Steve could no longer mobilize the energy or plan to initiate any behavior to remedy his current situation, even though he was troubled by the fact that he had become less and less active in every area: intellectual, social, emotional, and motor. He was increasingly disinterested in everything, and found himself constantly sitting by himself or [with] a similarly immobile group of peers, listening to high-volume rock music. He had become increasingly annoyed with everyone—including his peers, his parents, and his teachers—who demanded even the most reasonable of expectations from him. Increasingly he saw everyone and everything as a growing hassle. He had given up ideas of applying to college to pursue a career in social service, had instead decided during his senior year to become a keyboard player in a rock music group. That he had not played the piano since some early lessons during the third grade seemed to constitute only a minor problem for him if he could just "get himself to practice more."

Gilkeson noted three reversed d's and b's in Stephen's handwritten term paper, and promptly suggested a brain-wave test, since letter reversal is a classic sign of learning disabilities.

In addition to the standard hour-long electroencephalogram (EEG), Gilkeson used another half-hour of techniques he had developed for youngsters with learning disabilities, asking Stephen to perform various academic tasks. For example, Gilkeson told him: "When I give the signal, spell *bureau*—backwards." This is a difficult task for anyone. But Gilkeson was not so interested in the correctness of Stephen's answer as he was in seeing the brain-wave *response* to taxing and unfamiliar tasks.

The psychiatrist gave Stephen's EEG graphs to Dr. John Gardner, a neurologist and skilled encephalographer, who had never seen the patient. And, when the report came back, Gilkeson was fascinated. Stephen was seventeen. "But," said the psychiatrist, "his graphs might have been those of a seven- or eight-year-old—with a pronounced learning disability."

Gilkeson suspected that Stephen did not have a learning disability. The boy had given him a clue as to what the problem might be. "I don't admit it to anyone," Stephen had said, "but now pot bums me out, instead of making me high the way it did at first. Like, I used to be a master at one-liners. Now I just can't think of any. When I'm in a group it usually makes me paranoid because I seem so stupid. Also, my memory's going bad. I guess I'm really burned out." He had, he told Gilkeson, smoked marijuana four or five times a week for the past year.

Gilkeson decided to show Stephen the encephalographer's report, which began: *Abnormal EEG. Markedly immature for age, with excessive paroxysmal four to seven cps* [*cycles per second*] *Hz activity.* This type of slow-wave activity is associated with light sleep—even though Stephen had been awake during the entire examination.

"What does this mean?" Stephen asked. "Diffuse encephalopathologic process?"

"*Encephalo* means 'brain,' " Gilkeson told him. "*Pathologic* means 'sick.' Your EEG is typical of that of a severe 'learning disorder.' " But the psychiatrist suggested there might be an easy remedy. He asked Stephen to stop smoking pot for two months. The boy was so shaken that he agreed.

In eight weeks the EEG was repeated. It was notably improved, though not yet normal. "But," said Gilkeson, "there was real improvement in Stephen's grades, in his mood, his memory, his humor and in the increasing alacrity of his speech—which we had documented on the tape recorder. There was also a notable decreasing of irritability, depression and general 'flatness.' "

Encouraged, Stephen agreed to go for another two potless months—after which the encephologapher's report read: *Within normal limits for age.* Excited by this recovery, which, said Gilkeson, "showed not only on the EEG, but in Stephen's cognitive, emotional and behavioral gains," the psychiatrist decided to embark on a study, which is still in process. By February 1984, ninety pot-smoking teenagers had taken his specially developed EEG. Ranging in age from thirteen to eighteen, all came from the affluent suburbs of Cleveland. And all said they did not "do" other drugs. To qualify for the project, each subject had to have experienced marijuana highs at least two or three times a week for the four months preceding the EEG. But all were forbidden to smoke pot for at least twenty-four hours prior to the test.

Results: Thus far all but three of the EEGs were not only "markedly immature," like Stephen's, but were also dominated by slow alpha frequencies and an abnormal amount of even slower theta rhythms, "sufficient," said Gilkeson, "to be diagnostic of diffuse brain impairment. Some results were so abnormal that they were diagnosed as consistent with seizure disorders. In the additional section of academic tasks, none of these youngsters could speed up when challenged. Their brain waves failed to respond to these stimuli in the usual way, according to standardized norms."

By May 1984, of the ninety subjects thus far tested, some have refused to be retested. As one girl put it: "Seeing my EEG report was what scared me into getting off pot. Now that I'm doing so much better, why risk finding out that I still have an abnormal EEG?"

Among those who have been retested, a number have cleared (become normal). "Of even greater significance," says Dr. Gilkeson "are those who have progressed from abnormal to normal with abstinence—and a return to abnormal again when the youngster returned to chronic pot use." There are also some who have not cleared as yet. This may be because they are continuing to smoke pot, even though they say they have stopped, or because their EEGs were abnormal before they started pot smoking, or because there has been so much impairment that the damaged brain cells have not yet recovered. Thus far, the study indicates chronic brain impairment while pot smoking. It does not attest to permanent damage. "However," says Gilkeson, "this must remain a matter of grave concern."

In testifying about his ongoing study at the 1980 Senate hearings, Gilkeson pointed out, regarding the altered brain waves:

It is now generally accepted that the slower the frequency, the less cortical or cerebral-complex intellectual mental functioning is taking place as we know it. It is also important to recognize that the EEG continues to "mature" and speed up in frequency in general from birth to the age of 18 to 20 years of age. At this time it becomes rather specific to the individual and remains rather stable until the ages of 65 to 70 when slow wave and fast wave activities are seen again in more preponderance. The abundance of slow wave frequencies is the most common finding in moderate to severe brain insults and injuries, infections and trauma.

It is also true that changes in frequencies are also related to very definitive differences in cognitive functions, and the relative complexity and order of cognitive functions are quite clearly related to these changes in frequency.

With increasing slowing there is a universally accepted lowering of "alertness" and arousal. There is a lessened awareness and conscious experience of the sensing of time. There is less awareness of the specific sequence or order of events upon recall. There is a wandering of attention, and a decreasing richness and complexity of thought. . . . During these slow wave states there is much greater difficulty in sustaining continuous, sequential thought, without distractions and the occurrence of unrelated associations.

During his study of the pot-smoking teenagers, Gilkeson found that more than thirty scientists—using a wide range of methods of administration and recording—have come to similar conclusions. Dr. Turin Itel of New York Medical College, one of the foremost investigators of the effects of drugs on human EEGs, sums up: "Acute or chronic use of marijuana produces an EEG shift toward *slow*. This is definitely associated with impairment of cognitive functions and may be a physiological correlate of such symptoms as lack of desire and interest, the amotivational syndrome."

In May 1984, after ten years of clinical research on the subject of chronic cannabis use and its effects on the brain, Gilkeson said:

All recent work has confirmed that acute and chronic marijuana use lowers the brain's "arousal" transmitter substances. This, in turn, results in lowered cortical "energy" or activation. The lower the brain arousal, the less synapses are activated. They are both activated less, and less are activated. The less the synaptic transmission, the less complex the associations and the simpler the thought processes. New work in this area also shows that in animals and humans, cannabis can inhibit the influx of calcium across the membrane at the bouton. Calcium must be attached to the neurotransmitters in order for them to be released. Therefore, there is less transmitter available at the synapse to excite the next nerve, and pass on the message.

Gilkeson also pointed out that:

The chief reason that man is king of the animal kingdom is his ability to plan ahead. This type of planning is a major function of the pre-frontal lobe—which is two to three times larger and more complex in man than in the highest order of research primates. The monkeys in which Dr. Heath showed such dramatic brain cell damage had very small frontal lobes. However, damage in the cingulate gyrus and septal pathways leading to the monkeys' frontal lobes showed significant destruction. These are the pathways that take emotions and feelings from the "old brain" (limbic) area to the pre-frontal lobe—the planning area. The problem that showed in the monkeys' brain cells in this respect would presumably be far more extensive in man since the pre-frontal lobe is far larger.

I find that the first symptom of chronic pot use among adolescents is the change in the quality of their long-range planning. For instance, one chronic pot-smoking youngster dropped his plans for law school in favor of his new plan to become a guitar player in a rock group—though he had never played any instrument in his life. Another pot-smoker, aware of his memory impairment, said, "I don't really need my memory because I changed my plans. I'm not going to college anyway." That is *his* plan ahead.

Motivation, goal-directed behavior and judgment itself all are consistent with the concept that cells in the pre-frontal lobe have been inactivated by marijuana. With impairment of this part of the brain it is no wonder that the amotivational syndrome has long been so typical of the chronic pot-smoker.

People do "come back" when they quit the drug, but this can take time. Therefore, the former user should not be discouraged. I've seen cases where dramatic changes can't be seen until 18 months after the person stopped pot smoking.

Thus far, Dr. Robert Heath is the only scientist to have done research on marijuana and the brain using rhesus monkeys and humans (his many pot-smoking patients). He sums up on this subject:

People might drink rather heavily for twenty to thirty years and never get into serious trouble so far as alterations in their brains are concerned. But with marijuana it seems as though you have to use it only for a relatively short time in moderate to heavy use before persistent behavioral effects along with other evidence of brain damage begin to develop. Animal data confirm what many of us have suspected from clinical experience with marijuana users: namely, that this drug produces distinctive changes in the brain.

Chapter 11

The Immune System and Other Cellular Effects

Dr. Marietta Issidorides stared at the doctor in charge of the secret code. Only he knew the identities of the hashish smokers in the study. "Are you sure?" she repeated. "There are *no* female subjects?"

"Of course I'm sure," Dr. Boulougouris replied.

"That's something fantastic," Issidorides said softly. "Now we'll *really* start looking."

As with virtually all respected scientific cell studies, this one was "double blind"; only one person—someone having nothing to do with the laboratory study—knew the actual identities of the subjects and the controls, in this case, Dr. Boulougouris. His records, correlating the code numbers and the names, were kept under lock and key, not to be revealed until Issidorides had completed her investigations. (This prevents conscious or subconscious prejudice from affecting the grading and interpretation of results. While studying the cells, the researcher does not know whether they have come from a user or from a control.)

Issidorides knew that a small number of women used what Greeks call "the weed of the poor." If some of those women had been included as subjects, it might account for what she had seen under the microscope that morning. But now she had been told that all users and controls were men. In asking about the sex of the subjects, she was not asking that the code be broken. She merely wished to reconfirm the fact that all subjects and controls *were* men.

What had given rise to her question was this: In normal male blood cells, so-called "drumsticks"—small appendages on the nuclei—are extremely rare. In female blood cells, however, drumsticks are so common that they are regarded as a clear indication of cells from a girl or a woman.

Yet in the neutrophils (a type of white blood cell) of males that Issidorides had looked at that morning, a great profusion had had the "female sign." In fact, some of the blood-smear slides showed many more cells with the "female drumsticks" than are found in normal female blood. On the other hand, other slides had no female drumsticks on any of the nuclei. Was it possible that these normal cells had come from the non–hash-smoking controls, and that the "female sign" cells had come from the hashish smokers? Or did both controls and users share this peculiar cell symptom? She would not know the answer until all the planned cell studies on these users and nonusers were completed.

That process took two years, during which Issidorides examined thousands of white blood cells and sperm cells and recorded her observations in every detail. Though she used only ten subjects and controls for her sperm cell study (described in Chapter 9), she used thirty-eight hashish smokers and eighteen controls for her white-blood-cell study. The subjects had smoked hash for an average of sixteen years. They used no other drugs, but smoked moderate amounts of tobacco cigarettes and drank moderate amounts of alcohol. The controls in the study also used tobacco and alcohol, but no other drugs, and no hashish. Subjects and controls were carefully matched for age, place of upbringing, lifestyle, and occupation.

When the study was completed and Boulougouris turned over the coded records to Issidorides and her co-workers, the answer was clear. The cell changes were directly related to whether or not the men were long-term hashish smokers. The results were striking and conclusive. In normal human males, at most one drumstick appears per thousand cells. In the thousands of cells Issidorides had looked at from the non–hash-smoking male controls, she had not found a single drumstick. In normal female blood cells drumsticks show up in 1 to 7 percent of cells (one to seven drumsticks per hundred cells). *But in 61 percent of the male hash-smoking subjects, the "female sign" was seen in 8 to 16 percent of their cells—that is, in far greater profusion than in the normal female.*

"This," said Issidorides, "is certainly strong indication that cannabis causes a hormonal imbalance."

The mechanism that causes drumsticks to occur in the neutrophils of the male hash-users was not clear, although a French researcher, M. Bessis, had found that an increase in drumsticks in males was found in association with subtle pathological (disease) conditions.

It was also known that the drumstick phenomenon is related to estrogen levels. For example, in women, it had been shown that drumsticks increased during the pre-ovulatory cycle. But even *then* they did not increase to the degree Issidorides was seeing in many of the neutrophil nuclei of these male subjects. Did cannabinoids somehow produce female secondary sex characteristics in the white blood cells?

Issidorides had read of cases in which chronic male marijuana smokers had enlarged breasts, caused, it was thought, by increased secretion of the hormone prolactin. (Prolactin stimulates milk production in females.) The condition gradually disappeared after pot or hashish smoking was stopped. Was this another evidence of hormonal imbalance caused by cannabis? Might the causal factor be the same as that which had created the female drumsticks?

Another puzzling finding was the dramatic depletion of arginine (an essential amino acid) in the white blood cells and sperm cells of the long-term hashish-smokers. At a conference on cannabis held under the joint auspices of the Addiction Research Foundation (ARF) of Ontario, Canada, and the World Health Organization (WHO), Issidorides presented the results of her further investigations in this area. It was published in 1983 in the initial "Report of an ARF/WHO Scientific Meeting on Adverse Health and Behavior Consequences of Cannabis Use" under the subtitle "Possible Biochemical Mechanism," and was introduced by the editors in these words:

> Only one hypothesis is mentioned here in some detail, because it is recent and imaginative, and because it proposes a single explanation both for the deficiency in nuclear histone [a protein] synthesis and for the ultrastructural alterations encountered in the leukocytes [white blood cells] and spermatozoa of chronic human users of hashish. These cells are characterized by a depletion of the amino acid arginine and by abnormal chromatin condensation. According to this hypothesis, the biological effects observed in chronic cannabis users may be explained by arginine depletion which, in itself, can cause chromosomal aberrations, decreased sperm maturity and motility, defective ovulation, growth retardation, immunosuppression and the reactivation of latent viral infections and CNS [central nervous system] effects such as anorexia, motor incoordination, and lethargy.

In her studies of the long-term hash-smokers, Issidorides had found that there was a significant decrease of arginine in *all* of the abnormal-looking neutrophils of the hash-smokers. Amino acids are necessary for the body to manufacture proteins for growth or replacement due to aging. Twenty of them are considered essential to life, and arginine is one of them; it is an important key to the proper functioning of many body processes.

She had also found that the sperm cells of the hash-smokers were drastically deficient in arginine. Researchers working with humans and animals had shown that chronic pot use causes decreased sperm development and motility and decreased sperm maturity. Other scientists working in other areas had shown arginine deficiency to be a cause of sluggish and immature sperm. Since cannabis use resulted in arginine deficiency, might there be a causal link between cannabis and the effects of the lack of arginine on the sperm?

Issidorides's full exploration of the arginine hypothesis, covering many areas, was published in May 1984.

Both marijuana researchers and arginine researchers had independently demonstrated that arginine depletion causes defective ovulation.

As described in Chapters 8 and 9, cannabis researchers, working with animals, had shown that the drug causes growth retardation in the offspring of drug-exposed mothers or drug-exposed fathers. There were also clinical reports from pediatricians and others that youngsters who were chronic pot-smokers were often smaller, slighter, more "growth retarded" than was normal for their age. Arginine researchers had found that arginine depletion alone caused growth retardation.

Although CBD (cannabidiol) by itself, administered in large doses, may prove to be an antiepileptic agent, it is "street knowledge" that no epileptic should smoke grass because of the effects of THC. Doing so might bring on a seizure. Issidorides found published papers by leading neurologists who pointed out that arginine administration might protect a person from epileptic seizures.

Several investigators documented that during puberty, menstruation, and pregnancy, there are significantly increased demands for arginine in the healthy human. Marijuana researchers had established that THC causes a lowering of sex-hormone levels during these same periods. Could there be an interrelationship between the two?

Researchers have shown that in children, lack of arginine causes lethargy, apathy, depression, and motor incoordination.

Motor incoordination: Even pro-pot organizations agree it is dangerous to drive stoned—because of motor incoordination, among other driving impairments.

But perhaps the most sobering and significant possible correlations came in the area of genetic effects. Many papers report findings that arginine-rich histones (proteins) are important in the regulation of genetic structures and processes. If the regulator goes wrong, the results may be far-reaching— as far as future generations. Cannabis researchers (as we will see later in this chapter) had shown that chronic pot-smokers show distinct chromosomal abnormalities. And arginine researchers had shown that arginine deficiency causes chromosomal abnormalities.

Could there be a shared metabolic denominator present in cannabis-impaired cells that affects different types of cells in different ways: brain cells, immune-system cells, sperm cells? Different results, but a similar cause? Might arginine depletion be a key—or *the* key—to a "mechanism of action" responsible for a wide spectrum of cannabis impairments reported by both clinicians and marijuana researchers?

After the publication of her work on THC and arginine in 1984, Issidorides set to work on numerous experiments that may result in elevating her cannabis-arginine interaction hypothesis into a direct finding.

However, there are already two important sets of findings resulting from her study of long-term hashish-smokers that are distinctly classified as "solid science." One set concerns the sperm cells, already described in Chapter 9. The other set concerns the immune system.

Cells of the Immune System

In her study of the hashish smokers, Issidorides examined many hundreds of lymphocytes and neutrophils, two types of white blood cells that are part of the body's immune system. Lymphocytes, which constitute 20 to 30 percent of the white blood cells, multiply swiftly by dividing and mature with specific functions when a foreign substance, chemical organ transplant, or virus enters the body. They secrete "juices" or specific antibodies, which neutralize or reject the "enemy." In contrast, neutrophils don't divide; they are mature, motile cells. They attack a different type of enemy—usually bacteria—by extending cytoplasmic "protrusions" to surround, suck in, and destroy foreign invaders, a process known as *phagocytosis.*

The non–hash-smoking controls had fat, firm, healthy-looking cells of both varieties, but in the hash-smokers' lymphocytes and neutrophils the scientist found a preponderance of abnormal nuclei. (The nucleus, with its DNA, is the center of the cell's life and functional responsibilities, containing most of the cell's genetic material.) Most of the abnormal nuclei were also surrounded by impaired cell membrane, another of the most vital parts of a cell.

In the lymphocytes Issidorides found, for example, that many of the nuclei were compacted, which indicated a slowing of information exchange between RNA and DNA, the so-called "master modules of life." Among other things, inhibition of RNA and DNA production affects protein synthesis, which in turn affects the maintenance of the protein portions of the cell membrane.

Similarly, RNA is necessary for antibody production and for passing along DNA instructions for cell division. In the lymphocytes of the hash-smoking subjects virtually *none* of the nuclei had a normal appearance: 57 percent had orange-brown (in contrast to normal black) nuclei, while the remaining lymphocytes had yellow nuclei. This indicated a lower content of arginine-rich proteins, a deficiency that was not found in the cells of the controls.

In the neutrophils of the hash-smokers Issidorides found a dramatic change in the cell membrane, which made the cell look smaller, crumpled, and deformed. One effect of this membrane alteration may be an impaired ability to defend against bacteria and other foreign matter. The majority of the neutrophils examined from the long-term hash-smoking men looked abnormal, while the neutrophils in the non–hash-smoking controls looked healthy. (See picture on page 198.)

Issidorides sums up her findings on the immune-system cells:

> Our work shows that cannabis causes a weakening in the defense mechanisms. The long-term user may not have any overt disease, but his body may not be ready to meet an increased challenge. This could be regarded as a type of latent infirmity. The cells don't respond adequately. They're "stoned" too.
>
> It should also be remembered that all our subjects were carefully pre-screened. Anyone not healthy was eliminated. We will never know how many sickly subjects we might have found had we taken a random sampling of hash-smokers rather than selecting only well ones.

Another important immune-system study was published in 1974 by a pioneer pot researcher, Dr. Gabriel Nahas of the Columbia College of Physicians and Surgeons.

All of the immune system's white cells originate in the bone marrow. They migrate from the bone marrow to various lymphoid tissues such as the spleen, thymus, lymph nodes around the alimentary tract, and so on. At these points they become specialized in their functions.

About half the body's immune-system cells are lymphocytes; about 70 percent of these are transformed by the thymus gland into T-lymphocytes (*T* for *thymus*). They are the "signal corps" in the body's immune-system army, usually the first cells of the immune system to come in contact with whatever is invading the body: virus, fungus, bacteria, or invasive cancer. They circulate in the blood and when an "enemy" invades and begins to multiply, the T's go into action on several fronts at once. Some adhere to larger cells called monocytes and charge them up into a new division in the immune system army, the macrophages. The T's also busily produce

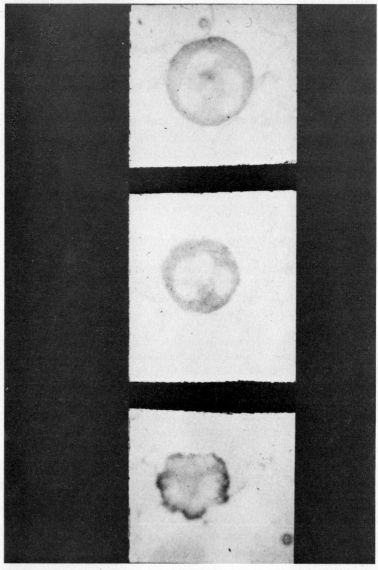

Neutrophils, a type of white blood cell in the human immune system. Those in the non–hash-smoking "controls" (*top*) looked healthy, with distinct nuclei and firm surface membrane ready to react to bacteria and other foreign invaders.

Of the thousands of neutrophils examined from the long-term hash-smokers, most looked unhealthy, although the extent of the damage varied (*middle* and *bottom*). They were smaller and "crumpled looking," with obvious changes in the cell membrane and the nuclei. These are abnormalities that, among other things, may affect the cell's ability to fight bacteria.

more T cells. And, on the third front, they signal the "chemical warfare agents," B-lymphocytes, to increase *their* numbers to produce and release antibodies.

Obviously, with all these roles to play, the T's are a vital ingredient of a healthy immune system. The T's increase their ranks by dividing very rapidly when they sense an enemy, such as viruses of all varieties, and cancer cells, which every one of us manufactures at one time or another. The T's act as a look-alert system for these cancer cells; when they spot one, or a clump of them, they charge in to do battle. Their strength lies in their numbers. It follows that if their dividing ability is decreased, their effectiveness is weakened.

The spleen is an important storage base for the T's, so when Dr. Nahas read a Swedish scientist's paper reporting that in animal studies, THC tended to lodge for days in the spleen, he wondered if THC affected the T's.

He rounded up fifty-one young marijuana smokers, all healthy young men. (No women were used because the menstrual cycles affects the production of T-lymphocytes.) All the subjects had smoked pot at least once a week; the average was several times a week. All had used the drug for at least a year; the average was four years. In addition, none had used other drugs, except alcohol. There was also a control group: eighty-one young men who did not smoke marijuana or use any other drug, except alcohol. The average age of the pot-smokers was twenty-two, and that of the controls, forty-four; this was deliberate, to give the pot-smokers an advantage over the controls, for the T-lymphocytes of young adults divide more actively than those of the middle-aged.

In this double-blind study, blood samples from both groups were fed into a machine called the Multiple Automatic Sample Harvester (MASH). Miniscule amounts of blood were dropped into an assembly line of tiny test tubes. When the researcher flicked a switch, MASH started to spin, sucking out the T-lymphocytes. The T's were then fed into a special computer, which counted them electronically and printed the results.

Results: The rate of division of T-lymphocytes averaged a startling 44 percent lower in the young pot-smokers than in the middle-aged controls.

Subsequent studies performed on subjects who were more carefully controlled to exclude other drugs did not show a similar fall in T-lymphocyte activity. Nahas pointed out: "The apparent inconsistencies may be due to the variability in the amount of marijuana consumed by users, the lack of standardized procedure used in each group and the differences in the various population of users."

The early study by Nahas initiated other investigations, which did indicate that THC interferes with the immune system in many ways. For example, Dr. Bruce Petersen and Dr. Louis Lemberger of Lilly Research Laboratories showed that human phagocytes (which engulf and digest foreign substances) were significantly reduced in number in pot-smokers compared to nonsmokers.

One immune-system finding may be of particular interest to the estimated twenty million Americans who have herpes simplex 2—and the millions more who are worried about contracting it.

In a 1979 study, Dr. Al Munson and other researchers at the Medical College of Virginia injected two thousand mice with herpes simplex virus, type 2. (In humans this is known as "the genital type.") Then they injected five hundred of the "herpes mice" with varying amounts of THC. Another five hundred got injections of varying amounts of marijuana extract. The one thousand control mice were injected with herpes virus only.

Results: The resistance of the THC and pot-extract mice was reduced about one hundred-fold. They all contracted herpes. However, the resistance was dose-related; which, in this case, meant that the more THC they received, the more deaths there were. The immune systems of the control mice remained intact.

In another study, these researchers compared the immunosuppressant effects of THC with two well-known immunosuppressants commonly used in transplant cases. One, a fairly potent steroid, flumenthazone, resulted in only a ten-fold decrease in resistance to herpes. The other, much more potent immunosuppressant, cyclophosphamide, decreased the immune system's resistance to herpes by 260-fold. Pot fell in between the two. Marijuana, however, is not "billed" as an immunosuppressant. Dr. Munson, chief researcher in this study, expressed concern that "exposure to marijuana could well lower resistance to infectious agents, including herpes."

Thus far, no human studies have been done on pot and herpes.

Some two hundred scientific papers have been published on marijuana and the immune system. Many animal studies have shown that marijuana impairs the immune system. In 1983, Dr. Arthur Zimmerman of the University of Toronto published a series of three papers in *Pharmacology* showing that both in the test tube and in the living animal (in this case mice), THC resulted in marked suppression of the immune system. In one of these studies, for example, Zimmerman found that a small dose of THC, 10 to 15 milligrams per kilogram (a human equivalency dose of two to four joints) injected for five days, suppressed the primary humoral immune response and the "memory aspect" of the humoral immunity. "This," said Dr. Zimmerman, "means that the antibodies which respond to a foreign body (germs and so on) are not called forth in a normal manner. In a normal situation, immune system cells remember and recognize a previous exposure to a specific foreign body, and they can quickly organize a defense system. But THC hampers this recognition and thus significantly suppresses and slows the response. This specific suppression effect was caused only by THC, not CBN or CBD."

Researchers who have done marijuana/immune-system studies on other animals—rabbits, rats, guinea pigs, and dogs—have also found that marijuana impairs the immune system.

As noted, not all *human* studies have shown that the immune system is affected by pot. But as an article in *Science* magazine pointed out, the studies with these negative findings used subjects who were neither long-term nor heavy users; it is unlikely that light, short-term use would affect the immune system.

Some human studies show that marijuana not only inhibits the ability of immune cells to recognize the encroachments of disease or a "foreign invader," it also suppresses the ability to take action once the encroachment is recognized. Says immunologist Dr. Robert McDonough, "That's like having a feeble, half-blind night watchman, taking his gun away from him—and then expecting him to function."

It should be remembered that different people react differently to the same amount of the same drug. In some people the T's and the B's may "come out fighting" even with heavy THC exposure, and the chronic pot-smoker may claim, "I've never been sick a day in my life." In other cases, the immune system of a healthy-seeming heavy pot smoker may "go down the tubes" all at once. And, in still other cases, the regular user seems to catch everything; infections take longer to heal, and conditions such as acne may be persistent.

Pediatrican Ingrid Lantner, who practices in a suburb of Cleveland, has long been aware of the effects pot smoking can have on young users. She comments:

We never used to *see* many sick teenagers. They're over the childhood diseases and usually in the prime of health. But now chronic young pot-smokers show up with a variety of symptoms including chest pains, chronic cough, bronchitis, persistent sore throat, fever, irregular menstrual periods, depression. And there are those who report that they just seem to get sick all the time.

Lantner often gives no medication. Her sole prescription: Cut out the pot and see what happens. When the patients do so, the symptoms usually disappear completely in four to twelve weeks, and do not reappear. "I'm convinced, from what I see every day," says Lantner, "that marijuana does affect the immune system."

Dr. Harold Voth, a well-known psychiatrist formerly on the faculty of the Menninger School of Psychiatry and chief of staff, the Topeka, Kansas, Veterans Medical Center, has treated or supervised the treatment of several thousand heavy pot-smokers. He says: "One of the telltale signs of the chronic pot-smoker is: They get sick a lot."

Dr. Gabriel Nahas sums up the situation in these words:

As regards marijuana's effects on the human immune system, there is at present a good deal of suggestive, but not conclusive, evidence that marijuana consumption may produce immune disability. Cannabis might be an immunodepressant, not an immuno*suppressant.* The final answer can only be documented by long-term epidemiological studies of marijuana smoking populations, and this has never been done.

Chromosome Damage

Dr. Akira Morishima of Columbia College of Physicians and Surgeons is an authority on cytogenetics, the branch of genetics concerned with cellular heredity. In 1973, Morishima did studies on chromosomes in the T-lymphocytes of twenty-five healthy adult males, aged eighteen to twenty-eight, who had smoked marijuana for an average of four years, ranging from one to ten joints a week.

Chromosomes are the submicroscopic particles of heredity packaged in the nucleus of every cell. Each individual chromosome is a rolled-up DNA tape of genetic instructions; all animals and plants have a particular number of chromosomes in each cell (e.g., twenty for corn cells, twenty-six for frogs). What Dr. Morishima found in his subjects was a dramatic increase in the number of cells with fewer than the normal human number of forty-six chromosomes—anywhere from thirty down to only *five!* The other chromosomes had disappeared or been destroyed. About one-third of the cells of the heavy pot smokers had less than the normal number of chromosomes. The young men who had the worst chromosome loss were those who smoked pot daily. Those whose abnormal cells were in the twenty- to thirty-chromosome range were the once-a-week or weekend smokers.

"I have done research on human cells for over two decades," said Morishima. "I have never found any other illegal drugs which had an effect similar to the DNA damage done by marijuana."

In a study published in 1980, Morishima showed that relatively small doses of THC in a test tube induced a three-fold increase in abnormal *movement* in chromosomes. This, in turn, resulted in abnormal cell division. Cell division is a delicate and complicated process in which the entire cell nucleus with all its chromosomes divides precisely in half to produce two new cells. But in marijuana users, Dr. Morishima found, the process was so botched that instead of creating two new identical nuclei, mutant (changed) nuclei were created through unequal division, which often included three or more nuclei formed from a single "parent." The mutant daughter cells thus created had differing amounts of DNA per cell. (See picture below).

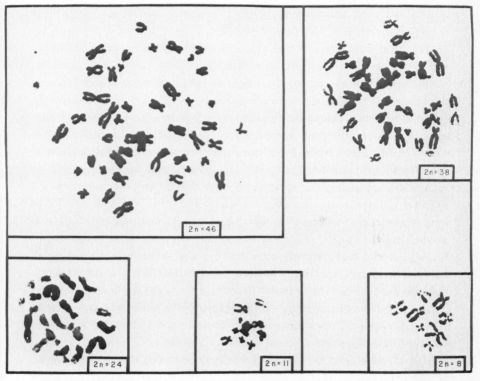

White blood cells of healthy adult males, who had been smoking pot for an average of four years, ranging from one to ten joints a week. Almost one-third of their cells had far less than the normal number of forty-six chromosomes—anywhere from thirty down to only *five*. The degree of damage correlated with the intensity of pot use.

Upper left panel from non–pot-smoker shows the normal number of forty-six chromosomes. All other panels show cells from marijuana smokers with fewer than the normal number. The chromosome-short cells, of course, had far less than the normal amount of DNA—the cell's most essential ingredient which has been termed the mastermodule of life itself.

Pot proponents frequently shrug off such findings by saying that aspirin, coffee, and alcohol also cause chromosome damage. Morishima repeated exactly the same test-tube procedure using similar quantities of salicylate (aspirin) and caffeine, and a heavily concentrated dose of alcohol—a thousand-fold more than the THC. Said Morishima, "If the BAC—blood alcohol content—reached that level in a human, it would kill the person." Results: None of these three produced any abnormal movement of chromosomes.

Morishima, who works with many drugs and chemicals, summed up:

> There are only a handful of chemicals which significantly disturb cell movement and division. But marijuana is the only drug routinely taken by humans which is known to disturb the process of cell division in this way. The accumulating body of evidence indicates that the cellular effects of marijuana are insidious, cumulative, and dangerous.

Dr. Morton Stenchever was chairman of the Department of Obstetrics and Gynecology of the University of Utah College of Medicine when he published a chromosome study on light to moderate users of marijuana in the January 1974 issue of the *American Journal of Obstetrics and Gynecology*. His subjects were twenty women and twenty-nine men. Of these, twenty-seven had used only marijuana; the rest had used other illegal drugs as well. The light smokers had used the drug once a week; the moderates had used it two or more times a week. The subjects had smoked pot for six months to nine years, averaging about three years, but none had smoked a joint for the five hours preceding the study, and some had abstained for as long as a month preceding the study. There were twenty non–pot-using controls.

All subjects and controls were healthy, and their nutrition was good. Subjects ranged in age from seventeen through thirty-four, average twenty-two. All were university students. The average age of the controls was twenty-eight—students and university staff members. None of the non–pot-smoking control group had been exposed to any drugs or medication for six months prior to the study, other than an occasional aspirin.

The chromosomes in white blood cells (leukocytes) were studied. Slides of the chromosome spreads were coded so the observer would not know whether they were from a subject or a control. All abnormal cells were photographed for careful analysis during the mitosic (cell division) stage—the time when chromosomes can be seen most clearly.

Five basic questions were asked during the study:

1. *Does marijuana cause chromosome damage?* In the controls, in every 100 cells there was an average of 1.2 with chromosome breaks. This was

more than doubled in the pot users: Out of every 100 cells, an average of 3.4 showed chromosome breaks. This represents considerable damage. The late Dr. Hardin Jones, a consultant to the Atomic Energy Commission as an expert in human radiation effects and chromosome damage, put it in these comparative terms: "This corresponds to the amount of breakage induced by high doses of ionizing radiation (150 roentgens)."

2. *Was there a significant "damage difference" between the light and moderate users?* No, the "lights" had a breakage rate of 3.2 cells per hundred; the moderates, 3.8 cells per hundred.

3. *Do male and female subjects respond differently with respect to chromosome-breakage effect?* No.

4. *Does the use of caffeine concurrently with marijuana have an additive chromosome-breakage effect?* No.

5. *Does the concurrent use of other drugs influence the extent of chromosome damage?* No. The twenty-two pot-smokers who also "did" other drugs had used barbiturates, amphetamines, tranquilizers, mescaline, LSD, and heroin. Chromosome damage in users of marijuana alone averaged 3.1 cells with breaks per 100; users of marijuana *and* other drugs averaged 3.7 cells with breaks per 100 cells. The difference was not statistically significant.

One interesting facet of these findings: A previous study by Stenchever had reported that LSD caused chromosome damage, which, given a good deal of media attention, had occasioned a drop in LSD use. However, later investigation showed that the LSD, dangerous though it was in other ways, did not cause chromosome breakage; the LSD users in the initial study were also pot-smokers. Stenchever's careful marijuana/chromosome study indicated that in the first study it had been pot, not LSD, that had caused the chromosome breakage.

Pot-smokers often claim that the so-called Jamaican Study (*Ganja in Jamaica*) showed no chromosome breaks in the cell studies. However, as Stenchever pointed out: "Only some twenty-five chromosome spreads per individual were scored: a very small number (most cell studies look at many hundreds of cell spreads per individual). Furthermore, control groups in our laboratory consistently have breakage rates of between 1 and 2 percent. That is what we find year after year. But the *control* group in the Jamaican study showed a much higher percent of chromosome breakage, which would imply that there were other factors at play." These might range from faulty technique to the fact that the control group had used marijuana in the past. Even Stenchever had problems finding controls who had never used marijuana. "I polled a hundred students," he said, "and ninety-eight had tried marijuana at least once."

Dr. Stenchever also pointed out that when increased chromosome breakage rates (more fragile chromosomes) run in the family, the incidence of cancer is higher:

> What you see in chromosome damage is the process of cell damage, particularly damage to the nucleus. This can injure the cell in such a way that it eludes the body's basic filtering defense mechanisms and leads to a neoplasm (tumor). We know that most cancers come from one cell— a cell which somehow eludes the body's defense mechanism—and there are probably some people who are more cancer-prone than others. Therefore, if chromosome damage takes place in these people, they are at greater risk of developing cancer than other people.

Cannabis and Cancer?

Missing chromosomes, moving chromosomes, broken chromosomes—all constitute genetic mutations. A mutation is a change in heredity material involving either a physical change in chromosomes or a fundamental structural change in genes. It has long been recognized that mutagenicity can be an indicator of carcinogenicity (the tendency to produce cancer).

In 1979 and 1980 Canadian researcher Dr. Arthur Zimmerman carried out standard tests for mutagenicity using three different cannabinoids.

Zimmerman, working with noted cancer researcher Dr. W. Robert Bruce of the Ontario Cancer Institute, gave THC to more than a hundred mice for five days. The dosages varied, ranging from the mouse equivalent of two to four joints a day. The researchers then looked at the shape of the sperm heads. In normal mice of this strain—commonly used for cancer research—about 1 percent of the sperm heads are abnormal. After the brief treatment with THC, the abnormal count increased to from 3 to 6 percent; the increase was dose-related. "Any increase above 3 percent," said Zimmerman, "is considered to be an indication of mutagenicity."

In a second test, Zimmerman gave mice the same doses for five days, then sacrificed them. A certain type of bone marrow cell (erythroblast—an "immature" red blood cell) was examined. "If you have a mutagen," said Zimmerman, "it causes a disruption of the mitotic event [cell-dividing process]—a damaged or broken chromosome may lag behind and form a small micronucleus—which has no role." Highly abnormal and readily identified, these micronuclei are used by researchers as an assessment for mutagenicity. In the controls, less than 1 percent of the cells had a micronucleus. In the THC-exposed cells, the incidence ranged from 2 to 10 percent. This also was dose-related.

He summed up:

> These standard tests for mutagenicity are relatively recent. If tobacco were to be introduced into our society today and were given these same tests and if it produced the same results, tobacco would surely be banned from use. The tests showed unequivocally that cannabinoids are detrimental to the cells.

Since cancer is "cells gone haywire," since cannabis creates such fundamental changes at the cellular level, and since pot has been shown to be mutagenic in numerous animal and human studies, it is strange that not more work has been done directly on the potential cancer-causing effects of the cannabinoids.

Dr. Josel Szepsenwol of the Department of Biological Sciences of Florida International University was the first researcher in the United States to do long-term cancer/cannabis studies on mice. In three studies from 1977 to 1982 he used small doses of two or three different cannabinoids—THC, cannabinol (CBN), and cannabidiol (CBD). Each mouse in all three experiments got a 20-microgram injection of one cannabinoid dissolved in .05 milliliter of sesame oil. In his first study, Szepsenwol gave the injections *only once a week*.

He injected 100 mice with prepared doses of THC, CBN or CBD for half the lifetime of each mouse. Result: 10 percent developed large malignant subcutaneous (under the skin) tumors at the point of injection (between the shoulder blades or in the groin). The controls were injected with the same amount of sesame oil, without a cannabinoid. None developed tumors.

In his second study, completed in 1981, Szepsenwol injected 216 mice with THC or CBN, once a week, as long as they remained alive. *Over 50 percent developed cancer,* including 10 percent with huge subcutaneous tumors at the point of injection, and 40 percent with "quite extensive" cancer of the lung. None of the control mice (sesame oil only) developed subcutaneous tumors; 4 percent got cancer of the lung, a normal number for this strain of mice.

In his third study, completed in 1982, the scientist used three cannabinoids; some mice got CBN, some got CBD, and some got THC. He gave the first injections to 172 baby mice at ages five days and twelve days, and then continued with weekly injections in the right groin until the mice were sacrificed. The same number of control mice received injections of sesame oil only. For five or six months all the mice seemed normal. Then, in the seventh or eighth month, 8 out of the 172 injected with cannabinoids developed synovial sarcomas. This type of cancerous tumor (developed from the synovial membrane of the joint) occurs quite frequently in humans, but in animals the condition is relatively rare.

Then, several weeks later, 4 of the mice developed another type of cancer also fairly common in humans, but relatively rare in animals: rhabdomyosarcomas, cancerous tumors in the skeletal muscles. Interestingly, tumors in the mice injected with the two nonpsychoactive cannabinoids grew larger than those in the mice injected with the psychoactive THC. None of the control mice developed any tumors.

When asked for a statement on the significance of his findings, Szepsenwol said: "The mice make the statement."

Effects on DNA and RNA

It sounds like the scrambling of letters in an anagram game: the effects of THC, CBN, or CBD on DNA and RNA—but these little letters contain the most sobering cellular aspects of all.

Aside from the reproductive cells—sperm and ova—all human cells contain forty-six chromosomes and thousands of genes—the same set as were in the single cell from which the individual's life began. Genes are made from the chemical deoxyribonucleic acid (DNA), which provides the basis for all life from a one-celled amoeba to a 100-trillion-celled human being. DNA carries the so-called genetic code, which acts as a blueprint for all cellular activity. The two specific functions of DNA are to duplicate itself and to produce messenger RNA, which gives rise to essential proteins (organic chemicals made up of amino acids).

This is a complicated process. Immunologist Dr. Robert J. McDonough puts it in these terms: "DNA may be described as 'the executive' dictating a letter (which even in chemical terms is called 'transcription') to the secretary, who takes the letter in shorthand. This letter is the messenger RNA. The shorthand letter is translated into the finished letter at the ribosome (the protein-producing 'factory'). Any misinterpretation of this message," says McDonough, "leads to a defective protein, which could lead to the death of the cell, or cancer. A cell can only express itself by the protein it produces."

Over a dozen research teams in the United States, Canada, France, and Israel have shown that marijuana and individual cannabinoids diminish the body's ability to synthesize DNA, RNA, and essential proteins.

Most of these studies were done with THC, but Dr. Gabriel Nahas compared the DNA-impairing effects of three cannabinoids. He took lymphocytes from non–pot-smokers and put them in a series of test tubes. Then he added a millionth of a gram of THC to some of the test tubes; the same amount of cannabinol (CBN) to other test tubes, and the same amount of cannabidiol (CBD) to a third set of test tubes. All the test tubes contained a milliliter of fluid. Result: The nonpsychoactive CBN and CBD were even more potent than THC in inhibiting DNA production.

Such results have been confirmed many times over in studies by other scientists. For example, Dr. Alexander Jakubovic, one of Canada's pioneer marijuana researchers, points out:

> From 1972 to 1978 we worked on the cellular effects of various psychoactive and non-psychoactive cannabinoids; those which are present in marijuana and also their metabolites. We showed that some of the non–mind-altering cannabinoids and their metabolites have much more toxic effect on some types of cells (such as testicular cells) than the psychoactive cannabinoids, notably delta-9-THC, or its main metabolite, 11-hydroxy-delta-9-THC. All of this means that the total package of cannabinoids in marijuana is far more damaging than the extremely worrying effects shown by researchers working with only one or two individual cannabinoids.
>
> Teenagers and pre-teens who are growing fast metabolize marijuana—and everything else—faster than an adult. Any interfering with the cellular metabolic processes can therefore be much more harmful to the youngsters than to the adult. The key molecules which are involved in the cellular metabolic processes are nucleic acids and proteins. Our findings showed that in the brain cells of rats, THC brought about significant inhibition of both the synthesis of nucleic acids and protein synthesis. Furthermore, when brain tissues of rats of different ages were used, the highest detriments occurred in the brain cells of the youngest rats. These comparative effects were clearly shown in electronmicroscopic studies of the ultrastructural changes in the brain cells. It should also be noted that after one dose of THC, both the ultrastructural and biochemical changes in the cells were completely reversible. However, with repeated doses, the brain cells find it much more difficult to "repair themselves." And, of course, those brain cells which are sufficiently damaged by repeated THC doses cannot regenerate as other cells do. They simply die.

Jakubovic makes another point on cell damage:

> Kids often say to their parents, "You have your alcohol. We have our pot." Of course, many youngsters use alcohol plus pot. However, let us separate the two for a moment. It takes at least two ounces of whiskey or two cans of beer or two glasses of wine to get you drunk. This means 24 grams of pure ethyl alcohol. And these 24 grams disappear completely

from the body in four or five hours. But only *ten thousandths of a gram of THC will make you high.* And the cannabinoids stay in the body for at least a week or two, often much longer. All that time they are irritating the cells. It's like having a piece of sand in your eye. THC and other cannabinoids or their metabolites are not substances that the cell is used to. No one knows what happens to the cannabinoids when tolerance sets in. But clearly, any foreign toxic chemical which stays in the body cells for a long time is dangerous. You don't feel it. It's not painful. But the cells have a hard time pushing it out. And in the case of a chronic pot-smoker who keeps overloading the cells with more and more cannabinoids, the cells of the body and the brain are fighting a losing battle.

In this chapter, as in the other chapters of Part Two, we have reported on only a handful of the research studies done. The more than three hundred studies on the effects of cannabinoids on animal and human cells that have been published in scientific journals since 1975 describe botched cell division, missing chromosomes, slowed cell growth, shrunken amounts of DNA, abnormal-sized cell nuclei, disturbed production of protein, and scrambled information from genes. With some effects (such as "female" drumsticks in male cells), scientists have not yet answered the question "What does it mean?" But many other studies make it apparent that cell damage provides the *pathological explanation* for pot's impairing effects.

Sir William Paton of Oxford University, a world-renowned pharmacologist, is Great Britain's pioneer researcher on marijuana's cellular effects. Paton says, "Even smoking moderate amounts of marijuana can cause various kinds of damage to body cells. This includes: actions on microsomes and mitochondria [cell filaments and granules], neurons [nerve cells], fibroblasts [connective tissue cells], white blood cells and on dividing cells, thus affecting cell metabolism, energy utilization, synthesis of cellular constituents, and immunological responses."

Dr. Marietta Issidorides puts it this way: "Cannabis affects the coping ability of everything from the single cell to the whole individual."

And Dr. Gabriel Nahas sums up:

Marijuana's impairing cellular effects on DNA can result in incomplete genetic information being transmitted to the offspring. This does not mean that babies of pot-smokers will have obvious birth defects. However, there is a great danger that there will be subtle changes in physical or psychological characteristics, which will not be detected until much later in life. Therefore, the marijuana smoker may be playing genetic roulette with unborn generations.

As for the user himself or herself, the many findings on various types of cellular damage caused by cannabis explain all the other damaging effects of the drug—on the brain, the lungs, the sex organs, the immune system. I call the cell damage done by regular pot smoking over the years "the slow erosion of life."

Chapter 12

Psychological Effects

We now move from the cell to the psyche, for the damage done by marijuana reaches from the lowest frontier of life—cells and submolecular DNA—to the highest levels of human existence—the mind, the personality. And, in the case of cannabis, damage to brain cells may well *result* in damage to the mind and the personality. As noted, the brain is one-third fat. Not only do the fat-soluble cannabinoids collect in brain cells, but, in addition, the other billions of body cells accumulate cannabinoids and continually release them into the bloodstream. Thus, the brain is not only treated to its own collected cannabinoids and their metabolites, but it is continually being blood-washed by new ones. In the case of the chronic pot-smoker, the slow and continual cannabinoid release from the cells means that there is a persisting "subclinical intoxication." As psychiatrist Roy Hart puts it: "The chronic pot user is, in fact, rarely sober. The cannabinoids keep plugging away at the very vitals of the brain cells and the drug continues to do a good measure of the thinking and talking."

We have seen the structural damage THC does to brain cells in the limbic area, and the relationship between these brain areas and specific psychological pot symptoms. Dr. Robert Heath has shown that, in rhesus monkeys, THC-caused cell damage in the hippocampus, medial amygdala, and cingulate gyrus is specifically correlated with hostile emotions such as aggression, rage, and fear—prominent symptoms of pot-induced paranoia. Other sites showing THC-caused cell impairment, including the paraventricular thalamus, are related to the typical pot symptoms of apathy and flatness.

Psychiatrist Robert Gilkeson, whose research concentrates on marijuana's effects on the frontal lobe, points out that complex brain functions need complex circuitry, which takes more neural connections. EEG and other studies clearly show that cannabinoids in the brain markedly decrease the activation of the brain circuits. "The psyche," says Gilkeson, "is just as cellularly dependent as sight or hearing."

Fair Oaks Hospital in Summit, New Jersey, is one of the few psychiatric hospitals in the country that specializes in the treatment of chronic marijuana users. In a letter in the *American Journal of Psychiatry*, psychiatrists Mark Gold, director of research, Charles Dackis, and A. Carter Pottash, of Fair Oaks Hospital expressed their concerns about the long-term effects of continual cannabinoid saturation of the brain:

> Psychiatric complications could readily result from constant exposure of these retained exogenous [from external sources] cannabinoid toxins. . . . Based upon our experience treating hundreds of chronic marijuana users, we believe that residual psychological effects are present and include memory, concentration and motivational impairment. We believe that the saturation of the brain by cannabinoids could lead to chronically altered subjective states, impaired cognitive functioning, and a re-definition of what is "normal" brain functioning. Such chronic alterations could effect personality changes which might be particularly harmful in developing children and adolescents.

Like the biological symptoms of pot impairment, the psychological symptoms are often insidious and subtle—although it is clear that the younger the user, the more rapidly the psychological symptoms show themselves. Parents often prefer to shrug off such symptoms as "It's only teenage!" And indeed, many of the symptoms of the pot-smoking teenager *can* be found in the literature describing typical adolescence. The difference is that cannabis exaggerates such symptoms, and they are usually not something the youngster "will grow out of"—not without help.

The Scope of the Problem

The prevalence and severity of psychiatric problems caused by cannabis can be partially gleaned from the fact that, after heroin, marijuana-related dysfunction has been the most frequent cause of admission to federally funded drug treatment facilities throughout the nation for years. Admission to these facilities—over five thousand marijuana cases a month—is voluntary. Half these patients began using pot at age fourteen or younger.

This statistic—the only one of its type available—remained constant from

213

1977 until October 1981, when the "block grant" program was inaugurated. States began collecting their own information, and most no longer reported to the federal government's drug-abuse reporting network, CODAP (Client Oriented Data Acquisition Process). Even during 1977 to 1981, only some two thousand federally funded facilities reported to CODAP; untold numbers of psychologists, psychiatrists, social workers, guidance counselors, and public and private treatment facilities dealing with drug abuse did not. One can only guess how many more unreported patients were psychologically dysfunctional because of chronic marijuana use.

It is revealing to look at a breakdown of the CODAP figures. The following are 1981 figures, the latest available to CODAP. Of people admitted into a federally funded drug treatment program, 47,675 persons reported a primary problem with marijuana:

- 75.3 percent were male, 24.7 percent female.

- 73.8 percent were white, 14.9 percent black, 8.9 percent hispanic, and 2.4 percent "other."

- 38.7 percent were under eighteen years of age, 16.3 percent between eighteen and nineteen, 23.4 percent between twenty and twenty-four, and 12.3 percent twenty-five and twenty-nine, over twenty-nine, 9.4.

- 60 percent were living with parents, 8 percent alone, 7 percent with a spouse, and 24 percent with "others." (Last available figures were for 1978.)

- 36.0 percent had first used marijuana before age fourteen, 29.9 percent at fourteen or fifteen, and 16.5 percent at sixteen or seventeen, 8.2 between eighteen and nineteen, and 3.7 between twenty and twenty-one.

- 27.6 percent said they did not have any other drug problem; 47.1 percent reported secondary problems with alcohol, 3.4 percent with hallucinogens, 8.1 percent with amphetamines, and 13.8 percent with various other drugs.

- Of those admitted to treatment for primary problems with sedatives, amphetamines, cocaine, and hallucinogens, more than 30 percent reported marijuana as a secondary drug problem.

According to the National Institute on Drug Abuse (NIDA),

If the number of people seeking treatment for marijuana in privately funded drug treatment clinics and psychiatric settings is about the same as in the federally funded clinics, it is possible to roughly estimate that each year approximately 60,000 persons, mostly white male teenagers who live with their parents, seek treatment for problems related to marijuana use. It is not possible to estimate how many more sought treatment in other settings.

The kind of treatment these young people receive will vary from clinic to clinic, but generally it involves out-patient drug-free therapy. The length of treatment averages four and a half months, and the rate of return to treatment is 19 percent.

According to Dr. Mitchell Rosenthal, director of Phoenix House, the nation's largest residential drug rehabilitation facility, "Today, mounting clinical evidence shows that among youngsters and young adults, marijuana may be causing one of the most massive psychiatric problems this nation has ever encountered."

Yet paradoxically, most of our treatment professionals seem ignorant of this psychiatric problem. Furthermore, many treatment facilities and individual drug-abuse professionals do not even accept the marijuana abuser who seeks help. They specialize in treating alcoholics, or those who use cocaine or heroin and other opiates. Other agencies and professionals dealing with drug abuse regard marijuana as a "soft drug" that "everybody does" and that, therefore, "doesn't count." Some who claim to insist that their outpatients remain drug-free overlook pot use when they screen for other drugs.

Dr. Robert DuPont, former director of NIDA and of the drug dependence section of the World Psychiatric Association, puts it this way:

Considering that marijuana is now used on a daily basis by about one out of every ten Americans eighteen to twenty-five, it is strange indeed that there has been almost no development of desperately needed treatment methods or facilities for youngsters and adults psychologically damaged by this drug; almost no place where a person can turn with the assurance that the treatment professional will be knowledgeable about the very specific problems of the marijuana-impaired personality, and the disrupted, often poisoned, family relationships this leads to.

In addition, there is very little effective treatment available for youngsters who are not yet pot-addicted or seriously impaired but who need help. They are often treated as though they and their families are psychoanalytic failures.

Joyce Nalepka, president of the National Federation of Parents for Drug-Free Youth, notes:

Since April 1980, when NFP was founded, we have received many hundreds of phone calls and letters from anguished and angry parents whose children were involved with marijuana either as beginning users, or moderate to heavy users. The parents had turned to professionals ranging from school guidance counselors to psychiatrists who were totally unaware of the specific symptoms of marijuana abuse, and their serious implications. In the case of "weekend smokers," the parents were almost invariably given this message: "Your child doesn't have a problem. You're overreacting. It's just a phase—something all kids do at that age."

In the case of youngsters exhibiting adverse symptoms of marijuana use, parents were usually made to feel that it was *their* fault, that the youngsters had "gone to pot" because they came from a "flawed family."

After dealing with countless parent groups for drug-free youth in every state of the nation, we know that there is no stereotype of family whose children get involved with drugs. A child from the most stable, loving middle- or upper-income family is almost as likely to get involved with marijuana as a ghetto child from a broken home.

It is essential, says Nalepka, that drug treatment professionals apprise themselves of the most up-to-date information on marijuana, including the mass of clinical reports—instead of waiting another fifteen years for epidemiological double-blind studies to be published.

Ask a parent whose child is strung out on marijuana about the intense psychological damage the drug is doing to that child—and to the entire family. Because of the generally poor track record treatment professionals have had on the marijuana front, often by the time a child does finally get into treatment, he or she is seriously addicted, and the child's family has become totally nonfunctional in trying to cope, totally battered.

Thus, our nation is shockingly ill equipped to treat and cure the massive psychiatric problems of our marijuana epidemic. Dr. Mark Gold points out one very good reason for this:

Most medical schools offer but minimal training in the area of drug abuse. Generally, during a psychiatric residency you spend one-third to one-sixth of the entire three-year period learning about schizophrenia—which affects 0.5 percent of our population—whereas many residents get no formal substance abuse training at all. Indeed, if you are a resident and wish to specialize in substance abuse, there are few options available to you. The number of residency training programs in this area are few and far between. Furthermore, there is no accrediting specialty board within medicine or psychiatry which is specifically concerned with substance abuse to enable parents or patients to identify which physicians have been trained in this area. *Substance abuse is now the number-one problem facing mental health professionals and physicians,* and it seems ridiculous that more time and energy is not spent in training these professionals to help prevent drug-related disease and disability, and to treat it when it occurs.

The Psychological Pot Portrait

The current treatment situation seems all the more astounding when we bear in mind that *the portrait of the pot-damaged personality has been clearly and accurately delineated for more than a decade.* What is more, the symptoms are so specific that the pot personality portrait drawn by psychiatrists aware of the problem in the early seventies is exactly the same as that reported by psychiatrists studying the problem today.

Consider, for example, the conclusion of psychiatrist A. J. Kornhabert in his paper "Marijuana in an Adolescent Psychiatric Outpatient Population," published in the *AMA Journal* in 1971:

> Marijuana-smoking adolescents seen as psychiatric outpatients showed a decrease in: attention, logical thinking, personal hygiene, performance in school, and participation in physical and social activities compared with their pre-marijuana status. These changes reversed when marijuana smoking was stopped.

Between 1965 and 1970, psychiatrists Harold Kolansky and William Moore studied thirty pot-smokers, aged thirteen to twenty-four, who habitually smoked marijuana at least twice a week but who did not use other drugs and who had not shown symptoms of emotional disorders prior to smoking marijuana. In their *AMA Journal* report, Kolansky and Moore listed a spate of symptoms, including:

> poor social judgment, poor attention span, poor concentration, confusion, anxiety, depression, apathy, passivity and, often, slowed and slurred speech. Many also exhibited an alteration of consciousness that included a split between an observing and an experiencing portion of the ego, inability to bring thoughts together, paranoid suspiciousness and regression to a more infantile state. In a few patients, hyperactivity, aggression and agitation were common. The symptoms were present even when the patients weren't "high" on the drug.

Over six hundred scientific papers have been published since 1970 on the harmful psychological, psychiatric, and psychosocial aspects of chronic marijuana use. Although the early studies draw the same basic pot profile we see today, current users smoke far more potent pot, smoke it more often, and start smoking at a younger age than their "foretokers" in the early 1970s. Consequently, additional dark features are being added to the profile.

For example, in 1982, Dr. Doris H. Milman, professor of pediatrics at the State University of New York, published a report on her study of twenty-

217

four teenagers. The IQs of the subjects ranged from above-average to superior. Seven youngsters were the sons and daughters of physicians. Drug use was the primary problem of all the youngsters, and marijuana was their primary drug of abuse. (Other drugs, with the exception of alcohol, were only used occasionally or experimentally on a once or twice basis.)

Milman describes symptoms seen by the psychiatrists reporting in the early 1970s, including:

> impaired recent memory and retrieval, attention deficits, altered time perception, drowsiness, indolence, withdrawal, anxiety and apprehension, feelings of depersonalization and derealization. . . . School failure following drug use; a change from a prior good to excellent school record was noted in 18 patients. Of those, half dropped out of high school or college, the dropout occurrences being in sharp contrast to intellectual ability . . .

However, Milman also noted more serious symptoms. For example,

> Suicidal ideation was a prominent finding, with overt gestures by one subject. A most significant fact is that only two subjects had a prior depressive history. Moreover, depressive symptoms, and in particular suicidal thinking, were reversed when cannabis use was even temporarily discontinued.
>
> The patients and their parents were particularly frightened by flashbacks and the occurrence of delusions. [A flashback is a spontaneous, involuntary recurrence of the feelings and perceptual state produced by the drug.] These states evoked unbearable anxiety, fear and agitation, requiring sedation with chlorpromazine. Flashbacks lasted up to four months after stopping the drug. Other researchers have found that marijuana can induce LSD, mescaline or PCP flashbacks in patients who have taken these drugs.
>
> The total of 11 instances out of 24 of schizophrenia and borderline schizophrenic personality was extremely high in relation to the absence of these categories in the predrug state. Personality traits and features also included a new finding of paranoia in addition to an increased incidence of depressive features.

We will examine some of these aspects in greater depth after a more careful delineation of the "pot personality." First, however, an important point should be made. Many claim that chronic pot use is a *result* of a personality disorder—not a *cause* of it. Therefore, they say, describing psychological symptoms is meaningless.

Naturally, in some cases, personality disorders may lead to marijuana use. However, treatment professionals continually see clear—and encouraging—proof that pot is usually the cause and not the result of a host of psychological manifestations.

In one respect, the solution is simple. Dr. Dean Parmelee, a director of adolescent in-patient services at Boston University Medical School, puts it this way: *"The clearest evidence that pot use causes the 'pot personality' is this: When the subject gives up the drug, the symptoms usually disappear completely and, in a matter of months, the youngster 'returns.' The real problem lies in getting the subject to give up the drug."*

Marijuana use is now so endemic in our society that no longer can we identify a pot-*prone* personality. Only one item remains as a "prone" factor: youth. Young users come from all strata of our society. However, after they become chronic pot-smokers, these widely diverse young users tend to slide into a melting pot of pot, and gel into a startling sameness, with a distinct and predictable pot-*induced* profile. As Dr. Parmelee points out:

> Not all kids have all the symptoms. In fact, some very bright youngsters with outgoing, goal-oriented personalities seem to be able to maintain their grades and activities for a few years. However, all users—regardless of age—gradually compromise their potential, their activities, and their life styles. And heavy *young* users eventually develop most, if not all, of the "pot personality" symptoms.

Psychiatrist Harold Voth of the Menninger School of Psychiatry and the Topeka, Kansas, Veterans' Medical Center, has studied the psychopathology of marijuana in depth since 1972. He paints the typical pot portrait based on what he has seen in his private patients, outpatients, and ward patients, and as borne out in clinical reports and studies published in scientific journals. Voth points out that it takes years of very heavy drinking to reach the point of psychological impairment that marijuana can induce in a matter of months, particularly in the case of the very young user. He notes that *the three impairments most specific to chronic marijuana use are impaired short-term memory, emotional flatness, and the amotivational—or "dropout"—syndrome.* This can progress from dropping out of sports, to dropping out of school, to dropping out of the family. A clear warning sign in the young user is a drop in grades. In some this can be gradual: A's and B's to B's and C's, followed, after a year or two, by an occasional D or F. In others, the effects can hit quickly. Voth mentions the case of a boy who was doing fine as a college freshman. Toward the end of the second semester, he started heavy pot smoking. He did not use other drugs and drank only an occasional beer. At the end of the year he flunked most of his subjects. Over the summer he quit pot, and when he came back for his sophomore year he got three A's and a B. "Initially," said Voth, "the young man refused to believe it was the marijuana. The element of denial that marijuana is affecting one adversely is one of the most common and most persistent aspects of the pot portrait."

How much pot brings on such impairments?

The more formed, stable, and mature the personality is, says Voth, the less likely there will be signs of personality impairment, although anyone who smokes three times a week or more will eventually lower his or her potential in a number of ways.

Voth enumerates more classic symptoms of the pot personality: "They lose their luster, their zest and zip. This is one of the first things to go, and it's slow to return after getting off the drug." Other signs are diminished willpower, a weakened hold on reality, and hostility toward authority—especially, in teenagers, the user's parents. There is an egoistic, narcissistic self-centeredness, coupled with a lack of caring about anyone or anything else—except procuring and smoking grass, and the "scene" that goes with it.

In addition, there is a tendency toward "less civilized behavior and a more dilapidated appearance." These, says Voth, are reflections of ego regression, a very characteristic marijuana symptom. There is also a social regression, manifested by isolation from the mainstream of life, and especially from the family.

The alienation from the more established aspects of society often has a delusional flavor, ranging from a high level of unwarranted suspiciousness to bouts of outright paranoia. Example: The high school sophomore in a new school who tells her parents that all the teachers are in a conspiracy against her. "They whisper to each other about me, and smile—but in a not nice way."

"Also," says Voth, "chronic marijuana use is linked to disheartening, dispirited depression and suicidal thoughts."

Voth agrees with other experts that the young user who cuts out all marijuana use completely for three months "will return to the youngster he or she once was. However, in some cases short-term memory takes a while to come back, and some never seem to get it back to its pre-pot sharpness. Also, *one common after-effect that can persist for many years is a lack of personal self-esteem.*"

In the final chapter of this book we discuss ways in which the young user *can* be successfully isolated from the drug for three months. Now, however, let us look in greater depth at some of the specific psychological and psychiatric symptoms of chronic marijuana use.

Behavioral Toxicity

The chronic "poisoning" of behavioral patterns is a marijuana-specific feature that apparently derives from the "time-release capsule" quality of the drug. Although other psychological symptoms of use are more evident among young users than adults, this one is just as notable in adult chronic users.

It can be understood most clearly by comparison to alcohol intoxication. If drunks behave in an aberrant or uncharacteristic fashion and then recall the behavior or are confronted with it when sober, they tend to disassociate themselves from the action or behavior ("I sure must have been bombed").

In the chronic marijuana user, on the other hand, there is a strange behavioral holdover. Drug-induced thinking and actions indulged in during the "high" are generally accepted, even stubbornly adhered to, in the sober state.

Furthermore, unlike the heavy drinker who generally "becomes himself again" when sober, *the underlying personality structure of the chronic pot smoker seems to change.* Psychiatrist John Meeks, medical director of the Psychiatric Institute of Montgomery County, Maryland, puts it this way:

> You can say of the "respectable" drunk, "I never realized that Charlie drank until I saw him sober one day!" But that insight can't occur to observers of the average adolescent dependent on pot. The problem is that if he or she smokes twice a week, sobering up—in a total sense— never occurs. For the first time in U.S. history we have a commonly used drug which affects the chronic user so that, even when not "high," he or she remains in a state of very subtle intoxication; in most cases, without even recognizing this "holdover" effect.

Kevin McEneaney of Phoenix House in New York City has dealt with hundreds of chronic pot-smoking teenagers and their parents. He points out:

> There is a peer–mind-set that happens when a kid is stoned and carries over to when he's sober. It's a kind of pollution of the mind with a new type of thinking. A parent may think he's talking to his kid. But he's not—he's talking to a stoned mind-set that says, for example, "It's okay for me to do this because everybody does it." Wild, almost irrational statements develop. For example: "All Jamaicans smoke pot—and it doesn't hurt them one bit." Sometimes this mind-set is dangerous, as in the case of the driver who insists: "I handle the car much better when I'm high."

This strange element of behavioral toxicity can be completely baffling to the person trying to "get through" to the pot smoker who is not high—who, indeed, may not have had a joint for two or three weeks. Instead of being *rational,* the user stubbornly adheres to the *rationale* he or she has developed for the pot-induced behavior.

As McEneaney puts it: "Pot smokers are defensive and overly sensitive about their drug. This can take a lot of faces, from pseudo-rational to verbal outrage. In any case, a curtain of denial comes down and it's very difficult to penetrate—until the user has been off the drug for a matter of months."

Psychiatrist Sidney Cohen of UCLA Medical School, who conducted one of the largest adult studies ever done of marijuana users, summed up:

> Of all the emerging concerns of parents, teachers, and physicians, the greatest may be the behavioral toxicity which sometimes accompanies even short-term heavy cannabis use (within three to six months). Subtle or pronounced modification of life-style and goal orientation may be observable within weeks of consistent use. Adolescents are particularly affected by drugs that diminish aspirations and purposeful behavior because their hopes and desires tend to be in a state of flux, and reformulation. When substances like cannabis are consumed during a fair part of one's waking hours, a discernible passivity and withdrawal from existing activities and interests sets in. It's to be expected that such demotivation will occur during the intoxication state. But I'm not really not speaking of that. With persistent cannabis use it carries over into the unintoxicated condition.

One eighteen-year-old who calls himself "an ex-pothead" put it this way: "Anyone who thinks that the effects of pot are gone after the high wears off might as well hang it up!"

Senility Symptoms in Young Pot Smokers

As we saw in Chapter 10, in brain-cell studies using teenage monkeys, Dr. Robert Heath found a dramatic increase in two cellular symptoms associated with old age in monkeys and in humans over seventy years of age—the dark swollen lipofusion granules, and the inclusion bodies (protein clots) in the nuclei. Other marijuana researchers working with other types of laboratory animals have observed similar brain-cell old-age symptoms in young animals. In recent years, psychiatrists have begun noting *behavioral* old-age symptoms in young chronic pot-smokers.

In a March 1980 paper Dr. Adam Sulkowski noted the carbon-copy similarities of psychological symptoms of marijuana intoxication and those of Alzheimer's disease. Sulkowski, a geriatric psychiatrist at the Bedford (Massachusetts) V.A. Medical Center and the Boston School of Medicine, defines Alzheimer's disease as "a horrible, progressive and irreversible disease otherwise known as 'pre-senile dementia' when it occurs before age 65, and 'senile dementia' when it occurs after that age." In his paper "Marijuana 'High': A Model of Senile Dementia?" Sulkowski suggested that the pot high might in fact be "a convenient, reversible and inexpensive laboratory model of Alzheimer's Disease."

Among the similarities between the young stoned pot-smoker and senile adults, Sulkowski noted the following:

• Marijuana is the only drug which *invariably* produces a specific alteration in time perception. During the "high," ten minutes may seem like an hour. Some gerontologists would consider *this* the "core" symptom of Alzheimer's disease.

• The munchies (erratic surges of appetite, particularly for sweets, junk food).

• Inappropriate behavior and inability to "self-correct."

Many of the senile symptoms in the chronic young pot-smoker extend past the high, into subacute intoxication. These, according to Sulkowski, include:

• Decreasing cognitive and intellectual function.

• Gradual decline of emotional life.

• Increased irritability.

• Increased stubbornness.

• Impaired short-term memory. This characteristic, so common among chronic young pot-smokers, is also specific to old age and senility. Old people may forget where they put their spectacles, but their long-term memory is frequently sharp and clear. However, chronic young pot-smokers with impaired short-term memory may also suffer long-term impairment. For example, a teenager may forget the telephone number of a girl he has been dating for a year, or he may forget his own telephone number, or his birthday.

• Frequent complaints of tiredness.

• A gradual decrease in the ability to perform complex tasks.

223

- A diminished ability to have accurate insights in self-evaluation.

- Loses track of time and dates.

- Becomes depressed, disoriented.

Sulkowski summed up with the hope that "some of the knowledge accumulated about marijuana in recent years could be used profitably in gerontologic [normal aging] and geriatric [pathological aging] research."

More research on old-age symptoms was completed in July 1981 by psychologist Stephen Williams of Houston, Texas. His study tested sixty teenaged pot-users who smoked daily but used no other drug. They were given a battery of psychological tests, which were repeated after six pot-free weeks in the hospital. Williams noted:

In old age we see a lot of people who are very depressed. We see various types of unrealistic thinking ranging from "peculiar responses" to paranoia. We see an unreasonable preoccupation with how one's body feels. We see obsessive compulsive tendencies, and inflexibility. All these symptoms were strikingly evident in our study of the teenage pot-smokers, and all these symptoms decreased markedly once the drug was out of the system.

For example, the standard MMPI (Minnesota Multiphasic Personality Inventory)—perhaps the most widely used psychological personality test in the U.S. today—showed that 42 percent of our subjects gave a significant number of "peculiar and unusual responses." Six drug-free weeks later this was down to 16 percent. Forty-one percent evidenced a significant number of paranoid responses—six drug-free weeks later, down to ten percent. Thirty-five percent showed an abnormal amount of obsessive compulsive tendencies—six weeks later, down to 19 percent. Seventeen percent showed hypochondriacal tendencies—commonly expressed in such terms as: I feel bummed out . . . weirded out. . . . I feel blah . . . I just feel bad all over. Six weeks later this was down to five percent. And thirty percent were abnormally depressed—six weeks later, down to six percent.

Depression is perhaps the most common and most uncomfortable psychological symptom among old people. It is usually associated with feelings of loss, such as loss of loved ones, of health, etc. The chief cause of depression among our teenage subjects was *also* loss; a tremendous loss of self-esteem. One good-looking, well-dressed sixteen-year-old put it this way: "I'm just like an empty shell. The surface of me looks the same as it did before. And people who don't know me think I'm all right. I'm the only one who knows that I'm all empty inside. There is nothing left that I like about myself. And pot did it." Marijuana was the only drug he used.

Another similarity to senility, with a sad difference, concerns nostalgia. Although both groups suffer from impaired short-term memory, an old person frequently has vivid recollections of early years accompanied by a keen, bitter-sweet nostalgia. When the youngster comes off the drug, his short-term memory usually returns. But he is now often hit by a sense of painful nostalgia— for a *lost* time: years never fully lived, because his relationship was not with childhood, but with drugs. He is now out of pace with his own chronology.

Sometimes older teenagers try to recapture these lost years. Dr. Jason Baron, medical director of Houston's Deer Park Hospital, which deals exclusively with drug abusers aged fourteen to twenty-five, reports:

> I've seen eighteen-year-olds who, when they get off pot, go through a short phase of playing with Barbie dolls or miniature cars, trying to experience a time they never knew. Fortunately, with adequate treatment, these youngsters can be taught new coping skills, which enable them, among other things, to recapture some of the essence of the lost years in a matter of weeks to months. But those who don't get help often experience a permanent void for the years they have "missed."

Interference with the Maturation Process

Ironically, given the precocious senility marijuana may cause in the teen-ager, it can at the same time cause a regression to a preteen immaturity. This is what psychiatrist Mitchell Rosenthal calls "interference with the maturation process." "The focus of my concern," he says,

> is pot's capacity to induce regression and, at times, irreversible immaturity. When youngsters need most to grow psychologically, they are pushed back toward infantalism by self-absorption and the desire for instant gratification. When they need most to learn how to *cope* with the emotional storms and squalls of the troubled teenage period, they are instead *copping out,* blowing their problems away with pot. When they need most to consider long-range goals, they are operating in a shrunken time-frame of days or hours. They are usually not aware of their psychological regression. Indeed, paradoxically, a great many young people see marijuana as the easy "cool" way to mature: the "with-it" way.

As one teenager, a former heavy pot-smoker, put it: "The messed-up, drugged-out kid is often viewed by other kids as a romantic figure. They respect him or her, and want to be like that."

Dr. Rosenthal predicts "drastic ramifications" of continued widespread adolescent marijuana use:

A sizable number of our young people will not mature as they should, will not make the intellectual gains they should during their growing years, will not become the capable and productive citizens our society needs. Instead, we can look forward to a growing population of immature, under-qualified adults, many of whom will be unable to live without economic, social and/or clinical support. We will have, in time, an unmanageable number of emotionally, socially and intellectually handicapped citizens.

The Four Stages

Too often, parents of pot-smoking teens or preteens do not recognize what their youngster is up to and into—until the child is so seriously involved with the drug that his life, as well as that of the family, has become a disaster. How can a parent recognize the symptoms early, when it is far easier to get the child to give up the drug?

Based on his studies of over five hundred chronic pot-smokers aged thirteen to seventeen, Dr. Miller Newton, program director of STRAIGHT, an adolescent drug treatment program in Florida, Georgia, and elsewhere, has come up with the first stage-by-stage description of what he terms "a highly communicable and progressive teenage disease."

Stage One—"Learning the Mood Swing"—Most kids refuse the offer of pot the first four to five times, but eventually make a personal choice to use drugs in response to peer pressure, in order to belong to the "in" group. They learn that pot, alcohol, and other drugs make you feel good with little or no initial consequences.

Stage Two—"Seeking the Mood Swing"—The kids get to like the euphoric feeling produced by pot and start to take the initiative to get their own money, their own space, and their own marijuana in order to get high. During this second stage, use moves from regular weekend to occasional weeknight, to regular weeknight, and getting high moves from a free choice to a compulsive need.

Stage Three—"Preoccupation with the Mood Swing"—Because of tolerance and increasing guilt and shame, the child becomes preoccupied with marijuana use. His or her life centers around obtaining drugs, getting high, and being a druggie.

Stage Four—"Use to Feel Normal"—The child can no longer experience the euphoric high from marijuana but must be under the influence of the drug just to function each day. Every area of life is a disaster. The kids—in teen terms—are "burn-outs" or "zombies."

Newton sums up:

Marijuana is the gateway drug, leading to this progressive deterioration. In Stage One or Two information and lots of alternative activities are often enough to get the child to give up the drug. In Stages Three and Four, he'll try to give it up, but can't—unless something happens in his life to give him strength; usually strong parental efforts which separate him from his environment.

The Marijuanaholic

Naturally, psychological symptoms caused by chronic pot use are not restricted to preteens and teenagers, even though this age group is the most vulnerable to the destructive effects of the drug.

In 1983 Dr. Mark Gold completed a study of one hundred "marijuanaholics" aged fifteen to forty; the majority were young adults who had started pot smoking in their teens. Gold is the director of research at Fair Oaks Hospital in Summit, New Jersey. In 1981, he was awarded the American Psychiatric Association's Foundation Prize for Research. In 1982, he became the first recipient of the Presidential Award of the National Association of Private Psychiatric Hospitals. He is also the recipient of a World Health Organization award for research, and a citation by the Presidential Commission for Mental Health.

Gold regards marijuana as "a dangerous drug of abuse whose use has been promoted by certain physicians and researchers who are 'professors' at minimizing the effects of the drug."

Dr. Gold's one hundred marijuanaholics had only used other drugs rarely, if at all, and had used none but pot for six months prior to their entry to Fair Oaks Hospital. Most smoked more than a joint a day. "They were," said Gold, "as pure marijuanaholics as you can find." During the study the subjects, confined to the hospital, were kept totally drug free. They were given marijuana urine tests daily, and *many tested positive for cannabinoids for forty days*—an impressive indication of the "accumulative cannabinoid factor." Most of the subjects, said Gold, had been on a "self-administered THC maintenance program for years."

Gold defines the marijuanaholic as "a person who is seriously disabled in numerous areas: psychological, physiological, and social." Psychologically, the person has some symptoms in each of five distinct categories:

1. *Physical-psychological problems.* Symptoms include chronic headaches, which, in some cases, last for days. During the drug-free period in the hospital,

227

the subjects' headaches disappeared. Also, although marijuana is said to "turn off the vomit center" in the brain, Gold's study shows that some heavy long-term users complain of nausea and even vomiting. "However," he says, "this is nothing like the traditional alcohol hangover—which is too bad, because a hangover is a warning signal."

Other symptoms include panic attacks—racing heart, sweating, palpitations, and heavy breathing, along with severe anxiety. Some heavy users also experience blackouts or loss of memory, which can run from a few minutes to a weekend. "Most heavy users," says Gold, "shrug off panic attacks as a 'bad trip.' However, they are, in fact, dramatic warning signals and should be taken seriously."

2. *Ego deterioration.* "Since most users consider marijuana to be 'like nothing,' " says Gold, "they don't attribute their inadequacies or failures to the drug, but to themselves. This is especially dangerous for youngsters from high-expectation families. The youngsters have high expectations for themselves, and they misdiagnose their pot-impaired performance in life as testimony to their lack of ability and self-worth. This puts them in a position where they must get help, or they can head into a severe depression, with concomitant suicide attempts. It's unusual to find an opiate addict who wants to die. But suicidal thoughts and attempts are common among marijuanaholics."

3. *Problems with drug control.* "If marijuana doesn't cause dependence," asks Gold, "why is it so hard to stop using?" He points out that people who do admit to marijuana dependence tend to trivialize it as not a physical addiction, merely a psychological one. There are, in fact, certain physical withdrawal symptoms: irritability, sleep-disturbance, and so on. However, because of the slow, continual release of cannabinoids into the system, there are no severe withdrawal symptoms, as with opiates. "But," says Gold, "at least we have treatments for severe physical withdrawal symptoms—*which is why psychological addiction is far more dangerous.* It lasts longer, and we have no easy or specific remedy for it. In effect, 100 percent of marijuanaholics have problems with drug control. Some, however, are able to define it in these terms: 'I've got to limit my use—otherwise, I'd go wild and smoke incessantly.'

"If marijuanaholics don't admit to the necessity for self-limitation," says Gold, "they go on continual—and sometimes continuous—pot binges. They'll light up their first joint when they roll out of bed in the morning, smoke three or four joints throughout the day, and another before they go to bed at night.

"Some marijuanaholics are as young as twelve or thirteen. And they tend to adhere to these patterns throughout high school and college (if they make it to college), and/or into their work years.

"Many teenagers in the United States are under the influence of marijuana twenty-four hours a day during their high school years. They become their own MD's (mood doctors). When they're nervous or depressed, they reach for a joint. Not only does this form of self-medicating keep them from developing normal problem-solving techniques; it also keeps them from getting help in psychiatric treatment."

Gold warns that *psychiatrists who have not studied the signs, symptoms, and dangers of chronic pot smoking fail to realize that it is virtually impossible to cure a chronic pot-smoker until he or she has completely given up marijuana.*

He also points out: "A number of treatment professionals are pot-smokers; indeed, at the time of the initial interview he or she may be under the influence of the drug. It is essential, therefore, to ask specifically about the professional's views on marijuana before engaging in treatment for yourself, your spouse, or your marijuana-using child. Unless you receive a clear and unambiguous answer concerning the physical and psychological health hazards of marijuana use, you might want to look elsewhere for a therapist."

(It is interesting to note in this regard that, according to the *Journal of the American Medical Association,* the incidence of alcoholism among physicians is the same as that of the general population. But the incidence of drug addiction among physicians—including psychiatrists—is many times greater than among the general population.)

4. *Social and family dysfunction.* Social dysfunction includes job or school difficulties, constant irritability and squabbling, losing friends, losing interest in social behavior. Family dysfunction means the serious disruption or poisoning of the normal fabric of family life by the marijuanaholic. The user may repeatedly promise spouse or parents to "cut down." "Unfortunately," says Gold, "lying is a classic symptom, and 'cutting down' may merely mean that less smoking is done at home. The user is simply changing the time and place of his pot smoking." Even if he feels somewhat guilty about it, he has a hard time stopping.

In the case of a child, the drug use itself can be a barrier between the user and the family, because it makes the youngster feel "if my family *knew* they wouldn't love me anymore," and because the common goals of the family are no longer those of the child, which are now centered around pot.

5. *Psychotic thinking.* Transient manifestations include "false beliefs" such as depersonalization (feeling "unreal"), and attributing personalized meaning to random natural happenings. These can be pleasant; for example, when seeing treetops blow in the breeze: "The trees are bowing to me." Or they can be frightening: "The cars were chasing me; they wanted to crush me."

Psychotic thinking also comes in other serious guises. These include manic-like psychosis, schizophrenic-like psychosis (disordered thinking), confusion psychosis (complete disorientation), and severe depression and a fear of dying. There is also a common acute paranoid psychosis, which tends to be short-lived. All of these can hit heavy users who have no personal or family history of psychosis prior to their pot-smoking. "*If* diagnosed correctly as cannabis-caused," says Gold, "even these dramatic symptoms disappear completely after pot use has been stopped. If misdiagnosed, and pot use continues, the psychotic symptoms are likely to continue as well."

Gold's marijuanaholic study resulted in two important new findings in the areas of psychological reversibility and addiction. Concerning reversibility, he found that although the young user is more at risk than the adult because all the important "tasks" of adolescence are impaired by heavy marijuana use, nevertheless, the user of eighteen or under is more resilient than the adult when it comes to throwing off the impairing psychological effects. Gold noted:

> Among youngsters, our study shows that with complete abstinence for an average of six months, there is return of concentration, attention, and memory to expected levels, as shown in a series of neuropsychological tests.
> This, however, was not true for older marijuanaholics. They were slower to rebound and, in some cases, particularly with respect to short-term memory loss, they do not appear to come back all the way. Furthermore, because older users are usually long-term users, they have made subtle changes in their lives that are hard to undo. For example, they slide into less demanding jobs, and find it hard to climb back.

Gold cites a typical case: An intensive-care-unit nurse became a heavy pot-smoker, and, because of her growing incompetence, was demoted to nurse's aide. She worked as an aide for five years before she stopped her drug use; by then, everyone in the hospital was used to her in the role of nurse's aide. She was not only scared to try "going back," but she was now out of touch.

"People around former users have become accustomed to treating them as though they are somewhat disabled. Their circle of friends has generally become limited to other heavy pot-smokers, so when they stop smoking they find they don't have any friends. A lot of adults have a lot of problems when they give up the drug." But, says Gold, "these problems are minimal compared to the escalating problems they face with continued heavy pot use."

Gold's second finding, concerning relapse, was surprising. It is well recognized that one beer or a single Scotch can send the recovering alcoholic hurtling back down the path of alcohol dependence. But it is generally assumed that if one stops smoking grass, he or she has proved control over "the weed," and can therefore start or stop at will.

This, Gold showed, is no more the case with the marijuanaholic than it is with the alcoholic. Even if the heavy pot-user has been off the drug for over a year, he or she is always at risk of relapse. As Gold put it,

> It may take many drug-free months of therapy until they are able to be released from the hospital. But two joints can set them on a marijuana binge and send them back, within two weeks' time, to where they were upon admission to the hospital. This reversion not only includes the number of joints smoked, but all the deleterious, sometimes devastating psychological symptoms as well.
>
> The chronic pot smoker who gives up the drug must realize that he or she will *always* be at risk of reversion to former pot-smoking patterns.

The reason for this is the principle called state dependency, which means that when you are in a *straight* state, the *intoxicated* state is "kind of fuzzy. You can't remember all the ramifications. You don't really believe the painful parts. If you do slip back, the opposite happens: The memories that are clearest are the drug memories. The straight memories fade. People will say, 'I'll just smoke one joint—again.' But this reactivates old 'joint-associated' memories and rituals."

> The major part of any chronic drug use is the life style that goes with it. There's even a certain pride associated with being an addict.
>
> What comes first in a straight society? Work, family, and (sometimes) God; the holy trinity. But what comes first to the drug user is the self. And the self also comes second and third.
>
> In the case of the recovering marijuanaholic, the memories of the drugged state are always there. They're just locked away. That's why some people need only to re-experience the drug once to get access to the drug-state memories—and to plummet back.

Followups done by Gold and his staff on recovered marijuana patients have confirmed a sad symptom seen by other psychiatrists: long-lasting feelings of inadequacy, which may persist for many months—even years—after giving up the drug. Gold puts it this way:

> At first, it's like being in a foreign country. You feel like an alien. And there's no orientation course on how to return.
> To say that it can sometimes take years for the marijuanaholic to integrate him- or herself into a straight society is not an understatement. By far the most long-lasting effect is the unjustified feeling of inadequacy. People look back to try to find a reason for and a message in what they have done. They often see their descent into drugs as evidence that they are somehow not as good or as strong as other friends or colleagues at work. But it doesn't necessarily mean this at all. It just means they made a mistake.
> *Realizing that these feelings of inadequacy are a leftover symptom of the drugged state can be a help. It's a result of the drug use, not a personality flaw.*

Further Psychiatric Effects

Two common unpleasant reactions may occur during the marijuana high. One is the previously noted panic attack, which can hit anyone from the experienced user who smokes a more potent joint than usual to the new user, youngster or adult. Psychiatrist David Janowsky of the University of California at San Diego describes it like this:

> Smokers suddenly feel they are losing control, or even losing their mind. Some feel suicidal. The treatment is "talking them down" with reassurance that the attack will subside when the high is over. And, usually, it does. But for parents unaware of the fact that pot has caused the condition, the experience can be as terrifying as it is for the youngster undergoing the attack.

The other, even more common, reaction is entering an acute paranoid state; this can start with episodes of intense suspiciousness, the state just preceding actual paranoid thinking.

Either of these reactions may be so severe that the person is taken to the hospital emergency room. However, usually when the high is over, the reaction disappears.

Dr. Doris Milman has been gathering data from her private psychiatric practice over the past twenty-one years. She notes:

> The psychological effects of cannabis have been known since antiquity. The most obvious is the cannabis-induced psychotic reaction, with delusional symptoms, disorientation, hallucinations, paranoia, and feelings of

depersonalization and derealization. The psychosis may be present acutely or insidiously, may be transient and wholly reversible, or it may be prolonged and chronic. *When chronic it is clinically indistinguishable from chronic psychosis of the schizophrenic or paranoid type.*

Since the symptoms are so close to other forms of psychoses, and since hospitals and treatment centers are still, in the main, not evaluating new admissions for the effects of marijuana, the symptoms are often misdiagnosed—leading to inappropriate diagnosis and management of the patient, with the wrong kinds of therapy and/or medication, as though the patient were suffering from a purely psychiatric illness rather than a drug-induced one. And, as Dr. Robert DuPont points out, "Since the patient often keeps right on with his pot smoking in the hospital, all the psychotic symptoms remain, even intensify."

Dr. DuPont also describes another type of cannabis-induced psychosis: "A person may have an underlying and frequently unmanifested vulnerability to a psychiatric illness such as schizophrenia. Marijuana can act in a 'lock and key fashion,' uncovering the previously hidden tendency. Then, in many cases, the newfound illness develops a life of its own."

As DuPont points out, millions of people carry within them a potential, latent pathology. "The likelihood of having this unleashed as a consequence of chronic marijuana smoking is quite great. It can even be unleashed after one or two joints. Anyone who has recovered from a psychiatric illness is especially vulnerable."

Psychiatrist José Carranza of Baylor College of Medicine in Houston, Texas, has treated a number of such cases; he notes that people with a family history of mental illness are especially susceptible to marijuana-induced psychosis. "Triggering of this sort," says Carranza, "does not appear to be related to the duration of pot smoking. It can, however, be related to high-potency pot, especially when smoked by a vulnerable new user. In some cases, a person may be saddled with a lifelong psychiatric illness, which might otherwise have remained dormant."

The psychiatric situation is further complicated by the fact that many patients *and* psychiatrists are unaware that pot can interfere with traditional antipsychotic medications. A typical example was "Jeffrey L.," a high school senior who smoked three or four joints a week. The boy was a good student, a leader. There was no indication of mental illness—until he suddenly began hearing voices. The diagnosis was schizophrenia. At age twenty-two, after his fourth hospitalization, he came to Carranza because he still had auditory hallucinations and other symptoms, despite pharmacological treatments.

When Carranza pointed out the possible relation between Jeff's psychosis and his pot smoking, the young man decided to stop. Several months later the medications proved effective in controlling his thinking disturbances and his auditory hallucinations.

"Many users," Carranza pointed out, "are unaware of the fact that cannabis is generally classified as a weak hallucinogen. The drug, therefore, can be expected to increase psychotic auditory and visual hallucinogenic symptoms."

Other investigators have noted that pot smoking can make a bona fide severe depression even worse, and a 1973 study by Dr. David Janowsky and his colleagues suggests a cause for this. Janowsky first showed that the neurotransmitter acetylcholine, a natural chemical in the brain, may be involved in actually causing depression. He then showed that even just one half-joint of pot "dramatically increases the mood-depressing actions of acetylcholine."

A different aspect of the problem of marijuana abuse has been addressed by Dr. Lawrence Kirstein, clinical director of Regent Hospital, a psychiatric hospital in New York City specializing in neuropsychiatric evaluation with particular emphasis on substance-abuse rehabilitation. Kirstein noted: "There are a large number of psychiatric patients who prefer to self-medicate their bona fide psychiatric symptoms with marijuana rather than with conventional medication therapies."

Kirstein further pointed out that the motivation for poor compliance with treatment has many origins. At least part of the failure to seek and comply with treatment is a direct effect of marijuana on motivation and judgment. A separate component of the problem is the relative social acceptance of marijuana abuse compared with the negative image of in-patient psychiatric treatment. And a third reason for failure to seek treatment is the antianxiety effect some patients attribute to marijuana.

Kirstein went on to say that for these patients, continued marijuana use becomes, in their view, the only means of avoiding the reality of social deterioration (loss of friends, alienation of family), academic and/or job deterioration, and increasing social isolation. Once these patients have been coerced into seeking treatment and continued marijuana abuse has been arrested, it can take weeks before a clear evaluation of a masked psychotic or mood disorder—or whatever underlying emotional disorder the patient had to begin with—becomes evident.

"The fact that some of these patients will return to marijuana abuse rather than comply with effective medical treatment," said Kirstein, "not only frustrates the family and clinician but bespeaks a poor long-term prognosis. Thus, these patients require appropriate treatment that not only addresses their psychiatric problem, but also emphasizes and reinforces a marijuana-free life style." For specific patients, Dr. Kirstein states, this not only requires involvement with a non–drug-using peer group, but also blood or urine marijuana testing.

⸙ The "Progression" Theory

Since 1975, the National High School Senior Survey has shown that about half the senior class uses marijuana to some degree, and half of *that* half also uses one or more other illegal drugs besides alcohol. These drugs include LSD, PCP, cocaine, Quaaludes, uppers, downers, even—to a small degree—heroin.

On the other hand, of the 50 percent of the senior class that does *not* use marijuana, virtually *none* are regular users of any other illegal drug. (As for alcohol, the survey consistently shows that the heavy pot-users are also the heavy drinkers, and the non–pot-smokers tend not to be heavy drinkers.)

A study called "Stages in Adolescent Involvement in Drug Use" by Dr. Denise Kandel of Columbia University and New York State Psychiatric Institute reported similar findings and stressed another interesting epidemiological facet.

Kandel's study was based on three large surveys of New York State high school students. The first, in the fall of 1971, was a random sampling of 8,209 students in eighteen high schools in all sections of the state—city, suburban, and rural. The teenagers answered a nineteen-page anonymous questionnaire concerning their legal and illegal drug use. (Note: Even though beer, wine, and hard liquor are illegal in most states for most high school students, for the sake of simple differentiation, Kandel refers to alcoholic beverages as legal drugs, along with cigarettes, because these are legal for most people in our society.)

In the spring of 1972, 7,255 students were requestioned in the same eighteen high schools. Of these, 5,468 were matched by code number to their previous questionnaires. The researchers subsequently contacted by mail, from class lists, all students in the participating senior classes after they graduated from high school. They were sent the questionnaire five to nine months after graduation. Of those who responded, 985 had answered the first two questionnaires.

Although the study was done in the early 1970s, before drug use had become as rampant among teenagers as it is today and before cocaine had become something of a commonplace among teenage drug-users, Kandel's study pointing out the progression factor from "legal" to "illegal drugs" holds as true today as it did over a decade ago. (The scientist's followup survey in 1980–81, when respondents were in their early 20's, attest to this.)

These were the three most important findings of the studies carried out in high school.

1. The "legal" drugs (alcohol and tobacco) were necessary intermediates between nonuse and marijuana. At that time, whereas 27 percent of high school students who smoked and drank progressed to marijuana during a school year, only 2 percent of those who had not used these legal drugs did so.

2. Marijuana, in turn, was a crucial step on the way to other illicit drugs. While 26 percent of marijuana users progressed to LSD, amphetamines, or heroin, only 1 percent of nondrug-users and 4 percent of alcohol and cigarette users did so. The same sequence was found in each of the four years in high school and in the year after graduation.

3. The reverse sequence held for regression of drug use. Illegal drug-users who gave up their current level of drug-taking do not step directly into nonuse "but only," says Kandel, "to lower categories of illegal drugs or to alcohol and cigarettes. This also applied to the large samples of graduated seniors."

Dr. Kandel's work clearly indicates that a child who smokes cigarettes or drinks beer will not necessarily become a pot-smoker and from there "springboard" on to other illicit drugs. However, in Kandel's study the progression from marijuana to other illicit drugs was one in every four cases in a six-month interval in a large group of teenagers fourteen to eighteen years old. On the other hand, according to this study, the fact that a youngster does *not* smoke cigarettes or drink makes it far less likely that he or she will smoke pot or become a regular user of other illicit drugs.

Other studies, including the annual National High School Senior Surveys, clearly show that the younger the cigarette and alcohol use starts, the more likely it is that the teenager will become a pot-smoker.

In a study done by research sociologists John O'Donnell and Richard Clayton, 2,510 men took part in a nationwide survey. The men were randomly selected from the records of the Selective Service System, which included every young man who had registered for the draft between 1964 and 1972, "to be representative of all men born in the years 1944 through 1954." Since the director of the Selective Service estimated that over 98 percent of young men in the United States had registered, "our sample," says Dr. Clayton, "is perfectly representative of the nineteen million males born between 1944 and 1954."

All the men in the sample were between twenty and thirty years old. Each man was personally interviewed about his drug use for over an hour. Only three drugs were looked at: marijuana, heroin, and cocaine.

The study showed that of those who had used marijuana at least 1,000 times, 73 percent graduated to cocaine, and 33 percent went all the way to heroin. One out of three of those who had used marijuana for the equivalent of once a day for three years had gone on to heroin!

On the other hand, of the 1,126 nonusers of marijuana, only 1 person had ever used heroin and only 1 had used cocaine.

Furthermore, "the stepping stone" was dose-related. Among those who had used marijuana 10 to 99 times, the percentage of heroin users was 4; it rose to 12 percent for those who had used marijuana 100 to 999 times. The dose-related step-up between heavy marijuana use and cocaine use was about the same. As noted, of the men who did not use marijuana, only 1 had used cocaine; also, of the 406 men who had used marijuana 1 to 9 times, only 4 had used cocaine (1 percent). Of the 342 men who had used marijuana 10 to 99 times, 24 had used cocaine (7 percent). Of the 325 men who had used pot 100 to 999 times, 120 (39 percent) had used cocaine. And of the 256 pot-smokers in the 1,000-or-more group, 186 (73 percent) had used cocaine.

Clayton and O'Donnell then did a study of a population where drugs of all types were easily available—Harlem and Spanish Harlem in New York City. This was a far smaller sample, but a randomly selected one. The researchers wondered whether easy availability would affect the step-up picture. It did not. Of the 48 non–pot-smokers, none had ever used cocaine. Of the 29 men who had used pot 1 to 9 times, 5 had used cocaine (17 percent). Of the 44 men who had used pot 10 to 99 times, 25 percent had used cocaine. Of the 44 men who had used pot 100 to 999 times, 52 percent had used cocaine. And of the 58 men who had smoked pot 1,000 or more times, 83 percent had used cocaine.

"This study," said Dr. Clayton, "showed the same sort of stair-step progression: the higher the use of marijuana, the higher the use of cocaine. The heroin pattern also showed the same sort of step-up progression."

The National High School Senior Surveys show the same dose-related progression. For example, in the 1980 survey, of those who did not smoke pot, .04 percent used cocaine. Of those who had smoked pot 10 to 19 times during the year, 11.7 percent had also used cocaine. Of those who had smoked pot 20 to 39 times during the year, 20.2 percent had used cocaine during the year. Of those who used pot 40 or more times, 52.9 percent had used cocaine. These figures are typical of other such "relationship" figures in recent years.

The connection seems clear. It is not that marijuana—or *any* other drug— contains pharmacological properties that make the user go on to other drugs. But, as with most other illegally used drugs, pot produces a physical and psychological tolerance. In order to reach the former "high," the heavy user must either go on to more and more marijuana and/or more and more potent pot, and/or must add to his or her drug "diet" by using other illegal drugs and/or legal drugs used illegally. And this polydrug use is now spreading to ever higher and ever lower age levels. "Also," as Dr. Clayton pointed out, "as one uses marijuana more frequently and looks for a more potent variety, one is forced to enter the illicit marketplace. Most dealers have a variety of wares to offer, and, like any salesman, they try to push their products. They are called 'pushers' for good reason."

Canadian psychiatrist Dr. Andrew Malcolm, one of the foremost clinical psychiatrists dealing with marijuana-using patients, stresses that cannabis significantly increases a young person's suggestibility, making him or her an easier target for people who are pushing other drugs. Given this increase in the pot-user's "suggestibility quotient," reinforced by the pusher's display of products, the step-up statistics should not be surprising.

As Dr. Clayton put it:

People who say there is no causal relationship between the use of marijuana and other illegal drugs because there is no pharmacological relationship are, in my view, just copping out. There are many social and environmental components of drug use which are as important, or more important, for us to consider in this context.

Why did the stepping-stone theory get shoved under the carpet for so long?

In October 1981, when testifying on the Clayton-O'Donnell paper before a senate subcommittee, Dr. William Pollin, director of the National Institute on Drug Abuse, said that the fact that some authorities have rejected these connections without any conclusive evidence to support their position "raises the suspicion that these experts did not examine the problem with the clinical objective detachment of scientists. Instead, they acted on behalf of the drug culture."

Suicide

Pot-smokers frequently point out that "marijuana never killed anybody" to "prove" its harmlessness when compared to certain drugs that can kill with an overdose. They also claim that pot is not physically addictive since, unlike other drugs, it does not have painful withdrawal symptoms. This is true. (As we have seen in Dr. Gold's studies, while withdrawal symptoms from marijuana do exist, they are not extreme, since the body cells act as tiny time-release capsules, slowly emitting the collected cannabinoids into the system long after the person has been completely off the drug.)

The part of the equation that may not be true is that "pot never killed anybody." The pot-high driver who crashes and dies is just as dead as the person who OD's and dies from other drug-related causes. As we will see in Dr. Sterling-Smith's study of drivers most responsible for fatal accidents, 16 percent were smoking pot before the accident (see Chapter 14). However, there is not much firm data on pot-*caused* traffic fatalities because of the time-release factor. At the present state of the art in testing body fluids, it is impossible to pinpoint the degree of pot impairment accurately, as we can with tests for alcohol.

Another demurral to the claim "pot never killed anyone" is the fact that tobacco cigarette smoking is considered the greatest cause of preventable death in America today. Since the constituents in both smokes are so similar— with marijuana more deleterious than tobacco in many ways—it may well be that in another decade or so we will begin to see marijuana-caused deaths from cancer and other diseases.

The third avenue in which pot may play a role contributing to death is suicide—the leading cause of death among college students today, and the second leading cause of death among fifteen- to nineteen-year-olds (after road fatalities).

According to the Surgeon General's Report, *Healthy People,* American teenagers are the *only* age group in the United States whose mortality rate has gone up during the past two decades. The chief reasons for this are due to drink- and drug-impaired driving, and drug-related suicide. The suicide rate among ten- to fourteen-year-old children has risen almost as fast as the rate among fifteen- to twenty-four-year-olds. Furthermore, there are a hundred attempted suicides among young people for every one that succeeds. Suicide rates among teenagers have tripled in the last two decades—which coincides with the epidemic of marijuana use among our young people.

This is not to say that marijuana use per se causes suicide. However, as we have seen, chronic pot use often leads to the use of other drugs and concommitant use of alcohol, which can sometimes cause unintended death; it can also lead to deep depression and other psychotic states—which *do* cause suicide. Professionals dealing with chronic young pot-smokers report that almost invariably these users have feelings of depression and thoughts of suicide; and when they get off the drug, suicidal thoughts almost invariably disappear. Dr. Harold Voth puts it like this: "Although chronic users deny that marijuana has affected their life adversely, at the same time they know that 'something's wrong' on many levels of their life, and this adds to the disheartening marijuana-induced depression, which very often includes suicidal thoughts."

One of Voth's patients, "Ted R.," was a typical example. A handsome and extremely popular A student, he started pot smoking at fourteen "because everybody did and I was curious." By sixteen, he was a daily user. By twenty, he was failing in college; beset by paranoia, panic, and despair, he often thought of suicide. He was voted by his friends as most likely to be "the first one to die within the next year." He went to Dr. Voth, got off pot, and stayed off. He returned to college in the fall—and proved his friends' prophecy wrong by graduating with honors.

Not all chronic pot-users caught in the morass of depression are that fortunate. Although no epidemiological studies—indeed, no studies of any sort—have been done on the impact of marijuana use on teenage suicide rates, a number of parents believe that marijuana *did* cause their children's deaths.

Among such parents are Mr. and Mrs. Bill Bufkin of Texas City, Texas, parents of Paul Hamilton Bufkin, an energetic, outgoing, popular eleventh-grader, on the football team and in the National Honor Society. (His worst grade was a B—in the seventh grade.)

In January 1980 Mr. and Mrs. Bufkin started noticing a personality change in their son. "It had gotten to where he couldn't sleep as well," Mrs. Bufkin said. "He was very jittery. And he seemed depressed. He'd never ever been depressed before."

In May, Paul told his mother that he'd been smoking pot and he thought that was what was wrong with him. He also thought he needed help in getting off the drug. Mrs. Bufkin took him to a doctor who said, "Well, you know, all kids take drugs."

"She was real light about it," Mrs. Bufkin remembers.

However, the doctor did hospitalize Paul to run some tests to determine if there were any physical problems. The test results showed only one abnormality: His bilirubin count was up. (Bilirubin is a pigment found in bile, blood, and urine.) But this, the doctor said, could not have caused his depressed condition.

Upon his release from the hospital, Paul was given a prescription for Mellaril to help him sleep. A few days later, on June 13, he took the whole bottle of pills.

He later told his mother: "I know it was the pot that made me do it." He also told her he never took any other drugs. Nor did he drink much: "Maybe three beers on a Saturday night, twice a month, that's all."

Frightened by his suicide attempt, Paul stopped smoking pot and within about two weeks, returned to the boy he had been.

About mid-August, his mother "noticed the personality change again. He became fidgety, sharp, and irritable." She asked him if he was smoking pot. Paul said: "No."

"He kept getting worse and worse," Mrs. Bufkin remembers. "And he kept lying to me. He'd say, 'I've got it wired, Mom, I'll be all right.' But later his friends told me that he had started smoking pot again. That he was smoking lots of joints every day, even between classes. And he rolled them real thick."

On September 24, 1980, Mrs. Bufkin picked up her little girl from dancing school, and returned home to find that her sixteen-year-old son had shot himself in the head with a gun he had borrowed from a friend for duck hunting.

In some cases marijuana plays the lead as a "stepping-stone" to the actual death. Mark Wilcox of Winter Haven, Florida, was one such case. His mother, Ruby Wilcox, says:

He was a bright, honest, trustworthy boy, when, at sixteen, he discovered marijuana. He grew a crop of it, five feet high, on the family beach. He told us it was catnip. One day my husband compared it to a picture in his plant book. That was our first contact with marijuana. To reassure us, Mark showed us literature he'd sent away for that "proved" that pot was harmless. As time went on, I'd tell him: "Mark, I can *see* what this drug is doing to you. I can see how you've changed." He had one answer. Sometimes he even shouted it at me. *"What makes you think you know more than the professional people?"*

Mark had been an achievement-oriented child—once the neighborhood voted him the most likely to be a millionaire before he was thirty. After two years of daily pot smoking he didn't care about anything—not his family, school, his future—nothing except getting stoned.

"To watch him change was devastating," Mrs. Wilcox said.

He turned into the opposite of what he had been. He became hostile, mixed-up, miserable. I knew, instinctively, that everything that was happening to him was caused by marijuana. Only I couldn't find any scientific information to back up my gut feelings.

We went through everything to get him help. We sent him to psychiatrists. Eight of them. But nobody would pay attention to the fact that he was a heavy marijuana user. They just brushed this aside as being unimportant. I felt it was *the* most important factor. We had no history of mental illness in our family. Mark's younger sister wasn't smoking pot, and she was doing just fine.

Mark only kept getting worse. We sent him to psychiatric hospitals. They gave him tranquilizers—and he became addicted to *them*.

Finally, I said, "Mark, I'll never put you in another hospital. I realize they're never going to help you. If you keep on smoking the marijuana, you're never going to get well."

He tried to stop, but what my husband and I didn't understand was that marijuana is a psychologically addicting drug. Had we understood the addiction, it might have been a different story.

On a spring afternoon in 1979, Mark was found dead in an orange grove. Mrs. Wilcox said, "we'll never know whether Mark's death was a suicide, or whether it was an accidental overdose of tranquilizers that actually killed him. But the son we knew started dying years ago when he became addicted to marijuana."

Kaye Blount of Barstow, Florida, was an A–B student, interested in music; she had won every honor a Girl Scout her age could win. She was the model child, until the age of twelve and a half when she started smoking pot.

"We watched her become just the opposite of what she had been," her mother said.

We tried to get her to give up the drug. But she insisted it was harmless. And she had all this literature to prove it—booklets put out by NORML and Do It Now. Friends supplied her with this "information" as well as with marijuana. She got into other drugs. We took her to a psychiatrist. It didn't help.

On October 31, 1980, I walked into the living room just as my daughter shot herself in the head. Six days later, she died. On that day she was exactly thirteen and a half years old.

The last entry in Kaye's diary was on October 29. In large letters on the top of the page she had written I HATE MYSELF. Below, in her normal handwriting, were these sentences: "I have hurt my Mom and my Daddy and sister. I love them but I have hurt them so much. There is no way that I can live with myself anymore."

Siblings as "Controls"

"Mark's younger sister wasn't smoking pot," Mrs. Wilcox had said. "And she was doing just fine."

This may be a very relevant comment, especially in light of constant claims that the parents, family tensions, and so on are the primary *cause* of a child's pot smoking. The sibling who grows up with the same parents and the same family tensions but who does not smoke marijuana can serve, therefore, as a kind of "control."

In a study published in 1981, Drs. Herbert Hendin, A. Pollinger, R. Ulman, and A. C. Carr of the Department of Psychiatry, New York Medical College, looked into this question. For their study titled "Adolescent Marijuana Abusers and Their Families," they interviewed at great length seventeen marijuana-abusing teenagers (eleven males, six females), their parents, and their siblings. About twenty-five interviews per family were conducted over a three-month period. Each family was then followed up at six-month intervals over a two-year period. In each case, a single interviewer saw each member of a particular family in individual interviews. All of the seventeen pot-smoking subjects were "daily or almost daily smokers with clearly established patterns of smoking marijuana throughout the day as well as during evening and nighttime hours. Marijuana constituted their primary, if not their sole, drug." The families were white; Catholic, Protestant, and Jewish; urban and suburban. There were no single-parent families. All the fathers were employed full-time; their occupations ranged from delivery-truck driver to corporate executive.

In describing family relationships of the seventeen subjects, the researchers wrote:

All of the marijuana-abusing adolescents had quite turbulent lives at home. In most cases their difficulties went well beyond the typical problems most youngsters have during adolescence. . . . These particular youngsters tended most often to be locked into destructive, angry-dependent relationships with their parents . . . characterized by a pattern of provocative and defiant behavior which infuriated and frustrated their parents at the same time. . . . Each of the youngsters, to one degree or another, refused to follow prescribed rules of conduct at home. Many insisted, for example, on coming home after school with friends whom they knew their parents did not want in their house. Most also consistently objected to helping with chores around the house. When they did agree to do their household jobs, they would often disappear without explanation before completing them.

The adolescent marijuana abusers smoked with their friends at special "hang outs," while riding around in cars, and at parties. Common leisure activities included throwing Frisbees and listening to music while high on marijuana. Traditional high school clubs and organizations, including athletics, were usually disavowed.

One aspect noted by the researchers was

consistent with research findings reported by others (Goode 1972; Jessor and Jessor 1975) that the marijuana-abusing participants in this study tended to have sexual experiences at an early age, significantly earlier than their non–drug-abusing siblings. All of the abusers—who ranged in age from 14 to 18—had had sexual intercourse. Virtually all of them, however, exhibited significant difficulties in establishing ongoing meaningful relationships.

Brief, intense attachments to friends of both sexes were commonly seen. Particularly in the case of boy-girl relationships, the youngsters' attachments were stormy and characterized by fights, breakups, reconciliations, and recriminations. For many of the girls, their relationships exposed them to considerable risk, including the risk of pregnancy. In spite of the frequency of sexual encounters, regular use of contraceptives was extremely rare, and several of the girls had had abortions. In addition, an attraction to physically abusive young men was fairly common among these girls, as was frequenting dangerous places. . . . The young men also appeared to have difficulty forming close relationships. For many, their marijuana use appeared to be related to this fact. Several spoke of increasing their use of marijuana in an attempt to deal with anxieties surrounding emotional and sexual intimacy.

In other areas, the researchers noted:

Sometimes, after telling their parents that they would call, they would stay out all night without calling. Agreements over how they would use the family car or money given them by their parents were often violated. Taking the family car out for a late night joy ride was a common activity for many of these adolescents. . . .

This type of defiance left many parents feeling that they had completely lost control of their children. The attempt to regain and reassert control . . . became a constant preoccupation for some of the parents. . . .

Physical violence toward parents or siblings was also not uncommon among these adolescents. One youngster . . . hit his mother in a fit of rage. . . . another regularly pummeled his younger brother when he was upset or angry at his parents.

Naturally, such behavior had a negative impact on the non–pot-smoking siblings. As one youngster put it, when asked by the interviewer about her present psychological problems: "My present psychological problem is my sister."

Nevertheless, despite the fact that a non–drug-using sibling might have a lower IQ than the drug-user, all the non–drug-users did better in school than the pot-smokers. Indeed, they did better in all areas of their lives.

The researchers summed up concerning the siblings:

The non–drug-abusers had generally learned how to get at least a minimal amount of gratification and support from their relationships with their parents. They expressed affection for at least one and often both of their parents, while anger if not outright hatred for one or both parents was most typically expressed by the marijuana abusers.

Although the siblings gave evidence that the disturbance in their families that had affected their marijuana-abusing siblings had also caused problems for them, they were significantly different from their brothers and sisters in their patterns of relatively high achievement, as well as in their lack of impulsiveness, self-destructiveness, and emotional liability. As a result, the non–drug-abusers were better able to meet parental and societal standards.

The seventeen families who agreed to participate in this study were offered free family and/or individual counseling. Some took advantage of this, and, with the help of the counseling, some of the youngsters gave up marijuana completely. They then acted as their own "controls," and the "pot personality" disappeared.

Others, like "Dave L.," continued their daily pot smoking. The researchers noted:

At 21, Dave, one of the brightest youngsters seen, is driving a cab irregularly, living on and off with several different friends, finding little satisfaction in personal and social relations, and centering his life around obtaining and smoking marijuana. Although he maintains sporadic contact with his parents, their interaction has not changed and Dave's current life seems merely to reinforce their view that he will never amount to anything.

How many Daves are there in this nation?

The researchers conclude:

Both the clinical interview material and the psychological test results obtained in this study unequivocally indicate the seriousness of marijuana abuse among adolescents. . . . Those adolescents who use the drug at the level of the 17 youngsters seen, clearly constitute a subgroup worthy of societal concern.

"The Most Pernicious Symptom"

The stories told by Mrs. Bufkin, Mrs. Wilcox, and Mrs. Blount have one crucial thing in common, in addition to the tragic outcomes and their root cause in marijuana. Mrs. Bufkin put it this way: "If only I'd known more about marijuana and what it can do to a child, I'm sure that my son would be alive today. If only I'd had the *information!*"

The information was there. Paul Bufkin killed himself in 1980, but some of the studies cited throughout this book were published as early as 1974; most had been published by 1980. "If only I'd known," Mrs. Bufkin said, "that you can have severe psychological effects from all that stuff being stored up in your brain!" Dr. Robert Heath published his first paper showing THC-caused brain-cell damage in 1973. If the information was there, why did the public not know about it? An answer lies in the most pernicious of all the psychological symptoms of marijuana use: the refusal of the chronic user to see that the drug is affecting him or her adversely.

Dr. Thomas Gleaton, one of the founders of the parent movement for drug-free youth, has spoken on the subject of drug abuse in general and marijuana in particular around the country, and has received reactions from all strata of the American public. He says:

The regular marijuana smoker seems to become one who is destined for life to defend this drug. Even those who stop smoking it continue to defend it—almost like a cult thing. People who get off Valium, for instance, or cocaine, or alcohol, or *any* other drug will tell you how bad it is. Marijuana is the only drug I know of which the person who has been harmed by it, typically not only refuses to admit that, but continues to defend it.

On the call-in talk shows invariably there are anonymous callers who first give a testimonial about how they've smoked regularly for a long period of time, and it has not affected them. But often in their speech patterns, and in their rationales, the detrimental effects they have suffered from their pot use is obvious.

Gleaton gave an example: A young man called in with his "commercial" on pot, which he had smoked for ten years and which had not affected him at all, he claimed. Then he said he had two questions. The first was did marijuana decrease the number of sperm cells. "Yes," replied Dr. Gleaton. The show host asked, "Okay, what's your second question?"

"My second question," said the caller, "is uh—uh—uh—"

The host mentioned that pot affected the short-term memory. Then, politely, he asked again, "Yes, sir, what's your second question?"

"There's nothing the matter with *my* memory!" said the caller. "My second question is uh—uh—uh— . . ."

Dr. Harold Voth summed up in these words:

Marijuana produces a wide spectrum of psychological symptoms. Some affect some people; some affect others. And there are those who seem to "get away with it" reasonably well, for a while. But there is one truly pernicious symptom—specifically related to marijuana—which seems to be evident in *every* chronic pot-user, youngster or adult. *This is the extraordinary refusal to accept the hard scientific evidence about the harmful effects of marijuana. The user will scoff at the evidence, twist it, pervert it, call it "reefer madness"—anything except look it straight in the face.*

This may be one reason much of the media have done shockingly little to relay the medical findings about the harmful effects of marijuana to the American public.

Dr. Mark Gold puts it this way: "Marijuana's most important psychological effects are addiction and denial—failure to recognize drug-related changes in medical, psychological, social, family, and work performance."

To sum up this chapter on the psychological effects of marijuana use, we turn to the American Medical Association. In its handbook *Drug Abuse: A Guide for the Primary Care Physician,* published in 1981, the AMA states:

Marijuana intoxication impairs learning, memory, thinking, comprehension and general intellectual performance. Even at "moderate" levels of social use, psychomotor performance (such as driving skill) is impaired. . . . Numerous studies show that enduring psychological impairment may result from heavy use. Large doses can induce frank hallucinations, delusions and paranoid feelings. Thinking becomes confused and disoriented, while depersonalization and altered time sense are accentuated. Euphoria may give way to anxiety reaching panic proportions. With sufficiently large doses, the clinical picture is that of a toxic psychosis, with hallucinations, depersonalization and loss of insight.

Chapter 13

Marijuana as Medicine?

The fact that marijuana is being used to treat cancer chemotherapy patients and glaucoma patients receives a great deal of publicity. There is also speculation about its uses for other ills ranging from anorexia to epilepsy to asthma. Actually, in all but a few studies only THC or another cannabinoid—not the crude drug marijuana—has been given. Thus far, the only *proven* hopeful and helpful use has been for cancer patients suffering from the effects of nausea and vomiting produced by their chemotherapy treatments.

THC and Cancer Chemotherapy

In June 1980 a strategic meeting was held in the offices of the Food and Drug Administration building in Bethesda, Maryland. Members of the FDA's oncologic drug advisory committee had gathered to discuss and vote on the proposal to make THC capsules available, through the federal government's National Cancer Institute (NCI), to oncologists (cancer specialists) throughout the country. One member of the committee could not attend the meeting: Dr. Charles Moertel, director of the Mayo Clinic's Comprehensive Cancer Center. However, Dr. Moertel had sent a letter expressing the strongest objections to the proposal. His objections were based on studies done at the Mayo Clinic, in New Zealand, and elsewhere, which showed that even if THC was effective as an antiemetic (antivomit agent) for young cancer patients who had had prior experience with marijuana, for older patients with no prior pot-smoking experience THC had, said Dr. Moertel, "all sorts of central nervous system side effects." And most cancer patients are older patients. He pointed out a chemotherapy study conducted in the

248

Netherlands that showed a 33 percent incidence of THC-induced hallucinations, some of them requiring psychiatric care.

The FDA committee, however, did not count Dr. Moertel's letter as "a vote"; and when the vote was taken, it turned out to be a tie. The chairman cast a tie-breaking vote in favor, and the FDA commissioner adopted the advisory board's recommendation that THC capsules be made available through NCI to all the cancer treatment clinics that are part of NCI's system—which includes virtually all the cancer treatment centers in the United States.

The purity of the THC in the pills is easily assured because it is synthetic, so it does not contain any other ingredient from marijuana, as "extracted THC" might. (Synthetic merely means that researchers have been able to copy the exact molecular structure of a substance so that it can be reproduced more efficiently, and at far less expense. Most of our effective medications are synthetic.) It has been clearly shown that it is the THC in marijuana that has a beneficial antinausea effect for some patients being treated by drug therapy for cancer. Although synthetic THC pills have a psychoactive effect that many patients find disorienting, at least cancer patients are spared the harmful effects of additional cannabinoids and other ingredients and impurities, including fungus, in smoked marijuana.

Moreover, *natural* THC, whether it's still in marijuana or has been extracted from it, is extremely unstable and loses potency over time. NCI points out that synthetic THC "can be manufactured as a pure substance in large quantities and precisely standardized to ensure constant potency."

According to a 1981 report in the *Journal of the American Medical Association,* about two hundred thousand Americans may be receiving chemotherapy treatments to combat cancer. Of these, about fifty thousand experience nausea as a result and, "while estimates vary, it is suggested that THC might help one half this group." But even synthetic THC has been shown by numerous studies to have harmful physical and psychological side effects for many patients. These can be so disturbing that many have chosen to give up the THC capsules and return to standard antiemetics such as Compazine.

Oncologists' reports as to the numbers of patients helped by THC vary from 30 to 50 percent; these are chiefly the younger patients. In one study comparing THC, a placebo, and Compazine, researchers found that the patients on THC pills did as well as but no better than those on Compazine. But the THC patients had many more side effects. The major THC toxicities noted by oncologists are incoordination, dizziness, ataxia (unstable gait), and paranoia. Also, according to a report by the Council on Scientific Affairs of the American Medical Association: "Older patients seem to respond less well than younger ones and to complain more about unpleasant drug-induced effects, such as drowsiness, hallucinations, anxiety, and tachycardia [rapid heartbeat]."

The AMA report noted that one encouraging study was done of fifty-five cancer chemotherapy patients who had not previously responded to standard antiemetic therapy, and pointed out: "It may well be that THC's usefulness as an antiemetic will be greatest among treatment failures."

Many cancer victims who do get help from THC feel, understandably, that consideration of any THC side effects must be subsidiary to the primary job of making the chemotherapy treatment more tolerable. There are, however, certain types of cancer chemotherapy drugs on which THC does not work at all. One such is higher doses of cisplatinum, a standard and very effective drug used against ovarian and testicular cancers, as well as lung, bladder, prostate, and other cancers.

Fortunately, there are promising alternatives to the THC capsules. According to an article by Sue Rusche in the U.S. *Journal on Drug and Alcohol Dependence:*

> The National Conference on the Therapeutic Applications of the Cannabinoids confirmed the view that delta-9-THC is at best an intermediate drug to be used while more effective anti-emetics are developed. Although THC does reduce the nausea of some cancer chemotherapy patients, the real promise seems to lie in several synthetic cannabinoid analogs [similar compounds with a slightly different chemical makeup] being developed in the research labs of pharmaceutical companies and university hospitals across the nation.
>
> In the words of Dr. Leo Hollister, Professor of Medicine and Psychiatry at Stanford University, who brought the meeting to a close, "The conference might easily have been called 'A Search for New Anti-emetics,' for this was clearly the focus of the whole meeting." In fact, the drug that generated the most interest at the conference—metoclopramide—is not a cannabinoid at all but one of a whole new generation of potential anti-nausea drugs from another family of compounds called benzamides.

Metoclopramide is now being tested in twelve cancer centers around the country. Tests have shown that large intravenous doses of this drug, as well as oral doses, reduces the incidence of nausea and vomiting produced by cisplatinum—one of the most "nausea and vomit-producing" anticancer drugs (on which THC has no effect). Not only did metoclopramide stop vomiting in 75 percent of the cases, but the physical side effects were minimal and there were no psychological side effects. Because the drug is also effective against nausea and emetic effects of other cancer chemotherapy drugs, it may turn out to be a far more useful antiemetic than THC.

250

Dr. George Hyman, a noted oncologist at Columbia College of Physicians and Surgeons, pointed out:

> Because THC is fat-soluble, it cannot be injected. Consequently, whether taken in pill form or in smoked marijuana, it is only 6 to 20 percent bioavailable [the amount of the active ingredient that enters the bloodstream]. Metoclopramide, on the other hand, is 100 percent bioavailable, because it can be given intravenously. Instead of "pushing" THC any further, a better answer would seem to be using a drug like metoclopramide, or its parent compound, alizapride, which has a proven margin of safety, a lower toxicity than THC, and far fewer side effects.

As had been noted by Dr. Moertel and many other oncologists, Hyman pointed out, "In my experience, the benefits of THC, when they do occur, are primarily in the under-thirty population (many of whom are users). Most cancer patients are over thirty. They often get no benefit from THC. All they get is the side effects."

Dr. Donald Sweet of the University of Chicago studied a number of cancer chemotherapy patients given synthetic THC pills; he said the drug provided only short-term antiemetic relief for most patients before they grew immune to it. Almost 20 percent of those in the program dropped out because they didn't like the side effects of the drug—namely getting high. But for a minority of patients, marijuana makes their symptoms disappear "like magic," Sweet said.

Some cancer patients claim that smoked marijuana is more effective than the synthetic THC pill, but a 1983 Georgia study found no significant difference: Smoked marijuana was 73 percent effective as an antiemetic; THC capsules were 76 percent effective.

Although synthetic THC pills are available to virtually all cancer chemotherapy patients who need them, and although marijuana joints are also available to patients via therapeutic research programs, the pro-pot lobby continues to downgrade "synthetic THC pills." It is true that the THC pill takes longer to have an effect than does smoked marijuana, for the inhalation route to the bloodstream is swifter than the oral route. Because of this, many oncologists suggest that patients take the THC capsule four hours prior to the chemotherapy treatment so that the antiemetic effects begin to work when the treatment starts.

One impurity avoided by using synthetic THC rather than smoked marijuana is fungus. In February 1981, Dr. Steven Kagen reported on fungi of the aspergillus family contained in both street pot and NIDA marijuana grown for researchers. "We have yet to find a sample of marijuana that does not have fungal organisms in it," Dr. Kagen said. "Blood samples of marijuana smokers and those who had never smoked pot were examined. Fifty-two percent of the smokers showed evidence in their blood of exposure to this fungus, compared to one percent of the nonsmokers. (These fungi are not found in tobacco cigarettes.)"

In noting that cancer patients often smoke marijuana to lessen the nausea associated with their drug therapy, Kagen wrote,

> While relieving the nausea, patients also expose themselves to fungal spores. This use of marijuana as an anti-emetic ought to be vigorously discouraged. In the lungs of a healthy person, the fungus is battled by the body's immune system. The result may be coughing, wheezing, congestion or a fever (which, in some cases, does not appear until three to 12 hours after smoking). But in persons with weak immune defenses, such as cancer patients being treated with chemotherapy, the same infection could cause death.

In March 1982, speaking at a conference on cannabinoid therapeutics sponsored by the Illinois Commission on Dangerous Drugs, Dr. William McGuire, of the University of Illinois Medical Center at Chicago, and a member of the Illinois Cancer Council, pointed out that use of THC as an antiemetic is still surrounded by a great deal of controversy. "Some feel it is categorically better than any standard antiemetic, some feel it is equal in effectiveness, but toxicity precludes its use, and others are convinced it is no better at all."

In 1982 a New Jersey pharmaceutical company, Unimed, filed a New Drug Application with the Food and Drug Administration to manufacture and market a synthetic THC capsule under the trade name Marinol. This is still in the development stage.

Also in 1982, the Eli Lilly Company in Indiana submitted a New Drug Application to FDA for approval to market Nabilone, a synthetic cannabinoid (but not THC) that Lilly has been developing over the past decade. Nabilone has already been approved in Canada, where it is marketed as an antiemetic under the trade name Cesemit. According to FDA, Nabilone has some psychoactive effects, similar to THC, and both Nabilone and Marinol have abuse potential.

As this book went to press, FDA approval for Nabilone and Marinol was under discussion. According to Dr. Sidney Cohen, "even if FDA approval is granted for Unimed's THC capsule, and for Nabilone, they will probably be supplanted soon by the newer drugs—even more efficacious than metoclopramide, but in that group of chemicals—which are now being prepared for marketing."

Glaucoma

Glaucoma is an eye disease characterized by increased pressure within the eye (intraocular pressure) and progressive damage to the optic nerve, which impairs vision and can lead to blindness. Treatment for glaucoma, either with drugs or surgery, is primarily aimed at lowering the pressure in an attempt to preserve vision.

Although there have been well-substantiated reports that smoking marijuana can lower intraocular pressure, it is not known whether visual function can be preserved. According to an article prepared by the federal government's National Eye Institute for the *Journal of the American Medical Association:*

> Reports of marijuana's effectiveness in reducing intraocular pressure in a few such [glaucoma] patients under carefully controlled experimental conditions may have led to serious consideration of this drug as a possible alternative to conventional therapy, particularly in patients who do not respond well to existing medications. These reports have also encouraged some glaucoma patients to assume that smoking marijuana may be beneficial for treating this eye disorder. Since no definitive clinical studies have been completed, this assumption is misleading and could result in serious ocular damage and systemic side effects.

Newspaper stories headlining marijuana—rather than THC drops—as a possible treatment for glaucoma have given the public the impression that glaucoma patients are puffing on joints of street pot. As Dr. Frank Newell, chairman of the Department of Ophthalmology at the University of Chicago, put it: "In order to reduce the intraocular pressure by this method, you'd have to smoke a joint every two hours—day and night."

Dr. John Bellows, director of the International Glaucoma Congress and the American Society of Contemporary Ophthalmology, points out that there are conventional remedies that are far more effective than THC eyedrops, without the possible harmful side effects—which may include nystagmoid movements ("dancing eye"); transitory loss of vision, corneal anesthesia (people tend not to notice—and not to remove—foreign particles, which could lead to infection), difficulty in focusing, pupil abnormalities, and decreased tearing (which, incidentally, is one reason many pot-smoking contact-lens–wearers often experience discomfort).

Dr. Coy Waller, a pioneer marijuana researcher, is studying the development of THC eyedrops for use by glaucoma patients. He points out: "Pilocarpine is one of the most effective drugs now used in the eye for the treatment of glaucoma. It comes from the leaves of the pilocarpus plant. It would be just as sensible to smoke pilocarpus leaves and take medical history back a hundred years, as it would be to smoke marijuana to get THC, instead of using synthetic THC eyedrops."

Dr. Edward Tocus, chief of the drug abuse staff for the Food and Drug Administration, points out that Waller and other researchers are using THC only as a stepping-stone to the development of THC-*related* eyedrops for glaucoma patients. THC itself is an irritant and, since it is not water-soluble, it is not suitable for use as eyedrops. However, the researchers are looking for a manmade THC analog—similar to the cannabinoid but different in chemical structure—which would be water-soluble, nonirritating, and effective. "So far," says Tocus, "scientists have not come up with anything along these lines."

In 1979 Robert Randall, who suffers from glaucoma and who is on the advisory board of NORML (National Organization for Reform of Marijuana Laws), sued NIDA for the right to be supplied with free NIDA joints as a research subject. He won the suit and has since received about seventy government-issued marijuana cigarettes a week. It is interesting to note that according to the FDA, despite his professed faith in marijuana as a cure for glaucoma, Randall continues to take traditionally prescribed medication for his disease.

Other Areas of Cannabis Research for Medical Uses

Dr. Sidney Cohen of the Neuropsychiatric Institute at UCLA may well be the most knowledgeable scientist in the United States in the area of marijuana components for medical use. Writing on "Marijuana as Medicine" in *Psychology Today* (April 1978), Cohen put pot's therapeutic history into perspective:

Like the ball of gum opium in the Turkish farmer's hut or the bottle of raw whisky in the American frontier cabin, cannabis has been for centuries, and remains, the staple medication of many remote Asian and African communities. Ancient Chinese, Persian, and Indian texts indicate that since prehistory cannabis has had hundreds of medicinal uses. In some instances, cannabis infusions, ointments, vapors or suppositories were probably no more than placebos. But in others they probably provided some symptomatic relief of pain, tension, loss of appetite, or insomnia. If this seems a small benefit, remember that until recent times, doctors knew only enough about tuberculosis, cholera, brain tumors, or indeed most other ailments to relieve the symptoms of these disorders and not enough to cure them.

Not until the latter half of the 19th century did clinicians begin systematic recording and reporting of their experiences with marijuana. Though no worse than other research of that era, their experimental methods were seriously defective by modern standards. . . .

Despite all the testimonials, marijuana began to slip into oblivion as a therapeutic agent. By the beginning of the 20th century, Western practitioners had almost stopped prescribing it. Working in a pharmacy after school during the late 20s and early 30s, I can remember the dusty bottle of "Fluidextract of Cannabis Sativa" on the shelf: the only time it was opened was to pour a few drops into the store's own remedy for corns— to color it green.

In May 1984, Dr. Cohen summed up for the author the present state of marijuana's therapeutic uses in these words:

> *For cancer chemotherapy patients:* I think we can say that THC is at least as good as Compazine. It also helps people that Compazine does not help, and therefore we should have it around. But I predict that THC will turn out to be a transitional drug for this purpose. Other more effective chemicals will replace it. Consequently, within a few years there should be no need for THC capsules or smoked marijuana for this purpose.
>
> *For glaucoma patients:* Although THC eyedrops do reduce intraocular pressure, at this point it looks as though the THC molecule is too irritating to the eyeball; therefore, use of THC eyedrops may not be possible. As far as smoked marijuana goes, it does appear to improve—though not to cure—the condition. However, glaucoma is particularly common among the elderly, many of whom cannot tolerate the intoxicating and disorienting effects produced by the drug.
>
> *Antiasthmatic:* As Dr. Donald Tashkin's studies clearly show, although marijuana smoking does cause initial brief bronchodilation, on continued smoking the irritant effects worsen the condition and, since asthma is a temporary constriction of the bronchial tubes, smoking marijuana is definitely contraindicated. The ideal solution would seem to be a THC aerosol, but THC researchers in Boston and Los Angeles have indicated that THC is so insoluble in fluid that it precipitates out; it doesn't stay in solution. Tiny globs of THC are deposited in the throat and are therefore ineffective in treating the bronchial passages in the lungs. Researchers have tried to develop a microspray with extremely small THC globules, which would penetrate into the bronchial tubes, but this was unsuccessful. No further work is being done in this area.

Pre-anesthetic: There is no evidence that supports THC for this use. This has therefore been abandoned on a research basis.

Appetite enhancer: Users report appetite is increased by cannabis (the "munchies"), yet studies only partially confirmed this.

Treatment for anorexia nervosa: In a study conducted by the National Institute of Health, THC was no better than diazepam in treating anorexia in a small number of patients, and some reported feeling paranoid with THC. (It should also be noted that diazepam has not been shown to be effective for this condition.)

Withdrawal from alcohol and opiates: Antabuse is a drug that produces a severe reaction when taken with alcohol. It is therefore sometimes used to discourage alcoholics from drinking. Marijuana, unlike some other drugs, can be taken with Antabuse; the two appear to be compatible. However, marijuana seems to play no role in alleviating the problems of withdrawal from alcohol. Nor have studies shown that it is effective in use for opiate withdrawal.

Epilepsy treatment: When you ask epileptics what smoking pot does for them, the reports are highly inconsistent. Some say that it brings on a seizure. Some say there is no improvement, and some say that it improves the condition. However, one of the cannabinoids, cannabidiol, has been found to be helpful in *grand mal* epilepsy. It elevates the seizure threshold. Studies have been done in Salt Lake City, Brazil, and in Israel. This is a promising area for research—especially since cannabidiol is nonpsychoactive.

Topical antibiotic: One study indicates that one cannabinoid, cannabichromene, may be an active antibiotic against certain types of bacteria when applied to the skin. It has no effect in this regard when swallowed or injected, or when marijuana is smoked; enzymes in the body destroy the effectiveness. But when cannabichromene is applied to the skin, the enzymes are not present. Thus far, cannabichromene has not been compared to standard suface antibiotics.

Muscle relaxant: Several studies done in the United States seemed to indicate that marijuana or THC was effective as a muscle relaxant, though neither did better in this area than standard muscle relaxants such as Baclofen. These were not double-blind studies. However, a more recent double-blind study completed in 1983 failed to show any effectiveness of marijuana or THC in this area.

Tumor growth retardant: Some animal work done at the University of Virginia during the mid-seventies indicated that THC had some tumor-suppressant effects. This, however, did not compare favorably with tumor-suppressant effects of cancer chemotherapy drugs. In fact, one cannabinoid, cannabidiol, has been found to enhance tumor growth to a moderate degree. When marijuana or THC is given for control of nausea or vomiting, it cannot be assumed that it has any cancer-controlling effects whatsoever. When marijuana is smoked, the cancer-enhancing effects of cannabidiol are probably neutralized by other cannbinoids, although no work has been done on this yet.

Dr. Cohen then addressed the question as to whether marijuana would ever become an accepted drug, approved by the FDA and stocked in pharmacies.

"Probably not," he said.

Marijuana is an unstable substance. It has a poor shelf life. It will be found to contain over a thousand chemicals—we only know of about four hundred–odd now but that's because we haven't been researching it very long—and it contains dozens of things that may not contribute to what we want it to do.

I can't think of very many drugs in the pharmacopoeia that are crude drugs any more [the whole plant, rather than the essential active ingredients]. We seem to have moved beyond the crude drug stage to extracting from them items we want to use, and then we have fewer problems with them.

Researchers around the country are working with cannabinoids to answer many important questions; for example, dosage levels, methods of administering the drug (nasal mist, suppository, injection, and so forth), why THC is an effective antiemetic for some people and not others in reducing nausea and vomiting after some kinds of chemotherapy treatment.

Meanwhile, other researchers are working on water soluble analogs, which will have more stability, greater dose reliability, longer shelf life—and fewer side effects.

"The Red Herring"

There is another aspect to "the marijuana as medicine" story, one that clouds the subject with controversy and confusion.

It started back in 1979. Keith Stroup, then director of NORML, summed it up succinctly when he was interviewed by reporters for the *Emory Wheel*, the student newspaper of Emory University in Atlanta, Georgia. In answer to the question "How is NORML utilizing the issue of marijuana treatment of chemotherapy patients?" Stroup replied, "We are trying to get marijuana reclassified medically. If we do that, and we'll do it in at least twenty states this year for chemotherapy patients, we'll be using the issue as a red herring to give marijuana a good name."

The story was duly reported in the university newspaper, but no one paid much attention.

Then, the following year, NORML advisory board member Robert Randall took another step along legal lines. He founded Alliance for Cannabis Therapeutics (ACT), an organization that would concentrate on promoting state laws legalizing marijuana—not THC alone—for medical uses. If THC, the single ingredient proven effective for some cancer chemotherapy patients, was "reclassified medically," this would leave "the weed" out on a limb.

"Reclassified medically" here means: changed from a Schedule I drug to a Schedule II drug. Schedule I drugs are controlled substances with no proven therapeutic value. Schedule II drugs are controlled substances that *have* proven therapeutic value, and that are approved by the Food and Drug Administration. This is the most restrictive schedule for marketed drugs.

Various avenues are available for rescheduling: The FDA and NIDA could decide to approve it, and so inform the Department of Health and Human Services; HHS in turn could forward the decision to the Drug Enforcement Administration, with the recommendation that it be implemented. Or Congress could pass a law to reschedule the drug. Once approved, a Schedule II drug can be legally prescribed by physicians "subject to approved conditions of use."

In May 1984, FDA's Dr. Edward C. Tocus explained it this way:

> If THC were approved by the FDA as a marketed drug, then it would be controlled in a manner identical to that of morphine—a Schedule II drug which is derived from opium, a Schedule I drug. Physicians who dispense morphine—or any Schedule II drug—must have a narcotics license. In addition, the drug must be kept in a locked cabinet by pharmacists, who must keep special records of its distribution. The records go to the U.S. Department of Justice.
>
> Marijuana itself will remain a Schedule I drug unless it is approved at some future time for some therapeutic purposes.

In any case, Stroup's statement about "getting the drug reclassified medically . . . in at least twenty states this year" perhaps did not reflect his intention, since the *states* cannot reclassify marijuana medically. Only Congress, the Food and Drug Administration, and/or the Drug Enforcement Administration can do this. Indeed, whether even the federal government can so reclassify THC is a controversial issue at this time. There would even be a problem in classifying an *analog* of THC as a Schedule II drug. The United States was one of many nations that signed the Psychotropic Convention Treaty of 1971, which limits use of delta-9-tetrahydrocannabinol (THC) itself and its analogs to medical and scientific purposes. If the FDA were to approve THC and recommend that it be changed to a Schedule II drug under the Controlled Substances Act, it is unclear at present whether THC would also have to be rescheduled under the Psychotropic Convention. If so, this would require individual action by the nations that are signatories of the treaty.

In addition to the Psychotropic Convention Treaty of 1971, the United States is one of seventy-four nations that signed the 1961 Single Convention Treaty on Narcotic Drugs, which classifies cannabis as a Schedule I drug.

Stroup had said, during another interview (*Playboy,* February 1977): "I think marijuana is substantially harmless and should be legalized. . . . Decriminalization is a kind of halfway stop—a cease fire. . . . We need laws that permit the user to grow his own marijuana—private cultivation." Both of these treaties stand in the way of NORML's goal.

NORML has fought the international treaties on two fronts: federal and state.

On the federal front, they held their own conference about the Single Convention Treaty, then published a paper that stated that, in the view of NORML's lawyers, the United States could legalize marijuana domestically— even if the drug did remain in Schedule I in international law. NORML also presented an administrative petition to the DEA to reschedule cannabis. In response, in May 1983 the Department of Health, Education and Welfare did a comprehensive review of the health aspects of cannabis, and the Drug Enforcement Administration did a review of the abuse potential. Both firmly decided to leave marijuana right where it was: in Schedule I.

NORML went to court on the matter—several times during a ten-year span. In June of 1982, the Court of Appeals in Washington, DC, ordered that the FDA report to the court four times a year on the progress of the recommendations to reschedule marijuana and THC.

In fighting for legalization via the state route, NORML has used the "marijuana as medicine" approach. By now this "red herring to give marijuana a good name" has proved successful in some thirty-two states, which have passed laws of various types "legalizing marijuana for medical uses."

Because of the federal and international laws in this regard, which no state can override, and because THC capsules are currently available to any oncologist who wishes to prescribe them, it might seem to be wasted effort and funds for NORML to try to get individual states to legalize marijuana for medical uses.

However, whenever "state legalization" occurs—*although cancer chemotherapy patients and glaucoma patients are actually not affected one way or the other*—countless newspapers and radio and TV newscasters announce

259

to millions of readers, listeners, and viewers that "legal pot" is now available in this or that state, further compounding the cannabis confusion and promoting the overall concept of legalizing marijuana for all pot-smokers.

The redundant aspect of the state laws was pointed out by Dr. Coy Waller, consultant to NIDA and the FDA for drugs of abuse:

"Legal marijuana" for research is being promoted in the United States, and state legislatures are passing laws to this effect. But the truth is that marijuana has been legal and available for human research projects under Investigative New Drug Applications (INDAs) approved by the Food and Drug Administration *since 1971,* or earlier, in certain cases. Thus, the state laws are totally unnecessary.

Dr. Robert DuPont put it this way:

For years "decriminalization" was the stalking horse for the marijuana lobby. Today "medical uses" has become the symbol behind which the pro-pot activists are marching. Their target is state legislatures. The fact is that no state legislation is needed in this area. Medical research on possible medical uses is well formed and ongoing. Federal laws are adequate. When and if medical uses are identified, the mechanism is available for making this product (or, more likely, purified components of marijuana) available.

The sad fact is that state legislatures have been targeted by the pro-pot lobby precisely because they generally lack the time and staff resources to sort through this type of issue, which is subject to emotional exploitation. Not only are such laws not needed, but passage of such laws is widely interpreted by the public, especially by youth, as a signal that pot is "okay" or, even worse, that it is "healthy."

Such warnings were, for the most part, unheeded.

As noted, the FDA has approved the distribution of NIDA joints to approved oncologists. Nevertheless, virtually all the thirty-two states passed "new" legislation stating that "now" legal marijuana would be available for therapeutic research purposes. Once each state passed such legislation, the pro-pot lobbies brought pressure to distribute free NIDA-grown joints to all cancer treatment centers in those states that had authorized it—despite the fact that most oncologists preferred to prescribe the THC capsule rather than smoked marijuana. This new NORML-engendered publicity further enhanced the image of "legal pot."

Some of the state laws went so far as to authorize the use of seized street marijuana in the event that the National Cancer Institute was unable to provide an adequate supply of NIDA-grown marijuana cigarettes. Not only was this totally unnecessary, but using seized marijuana in experimental medical research violates several federal statutes designed to protect unwitting patients from the administration of unapproved drugs.

In 1980 the pro-pot lobbies took another step along the legalization route. Working through certain congressmen, they insisted that NIDA grow an extra crop of marijuana to meet the projected demands in those states that had "legalized" NIDA-grown marijuana joints for cancer chemotherapy patients. This also proved totally unnecessary. For example, in California, officials estimated they would need three million NIDA marijuana joints. NIDA initially shipped thirty thousand marijuana cigarettes to California to get them started. One year later, those thirty thousand had not yet been used up. Actual consumption has since stabilized at six thousand joints a year.

When the new law was passed in Georgia, notices were sent to all thirteen thousand physicians registered in the state announcing the availability of the NIDA joints for cancer chemotherapy patients. Georgia officials estimated that at least a thousand cancer patients would enroll in the therapeutic research program, in which they would be supplied free NIDA joints. A year later, the total number of applicants was eighty.

Despite such striking statistics, in 1981 the pro-pot lobby was able to get such respected U.S. Congressmen and -women as Millicent Fenwick, Stewart McKinney, Hamilton Fish, and Newt Gingrich to back a bill (HR 4498) aimed at *legalizing the domestic cultivation* of marijuana for use by cancer chemotherapy patients. In light of the fact that NIDA had by then stockpiled enough marijuana for 2.5 million cigarettes, the bill appeared to be another political ploy to "down-schedule" marijuana, opening a further door to legalization.

On October 13, 1981, NIDA issued a report to the media in order to clarify the situation in regard to HR 4498. The release said in part:

> The main argument for [HR 4498] is an alleged lack of available material for use in therapeutic research projects. In fact, we are faced with an overabundance of material which could be a potentially serious storage problem. . . . A total inventory of cannabis sufficient for over 2,500,000 cigarettes is thus in hand or will be by mid-November when the present harvest is complete.
>
> Our rate of distribution of marijuana is less than 5,000 cigarettes per month for all research including therapeutics. The largest state program under way is California which uses approximately 500 cigarettes per week. Lesser amounts are used by Georgia, Florida, Oregon, New Mexico and Michigan. A study on chemotherapeutic use of marijuana in New York State which is planned to start soon projects a use of approximately 1,200 cigarettes per month depending on patient response. . . .

We have a tremendous excess of cannabis at this time. With no projections of a large change of consumption we could be faced with the necessity of destroying some material to make room for the new crop.

The NIDA statement was largely unreported. The following day the *Atlanta Constitution* was one of the relatively few newspapers to report accurately on the subject:

Unsubstantiated and untruthful medical claims are cited as justification for legalizing domestic cultivation of marijuana. The result is that seriously ill patients are being exploited in the name of legal pot. . . . This is a dangerous bill about a dangerous drug. It should be exposed for what it is: an effort to legalize marijuana through perpetuating a myth that marijuana cigarettes are safe and effective for medical uses.

This particular bill (HR 4498) died. But in 1983, Representative Stuart McKinney of Connecticut introduced a new, almost identical bill, HR 2282, which, the *New York Times* reported, "would enable doctors to prescribe marijuana to patients who need the drug. . . . Mr. McKinney's bill . . . proposes to reclassify the drug by amending the Controlled Substances Act. Marijuana is available now only for research purposes, and then only after approval of a 68-page application."

According to Dr. Ed Tocus of the FDA, whose department receives such applications:

This statement is a little exaggerated. What happens is, the doctor phones or writes the FDA and receives a two-page form. He or she submits a research protocol, which may be as long or as short as desired. Nor need the protocol involve original research. It's simply that when we distribute the free THC pills and/or NIDA marijuana we want to know what results have been achieved. Results need be submitted to the FDA periodically.

The *New York Times* story did not mention the availability of THC capsules. But a *Washington Post* story did. Indeed, it was headlined MEDICAL SUBSTITUTE FOR MARIJUANA WON'T WORK. The author was NORML advisory board member and ACT co-director Robert Randall. The article stated that "by design or gross mismanagement, the government has promised the states supplies of marijuana which do not exist; instead, federal agencies intend to force the states to accept TCH (*sic*). . . . NIDA had only enough marijuana on hand for fewer than 250 individuals."

This story ran on June 29, 1980, and was then syndicated by the *Washington Post* and appeared in major newspapers throughout the United States. On July 22, 1980, Dr. Carlton Turner, then director of the NIDA Marijuana Project at the University of Mississippi, wrote to Benjamin Bradlee, executive editor of the *Washington Post,* a four-and-a-half-page single-spaced refutation of the points made by Randall. After rebutting a host of inaccuracies, Turner concluded, "Perhaps the grossest misconception and fallacy in this whole article is 'that NIDA had only enough marijuana on hand for fewer than 250 individuals.' This is untrue; in fact, an out and out lie."

Turner pointed out also: "There is not a researcher, certainly not this one, who would deny a cancer patient, or anyone else in a life-threatening situation, the opportunity to smoke a cannabis cigarette if it would be beneficial. However, to then use this act as a 'calling card' to promote marijuana as a good substance is outside the realm of reality."

Dr. Turner's letter was not published by the *Washington Post,* or by any of the newspapers that carried Robert Randall's story. As Turner himself had noted: "You may not choose to publish this letter. In fact, even if you do, the damage has already been done by the original article."

It is well known that by the time the headlines extolling "legal pot" . . . "pot pills" . . . "marijuana as medicine," etc., sift down to the schoolyard, it is often interpreted by kids to mean that "pot cures cancer" . . . "pot cures nearsightedness" . . . and even, "pot is good for you, like vitamins."

The damage caused by misinformation and misinterpretation may be surmised by the following case history.

Dr. Eugene McCormick of Wellington, Kansas, reported on a patient named Joey, who started pot smoking at age twelve. He had asthma and had read that pot was good for the condition. "I told him," said McCormick, "that this had been a finding for short-term use. But it had been shown in studies by the same scientist, Dr. Donald Tashkin of UCLA, that long-term marijuana smoking was extremely harmful for asthmatics. I begged him to give up the drug."

Then Joey and his family moved to Mississippi. Three days after his eighteenth birthday, the boy died. His mother sent Dr. McCormick the final diagnosis after the autopsy: asthma with chronic obstructive pulmonary disease (COPD). "COPD," said McCormick, "is very uncommon for young people, but common in people of forty-pack-years [people who have smoked a pack of cigarettes a day for forty years]. The pathologist also stated: 'The lung showed severe changes . . . with marked thickening of the walls of the bronchial tubes, as though he were a man of seventy-five.'

"That extent of damage," said Dr. McCormick, "would be very rare from the asthma alone. Indeed, I have never heard of it. Such severe damage would require some additional toxic substance, such as marijuana."

Later, Dr. McCormick met Joey's sister, who told him the boy had remained a daily pot-smoker until the day he died. "Joey insisted marijuana couldn't be harmful," she said, "because they were even using it to cure cancer."

Chapter 14

Marijuana and Driving

Three sets of statistics make marijuana and driving a subject of urgent national concern.

- Over one out of every four Americans aged eighteen to twenty-five has smoked marijuana within the past thirty days.

- Surveys reported by the National Institute on Drug Abuse show that "60 to 80 percent of marijuana users questioned indicated that they sometimes drive while cannabis intoxicated."

- Over seventy studies done since 1971 show that marijuana—like alcohol—seriously impairs driving; in some respects, marijuana is even more impairing than alcohol.

With alcohol, at least the roadside "breath tests" act as a deterrent. Every state has laws that define the drunk driver for the purposes of prosecution. For marijuana intoxication, however, there is no inexpensive, easy-to-use roadside test for impairment. NIDA-funded researchers are working hard to develop one (see Chapter 17), but, according to Dr. Richard Hawks, the person at NIDA responsible for this specific area, "We are probably several years away from coming up with a viable roadside test that can give precise THC levels at the time of the arrest." If such a test is developed, it will still probably be years before states pass laws concerning legal pot-impairment levels. (It was several decades after the BAC—Blood Alcohol Concentration test—was developed before states passed laws concerning specific levels of alcohol-impaired driving.) We are, consequently, in a legal limbo as far as the pot-high driver is concerned.

At last—and at least—alcohol is being recognized as a highway hazard worthy of concerted national effort. Two national citizen activist groups are doing an amazing job of stirring up concern and action on the drunk driving front: RID (Remove Intoxicated Drivers) and MADD (Mothers Against Drunk Drivers). In 1982, President Reagan set up a National Commission on Drunk Driving to study the problem and make recommendations. In over half the states, governors have formed their own drunk driving commissions to address the problem statewide, and the media are doing a responsible and effective job in focusing public concern on this issue.

But while all this essential attention has been given to the problem of the drunk driver, virtually nothing is being said or done about the pot-high driver. And this, according to police officials, gives an implied message to the marijuana user: It must be okay to drive stoned; otherwise, why wouldn't the government or anyone else be saying anything about it, in conjunction with these drunk-driver campaigns?

This one facet of the health-hazard picture is probably the only one on which pro- and anti-pot forces agree: Marijuana and driving do not mix. NORML, the National Organization for the Reform of Marijuana Laws, states in its official policy, "NORML strongly discourages the driving of automobiles or other vehicles while under the influence of marijuana or any other drug, and recognizes the legitimate public interest in prohibiting such conduct."

But the message is not getting across. The legitimate public interest is not being protected. And every day untold numbers of pot-high drivers are endangering their own lives as well as the lives of others.

It may be coincidental, but highway deaths in the United States increased 45 percent between 1961 and 1971. This increase first appeared in college-aged persons, in later years spreading to younger and older age groups— which exactly corresponded with the ages affected during that decade by the burgeoning marijuana movement in this country.

There is, however, nothing coincidental about the research studies and statistics on marijuana-impaired driving, and on traffic accidents and arrests for DUID (driving under the influence of drugs). And these findings provide the basis for the *only* deterrent we have right now: educating the public in general, and the pot-smoker in particular, as to the very specific hazards of driving high.

The first step is recognition of the problem.

Specific Pot-Caused Driving Impairments

Sobering enough is the fact that numerous research studies show that marijuana effects can be just as driver-impairing as the effects of alcohol, and in some cases more so.

There are, however, *seven additional danger factors.* These seven factors are specific to marijuana and do not generally occur with the alcohol-impaired driver.

First, there is the *pleasure factor.* Highway officials, drug treatment professionals, research scientists, police chiefs, and medical examiners express profound concern about marijuana's mounting impact on our massive national highway problem. What perhaps worries them most is the fact that many pot-smokers say they often drive high—because they *enjoy* doing so.

Ed Moses is a drug-abuse counselor who works with teenagers throughout Missouri. "Hundreds of kids have given me this message," he said. "They tell me, 'I like what my drug does to me when I'm driving,' or 'I get more *into* my driving when I'm stoned'—like they get more *into* their music. Some of them tell me that because their perceptions and reactions are distorted, they find it *challenging* to drive under the influence of marijuana."

One pot-smoker was so anxious to communicate the pleasure of "losing the whole boring reality of the Jersey Turnpike" that he wrote a poem to express the exuberant highway high:

Wheels are flying, sun is shining, tunes are running through your head / And that road stretches on and out / Turn it up sing and shout / Color flash hill and turn / Forward motion constant burn / From here to there without a care / Speed by, fly high stay right / Watch the light dynamite / Let your fancy flow, let your hair blow / On and on you go / Many thoughts many feelings / Down the road down the road / Whooooooooooooosh—gone.

A second danger factor is *behavioral toxicity,* the carryover into the sober state of the "magical thinking" that occurred in the stoned state. This is particularly dangerous when it comes to the pot-high driver. For example, if he smokes a joint while tooling along the highway and thinks he's driving better, this total misconception may well stay with him when he's *not* stoned. Therefore, next time he gets behind the wheel he "tokes" (smokes pot) so that he will "drive better."

How many alcohol consumers claim "I drive better when I'm drunk"? Virtually none. Yet pot-smokers commonly insist, "I drive better stoned because I don't take chances." Studies have shown, however, that "marijuana creates the greatest deficit in a driver's ability to perceive and respond to dangers from the environment." The driver who cannot perceive dangers cannot be counted on to avoid them.

Many pot-smokers close their eyes to their driving impairments, or view them through "rose-colored sunglasses." This was brought out statistically in a 1970 study organized by Dr. Joseph Davis, the chief medical examiner in Dade County, Florida. Questionnaires concerning marijuana and driving were sent to students in a local junior college, an undergraduate university, a medical school, and a law school. There were 571 replies. In every driving category, former users and infrequent users sharply downgraded their ability to perform while stoned. But chronic pot-smokers gave themselves quite good grades. For example, "ability to keep the vehicle under control" was downgraded by 65 percent of former users, and by only 18 percent of chronic users.

Despite their cheery assessments, 53 percent of the chronic users had been stopped by police for driving under the influence of drugs—compared to 17 percent of the former and infrequent users. Twenty-two percent of the chronic users had been charged with three or more violations, compared with 2.3 percent of nonusers. And 8 percent of the chronic users had had their licenses revoked, compared to only 1 percent of the nonusers.

Hugh Alcott, project manager of the California Department of Corrections' Special Narcotics Section, deals with some five thousand drug-abusing adults every year. He pointed out another example of "magical thinking":

A lot of people who've had too much to drink, and know their driving will be affected, smoke a joint "so they can drive better." They actually believe that marijuana acts as an *antidote* to the effects of alcohol! All the pot does, of course, is to make them *feel* they're driving better. In fact, their driving is far more impaired than if they'd used alcohol alone.

Bruce Bomier is executive director of the Minnesota Behavioral Institute, which administers a statewide educational program aimed at marijuana users. He said:

We've interviewed about 1,000 people arrested for marijuana possession in Minnesota. Their average age was 19. Over 25 percent thought that marijuana would improve their hand-motor coordination. About the same number thought it had no effect at all on their driving. Marijuana intoxication can be subtle. Therefore, many people are not really sensitive to the fact that their perceptions *are* distorted.

A third factor that adds to the danger of the pot-high driver is the *ability to "hide the high."*

The alcohol-impaired driver usually finds it hard to hide the condition, if stopped by the police. But the pot-high driver can often "come down" and carry on a seemingly normal conversation with a police officer, and thus escape detection.

This was illustrated by one of Dr. Davis' students, who taped the roadway reactions of a friend who had smoked 2½ joints before taking the wheel. An excerpt: "I feel like I'm going around the edge of a teacup. It's like I'm going to roll right off. Oh, it's like I'm going straight down. [The road was actually flat.] I can't possibly drive now because I'm driving on my head. I have to get off the road."

He did pull off the road. A highway patrolman came over to see why the car had stopped. The young man explained he had driven a long way, was tired, and was about to change places with his friend. The policeman left. He had not detected or suspected that the driver was incapable of operating the car. The student put it this way: "He was dumb because I was really wrecked!"

This ability to hide the high gives many pot-smokers confidence that they can drive stoned and be "home free." One such self-assured driver was Andre McNicoll, a thirty-year-old medical sociologist in Ottawa, Canada.

One summer evening McNicoll was at a friend's house, rapping and smoking a few joints. "I was a purist," he said. "I never touched alcohol. I was delighted to have discovered this harmless pleasurable substance called pot, which I'd been smoking daily for three years." Around ten o'clock he borrowed his friend's car because, as he put it:

I loved the dreamlike experience of driving stoned. And I was sure I could handle whatever might turn up on the road—including a cop.

This time, as I drove down Sherbooke, one of the busiest streets in the city, the pleasure burst in a total psychedelic experience. All I could see was a myriad of tiny dancing lights. I was so totally spaced out that I had no awareness of even being in a car, much less driving one.

When a traffic light turned red, McNicoll did not notice. He crashed into a small car that had stopped for the light. McNicoll hit his head on the steering wheel, got out, danced a little jig, walked away, and wandered around the city for hours. "I knew something had happened. But I didn't know what. It was terrifying."

Around 4:00 A.M. he remembered, and turned himself in to the police. He learned that he had wrecked his friend's car, and had totally demolished the small Datsun in front of him—which had, in turn, crashed into the Ford sedan in front of *it*. Miraculously, no one had been seriously injured.

"That night," said McNicoll, "started me thinking about this 'harmless pleasurable substance.' But it took a few more experiences that *were* really tragic before I was able to 'get off the pot' for good."

The fourth additional danger factor is that *it's far easier to light up a joint at the wheel than to take a drink while driving*. The drug paraphernalia industry aids in this endeavor by selling such devices as a pot pipe that attaches to the dashboard, with plastic tubing to reach the driver's mouth for "no-hands toking." There are other devices specially tailored for the motorcyclist. One full-color, full-page ad in a motorcycle magazine features such a product being used by a man on a motorcycle, his hair streaming back in the wind. The large headline reads: WHO SEZ YOU CAN'T SMOKE AT 60 M.P.H.?" The ad extols the pleasures of smoking "your doobie" while speeding. (Doobie is a street name for a cigar-sized joint.) "Hey, and guess what . . . no more ashes in your eyes."

The fifth additional danger is the *time-of-day factor*. Alcohol-involved accidents occur chiefly on weekend nights, but pot-smoking drivers take to the roads all through the week, day and night.

The sixth danger factor, as noted in the NIDA *Marijuana and Health* report, is this: "A person may attempt to drive without realizing that *functioning is still impaired—even though he or she no longer feels 'high.'* " One driving-simulator study showed "that a marked decrement was still present five to six hours after intake. . . . Some subjects noticed a definite effect eight to ten hours after intake, and a discrete late effect as long as twenty-four hours later."

The seventh danger may be termed *the unexpected factor*. Many chronic pot-smokers report that a few puffs of "good pot" (with a high THC content) can result in a sudden, intense high. If this happens on the highway, it can be frightening and dangerous. As one user put it: "I hadn't smoked all day. I lit up a 'j' to take away that monotony of driving for miles and miles. But suddenly after a few tokes, I didn't know if the car was actually drifting, or whether I was drifting. I knew I'd lost some degree of control. And when you're on a superhighway, you have very little margin for error."

The flashback is another form of unexpected impairment. If the driver has previously taken LSD, PCP, or mescaline, a few tokes of a joint can trigger a flashback to that drug experience. The person at the wheel may suddenly find himself "tripping"—even though he or she might not have used a hallucinogenic drug for three months.

Other Pot-Caused Driving Impairments

These seven special dangers relate only to the marijuana-impaired driver, not to the drunk driver. But there is also a whole spectrum of driving impairments that affect both the drunk driver and the pot-high driver, in different ways and in varying degrees.

Numerous research studies on the subject have been done in the United States and abroad (notably in Canada, Great Britain, Australia, New Zealand, Sweden, Denmark, Finland, and Switzerland). Results found by research scientists in one country have been replicated in other countries. Some of the old and overly simple studies (often quoted by dedicated pot-smokers) failed to turn up meaningful evidence regarding impairment. However, the later, carefully controlled studies tell quite another story.

As noted, over seventy such studies have been done in the United States since 1971, when, for the first time, "NIDA marijuana" was made available to researchers. Most subjects in these studies were given "NIDA cigarettes" with a THC content ranging from 1 to 2 percent. It should be remembered that much of the marijuana now being smoked by drivers today is far more potent than that used by these researchers. Furthermore, subjects in driving-simulator experiments generally smoke one or, at most, two joints prior to the test, whereas young people driving home after school, or after "partying" or a rock concert, often smoke more than this, and many may continue to "toke" on the road.

In a typical driving-simulator experiment, the subject sits in the front half of an actual car body, facing a wide screen on which a film is projected. Some experiments focus on one driving component. Others are general, having the subject "drive" through normal and emergency conditions on city and suburban streets, country roads and highways. Driving errors are scored for steering in the wrong direction; inappropriately braking, accelerating, or using the turn signal; speeding, and so forth. For each test there are "controls," who smoke placebos from which the THC is removed. (The drivers often think these are joints of pot with a low THC content.) Subjects sometimes act as their own controls by taking the same test at different times, once after smoking a placebo.

Dr. Herbert Moskowitz, a research psychologist at UCLA, has probably done the most work over the longest period of time on marijuana and simulated-driving studies. In summing up the wide range of findings, he said: "The preponderance of evidence indicates that marijuana impairs skills performance, perceptual processes, attention, and tracking behavior. *All important components of driving and skills performance are thus clearly affected."*

Some of these components,—for example: *"search and recognition"* abilities—are impaired after one joint. Driving requires a full awareness of the environment and full command of a variety of skills. But after one joint the driver may become totally involved with only one facet of driving, or with music from the car radio, or with a private reverie, so he or she might simply not notice a car exiting from a crossroad or a pedestrian who has stepped into the street.

One joint can also result in *expansion of the time-speed sense.* In the words of John M. Clark, Jr., former vice president of the automotive research division of the Southwest Research Institute: "It's like operating with a faulty speedometer. The marijuana-intoxicated driver often *thinks* he is traveling only forty miles per hour, when in fact he is doing eighty or ninety."

Other impairments, such as *tracking performance,* were "significant" at dose levels equal to two street joints. The driver may imagine he is keeping the car in the correct lane when in fact he is weaving in a bizarre manner. (In one study, a pot-high driver said he was going to "bring himself down and stop weaving back and forth." His observer noted: "The driver *thinks* he is controlling the car now, but in fact he is continuing to weave.") Sometimes tracking ability is so impaired that the driver proceeds the wrong way on a one-way highway.

Moskowitz and other researchers also found the following impairments caused by marijuana intoxication:

* *Impairment of peripheral-vision signal detection.* The driver, for example, might not pick up the fact that another car was trying to pass, and might suddenly turn—into a passing car.

* *Impairment of central-vision signal detection.* The driver might not start the car when a green light comes on, might drive through a red light, or might fail to recognize the red and white "no entry" sign and find himself in a head-on collision course with another car.

* *Impairment of time reaction.* Inability to brake quickly in rush-hour traffic, or to move over quickly if another driver cuts in ahead. Subjects have trouble maintaining a steady speed, which can be especially dangerous among fast-moving cars on an expressway.

* *Impairment of night driving abilities.* Marked increase in time needed to recover from glare. Trouble in "placing" lights, particularly on a dark

country road. ("Is that oncoming car far away? or very close? Is that a stationary traffic light—or a light coming toward me?")

• *Impairment of short-term memory function and information storage.* The driver may forget where to get off the highway, or which crossroad to take—on a route he or she knows well.

• *Impairment of manipulative and coordination skills.* Difficulty in backing, turning around, passing another car, getting on or off a crowded expressway, weaving in and out of traffic, or even maneuvering around a parked truck on a crowded city street.

In addition, researchers have found pot-smoking drivers have *impaired instantaneous judgment abilities, impaired concentration, impaired stability, impaired vigilance, impaired auditory signal detection, and impaired interpretation.*

Most of these results came from simulated driving tests. And, as Dr. Moskowitz pointed out: "People drive *better* under simulated driving test conditions than they drive normally." Even so, it is unlikely many tests will be done in actual driving conditions.

There was one, however. It was carried out by a Canadian, Dr. Harry Klonoff, professor of psychiatry at the University of Vancouver. "No wonder no one's ever tried it again," he said. "The logistics for arranging the study were horrendous. We had to get clearances from all the various law enforcement agencies, plus full liability insurance from a private agency—which was no easy matter!"

As subjects Dr. Klonoff chose 102 "psychologically stable" Vancouver University students, male and female. All had used marijuana before. One third were given one joint of government-supplied marijuana; one third were given two joints; the third group were given placebos. Dual-control cars were used, and each subject was accompanied by a trained observer from the licensing bureau. Neither drivers nor observers knew who had received pot or placebos.

All 102 students drove through a closed course with no other traffic, wending their way through two tunnels, one funnel, and a set-up of cones. Thirty-eight students also drove a seven-mile route from the university campus through the traffic-heavy downtown area and back. They were rated according to the system used by the Department of Motor Vehicles in examining drivers for licensing, which includes both skills and behavioral components.

When the scores were computed, overall figures showed that *those who had received the one-joint dose had a 42 percent significant decline in general driving skills. Those who received the two-joint dose had a 63 percent significant decline in driving skills.* "Unusual driving behavior," Dr. Klonoff reported, "included the missing of traffic lights or stop signs, engagement in passing maneuvers without sufficient caution, poor handling of the vehicle with respect to traffic flow, unawareness of pedestrians or stationary vehicles, preoccupation at traffic signals, and lack of response to green lights."

Of the eleven behavioral components tested, the three areas of greatest vulnerability were *judgment, care while driving,* and *concentration*—despite the fact that many of the subjects later admitted that they were paying special attention to their driving, since an observer was sitting beside them, marking their every move. Some also said they were "biased": They wanted to *prove* that pot had no impairing effects on driving. Since presumably some of the scores were improved because of the special attention to their driving accorded by the "biased" students, the overall dramatic decline in scores is even more startling.

"It is evident," Klonoff concluded in his official report, "that the smoking of marijuana does have a detrimental effect on driving skills and performance in a restricted driving area, *and that this effect is even greater under normal conditions of driving on city streets.*"

Another driving/pot test, less scientific but interesting nonetheless, was conducted by the magazine *Car and Driver.* The results were published in an article by Mike Knepper in the June 1980 issue. The subjects were experienced pot-smokers who took *only two "hits" of a street joint (two deep puffs)* before driving a 1980 Chevrolet Citation two-door four-speed through a slalom course to test dexterity, and a lane change to test reaction time. The slalom course used nine pylons set seventy-five feet apart. The lane change test was patterned after a General Motors test. There were five sets of runs per driver and the drivers took repeated "tokes" (puffs of a marijuana cigarette).

The article was titled "Puff, the Dangerous Driver." The conclusion of the study: "Doping and driving don't mix."

Here are comments by the subjects interviewed for the article:

Rich Ceppos: What I realized from our afternoon trip to nirvana is that marijuana erodes driving skills in a far more subtle way than alcohol. And the problem wasn't one of execution so much as a simple lapse of concentration. Behind the wheel, I progressively felt more like an observer than a participant and I paid less and less attention to driving the return loops. There was, after all, so much else worth considering: the Southern California sky was particularly blue; the distant, snowcapped mountains were captivating. I dwelt on the tree overhanging the return road. I studied the texture and color of the pavement with great interest. It was obvious that once I was solidly stoned my concentration and decision-making abilities were seriously watered down. Focusing my attention on the long-term effort of piloting an automobile was work, and, hey, work was the last thing in the world I wanted to do. That was no problem within the artificial confines of the proving ground, of course. But real-world driving, just getting from point a to point b, is a deceptively complex process, fraught with chance happenings and judgment calls. What if the return road had been a real street, and, while I was momentarily absorbed in communicating with the cosmos, a kid on a skateboard had shot out in front of me? What if a car had swerved into my lane? Would I have had the presence of mind to make the right decisions, take the right evasive action? To tell the truth, I'm not sure.

And I *can* tell you this: When it came time to drive home, this space cadet was more than happy to let someone else deal with it. I advise you to do the same.

Stephen Smith: What would have happened if I'd had to deal with the random warp and woof of real traffic for, say, 45 minutes? Could I stay focused that long after partying all night? If you're stoned enough to hallucinate or drift into fantasy, your driving might well be impeccable— save one tiny detail. Something like losing track of the aggressively driven "National Casket Co." eighteen-wheeler on your right flank. Something fatal.

There must be some penalty for driving around with your reality out of whack. Maybe dope just puts you in a better frame of mind to accept the inevitable accident.

Don Sherman: Within three minutes of my first tokes of marijuana, various sensory alarms started to trip all over my body. My fingertips tingled, my mouth started to parch. And the clock slowed way down, all on two light hits. I seemed to be more conscious of ragged steering action and bad timing. I got lost a lot between exercises, and at one point charged toward the lane-change entrance 10 mph too fast. More dope didn't alter the initial buzz much, but I gradually mellowed out into a semi-conscious zombie-like trance. The time-extension syndrome made me feel as if I had minutes rather than microseconds to react to the left or right instructions. I learned that I can control a car under the influence of marijuana. I also realized that the really impossible task is staying awake to do so. Dope will kill your long-term concentration. And probably you too, if you're foolish enough to dope and drive.

Pot *Plus* Alcohol

Back in 1974, when Dr. Klonoff interviewed his Vancouver students prior to the driving test, he learned that 64 percent of them often used alcohol in combination with pot before driving. This trend rose sharply during the past decade in both Canada and the United States.

Today many parents prefer to think that their child only smokes pot—*instead* of drinking. Unfortunately, this is not likely to be the case. Virtually all recent city, suburban, rural, county, state, and national drug-abuse surveys show that marijuana and alcohol are not an either/or proposition. Most pot-smokers also drink; and they often drink while they "toke" (smoke pot). Furthermore, they often do both prior to driving.

The most popular type of party among high school and college-aged young people today is "the keg." The host buys a keg of beer. Guests drop in, paying a dollar or two each for all the beer they can drink. They also smoke pot—often the equivalent of two to three joints. Then they drive home.

Many parents like the idea of a keg party. It costs nothing, and sounds harmless enough. ("It's only *beer,* Mom!") And, pleased to get away from the blasting rock, many honor their kids' insistent request to "go to the movies or something" while the party's on. If, when they return home, the parents are aware of the sweet smell of marijuana hovering in the room, they're usually only too ready to believe their youngster's shoulder-shrugging response: "A joint was passed around, and a few people took a drag or two. Big deal."

But it *is* a "big deal." Dual use statistics are sobering indeed. For example, according to the 1983 National High School Senior Survey, *70 percent* of twelfth-graders who had smoked pot at all during the year say that they have used alcohol at the same time. Twenty-one percent said they'd used both at the same time "most of the time or every time." And about one in four daily pot-smokers are also daily drinkers.

What impact does this have on driving? How impairing *is* the mix of pot plus alcohol?

In a study published in June 1980, Dr. Moskowitz and Dr. Marcelline Burns of the Southern California Research Institute tested twelve healthy men (average age 26½) who used pot no more than twice a week, and who did not "do" other drugs. The subjects performed a series of laboratory "tasks," each related to a specific driving component such as tracking or information processing. Each subject was tested, at different times, under

276

eight different "double-blind" conditions. (No one knew what he was getting when.) The conditions ranged from low alcohol, .05 BAC, and placebo marijuana (a joint with the THC removed) to placebo alcohol (orange juice with a few drops of vodka floated on top to give the appearance of a "spiked" drink) plus two marijuana cigarettes.

Following this study, Dr. Moskowitz and Dr. Alison Smiley did a similar study, but this time the subjects "drove" for twenty-one miles in a driving simulator.

The results of both studies were virtually the same. The "alcohol onlys" showed the well-recognized alcohol-caused driving impairments of *reaction time, coordination, visual awareness, attention, judgment, and information processing.* The "pot onlys" showed the same long list of driving impairments that Moskowitz and other researchers had shown in previous studies.

But the result of *dual use* of alcohol and pot was, said Moskowitz, "essentially *additive*" (One plus one equals two—a *doubling* of impairment). These results duplicated previous laboratory studies done in this area in the United States and abroad.

The impairments from alcohol and from marijuana were not always similar, and in some tasks added up to real double trouble for the driver. "For example," said Moskowitz:

> driving is obviously a multi-task process. You must be able to do two or more things simultaneously. Alcohol impairs this ability in one way, and marijuana in another way. The drunk driver tends to concentrate on one driving element, to the exclusion of everything else. By sticking close to the center line for reference, the driver can keep the car from weaving, but may be totally unable to attend to any unexpected highway happening. The pot-high driver, on the other hand, appears to have brief total "dropouts" in attention concerning all facets of driving. Thus working together—and against each other—alcohol and marijuana undermine the ability of the driver to process the roadway information necessary to control the vehicle safely.

Moskowitz summed up both his studies by saying: "Drivers under the combined influence of alcohol and marijuana have a greatly increased likelihood of initiating an accident."

In August 1980, Dr. Lawrence Sutton became the first U.S. researcher to test the effects of marijuana and alcohol in a "closed" driving course. Sutton, executive director of Pittsburgh's Institute for Driver Research and Substance Abuse, selected nine healthy young male students from the University of Pittsburgh. All were experienced drivers, pot-smokers, and drinkers.

Each drove on four successive afternoons, under four different "conditions": pot (one joint) plus alcohol; placebo alcohol plus one joint; placebo joint plus alcohol; placebo alcohol plus placebo joint.

During the thirty-six driving trials, which included common procedures for a driver's license examination in Pennsylvania, an experienced highway patrol officer, Donald Dolfi, followed the subjects in his own car, noting their performance. He "pulled over" those drivers to whom he would have given a "DUI" (driving under the influence) citation—if they'd been on the road.

When it was completed, Dolfi said to Sutton, "I guess I spoiled your study. I only pulled over fifteen drivers." But when the double blind code was revealed the result showed that of the fifteen "pulled over" by Dolfi, one bad driver had taken only placebos, three had had "marijuana only," and two had had "alcohol only." But all nine—100 percent—*of the alcohol-plus-marijuana drivers had been pulled over.*

"This result," said Sutton, "was quite startling. In the patrol officer's trained eye, *all* of the drivers who had received one marijuana cigarette plus a low dose of alcohol were too intoxicated to be on the road." (The .06 BAC level of these drivers could have been created by as little as two 12-ounce cans of beer.)

When the subjects' objective performance evaluations were codified (number of stop signs missed, number of pylons hit, weaving across the line, and so on), they produced similar statistical results.

The results of Dr. Sutton's study show that the impairments caused by pot plus alcohol may be more than additive. They may be synergistic, that is, one drug potentiates ("fires up") the other; so that one plus one equals three or four on the impairment scale.

A further noteworthy factor: If they had been on the highway, none of these drivers could have been prosecuted for DUI—Driving Under the Influence—since a Blood Alcohol Concentration level of .10 is the legal definition of the drunk driver in all but two states. (Note: Some law enforcement agencies use the term DUI—Driving Under the Influence; some use DWI—Driving While Intoxicated. DUID means, specifically, Driving Under the Influence of Drugs.) Since they were below the legal alcohol level and there is as yet no viable roadside test for the pot-high driver, all fifteen drivers pulled over for DUI by Officer Dolfi would therefore have been "home free," unless, of course, they had injured or killed themselves, or others.

By far the most definitive study on the impairing effects of pot plus alcohol on driving was done by Victor Reeve of the California Department of Justice.

It was conducted in 1981 at the California Highway Patrol Academy near Sacramento, which has an elaborate test-driving area used for training cadets.

As subjects, Reeve and his researchers chose, as he put it, "a select group, potentially quite different from the population of individuals who drive while impaired by marijuana." The one hundred volunteers were male U.S. citizens aged twenty-one to thirty-five, in good health, with relatively good driving records—and no felony convictions. They were moderate users of alcohol, and had smoked pot for at least two years prior to the test. Their recent use had been "one to seven average-potency 'joints' weekly for the past three months; not more than one daily." And they were not to have used any other drug. (This was double-checked in each case by urine and blood tests.) Nor were they allowed any alcohol, pot, or any other drug from 8:00 A.M. on the morning of the day preceding the test. (This also was blood- and urine-tested, and a few subjects were disqualified because they had disobeyed.)

Each subject was given two training drives on the course to familiarize himself with what he would be expected to do when the experiment was underway. Each subject, for example, was carefully drilled on how to perform the skills test and the various maneuvers involved in negotiating the course. Having performed that drive, the subject then performed a "baseline drive" while he was not under the influence of marijuana and alcohol. "This," said Reeve, "functioned as the reference point drive for any future drives by that subject."

Each subject drove the course five times, under the same "conditions" each time but no one knew which "dose" he was getting. The controls got placebo alcohol (orange juice with a few drops of vodka floating on top) and placebo marijuana (a joint with the THC removed). The Marijuana Only drivers got a low potency joint (1.9 percent THC) and placebo alcohol. The Alcohol Onlys got a placebo joint plus orange juice with sufficient vodka to produce a BAC (Blood Alcohol Concentration) level of .06 to .08. This alcohol dose was comparable to a 160-pound man drinking four to five beers within half an hour, or four to five 4-ounce glasses of wine, or four to five shot glasses of whiskey, all of which contain the same amount of ethyl alcohol. The Dual Use group got the low-potency joint, plus the same alcohol dose as the Alcohol Only group.

Since .10 BAC is the legal definition of the drunk driver in almost all states, why did Reeve work with a lower level? Since street pot averages 3 to 4 percent THC, why use pot with such a relatively low potency?

Reeve noted: "We wanted to look at what we considered borderline impairment levels. We didn't want people drunk or stoned. We wanted the type of impairment you normally encounter on the highway. We were also hoping to have a comparable impairment effect from both drugs."

During the actual experiment each subject drove the course five times. Each drive took twenty minutes, with time out in between during which the subject was evaluated in numerous ways.

To help measure driving impairments, each car had special instruments including two video cameras. One camera, on the roof, documented the movement of the car around the course. The other, in the trunk, focussed on sensors which measured what the vehicle was doing; accelerating, braking, turning, and so on. Both cameras provided ongoing coverage during the entire twenty minutes of each drive. The other instruments recorded the position of the car every tenth of a second as it moved through all phases of the test.

Each driver was accompanied by a human evaluator from the Department of Motor Vehicles who took careful notes, answering six pages of standardized check sheets on the subject's performance. In addition, on the "extended drive" portion of the test (a two-mile looping course that simulated rural country driving), a trained highway patrol officer trailed each car in an unmarked vehicle. The officer evaluated driving performance on a rating sheet and provided a taped commentary on the driver's performance. Neither officer nor examiner knew which "dose" his subject had been given.

At the conclusion of each twenty-minute drive, each subject was asked to perform a roadside dexterity test, a critical tracking task, and a time estimation task. (He had been trained to do both of the latter tests in his "straight state" on previous days.) Also, each was asked to fill out his own subjective evaluation sheet.

Urine tests for marijuana metabolites were taken prior to each drive, and four hours after the drive, and blood and breath samples for alcohol were taken at hourly intervals before and after the doses of pot and alcohol were given. The subjects also were checked by a medical team after each drive for pulse, blood pressure, general well-being, and so on. Then all this mass of information was fed into computers.

Findings showed important correlations between objective tests of driver performance (done by instruments) and the subjective evaluations of the examiners who rode in the vehicles with the drivers and the California Highway Patrol officers who observed the vehicles and then gave field sobriety tests to the drivers.

So far as the self-evaluations of the pot- and alcohol-impaired drivers were concerned, initially they were accurate; but they became less accurate after the first hour. When people take a drug, "like alcohol and/or marijuana," said Reeve,

> they feel the impact on the brain. Then they become more used to the effect and don't notice it. Consequently, they feel they are quite sober and in control of the car—when in fact they are not.
>
> Since THC is fat-soluble, there is a longer delay in terms of its reaching its maximum effects. The initial surge of the high that the smoker feels does not necessarily occur at the same time as the impairment factor. You can smoke a joint at a party and figure a half hour later that you've "come down" and it's safe to drive home—but in actual fact you are at the greatest point of impairment so far as driving is concerned. And if you throw alcohol into the picture you *really* don't know where you're at in terms of impairment!

Reeve pointed out that on initial smoking, before the first deep inhalation is released, the effects are felt in the brain. But after the first surge of THC into the blood, the fat-solubility factor may come into play and delay the maximum driving-impairment effects.

On the other hand, once alcohol hits the bloodstream, the impairment effects are felt at once. "Also," says Reeve, "there is not the tremendous surge of alcohol in the blood, as *is* the case with marijuana. The effects of alcohol on the brain and the impairment level tend to parallel one another. This is not true with marijuana. With pot, there is no parallel. When you feel yourself 'coming down,' actually your impairment level is going up."

Reeve first observed this phenomenon in 1979 and 1980 when he and Dr. Leo Hollister did field sobriety tests with sixty healthy male and female pot-smokers aged twenty-one to sixty in a study at the Palo Alto, California, Veterans' Administration Hospital. They tested drivers and found they were more impaired half an hour after smoking than they were after ten minutes. There was an even more pronounced effect on the fifty- and sixty-year-old drivers than on the younger people.

Reeve's study also showed that although the moderate or the chronic pot-user becomes acclimatized to the effects of the drug and does not feel them, this *tolerance does not affect driving impairment.* In other words, although the experienced pot-smoker doesn't *feel* high, his or her driving may be just as impaired as it was when he or she was a "naive" (or beginning) pot-smoker. (This is not true of some other drugs where tolerance to the drug also brings tolerance to its driver-impairing effects.)

Another surprising finding in Reeve's driving-impairment study was the *duration* of the drug effects. The researchers found that—although the alcohol levels had declined and the THC levels had dropped—after four hours the subject had still not returned to baseline driving performance. Even when alcohol levels had dropped to .02 BAC, the subjects did not return to their baseline performance (.02 BAC can be reached after one 12-ounce can of beer). Reeve noted that drinking one can of beer does not usually cause any driving decrement. However, he said, "if one drinks four or five beers and gets to .08 or higher and then—through time and metabolism of the alcohol—comes down to .02, driving will be affected because the person is fighting off the effects of the poisoning of the system. Some of the metabolites of ethyl alcohol are more toxic than the alcohol itself."

As far as the marijuana-caused driving impairments went, "We were surprised," said Reeve, "to see the degree of impairment that we did after four hours. In laboratory settings researchers have seen impairment as long as twelve hours. We ran our tests only for four hours because the subjects were getting tired. However, it was not fatigue which accounted for the continued impairment because the control group, who were just as tired, showed nonetheless a progressive improvement, because of practice." (They, of course, had the same initial practice—the familiarization and baseline drives—as the marijuana and alcohol subjects. The remaining practice came during the five test drives.)

In some instances, the performance of the Marijuana Only people became reckless. In other cases, their performance became more cautious. "However," said Reeve, "this does not necessarily mean safe driving. If they happen to be driving slowly and cautiously in the fast lane, that's certainly not safe driving behavior."

The Marijuana Only drivers did things a little differently from the Alcohol Only group. "For example," said Reeve,

> when a person is driving after smoking a joint, he'll just kind of sit back and let the car pull through the tasks by itself. This may not emerge as a problem until the driver is confronted by an unexpected maneuver or sudden curve, or if he has to change directions or something out of the ordinary happens. In the course, we had a detour with an S-curve. As the driver came out of the curve, he had to maneuver the car carefully to keep it in its lane. The marijuana driver usually failed to maintain his lane position; he would either go out into the oncoming traffic or cut the corner too short and drop a wheel or two into the gravel. There was a very pronounced effect. The alcohol-impaired driver generally performed better in this particular skills test than the pot-impaired driver.

In the case of forced lane changes, the marijuana-impaired driver generally maneuvered at a slower speed, and with fewer errors, than the alcohol-impaired driver. "But," said Reeve, "this would not be unexpected in the case of the pot-impaired driver who was relaxing and letting the car do its thing. The alcohol-impaired driver would rush it, push it, make more mistakes."

The study also found that the effects of marijuana and alcohol were additive (one marijuana impairment plus one alcohol impairment equals a doubly impaired driver). Furthermore, the impairments shown by the alcohol group and the impairments shown by the marijuana group were *all* present in the dual-use group. (Some drugs may counteract each other, lessening the deleterious impact of either drug. This was *not* the case with the marijuana/alcohol impairments.)

"For example," said Reeve, "with the Two-Treatment group you have an impaired driver who has trouble tracking his car and trouble estimating time and speed (both of which come from marijuana) *combined with* trouble in tracking and reckless driving, which is symptomatic of alcohol impairment. It's quite a combination to stir together!"

In addition to additive effects, in some of the tasks or skills a synergistic effect was noted: One plus one equaled a five or six on the impairment scale. "For example," said Reeve, "we saw this synergistic effect in driving the car backward, as one would have to do in order to maneuver into a parking space or backing out of a garage or driveway."

By June 1983, the forty million data points had been computerized and studied, and two of the most surprising findings were revealed:

1. The impairment level of the Marijuana Only drivers came closer to that of the Dual Use group than did that of the Alcohol Only group. In other words, one relatively *low-potency "NIDA joint" (1.9 percent THC) was more driver-impairing than alcohol resulting in a .06 or .08 BAC.*

2. *The initial surge of the high that the smoker feels does not necessarily occur at the same time as the maximum impairment level.* In fact, although the Marijuana Only drivers were definitely impaired when high, *their driving was even more impaired a half hour after they had "come down" and felt themselves to be completely unaffected by the drug.*

"All of this means," said Reeve, "that the combination of pot plus alcohol can lead to some totally unexpected and dangerous situations—even for the driver who thinks he is being careful." He summed up:

We must remember that the group of pot-smokers that is most prevalent out there on the highway is the group that uses alcohol along with marijuana. Our national level of concern *must* be elevated beyond that of the drunk driver. The many millions of pot-smoking drivers who also drink are a doubly dangerous highway hazard, and many of the dangers lie in the areas of the unknown and the unexpected. We would strongly recommend that these drugs never be used together in any concentration whatever before or while driving. Furthermore, from what we and other researchers have shown, the potential for a hazardous driving situation is greatly increased by the use of either drug.

Ed Moses had this observation on the subject:

You see it all the time, kids go into a bar, drink for a while. Then they come out and smoke pot in the parking lot—before driving home. And what some of them are going to now is liquid hash oil—with up to 40 percent THC. Pro-drug magazines have mail-order ads for liquid hash-oil cookers. Kid make their own hash oil out of marijuana. Some spike up a joint with hash oil. Others inject hash oil into tobacco cigarettes, so they can look legal and get stoned.

We may soon look back on the "good old days" when we only had alcohol to worry about as a roadway hazard. According to AA, only 12 percent of our adult population drink to become intoxicated. But with almost all pot-smokers, their only reason for using the drug is to get high.

It should be remembered that the THC potency of the government-issued "NIDA marijuana" used by Reeve, Sutton, Moskowitz, and other U.S. researchers—about 2 percent—was lower in potency than that used by most pot-smoking drivers today, when street pot averages 3 to 4 percent THC.

Also, as noted, the increasingly popular U.S.–grown sinsemilla is often 8 percent THC or more—which makes it rank among the most potent types of cannabis in the world.

Pot's Impact on Driving Arrests for DUIs, Accidents, and Fatalities

What impact does driving high have on traffic accidents and fatalities? Because we've had the Blood Alcohol Concentration (BAC) test for many years, we know from police reports throughout the nation that about half the traffic fatalities that occur every year are alcohol-related. Since we have no viable roadside test for marijuana, there are no comparable national or statewide figures available, nor will there be any in the foreseeable future. We must therefore rely on the results of studies and surveys to get some idea of what may actually be happening on the highways as a result of pot-high drivers.

The largest study ever undertaken in this area was also done by Victor Reeve and his associates at the California Department of Justice. It was a thirty-month statewide study, begun in late 1976. The decision to undertake this large project was influenced by some ominous statistics. According to a comprehensive report published by an assortment of California state agencies and departments, *in the first six months following decriminalization in California in 1976, arrests for driving under the influence of drugs increased 46.2 percent in the case of adults, and 71.4 percent in the case of juveniles.* The state's Department of Justice further pointed out that "although California licensed drivers represent 10 percent of the nation's total, the number of impaired driving arrests in California now number almost 30 percent of the nation's total."

Reeve's statewide study was the first large-scale research project ever undertaken to see whether *chemically validated evidence* existed to relate marijuana smoking to traffic arrests for impaired driving. The study was made possible by the fact that an eminently accurate process had been developed whereby THC metabolites *in the blood* could be recognized when analyzed via a sophisticated, yet not unduly expensive, radioimmunoassay (RIA) laboratory technique (see Chapter 17). The problem was, how many drivers arrested for DWI (driving while intoxicated—by alcohol and/or drugs) would *agree* to have a blood sample taken? Urine tests were "offered," but only blood was used. Since marijuana was an illegal drug, presumably most pot-smokers would choose to have an alcohol breath test, particularly if they had not been drinking alcohol, or if they had not had enough to reach the state's legal impairment level: .10 BAC. (Each arrested driver was free to select the type of test he or she wished to have; those who refused to have any test were subject to license revocation for a matter of months.)

Despite this initial handicap to their study, the researchers went ahead. As a first step, a legal opinion was sought from the State Attorney General's Office. The specifics of the plan were set forth: The research study would be statewide, covering forty-six of the fifty-eight counties in California. Police would submit blood samples from drivers arrested in traffic accidents as DUIs. An anonymous random sampling of blood specimens would then be tested for THC content. Each would receive a code number; the code would be broken only when the study was completed. There would be no possible way that the courts, law enforcement agencies, the driver—or even the researchers conducting the study—could ever link the arrest sheet and the blood results. On this basis, the project received a legal green light.

Since each year the California Highway Patrol routinely submitted to the Justice Department blood samples from some 19,000 to 25,000 drivers who had been arrested for DUI, these were available for testing. Of the 65,000 DUIs arrested during the year of the study—1978–79—only a little over one in three had chosen to give a blood sample rather than a breath or urine sample.

Victor Reeve noted:

> How many of *those* arrested drivers might have been marijuana-impaired we will never know. But presumably those with no drugs in their system would have been more prone to provide a blood sample than those who had used marijuana.
>
> There are two reasons those arrested for DUI who knew they had used no drugs or alcohol would be more than willing to have a blood test. First, in about 99 percent of DUI arrests when there *is* evidence of alcohol and/or drugs in the body, courts will convict. The drug-free suspect would have irrefutably demonstrated DUI innocence to the court. Second, some of the arrested drivers were involved in accidents. Most insurance companies will not cover a driver who has caused an accident if he or she has chemically validated evidence of alcohol and/or drugs in the system. Also, if an insurance company becomes aware of a DUI conviction they frequently automatically cancel the policy, even if there has been no accident. The person is put into an assigned risk category— with very high rates. In some cases, when the person was involved in an accident, he or she may not be reinsured. This is especially true in the case of repeat offenders.
>
> Those who had been smoking marijuana but had not been drinking in any notable amount would presumably have been far more likely to opt for an alcohol breath sample, than a blood test.

The researchers randomly selected 1,792 blood samples from the 19,000 DUI drivers and sent them to Los Angeles for RIA analysis. Result: Of those arrested who had no detectable blood level of alcohol, *24 percent had sufficient THC in their blood to indicate marijuana impairment.*

High as this figure was, as Victor Reeve pointed out,

> It must be regarded as conservative, not only because forty thousand of the arrested drivers had refused to give a blood sample, but also because THC doesn't stay around long in blood. In two to four hours it drops below all levels that we could detect in our laboratories at that time. [More sensitive techniques have been developed since.] It sometimes took two hours or more between the time of the arrest and the drawing of blood in the closest clinical laboratory. Therefore, it's very possible that we missed some low level consumption—which may have caused driving impairment.

Another significant finding resulted from the roadside dexterity test given to all of the drivers. Some of the drivers with alcohol only in their blood had passed the test; Reeve noted that some people with .10 BAC can pass this test. They develop tolerance to the drug, and some can adjust to the effects of alcohol for the many single-attention tasks in these tests. They usually cannot do all the dual-attention tasks.

Although some of the drivers arrested for DUI with alcohol only in their blood had passed the roadside dexterity test, *100 percent of the drivers arrested for DUI who had no alcohol in their blood but who showed positive for marijuana had failed the roadside dexterity test.* This indicated that the driving impairment had come from pot.

The California study, published in 1979, looked predominantly at arrested drivers who had not caused an accident.

In 1980, a two-year study done by Dr. Joerg Pirl and Dr. John Spikes was reported by the Department of Public Health in Chicago. The researchers, who were medical examiners, had examined the blood of 158 *fatally* injured drivers. A complex but extremely accurate procedure known as gas chromatography/mass spectrometry (GC/MS) was used to determine precise amounts of cannabinoids in the blood. Result: Twenty percent of the dead drivers had detectable blood levels of THC.

Another study of "fatals" was done in Ontario, Canada, in 1980. The subjects were 484 drivers and pedestrians killed in car accidents. Their blood and urine were screened. More than 55 percent were positive for alcohol. Of those positive for drugs (26 percent), nearly half (46 percent) were pot-positive, although most of those tested were by urine rather than blood tests, so time of intoxication could not be pinpointed.

Earlier studies had used other methods of looking at the "accident quotient" of pot-high drivers.

In 1968 researchers in the state of Washington surveyed the driving records of people arrested for illegal drug use. The records were compared to a demographically matched control group of non–drug-users (matched for income level, type of job, type of car, level of education, sex, age, number of years of driving, and so forth). It was found that *the pot-users had up to 39 percent more traffic accidents and traffic violations than non-users.* The three most prevalent traffic violations among the pot-smokers were reckless driving, failure to yield, and failure to stop.

287

A different type of survey was done in the Boston area in 1975. The Boston University Traffic Accident Research Team, headed by Dr. Robert Sterling-Smith, did in-depth interviews with friends, family, domestic and professional associates—and passengers—of 267 drivers deemed "most responsible for a fatal accident." In cases where the driver had survived, he or she was also interviewed by the researchers. Each interview took at least an hour, and covered a list of three hundred information points.

Result: Sixteen percent of the 267 drivers were known to have been smoking marijuana prior to the fatal accident. The study summed up: "Marijuana smokers were over-represented in fatal highway accidents when compared to a control group of 801 randomly selected drivers carefully matched with the 267 for sex, age and town of residence."

Are teenagers aware of the dangers of driving high?

A first-of-its-kind sixteen-state survey was published in July 1981 by the American Automobile Association's Foundation for Traffic Safety. Fifty-five hundred students in a hundred high schools answered detailed questionnaires on this subject. Well over half the pot-smokers said that marijuana has harmful effects on steering, braking, making decisions, reacting to any emergency, and obeying traffic signs and signals; 67.7 percent said marijuana harms the ability to "stay in one lane," and 71.7 percent said it harms the ability to pay attention.

In addition, 69.5 percent said that marijuana plus alcohol had worse effects on driving than did alcohol alone. Nevertheless, the general feeling was, "Driving high is okay for me. I can handle it."

It became clear from this and other surveys that after obtaining a license and with it the privacy of a car, this became a favorite location for pot smoking.

Many teenage drivers regard the ride home as part of the "partying." They often drink and smoke pot en route. Sometimes the party ends abruptly, and forever. For example, a boy in Bethesda, Maryland, was given a car for his sixteenth birthday. After a party at home he and four friends went into the woods to drink beer and smoke pot and hashish. Then they decided to try out the new car. Laughing and high, they hurtled off down the highway. At a curve in the road the driver stepped on the accelerator instead of the brakes, and the car crashed into a metal guardrail. Three of the youngsters were badly hurt. One girl was in a body cast for months. The birthday boy and his best friend were killed.

Since "dual use" is increasing, and since the impairing effects of pot plus alcohol are far worse than either drug used alone, the shadow cast over our roadway future is dark indeed.

What Can Be Done?

Shockingly little has been done about the pot-high driver. However, in a few places a few people have taken effective steps along the don't-drive-stoned legal route. A look at what they are doing may provide helpful leads for those who would pursue this subject.

Some states have laws in which an open liquor bottle in the car of a DUI is considered *prima facie* evidence of a crime. Minnesota also has an "open baggie" law. Anyone with any amount of marijuana in the car—whether smoking it or not—is considered to have committed a crime.

What happens in Minnesota to someone found in possession of marijuana in a car? The driver is held responsible. He or she must attend the state's mandatory four- to five-hour course on the health—and driving—hazards of pot smoking, which is given in forty-eight different localities throughout the state by instructors trained at the Minnesota Institute in Anoka.

In most states police overlook personal possession of small amounts of marijuana. In Minnesota they often do *not* overlook this, especially if pot is found in cars. Minnesota police tend to arrest *young* users, whom they want to help, not hurt. The mandatory "pot course" offers this opportunity: The average age of those taking the course is nineteen. Forty percent of those taking the course have been involved in one car-related citation or another.

First offenders who have *not* injured anyone *must* be sent to the institute's "marijuana education course." This is a "summary disposition" without criminal penalties; the arresting officer need not even appear in court. However, if the driver was involved in an accident or was driving recklessly "in a serious way," he or she is treated within the criminal justice framework.

Bruce Bomier, director of the course, expresses the state philosophy:

In view of the fact that there's been a very permissive sentiment about marijuana, and very little solid information given out about the dangers of driving high, *we have a responsibility* to make sure that users understand the health and driving hazards involved in marijuana use. We also explain what a second offense will mean in terms of having a criminal record, etc.

But if they "cross the line" a second time—after the community has

explained to them how they are endangering themselves and others—
then we have a responsibility to the community to be firm. A second
possession offense in Minnesota usually means a fine of up to $500 and
incarceration over a series of weekends in a county jail or work farm
(with lock-up cells for the night).

A recent evaluation study of 3,255 of the program participants showed
that "two thirds indicated that in the future they would make positive changes
relative to their use of marijuana and alcohol."

The program does *not* apply to a pot-smoker responsible for death or
injury on the highway. Minnesota judges, in fact, tend to be tough on pot-
smoking drivers or reckless drivers found with marijuana in the car when
they cause accidents. The judges have been thoroughly briefed on the driving
impairments caused by this drug. During two statewide sessions in 1979
and 1981 all municipal and county court judges in Minnesota were addressed
on the subject of the pot-impaired driver by Bruce Bomier.

In most states all judges meet once or twice a year. This offers an excellent
opportunity for an expert on marijuana and driving to address the judges.
Judicial understanding of the hazards involved in driving high is essential
in order for a fair, uniform, and effective system of penalties to evolve within
the state.

An interesting use of marijuana urine testing of parolees in Albany, Georgia, is described in Part Three of this book under Marijuana Detection Tests:
The Criminal Justice System. This pilot project program, which can easily
be adapted or adopted by any town, city, or county, has had statistically
very significant results that go far beyond dramatic improvement in traffic
arrests, accidents, injuries, and fatalities.

Another possible legal avenue: State legislators can pass a law prescribing
a thousand-dollar fine and/or other mandatory penalty for possession of
any cannabis product in a vehicle (marijuana, hash, or hash oil). Whether
the driver was smoking would not matter. Whether he or she was high
would not matter. What *would* matter is that a message gets across very
quickly to the general public: There must be something dangerous about
mixing pot and driving. Otherwise, why this tough legislation?

If passed, the legislation would, of course, have no effect on the person
who "parties," smokes a few joints, and then gets behind the steering wheel.
However, the legislation should help deter some of the drivers who enjoy
lighting up a "j" when they're behind the wheel.

Legislation can mandate penalties for failing roadside dexterity tests, for positive results in blood or urine tests for marijuana (or for refusing such tests), or for having pot in the car. Unfortunately, however, because we do not yet have an easy-to-use and inexpensive roadside test that can ascertain marijuana *impairment,* it is obvious that the legal route for punishing the pot-high driver is largely unavailable.

But one route is wide open: education. And it has numerous byways as well as superhighways that can be taken by governmental organizations, foundations, and private groups. Obviously, coordination of effort would greatly increase the impact of the message, which, after all, is a simple one: It's dangerous to drive after or while smoking marijuana. At a statewide level, for example, the Office of Traffic Safety, the Department of Alcohol and Drug Abuse, the Department of Justice, the Department of Education, and the Department of Motor of Vehicles, by working together, can achieve massive educational results—quickly.

Driving schools present an obvious education outlet; however, sometimes the instructors need instructing. (One young man taking a driving course in Manhattan was offered a joint by his instructor "to relax.")

Local school boards and PTAs/PTOs can ensure that information on the hazards of driving stoned is incorporated into high school driving courses. (See Appendix for several excellent films and books in this area.)

An information campaign can start where road users are most likely to get the message: brochures handed out at toll booths, gas stations, garages. Car-users are a captive audience and "spot warnings" can be tailored to a range of radio programs from early morning news to late night disk jockeys (many of whom now serve as on-air pot promoters). The AAA and National Safety Council might inaugurate a nationwide information campaign. And it would behoove insurance companies to help spread the word.

The Canadian government has taken an impressive step in this direction. In March 1983, Canada's Department of Health and Welfare published a twenty-two-page booklet on cannabis. It is free, and widely advertised in TV commercials. Every Canadian parent of children and teenagers received a mailing describing the booklet, "Stay Real," with information on how to obtain it (see Resource list). Three hundred thousand copies were ordered in the first fifty days. Under the heading "Safety Hazards," the booklet includes this statement:

> Cannabis intoxication can pose serious safety risks while riding a bicycle, operating machinery, or even crossing a busy street. But the most significant safety risk comes from trying to drive while stoned. To make matters worse, people who are under the influence may be unaware of their im-

paired performance, and may believe that they can drive just as well as, if not better than, when they are not.

In 1982, the Canadian Medical Association passed a resolution recommending that doctors should have the right to take blood samples from impaired drivers without their consent—when the person was involved in an accident. (Until new methods are perfected, blood tests remain the only way to measure the *level* of cannabinoids in the system of the pot-high driver—and thus to measure, to some degree, marijuana-caused driving impairment.) The sponsor of the resolution, Dr. Robert MacMillan, answered the question of violation of civil rights by commenting: "The resolution speaks to the rights of the guy who is run over." The legislation is now being considered by the Canadian government.

Dr. MacMillan pointed out that this proposed legislation should be of interest to the many millions concerned about the problem of the drunk driver, since often an injured driver, unable to take a breath test for alcohol impairment, is rushed to the hospital—where the tests can be done easily. If no alcohol blood test is obtained, there is no chemically validated legal evidence to present in court.

On December 19, 1983, the governor general of Canada in the government's Throne Speech (which outlines legislation to be put before the House of Commons in early 1984) noted:

> Police could telephone judges to obtain warrants allowing doctors to take blood samples from unconscious people they suspect are drunk drivers. This would be done only when someone is killed or injured. . . . Mark MacGuigan [Canada's Justice Minister] said blood tests could also be used to detect the presence of drugs as well as alcohol even though there is no scientifically proven level at which a driver could legally be considered impaired by drugs.

This proposed legislation makes clear the importance of coordinating the antidrunk *and* -drugged-driving campaigns. Since the symptoms and the results are interconnected, so should the solutions be interconnected. As Keith Cowan, a Canadian government consultant on drug education, put it: "Government and private agencies should warn the public against the use of pot before or while driving—as *part* of their excellent anti-drinking and driving 'advertisement campaigns.' "

Many anti–drunk-driving activists do not want the marijuana issue to ride the coattails of their endeavors. "Let us tackle the drunk driving battle first," they say. "When we win it, then we can look at marijuana and other drugs and driving."

But "then" will be too late for those who have been killed or maimed by the driver who is stoned on marijuana, or who is doubly impaired by the mix of pot plus alcohol, or the increasingly common combination of marijuana plus other driver-impairing drugs.

We should have started on the educational route yesterday. But today is at least better than tomorrow.

PART THREE

WHAT IS BEING DONE ABOUT IT?

Chapter 15

A Brief Overview

What is being done about it? This question is the theme of the third section of this book.

Unfortunately, the basic answer can be summed up in two words: *Not much.*

Nevertheless, it is vitally important to examine what *is* being done, for in doing so we also see what can be done and how to do it.

It is also important that we are not lulled into the comfortable assurance that the situation is being taken care of . . . the pot epidemic is receding . . . we can all sit back now and "let George do it."

Remember that in too many cases and for far too long, George has also been sitting back.

In addition, it is important to keep the following fact in mind: Although the situation is improving somewhat, U.S. cannabis-consumption figures are still higher than those of any other country in the developed world.

We will now look at what is being done about it—for there is something each of us and all of us can do to improve the situation for ourselves, for our children, our schools, our neighborhoods, our towns, our counties. Part Three describes pilot projects that are working in various areas. Beginnings are finally being made. And these beginnings offer valuable ways to go for those who have not yet begun.

Chapter 16, "The Federal Strategy," is the one most likely to evoke the "let George do it" feeling full force. The concerted and coordinated effort being made by the federal government is more dramatic and effective than any ever undertaken before against our national drug-abuse epidemic in general, and marijuana in particular. But—commendable though the effort is—

it is obviously underfunded, understaffed, and in drastic need of cooperation and input from all segments of our society.

There are two chief thrusts to the federal government's program; one attacks the demand, the other, the supply. Since there have been numerous books and articles on drug smuggling (many of them making it sound quite an exciting enterprise), we will not deal with this aspect of the subject in our discussion of the supply.

Furthermore, because of lack of space, we will not deal with the long-unsung heroes in the war against drug abuse: narcotics agents. Decades before our nation was even aware of the term "drug epidemic," federal, state, and local narcotics agents were risking their lives, often going undercover with a consequent disruption of their personal lives and those of their families. For years, they have been in the front lines fighting the battle with little or no recognition from the rest of society.

Chapter 17 concerns an important "weapon" in the battle against drug abuse: the new marijuana-detection breakthrough, with the emphasis on urine testing.

In Chapters 18, 19, and 20 we will turn to the three specific areas we covered in Part One—the schools, the armed forces, and the workplace—to see what is being done about the marijuana epidemic. The armed forces have responded to the drug threat with organization, determination, and dedication. The pilot projects presented in the other two sections must be regarded as merely drops in the ocean. The drops, however, are well worth recording, for they illustrate effective efforts of dealing with these two vast drug-logged areas of our society.

Chapter 21 describes the impressive statewide effort called the Texans' War on Drugs, which started with a governor's directive and now encompasses broad spectrums of Texan society. It has proven to be so effective that it is being emulated by several other states.

Our final chapter concerns the parent movement for drug-free youth, a unique grassroots movement. It is so effective that many—from politicians to educators—are now passing the buck: "Let the parents do it." But those in the parents' movement are well aware that only through coordinated efforts of all areas of our society can we win this battle.

Chapter 16

The Federal Strategy

The war against drugs takes place on many fronts. In this chapter we will look at what is being done at the federal level.

A clue to the Reagan administration's position on pot was the appointment of Dr. Carlton Turner as director of the White House Drug Abuse Policy Office. Turner's views on marijuana were well known. As the ten-year director of the federal marijuana research project in Mississippi, he had spoken out frequently on the subject of pot's health hazards. Indeed, Turner was the first White House drug policy appointee whose primary expertise was in this area; previous appointees focused on heroin addiction.

For the first time, serious and concerted attention would be given to the matter of marijuana, on both the supply and the demand sides. Turner's appointment as director of the Drug Abuse Policy Office (and later elevation to special assistant to the president for drug abuse policy) meant that not only would he advise the president on what national drug-abuse policy ought to be, but he would have the authority to ensure that thirty-three federal agencies with major responsibilities for drug trafficking and drug-abuse prevention would carry out the president's policies.

On October 5, 1982, Turner issued the official 1982 "Federal Strategy for Prevention of Drug Abuse and Drug Trafficking," the program President Reagan and Turner had promised the nation at the June 24 briefing in the White House Rose Garden (see Chapter 1). This seventy-six-page policy document was presented to Congress and sent to all government agencies with drug responsibilities; it also went to all state governors, attorneys general, appropriate civic and professional organizations, and to any private individuals who requested it.

Past strategies of other administrations had given highest priority to the "most dangerous drugs" (principally heroin), but the 1982 document stated:

> Programs must also respond to the large numbers of people and families who are suffering the direct and indirect effects of other drugs of abuse, including marijuana and alcohol. In 1982, *the effects of drug abuse are being felt in nearly every family and every community throughout the United States.* This broad social impact requires greater attention to the entire spectrum of drug abuse and requires feasible health and law enforcement priorities which address the drug problems in each geographic area.
>
> The 1982 strategy does not attempt to dictate from a national level the relative priorities for local responses to drug problems. While drug abuse is a menace to our entire society, the drug problems of a large city may be quite different from those of a small town. Each locality must determine its own priorities and must have the flexibility to fashion appropriate responses if we are to be effective in reducing drug abuse. [Emphasis added.]

Nine cabinet departments and thirty-three federal agencies were involved in the broad national effort. The president's budget for 1983 requested and received from Congress almost one billion dollars ($901.4 million) to support federal drug-abuse programs and to provide states with "block grants" so that they could help control how and where their federal substance-abuse funding should be spent.

Many wondered how the job could be done, since the budgets of various departments had been cut. Turner stressed that the operative word was not *cut* but *readjusted.* He put it this way: "By getting more agencies involved that have never been involved before, and by giving the drug issue higher priority in all the agencies which *are* involved . . . we'll be able to do a lot more than we have been doing with the budget that does exist."

The federal strategy is to attack the nation's drug-abuse epidemic by *coordinated and concerted efforts* to cut down on the supply, as well as by cutting down on the demand for drugs. Let us first look at the many-faceted attack on the supply.

The South Florida Task Force

A major ingredient of the new strategy went into operation before the document was published: the South Florida Task Force, which was a response to cries for help from citizens' groups (notably Miami Citizens Against Crime in drug-flooded Miami), and to reports from government agencies that 80 to 90 percent of the country's marijuana and cocaine entered the United States through southern Florida. Some authorities estimated that annual drug smuggling in south Florida alone was a seven-billion-dollar business.

The task force, under the leadership of Vice President Bush, went into full-scale operation in March 1982 with a nine-million-dollar budget. It was both an interdiction and an investigative force, created to bring all available federal resources to bear against drug traffickers who had been using the state as a virtual free port of entry. The interdiction staffs of local federal agencies were beefed up, and the subsequent coordination of efforts of various services was to prove a new keynote in many areas of the federal strategy. The South Florida Task Force not only set a pattern but also proved the efficacy of the approach. In addition to the DEA, the FBI, and the Border Patrol, other agencies that cooperated in the interdiction effort included the U.S. Customs Service; U.S. Coast Guard; Federal Aviation Administration; Internal Revenue Service; Bureau of Alcohol, Tobacco and Firearms; the U.S. Attorney's Office; U.S. military personnel; and state and local authorities. Army Cobra helicopters and two Navy E-2C Hawkeyes (planes with advanced look-down radar capabilities) were also used in the effort. In addition, the Coast Guard was assigned five more vessels for narcotics patrols.

The results were impressive indeed. In the course of a few months, the South Florida Task Force made more than six hundred arrests; they seized $7.9 million in assets of the drug smugglers—including forty-five vessels— and they seized more than sixteen hundred pounds of cocaine, nearly one million pounds of marijuana, and seventy-seven thousand doses of methaqualone (Quaaludes).

Statistically speaking, this meant that for the first half of 1982, drug-related arrests in Florida were up more than 40 percent over the same period in 1981. The amount of marijuana seized was up about 80 percent, and the amount of cocaine, about 120 percent.

The task force's interdiction efforts also affected other areas of the local drug-smuggling picture. A Miami DEA agent put it this way: "We have been able to work on long-range conspiracy cases and undercover probes we might not have had time for when we were running down to the docks every day meeting pot ships." These cases included investigations over several months resulting in the roundup of narcotics money-laundering rings and other types of smuggling operations. Furthermore, the local public coffers were enriched by the confiscations. For instance, Fort Lauderdale opened a new $1 million jail, and according to Jeff Hockman, the city's special counsel, "The entire construction cost was paid for by the dopers."

On May 1, 1982, the *New York Times* ran a story that began: "A federal task force assembled to assist Miami in its struggle against narcotics smuggling has apparently reduced the tide to a trickle."

The South Florida Task Force galvanized community spirit in south Florida and brought, for the first time, optimism about the government's ability to deal with drugs and crime.

Other areas of the East Coast, from Maine on down, were less thrilled with the effects of the South Florida Task Force efforts—for the smugglers did not turn tail, they merely turned elsewhere. The normal routes of the drug traffickers were disrupted, so they moved up the coast. The disruption, according to Charles Rinkevich, then coordinator of the South Florida Task Force, "causes the traffickers to use other routes, larger aircraft and larger ships, to cover longer distances and to spend more time in transit. And therefore," he said, "there is more opportunity to nail them and therefore it's good for our side." But other coastal areas, now drug-flooded, took a dim view of this type of optimism.

However, help was on the way.

The Twelve Task Forces

In 1983, a new and important part of the federal strategy went into effect: twelve regional task forces that covered not only the coastal areas, but the entire nation (see Appendix). Unlike the South Florida Task Force, which includes interdiction and investigation, *these* task forces—officially known as Organized Crime/Drug Enforcement Task Forces (OCDE)—are concerned only with investigating and prosecuting drug trafficking by organized criminal groups within their areas. The twelve OCDE Task Forces are composed of investigators from the Drug Enforcement Administration, the FBI, the Treasury Department, and other enforcement experts who work together as teams. In addition, $127.5 million was approved by Congress to support the new program and its staff of more than twelve hundred additional specialists, plus a support staff of four hundred.

The twelve task forces concentrate on networks of distribution, the bigtime operators, rather than on street sales and pushers. One Justice Department official summed up like this: "We are choosing cases that are complex; cases that involve wiretaps, investigative grand juries, financial transactions, and large organizations. We're not going after the powder-on-the-table, bodies-on-the-floor type cases. We're going after the people at the top who may never even see the drugs, and when we get them, the indictments may not even include drug charges."

In many instances, the ultimate charges may be for tax evasion. The I.R.S.; Customs; Alcohol, Tobacco and Firearms; U.S. marshals; U.S. attorneys; and the Coast Guard may all be involved, but in all cases the two prime "movers and shakers" are the DEA and the FBI. We will look later in greater detail at the new cooperation between these two agencies.

Often arrests in one task force area lead directly to arrests in other areas. For example, in September 1983, because of the work of the task force in the New York City area, warrants were issued for twenty-three people accused of operating two drug rings in New York, Cleveland, Pittsburgh, and Detroit; four separate organized crime families were involved.

Said FBI Director William Webster:

Besides ruining the lives of countless Americans, the drug cartels and organized criminal groups have tentacles probing into our system of government. Drug trafficking is big business, and drug traffickers can afford to offer public officials very tempting bribes to get them to look the other way, to be somewhere else, to ignore illegal activities going on in their own communities, and to provide early warning systems for the drug operators whenever law enforcement is getting too close. . . . Narcotics operations of the magnitude that we're dealing with could not function in this country without the cooperation of corrupt public officials. As we have closed off their old trade routes, narcotics traffickers have sought new ports of entry for their drugs, and we've seen the problem of drug-related corruption spread from urban areas to rural communities.

As the head of the National Sheriff's Association pointed out: "Think about the problem we have. Ask yourself the question, 'How long does it take a nine-thousand-dollar-a-year sheriff or deputy sheriff to save the fifty thousand dollars that he can make in one night or one week, simply by being somewhere else?' "

"The lure of tremendous profits," said FBI's Webster, "has spawned corruption among businessmen, judges, municipal officials, police officers, and government prosecutors, as well as elected officials. Hardly a week goes by that I don't receive a report of some kind of arrest, indictment, or conviction involving public officials and drugs."

Such testimony gives but a taste of the massive problems confronted by our law enforcement bodies in their battle to stem the influx of illegal drugs.

It is obvious that each branch needs all the help it can get—from all the others.

The Rest of the Network

The National Narcotics Border Interdiction System

Known as NNBIS (pronounced EN-bis), the National Narcotics Border Interdiction System went into operation in March 1983. Whereas the twelve task forces are concerned primarily with drug traffickers and organized crime, NNBIS is concerned strictly with stopping drug smuggling into the United States. It is, in effect, the interdiction portion of the South Florida Task Force expanded to our borders nationwide. Its executive board is chaired by the vice president, and its task is to coordinate the work of those federal agencies with existing responsibilities and capabilities for interdiction of sea-borne, airborne, and cross-border importation of narcotics. NNBIS complements, but does not replicate, the duties of the regional OC/DE Task Forces, which are operated by the Department of Justice.

NNBIS's impressive cabinet-level executive board includes the secretary of state, secretary of the treasury, secretary of defense, attorney general, secretary of transportation, counselor to the president, director of the Central Intelligence Agency (CIA), and the director of the White House Drug Abuse Policy Office.

In addition, there is the equally impressive coordinating board which includes the secretaries of the army, navy, and air force, the deputy director of the CIA, associate attorney general, administrator of the DEA, administrator of the Bureau of Alcohol, Tobacco and Firearms, and the director of the FBI. The two boards meet regularly to provide central coordination and high-level direction designed to strengthen interdiction efforts along all of our borders.

Although the South Florida Task Force, the twelve task forces, and NNBIS provide a coordinated, ongoing cooperation of law enforcement forces, the federal effort does not stop with these three. Two more separate entities operate on interagency lines: EPIC and the LECCs.

The El Paso Intelligence Center

EPIC is managed by the DEA with participation by eight other federal agencies. In addition to personnel, EPIC is also the major headquarters for all the computers of all the federal law enforcement agencies, which busily "talk to each other," trading information.

The Law Enforcement Coordinating Committees

LECCs in each of the ninety-four federal judicial districts provide a network covering the entire nation. The LECCs, formed at the direction of Attorney General William French Smith, draw up plans to focus all available resources on the most serious crimes in each district, at the local, state, and federal levels.

The LECCs began operating by January 1982, about the same time that the South Florida Task Force went into action. The committees include top law enforcement officials in each judicial district; sheriffs, chief prosecutors, often the heads of prisons; people representing any military installation in the district; as well as locally based federal agents from the FBI; Alcohol, Tobacco and Firearms; U.S. Marshals; Customs, and so on.

The LECCs also deal with matters other than drug abuse, including white-collar crime, public corruption, fraud, and violent crime. At the start of their operation, a poll was taken of all LECCs to establish the top law enforcement priority in each district. Since ninety-three of the ninety-four districts reported that their top priority was narcotics, that has been a major focus of all the LECCs.

Every LECC is mandated to have a subcommittee on narcotics. The twelve task forces guidelines specify that each of *their* districts must have a District Law Enforcement Coordination Group, which must have a link to the LECC in that district.

Judith Friedman, special counsel in the executive office for U.S. attorneys and the administrator of the LECC program nationwide, summed up by saying:

> The real thrust of this administration has been to have local, state, and federal law enforcement agencies cooperate and share resources—instead of stepping on each other's toes, as frequently happened previously. Each organization, however, has its own specific mission and function. The twelve task forces are entirely "operational" units. They are there to "make cases." The LECCs are there to coordinate strategies and policies to facilitate cooperation among the different levels of law enforcement in their respective districts, as well as to develop and implement joint operations.

The DEA plus the FBI

To gain more insight into what interagency cooperation in the drug trafficking area really means, let us take a closer look at two of the most important agencies in this area.

The Drug Enforcement Administration was created in July 1973 by a merger of four existing federal narcotics law enforcement agencies. DEA is the primary federal narcotics law enforcement agency. (U.S. Customs and the U.S. Coast Guard are the primary narcotics interdiction agencies.) DEA's task is, for the most part, investigative.

DEA has some four thousand employees, about half of whom are special agents. Their particular mission is to arrest those who traffic illegally in drugs, to disrupt the organization and, whenever possible, to seize the substances being trafficked.

The agency also operates overseas with over 170 special agents in more than forty countries. The DEA agents share intelligence with agents in their host country and they help train agents. However, when operating overseas, they may not make arrests.

In January 1982, drug law enforcement took a new direction. As part of the federal strategy, the attorney general gave to the FBI, for the first time, concurrent jurisdiction in narcotics law enforcement. This means that the FBI is authorized to investigate the same violations of the 1970 Controlled Substances Act that DEA is authorized to investigate. Since the FBI has 59 field offices and about 450 satellite offices—compared to DEA's less than 30 field offices—this factor alone greatly expands the manpower available for narcotics investigation cases. The administrator of DEA, who heretofore reported directly to the attorney general, now reports *through* the FBI director, which further ties the two agencies together.

"At first," said DEA's Bob Feldkamp, "we weren't sure how this would shake down. But it's worked out very well. For example, prior to January 1982, the FBI was involved with DEA in only 15 joint narcotics cases. By October 1983, the two agencies were working 540 cases together."

Wiretaps provide just one example of the benefits of working together. Says Feldkamp, "Wiretaps are one of the basic tools of narcotics law enforcement. But they're tremendously time-consuming and manpower intensive." Wiretaps require surveillance to see when the individual to be "tapped" comes into the vacinity of the microphone. The microphone must be monitored consistently, and the tapes transcribed. The FBI had been successful in using wiretap techniques in many sophisticated long-term investigations—techniques that are now applied to narcotics cases as well. The DEA has rarely had personnel available to "sit on a wire." But, within one year, utilizing the considerable manpower of the FBI, there was a 148-percent increase in the number of federal court-authorized wiretaps for narcotics law enforcement.

Generally, the agency that initiates the case "runs" it. DEA agents are often assigned to work out of FBI offices, and vice versa. The two agencies are now cross-training each other's agents for the first time: FBI agents are trained in narcotics work in DEA's federal training center in Glynco, Georgia, and the FBI is training DEA agents at their training center in Quantico, Virginia, in some of their sophisticated techniques such as tracing the flow of money.

This money-flow aspect is one of the primary new directions the battle is taking. In one case, for example, code-named "Bancoshares," the FBI discovered that a number of Colombian drug operations were laundering their funds in South Florida before they put it into the banks. So the FBI formed an undercover operation to go into the laundry business. In less than a year and a half, about eight undercover agents laundered over $170 million in cash. When the operation ended, they had indicted about thirty-six key players of a number of Colombian drug cartels. They seized $6 million in cash, $11 million in bank accounts, numerous airplanes, automobiles, and a forty-six-hundred-acre ranch valued at more than $4 million.

The DEA and FBI now trace assets of the traffickers through stricter banking laws. They are also working in the offshore banking-haven areas.

The Internal Revenue Service (IRS) is a part of each of the twelve task forces. IRS gets flagged in a number of ways. For example, banking laws require that any deposit of ten thousand dollars or more must be reported to the Treasury Department, which includes the IRS. If a bank gets dozens of such deposits from a single individual, the IRS tips off DEA or FBI.

The DEA, FBI, Customs, IRS, and other agencies also use computers, which notify each other of patterns—for instance, when wire transfers of money are made regularly from a bank in Florida to a bank in the Cayman Islands or a bank in Italy.

The computers are also tied in to FAA (Federal Aviation Administration) relating to flight plans. Even illegal planes usually file flight plans, as major traffickers generally use commercial airports. Shipping routes must also be filed. If a ship from Colombia, for example, is pursuing an erratic course and looks suspect, our intelligence in Colombia will put details of the ship into a computer; it may then be surveilled by the U.S. Customs or Coast Guard, and perhaps the DEA.

In September 1983, speaking of the FBI's entrance into the drug investigations area, Director Webster noted: "During the initial period of DEA–FBI cooperation, FBI drug investigations increased from about a hundred to more than fifteen hundred quality drug investigations, with over five hundred of these being jointly operated with the Drug Enforcement Administration."

Both FBI Director William Webster and DEA Administrator Francis Mullen, Jr., agree that narcotics trafficking is the number-one crime problem facing the United States.

Mullen points out that although the DEA is achieving more narcotics convictions than ever before, law enforcement is just a holding action:

> It takes months, often years, to identify a drug-trafficking organization, to infiltrate it, and subsequently to immobilize it. We have found drug money laundering operations which process approximately $1,000,000 a day.
>
> We could be the answer, if we had 100,000 drug agents. But the real answer has to be eliminating the supply *and* the demand.

New Legislation in the Anti-Drug Battle

The federal strategy has received an important assist in eliminating supply via three new areas of legislation.

An Assist from the Military

Military assistance to civilian law enforcement authorities in identifying the drug traffic was made possible on November 28, 1981, when a change in the Posse Comitatus Act of 1878 was signed into law. The 1878 law prohibited the military from becoming involved in civilian matters. This is a sound concept generally but a distinct handicap when dealing with illegal drug traffickers who have sophisticated surveillance equipment of a type that the DEA, Coast Guard, Customs, and local law enforcement would never be able to afford. However, the U.S. Air Force, for example, has sophisticated surveillance equipment—also of a type that could never be afforded by DEA, Coast Guard, Customs, and local law enforcement authorities.

The 1981 change passed by Congress provides a limited exception to the doctrine of military noninvolvement in civilian law enforcement. Public Law 97–86 allows for the greater loan of equipment, training assistance, and sharing of information on the movement of air and sea traffic outside the land area of the United States. The up-to-date equipment and expertise of our military can now be used against the sophisticated measures taken by illegal traffickers. This means, for example, that if an Air Force plane sights a suspicious aircraft or ship while conducting normal military operations, this information can be turned over at once to the Coast Guard, DEA, and/or the local authorities. There is no provision for search, seizure, or arrest. Someone from DEA, Customs, or the Coast Guard must be present to do this job—but they *can* go out to the "mother ship" (which carries the drugs) on a military plane or ship.

The 1982 IRS Tax Disclosure Amendment

On September 3, 1982, a law was enacted removing restrictions on the IRS from sharing with other law enforcement branches intelligence on criminal activities uncovered by IRS agents.

IRS had always shared such information until an amendment to the Tax Reform Act of 1976 placed restrictions on federal investigators and prosecutors seeking access to tax information for use in cases of serious nontax crime. When the Tax Reform Act cut off all major information from the IRS to the FBI and DEA, narcotics traffickers hid behind its provisions. However, since the 1982 Tax Disclosure Act, when huge amounts of money with no explained source show up, the IRS can share this information with other federal authorities.

Included in the disclosure amendment are safeguards. For example, the amendment allows the IRS to cooperate and exchange information only under a very carefully restricted legislative scheme involving court orders and formal requests concerning criminals who earn their money from illegal means. In order to obtain information, reasons must be presented to show that there is "reasonable cause" to believe that the information would be relevant to a matter related to the commission of a criminal act (the same standards that are required for the authorization of a wiretap).

Civil Forfeiture of Illegal Drug Profits

Forfeiture is the taking by the government of property illegally used or acquired, without compensating the owner. The 1978 federal Civil Forfeiture Law provides that all monies and other assets acquired from the illegal drug trade shall be subject to civil forfeiture.

From 1978 to 1981, the DEA seized property worth $268 million from the drug trade, a portion of which was turned over to the federal treasury. Only *money* from impounded bank accounts, sale of property, and so on need be turned over to the treasury; such items as cars and planes, which can be directly converted to law enforcement use, are allocated to the agency that breaks the case.

This law is a two-sided tool: It can act as a deterrent to the drug trafficker, who may begin to consider the possibility that crime does not pay, when everything he paid *for* with illicit drug profits—his villa, his limousine, his yacht—is confiscated, and his bank account reads $00.00. On the other hand, his crime *does* help pay law enforcement costs in tracking down drug traffickers and bringing them to trial.

Furthermore, local communities are finding that this law also allows them to apply some of these forfeiture funds to such positive uses as work in drug prevention in schools and defraying costs of treatment in drug-abuse facilities, as well as to support law enforcement efforts in the narcotics area.

Let us look at how the law works for federal law enforcement agencies, and at how states, counties, and cities are availing themselves of this new avenue of much-needed funding to combat drug abuse and its many-tentacled ills.

Under this law, all monies used in, and all assets acquired from, the illicit drug trade belong to the United States government and are subject to civil seizure under the forfeiture power. In effect, Congress has authorized federal attorneys to file civil lawsuits asserting the government's right to such property.

Perhaps the most important point concerning civil forfeiture suits is this: The property—not the person—is the defendant. However, the person can choose to have his or her day in court concerning the property.

In the case of federal seizures, if a federal agency (DEA, FBI, Customs, Coast Guard) has probable cause to believe that property has been used in violation of the law, that property is subject to a civil forfeiture suit. If the land, the house, the bank account has been traded in a drug exchange or can be shown to have been purchased with drug money, then the house, the property, the bank account is subject to forfeiture.

If the human owner claims that the property or money assets that the government is seeking have not been acquired by or used in violation of the law, he or she may contest the forfeiture in the U.S. District Court, retain a lawyer, and have the case tried before a judge and/or jury.

Under state laws, the same principles hold. The property is the defendant. In most states a judge is always involved in the forfeiture process. Each state procedure is somewhat different, but most states do not have administrative forfeiture. In any case, the owner of the property or assets can defend the property in court, or get a lawyer to do so, if he or she wishes.

Forfeiture can range from the multimillion-dollar assets of a drug traffickers' money, bank account, and property to the fishing speedboat caught with a load of marijuana offloaded from a mother ship. At the time this book went to press, there was a bill before Congress to allow profits from drug forfeitures to be used by the "seizing agency" to pay informants who furnish information that leads to forfeiture, and to pay expenses in regard to such forfeiture. This would be a twenty-million-dollar revolving fund; the rest of the forfeiture assets would continue to be deposited in the U.S. Treasury to help pay such "general receipts" as Social Security, federal retirement, and welfare. The seizing agency would continue to appropriate such items as cars, boats, and planes that had belonged to the trafficker.

The states have more freedom than the federal government to use forfeiture assets to pay for narcotics law enforcement and drug treatment and prevention costs.

In 1981, Harry Myers, associate chief counsel of the Drug Enforcement Administration (and the man who wrote the original federal forfeiture law passed by Congress in 1978) wrote a model Forfeiture of Drug Profits Act, which consists of an amendment to the civil forfeiture section of the Uniform Controlled Substances Act, now enforced in forty-seven states. "Model law" means one that is recommended for use by states, counties, or other jurisdictions. (See Appendix, p. 494, for information on obtaining a copy of the model Forfeiture of Drug Profits Act.)

Aside from money allocations, there is basically no difference between the federal law and the model state law.

When enacted by a state legislature, the law would permit the state to seize, civilly forfeit, and deposit in their treasuries:

- All monies and property used by drug dealers to buy contraband drugs.

- All property bought by drug dealers with the profits from drug dealing.

- All monies used by drug dealers to facilitate any drug law violation.

By May 1984, according to information supplied to DEA, more than a dozen states had enacted model state asset seizure acts that are very close to the recommended federal act, and that permits them to use forfeited assets in their activities against drug traffickers. Twenty-six other states had enacted legislation containing some features of the model act. These features allow the law enforcement agencies in these states to place suitable property formerly owned by the traffickers (such as vehicles, vessels, aircraft) into official government use. Other features allow property to be sold and the proceeds placed in state and local treasuries, or, in some states such as Florida, to be used in drug enforcement and prevention activities. In addition, some cities and localities either have passed or are considering passing local asset-forfeiture statutes.

As this book went to press, the following states had not yet enacted any type of forfeiture of assets statutes in the drug area: Connecticut, Delaware, Indiana, Kansas, Minnesota, Nebraska, New York, North Carolina, North Dakota, Ohio, Oregon, Vermont, West Virginia, and Wisconsin.

On January 6, 1983, *USA Today* ran a story headlined DRUG CONTRABAND PAYS OFF FOR STATES. It included the following figures on the value of seizures in a single year, 1982:

- Florida: $3 million, including two high-speed boats now used for drug patrols.

- Maine: $3 million, including a ship that can carry ninety.

- Washington: $59,600 in vehicles now used by the police.

- Alabama: $2.5 million, including $32,000 in jewelry.

- Georgia: $400,000 in equipment, including a $200,000 shrimp boat.

- Oregon: Over $200,000, including a $150,000 airplane.

- Federal drug enforcers (including DEA, FBI, Customs, IRS) seized more than $200 million in 1982—up 2000 percent in four years—in illegal profits of drug traffickers.

One year later, in May 1984, Bob A. Ricks, chief counsel of the Drug Enforcement Administration, stressed the importance of local communities passing this type of legislation. Said Ricks:

Every community should seriously consider enacting a law based upon this model Forfeiture of Drug Profits Act. It is a civil statute which is easier to apply than traditional criminal punishments. It takes us one step closer to a society where crime does not pay. It raids the treasuries of organized drug traffickers to disrupt their illegal businesses. And it is a great source of revenue. Under this law most communities return confiscated drug money to law enforcement without draining public treasuries. For example, a small police department in Texas recently seized a drug dealer's farm, worth $500,000. One town in Florida has seized more than $3,000,000 worth of drug dealers' properties within the last few years. Both these communities had previously passed the model Forfeiture of Drug Profits Act and were therefore able to channel these funds directly into their law enforcement efforts.

Other Legislation

The administration is renewing its efforts for passage by Congress of further essential federal criminal law reforms. These include:

• Bail reform, to make certain that persons who are a danger to the community or who are likely to flee will be held in custody. This, of course, has particular relevance to drug traffickers, who frequently are able to post large cash bonds and then vanish.

• Sentencing reform, to make certain that sentences are appropriate for the seriousness of the offense—and to assure that sentences are actually served instead of being made meaningless by ill-considered probation or parole.

• Revision of the exclusionary rule, so that sound, important cases are not lost because of minor technicalities.

Domestic Eradication of Marijuana

Since 1979 law enforcement officials have become increasingly aware of a new and ever-growing area of concern: the "homegrown" product.

By 1984, not only was marijuana grown illegally in every state, but a high proportion of it was cultivated using the "sinsemilla technique," which results in marijuana of greater THC potency and, consequently, higher prices for the grower.

The growth of this illegal industry is attested to by these figures: In 1981 the DEA estimated that some 1,200 metric tons of marijuana were grown in the United States. However, in 1982 DEA and other law enforcement bodies eradicated 1,653 metric tons, or 3.6 million pounds, of marketable marijuana. This meant that 38 percent more marijuana had been *eradicated* than the DEA had previously believed *existed*.

Although a total U.S. marijuana production figure is not easily determined, these statistics reveal that the United States is becoming a major source of the drug. It is estimated that some 20 percent of the pot consumed in the United States is now grown here.

Since 1979, DEA has supported marijuana-eradication efforts by state and local law enforcement agencies in California and Hawaii. By 1981, seven states were involved with the DEA in a "Domestic Marijuana Eradication/ Suppression Program." In 1982 this increased to twenty-five states, and by 1983 it was forty states. DEA's role in this cooperative venture is to encourage state efforts and to contribute—within resource limitations—funding, training, and investigative and aircraft resources to support the efforts of state and local law enforcement agencies in domestic marijuana eradication.

In addition, DEA has four Marijuana Aerial Observer Schools in which state and local officers receive training in detecting marijuana from the air and in related eradication skills. DEA also supports aerial observer schools conducted by states including Florida, Mississippi, California, and Texas.

Other federal agencies are also cooperating in the domestic eradication effort. In 1982, the U.S. Forest Service and the Bureau of Land Management became actively involved in domestic marijuana eradication, as a result of increased cultivation in national forests. Their efforts have generally been coordinated with DEA. Also in 1982, the National Guard in Hawaii and in Arkansas provided essential helicopter support to marijuana-eradication efforts in those states. New Mexico activated the National Guard to help manually destroy a field of marijuana covering approximately fifty acres. The federal policy is to encourage the states to seek the assistance of their National Guard in eradication efforts.

All these operations were undertaken with a minimum of fanfare. But when aerial paraquat spraying of marijuana on federal land entered the picture in the summer of 1983, the situation exploded into what one DEA official termed a "circus." Let us take a closer look at this complicated and controversial subject.

Paraquat

Marijuana can obviously be controlled most effectively at the initial point of production by eradication of the cannabis plants while growing, for once the illicit crop has been harvested and sent on its way, the problem of discovering and intercepting it is manifold. Law enforcement officials estimate that some 90 percent of the pot entering the United States remains undetected. The use of the herbicide paraquat is one effective way to eradicate cannabis before it is harvested and shipped.

This fact was clearly borne out when Mexico started using paraquat in its marijuana-eradication program in 1975. For the next three years the United States contributed some thirty million dollars a year to this program, and to a spraying program for eradication of poppies via another herbicide, 2,4-D. U.S. dollars were used solely for indirect support, such as for purchase and maintenance of the aircraft. The herbicides themselves were purchased directly by the government of Mexico.

The result of this dual program: *a 70 percent reduction* in marijuana coming in from Mexico, according to U.S. law enforcement confiscation figures. (The poppy eradication program was also highly successful, resulting in a sharp decline of importation of Mexican heroin into the United States.)

Before Mexico started its paraquat/pot-eradication program, that country supplied about 85 percent of all the marijuana coming into the United States.

314

By 1979, Mexican marijuana accounted for only 11 percent of the U.S. supply.

Paraquat is one of the most effective and widely used herbicides in the world. It is a broad-leaf weed killer, and cannabis is a broad-leaf weed. It appears to react within plant cells in concert with sunlight to speed up the process of photosynthesis, causing the leaves to wilt and die.

In July 1979, a United Nations Narcotics Laboratory study group composed of experts from around the world convened in Geneva to consider a variety of methods for the eradication of illicit narcotic crops. Concerning cannabis, their report stated:

> Paraquat provides effective control of cannabis. . . . It produces the most rapid response of any of the chemicals that have been tested. As for the environmental impact, drift of paraquat to nearby vegetation may cause visible necrotic spots, but under ordinary circumstances damage would be minimal. Paraquat persists in the soil for long periods, but it is not biologically available because it is rapidly adsorbed [bound to the surface of] soil particles.

The U.N. study group also noted that paraquat is not toxic to plants or animals in this form. In addition, the adsorbed herbicide is readily deactivated by sunlight and microorganisms. It also decomposes and loses its herbicidal effect when stored for long periods and when heated. Furthermore, paraquat does not leach out into the soil and contaminate nearby rivers and streams.

The history of paraquat spraying is interesting, and little known. Paraquat was developed in England in the late 1950s, and has been widely used in the United States since 1962 as a herbicide. *Some four million pounds of paraquat have been sprayed over some 10.7 million acres in this country every year*—applied via manual spraying, usually from a backpack, spraying from a truck, and aerial spraying. It is used:

• As a directed spray in certain areas of orchards (peaches, pears, almonds, walnuts, sour cherries), vineyards, and fields of guava, passion fruit, pineapple, small berries, grain sorghum, and field corn.

• As a weed-killer before crops come up in fields of corn, lettuce, melons, peppers, sugar beets, tomatoes, barley, wheat, asparagus, cotton, soybeans.

• In pasture and range reseeding, preharvest vine killing for potatoes, and for direct application as a defoliant for soybeans, sunflowers, and sugarcane.

315

- For nonagricultural applications, such as along public roadways, railroads, and electric utility stations rights-of-way.

Like any effective herbicide, paraquat is highly toxic. Accidental or suicidal ingestion of a very small dose (less than one teaspoon) of concentrated paraquat may produce irreversible progressive lung fibrosis. Yet, since paraquat has been used in the United States for over two decades according to label directions there were few problems and no special attention was paid to the product by the public—until it was used to kill cannabis and reduce the supply of marijuana.

When paraquat-spraying in Mexico shriveled the Mexican share of the marijuana market in the United States from 85 percent to 11 percent, other nations, notably Colombia, moved in to fill the pot-gap. Clearly, if *other* foreign nations that grew cannabis and exported it in bulk could also be persuaded to use paraquat, the pot epidemic pervading the United States and numerous other nations could be sharply reversed—with minimal cost and maximum efficiency.

Interestingly, it was a 1978 letter by Dr. Carlton Turner published in the *Journal of the American Medical Association* that offered pot advocates "a way out." Turner was then director of the Federal Marijuana Project at the University of Mississippi. As noted in Chapter 6, one of the ongoing responsibilities of this project was to analyze street samples of confiscated pot submitted by DEA and others. In his letter Turner noted that 21 of 61 marijuana samples confiscated in California, Arizona, and Texas from October 1976 through August 1977 contained paraquat, in concentrations ranging from 3.3 parts per million (ppm) to 2,364 ppm. Over half had less than 100 ppm, despite the fact that during those early years of cannabis spraying in Mexico, plants were doused with far more of the herbicide than was necessary to kill them. (The Mexican authorities soon learned that the job could be done just as effectively using far less of the weed killer.)

The federal Centers for Disease Control (CDC) in Atlanta, Georgia, then did a study of 910 street samples, and found that 3.6 percent contained paraquat, ranging from 10 to 461 ppm.

What did these ppm's mean in terms of possible danger to pot-smokers?

A 1978 study done by Dr. Richard Hawks at NIDA showed that 99.8 percent of the paraquat was burned off in the smoking process. Only 0.2 percent passed unchanged into the smoke. A further study by the Department of Health, Education and Welfare hypothesized that if a person smoked five joints a day every day for a year, and if each joint contained 500 ppm, permanent lung fibrosis could develop. (Fibrosis is a condition that reduces the capacity of the lungs to absorb oxygen.)

Despite the near impossibility of anyone's happening to have smoked five joints every day, every one of which happened to be contaminated with 500 or more ppm of paraquat, and despite the fact that no clinical case of lung damage due to paraquat was found by the CDC in any of the cases reported to the agency or in any of the cases examined by the CDC of people who had anonymously submitted marijuana samples for paraquat testing, the Great Paraquat Scare of 1978 flared full force.

According to the White House Drug Abuse Policy Office, hundreds of thousands of anti–paraquat-spraying telegrams, calls, and letters were received on the subject in Congress and in the White House in a matter of months. Virtually no letters were received favoring paraquat spraying.

As a result, Congress, in the so-called Percy Amendment, placed restrictions on U.S. support to foreign governments using paraquat for the eradication of cannabis. This meant that Mexico—or any other nation that sprayed cannabis plants with paraquat—would no longer be entitled to receive U.S. foreign aid for this purpose.

No nations started paraquat spraying. However, the government of Mexico, which regarded cannabis as a threat to the health and well-being of its own people and which had noted no adverse environmental or health effects from paraquat, continued its eradication campaign. In doing so, Mexico also continued its role as the only western-hemisphere nation fulfilling its *obligation* as a signatory to the Single Convention on Narcotic Drugs, which requires nations to control the domestic production of marijuana.

Certainly the United States was not fulfilling these requirements. We tried to encourage other nations to do so, suggesting paraquat spraying as the most effective and cost-effective means of killing their cannabis crops. But these suggestions fell, understandably, on deaf ears—since we were not using the herbicide ourselves and, what is more, were not aiding the funding of nations that did so.

Meanwhile, further research was done on the matter of paraquat-sprayed cannabis. It became clear that the initial theory about joints with 500 ppm could not be substantiated, and many questions arose as to the validity of these 1978 HEW studies. By 1980, when the House Select Committee on Narcotics Abuse and Control held hearings on paraquat, the CDC still had not a single case to report of any lung damage attributable to smoking paraquat-contaminated pot. (An estimated 10 percent of the U.S. imported supply was still coming from Mexico—so there was paraquat-sprayed pot "on the market.")

At the same time, new research kept emanating from the scientific community which clearly showed the lung damage pot smoking itself could do, as well as the other types of biological and psychological damage described in Part Two of this book.

Consequently, the U.S. State Department's Bureau of International Narcotics Matters did an environmental impact statement (EIS) on the use of paraquat to eradicate cannabis plants. This was conducted under the National Environmental Policy Act (NEPA) "to determine the health impacts in the United States from paraquat spraying of marijuana *in foreign countries.*" (Emphasis added.)

Paraquat was not the only alternative considered. As noted in the summary of the Final Environmental Impact Statement (FEIS), the study considered

the various alternatives available to the U.S. which could be utilized in a cannabis control program, namely: no action; alternative eradication techniques; use of alternative herbicides; the use of a marking agent in conjunction with a herbicide, when available; increased enforcement efforts; different land use programs; legalization; and aerial application of paraquat, the proposed action.

The summary concluded: "The available information indicates that none of the proposed alternatives would be as effective as the proposed activity in swiftly eliminating U.S.-bound export sources of marijuana in Western Hemisphere nations."

The summary also pointed out that

available evidence indicates . . . even heavy marijuana users are unlikely to exceed the NOEL [No Observable Effect Level]. . . . If the proposed program is accompanied by concurrent companion efforts in the major marijuana producing states of the U.S. no significant increase in domestic marijuana production is likely to occur.

The principal result from the proposed program would be a reduction in U.S. imports of marijuana by as much as 70 percent of the U.S. supply (judged by the success of the Mexican program), assuming all source nations have simultaneous programs. This would decrease access to the drug by reducing the supply and increasing the cost. This result, in turn, will reduce the adverse health effects to current marijuana smokers. This is the goal of the proposed activity and the principal environmental impact.

Based on the findings of the FEIS, the CDC, NIDA, and other agencies, on December 15, 1981, Congress repealed the Percy Amendment and appropriated $37.7 million each year for fiscal years 1982 and 1983 for renewed use of herbicides in international narcotics control.

The Public Health Services of the Department of Health and Human Services (successor to HEW, which had issued the preliminary paraquat/pot report in 1978) reviewed the matter from a public health standpoint and issued a report, which stated that "the Public Health Service (PHS) strongly supports the program for eradication of cannabis in the Foreign Western Hemisphere Nations."

And on December 21, 1983, a Public Notice appeared, signed by Dominick DiCarlo, assistant secretary for international narcotics matters, stating that the United States would once again "support efforts of foreign Western Hemisphere nations to eradicate cannabis by applying the herbicide paraquat." DiCarlo further pointed out that

> the overall benefits of using paraquat would significantly outweigh the potential problems of the herbicide. The possible risk of paraquat lung damage to drug users is virtually nonexistent. On the other hand, the overall public health benefit of a marijuana reduction program is very great. We estimate that marijuana supplies from foreign countries may be permanently reduced by as much as 60–70 percent if herbicide eradication is conducted. This represents an aggregate public health benefit in itself. Further, as with any commodity, reduced supplies results in higher prices. This would be particularly important with regard to school children who would be less likely to afford a drug price increase. Additionally, reduction in crime and law enforcement efforts to control marijuana trafficking should also result from a paraquat program.

Since our government was now so officially enthusiastic about funding other countries who wished to spray their cannabis crops with paraquat, it was obvious that we should set an example ourselves.

DEA examined the proposed use of paraquat to control marijuana on public lands in the United States and concluded that the spraying program would have no significant impact on the human environment. Therefore, DEA concluded that the National Environmental Policy Act did not require the preparation of an Environmental Impact Statement on this proposed program, especially in view of the fact that the State Department had recently prepared two Environmental Impact Statements on the use of paraquat to eradicate cannabis in the Western Hemisphere. Furthermore, DEA's proposed program contained detailed guidelines for the selection of appropriate target sites to minimize any possible adverse environmental impact. The guidelines also required that all cannabis plants large enough to be harvested would be destroyed—thus eliminating any chance that contaminated marijuana could reach pot smokers.

On August 12, 1983, the DEA sprayed seventy cannabis plants in the Chattahoochee National Forest in Georgia, using 1.5 pounds of paraquat. The matter made irate headlines in newspapers and news magazines, TV and radio newscasts across the nation.

A relatively few media sources did an accurate reporting job. One such was the *Atlanta Constitution*, which reported that 50,000 to 80,000 gallons of paraquat had been used on 312,000 acres of Georgia farmland in 1982 by backpack, vehicle, and aerial spraying, with no known ill effects.

Nonetheless, a Georgia citizen's group (North Georgia Citizens Opposed to Paraquat Spraying) filed a fifteen-million-dollar damage suit against the federal government, and a federal judge in Georgia issued a temporary restraining order prohibiting DEA from spraying any more cannabis plants in the Chattahoochee National Forest.

On August 19, 1983, the DEA moved on to Kentucky and sprayed 210 cannabis plants in Daniel Boone National Forest. All the plants were fifteen to eighteen feet high. This resulted in opposition and another lawsuit in Kentucky.

On August 31, 1983, NORML filed a lawsuit against DEA demanding an immediate halt to the spraying of paraquat to eradicate marijuana anywhere in the United States, together with thirty million dollars in punitive damages. NORML argued, among other things, that the spraying program constituted "a massive invasion of the constitutional and civil rights of plaintiff's members, including the right to be free of Cruel and Unusual Punishment and the Right of Privacy."

On that same day, the Sierra Club, a century-old environmentalist group with some 350,000 members, filed a lawsuit against DEA. It sought only to halt the spraying of marijuana on public lands.

Judge June Green of the U.S. District Court for the District of Columbia ordered that the NORML and the Sierra Club cases against DEA be consolidated. On September 13, 1983, Judge Green issued a temporary injunction preventing DEA from spraying paraquat to eradicate marijuana on public lands until a full hearing could be held. Settlement discussions followed between the Sierra Club, NORML, and the DEA. The result of this was that on November 8, 1983, a consent judgment was entered. DEA agreed not to use paraquat to eradicate marijuana on public lands until it had prepared an Environmental Impact Statement (EIS). NORML abandoned its claim for the thirty-million-dollar damages. (This settlement, in effect, resolved all questions raised in the Georgia and Kentucky lawsuits.)

In January 1984, the DEA undertook to prepare an Environmental Impact Statement on alternate methods of eradication of cannabis on federal lands, which ranged from fire to machetes, paraquat, and other herbicides.

On January 6, the government began the process for an EIS, starting with four "scoping sessions" (public meetings) in Atlanta, Georgia; Spokane, Washington; Denver, Colorado; and Washington, DC. At these four meetings, members of the public were given the opportunity to raise questions and express their views on herbicide spraying of marijuana on federal lands. After that, a private outside contractor selected to conduct the EIS made an extensive study of the situation, bearing in mind the questions and statements made at the scoping sessions. They then wrote a detailed report, to be made available to anyone wishing to comment on it. The EIS contractor then helped DEA to prepare a draft EIS which will be made available to the public for comments before it is finalized.

At the time this book went to press, the Environmental Impact Statement had not been completed. When completed, it will not be reviewed by any court unless someone files a new lawsuit challenging the accuracy of the EIS.

It should be noted that the EIS and Judge Green's ruling apply only to federal agencies and federal lands—states are not affected by it. Some states require environmental impact studies, and some don't. For example, in 1982, 3,262 cannabis plants in Florida's Red Bay area were sprayed with paraquat via trucks and backpack. NORML filed suit to try to stop the spraying program, claiming that an Environmental Impact Statement should have been prepared. A federal District Court judge in the District of Columbia rejected that claim, holding that Florida's spraying program was a state rather than a federal action and therefore the National Environmental Policy Act did not apply.

There was another side to the story of pot-growing on federal lands. On June 23, 1983, the U.S. Forest Service issued *its* assessment of the government's action in spraying paraquat on cannabis grown in national forests.

During 1982, about 6,000 cannabis cultivation sites were identified within the National Forests. These sites supported from 14 plants to 4,410 plants. Investigations indicate that cannabis is currently growing in most of the 155 National Forests. The popularity of the National Forests for this illegal activity is attributable to two facts: 1) many of the forests encompass remote areas and 2) because the forests are public lands, cannabis growers cannot be identified on the basis of land ownership.

The Forest Service's concerns regarding the cultivation of cannabis within the National Forests include 1) illegality of the activity and 2) safety of visitors and employees. Last year, more than 250 incidents were reported in which National Forest visitors and Forest Service employees were threatened by people suspected of growing or protecting cannabis plantations. These incidents ranged from the firing of warning shots to verbal harassment. Numerous booby traps and other security devices used by cannabis growers to protect their crops have also been encountered. Some of these devices could fatally injure anyone who inadvertently triggered them. Furthermore, as part of their cultivation activities, cannabis growers also use high concentrations of herbicides and pesticides, divert streams and destroy wildlife that might damage their crops. These activities can have serious negative impacts on the effective management of the National Forests.

The Forest Service believes the situation demands aggressive action. Enforcement agencies should eradicate cannabis using the most effective legal methods available, whether by mechanical means or by the use of herbicides.

An affidavit submitted to the U.S. District Court for the District of Columbia on September 7, 1983, presented further insights into the problem. Ernest V. Andersen, leader of law enforcement in fiscal and accounting management in the Washington, DC, office of the Forest Service, noted that not only had there been a dramatic increase in the use of the national forests to grow cannabis illicitly over the past three years, but "there has been an even more dramatic influence on visitors to the National Forests and on Forest Service employees." He further pointed out that "the street value of these illicit crops is as much as $2,000 per plant or more. Due to this value, some growers take extreme measures of protection. These measures include armed guards, guard dogs, and various sabotage devices."

Other Forest Service officials, when testifying, had been more explicit about these sabotage devices, which included "a trip wire set to release an armed hand grenade, booby traps including fish hooks set at eye level, crowbars set to fire if a wire is tripped, punji sticks set in the ground, and rattlesnakes, some with rattles removed, to guard the cannabis plants." It was also pointed out at a July 1983 hearing held by the House Select Committee on Narcotics Abuse and Control that "the last seven murders in Humboldt County, California, were directly related to illegal farming of marijuana on national and state wilderness lands."

Forest Service officials also testified that "in 1980 there were reports from the Forest Service regions that the on-site danger was so great that public use was essentially excluded on 220,000 acres. By 1982 the acreage so impacted was reported to be 1,534,000."

But humans were not the only "users" of the national forests adversely affected by the cannabis growers. In his September 7, 1983, affidavit submitted to the U.S. District Court, for the District of Columbia, the Forest Service's Ernest Andersen noted:

> In addition to the direct social effects and long-term effects on the morale and productivity of Forest Service employees, substantial environmental damage is common. One example is . . . the placement of large quantities of rodenticides adjacent to the plants. . . . This outdoor placement of poisons designed only for indoor use allows the poisons to enter the soil and the food chain of wild carnivores. Another example is the heavy use of nitrogen fertilizers which leach into nearby streams. These super-rich streams produce substantial aquatic growth. This aquatic growth removes most of the dissolved oxygen from the streams, which kills the fish life. This problem is most severe in the West.

Forest Service officials in California pointed out that in some cases the rodenticides and pesticides used by the California growers to protect their cannabis crops had leached into nearby streams and had kept the salmon and steelhead from spawning.

In view of these factors, it seemed puzzling to some people that the Sierra Club, representing forest and wildlife lovers, should be connected with NORML in a lawsuit aimed at stopping paraquat spraying in national forest lands.

When asked about this on January 18, 1984, Denny Shaffer, president of the Sierra Club, stressed that "there was no relation at all between the Sierra Club and NORML."

> It's purely coincidental that we have a joint lawsuit—if, indeed, it *is* a joint lawsuit. This concern about aerial paraquat-spraying was generated from members of the organization, and the lawsuit was approved by our officers. Our involvement had to do with marijuana only in that it was a substance being sprayed in the national forests. Our objection was to aerial spraying of anything in the forests, for any reason, particularly since, in our judgment, the job could be done in more discriminating ways, by hand. Our concern is the effect the herbicide would have on other plants, animals, and/or humans.

When asked about the pesticides and rodenticides being used by the marijuana growers in national forests, and their effects on the spawning of salmon and steelhead, as well as wildlife, Mr. Shaffer said, "If the assumption is correct, we would not feel good about that either."

Dr. Carlton Turner summed up the paraquat-spraying situation: "I'm disappointed that a great hue and cry occurs only when we attempt to get

323

rid of a weed that threatens to destroy our society. When the red herrings are sorted out, paraquat is not the issue; marijuana is."

Attacking the Demand

"We must," said Carlton Turner,

attack both supply and demand; take the customers away from the drug dealers, as well as take drugs away from the customers. We want to institutionalize prevention in the private sector; get people involved on their own, so that the prevention efforts are lasting and, no matter who is in the White House, the commitment to and the momentum of drug-abuse prevention will continue.

As we will see, this aspect of the federal strategy has resulted in effective prevention programs, ranging in diversity from the involvement of national sports associations to a national program featuring an excellent antidrug comic book for grade-school children—one that does not occasion sneers and smirks, as prior efforts along these lines were wont to do.

The federal strategy has three parts aimed at reducing use from the demand side: education and prevention, detoxication and treatment, and research. In this chapter we will deal chiefly with the education and prevention section.

The strategy calls for a major organizational effort within each state to develop and coordinate a statewide prevention effort. The program developed by the state of Texas is used as an outstanding example that can serve as a model for other states (see Chaptei 21). Each state governor is urged to identify and use community leaders to advise and assist with drug- and alcohol-abuse prevention and control activities in their states. Governors, it was hoped, could—and would—serve as a focal point for developing initiatives and supporting volunteer activities in the private sector.

In the final section of this chapter we will discuss the federal approach of turning over federal funds for drug-abuse treatment, prevention, and early intervention programs so that each state can have far more control over how and where these funds are spent. Because of this so-called block grant program, NIDA's prevention budget was cut back from $16 million in 1981 (prior to the block grants) to about $832,000 in 1983 (the $16 million was put into the block grant program). NIDA still issues such informational aids as booklets, leaflets, and film strips. In 1983 it launched a new program called "Just Say No," with radio and television public service announcements (PSAs), newspaper and magazine print ads, posters, buttons, pamphlets, and ads in transit stations. The campaign is targeted in large part at marijuana and aims to motivate young people to "just say no" when a drug is offered to them. In 1983 NIDA also produced a program called "It's a FACT . . . Pot Hurts," aimed at youngsters ages eleven to thirteen. This nationwide campaign includes posters and booklets on the negative social and health effects of marijuana, as well as PSAs featuring kids telling other kids why "pot hurts."

However, according to Dr. Jean Paul Smith, NIDA's deputy associate director for science, "NIDA's principal activity now is to initiate and fund research on drugs that are related to the dependence process." In fiscal year 1980 NIDA spent $4.118 million for marijuana research, 10 percent of its total research budget. In FY 1981 it was $4.88 million (12 percent); for FY 1983 it was $4.754 million (11 percent). "In our marijuana research," says Smith, "the major area of our concern is the consequences of long-term chronic use of the drug."

ACTION

The federal agency that has come to the fore in the area of prevention is ACTION, which aids and stimulates the concept of volunteerism. ACTION has existed for many years, but its drug prevention program was just set up in 1981 as a new initiative by the agency's director, Tom Pauken.

There are two major thrusts to the ACTION prevention program. The first is to help support national drug-information resource centers. PRIDE (Parent Resource Institute for Drug Education) is ACTION's major grant recipient. This includes support for some of PRIDE's staff, including the youth coordinator who provides drug-abuse information for youth throughout the country, and helps them form groups for drug-free youth, which are now emerging in many states. ACTION also funds some of PRIDE's resource material and their national toll-free number (800–241–9746), so that anyone can call at any time and receive up-to-date information on drug research as well as material on how to form a parent group for drug-free youth. (The number is *not* an emergency hotline for parents whose children are having problems with drugs.)

ACTION gives an annual grant to Families in Action (no "relation") to maintain its Drug Information Center, which contains over a hundred thousand documents, and to publish *Drug Abuse Update*, a quarterly publication that abstracts current information collected at the center (see Resource list). ACTION has also given grants to the American Council for Drug Education, enabling them, for example, to publish nine brochures on marijuana and one on cocaine (see Resource list).

ACTION's second major thrust is to encourage the statewide networking of parent groups for drug-free youth. Said Brian Vogt, special assistant to the director, "In each state we try to fund what the parent groups need most—which can differ in each case. For example, in 1983 we gave a grant of about twenty-five thousand dollars to PAN (Parents in Action in Nebraska) in North Platte. They set up a network, emphasizing the organizing of new parent groups in rural areas of the state."

ACTION does not give grants to individual parent groups. "We don't have the funding for this," says Vogt. "Therefore, we concentrate on helping established groups who are networking their state."

On March 22, 1982, ACTION sponsored a first-of-its-kind day-long program at the White House, hosted by Nancy Reagan. Some three hundred leaders of private-sector/national organizations and businesses attended the White House briefing on "Drug Use and the Family." Some of these leaders became actively involved in the drug prevention area as a direct result of the White House briefing. One of the most effective and far-reaching of the programs that had its genesis at the briefing was:

Pharmacists Against Drug Abuse (PADA)

Among the corporate leaders who attended the White House briefing was Jack O'Brien, president of McNeil Pharmaceutical, one of the nation's leading research-oriented pharmaceutical manufacturers. He was so moved by the facts and information presented that day by Carlton Turner and others and so impressed by the magnitude of the problem that before he left the White House he promised Nancy Reagan that "McNeil Pharmaceutical would do something." And it did.

In November 1982, it started a program entitled Pharmacists Against Drug Abuse (PADA), which distributes through pharmacies a free brochure called "The Kinds of Drugs Kids Are Getting Into." This brochure focuses on marijuana, alcohol, and cocaine and also includes a section on PCP which "is usually smoked in tobacco or marijuana cigarettes—which is why it is sometimes sold as 'superpot.' "

In addition, the brochure contains some answers to these pertinent questions: "Can You Spot a Kid Who's Getting into Drugs?" and "What Can a Parent Do?"

During the program's first year, PADA spread throughout New England as a pilot project for the nation.

Pharmacists are experts on drugs, and as communities became aware of this source of local expertise, pharmacists were invited to speak at local meetings. The problem was, however, that although they could speak on all manner of legal drugs—including legal drugs used illegally—most pharmacists knew very little about illegal drugs. PADA responded to this need in two ways. The first was a twenty-page publication with accompanying slides, developed and written by Albert P. Catalbo, McNeil Pharmaceutical's director of professional pharmacy relations, titled *Pharmacists Against Drug Abuse: Speeches for Adult and Youth Audiences.* The speeches for both youth and adult audiences begin with the same sentence: "What if I were to tell you that thirty million Americans between the ages of twelve and twenty-five are guinea pigs in an experiment where they are given a potent drug that has immediate, serious effects on their health—and is suspected of having still more serious long-term effects? . . . That drug, of course, is marijuana." The ten pages on pot that follow are well-researched, well-presented, and eminently accurate.

This presentation, funded by McNeil Pharmaceutical, is available free of charge from state pharmaceutical associations. Also available from the same sources, and also free, is *A Pharmacist's Guide to Drug Abuse,* which focuses on marijuana, alcohol, cigarettes, and cocaine, with a six-page section on other drugs, and a six-page section headed "What Can I Do?" with specific suggestions for groups including pharmacists, parent groups, civic groups, and senior citizens.

On April 27, 1984, the PADA program was launched nationwide. Every one of the retail pharmacies in the United States—independents and chains—received a free packet from the PADA Foundation, founded and, to a large extent, funded by McNeil Pharmaceutical and their parent organization, Johnson & Johnson. The packet contained a fifty-page manual to raise the pharmacist's level of expertise on drugs of abuse, both illicit and licit, from cigarettes to heroin; a kit consisting of 150 brochures and a letter from Al Catalbo explaining the program. Initial distribution was 8.25 million brochures, and an additional 17 million went to pharmacy wholesalers so that pharmacies could replenish their free supply. The kit also contained a counter display easel, a window banner, four camera-ready print ads, and two "pocket savers" for ball-point pens which read, ASK ME ABOUT DRUG ABUSE. In addition, a description of this first-of-its-kind nationwide program appeared in all pharmaceutical trade journals and, in May 1984, all major radio and television stations in the United States received a public service announcement, funded by PADA featuring actor Michael Landon, national spokesperson for PADA, to inform the public that the free brochures were now available in all pharmacies.

Says Catalbo:

PADA encourages pharmacists who are becoming active in the community to speak with local police narcotics officers and enforcement officers, school principals, teachers and school nurses, drug and alcohol abuse counselors, and emergency room personnel in order to gain a more complete understanding of the problems that exist in that particular community, so they can personalize their presentation when they speak before groups.

A 1983 survey in the New England area, where McNeil first introduced its program, showed that about one in ten pharmacists who received PADA material became further involved in community efforts to reverse the local tide of youth drug abuse. In some communities pharmacists are now teaching drug education programs in the local school system.

The National Sports Drug and Alcohol Education Program

In February 1982 Dr. Carlton Turner and Joe Band, special assistant to the deputy assistant U.S. Attorney General, decided to try to bring all the national professional sports organizations together under one umbrella organization with the logo "Team Up Against Drugs." The program they planned would use drug-free athletes with high visibility to project a positive role model for young people—and adults.

On December 16, 1982, commissioners and representatives of the major sports organizations in the United States met with President and Mrs. Reagan, Carlton Turner, and Joe Band in the State Room of the White House. Among those represented were the National Hockey League (NHL), the National Basketball Association (NBA), National Football League (NFL), the United States Football League (USFL), U.S. Tennis and Lawn Association, Professional Golf Association (PGA), National American Soccer League, Major Indoor Soccer League, and Ladies' Professional Golf Association (LPGA).

Mark Murphy of the NFL Washington Redskins and Julius "Doc" Irving of the NBA Philadelphia 76ers were named co-chairmen of the National Sports Drug and Alcohol Education Program.

In January 1983 NFL Commissioner Pete Rozelle and Mrs. Reagan filmed a thirty-second television public service announcement aired during halftime of Superbowl XVII. This kicked off the Team Up Against Drugs campaign nationwide. On December 17, 1983, at halftime during the New York Giants–Washington Redskins game, Redskins' owner Jack Kent Cooke presented Joyce Nalepka, senior vice president of the National Federation of Parents for Drug-Free Youth (NFP) with a check for forty thousand dollars from NFL Charities to provide initial funding for NFP's national speakers' bureau, and—not incidentally—to provide NFP with invaluable publicity, for the presentation was made before an estimated thirty million television viewers. (By early 1984 the new NFP/Nancy Reagan Speakers' Bureau was providing speakers for national, state, and local conferences, in-service teacher training, consultants to community groups in prevention efforts, awareness meetings and workshops—and to talk to students.) And in 1983 Topps Chewing Gum, Inc., put "Team Up Against Drugs!" on fifteen million bubble-gum wrappers.

The Keebler Comics Program

Inspired by the *Weekly Reader* national survey that showed that one-quarter of our fourth-graders felt peer pressure to smoke pot, the White House Drug Abuse Policy Office and Keebler/DC Comics decided to try to address the problem in a comic book for fourth-, fifth-, and sixth-graders, plus a Teacher's Guide with an introduction by Dr. Carlton Turner.

The thirty-two-page comic book "The New Teen Titans" is replete with examples of the not-so-comic results that can come from youth drug abuse.

Exciting and involving, "The New Teen Titans" incorporates solid information on the health hazards of marijuana and other drugs. The back page contains a declaration to remain drug-free, complete with spaces for signatures by the reader and a witness, plus a separate "Certificate of Heroism, awarded to _____ , for participation in the President's Drug Awareness Program," signed by Nancy Reagan.

In 1983 the Department of Education sent a million copies of "The New Teen Titans" free to thirty-five thousand elementary schools, and Keebler/DC Comics distributed another million copies free to fourth-, fifth-, and sixth-graders throughout the nation.

It obviously takes more than a comic book to help a child say no and continue to say no to the peer pressure he or she will continually experience in junior high and high school. In some states the prevention and early intervention segments of the federal block grant program are helping to fill the knowledge vacuum about the health hazards of drugs; accurate information has been found one of the most important factors in giving a youngster the strength to remain drug-free.

In the final segment of this chapter let us look at an all-important part of the federal strategy, which operates in the area of reducing the demand.

The Block Grant Program

There is much confusion about this program, on the part of both its adherents and its adversaries. Much of the confusion emanates from the inaccurate understanding of the figures involved. Since these programs are now responsible for most of the prevention, early intervention, and treatment programs in each of the states, it is important to understand how the "dollar pie" is divided. (At least it is important if you are a member of a parent group or other organization concerned with drug abuse.)

In the 1970s, the federal government developed a system of statewide drug- and alcohol-abuse services, and state prevention coordinators were placed in almost every state and territory. (See Appendix for addresses of state prevention coordinators.) Most of the funding for these programs came from the federal government—replete with federal specifications on where and how this money was to be spent, and multiple federal reporting requirements.

In 1981, this money was, in effect, turned over to the states in block grants. This did not mean that each state was free to spend its block grant money how and where it wished within the state; it meant that states now assumed official responsibility for many of the functions they were already carrying out. And it meant that each state had more flexibility to target funds to specific areas. The federal thinking was that states were in a better position than the federal government to determine their own needs in the substance-abuse and mental health areas, and to respond accordingly.

However, to assure that, for example, a governor who was intensely interested in alcohol abuse should not decimate the drug-abuse and mental health programs by channeling a disproportionate amount of money into the alcohol programs, Congress put strictures on the dispensation of the dollars. In 1982, the first year the block program went into full operation, the amount given each state by the federal government was proportionately based on what the federal government had been spending in that state in the three separate areas of alcohol, drug abuse, and mental health in pre–block grant years.

The law specified that a state could not spend less than 35 percent of the total alcohol/drug fund on either its alcohol- or drug-abuse programs. They could spend more than 35 percent, but not less. This meant, for example, that a state given forty million dollars in its block grant from the federal government, of which twenty million dollars had to be allocated to its mental health programs because of the pre–block grant formula for dividing the pie, would have twenty million for its alcohol- and drug-abuse programs. Of this, it could spend as much as 65 percent, or thirteen million, on its drug-abuse programs—which meant that it would have the minimum 35 percent of the alcohol/drug fund for its alcohol programs.

The law further specified that of the money spent for alcohol or for drugs, 20 percent had to be spent on prevention or early intervention. (Therefore, in our hypothetical case, at least $2.6 million would be spent on drug abuse prevention and early intervention.)

The law provided that, starting in 1984, the states have some discretionary power to take up to 15 percent of their total block grant allocations and retarget it to alcohol, drug abuse, or mental health programs. For example, if a state has a pressing need for more money to aid in the drug abuse area, it is entitled to take some of the money from the alcohol and/or mental health programs. The remaining 85 percent of the dollar pie still has to be allocated according to the formula noted above.

There is another way further dollars can be directed to a crisis area. The alcohol, drug abuse, and mental health block grant is only one of three block grants each state receives for health services. The other two are preventive health and health services, and primary care (which includes, for example, community health centers). The law allows each state to take up to 7 percent of any block grant allocation and shift it to any other block grant.

According to an official in the Department of Health and Human Services who deals with the three block grant programs daily:

Although most states receive less total dollars than they had before the block grant program went into effect, they have more freedom now in allocating these dollars. Also, they are freed from the multiple federal reporting requirements, and freed from numerous federal program requirements that had previously restricted the number and type of programs that could have received federal dollars. The evidence we have indicates that, although states wish there was more money coming in from the federal government, on the whole they like the block grant program.

President Reagan put it like this:

By 1988, the States will be in complete control of over 40 federal grant programs. . . . We will be establishing a realignment that will end cumbersome administration and spiraling costs at the federal level, while we insure that these programs will be more responsive to both the people they are meant to help, and the people who pay for them.

A Closing Quote

At the start of her campaign against youth drug abuse, some suggested that Nancy Reagan's involvement was purely political—a public relations gesture to give her a more positive image. But such comments are rarely heard from those who have heard her speak on the subject. And many millions *have* heard her—on television programs ranging from a week-long series on youth drug abuse, which she co-hosted on *Good Morning America,* to "The Chemical People," a two-hour program she hosted, which was seen on PBS stations throughout the nation as well as at some ten thousand town meetings, where local people gathered to form task forces to address the problem in their community. In addition, thousands have heard her in person as she travels to many corners of the country to visit treatment centers, and to speak to parents, teachers, drug treatment professionals—and children. She has probably become the single person most recognized by the American public as having sounded the alarm about youth drug abuse. Her sincerity, her concern are obvious. She minces no words. "We are in danger," she says, "of losing a whole generation of our children to the drug culture."

The following sentences, often used by Mrs. Reagan, are apt ones with which to close this chapter on the federal strategy, for they make one tragic aspect tellingly clear: Despite the fact that this administration has done more than any other in combating drug abuse from both the supply and the demand sides; despite the fact that many new approaches, such as the twelve task forces, are operating effectively; despite the fact that Americans are beginning to wake up and realize that we have a dangerous drug problem that must be addressed—still we are only at the beginning of the battle.

Mrs. Reagan puts the drug-abuse crisis in these words:

> Right now, it is like one of those dread diseases for which there is no cure. It crosses all boundaries. Rich and poor are not immune; neither are the educated or non-educated, black or white. Drugs have invaded the cities and suburbs all across America, as well as the rural areas. No section of our country is safe from the threat. And the victims are getting younger all the time. No one can assure any longer that it is always someone else's child who is on drugs.

But, after accurately outlining the grim picture, Nancy Reagan often ends a speech with these words:

"I come here today to thank you for what you are accomplishing. And to tell you to hang in there—together we will make it!"

Chapter 17

Marijuana
Detection Tests

There is one important ingredient in the prevention section of the federal strategy, in the armed forces' War on Drugs, and in the struggle of parents to bring up children drug-free. This is the ability to test chemically for marijuana use. As the understanding of the health hazards of this drug increases, so does interest in methods of determining pot use. It is therefore important to look at the various approaches science has come up with in this area. Let us look first at the underlying factors we must understand before examining the specific marijuana detection tests now available.

Currently there are three types of detection tests on the market: urine tests, blood tests, and a saliva test.

Only the blood and saliva tests can determine recent use, because it takes several hours for the metabolites of THC and other cannabinoids to get from the lungs to the urine. In addition, because of the fat-solubility factor, cannabinoids and their metabolites are continually being released back into the bloodstream. Therefore, a person may show pot positive on a urine detection test because he or she has smoked a joint on the average of two to three days prior to the test. The nearer to the time of pot-smoking that the test is taken, the more likely it is to show positive. After two to four days, the test is still likely to show positive, but in some cases it can show positive up to two weeks later or more, depending on the strength of the joint, on how much the person chronically smokes, metabolism, and other factors.

The reason cannabinoids *can* show up in the urine in two hours is this: Not all of them and their metabolites are "absorbed" by the fatty sections of the cells and by fatty organs. After each joint is smoked, a small percentage of the THC is carried in the bloodstream to the liver, where enzymes transform it into many metabolites. The most prevalent of the delta-9 metabolites is

9-carboxy-THC, which is detectable in the blood for many hours, much longer than the THC itself. This and other metabolites are turned by the liver into a conjugate—a water-soluble complex that is then excreted, mostly in the feces, but about one-third in the urine.

The marijuana detection tests based on blood samples are, however, quite another matter. Delta-9-THC shows up in the blood as soon as one starts smoking a joint. Levels sink in four to six hours. But, as THC levels are sinking, the levels of THC metabolites—9-carboxy-THC and others—are slowly rising in the blood. Therefore, blood tests *can* ascertain marijuana use for several hours after a joint has been smoked. Indeed, if you see delta-9-THC itself in the blood, it probably means use at least within the past two to four hours, because after that THC is detectable only by very sensitive research methods.

As for the saliva test, it can only detect the THC up to three to five hours after the person has smoked, depending on food and drink intake.

At present, none of the detection tests can accurately test impairment levels. Consequently, none can be used as a roadside test for the marijuana-impaired driver—except as circumstantial evidence, as we will see later in this chapter.

Let us examine the various types of tests, the legal implications of testing for marijuana use, and, finally, those areas in which the urine test in particular is being, or can be, used with greatest benefit. It should be noted that the ability to detect marijuana use in its earliest stages means it can be found at the time when treatment can be most successful and least costly, and damage can be held to a minimum.

Types of Tests

The GC/MS

Gas chromotography/mass spectrometry (GC/MS, or simply "mass spec") was developed in the early seventies and is the most sensitive test now available. It can be used for many body fluids and tissues, including both blood and urine, and can detect cannabinoids at less than 1 nanogram per milliliter—1 ng/ml. (A nanogram is a millionth of a gram. A milliliter is a thousandth of a liter.)

Because of its extreme sensitivity, the GC/MS blood test comes close to being able to ascertain impairment and/or intoxication—since it can indicate the levels of 1 ng/ml on up to many hundreds. Presumably, the more delta-9-THC, the greater the impairment.

However, the GC/MS equipment usually costs as much as fifty thousand dollars and can be as much as half a million dollars. Also, the test must be done by a well-trained technician. Each sample costs about thirty dollars or more to analyze. Because of its expense, the GC/MS is rarely used as a first-time test. It is used in research, by medical examiners, and for corroboration purposes in the case of tests already classified as "pot positive."

Radioimmunoassay (RIA)

The radioimmunoassay (RIA) technique was developed in the late 1960s. It evolved when scientists were able to generate antibodies to specific substances and combine them with a radioactive tracer for those substances. The RIA for THC is based on immunochemical recognition of a cannabinoid metabolite. (*Immunochemical* means identifying a chemical substance through immunological means.) In this case, RIA uses an antibody most strongly directed toward the delta-9-THC metabolite, 9-carboxy acid. This is the metabolite usually found in the highest concentration in the body, and it stays in the body much longer than the THC cannabinoid itself.

The RIA technique is for both blood and urine testing, and these tests are now marketed by several companies; among these is Roche Diagnostics Systems, a division of Hoffman La Roche of Nutley, New Jersey, one of the largest pharmaceutical companies in the world. In 1982, it began marketing an RIA kit to detect cannabinoids in the urine.

The Roche Abuscreen for Cannabinoids (often called the Roche RIA) utilizes the radioactive isotope of iodine. For each urine screen there are three vials, each containing a different reagent (a radioactive chemical tag). One contains the antibody to 9-carboxy-THC. The second contains the radioactive isotope labeled "THC metabolite." The two are added in measured amounts in a test tube, where they will combine chemically; then the sample of the person's urine is added. If the urine contains the THC metabolite, it also combines with the antibody, competing with the radioactive-labeled metabolite. Measuring the amount of competitive reaction that takes place when the third reagent is added will provide a direct measure of the quantity of metabolites present in the person's sample. But this does not mean that the Roche RIA (or any other immunological test) can test for intoxication, or that it can be directly correlated with degree of use. For example, a sample taken from an occasional user immediately after he or she has smoked a joint may have a higher level than a sample from a chronic user whose urine was taken many hours after last smoking a joint.

The manufacturer claims that the sensitivity of the Roche Abuscreen for Cannabinoids is five nanograms per milliliter. Also according to the manufacturer, all clinical trials have shown excellent correlation of results between the Abuscreen and the highly sensitive GC/MS. Indeed, the manufacturer claims virtually 100 percent accuracy for the test itself. However, Roche recommends that a confirmation test be used when the situation concerns a decision such as job jeopardy, to rule out the possibility of human, methodology, or other error.

All four services of the armed forces use the Abuscreen for Cannabinoids as their primary screen in the laboratories. The military has elected to use a cutoff of 100 ng/ml to eliminate any possible claim of interference from passive inhalation as well as to provide a high degree of correlation with the GLC (gas liquid chromotography), which, at the time the 100 ng/ml decision was made, was the confirmatory test in use (it has a sensitivity of 25–30 ng/ml).

Note: The typical NIDA joint of 2 percent THC produces blood levels of about 50 ng/ml about fifteen minutes after smoking, and urine levels from 50 to several hundred ng/ml several hours after smoking. Detectable levels of the NIDA joint may appear in the urine for several days after smoking, depending on the analysis method used.

Although the military uses it qualitatively (for a yes or no answer), the Abuscreen for Cannabinoids is being used by others, such as clinical facilities, quantitatively, to determine how many metabolites are present. (The Abuscreen user has the alternative of selecting a lower cutoff.)

The Roche Abuscreen for Cannabinoids costs about $1.50 per test. It requires a trained technician to perform the procedure, which must be done in a laboratory. Most laboratories and many hospitals already have the equipment for doing Abuscreen testing for other drugs. The same equipment is used for the Abuscreen for Cannabinoids. The price of the basic equipment varies from several hundred dollars to ten thousand dollars or more, depending on the degree of automation desired.

Syva's EMIT Cannabinoid Assays

In 1979 another method was developed, also based on antibodies; this system, unlike the Roche RIA, uses an enzyme label rather than a radioactive tracer. Called the EMIT Cannabinoid Assay, it was designed for existing Syva instruments already widely used in hospitals and laboratories for detecting therapeutic drugs and also a number of illicit drugs (such as cocaine and opiates) in urine and blood serum. (Syva has been in the drug detection business since 1972.)

The EMIT system comes in two forms. The instrument system called Syva Drug Screening System (sometimes known as the EMIT d.a.u.), which costs in various degrees of automation from six thousand to twenty thousand dollars, contains the instrumentation to run the EMIT chemistry. The cost of each individual marijuana test using this system is a dollar-fifty to two dollars.

Syva also has a portable system called the EMIT/ST Drug Detection System, for physicians or technicians initially trained by a Syva representative. This easy-to-use instrument, small enough to fit into an attache case, costs about thirty-three-hundred dollars. It can detect opiates, diazepam (Valium), PCP, barbiturates, methaqualone, amphetamines, methadone, ethyl alcohol—and cannabinoids. It prints out individual results in ninety seconds. Each test costs about three dollars.

According to the manufacturer, Syva's sensitivity range is similar to that of the Roche RIA (the Abuscreen). Also, according to the manufacturer, both the EMIT assays have a greater than 99 percent reliability rating.

The Immunalysis RIAs

These tests were developed by Dr. Stanley Gross and his associates in Glendale, California. Separate kits are available to detect marijuana in either blood or urine. The RIA blood test was approved by the FDA in October 1979. The Immunalysis urine test was approved by FDA in January 1984. According to the manufacturer, both tests can measure concentrations of cannabinoids or their metabolites in blood or urine to a level of 5 ng/ml. As we have seen, urine levels are not related to impairment; they merely indicate presence. But a positive THC blood level probably indicates recent use, since after two to four hours the THC itself is metabolized and is no longer detectable. It may be said, therefore, that *THC is the key* to recent use.

The equipment needed for both the Immunalysis urine and blood tests can be found in virtually all hospital and forensic labs that have RIA equipment for routine tests for drugs and hormones. The price for both blood and urine tests range from ten dollars to thirty dollars.

The Saliva Test

This test was also developed by Dr. Gross and Dr. Emory Zimmerman, professors of anatomy at UCLA, and by their associates Dr. James Soares and Dr. James Grant. When this book went to press, the test had no trade-marked name but was known rather formally as the Non-Invasive Test for Recent Use of Marijuana.

Urine tests are noninvasive, but, as noted, cannot test for recent use. The saliva test, however, can *only* test for recent use. After five hours the saliva becomes negative for THC. However, even though the sample must be collected within five hours of use, the test itself can be done up to a week or more later.

The saliva test works like this: A cotton swab is rubbed on the tongue or elsewhere in the mouth. The "collection" is then liquefied in a test tube—a plastic inch-high vial filled with a solvent. This is taken to a laboratory and tested on the RIA equipment. Test results available within a few hours show whether the sample is positive or negative for THC.

This test, approved by FDA in the spring of 1983, is being marketed through Metpath in Teterboro, New Jersey. Before receiving FDA approval the test had been shown to be 100 percent accurate in field clinical trials: There were no false positives and no false negatives despite the fact that the researchers attempted to see if the results could be altered by medications, alcohol, and foods strong in acid such as pizza.

Dr. Gross hopes that ultimately the saliva test will evolve into a fluoro-metric roadside detection system that any police officer can use on the spot for a driver suspected of being marijuana-impaired. At present pot-high drivers sometimes take a quick sip of whiskey or beer so police will smell alcohol and take them in for a Breathalyzer test. When their blood alcohol content (BAC) reads .00, the impaired drivers are released—because the police now have no easy, inexpensive, accurate method of testing for recent marijuana use. One day the "pot saliva test" may take its place alongside the alcohol Breathalyzer, although at present it cannot ascertain degree of impairment.

Other researchers are currently investigating the marijuana-saliva tests. The saliva test offers the best chance for the development of a roadside presumptive screening test to let the officer know whether a blood test should be taken. At the present time, only the blood test can test for intoxication.

Nevertheless, the saliva test might one day be used to provide circumstantial evidence if the driver is found pot positive *and* fails the roadside dexterity test, *and* if an alcohol test shows a BAC well below the legal alcohol-impairment level. Also, the test might be used—as the alcohol Breathalyzer is now—for its "refusal factor." If an impaired driver, with other signs of marijuana use and/or impairment, refuses to take the "pot saliva test," this might be used in court as circumstantial evidence.

But there is no inexpensive marijuana roadside test even on the horizon that can do what the alcohol breath test and blood test can do—test impairment levels.

Meanwhile, marijuana detection tests—particularly urine tests—have important current applications in other areas, which we will examine along with the legal ramifications of their use. First, however, let us look at a few questions that crop up frequently concerning urine detection tests for marijuana.

Urine Testing: Q. and A.

Q. Can any of these tests be bought by private individuals?

A. No. Manufacturers of the various urine tests sell their products to licensed professional clinical laboratories. (There are some twelve thousand such labs in the United States, most of which are equipped to process one or more of the marijuana urine tests.) Manufacturers also sell to hospitals, physicians, law enforcement bodies, the armed forces, drug-abuse treatment centers, and so forth.

Q. What about passive inhalation?

A. The best systematic study done in this area was published by Dr. Mario Perez-Reyes at the University of North Carolina, in *Clinical Pharmacology and Therapeutics* in 1983. He put six subjects in a medium-sized station wagon with the windows tightly closed. Four were smoking pot (NIDA joints); the other two were not. The car was soon filled with pot smoke, and the six subjects remained in it for one hour. Result: The urine screens of the nonsmokers showed one cannabinoid positive just above 20 ng/ml in a specimen taken within four hours. The other was below 20 ng/ml.

The armed forces use a cutoff level of 100 ng/ml as registering positive; the workplace and other organizations usually use from 50 to 100 ng/ml. Readings below this are automatically classified as negative. Dr. Perez-Reyes commented:

> It is highly unlikely that in a real-life situation anyone would be in a car for one hour with the windows tightly closed while four others were smoking pot simultaneously. It was extremely uncomfortable for the subjects in my study to remain in the car for one hour. Even in a rock concert you are in a large auditorium with windows open and air moving. Thus, there would not be the concentration of marijuana smoke in the air that I achieved in my experiment. Consequently, claims that urines registering above 50 ng/ml are due to passive inhalation at rock concerts, at parties, etc., are erroneous.

In another but similar experiment, Dr. Perez-Reyes put subjects in a small room and exposed two nonusers to NIDA joints smoked by four pot smokers for one hour on three consecutive days. Only after three days of exposure did one of the nonusers show the same low pot-positive level as had been shown in the car experiment. But this level was found only at the first voiding after exposure. Subsequent voidings showed no positive cannabinoid readings among the nonsmokers.

Q. Can urine be diluted when the subject drinks quantities of liquid prior to a urine test?

A. According to some researchers, the answer is yes—when the cutoff level is as high as 100 ng/ml. In other screens, where the cutoff is lower, the answer, presumably, is no. In any event, the cannabinoids are most concentrated in the "first urine of the day."

Q. Is the 100 ng/ml level satisfactory?

A. According to Dr. Sidney Cohen, a noted marijuana researcher, the 100 ng/ml cutoff point is considered too high by some authorities, who recommend that it should be reduced to 20 or 50 ng/ml. However, it has the advantage of practically eliminating the possibility of a false positive. It is true that some people who have smoked recently will not be detected at this level, so that false negatives are likely. The 100 ng/ml level also rules out the possibility of the passive smoker's being found positive. For legal purposes it seems preferable to set the cutoff level a little higher than a little lower.

Q. What if the marijuana is swallowed?

A. Marijuana will begin to appear in the urine about sixty minutes later.

Q. Who shows higher levels in urine after smoking the same amount, the daily user or the infrequent user?

A. The daily user, partly due to more efficient smoking and partly due to fat-storage, which results in higher levels of cannabinoid metabolites in the urine.

Q. There has been controversy about the accuracy of urine testing. Has this been resolved?

A. For an answer to this prevalent question we turned to Dr. Robert Willette, former chief of the Research Technology Branch at NIDA, under whose auspices much of the marijuana detection research was done. Willette is now director of Duo Research, a division of Research Designs, Inc., Annapolis, Maryland, and currently serves as a consultant to business and government agencies in the area of urinalysis and drug research. Says Willette:

There is nothing unique about the assays currently available for cannabinoids. They all follow conventional methodologies, most of which have been available for other drugs for many years. The matter of testing is clearly an area where analytical chemistry and assay developers have been put to the test of public scrutiny. Because of the controversies that surround marijuana use, the assays in current use have not had the time to find universal acceptance. As their use is increased and additional experience and data are acquired, they should take their place with other routine assays.

The available evidence does support, however, that the various marijuana urine tests are sufficiently accurate and valid to be used when the proper precautions are followed.

Legal Implications of Urine Testing

With the development of rapid-response urine tests to identify the presence of opiates and certain other commonly abused drugs, the use of such tests became standard in much of the drug-abuse treatment industry and in parts of the criminal justice system. Indeed, federal methadone regulations *require* urine testing of program participants as a condition of federal funding. As more drug treatment clients were referred to treatment from the criminal justice system, often on the basis of "dirty" urines (containing evidence of illegal use of drugs), considerable attention was given to analyzing the legal implications of urine testing. As urine testing programs grew more numerous, there was general acknowledgment that they would be challenged and that the courts would decide the extent to which mandatory urine testing was permissible. Somewhat surprisingly, the expected legal challenges never materialized.

However, it is clear that the legality of urine testing for *marijuana* use is coming under intense scrutiny, and that it will vary depending on the extent and circumstances of the testing and the use made of information collected. In a conference on marijuana urine testing held in Bethesda, Maryland, in December 1980, Nancy Winstra, chief counsel at Michael Reese Hospital, summed up the legal perspective by pointing out that in determining the probable legality of any specific marijuana testing program, several aspects of the program must be analyzed. The questions to be asked, said Ms. Winstra, include:

• *Who is being tested?* Possible groups to be tested include persons arrested for a variety of crimes, including, where applicable, public inebriation or disorderly conduct; persons charged with various traffic offenses, including driving while intoxicated; probationers and parolees; school children; athletes; or virtually any other subgroup. The broader the net of testing extends, the more difficult it will be to support the legality of the program.

• *Who is doing the testing?* Testing could be done by law enforcement officials, public health officials, regulatory agencies, or others. The extent to which testing is done only by qualified individuals and under appropriate conditions will impact on the legality of any testing program.

• *Why is the testing being done?* Testing may be done to identify marijuana users for subsequent criminal or civil enforcement action; to identify candidates for treatment; to screen job applicants; to assess blame in vehicular accidents; to reduce accidents; or simply to obtain information on the extent of marijuana use. Testing to identify users, with no followup, raises ethical problems. Testing to refer to treatment is valid only if treatment is available and efficacious.

The applicability of several legal principles must be assessed to determine whether any particular testing program would be likely to withstand legal challenge. Ms. Winstra said the core issues are the following:

• *Privacy.* Although the Constitution does not explicitly mention any right of privacy, the protections of the Constitution have been held to extend to certain areas or "penumbras" of privacy. Wrongful intrusion into one's personal affairs and private activities constitutes an invasion of privacy. It is only when the individual's conduct begins to affect a third party or society at large that intervention into the "zone of privacy" becomes warranted.

• *Due process.* The due process clause of the Fourteenth Amendment requires that persons not be deprived of life, liberty, or property without due process of law. In order for a testing procedure to withstand a due-process challenge, it would be necessary that the tests be conducted in accordance with sound medical procedures and that the degree of bodily invasion be as minimal as possible under the circumstances. Based on the case of *Rochin* v. *California,* it is unlikely that requiring arrested individuals to provide voluntarily expelled urine specimens would violate the due-process clause.

• *Self-incrimination.* The courts have generally limited the protection against self-incrimination to testimonial evidence and have held that physical evidence, including body fluids, is not protected under the Fifth Amendment. The key case in this area is *Schmerber* v. *California.* On this basis it seems unlikely that courts would refuse to allow as evidence the fact that a defendant has refused to submit to chemical testing.

Other lawyers caution that despite the scientific advances and the promising future urine tests have for detecting drug abuse, the reliability of urine screens has yet to be firmly determined and accepted in the courts. They point out that the technology is still relatively new. No urine test now marketed claims to be 100 percent accurate, except in clinical tests. In actual use, lab equipment can malfunction. Technicians can make mistakes. No machine, no human, is infallible. Consequently, when jobs, careers, or reputations are at stake, total reliance should never be placed upon a urine test. Positive test results, they say, must always be combined with some additional proof of drug use before it is safe to conclude that someone uses illicit drugs.

Conclusion: The likelihood of withstanding a legal challenge will be greatest if the test program is narrowly drawn and its focus rehabilitative rather than punitive.

Now for a closer look at specific areas in which the marijuana urine test has thus far been used with notably positive results. (We will include a discussion of urine testing in the armed forces in Chapter 19.)

Use in the Criminal Justice System

Criminal justice systems, including those of Oregon, Missouri, and Alaska, are now using the marijuana urine test. But perhaps the most impressive results to date have been obtained in the town of Albany, Georgia, population 103,000. Albany is the center of a vast farming area; it is also a rail transportation hub, with an excellent industrial base. It is therefore typical, in many ways, of countless American towns.

In July 1980, Dan MacDougald, Jr., a lawyer who was then director of the Social Research Laboratories in Atlanta, was selected by ten Superior Court judges to serve as director of their new Advisory Council for Probation, a special agency created by the governor to help improve probation operations in Georgia. After finding out as much as he could about the new urine testing program for use in the armed forces, MacDougald adapted the program for civilian use in conjunction with special conditions of probation. He had long believed that if you want to improve the local crime picture, you must *improve the crime deterrents of probation,* and he saw the urine test as a possible deterrent tool—*if* judges tied urine testing into their probation contracts.

All judges in every state are empowered to write special stipulations

343

into their own probation contracts. "The judge," says MacDougald, "has the most effective deterrent power of anyone in the community. Furthermore, the stipulations in the probation contracts need not be applicable only to probationers, but to anyone out on bail or parole, or under a suspended sentence from a court without a probation department."

This can be quite a sizable population. MacDougald points out that the number of criminals carried on the state crime information systems is generally about 5 percent of a state's population. But at any given time, only one-tenth of the criminals in the state are in prisons or jails—which are badly overcrowded. This leaves about 90 percent of all convicted offenders free in our communities. And the large majority of these are placed on probation.

In Albany some twenty thousand court cases are processed each year (which does not mean, of course, that one in five Albany citizens go to court, since many cases are brought against the same individual). Albany's arrest figures are typical of those of any town its size.

On July 1, 1981—the same day that the armed forces initiated their new marijuana testing program—Albany initiated *its* program. Syva's EMIT equipment was installed in the sheriff's office, and a deputy sheriff was trained by Syva and assigned to do the urine testing. The key to the program was a clause in the probation contract authorizing revocation of probation if evidence of illegal drugs was found in the probationer's urine. Only pot was tested for in Albany, for two reasons: one, to save money, and two, because a program run in Albany in the mid-seventies had succeeded in getting heroin dealers and users out of town, leaving pot and cocaine as Albany's chief drugs of abuse. However, if other drugs were suspected, the probationer's urine sample was sent to the state crime lab for analysis.

According to the probation contract, the probationer must take the urine test whenever requested to do so by a probation officer or a law enforcement officer. If the urine shows pot positive the first time, the probationer can be put in jail for seven days. (MacDougald termed this "motivational therapy.") If the urine tested pot positive for a second time in sixty days, the sentence could be ninety days in jail. (This MacDougald called "detoxification therapy.") A third pot positive while on probation could mean prison for a term of years selected by the court, not to exceed the term of probation. The same formula was generally applied to other drugs of abuse. If the defendant disputed the results, the sample was sent to the state crime lab for substantiation by GC/MS or other chemical methods. (By January 1984, all positives had been substantiated.)

When the police and sheriff's log books were studied ten months after the program started, the percentage of those who were pot positive had dropped from 62.5, at the beginning of the program, to 17.9. Eight months later it dropped to 10.5 percent, where it stabilized. In the first eighteen months of the program, only two people were sent to prison as three-time losers.

There were other results. Crime dropped, particularly burglaries. For example, from February to June 1982, burglaries averaged 13 percent less than in the corresponding quarter for the three years prior to the pot/probation program. The program was applied only to felons (committers of major crimes), not to misdemeanants (minor offenses such as shoplifting and writing bad checks). Thus, the misdemeanants acted as a type of "control" in the experiment. The number of misdemeanors went up significantly from February to June 1982, but felony warrants of all types went down 42 percent during those same months, during which the pot/probation contract was being strictly enforced.

Furthermore, traffic department figures showed that Albany's DUI (driving under the influence) figures had dropped 23 percent in the first quarter of 1982, compared to the same quarter in 1981, before the pot/probation program started. In other areas of the state DUI figures had stayed the same or had risen during the same period. Also, when compared to the same period the previous year, traffic-related injuries declined 8.1 percent, DUI accidents declined 10.6 percent, and economic damage from traffic accidents declined 15.2 percent. During this period no additional special regulations concerning traffic safety or law enforcement had been implemented. (In September 1982, strong drunk driving laws were initiated, which increased the improvement still further.)

Another statistic attributed to the marijuana testing program was this: New cases coming to the mental health department declined 15 percent from the first half of 1981 to the corresponding period in 1982. Psychologist Wilber McCarty, the court diagnostician who delivers pre-sentence evaluations to the court and reports on the progress of correctional therapy, said that probationer-patients were "getting better faster. In fact, it looks as though there's an across-the-board community benefit resulting from the pot/probation enforcement program in Albany."

On January 19, 1984, a Syva company representative reported to the Dougherty County police (the borders of Albany and Dougherty County are identical) that "urine testing of probationers is becoming very, very popular in other areas, and it's all traceable to this program initiated by Albany, Georgia."

The pot/probation program cost Albany taxpayers about $8,000 in 1981 for the Syva EMIT equipment, and about $8,000 a year thereafter for test supplies and for the equipment maintenance contract. By the end of the first six months of the program, there was an economic reduction in traffic damage in Albany of $684,000 as calculated from a National Safety Council formula. And that was just one of the cost savings to the community during that period.

Because of the success of the program, in October 1983 the probation contract for burglars was expanded to include two other elements: 1) the urine test would now be used in conjunction with a Psychological Stress Evaluator (PSE), which differed from the simple polygraph ("lie detector") test in that it was used as a rehabilitative teaching instrument for the offender, and 2) court-ordered disulfiram (Antabuse) for those with an alcohol problem. (Burglar-probationers who did not take the disulfiram on time—as administered by the County Health Department—were sent to jail for seven days under the stipulations of the probation contract.)

The results of this triple-threat probation program aimed at burglars: As noted in a report made January 19, 1984, by Albany's Chief Judge Asa B. Kelley, chairman of the state's Advisory Council on Probation, to the governor, burglary arrests dropped 74 percent, and the jail population dropped 51 percent from April 1982 to January 1984, "obviating," as Kelley put it, "the necessity for a new $10,000,000 to $12,000,000 jail facility which had been planned because of overcrowding." The Albany jail is no longer over-crowded.

In addition, in December 1983, Dr. Richard Anson, director of research at the Criminal Justice Institute at Albany State University, evaluated the results of Albany's tri-faceted Burglar Probation Program. He selected four Georgia counties as a control group. Dougherty (i.e., Albany's) County burglary figures were well below those of the control counties. Furthermore, in January 1984 the State Probation Department figures revealed that new reported crimes by Dougherty County probationers had dropped 34 percent in fiscal year 1983, compared to FY 1982. However, for the state at large there was 37 percent *increase* in reported new crimes by probationers!

"What works in Albany, Georgia," said Dan MacDougald,

> could work in any other town or community (though it may not work in large urban areas)—if all probationers were on a computer, and if every probation contract involved the automatic right to test the urine of any probationer, and to revoke probation for illegal use of drugs. In communities in which drugs other than pot are the prevailing problem,

the same urine testing equipment, for a few dollars more per test, can test for other commonly used illegal drugs, and for a variety of legal drugs which are often used illegally.

I've been working in this area since 1967, and these special conditions of probation enforced by the police provide the first genuine hope I've seen. This program can make a real impact in rehabilitating convicted criminals and in reduction of crime in communities.

Use in Drug Treatment Programs

Dr. Herbert Kleber, professor of psychiatry at Yale Medical School and director of the substance abuse treatment unit of the Connecticut Mental Health Center, gave this overview of uses and contributions of the urine pot test in drug treatment programs:

Therapeutic communities in general have condemned marijuana use, and forbidden it among their patients. It is, of course, difficult in treatment programs to forbid behavior where transgressions cannot be monitored with some regularity and where it is often an accident if the abuse in question is detected. Forbidden behavior, if constantly practiced, tends to create a climate of disrespect for the rules of the organization in general, as well as creating a climate of unfairness for the occasional individual who gets caught and who can rightfully say that he or she is being a scapegoat because many other people are doing the forbidden behavior.

The presence of a reliable, inexpensive, and easily performed test for marijuana changes this picture. Many residential therapeutic communities find the urine testing technique a useful tool to enforce the prohibition they already believe in. Residents can be checked for marijuana use after weekend passes or trips into the community.

Regarding outpatient adolescent programs, current indices of use indicate that most of their clients will use marijuana at least occasionally and a substantial number on a regular basis. The urine test makes it possible for programs to detect such use. Marijuana will become an additional proscribed drug and transgressions will have to be dealt with by the therapeutic regimen.

Use by Pediatricians

Dr. Donald Ian Macdonald of Clearwater, Florida, former president of the Florida Pediatric Society, has been a practicing pediatrician for eighteen years. At the time this book went to press, he had been nominated as President Reagan's appointee to be head of the federal Alcohol, Drug Abuse and Mental Health Administration (ADAMHA), which is the parent agency of NIDA, the National Institute of Alcohol and Alcoholism, and the National Institute of Mental Health. Macdonald is also one of the first pediatricians in the country to have used the EMIT Cannabinoid assay on a regular basis. He found he could often skip a whole series of steps in diagnosing many of his patients by using the urine test. Says Macdonald,

> The ones that I'd been missing were the kids brought in by their parents because they were chronically fatigued. And I was testing them for mono, for anemia, for hepatitis; or there was the kid with cough, sore throat, red eyes, and I went through the whole business of chest X rays, sinus X rays, nasal decongestents—and never once thought that this twelve-year-old was smoking pot. But with the urine test I could say, "I don't know if this is the cause of his symptoms, but I would suspect that it's related because he sure is showing pot positive urines."

Macdonald found that in terms of diagnosis, the marijuana urine test is "as valuable as a whole load of other tests that we do routinely."

Another use is early diagnosis. As he puts it: "A burnout is easy to diagnose. But how about a kid of thirteen or fourteen who's starting to play around with grass? With early diagnosis and intervention, treatment can begin before the patient gets to an *easily* diagnosed stage."

Bill Barton, the first president of the National Federation of Parents for Drug-free Youth, puts it this way:

> Early intervention is exceedingly important. I am convinced that if my wife and I had known earlier that our daughter was using marijuana, the problem would have been far easier to solve. My wife and I are very observant people. We spend a lot of time with our kids. We thought we knew what they were doing all the time when in fact we didn't know what they were doing at all. If that simple pot urine test had come along when Tracy was thirteen, our job would've been much easier. And I think that we are no different from other parents in the country.

Dr. Macdonald points out another factor that makes the "pot test" especially useful for pediatricians:

> The fact that marijuana lasts in the body so long is very convenient. You don't have to catch the child stoned or intoxicated. You can check his urine almost any time. Even if he only smokes once a week, he's frequently going to come up with a positive urine. And, incidentally, when a youngster *knows* he's only had one joint a few days ago, and he sees the test come up pot positive, this can be an impressive educational experience. He sees clearly that his body is being continuously exposed to the chemicals in marijuana. The long half-life of this drug and the

fat-solubility factor are not just words in a book, or a speech from a pediatrician. They're what's going on in his own body.

Another use is for followup with kids who say to their parents, "Look, that pot was there because someone gave me a brownie and it did taste sort of funny," or "I tried it once, but I'm not going to try it again." There are a lot of parents who want to bring in their youngster's urine to see if the kid is really doing what he's says.

About the issue of confidentiality, Macdonald says:

I believe that as soon as the physician knows a kid's involved with pot, the parent should be involved. Often a child needs much more than the doctor's help to get off the drug.

I'm also concerned about *parental rights and responsibility.* I think parents have a right to know about what their kids are doing. And they have a responsibility to protect them.

I also believe that this is a communicable disease. A youngster gets it because other kids are doing it—and the legal precedent for testing for communicable diseases exists. A pregnant woman has to have a VD test before her baby is born. They test food service workers and school personnel for TB. A kid on pot is involved with something that he's going to spread to his peers, and I think we have a responsibility to protect those peers.

The cannabinoid assay, according to Macdonald, has these specific pediatric uses:

• *For sick children.* For example, respiratory-tract symptoms are often pot-related; so is precordial pain (chest pain), which is often alarming to a pot-smoking youngster. In such cases, a cannabinoid screen may be more helpful—and less expensive—than chest X rays, throat cultures, nasal smears, and therapeutic trials of cough medicines and antihistamines.

• *For children with behavioral problems.* Adolescents with a variety of behavioral problems are often doing drugs, and many of these problems are caused by drug use; not vice versa. Removing a child from drugs often makes the symptoms disappear. On the other hand, counseling a child who continues to do drugs is usually doomed to failure. The sometimes subtle changes may initially consist of no more than the dropping of extracurricular activities or hobbies or just expressing boredom about school. Lack of motivation can be an important indicator of significant drug involvement. Because chemical dependency is a *progressive* disease, early diagnosis is most important.

• *For annual check-ups.* Treatment programs for chemical dependency are usually expensive and time consuming, and often have high dropout and recidivism rates. A better answer lies in prevention or detection and intervention in early stages of involvement. Parental awareness and adolescent denial can both be addressed by a reliable screening examination, done with prior parental approval.

- *For followup.* This test is an excellent tool in monitoring those children who have been drug-users but have agreed to quit.

"When a pediatrician gives parents news of a pot-positive result, it should be done very carefully," says Macdonald. "Suggesting pot as the cause of a child's problems—as most parents see it—is not a diagnosis, it's an accusation. And they go the standard reaction route of denial, guilt and anger."

Bob Kramer, current president of the National Federation of Parents for Drug-Free Youth, adds this insight: "The urine test can deal effectively with a pervasive dual problem: parental denial on the one hand ('Not *my* kid!'), and, on the other hand, parental hopelessness. If, with this test, we can catch pot use at a much earlier stage, the terrible feelings of hopelessness and helplessness would not be nearly as great, since it would be a lot easier for the parent to intervene successfully with the child."

Is a pediatrician or family physician obligated to ask parental permission before testing for marijuana? Says MacDonald,

> I believe that if the symptoms point to drug use, parents should be told that one of the possible causes of the child's problems may be marijuana and an easy way to check this is to do a urine screen.
>
> It is important to point out to the parents why you are concerned, and remind them that your job is to assist them in keeping their children free of disease and to treat disease when present. Accurate diagnosis must precede advice and therapy. If the parents still say no, you can ask them why; they don't say no when you tell them the child needs a chest X ray or a blood culture or any other sort of lab work. Sit down and talk it out. Explain that's how medicine is done. Lab work helps rule out possibilities. And because of the expense of lab work, you try to start with the most likely possibilities. If parents continue to refuse, you might do some of the other tests. And if they all come back negative and the child's symptoms are still evident, the parents are then usually willing to test for marijuana use.

Macdonald warns, however, that there are dangers in leaning too heavily on the test: the possibility of a false negative, or the children whose main drug is alcohol, or other substances, and who have the same clinical picture as the chronic pot-smoker. In such cases, the negative marijuana urine screen may further feed the denial syndrome so often seen in parents.

Macdonald summed up the urine test as it pertains to use by pediatricians:

> From the broad spectrum of positive results I have had after a pot test shows positive, I would say that the pediatrician who uses the test routinely will find he has got a lot more kids smoking pot than he thought he did, and he'll also find that he has been helped with a lot of perplexing behavioral and physical diagnoses.

Macdonald is very concerned about the "youngest patient—the fetus." He feels that obstetricians should also be aware of the value of urine screening:

> I would like to see more obstetricians being more concerned about the risks to the fetus of marijuana smoking during pregnancy, and spending more time in educating their patients about these risks. Many mothers have given up drinking during pregnancy. If those who smoke marijuana realized the hazards to their baby, they would undoubtedly be more apt to give up pot smoking as well.

Urine Testing and the Schools

For years our teachers and school administrators have had to cope with the many destructive effects marijuana has upon large portions of their class populations. In many areas they still cope with this—and cope alone. Parents generally don't want to hear about the fact that the school their youngster attends is an open marketplace for drugs.

Dr. Herbert Kleber serves as a psychiatric consultant to several private schools. He points out that

> marijuana availability is not just physical availability; it's also perceived psychological availability. One of the things that affects perceived psychological availability is the perception of what will happen if you use. If there's a fairly certain idea of being caught, and if the consequences are unpleasant enough, it changes the availability. Even though the drug may be present in the environment, it's no longer perceived as available.

One of the schools for which Kleber is a consultant has a get-tough policy: If you get caught once using alcohol or marijuana, you are put on final warning, which lasts for that whole school year. If you're caught intoxicated again, you are expelled. "Last year," says Kleber, "they lost forty kids out of a population of nine hundred, for alcohol and drugs. Perhaps it would be a better idea if the kids on probation had to report to the infirmary every ten days for a urine test. That would take away some of the Russian roulette element that now exists. And maybe they wouldn't get expelled."

Dr. Richard Hawley, dean of students at University School, a private school in Cleveland, Ohio, has lectured widely throughout the country on the health hazards of marijuana and its impact on education. Hawley points out that it is often difficult for school personnel to talk frankly with students whose marijuana use is suspected or apparent. Such students often fear disciplinary reprisals if they admit their marijuana involvement. Therefore, counselors and teachers who would like to demonstrate the relationship between a student's marijuana use and specific problem behavior would be aided considerably by having their observations confirmed (or not) by a urine test.

Hawley suggests the following process, which can be of benefit to school and student:

1. A teacher or counselor identifies a student problem he or she either knows or suspects to be marijuana-related, and shares the concern with the student in a nondisciplinary setting.

2. The teacher/counselor contacts (directly or through appropriate school personnel) the family of the student to discuss the problem, and proposes that the parents have the student urine-tested for recent marijuana use by a physican (ideally as part of a general physical examination).

3. If the test results are positive, the counselor, family, and student can further explore the relationship between marijuana use and the problems that have arisen in school.

Hawley points out that such a process has the advantage of not being too aversive for students and their families. To be effective, however, it requires informed, observing, committed teachers and counselors, and formation of a school-parent-physician partnership.

Hawley suggests that such a program should always be supplemented by information incorporated in science or health classes on the health hazards of marijuana use. He points out: "Most youngsters *are* interested in their own health—especially if you don't come on from the disciplinary standpoint first. Tell the kid what you've learned about pot and get him engaged in the process of figuring out what's going on with him. That kid then becomes a partner in research about the whole thing."

Chapter 18

Schools: Successful Programs

Schools, for the most part, are still doing little or nothing about drug abuse. The common shrug-off is "They're not *our* kids. Let their parents deal with it." Or "Drugs are no problem in *our* school. Somewhere else maybe. But not *here.*" A problem not acknowledged need not be dealt with. However, some schools have faced up to the situation and have taken firm action—with impressive results.

One effective approach was used in Essex County, New Jersey. First, undercover agents were brought in to determine the extent of school drug abuse in two high schools. The results were so startling that Essex County took the matter one dramatic step further—they presented the situation to a grand jury.

This happened in Essex County, New Jersey. But it could have happened in Any County, Anywhere, U.S.A. It happened in 1979. But it is happening today. Everywhere. And unless your local school has already faced up to the drug problem and has taken determined steps to deal with it, what the citizens on the Essex County grand jury saw and heard in 1979 might well be what you would see and hear today if you were selected to be on a grand jury to investigate drug use in your local schools.

There were twenty-three citizens in the Essex County grand jury room, chosen by lot. They stared at the screen, watching a videotape taken by an undercover narcotics agent of a small group of youngsters—some sitting, some standing, all smoking—behind a hedge thirty feet from the local high school. A tall, neatly dressed teenager ambled into focus. He carried a large paper bag. And suddenly, as if on signal, dozens of kids were swarming around him. He distributed small plastic bags. Money changed hands. Several youngsters swallowed pills they had just bought. Others started rolling joints. The dealer left. His paper bag was empty.

Richard Roberts, then assistant prosecutor and director of the Essex County Bureau of Narcotics, stood by the screen and identified the scene. "This film was taken at seven-thirty in the morning outside Irvington High School. It could have been taken at any of the high schools in our county. On any day before school. Or after school. Or at recess. Or lunchtime."

A jury member asked: "What kind of pills was that kid selling?"

"Could have been anything," said Roberts. "Uppers and Quaaludes are very in this season. Also, the use of cocaine is increasing. And selling and smoking pot is accepted as a natural part of life. These youngsters on the screen are fourteen to eighteen years old. You'll be hearing testimony about pot-smokers in the fourth and fifth grades."

Irvington, New Jersey, is a suburban community of white middle-class families, most of whom live in comfortable private homes on tree-shaded streets: a typical American community. And the videotape depicted a typical American schoolground scene.

The grand jury then heard the testimony of an undercover agent who had worked for three months as a janitor in another suburban school, Bloomfield High, in an upper-middle-class community. He testified that 30 percent of the students "smoke marijuana constantly. Every morning I swept up large amounts of partially smoked marijuana cigarette butts in the school hallway. And, at any time of the day, there were butts on the floor." The next witness was the principal of that school, who had not heard the testimony of the janitor. He stated that marijuana was not a problem in *his* school.

The hearings went on for four months. During the preceding eight months, Roberts and other investigators had interviewed witnesses from all over the state of New Jersey. The grand jury heard testimony from 117 witnesses, including parents, students, school officials, law enforcement officers, judges, doctors—and teenage drug dealers who worked the grade schools and junior highs. Patricia Joiner from the Office of Drug Education of the Newark Board of Education testified that "recently we have been receiving more reports from the elementary and secondary level as opposed to the high school level, which has not been so in the past." Junior high school students spoke about the smell of pot in the stairwells and hallways. "In the bathroom," said one fourteen-year-old, "the pot smells so strong that you can't breathe. You wait till you get home to go to the bathroom."

Among those who testified were drug experts from the federal government, who painted a clear and convincing picture of drug abuse among school children in the country as a whole.

On March 7, 1979, the grand jury issued its presentment. They had been charged with the responsibility of determining whether or not a condition of serious drug abuse existed in the local school system. They were asked to present the facts, not to prosecute—although certain administrators came perilously close to indictment. The jury charged that in the face of first-hand evidence to the contrary, approximately one-third of the high school principals claimed no drug problem existed in their schools.

"And," Assistant Prosecutor Roberts added, "among parents, the situation was generally just as bleak."

The sixty-page grand jury presentment started off with these words:

We, the members of this Grand Jury, are lay people who constitute a cross-section of the population of Essex County. We are black, white, rich, poor, conservative, moderate and liberal. While digesting four months of testimony, our emotions have run the gamut from shock to disbelief, anger, fear and finally resolve: resolve to alert the public to the danger that is facing our society; resolve to make meaningful recommendations; resolve to insist that our voices be heard.

It appears the drug problem in this county is typical of what is happening to our young people throughout the nation. The lack of recognition and the inability to coordinate corrective efforts are a national disgrace. Our schools have become the main marketplace for drugs, and almost any drug is available.

We feel we have barely scratched the surface in observing the totality of the problem, and understanding its tragic implications. It is sometimes difficult to translate the facts into real human emotions. We only wish that all of those who read this report could have had the opportunity, as we did, to view young people who testified how they used, bought and sold drugs in school, and remained high for a great deal of time during their school experience. We hope you can imagine the human tragedy of a young person who seems to have lost his way . . .

Many of the jury's concrete recommendations have been implemented in Essex County. And they have been adopted in other communities. The prosecutor in Passaic, New Jersey, told the county's superintendent of schools that they did not need a grand jury investigation; they would take the Essex County recommendations and go with them.

For example, as a direct result of the grand jury investigation, the New Jersey State Assembly and Legislature passed a bill mandating drug education in every school and in every grade from kindergarten to twelfth. (This, as may be expected, is working in some schools better than others; but all schools have some sort of drug education.)

In 1981 New Jersey legislators passed the Model Paraphernalia Law, forbidding the manufacture and sale of drug paraphernalia in the entire state (see Appendix). In addition, as a direct result of the grand jury investigation, a statewide investigation of drugs in the schools was started by the attorney general, the commissioner of education created a Drug Awareness Task Force, and the New Jersey State PTA was the first to take on the drug issue as its number-one priority throughout the state; also, over one hundred parent groups for drug-free youth were formed throughout New Jersey.

The grand jury investigation served to create a sympathetic, understanding, and cooperative New Jersey State Legislature, which has now revamped and updated drug laws ranging from increased penalties for marijuana growing to new legislation for "look-alike" pills. Most important, the school-drug problem in New Jersey is no longer being swept under the rug.

Gerri Silverman's Fifth- and Sixth-Grade Program

Perhaps the single most dynamic force to emerge in the state as a direct result of the grand jury investigation was a suburban housewife from Short Hills, New Jersey, named Gerri Silverman. It was in large measure through Silverman's efforts that the first set of anti–drug paraphernalia laws passed locally and were introduced into the legislature in 1979. She then began drug-awareness programs for parents and in-service teacher-training programs. "However," said Silverman, "at the end of 1981 I suddenly realized that the real answer in turning around the drug epidemic was not so much in intervention—which occurs in junior and senior high, but in prevention—which begins in grade school."

She therefore created a drug education program called "It's Your Decision," aimed at fifth- and sixth-graders. Strictly on a volunteer basis, she took her one-woman program throughout every county in the state as well as to schools in New York, Pennsylvania, and New Hampshire. Within two years she had spoken to over ten thousand fifth- and sixth-graders in over two hundred schools.

The program is roughly an hour and a half long. She starts by asking, "What's the number-one drug in your community?" The answer invariably is: "Marijuana." She asks for other names for the drug and the kids shout out: "Tea, Grass, Pot, Weed, Maryjane, Dope, Reefer, Joints, Maui Wowie, Colombian Gold, Acapulco Gold, MJ." The list goes on and on. "How many of you have ever seen marijuana?" At least a third, sometimes half the children raise their hands.

The program involves the youngsters in their own learning experience.

For example, Silverman illustrates the fat-solubility factor by using a white sponge. She tells the youngsters, "You have two very fatty organs in your body. Where are they?" (Nobody knows.) "One is your reproductive organs," and she describes the lowered testosterone level, and the fact that females eggs may be damaged by THC collected in the ovaries. "The other fatty organ is the brain." A child comes up and dips the sponge in red food coloring, which represents the THC in marijuana. Another child pours a pitcher of water over the sponge. But only some of the coloring comes out. "Half the THC and other chemicals someone may smoke at a pot party on a Friday night is still there a week later," says Silverman. "Now if the person smokes another joint the next week, the THC accumulates. The body is never drug free."

Each point Silverman makes is related to an experiment, a game, a device. But all the information hits home. At the end of each session she suggests, "How about making a poster: 'Coming Soon to Senior High, the Drug-Free Class of 19___.' All sign your names to it. Take the poster with you into Junior High and right straight through till you're seniors." (Many classes do make such a poster.)

Then she says, "What if every kid in the fifth and sixth grade in your town decided not to do drugs? By the time you reach high school you could turn the problem around in your town."

"You can see it dawning in their faces," Silverman says. "*They* are the answer to the problem. They can make a turnaround in their town." Then she asks: "What if every fifth- and sixth-grader had the same program in our state? Could we turn the state of New Jersey around?"

They shout: "Yes." They go out determined to keep peer pressure on each other—*not* to begin.

Does it work? No surveys have been made. But four years ago the schools in Millburn/Short Hills, Gerri's community, were replicas of Bloomfield High and Irvington High, the schools examined in the Essex County grand jury hearings. Now, after Gerri's program, which has reached every single fifth- and sixth-grader in the community and which is followed up each year by teachers and nurses so that the children get continuing reinforcement, the feeling among school administrators, teachers, parents, and kids is that there has been a tremendous reduction of drug use in the junior high. A typical reaction came from two sisters, one a senior at Millburn High School, the other an eighth-grader at the junior high. In January 1984 the older sister recalled, "When I came into junior high, anybody who wanted drugs could get them anytime at school."

The younger sister said, "I wouldn't even know where to find drugs if I wanted them—which I certainly *don't!*"

In addition to her fifth- and sixth-grade programs, Silverman has organized a community drug awareness committee through the Millburn PTAs. In 1982 the committee began an annual Drug Awareness Week, which includes publication of full-page ads in two newspapers covering eleven communities ("Our Community Is Getting It Together. How About Yours?"); separate programs on drug awareness for junior and senior high students, for their teachers and for their parents; a walkathon called "Life—Be In It" to get people from kindergarteners to senior citizens out and participating; and a special marathon event at each of the junior and senior highs. In addition, each year a mailing with drug-abuse information is made to all families in the community. "It's a lot of work," said Silverman. "But sparing one child, one family, from the agony of drug abuse makes it all worthwhile.

"My dream," she says, "is a volunteer drug-awareness program throughout the United States aimed at every fifth- and sixth-grader in our nation. I truly believe that if this were done, we could turn this epidemic around in a matter of four years."

For information about a written script, and audio and video cassettes of Silverman's fifth- and sixth-grade program, write Gerri Silverman, 23 Audubon Street, Short Hills, New Jersey 07078.

Me-ology

This prevention program is primarily aimed at sixth-graders, but unlike Silverman's "one woman show," Me-ology comes replete with 18 carefully structured lessons, workbooks, teacher guides—and three-day training seminars which are required for all teachers who wish to use the course.

It began in 1978 when Charles Mendez, Jr., president of a small family foundation in Tampa, Florida, said to Elizabeth McConnell, a guidance counselor, "Don't you think the best way to immunize kids to the use of drugs would be to teach them what drugs do to the body—and how great it is to be healthy? When *we* went to school health education meant talking about Mr. Floss for your teeth and that was about the level of it. But health *could* be made fun."

McConnell—known as "BJ"—agreed enthusiastically. And she and Mendez set out to create a "fun program"—aimed at the most serious problem in the community: rampant drug abuse among youth.

The program, developed in the main by "BJ", and funded at first entirely by the C. E. Mendez Foundation, started in 1979 with two teachers. By 1981 there were 7 full-time Me-ology teachers and the program had been given to 10,733 sixth-graders. Evaluations and follow-up surveys in school showed that children who'd had the course were 50 percent less likely to have a drug-related incident in school than the non-Me-ologers. (The definition of drugs included cigarettes and alcohol.)

The first few sessions of Me-ology are health oriented—with plenty of enthusiastic student participation and little said about drugs. In the first lesson, for example, each kid is given an imaginary car. "There's only one hitch. You have to keep this car for the rest of your life." The moral comes quickly to the fore. "Your body is the neatest machine you'll ever have. Why would you take better care of a car than your own body?" This is the basic concept of the course which gives rise to the name: Me-ology: the study of—*me*.

From that starting springboard, students are better equipped to face peer pressure—the next segment of the course. Says McConnell, "In the sixth grade, kids are fascinated by the idea that there *is* a thing called peer pressure. They've experienced it—without knowing that it's a whole aspect of behavior which they can learn how to handle. We structure it for them so, for example, the next time other kids are standing around with a lit joint and taunting, 'What's the matter? You chicken or something?' a recognition light will go off. 'Wow, this is just what the teacher was talking about!' "

When the teacher walks into a class during the "peer pressure and decision-making classes," she says, "Okay, who got peer pressure last week and what did you do about it?"

Then, with games, with cards, with acting-out situations, kids practice how to say No to drugs—with most emphasis given to pot since that is the drug with most mystique to sixth-graders. Each of the remaining 14 weeks is devoted to a single psychoactive drug category, including tobacco, alcohol, and look-alikes (street drugs made to look like those prescription pills which have psychoactive effects). But at least 15 minutes of each hour is given over to reinforcing what has been learned about peer pressure and decision-making.

In 1982, BJ decided that the youngsters who'd had the Me-ology course in 1979 were now entering the ninth grade and no doubt needed a "booster shot." Her staff developed an eight-hour course called "Choices." Marijuana had its own day, as did alcohol, cigarettes, peer pressure, and decision-making.

In 1983, Mrs. Elaine Shimberg, a Tampa resident, mother of five, and co-founder with her husband of the Shimberg Foundation, said: "Teaching kids without teaching parents is like clapping with one hand." Therefore, the foundation funded a program for parents called Choices and Challenges, an eight-week course held once a week for five hours. Says McConnell: "The kids are so enthusiastic after taking the Me-ology course that the parents get interested too."

By May 1984 the program had spread to cities in nine other states, over three hundred teachers had taken the three-day seminar, and many thousands of parents and sixth- and ninth-grade children had completed the course. The kids' "evaluation" was summed up by a sixth-grader in Bridgeport, Connecticut, who said: "Me-ology taught me I'm too good to do drugs!"

For further information, write Elizabeth McConnell, Executive Director, C. E. Mendez Foundation, P.O. Box 10059, Tampa, Florida, 33679. Telephone: (813) 875-2579.

Northside High

Another approach was taken by an individual school in Atlanta, Georgia—Northside High, which principal Bill Rudolph describes as "a microcosm of the city." The fourteen hundred students *are* from poor, middle-income, and wealthy homes, and "exactly half and half" (black and white)—assured through voluntary busing.

In 1977, when thirty-three-year-old Rudolph came in as principal, as he put it,

> Pot was openly used. Marijuana was growing in the library. Kids were blowing pot into the air conditioning system to turn the whole school on. The odor of marijuana was obvious in the bathrooms and sometimes in the halls. Students talked openly about getting high. They'd cut classes and go into the wooded area behind school to get stoned. We also had reason to believe that hard drugs were being used.
>
> All I knew at that time was that pot smoking was against the law. I didn't *think* it was harmless. Deep down I felt it was deleterious. But until one of the mothers brought me a few *Reader's Digest* articles—I was in total ignorance of the facts.

So, it turned out, were the students, who were getting much of their drug information through mail-order books advertised in *High Times*. "These books," read one mail-order ad, "represent some of the best and most accurate information available about how to grow, prepare, manufacture and consume psychoactive substances."

Rudolph's first step was to publish the first "Northside High Student

Handbook," twenty-two pages, which contained one sentence about drugs: *Students found in possession of any illegal drug will be dealt with by the appropriate authorities.*

"We felt if we had an assembly about this, we might get booed out of the place. So we relied on word of mouth to get the message across: that we meant to enforce the law. The students took a wait-look-and-see attitude. There was no overt opposition. They didn't come to me and say, 'You can't do it'—because they knew damn well I could."

The first youngsters to get caught on the new law were smoking pot in the church parking lot across from the school. The kids protested, "We're not on school property!" Rudolph told them, "It's during the school day, and if I can't press charges as school principal, I will do it as a citizen."

He took them to his office and called the police—who charged them with possession of less than one ounce of marijuana. The youngsters were also suspended for a few days. Said Rudolph:

> If I was going to get flak from the parents, *this* is where I expected it to happen—because the parents of these particular kids were very influential in the community. But instead I got their support. It was silent support. Some of the parents came privately to thank me for being concerned enough about the situation to do something about it.

Rudolph's two assistant principals and a few of the male faculty members were on constant lookout. "When we saw someone starting to roll a joint, or pass a joint from friend to friend, we'd bring them into my office and call the police. If the police felt we had enough evidence, we'd prosecute. In almost all cases the youngster was remanded to the custody of the parents."

The school also inaugurated medically accurate drug education courses, focusing on marijuana. In addition, Rudolph "tightened up all along the line. The school went from permissive to very structured."

Rudolph noted, "When I first came to the school in the first quarter of 1977 we averaged 5000 tardies a day. In other words, there were tardies in half of all the classes every day. Furthermore, we were only feeding 250 kids in the cafeteria at lunchtime. The rest—about 1500 youngsters—were all leaving school at lunchtime and no one knew where they were. Two years later we averaged less than 70 tardies a day, and we could account for all the students at lunchtime."

By 1981, there was very little pot smoking during the school day.

Furthermore, although the enrollment of the school stayed the same, there was a significant change in the type of elective courses students were taking: a sharp decrease in woodworking, shop, and home economics—and a 300 percent enrollment increase in physics, a 24 percent increase in chemistry, a 25 percent increase in Latin, a 30 percent increase in the four other languages offered, and a measurable increase in all other academic areas, including the honors courses. Within two years, the school had shown significant academic improvement in reading, composition, and math, as tested by the state standardized achievement test. And Northside High had the highest achievement level in the city of Atlanta.

In addition, there was a 100 percent increase in the number of students going out for football practice, a 300 percent increase in the number of youngsters who tried out for the basketball team, a 500 percent increase in the number going out for track. "Many of our teams did very well," said Rudolph, "and there was a significant increase in the number of kids who turned out to watch the games."

From the start, an important ingredient had been integrated into Northside High's drug prevention system: parents. Rudolph put it this way: "Most educators only allow parents to have decisions on situations when the educators don't care where the decision goes in any case. There is a vested interest in the educational system to exclude parents." The school not only produced an annual student handbook, but one for the staff and a newsletter mailed to all parents. In all of these, the consequences of drug and alcohol use were clearly spelled out. Said Rudolph: "We found that most parents were shaky about consequences—and tried to straddle the fence from both sides. They now were told, along with their children, that the consequences of drug use would be arrest, and the consequences of being late would be detention." One result of this clear spelling out of the rules was that, said Rudolph, "We didn't have fourteen-year-olds telling us what to do. Parents were beginning to regain control of their children, and children were beginning to respect the word 'no.'

"Furthermore," said Rudolph, "teachers did not need to be policemen. They were not asked to deal with stoned or intoxicated students or even to suggest that students were under the influence. If a teacher noticed a student who seemed to have problems in the class, the situation was reported to the administrator, who dealt with it. I didn't ask my teachers for support in this. They are employees of the school system, and I insisted on it.

"If a student was found to be intoxicated and there was no physical evidence such as a joint or pills or a bottle, parents were asked to come to school and to assume the responsibility for intervening with their children. We told them we did not want the student to return to school until the problem was resolved. But if there was physical evidence we would prosecute."

In addition to their academic and sports achievements, Northside High serves as a magnet school for the performing arts—which means that talented youngsters from throughout Atlanta may attend Northside for its academic as well as its performing arts program. The school has developed such professional quality actors, singers, and dancers that, as part of the performing arts program, groups of Northside High students have performed throughout the United States and Europe and they premiered the exuberant "Coke is it" TV singing commercial in 1982.

By 1982 there was only one drug-related incident during the entire school year. That year Northside High received a ten-thousand-dollar award from the Rockefeller Foundation as the best performing arts high school in the country. And in April 1984 they won a Carnegie Foundation grant for their continued improvement in their academic program.

STAMP (Students Teaching About Marijuana Problems)

Another project was completely organized by sixth-grader Billy Coletti of St. Petersburg, Florida, who got the idea when he was attending a parent group conference in Atlanta, Georgia, in 1979 with his mother, Shirley, executive director of Operation PAR (Parental Awareness and Responsibility). Billy recalls, "While I was sitting listening to everybody saying 'get involved, start a parent group,' I said to myself, 'Hey, I'm a normal kid, why don't I start up my own program?' So I began scribbling on a piece of paper thinking up a name and I came up with STAMP."

Bill's idea was a six-week program using two other students in the sixth grade to inform the fourth-, fifth-, and sixth-graders

about marijuana and other drugs, like inhalants, and alcohol. I didn't go into "big drugs" like heroin and things like that. I had plenty of information from my mom about marijuana and its problems and the effects on the human body, and I had good information about inhalants and alcohol, too. For the first week, I educated two friends who were going to help me. We went to my house each day after school and I gave them information, and let them read pamphlets and books that I had gotten from my mom.

Then I went to the principal of my school, Canterbury School of Florida in St. Petersburg [a private school]. First the principal didn't think I could do it, and that I would give misleading information. But when I gave her some idea of how much I knew and how I was going to present it, she gave me the go-ahead, if each of the teachers approved. So I had to go to each of them. Then me and my two friends went into the fourth-grade class, for two days a week for five weeks, during the sixth-graders' lunch period (so we lost our lunch time). The first day we were extremely nervous as to how the kids were going to accept it. But we were absolutely amazed by their attention and their wanting to learn. At the end of the first day we left ten minutes for questions— but we ran twenty minutes because they had so many questions. That was really exciting and good encouragement to keep on going.

Our Monday and Wednesday lunch hours were for the fourth grade. Our Tuesday and Thursday lunch hours were for the fifth grade. And in the sixth grade the teacher turned over an hour to us and called it the Drug Awareness Class; that was every Friday—*not* during our lunch.

The fifth-graders thought they were really cool and they didn't want to listen to a stupid sixth-grader. But as soon as we got started they livened up and gave more attention. Their reaction was one of wanting to know.

The sixth grade was the hardest because those were all of our friends. They snickered and stuff. I made up work sheets and they would look for things wrong with them and try to embarrass me. But after the first three times they sort of said, "Hey, these guys know what they're talking about!" And they began to listen. The sixth grade was more conscious of marijuana than alcohol and inhalants. They knew more about it and were exposed to it more than the fourth-graders. But there sure was plenty they didn't know about the drug being bad for you. And after my program they were educated to the subject and could make a better decision. A lot of them told me, "I don't want this to happen to me. I'm not even going to try it!" This is what the fifth- and the fourth-graders had told me, too.

Billy graduated from Canterbury in 1980, and went on to Lakewood High—

a big public school of fourteen hundred kids. I started STAMP again so that students wouldn't have to have the pressures of going to a party and knowing that marijuana was going to be there and knowing that if you don't do any you're going to be laughed at or called chicken or something worse. Now I'm talking about the health hazards of marijuana and some other drugs and in addition, STAMP presents drug-free alternatives for kids who don't want to get stoned all the time.

I've had calls from a couple of parents in other states who want to know how their kids can start up a STAMP program in their school. I hope more kids will start up a similar program because it is really helpful. Kids know what they're talking about because they know what's *really* going on at school and at parties. But the most important thing is that you have to have accurate scientific information—because if you give misleading information you're doing more harm than good.

In May 1983 Billy spoke on STAMP at the Florida Alcohol and Drug Abuse Workshop in Sarasota, Florida. He wrote up his program for this meeting, and it is available by writing: Billy Coletti, at address below. Send two dollars to cover printing and mailing.

In November 1984 Billy started Florida Informed Teens (FIT). "It's a pretty neat name," said Billy, "because we stress fitness as one of the alternatives to drugs." The organization started with ten high school students from three different schools. They printed a brochure which included these sentences: "FIT members acquire leadership skills. They help organize drug and alcohol prevention activities in their community. It's an organization led by youth, for youth, with adults acting as advisors." As of May 1984, FIT had seven thriving groups throughout Florida. For information on how to set up a FIT Program in your community, send two dollars to Billy Coletti, 6613 49th St. N., Pinellas Park, Florida, 33565.

The Canadian Headmasters

Perhaps the most impressive school-generated effort of all is that of the Canadian headmasters, who have, thus far, done far more than their counterparts in the United States to develop drug education programs, which are used in an increasing number of schools all across Canada.

One of the leaders in the headmasters' efforts is Fred Burford, president of Ontario's Council on Drug Abuse and chairman of the Headmasters Council's Marijuana Committee of Ontario. Burford said,

> Our concentrated effort started in Ontario in 1977. With growing knowledge of the more recent scientific findings concerning the adverse health effects of marijuana, our first energies were devoted exclusively to influencing proposed federal changes in legislation; the government was considering decriminalizing marijuana. The Ontario Secondary School Headmasters' Council, which represented 1,500 headmasters, was able to enlist the support of the Canadian Association of Principals, with a membership of 12,000 across the country. We wrote letters and many headmasters personally saw members of Parliament across Canada. In Ottawa our headmasters' committee visited the Minister of Health, the Minister of Justice, and the Solicitor General, and we worked as well to obtain the support of the organizations outside the educational field, including the Ontario Chiefs of Police, the Canadian Home and School Association, the Catholic Women's League, etc. We were, in fact, the catalyst for the concerned majority of the public, and thus far decriminalization has not taken place.

MARIJUANA ALERT

The headmasters in Canada have proven to be the most active and effective single group in the country in this regard. Unquestionably the pressure exerted by the Canadian headmasters in 1982 and 1983 helped greatly in encouraging the federal government to promulgate its 1983 nationwide public education program on marijuana, with its excellent *Stay Real* booklet—in English and French—on the health hazards of cannabis; an announcement of the availability of the free booklet was mailed by the Canadian government to all parents of school-aged children in the country. The availability of the free booklet was also widely advertised on national television.

Since 1980 Canadian headmasters and teachers have also been working to develop effective health education programs in the schools. Their aim is to cover grades K through 12. (In Ontario it's K through 13, as they have an additional year of high school.) For example, the headmasters of Windsor, Ontario, have implemented a drug education program called SLAP (Straight Look at Pot), which gives current accurate information about marijuana to all students in secondary schools in Windsor. This is done through the initiative and the involvement of the headmasters of Windsor, with the cooperation of their teachers.

The headmasters in Canada have, in effect, developed a network of action on the marijuana front which is having an impact on the entire nation.

The U.S. schools lag far behind in this area. However, since more public attention has been and is being focused on pot-smoking youth in junior high and high schools than on any other segment of our society, it is to be hoped that more schools—with the concerted cooperation of parents and local government—will adopt responsible and effective overall strategies. The way has been shown. The benefits are clear.

But for most schools in the United States the step now to be taken is the hardest. That step is: To begin.

Chapter 19

The Armed Forces

Civilians combating the drug problem may find hope and help in the success the armed forces are having, for—as shown in all questionnaire surveys taken prior to 1982—the drug problem in the armed forces was even worse than that in other areas of our national life. Yet, within a single year, 1981/82, they succeeded in cutting back drug use to an amazing degree. There are many aspects to this story, but the clearest evidence that it is indeed a success story comes in two sets of statistics.

In 1980 the military did a worldwide drug-abuse survey of armed forces personnel, with dismal results. (See Chapter 4, the Burt and Biegel survey.)

The second "Department of Defense Worldwide Survey of Non-Medical Drug and Alcohol Use among Military Personnel" was taken two years later, from September to November 1982, by the Research Triangle Institute. The results were published in June 1983. They were as follows: Drug abuse (virtually synonymous with marijuana use) had been *reduced by*

- 62 percent in the navy.
- 58 percent in the marines.
- 26 percent in the air force.
- 22 percent in the army.

This is all the more remarkable in view of the fact that not only did armed forces personnel have "reasons to do drugs" that did not apply to the civilian population (see Chapter 4), but, according to all local, state, and national surveys, the prevalence of abuse of drugs varies considerably by age, sex, marital status, and educational level. The highest risk group for both drug and alcohol problems consists of young, single males—precisely the population from which the armed forces recruit.

True, in some respects the armed forces have "advantages" in dealing with the drug-abuse situation that civilians do not have. Military life is highly cohesive and structured; refusal to obey orders can result in a court martial. Also, military personnel must abide by "rules of the organization" twenty-four hours a day, as compared to rules operating eight hours a day in the workplace or six hours a day in the schools. On the other hand, some aspects of the armed forces' war against drug use in the services can be adopted or adapted by civilians—from school authorities to employers. It is therefore important to take a close look at what the services are doing to achieve their successes.

Since this book concerns marijuana, we will look in depth at the effects of the armed forces policies—and actions—as they pertain in particular to that drug. But, as the survey shows, the program had a positive impact on the use of almost all of the illegal drugs, and legal drugs used illegally.

In both the 1980 and 1982 surveys, virtually all military personnel who used illegal drugs used marijuana. Some stuck to pot exclusively; most included other drugs. The survey researchers put it this way: "In general, changes in marijuana use were similar to the changes observed for use of any drugs. This is explained by the fact that marijuana is the drug used most frequently and accounts to a large extent for the general pattern of overall drug use."

Concerning current use of marijuana ("in the past 30 days"), the 1980 survey showed that military and civilian use rates were about the same: more than one in every three persons between the ages of eighteen and twenty-four. By 1982, current use in the civilian population was reduced to 27.4 percent. But in the military, the survey researchers reported that in 1982 there was a significant decline in current marijuana use for all military personnel to *16 percent*. Much of this was accounted for by the significant decrease in use among E-1 through E-5 personnel, from 37 percent to 22 percent.

The survey summary also noted that:

• Significant decreases in marijuana use were observed between 1980 and 1982 for all services, especially the navy and the marines. The air force and the army decreases were less, but still significant. (It should be noted, however, that the army and air force did not begin using urine test results for disciplinary purposes until nine to twelve months after the navy and the marines did.)

• Comparison of 1980 and 1982 levels of use among E-1s through E-5s for individual drugs showed an overall pattern of reductions for each drug. Significant decreases in use occurred for all drugs except PCP and heroin, which had had minimal usage rates even in 1980.

• Reports of diminished work performance due to drug use decreased significantly for total DOD (Department of Defense) from 41 to 21 percent. Each of the indicators of diminished performance showed a significant reduction at the total DOD level, and each service showed a corresponding significant reduction.

It should also be noted that another survey, done by the firm of Booz, Allen, and Hamilton, was ordered by the navy to see whether the "self-reporting" statistics held up when compared to a random urinalysis survey. The urine tests were done in the summer of 1982 on navy men and women in San Diego, California, and Norfolk, Virginia, the Navy's two major port installations. Results: There was only a 1 percent differential between the chemical (urine) survey and the self-reporting survey.

We will look more closely at how the remarkable drops in drug usage were achieved by each of the services. However, since urine testing played, and continues to play, a major role in the success rate of all four services, let us first look at this subject with its special ramifications regarding the military.

The Military Use of Urine Testing

The urinalysis testing program in the armed forces began in 1971 with an executive order by President Nixon: The armed forces were to conduct a program to identify soldiers using heroin who were in Vietnam or had returned from Vietnam. There was random testing for several years, starting with heroin and then continuing with other drugs—barbiturates, amphetamines, Quaaludes, and, some years later, cocaine. Marijuana was not included—for the very good reason that the tests for cannabis did not yet exist. In 1975 Congress stopped all random urine testing because it was not cost effective; there was too much testing going on, and too few users being identified.

This was followed by a program of urine testing that was basically incident-related, for individuals who "called attention to themselves" in a manner that seemed to be drug-related. However, as a result of a court ruling in 1974 (*Pvt. Ruiz* v. *The United States*), the U.S. Court of Military Appeals determined that positive results from urine testing could not be used as a cause for disciplinary action or to "characterize discharge." This decision was based on the "self-incrimination" right. The only action that could be taken was to put the person into a rehabilitation program, or to give him or her an honorable discharge. If the person refused to enter a rehab program, he or she would receive an honorable discharge—replete with all a veteran's benefits.

This ruling did not sit too well with commanders. Military personnel who worked hard for four years received honorable discharges at the end of their service; now drug-abusers who refused treatment could receive the same honorable discharge. Furthermore, many drug-users who wanted out opted for this quick and easy urine-test method to get their discharge; there were cases of people taking up drugs as a way out.

In 1980 another court case changed all this (*Armstrong* v. *The United States*). This time the U.S. Court of Military Appeals ruled that the Fifth Amendment did not apply to body fluids, which were evidence in and of themselves. If body fluids were procured under legal search circumstances, they were admissible. (There are several pages of military law devoted to specific instances under which searches can be conducted.) If urine samples were taken under the proper search conditions, and if the findings were positive, the results *could* be used as evidence for disciplinary action or to characterize a discharge. Random testing was also once again permitted.

Maj. R. Dennis Smith of the Department of Defense Drug and Alcohol Abuse Program was the "man at the Pentagon" directly in charge of developing policy for the armed forces urine-testing program. He put it this way: "Our policy is that we do not call a test positive until it has been confirmed by two independent methodologies. It is just as important to us not to misidentify nonusers as it is to identify users."

If the initial test, an RIA or an EMIT, is positive, but the corroborative test, a GLC (gas liquid chromatography) or a GC/MS (Gas Chromotography/mass spectrometry) is negative, then the commander of the person's unit will be told the test was pot-negative.

It should be stressed in regard to urine testing that nobody is *automatically* out. The military review process means that a legal process is followed in separating each individual from the service. Each case is reviewed by military authorities, which involves written reports. Then the case is reviewed throughout the chain of command. Some cases may take thirty days; some take many months. For example, one case concerned a sailor who lived with his sister when on shore leave. Returning to the ship, his urine was random-sampled—and showed pot-positive. He was stunned, and insisted he never did drugs. His CO believed him, and set several investigators on the case. It turned out that the sailor's sister was a pot-smoker, and had baked up some marijuana in brownies—which the sailor had unwittingly eaten. He was cleared. The case was closed. But he was advised not to stay with his sister during subsequent shore leaves.

Another possible problem was "switched samples." The armed forces instituted a policy of "observed urines" from the beginning, but commanders who did not follow these instructions found that enlisted men were, for example, purchasing a vial of baby's urine for twenty-five dollars and hiding it in their shirts for use if called upon to produce. Since there were complaints and law cases emanating from some who insisted that urines had been switched and that *theirs* had been falsely labeled pot-positive, the urine is packaged and labeled in front of the donor, who "signs for it." There is no more question of switched or adulterated specimens. Now virtually everyone follows the observed urine policies.

Urine can be requested under one of three circumstances:

• *Random sampling.* Because everyone has the same "opportunity" to be selected, disciplinary action can be taken if the positives are corroborated. (In 1983 the Court of Military Appeals found that even random sampling of personnel coming back on duty from an extended leave was legal. The court upheld the navy's right to try a petty officer who had returned from duty after a thirty-day leave—with a pot-positive urine.)

• *If there is probable cause.* If, for example, a sniff dog "points" by a bunk and a baggie of pot is discovered beneath the sleeping seaman's pillow, this is probable cause. Again, disciplinary action can be taken.

• *A command-directed urine test.* If a CO suspects an individual, but the situation falls short of probable cause, the test can be ordered. In this case, even if the test is positive, no disciplinary action can be taken—because there was not clear probable cause. However, if the individual is in a critical position, such as on watch, the CO can remove him or her from this position.

(There is no current policy concerning urinalysis screening programs for the civilian employees working for the military.)

Each of the services uses urine testing as an integral part of its program. None use the test for screening prior to induction. However, if would-be recruits have a history of drug or alcohol addiction, or if they have a criminal record that includes drugs, they are not accepted. Recruits in all services are told that drug use will not be tolerated, and those entering the navy or marines are informed that they will receive a urine screen in thirty days—time enough for evidence of "civilian pot use" to clear from the body. If they then show pot-positive, the urine is sent for a corroborative test. And, if this test seconds the verdict, the new recruit promptly becomes an ex-recruit. However, if the sailor or marine shows up pot-positive for the *first* time *after* the initial induction period, then a second chance is given.

The army and air force do not do the thirty-day urine screening.

The pot-positive policies concerning enlisted men differ with each service, and the handling differs somewhat according to each commanding officer, and according to each case. But there is no such leeway for commissioned or noncommissioned officers. In the army, navy, marines, or air force, if they are pot-positive, corroborated by a second test, they are, in most cases, separated from the service.

Maj. Smith sums up: "The marijuana urine testing is helping immeasurably in our goal of reducing drug use in the U.S. military."

The use of urine testing is only one part of the success pattern, albeit an essential part. Another essential and concommitant ingredient is the firm no-drugs message, which starts with the top brass and is heard and acted upon, with no mixed signals, down the entire chain of command.

According to Dr. John Johns, former deputy assistant secretary of defense, "We are the only armed forces in the western world that has addressed this problem head on."

Let us now look at how each of the services *has* addressed the problem.

The Army

There was good reason for the fact that the army's drug use—and/or pot-use figures—did not show the same impressively lowered 1982 ratings as the other services. As we will see, the greatest single deterrent factor in the war against drugs waged by all the services is urine testing. The army started its firm antidrug crackdown somewhat later than the other services. Furthermore, the army did not institute its marijuana urine testing for disciplinary purposes until September 1982, and the second Worldwide Drug Abuse Survey was done in September to November 1982. Colonel Patrick O'Meara, former chief of the army's Drug and Alcohol Abuse Policy Office, summed up: "We may have started our all-out efforts later. But we are catching up fast!"

When a would-be army recruit first comes to the recruiting station, he or she is asked about past drug use, and is also asked to fill out a questionnaire that contains questions about drug use; for example, "Have you used drugs within the last 90 days, including marijuana?" If, in the personal interview and/or in the questionnaire, the would-be recruit admits to being a user of marijuana, but not habitually, he or she is sent for a further assessment by a doctor at the MEPS (Military Entrance and Processing Station). The M.D. gives a yes or no vote, which determines whether the sometime smoker may enter the army. Once in the service, being caught in possession of marijuana is a court-martial offense. The outcome of the case depends on the soldier's past record and on the amount of pot involved.

If a soldier is suspected by the commanding officer of being a pot-user, and if the officer feels there is "probable cause" to ask for a urine screen, he or she may do so. Probable cause, according to Colonel O'Meara, "can mean red eyes, staggering gait, inability to perform the job, no indication of alcohol, and other previous incidents." The commanding officer may then direct the soldier to the nearest urine collection station, usually under the supervision of a noncommissioned officer. Said Colonel O'Meara: "Our laboratories are charged to check every specimen that comes in for marijuana. Some laboratories also 'pulse test' for at least one other drug. That one other drug is changed from time to time, depending on the area of the country, and the drug usage in that area. In Germany, urines are checked for all drugs, from marijuana to heroin."

If Soldier X is positive on the initial test and the corroborative test, the unit commander is notified. The commander sends the soldier to one of the army's ADAPCPs (Alcohol and Drug Abuse Prevention and Control Program); there are 187 ADAPCPs in the U.S. Army. The soldier is interviewed to determine whether he or she is dependent on a drug; to see if there are other drugs involved, including alcohol; to decide what his or her prognosis for rehabilitation may be. Then the ADAPCP office calls the commander and both of them, in consultation, determine whether Soldier X should be rehabilitated; i.e., whether he or she has the potential for further military service. The soldier is not involved in this process.

In the event that Soldier X does possess potential, the army provides a rehabilitation program consisting of three tracks. Track One is a minimum of twelve hours of education and group counseling. The size of the group does not exceed fourteen to fifteen persons, and family participation is encouraged.

Track Two is for the individual with a fairly serious problem. It involves all the elements in Track One as well as individual counseling and attention, and group therapy. The maximum time for Track Two is one year. The soldiers are generally working in their units while they are "tracking"; they have counseling in their off-duty hours and in the evenings.

Track Three applies to six-week in-patient treatment facilities, primarily for curing alcoholics.

Each ADAPCP has a clinical director with a background in drug- and alcohol-abuse counseling; an education coordinator; and a civilian coordinator. There are additional counselors to handle the one-to-one workload. Over two thousand military and civilian personnel are working in ADAPCPs.

If the soldier refuses to go into "the track," he or she is, in effect, refusing a direct order from a commanding officer; this is a court-martial offense. It may result in a discharge—honorable or less-than-honorable. "But," says O'Meara, "I am not aware of any cases where an individual has refused to go into treatment because of marijuana. It does happen sometimes in the case of alcohol addiction."

Although some people may enter the army with the mistaken illusion that marijuana is not a drug, merely a recreational pastime, they do not retain this view for long. Says O'Meara, "This office has used every possible means to get the word out that illegal drugs, including marijuana, are not condoned in the army. We use the armed forces radio and television service, the Army News Service, the *Army Times,* and our own bulletins. In all of our publications we have talked about the physical and psychological health hazards of marijuana use."

On August 17, 1982, Secretary of the Army John O. Marsh, Jr., and Army Chief of Staff General E. C. Meyer signed a memorandum for all personnel: The Army Alcohol and Drug Abuse Policy Statement. "There is no place in the Army for abuse of alcohol or drugs. It affects the morale, discipline, health and safety not only of our soldiers and civilian employees, but also of their families, friends, and co-workers."

This policy is being translated into effective action. Furthermore, as Colonel O'Meara puts it, "We have lots of things coming down the pike that will help even further. One thing we're working on is in the area of the army family, and what help we can give them regarding drug use by a soldier's spouse or child."

The Air Force

As evidenced by both sets of worldwide statistics, in 1980 and 1982, drug use in the air force was far lower than in the other services; in fact, it was lower than in the civilian population in the eighteen-to-twenty-five age group. Lt. Col. Jack Killeen, formerly in the office of the Secretary of Defense, points out that there are several reasons for this. One is demographics. The air force tends to be somewhat older than the other services, more female, to have a higher educational level and a larger percentage of married personnel; it is the young, single male who has not gone to college who is the most "at risk" of becoming a drug-user.

"It is our judgment," says Colonel Killeen,

that the other chief reason for the lower use figures in the air force is accounted for by our drug and alcohol abuse program, which we started in 1971. We have sustained steady emphasis since that time—without the peaks and valleys of interest which occurred in the other services. For example, since 1971 we have had trained drug/alcohol abuse-prevention professionals in the air force. This has made a significant difference.

We have high standards of whom we take in the air force. Applicants are asked about drug use. We accept experimental marijuana users—which means very limited lifetime use. But, since the mid-seventies, applicants have been required to sign a document acknowledging their awareness of the fact that the air force does not tolerate drug or alcohol abuse, *on or off duty,* and should they be caught, they will be subject to disciplinary action which can include separation from the service. With the advent of urine testing we were able to crack down even more.

Random urine testing did not prove cost-effective for the air force; therefore, testing is now targeted to incidents that may be related to drug abuse, such as car accidents, erratic driving, unexplained lowered duty performance, petty theft, or disrespect for superior NCOs.

Like those of the other services, the air force program has its treatment and its drug education/prevention components. Its "hardnosed component" includes drug detection dogs and undercover investigators.

One feature of the air force prevention program is this: When airmen and women report for their first assignment, and for each new assignment thereafter, they are required to attend a four-hour course in drug and alcohol education within sixty days. The focus is on the drug and alcohol situation on the base and in the local community. Drug-prevention education has also been integrated into other areas of professional military education given by the air force. "This means," says Killeen, "that in order to get promoted, individuals must attend training to learn those things they have to know to attain the next rank. This goes from NCOs to general officers."

Since the army "started late" and the air force "started early," we will look in greater depth at the two services that came from far behind and within a single year achieved spectacular reductions of drug (pot) use: 62 percent in the navy, and 58 percent in the marines.

The Navy

The navy and the marines' all-out war on drugs was precipitated by two events.

The first was the 1980 Worldwide Drug Abuse Survey, released on November 14, 1980, which resulted in national headlines for these two services because of their extraordinarily high drug use. (Current pot use in the army was 40 percent, in the air force 20 percent, in the navy 47 percent, and in the marines 47 percent.)

The second event occured six months later: A Navy jet crashed onto the USS *Nimitz;* fourteen people were killed, another forty-four seriously injured, and twenty aircraft were damaged at a cost of over $100 million. Six of the dead sailors had cannabinoids in their urine.

As noted in a report to Congress, although there was no evidence that the six men were in any way responsible for the crash,

> the relevancy of this information becomes more pronounced when considered with the fact that the *USS Nimitz* had been at sea for 11 days prior to the accident and the DOD worldwide survey that shows 26 percent of the Navy E-1 to E-5 population reporting that they were "high while working." In addition, nearly one-half of all E-1 to E-5 respondents in the worldwide survey who indicated that this had occurred, reported experiencing this on 40 or more days during the preceding 12 months.

On July 9, 1981, two months after the *Nimitz* tragedy, Adm. Thomas B. Hayward inaugurated the navy's new Get Tough on Drugs Policy in a wireless message, which had navywide coverage. Included in Hayward's now-historic twelve-minute videotape were these no-holds-barred sentences:

> There is something going on in our ranks today that must be stamped out and stamped out fast, because there is no room for such conduct in our profession. . . . You've all seen it in the news and in political cartoons over the past several weeks. A Navy "sky-high" . . . "spaced out" on the job. Let me tell you, this kind of image of our Navy makes me

furious. . . . But the trouble is, we do have a problem. Looking at me right now on the screen are tens of thousands of young men and women wearing the uniform of the U.S. Navy who are recklessly and carelessly using drugs. . . . Some of you are hooked and won't admit it. . . . Some of you have become drug dependent and your performance is on the way down. . . . Some of you are just doing it for kicks, to get away with something, to be part of a different generation.

So I have two messages I wish to get across today—a message for those of you who are using drugs—and a message for those of you not on drugs.

For those using drugs, on liberty, at home, on the base, aboard ship, in your squadron, at work, my message is . . . "We're out to help you or to hammer you—take your choice.". . . Believe me, my policy is a "get tough" one. That policy is going to be transmitted down through the chain of command until every one of you feels it in your bones. . . . We're going to stamp out the abuse of drugs in our Navy fast.

To those not on drugs, the admiral's message was:

All it takes is your accepting one simple set of standards: "Not here"— "not on my watch"—"not in my division"—"not on my ship or in my squadron"—"not in my Navy." My request to each of you is that we do a turn—180 degrees—from our present stance of indifference, passivity and non-responsibility—"it's not my problem"—to one of commitment, activity and accepting that responsibility which clearly is ours. . . . Our pride in what we are doing, our professionalism in seeing to it that the job is done as well as we know how, rebel against those who think it's okay to mess around with drugs—it's okay to feel high on the job—it's okay to treat life in the Navy as just another job. The heck it is—*not in our Navy!*

Many firm words condemning drug abuse had been spoken by many members of the top brass in all of the services over many years. But Hayward's words were backed by action—on many fronts at once. The navy's War on Drugs became fully operational in February 1982. It focused on E-1s to E-5s, since surveys had shows that drug use among those grades was five times more likely than in other grades. The following are some of the fronts in the navy's war.

The Drug Abuse Education Program

The education program, in fact, begins prior to enlistment, for the navy shows a videotape to prospective recruits and their parents, informing them of the navy's policies on drug use. It is made very clear that this includes marijuana use—and why. A thirty-six hour education program alerts all navy personnel to the dangers of each illegal drug, and legal drug illegally used. In addition, there are videotapes for fleetwide distribution, and packages of anti–drug- and alcohol-abuse literature mailed to shore stations and ships at sea. All formal training schools have curricula that specifically cover the problems of drug and alcohol abuse, and include the latest authoritative information on substance abuse "to improve leader knowledge and effectiveness."

Rear Adm. Paul J. Mulloy, director of the navy's Human Resources Management Division (which includes the Division of Substance Abuse) puts it this way: "Our best weapon against drug abuse is information in any and all forms."

The Drug-Detection Dog Program

In 1980 the Navy had fifty-three drug-detection dogs. By September 1983 there were over two hundred dog teams; during the first half of 1983 they completed over fifty-two thousand searches at base entry points, on board ships, in barracks, warehouses, storage buildings, and aircraft. The dogs do double duty: detection and deterrence. Said Mulloy: "Drugs often 'went over the side' when the dogs came aboard."

Most of the dogs are large—German shepherds, Labrador retrievers, or German shorthair pointers. But some are small beagles, which can be lifted up to bunks and other overhead areas to sniff out drugs. Virtually all the dogs are trained to sit, or point, when they sniff the more readily available and heavily used substances, which of course includes marijuana.

"Dogs in the mailroom" became of prime importance after postal regulations were changed at the request of Congress in July 1982 in order to allow a military commander overseas or on the high seas to inspect or search the mails if he or she felt there was cause to believe that a letter or parcel contained drugs. Prior to that a letter or package could be opened only when permission was given by a U.S. postal inspector or federal magistrate— a difficult requirement when at sea. Now mail is fluroscoped for evidence of drugs, and dogs are used. If the dog points or "alerts" at a letter or package, the mail-room petty officer requests permission from the commanding officer to open the letter. Then, if drugs are found, one of several courses of action may be taken. A large quantity of drugs would indicate that the person is not merely a user, but also a dealer. The CO would, in all likelihood, let the individual receive the package and commence sales. The dealer would then be apprehended "in the act." In other cases, the CO may ask the recipient to open the package or letter in front of him or her. The new mail laws, plus the detection dogs, have had a tremendous effect in eliminating use of the mail as a conduit for illegal drug traffic to ships at sea.

The Naval Investigative Service (NIS)

Between August 1982 and August 1983, the Naval Investigative Service initiated 6,136 narcotics investigations. Their "territory" includes the Port Visit Program, in which NIS agents go into a port city before a carrier arrives. (The port stops of naval vessels are classified information.) Navy agents, in cooperation with local law enforcement personnel, make buys followed by arrests, so that before the ship gets into port, many—hopefully most—of the drug dealers are in jail. This is an effective program, especially in view of the fact that NIS activities are curtailed by the limited number of agents available. As one law enforcement official put it: "You have two dozen agents going into Hong Kong or Pattaya Beach (Thailand) or Naples . . . trying to clean up the city so that when a carrier shows up with five thousand men on board, five hundred of whom may be looking to buy, they'll have a hard time trying to find drugs."

The Master at Arms Mobile Training Team

Masters at Arms (MAAs) are commensurate with military police in the army. They set up workshops for the law enforcement personnel on the ships and the stations, showing, for example, different methods of smuggling, concealing, and using drugs on board. This program gives the local law enforcement naval personnel the latest information on law enforcement aspects of drug abuse.

Urine Testing

Despite the other important facets of the navy's detection/deterrence program, this one remains the most important. When "the war" started, the navy was processing some 120,000 urine specimens a year. By October 1983 they were processing 1.2 million. Every sample is tested for six drugs; five may vary—but every urine sample is tested for marijuana.

In 1980 the navy had a total of twenty portable testing kits, and no real plan of action to use them. By October 1983, they had five hundred kits in the field, on ships, shore stations, aviation squadrons, on submarines. The kits were used for primary screening. But, since the armed forces have a firm policy requiring a second confirmation test for each positive urine, the four small laboratories that were used in 1981 were expanded to five large labs by October 1983, each near a large navy base in the United States. The staff in these labs was increased some 300 percent, and the latest equipment was installed, costing almost 25 million dollars. In 1984, the Navy switched from GLC for its confirmation tests to the more expensive—and more sensitive—GC/MS.

Now, according to Lt. Comdr. Larry Ledford of the navy's Substance Abuse Office (manned by a staff of thirty), "Virtually all members of the Navy can be urine tested. In those locations or on those ships where a portable kit is not available, urine samples are collected and sent to a navy lab."

On October 4, 1983, in testifying before Congress on the navy's War on Drugs, Admiral Mulloy told members of the Senate Subcommittee on Defense Manpower and Personnel and Defense Preparedness:

> Not only do we perform a urine screening test and confirmatory test, monitor procedures and output through a rigorous quality control program, but, most importantly, we rely on the Commanding Officer's judgment in weighing all factors in a case, before substantiating and prosecuting drug abuse. We have had some lab mistakes and will probably never completely eliminate them. But in every case, we rectify if there is any doubt, and resolve in favor of the individual. In 11½ months of fiscal year 1983, we have had an error rate of .002 percent. But because of the potentially serious consequences of a determination, we are constantly working to improve even that low rate and ensure that each Navy individual suspected of drug abuse gets a fair and just hearing, and due process. In resolving cases, we "err" in favor of the individual while aggressively pursuing our goal of a drug-free Navy.

Mulloy also pointed out to the Senate Armed Services Committee that in 1983, based on the positive urine samples in the navy laboratories, marijuana use in the navy had dropped to 12 percent.

Another important deterrent aspect of the navy's War on Drugs is this: When a decision is made on a case, the results are not kept secret. Although the name of the offender is never published, the "Plan of the Day," a mimeographed or printed sheet distributed or posted for all to see, includes—amid such items as the movie of the night and notice of examination dates—the outcome of either nonjudicial punishment or court-martial proceedings against an individual who has been involved with drugs. For example: These items appeared in August 1983:

• Lieutenant (Junior Grade)/USN. General court-martial for possession and distribution of 26 grams of marijuana. Sentenced to confinement at hard labor for 14 months. Total forfeiture of all pay and allowances, and dismissed from the naval service.

• Petty officer third class/USNR on active duty. Special court-martial for possession of marijuana. Sentenced to confinement at hard labor for three months, reduction to grade E-1 and bad conduct discharge.

- Seaman Recruit/USN. Special court-martial for distribution of marijuana, sentenced to confinement at hard labor for five months, forfeiture of $382 per month for four months, and bad conduct discharge.

Since 1981 the navy has had a Voluntary Self-Referral Program. Any enlisted person or officer who requests help with a drug or alcohol problem will be afforded treatment on one of three levels, similar to the army's "three track" program.

Admiral Mulloy's Human Resources Management Division includes the Family Services Division and the Health and Physical Readiness Division—which also play a part in the navy's War on Drugs. For example, the Navy's Family Service Centers (FSC) are available to some 85 percent of navy personnel. The FSCs assist the dependents of navy personnel in counseling ranging from financial management to substance abuse—which includes help for drug-abusing members of a sailor's family.

The matter of drug-using dependents is a two-way street. A strong deterrent to dependents' drug use is this: A sailor can be removed from housing on base because of drug involvement by dependents. Also, dependents can be barred from the base as a result of drug violations.

Furthermore, according to Lt. Comdr. Deborah Burnette, deputy assistant for public affairs at the Navy Military Personnel Command in Washington, DC,

All the services are now working with local citizen groups, including parent groups, youth groups, and law enforcement officials, in areas where there are military bases in order to educate and also to curb availability of illegal drugs in the community. Participation by military people in the local communities has increased noticeably since early 1982. This is an unusual development for military people, but as awareness of the drug problem is increased among the military they, for example, became concerned about their own youngsters, who are attending local schools, a local Y, and who work, study and play in the community.

An intergral part of the navy's antidrug program is the Health and Physical Readiness Program, which provides alternatives to substance abuse by encouraging healthy lifestyles and physical fitness training programs, which include substance abuse prevention.

The success of the navy's War on Drugs can be summed up by two statistics:

- Between 1980 and 1982 the Navy cut pot use in half—the most dramatic reduction seen in any of the services.

- The navy's War on Drugs program officially started in February 1982. The second Worldwide Drug Abuse Survey was done from September to November 1982. The navy had achieved its drug-use reductions in eight to ten months!

Furthermore, the program impacted on areas beyond specific drug-use figures. On November 10, 1983, Senator Paula Hawkins, chairperson of the U.S. Senate Drug Abuse Caucus, put it this way:

> By far the Navy has achieved the most dramatic results in reducing drug abuse levels. . . . The Navy is also achieving increases in overall unit operational readiness, personnel readiness, retention (people signing up for another tour of duty) and recruiting. . . . The peer responsibility in attacking the problem of drug abuse cannot be underestimated.

That same month, November 1983, *SSAM,* a monthly publication put out by civilians for the military, ran a series of letters on the subject—in response to one from a user with gripes about the navy's War on Drugs. An E-4 wrote:

> I don't object to urinalysis or searches of any kind. I also know from experience that marijuana does cause damage to a person's state of mind. My memory has improved over the past four years since I smoked my last joint. It is not as up-to-par as it was before I ever heard of marijuana, but it has improved.

Another E-4 wrote:

> I learned the hard way. Marijuana has no place in the military; they are serious about it and they will find *you* sooner or later. I only wish that I had seen the obvious sooner. I am one of the lucky ones who still has a job. I'll prove myself again. But I'll never risk it all again for a high.

An E-5 wrote:

> As a civilian, I smoked marijuana and hash regularly. I did every other form of drug available. There are three years of my life that I remember very little about—the three years that I was a drug abuser. I came into the Navy on a drug waiver and my first goal was never to abuse any type of drug again. And reaching that goal was so easy! I've never felt cleaner or stronger in my life.

The Marines

The program of the U.S. Marines is almost a duplicate of the navy's, except that in a few areas it is "even more so."

The marines' War on Drugs also went into action on February 1, 1982—after a call to arms from Comm. Gen. Robert E. Barrow—top man in the marines. "My aim," said the general, "is to have a *drug-free Marine Corps.* Marines who persist in the use of illegal drugs will be separated from the Marine Corps." He also announced:

> From now on, *I* am "the" drug and alcohol abuse officer in the Marine Corps. . . . When I make my rounds, I will expect to see positive results. A total leadership effort involving full participation by all officers and NCOs is required. Marine Corps leadership at all levels must be thoroughly knowledgeable on the drug problem.

Since then all marine officers have received intensive awareness training (plus "updates") in the substance-abuse area. All E-5s are required to take a written test, which includes twenty-two multiple-choice questions on substance abuse. In addition, the marines, along with the navy, frequently sponsor programs for enlisted personnel and officers on substance abuse. According to military personnel in this area, the subject that interests enlisted personnel most is marijuana—the harm it can do. Said Lt. Col. Marguerite Campbell, chief of the marines' Drug and Alcohol Section, "The questions after the marijuana sessions generally include: 'Why don't the high schools teach us about this?' 'Why haven't I heard this before?' "

Perhaps the single most noteworthy marijuana program sponsored by the navy and the marines was the lecture tour of Dr. Harold Voth, rear admiral, Medical Corps, U.S. Naval Reserve, with thirty-nine years in the service. Voth is also chief of staff of the Veterans Administration Hospital in Topeka, professor of psychiatry at the University of Kansas School of Medicine, on the faculty of the Menninger School of Psychiatry, and a practicing psychiatrist who has specialized in the psychopathology of marijuana-using patients for over a decade.

In 1982 he traveled thousands of miles to lecture aboard ships and at naval and marine bases. On one trip he gave eighteen lectures in three days, speaking to audiences of two hundred to five hundred each time. In his talks he stressed two themes: the physical and psychological health hazards of marijuana, and the "wounded marine" or "peer responsibility concept." In lecturing to the Marine Corps General Officer Symposium, he put it this way: "Marines are noted for saving their wounded. You've got to have the same sense of responsibility when it comes to helping a marine wounded by drug abuse. *A drug-using serviceman is a wounded man. If he cannot save himself, and most substance abusers can't, then others must save him.*"

Central to the concept is the acknowledgment of the existence of a battlefield whereon non–drug-users fight for the recovery of the drug-users—the walking wounded of the peacetime armed services.

According to Lieutenant Colonel Campbell,

> From all reports, the attitude about the drug-user has changed in the marines. Our war on drugs is achieving a new realization among our men and women—that each marine *has* the responsibility to help save a comrade who is a drug-user by the encouragement to understand that any marine who recognizes his or her drug problem, and who is sincere in trying to solve it, has half the battle won. Whether the person sees his CO, the drug and alcohol control officer, or the local drug/alcohol counselor, the first step toward becoming a healthy and productive marine is to seek help.
>
> If the peer-encouragement to seek help gets nowhere, marines are beginning to understand that an anonymous phone call to, or conference with, the CO or other appropriate person is not the act of a "fink" or a "narc," but instead that of a responsible friend taking the single most important initial step in helping the drug-user recover.
>
> Most marines also now understand that everyone who enters the service has the *right* to a drug-free environment, and we are determined to protect the rights of the drug-free.

How well do the marines' knowledge-plus-deterrence policies hold up in time of emergency? The programs were well tested when marines were sent to Lebanon—known as one of the hashish capitals of the world. All systems were "set to go" regarding the doing of drugs, notably hashish. The marines were lonely, bored, had excessive free time. They were, in the main, single males, E-1s to E-5s. Furthermore, they were surrounded by daily and nightly twenty-four-hour opportunities for a low-priced escape into a "hash high."

Yet they had been warned that every marine returning from Lebanon would be given a urine test. (If all members of a ship or unit are tested, this procedure has been upheld in court as being just as legal as random testing.) The urine samples were taken aboard ship, and flown to the laboratories—arriving in the States before their donors did.

In the 1980 Worldwide Survey of Nonmedical Drug Use, the marines had the highest percentage of pot use of any of the services: 51 percent of E-1 through E-5 marines had used marijuana during the past 30 days; 25 percent of E-1s through E-5s had been "high while working," and half this number reported "experiencing this on 40 or more days during the preceding 12 months." Furthermore, one in every four enlisted marines reported being "high more than one day at a time," and 13 percent self-estimated that the high had resulted in lowered performance on duty. (Their officers might have upped this figure considerably, since one symptom of marijuana abuse is that the user feels he or she is "doing just fine.")

How many marines returning from Lebanon—"the hashish capital"—had cannabinoids in their urine?

One percent.

Chapter 20

The Workplace:
Successful Programs

Compared to schools and the armed forces, the workplace has perhaps dragged its feet the most when it comes to facing up to the problems of drug abuse. "But," says Peter Bensinger, a specialist in the subject of drug abuse in industry, "the first important sign of progress is the recognition of the problem."

Once recognized, employers are handling the matter in a variety of ways.

Employee Assistance Programs

Addressing the drug problem is not as difficult as it may initially sound, for, in many cases, the structure for doing so is already in place in the form of EAPs (Employee Assistance Programs), which have existed for years to help employees with alcohol problems.

According to Dr. William Mayer, former administrator of the federal government's Alcohol, Drug Abuse and Mental Health Administration (ADAMHA), "From 1972 to 1982 there was a growth in the Employee Assistance Programs from fewer than 300 to more than 5,500. Twelve percent of all firms in the U.S. have EAPs, and 70 percent of those programs now assist in problems of drug abuse as well as alcohol abuse."

Ed Johnson is corporate manager of Firestone's EAPs in over thirty-five work locations in the United States. Firestone was one of the first large companies in the country to include drug abuse along with alcohol abuse in their EAPs. Johnson notes:

Firestone's program is not based on bloodshot eyes or smelling breath— if we used that type of approach we'd be running a witchhunt. We base

386

our approach on work deterioration and absenteeism. We spend a lot of time training our supervisors not to be amateur diagnosticians; to stick strictly to work performance criteria. We find that the average drug-abuser in the workforce is working at about 65 percent of his or her potential, so they're often not hard to spot. For example, if the blue-collar worker who should be producing 20 widgets (wheel rims) per hour is only producing 12 or 15, you can tell almost instantly what his rate of production is. When he does this continually day after day, the whole section or department suffers because their unit is not cost effective, and the supervisor suffers because his boss is getting on him. The supervisor then has a valid reason to say to the employee: "You've got problems which are beyond my scope and I'm going to suggest that you see the people at the EAP." (There is an EAP representative in all the branches.) The EAP makes the evaluation; then refers the worker to appropriate community resources.

When the employee comes back to work, he usually returns at about 115 percent of production standards because he's grateful that he's off drugs and he's grateful to the company for helping him to get off. None of us likes to be dependent on drugs.

Johnson also points out,

Marijuana affects production for hours after the worker comes down from the high. This ranges from the blue-collar worker who is applying treads to a tire and can't get them aligned straight before the tire is molded in the machine, to the executive who studies a piece of paper for several hours trying to make a logical decision—but his brain is muddled. He may make the wrong decision—but usually it's no decision at all. This man or woman is showing on-the-job absenteeism. He or she is there physically, but not mentally.

He sums up:

We have often said that at Firestone we have, and work with, an 85/15 syndrome. In other words, 85 percent of our employees never give us any problem—15 percent do—and that 15 percent is where our [EAP] efforts are concentrated. Over a period of time we identify and intervene with 85 percent of that 15 percent factor, and approximately 85 percent that we identify respond favorably; 15 percent do not—they become our recidivists. Eventually we will get a response from approximately 85 percent of that 15 percent—the balance quit, are terminated, or die.

Some large companies and factories have their own EAPs. In most cases, the purpose of an employee counseling services program is to identify the nature of the problem, not to provide treatment. The employee is referred by the counselor to an outside community resource for the necessary treatment.

One of the most frequently used drug treatment approaches is the establishment of a consortium of small agencies. In this arrangement, agencies join together and, through a formal contractual agreement with a private organization, establish an appropriate program for their employees.

Often the drug-abuser is given a leave of absence with a promise of reinstatement when he or she is drug-free. Insurance and other benefits continue during this period. More and more unions are asking for, and receiving, drug-treatment coverage in company health insurance policies.

Overall, according to Senator Paula Hawkins, then head of the U.S. Senate Drug Abuse Caucus, the success ratio of EAPs falls between 50 and 70 percent.

Peter Bensinger has this to say about EAPs: "They are a step in the right direction, but we must realize that most often they deal only with the end stages when the price is already high for the individual and for the company. Very few people in industry are doing anything about identifying the marijuana user earlier. That's why the urine test is so important."

Undercover Agents

Another approach to the problem of drug use and drug-dealing on the job is the hiring of undercover agents. Positive results are often quick to come. For example, when rising operating costs and extremely late shipments pushed a division of Armco's National Supply Company into the red, undercover agents were called in. A six-month investigation led to the arrest of some twenty-five employees on drug violations—including a few supervisors. The "kingpin" of the operation was a quality-control inspector with twenty-five years of service.

One week later, minor accidents had decreased by two-thirds and productivity was up 15 percent. Within three months, the plant was back in the black. Quality improved noticeably, and employee turnover, which had been running about 30 percent, declined substantially.

Some firms are reluctant to investigate drug use, fearing the resultant publicity will impact badly on the firm name and products. Often, however, the opposite is the case. For example, in June 1980, Compugraphic Corporation of Wilmington, Massachusetts, the largest manufacturer of typesetting equipment for the printing and publishing industries throughout the world, identified workers who were selling drugs on the premises. The company had called in undercover narcotics agents, but with instructions that the company name be kept out of the papers. Thirteen employees were arrested; their drug ring had taken in an estimated forty thousand dollars a month. Somehow, the news was leaked. But the headlines resulted in such favorable reaction from the public that Compugraphic employee morale soared; some workers even sported T-shirts reading "We survived the C-G bust!"

David R. Dearborn, former director of investigations and now assistant vice president of Pinkerton, puts it this way:

> One thing is certain: Those firms and industries who use the difficulty in "fingering" drug-users as an excuse to avoid addressing the problem do not receive the general approval of their employees. Quite the contrary. In nine out of ten cases where our investigations have exposed drug problems, the overall spirit of the shop seems to lift up because they're glad somebody has finally done something about the matter.

Though employee morale may be raised after dismissal of drug-involved workers, quick firing is not necessarily the best solution for those workers, or for the public in general. As Peter Bensinger points out: "Quick firing merely 'dumps' the drug user onto another employer—or onto welfare. A far better approach for all concerned is employee assistance and rehabilitation."

Self-Referral

Some companies have stressed the importance of self-referral for employees and their dependents, before a serious problem develops in the home or workplace. A cornerstone of ensuring maximum utilization of the EAP and the self-referral programs rests in the dual task of educating employees about the helpful nature of the programs while simultaneously assuring them that their jobs will not be in jeopardy because of participation. The Stroh Brewery accomplished this through a continuous barrage of company/union newsletter articles, posters, testimonials of successfully treated employees, annual employee training sessions, and letters to employees' homes. A strict adherence to the privacy and anonymity of program participation helped dispel fears that referral would adversely affect an employee's work status.

Stroh has encouraged innovative steps to reach employees at times of crisis by supporting the establishment of a twenty-four-hour, seven-day-a-week EAP hot line, as well as offering educational seminars to draw family members into the program office. The company has also established a joint labor/management advisory committee.

Union/Management Cooperation

The importance of union/management cooperation in the drug abuse area cannot be overestimated. Sometimes the recovery programs start with the union. For example, Local 933, the largest United Auto Workers local in Indiana, was the first UAW local in the state to start an alcohol recovery program. Three years later, in 1973, they expanded the program to include drug abuse as well. Their referrals come from first-line supervisors, (those who *directly* supervise workers), the medical department, from family members of the employee, and in some cases from the court system. One important part of this union program is the "supportive activities" at the union hall. On Mondays there is a support group for families of "troubled employees"; on Wednesdays, a Narcotics Anonymous meeting; on Thursdays, open Alcoholics Anonymous, Al-Anon and Al-Teen meetings; and on Fridays, another family support group.

According to Llosy Liscomb, union representative in the EAP, "Prior to 1978, what we had was a union-oriented program. We were successful in what we were doing but the effectiveness of our program has greatly increased due to the fact that management has joined our efforts, and we now have a joint program." Liscomb also pointed out that in 1978, the program moved away from the personnel department and was put under the medical department. That move made the program more effective due to the emphasis on the medical aspect, and the department's established respect for confidential material.

Other Approaches

Ira Lipman, president of the security services company Guardsmark, believes that another way for companies to attack the problem is by offering financial incentives to workers in departments where drug use is heavy. "Eliminate lost time, absenteeism and malingering by having incentives based on productivity," he says. "Drug users would have to straighten up because of pressure from their peers."

A different method was used by C. Gregory Thomas, general manager of a wood-products manufacturing plant in Edwardsville, Illinois. In a small plant like this, the recognition factor is not difficult. Mr. Thomas recalls:

I could smell it on their clothes. Their eyes were bloodshot and glassy. They had little "pot areas" in our 150,000-square-foot warehouse facilities. I would find marijuana seeds and roaches [butts]. I would also see the results of the pot smoking. Their level of concentration was very poor. In most cases employees have to read an order, go into the warehouse, and select the materials the order calls for. They can't take the order with them because others are using it at the same time. The orders are not complicated, but the pot-smokers would have to come back several times to reread the order because they'd forgotten the numbers while crossing to the warehouse, or else they'd bring back the wrong things. Also, their judgment was affected. For example, they'd drill too large a hole. And carelessness became a big—and expensive—factor. They often shipped a load of kitchen cabinets or furniture to the wrong place. The men smoked during their two breaks. And after the breaks they were more irritable. The slightest reprimand would make them turn surly. Sometimes they threatened to beat up the foreman.

At first, I spent a lot of time trying to talk them out of their pot using—at least before and during work. This did no good at all.

Then Thomas hit on a method of handling the situation. When the young workers drop out or are fired, he replaces them with men age forty or older. "That way," he says, "I'm pretty sure I don't end up with pot smokers. Everything's going just fine at our plant now."

Some companies have dismissed employees for off-site use. For example, the Virginia Electric Power Company learned that at its Surry Nuclear Plant a number of security guards were using marijuana on the way to work and off duty. They decided to dismiss these employees, and then published a rule stating that off-duty use of drugs could be cause for disciplinary action up to and including dismissal, if it affected job performance or the public's confidence in the integrity of the company and its employees.

Health Promotion Programs

A relatively new prevention approach is the concept of health promotion programs. A 1980 survey showed that among U.S. companies employing more than one hundred people, some six hundred such programs had been started. Some stress physical fitness; some include smoking cessation, hypertension control, nutrition, weight loss, stress management—and drug and alcohol control.

One essential ingredient of the health promotion program should be information on the health hazards of marijuana and other drugs. Indeed, this is the first item in Peter Bensinger's list of the five ingredients essential to the success of any program to eliminate drug abuse in the workplace:

1. Accurate information on marijuana and other drugs made available to every employee.

2. A clear statement of company policy on drug use, including penalties.

3. Training for supervisors: "Know your people" is the key.

4. Reaching out to the unions. Before the policy is issued, unions should be invited to comment on it, not to make the policy, but to provide the essential communication link.

5. The law enforcement community should also be involved. "In my view," says Bensinger, "a company cannot take the position, 'Well, we can decide what drugs we will report to the police, and what we won't.' Employees cannot violate the law."

The Supervisor's Role

In large plants or organizations, a vital key to the success of most types of effective drug-abuse programs is the role of supervisors. They are in the best position to spot the potential substance-abuser—and to do something about it. But unless they are made to feel responsible and unless they are specifically trained in how to address the problem, they frequently close their eyes to it, or pass the buck. As Joseph Taylor, director of investigations for Burns International Security Services, put it:

> The supervisors may suspect something is going on, but they don't know how to come to grips with it. Other supervisors want to avoid getting involved and creating antagonisms. And some supervisors sell stuff to users in the plant.
>
> But perhaps what is most common are supervisors who have not been exposed to the drug culture, and feel uncomfortable about involving themselves in it in any way. So they don't act—even though they know what is going on. Other workers won't report on the drug abusers if the supervisor does nothing. The result is that the employer knows nothing about drug use among his workers.

On the other hand, if supervisors are trained in workshops or seminars, they usually prove a responsible and essential link in the chain of curing the employee drug-abuser. In such workshops, supervisors learn that the earlier the abuser is spotted, the more likely it is that he or she can be helped, and the easier the rehabilitation job will be.

According to one excellent booklet on the subject, "The Supervisor's Handbook on Substance Abuse," "It must also be stressed that supervisors or executives in a business firm should not attempt to diagnose or counsel. This must be left to the professionals. The supervisor's role is to pinpoint the drug-abusing worker."

One prime clue is absenteeism. This is such a clearcut signal that some firms have been successful in spotting drug-abusers simply by keeping a running record of absenteeism. General Motors' medical director Dr. Robert Wiencek says, "If I were to make a single recommendation to every firm in America in this regard, I would say track absenteeism accurately. Instead of calling in sick, many workers say, 'I'm going to take this as a vacation day.' If it's every Monday—you can wonder."

Other signs, signals, or symptoms of drug use include:

• Increasing lateness, extended lunch periods, more frequent trips to the toilet, and unexplained disappearances from the job.

• Falling asleep on the job.

• Careless handling and maintenance of machinery, disregard for safety, including the safety of co-workers.

• Deterioration of work performance, which can include inconsistent quality of work, lowered productivity, poor memory, faulty concentration, spasmodic work pace, neglect of details, chronic fatigue.

• Changes in attitude, which can include a change in personality (a chatty person who clams up, or vice versa), putting the blame on others, irritability and hostility, inability to accept justified criticism. Frequently the supervisor and even co-workers are deliberately avoided. The "caring less about everything" syndrome—including personal appearance. There is often a detectable difference in the drug-abuser's gait and sometimes a difference in the eyes. (Red eyes are often an indication of pot use.)

• Co-workers may show signs of poor morale, a result of resentment toward the drug-abuser, plus the confusion of trying to cover up for him or her.

Workshops and handbooks for supervisors also make it clear that once the potential drug-user has been identified, supervisors should not confront the person with a charge or even mention the matter. Instead they should talk to the employee *about the decline in work performance,* and have documentable evidence (such as specific notes on such matters as absenteeism, mistakes, and failure to meet deadlines). This first approach should be "low key," merely a job evaluation session—but without sympathetic or apologetic overtones.

If, after this warning, a second session is necessary, the supervisor should make the employee fully aware of the company's policies regarding treatment for drug and/or alcohol abuse, and the confidentiality of such treatment. The employee should be encouraged to go to the designated department for further consultation. If he or she does not take advantage of this opportunity, the supervisor must make it clear that *this* choice can result in a job action.

According to the "Supervisor's Handbook on Substance Abuse,"

When the abuser finally agrees, or is obliged to accept treatment, the supervisor should make the appointment, offer encouragement, express optimism for the outcome and schedule follow-up interviews to discuss progress. No one likes fingering a friend or a colleague. But the critical point to remember is that the supervisor is not helping the individual abuser by neglecting the problem, and is certainly not upholding his or her responsibility to the organization and to the people within the company who have come to depend upon each other.

What happens when the employee goes for counseling? Increasingly, urine tests are given, along with a complete physical. Drug-abuse counseling— with job jeopardy as a prime reason for continuing the treatment—results in a high percentage of cures. (As noted by Firestone's EAP director Ed Johnson, "In our case, 85 percent of our workers return to their jobs drug-free.")

Other Important Considerations

One essential for employers to look into prior to—or even while—embarking on an EAP and/or outside treatment program is this: What is the attitude of the treatment professionals toward marijuana?

Ed Johnson and Peter Bensinger both make this point: Many drug-abuse treatment professionals do not understand or know how to treat the marijuana-abusing employee. Bensinger puts it this way: "They tend to treat the employee for his or her alcohol and/or other drug problems and to shrug off marijuana as a 'soft' or recreational drug.

"The term 'soft' vs. 'hard' drugs," says Bensinger, "implies that one type of use is more acceptable than another. It gives a wrong and totally inaccurate signal."

Bensinger also points out that many treatment professionals as well as middle- and upper-management people may have experimented with marijuana a decade ago, and found it to be mild. "They don't realize that today's marijuana is ten times as strong."

If the treatment professional does "not bother about" marijuana—and many do not—the user becomes increasingly dependent psychologically upon his joints. Furthermore, not dealing with marijuana will mean a continued lack of energy, lack of vigilance, short-term memory loss, and so on, plus the pernicious danger of acting against company policy, which prohibits illegal drug use on company time and which prohibits employees from working under the influence of alcohol and drugs. Also, if the employee is using drugs in addition to marijuana, any treatment being directed at these drugs, including alcohol, will be compromised. Says Bensinger,

> Companies should ensure that treatment professionals not only discourage the use of all drugs but do not look the other way with personal philosophies or opinions that are contrary to the law, and to the important health research now available on marijuana.
>
> It is *essential,* before employing an outside treatment professional or firm, that this question on marijuana be fully addressed.

Another important consideration is this: Dismissal from the treatment program as drug-free does not automatically mean that the former user has no more problems on this score. As noted in Chapter 12, the chronic user has often become involved in a drug-centered way of life, and has adopted a different set of values from those in the "straight" world. Returning to work straight, he or she feels like a foreigner in a strange country. Not only that, he or she must overcome the earlier stigma of having been a drug-abuser. "The Supervisor's Handbook on Substance Abuse" points out in this regard:

> Sympathy and over-protectiveness should play no part in deciding work assignments since this may only reinforce the stigma and the attitude that the drug abuser is somehow "different." On the one hand the problem employee should not be given preferential treatment. On the other hand, one short period of treatment does not constitute full recovery. Drug abusers returning to the working place often have feelings of guilt and low self-esteem. Regaining the respect of others thus becomes doubly important. Just as the supervisor is not expected to dismiss poor working quality in a person being rehabilitated, so he or she should not neglect good work when it is apparent.
>
> Such reinforcement, when it is honest and deserved, can be of immeasurable value to the returning employee. The supervisor may notice rough spots along the way. He or she may spot in the user changes in mood, difficulty in coping with routine situations, lack of interest in the duties at hand or strained relationships. These may be danger signs on the road to recovery and so the supervisor should remain understanding but alert.

A slip does not necessarily mean that treatment has failed. In certain instances, it may serve as a reminder to the abuser that he or she is simply unable to continue drug use and at the same time recover.

Cost-Effectiveness

Programs aimed at combating and conquering the problems of drug use in the workplace may be expensive, but they are dramatically cost-effective. As an example, in 1972, GM and the United Automobile Workers embarked on a joint corporation-wide alcoholism recovery program, which was later expanded to include drugs, and now covers over 130 GM plants in North America. It begins with a pre-employment urine screening for drugs. Says Medical Director Dr. Robert Wiencek, "We would not generally hire anyone who is an active user of drugs."

One of the shop and safety rules approved by GM's union and management is that the sale, possession, or use of illicit drugs on the premises is specifically prohibited and subject to disciplinary action, which ranges from being sent home without pay to discharge—depending on the number and seriousness of the offenses. However, Wiencek notes, "Instead of saying, 'Give up pot, or we'll fire you,' our approach generally is 'We don't want to fire you because we need you, so how can we help?' "

Studies GM conducted before treatment showed that the drug-dependent employees experienced twice as many occupational injuries as the non–drug-dependent employees. They had a higher number of days of unexcused absence, and visited the medical department fifteen times more often for nonoccupational complaints. After five months of treatment, the occupational injury rate dropped to a level comparable to that of the nonuser. Visits to the medical department for nonoccupational complaints remained only slightly higher than for the nonuser. (This rate remained higher partially because they continued to have psychosomatic complaints of unknown etiology—or cause.) And after five months of treatment there was an overall average reduction in absenteeism of 80.6 percent.

GM is one of the pioneers in drug-abuse treatment in industry, and since their program began in 1972, well over fifty thousand employees have been referred for help, or have sought it on their own. A cost-effectiveness study conducted for GM by research consultants from the University of Michigan found that during the first year after entry into the program, there was a 40 percent reduction in lost time among participants. Sickness and accident-benefits utilization for the same group was reduced by 60 percent. Grievances were cut as much as 50 percent. Disciplinary action taken by management against the former drug-user was cut in half. Occupational injuries were also reduced by 50 percent.

The researchers figured that GM was getting better than a two-for-one return on their money. For every dollar spent by GM for treatment of employees in the program, more than two dollars were being returned to the company within a period of three years. The rate of return was based solely on savings due to improvements in attendance and reductions in the use of sickness and accident benefits. Obviously, there were savings in other areas as well.

Since $65 billion per year is being lost through drug and alcohol use in the workplace, it is clear that individual companies can save substantial sums of money by recognizing the problem and by addressing it in constructive ways.

Furthermore, the programs prove "cost effective" for the former drug-user as well. Perry Izenson, director of Pot Smokers Anonymous in New York City, has an overall view on this aspect of the subject. She says:

> People who come to see us are a cross-section of the job population: physicians, cab drivers, crane operators, teachers. You name it, they've been here. When they graduate we tell them not to smoke for one year and if that year was not far more productive than five previous years when they were smoking, we invite them to take up pot again. Seventy-five percent of our graduates keep off the drug. And virtually all of them say their lives, including their job performance, have dramatically improved.
>
> We've treated well over a thousand people since we started in 1978. Most people who come in do not see themselves as having any problem professionally. They came in because of other problems with the drug—for example, a wife who says "Stop pot smoking or I'm going to get a divorce." Something subtle like that.
>
> But when they *do* stop, they realize all the things pot was preventing them from doing. They find they become much more productive—in the workplace as well as other ways. This is seen most dramatically in salesmen because they work on commission. It's not uncommon for them to triple their income within a year after they've given up pot smoking completely.

In December 1983 the television program *Wall Street Week* did an exposé on rampant cocaine use among Wall Street brokerage employees, making the point that firms were doing little or nothing about addressing the problem since they felt if it became known that their employees were users, investors would take their business to a competitor.

This same fear can be found among employers in innumerable businesses and industries. However, as pointed out earlier, often the reverse happens: The public trust in the company is enhanced by the firm anti–drug-use policies. And, in addition, the morale of the non–drug-using employees is almost invariably lifted. Companies willing to recognize these two positive factors often falter at the next-step excuse. Drug use in the workplace is so pervasive that to deal with it effectively seems a virtual impossibility. Firms therefore choose the other alternative: They do nothing.

They fail to realize that they hold in their hands the most strategic card of all in curing the civilian drug-abuser. The trump card held by every civilian employer is job jeopardy. As Peter Bensinger puts it:

> One characteristic typical of drug-users is their tremendous dependence on their job. They initially feel that they need the paycheck to feed their habit. Then, when the rehabilitative process begins, it has been found that—with the threat of job action as the prime motivator—they will respond and change their behavior far more readily than they will from home, family, friends, church or any other type of influence. *Job jeopardy has clearly been found to be the single most effective tool that we have in the rehabilitation of the drug-user.*

Chapter 21

The Texans' War on Drugs

It's a no-holds-barred name, which might be considered "typically Texan." But what makes it unique is the fact that not only do Texans mean it, but they are doing more about it than any state in the nation. Within two years Texans organized a remarkable all-action network of existing organizations working together in an integrated antidrug effort, fired and inspired, and to some extent funded, by a superstructure of a brand-new network headed by some of the most effective movers and shakers in the state.

Whereas action in other states started—and for the most part remains—at the grassroots level, an almost all-volunteer effort, the Texas operation started "at the top," although it too is an almost all-volunteer effort.

The success of the Texans' War on Drugs has not only had great impact in that state, but has had national—even international—ramifications. Other states, impressed by what Texas has done, are starting to emulate its system. And at their April 1982 meeting the International Association of Lions Clubs, inspired by the Texans' War on Drugs, adopted drug-abuse education and prevention as a primary program for their 35,837 Lions Clubs, 4,042 Lioness Clubs, and 3,656 Leo Clubs in 157 countries around the world—the first international service organization to adopt drug-abuse prevention as an intensive program.

It started in 1979 when the new governor, William Clements, asked Texas multimillionaire H. Ross Perot to head a volunteer committee to address the problem of drug abuse—which Clements had realized, when campaigning, was of primary concern to the people of Texas.

Perot and two partners had founded Electronic Data Systems (EDS) with a thousand dollars in savings and a staff of two. Within six years all three had become multimillionaires. As a founder of a firm with eighty-five hundred employees, which operated in forty-nine states and four foreign countries, Perot knew how to organize a successful business, but as he told the governor, he didn't know a thing about drugs.

The other seventeen members of the newly named Texans' War on Drugs Committee knew as little about drug abuse as their chairman. But each was well known in his or her area, and all had a history of producing results in their business and civic activities. It was a nonpolitical bipartisan group, and it had nothing to do with existing state drug-abuse agencies—which continued their activities, primarily in the treatment area.

The committee had four mandates from the governor:

1. Get the children of Texas off drugs and keep them off.

2. Make Texas the worst state in the United States for major drug dealers to operate in.

3. Thoroughly research this problem and develop specific programs, involving prevention, treatment, law enforcement, and needed legislation.

4. Make sure that justice is administered even-handedly.

The committee first spent a year and a half on Number 3. As Perot put it: "Before we do anything about this problem, we're going to learn everything we can about it." They met with judges and prosecutors across the state, and with Coast Guard and drug enforcement officers at the federal, state, and local levels. They visited treatment centers and state mental institutions where children and adults were being treated for drug use, interviewing staff and patients. They interviewed school children who were using drugs. They looked at the figures—more high school seniors smoking pot daily than using alcohol daily (including beer); more seventeen-year-olds smoking marijuana than tobacco cigarettes. And they compared those figures to 1964, when only 2 percent of young people in the United States had ever used marijuana or any other illegal drug.

They studied the effects of pot and other drugs on users, children in particular. Perot spent a week at NIDA. Then the committee visited marijuana researchers and attended conferences, where they videotaped the scientists who presented material. They concluded, in Perot's words, "that the evidence is overwhelming that continuous use of drugs, particularly by young people while their minds and bodies are still growing and developing, has devastating long-term effects."

The committee also studied the international flow of drug traffic. Perot visited Colombia, interviewing government officials. He and other committee members talked to convicted drug smugglers in Texas jails and prisons, learning that roughly 80 percent of all Texas prisoners were involved with drug-related crime. They learned that Texas had two of the top three smuggling airports in the United States: Dallas/Ft. Worth and Houston (the third was Miami). They learned that even college girls were acting as "mules": transporting such compact drugs as heroin and cocaine inside their bodies. The students were generally given a free round-trip ticket to Mexico, plus two hundred dollars for the hazardous weekend jaunt.

They learned, furthermore, that Texas, with its eight hundred miles of sea coast and eleven hundred miles of land border with Mexico, plus its vast wide-open spaces, "accommodated" an estimated fifty illegal aircraft a day, flying across the border carrying drugs; about 80 percent of this was marijuana. Convicted air smugglers informed them that planes were often stolen, flown to Mexico, returned loaded with pot, thoroughly cleaned, and put back in the hangar. In some cases the owner never knew it had been taken.

After studying the situation in the state, the committee went outside the state to find other drug-abuse and -prevention programs that were working and that could be imported into Texas. They investigated numerous private and government-funded drug-prevention programs, but found only one that they felt was both effective and cost-effective—the fledgling parent movement in Atlanta, Georgia, and Naples, Florida (described in Chapter 22).

As Perot put it: "We studied some federal programs that had gone through millions of dollars to keep children off drugs and hadn't produced anything. So we decided that money wasn't the key to the whole thing; that the proper program, organized around the family and the child's circle of friends, and the parents of those children, was the key."

Aside from the parent movement, which the Texans copied "verbatim," they worked out new organizational strategies for their coming campaign. The first was to get the drug laws changed. A legislative subcommittee was formed. The committee analyzed the existing drug laws; then it rewrote them so that Texas would, according to the governor's mandate, have the toughest drug laws in the United States. They came up with five proposals, called the Texans' War on Drugs Legislative Package.

The legislature was going into session—for twenty weeks—in January 1981. In Texas the legislature meets only every two years, so the committee had to get its package of laws passed or wait two years. Another difficulty was that the legislation was so tough that even those who drafted it felt the package of five didn't have a prayer of getting passed.

Perot first turned to two well-organized groups of women who were already recognized as leaders in their communities; the 15,500-member, twenty-two-chapter Junior League; and the 7,500-member, sixty-six-chapter Texas Medical Association Auxiliary, composed entirely of doctors' wives.

In September 1980, Perot invited two delegates from every Junior League in Texas, plus their president, to a first-of-its-kind seminar in Dallas, during which they heard a host of experts speak.

The Leaguers went home inspired and fired with zeal to work with TWOD (Texans' War on Drugs). The next week there was a repeat performance with a new audience, the doctors' wives; again delegates were flown in for a seminar. Then they went back to their respective communities, and the majority of them immediately began to organize town rallies concerned with drug abuse. As Perot put it:

"The Junior Leagues and the Texas Medical Auxiliary organized at the grassroots level and did an incredible job in three months—between September and December. We held drug rallies in cities of any size all across Texas. And there was tremendous interest. Parents were concerned. Children were concerned. It was a perfect environment to make changes."

There were three main thrusts to the rallies: first, to tell people about the scientific findings concerning the physical and psychological health hazards of marijuana; second, to educate them about setting up parent groups; third, to let them know that their help was needed to get the legislative package passed.

"Then," said Perot, "along came the Texas PTA, 750,000 strong, and said, 'How can we help?' " Connie Miller, the then-PTA-state president and Perot, Tom Marquez, and a few other committee members arranged press conferences all over the state to announce that the PTA was joining in the Texans' War on Drugs effort, along with the Junior League and the doctors' wives—all working together for the first time in their history toward a single end: to get the kids of Texas off drugs and keep them off.

Meanwhile, in Austin, the five Texans' War on Drugs bills had to pass through a series of committees. Each bill required six major voting events, three in the Senate, three in the House. And for twenty weeks, from January through May 1981, busloads of citizens, mostly women, kept arriving from all over the state: JLs, parents, teachers, doctors' wives, and others came to lobby their legislators to vote for the package. In addition, each of the legislators was bombarded with mail from constituents. Before the legislature had even opened for business in December 1980, four thousand letters had been received on the subject. Between December and May, over one hundred thousand letters were received. Experienced legislative observers said that this was more mail on a single issue than had ever been received in the history of the Texas legislature.

Finally, on the final day of the legislature, June 1, 1981, the last bill of the package was voted into law. Each was signed by the governor and four became effective in September 1981; the fifth and final bill, Triplicate Prescription, became effective in January 1982. These were the five bills:

- *Delivery to minors.* This law significantly toughens penalties against adults who deliver marijuana or controlled substances to persons seventeen years of age or younger. No deferred adjudications will be permitted, assuring that persons convicted of delivering these drugs to minors cannot avoid a felony conviction record.

- *Trafficking.* This statute significantly toughens penalties for possession or delivery of large, commercial quantities of illegal drugs. It broadens the circumstances under which vehicles, vessels, and airplanes can be seized in connection with drug enforcement activity and makes it possible to seize all proceeds derived from illegal drug-related criminal activity, to obtain forfeitures if the right to seizure can be proved by a "preponderance of the evidence," rather than "beyond a reasonable doubt." It provides for money seized by law enforcement authorities to be retained by the seizing authority for later use in drug enforcement. It also establishes penalties for knowingly financing, or investing in, illegal drug-related activities.

- *Drug paraphernalia.* This law prohibits the manufacture, delivery, and possession of "drug paraphernalia." It also provides for the seizure and forfeiture of drug paraphernalia; consequently it should be possible to close down the "head shops" by seizing and confiscating their inventory of drug paraphernalia.

- *Professional license revocation.* This law permits the licenses of health care professionals convicted of drug-related felony crimes to be revoked on an immediate basis, in contrast to previous law, under which delays of up to two years have been experienced.

- *Triplicate prescriptions.* Under this law, the Department of Public Safety (DPS) requires prescriptions for Schedule II Drugs (including opium derivative drugs, amphetamines, barbiturates, and methaqualone or Quaaludes) to be written and filled using a triplicate form, with one copy for the M.D., one for the pharmacist, and one sent to DPS for computer analysis.

This program is an effective investigative tool to find the "pill pusher" doctors and pharmacists, and serves as an extremely effective deterrent against such illegal activities by health care professionals. The computer also "spits out" the name of the person who visits numerous M.D.'s and gets the same prescription filled in different drug stores.

Many all-out campaigns fizzle once the goal has been reached and won. This was not the case with Texans' War on Drugs—for the legislative package was only one of the goals. Jo White, TWOD's administrative assistant, put it this way:

> From the beginning, TWOD and the Texans' War on Drugs Committee have had a three-pronged approach: legislative action, law enforcement, and an educational approach for citizens—education being the top priority. The legislative package was a triumph. Law enforcement action is ongoing and has achieved a far greater degree of coordination and effectiveness than prior to TWOD. And as far as the education accomplishments, particularly on the health hazards of marijuana, these achievements have progressed in three short years, beyond our wildest hopes.

Let us look now at the educational part of the TWOD picture.

In June 1979, Tom Marquez, who had been one of Perot's two partners back in the one-thousand-dollar-down days when they started Electronic Data Systems, and who was one of the seventeen TWOD Committee members, became director of the education subcommittee. Although there were four multimillionaires on the TWOD Committee, it was obvious that the statewide educational effort would need government funding. And since, in Texas, government funding precludes all lobbying activities, a separate education committee was set up that would be concerned only with drug education and prevention. It was first called DARE (Drug Abuse Research and Education) to differentiate it from the rest of TWOD. However, since everyone persisted in referring to DARE as Texans' War on Drugs, the name DARE was dropped and the government-funded education arm was henceforth called merely Texans' War on Drugs, as differentiated from the privately funded efforts, which *could* involve lobbying. These remained under the umbrella title Texans' War on Drugs *Committee*. Texans' War on Drugs was funded from the Governor's Office of General Counsel and Criminal Justice—to the scarcely munificent tune of some six hundred thousand dollars the first and subsequent years.

For executive director of Texans' War on Drugs, Perot and Marquez selected a retired U.S. Air Force brigadier general, Robinson Risner, a jet ace, holder of two air force crosses and a survivor of 7½ years in a North Vietnam prisoner of war camp. Risner had vowed while in prison that when he returned to the United States he would work with young people—and the war on drugs was his chance to do just that.

Under Risner's leadership, TWOD set out to raise the awareness of every person in Texas, beginning at the community level. The state was divided into six regions, with an office in each region. A paid staff of four ran the central office in Austin with a youth coordinator, a minority coordinator, and a PTA coordinator added later to work the entire state. Many hundreds of presentations were made describing the drug problem, the social pressures that encourage such behavior, and the social, psychological, and physiological consequences of drug abuse, particularly marijuana.

At the same time, the Junior Leagues, the Medical Auxiliary chapters, and the PTAs had continued working separately and together in a statewide effort to increase drug awareness and prevention efforts in their local communities.

Many, if not most, of the Junior Leagues became actively involved with drug awareness and prevention programs, concentrating in the main on prevention programs in the grade schools, junior high, and high schools. In El Paso, for example, a contractual relationship was worked out among the school district, the local parent organization called Families in Action, and the Junior League to provide drug education in the elementary schools— all on a volunteer basis. Many leagues worked with their school systems to devise better ways of dealing with drug education. Others joined their local PTAs in offering training and awareness programs. Some researched effective alternatives to drug abuse. Some formed speakers' bureaus; others pursued media involvement. And, on an individual basis, many Junior League members formed parent support groups to set common guidelines for their children to follow.

The Texas Medical Association Auxiliary (TMAA) also established speakers' bureaus. When "the doctor's wife" spoke at a local meeting she had a built-in credibility quotient. In addition, TMAA chapters formed parent groups and held seminars for nurses and doctors (offering continuing-education credit); they sponsored poster contests in schools, manned booths at health fairs, and formed networks and coalitions with PTAs and Junior Leagues. Many communities incorporated groups of "Parents for Drug Awareness"—in which members of the three organizations worked closely together for the first time. By April 1983, in the city of El Paso alone, their coalition had addressed over seven thousand people in two hundred different programs and their newsletter went regularly to some twenty-two thousand people. A typical TMAA chapter in Angelica County worked with its service league, local school district, PTA, police department, mayor, sheriff's department, and alcohol-abuse group to reach the entire community through a seminar, establishment of a parent/peer group, and supplying speakers for programs.

While its locals were busy, the state TMAA put out a publication, *Impact of the War on Drugs,* which goes to all TMAA and TWOD leaders throughout the state. They wrote, published, and by April 1983 had distributed over two hundred thousand copies in English and over fifty thousand in Spanish of a leaflet called "The Dirty Dozen: 12 Things You Need to Know about Marijuana." They wrote the script for a puppet show called "Fonzie and Friends" for grade-schoolers, and they produced the puppets for sale at cost. In many areas high school students put on the show for grade-schoolers. The TMAA also produced a filmstrip designed for second- to fourth-graders.

They have sold thousands of STOP POT T-shirts and bright green bumper stickers and, says Amy Wilson, "Our materials are used successfully by auxiliaries in other states." (For information on TMAA materials, write TMAA, 1801 North Lamar Boulevard, Austin, Texas 78701.)

The Texas PTA, with over one hundred councils and some twenty-four hundred local units, has also worked diligently in cooperation with TWOD across the state. In 1982, at the suggestion of PTA and TWOD, the Texas State Board of Education pointed out to health textbook publishers that their material on marijuana was outdated and would therefore be confusing to youngsters who were being presented with the latest scientific information by PTAs, parent groups, and others. The publishers have since rewritten the marijuana sections of the textbooks concerning drug abuse.

Other statewide organizations joined the Texans' War on Drugs' ranks. One was the 22,680-member Texas Extension Homemakers' Association, which follows the lead of the other networked groups with speakers' groups, teachers' in-service training, and so on. In addition, the association specializes in "court-watching" cases that involve drugs to see that offenders do not get off without receiving the full penalty that fits the crime. TWOD has published an excellent thirty-eight-page "Court Watcher's Manual," which can be helpful in a similar program in any community or state. (For address of this and other TWOD organizations with helpful material, see Resource list for Chapter 21.)

In August 1981, the state Lions organization officially adopted the goals of Texans' War on Drugs. The connection between TWOD and the world's largest men's service organization, with some 1.4 million members in 157 countries, was forged by the president of Lions International, who happened to be an attorney from Ballinger, Texas, Everett J. "Ebb" Grindstaff. Key Lions leaders in Texas began working with Grindstaff to adopt the drug-abuse prevention program internationally. With the help of TWOD, the Lions developed a color slide show and script on the harmful effects of marijuana, and began giving awareness programs, on the neighborhood level, internationally. In spring 1983 they developed a plan and materials to involve the Leo Clubs and the young Lions to work in the area of drug prevention in their communities around the world.

Another Lion who had been working for years in the area of youth drug abuse was John Hall, now state coordinator of Texans' War on Drugs/Lions International. In April 1983, Hall made this statement: "For a decade I have worked extensively with state, county, school, and city organizations that were supposedly working on drug prevention in various areas. We get far more effectiveness return on our prevention when working in association with Texans' War on Drugs than with all the other agencies combined."

From all corners of the state and from all constituencies similar comments are heard concerning the unique operation that has woven volunteers of Texas into a cohesive and effective network. The effort started off with such urgency that no one thought to make a "baseline survey" of drug abuse in the state. And the effort has continued at such an intensive pace that no one has stopped to make a survey. But statements can sometimes be as telling as statistics. Here are a few, which are typical.

B. D. Martin, past president, Texas Narcotics Officers Association:

I cannot say enough about accomplishments of Texans' War on Drugs. For years narcotics officers worked long hours attempting to arrest and subdue the drug problems without any recognition. Now, because of the increased citizens' awareness regarding all facets of this problem, there has been, for the first time, appreciation and understanding of our job. This has meant a great deal to narcotics officers who no longer feel they are "out there all alone." Furthermore, what was considered before to be a law enforcement problem is now viewed as a community problem, and law enforcement is benefiting greatly from community support.

Ella Prichard, president of Coastal Bend [Texas] Families in Action:

In the two years since I have been involved at the local level, I have seen the tremendous impact TWOD has had. Students are now telling us that drug use is no longer a problem at the high school level. The "druggers" are in their own isolated group; they are outcasts—not the respected group they used to be, and non–drug-users are not confronted with drugs.

Also, for the first time in Texas we as amateurs are being recognized as a voice of authority on drug issues. We are regularly contacted by the media, school district, law enforcement personnel, elected officials, even—occasionally—the treatment agencies for our opinions and help.

Steve Glenn, Sr., chairman, Deer Park [a Houston suburb] War on Drugs Committee:

Before Texans' War on Drugs, our town refused to even address our drug problem. City fathers, church leaders, school officials, and parents would not, or could not, begin to attack the epidemic in our city. Law enforcement agencies were understandably tired of being blamed. Parents felt that the situation was hopeless.

In just two short years we have grown from zero to over fifty parent groups. We have established a student awareness group in all eleven of our schools, held several hours of in-service training for all school employees, developed parent leadership and awareness through a series of evening meetings, and instituted a K–12 drug and alcohol abuse curriculum in our schools. In April 1983, we employed a certified drug counselor for our secondary schools. In addition, and with the day-to-day support of Texans' War on Drugs, we have held training seminars for area police and juvenile officers, city council members, and school board members. Working with volunteers from surrounding communities, we have assisted in establishing War-on-Drugs committees in LaPorte, Pasadena, Baytown, and Clear Lake. Our local committee, with an active membership of one just one year ago, has grown to include 389 families on our active roll, over fifty industries, forty churches, and many other individuals. Our organization has given drug information speeches to over forty thousand individuals since 1981.

What happened? Why has this one little community [population 25,000] suddenly come alive? Why are we finally united in this cause? The answer is easy: Texans' War on Drugs. Their leadership at the state level and at the regional level has been inspirational to parents everywhere. Not only did they cause an amazing increase in drug awareness, they held training sessions during which the latest research in drugs, particularly marijuana, was shared. We at the local level finally had answers. In addition, the TWOD went to the legislature to see that several much-needed pieces of legislation were passed. They supplied printed material, videotapes, newsletters and, most importantly, moral support. As a school administrator I can honestly say that there is a subtle change of attitude on the part of our students. The peer pressure is beginning to change from "it's okay to do your own thing" to "we care, please don't do drugs." Our kids are better informed and more aware that they must join this fight against drug abuse. It is no longer *cool* to do drugs in Deer Park, Texas. Kids are reaching out to kids. Our community has stopped pointing fingers and has joined hands. Thanks mainly to the leadership of Texans' War on Drugs, we are on our way to fulfilling our goal—making "Deer Park Drug Proof."

Another front on which the Texans' War on Drugs is being fought is in the Mexican-American and the black communities, which embrace one out of every three people in Texas (21 percent Hispanics, 12 percent blacks). In 1982, Ricardo Loera, a Mexican-American, a teacher, and an educational consultant, was hired as TWOD's minorities coordinator. The job is not easy, "although," says Loera, "from what I hear is happening in other states, Texas is leading in the number of minority groups involved." When he speaks in schools, Loera talks chiefly about the health hazards of marijuana. "The kids are invariably surprised to hear that there *are* health hazards. Usually the young teachers are also surprised. All they've heard is: 'If you smoke this, you'll feel good.' "

One problem has been lack of teaching materials in Spanish. But TWOD's minorities coordinator now has a standard training guide in Spanish put out by TWOD, which contains information on marijuana research findings as well as information on other drugs.

By March 31, 1984—within just 3½ years—Texans' War on Drugs had

- Made 4,305 community/media presentations.
- Conducted 227 PTA Drug Awareness Workshops.
- Conducted 99 Teacher In-Service Training Sessions.
- Conducted 23 Drugs-in-the-Workplace Workshops
- Conducted 31 PTO (Parent-Teachers Organizations) and PTC (Parent-Teacher Club) School Workshops.
- Conducted 19 Parenting Education Workshops.
- Conducted 33 Law Enforcement Seminars.
- Conducted 449 miscellaneous Drug Awareness Workshops (civic groups, industry, and so on).
- Organized 167 Steering Committees.
- Organized 187 Community Coalitions.
- Organized 277 known parent peer groups (parents whose children are friends).
- Organized 73 Youth Against Drug groups.
- Organized 66 Speakers' Bureaus.

According to Jo White, who assisted Robinson Risner in organizing the statewide program, "Texans' War on Drugs has now grown into an international model providing guidelines and assistance to other states and nations. Our organizational packet has gone out to people in a number of countries who requested it, including Australia, New Zealand, Colombia, and Sweden."

What has happened in Texas can happen in any state, and it is beginning to happen in others. In Mississippi, the program is called DREAM (Drug Research Education Association in Mississippi). It is a statewide program started in September 1981, patterned on the Texans' War on Drugs. Mississippi became the second state in the nation to organize in this manner.

Kentucky was the third. On March 4, 1983, Governor John Y. Brown, Jr., announced a new half-million-dollar drug-abuse prevention program called the Kentucky War on Drugs. He chose his predecessor, former governor Julian M. Carroll, to run it. Modeled on the Texans' War on Drugs, the Kentucky version has similar goals; it received a quarter of a million dollars in state funds in 1983, from the budgets of the state education, justice, and human resources cabinets. The rest of the money came from private contributions. Like the Texans' War on Drugs, it is organized independently of government as a private corporation with directors from businesses, churches, schools, and law enforcement agencies. Governor Brown mandated that the Kentucky program focus on teaching students and law-enforcement officers about drugs, as well as recommending changes in state drug laws.

Ross Perot is convinced that every state can wage its own networked and coordinated War on Drugs. He has one prime piece of advice: "The best way to get the whole country going is to go through the governors."

It is clearly working in Texas, a well-organized network that goes from the top down, and, almost simultaneously, from the bottom up.

In our final chapter we will look at what is happening in the rest of the country in one of the most unique and successful *grassroots* movements this nation has ever known: parents for drug-free youth.

Chapter 22

The Parent Movement
for Drug-Free Youth

Most parents still have a head-in-the-sand posture about youth drug abuse: "Not my kid," or "It's just teenage. He'll grow out of it." If a situation is not seen, it need not be acted upon. Since they do not know what action to take, the easiest course is to turn their backs. There is also a stifling apathy that seems to encase many parents on the subject of youth drug abuse.

A typical drug-awareness survey of youth was made in 1982 in Anderson Township, an upper- and middle-income community in the suburbs of Cincinnati. The ratio of students who said they used drugs and alcohol ranged from 38 percent in the sixth grade to 89 percent in the senior class. But only 8 percent of the parents of those same youngsters thought their children used drugs at all, and then only "occasionally."

Fortunately for our nation's youth and, consequently, for our nation's future, one force is not only aware of the proportions of this epidemic, but is actively doing something about it—and, what is more, is succeeding.

Armed with current scientific information and fierce determination, over four thousand parent groups have formed to battle drug use among teenagers and preteens. It is a nationwide grassroots movement, born of desperation. Politically, the parent groups span the spectrum—from ultra-liberal to arch-conservative. All religions are represented. And, although it started as a middle-class movement, groups of wealthy and ghetto parents have emerged. It would, in fact, be hard to find a nationwide movement with more diversity, for the parents are united on one thing only: They want their children to grow up drug-free.

There are parent groups in every state, ranging from Families in Action in Ketchikan, Alaska, the state in which pot is grown as openly as geraniums in window boxes, to Parents Against Drugs in South Logan, Utah, the state in which the predominant Mormon religion has long taught abstinence from *any* use of alcohol and illegal drugs.

The groups range in size from 10 Concerned Parents who meet in a schoolroom in the farming community of Island, Kentucky (population 603), to **PRIDE** Omaha, with over 800 members. The individual groups have many different names, many different approaches, many different types of successes, and some failures. But virtually all have the same cornerstone: They educate themselves about the health hazards of marijuana. Indeed, the parent movement is the only one in the country to have taken active, organized steps aimed first and foremost at stopping marijuana use. There are four chief reasons for this.

1. Marijuana is, of course, the illegal drug used by most kids who use drugs. In fact, until 1982 national surveys showed that more teenagers smoked pot than tobacco cigarettes.

2. For years, watching their children change and deteriorate, parents had the "gut feeling" that pot was doing it—despite the fact that pediatricians, psychologists, school guidance counselors, and other professionals assured them that they were "overreacting"—that marijuana was "nothing to worry about." Throughout the country parents went respectfully to the experts, and gradually discovered that many of the experts had, in effect, sold the kids out. Indeed, some were fostering an incredible concept: Teach children "the responsible use of drugs." For years, operating alone, parents were cowed, confused, humiliated. They did not know where to turn or what to do in their anguish and despair about their drug-using children. Then they began learning that there were other parents across the street, down the block, who were going through the same agonies. The parents began to get together, giving each other strength. And the strength of their own convictions about what was happening to their kids had more meaning to them and offered more hope and help than the advice they heard from the "experts."

3. The parents learned—on their own—that marijuana had serious biological and psychological hazards. Indeed, it has been parents' bringing magazine articles and scientific papers on the subject to their pediatricians and family doctors that has succeeded in awakening many in

the medical profession about the damage this drug is doing to young people. Before the parent movement began generating pressure on them, relatively few pediatricians or family physicians troubled even to ask their young patients about illegal drug use. Parents also brought up-to-date magazine articles about marijuana to guidance counselors, psychiatrists, and psychologists—even drug-abuse professionals—which helped to awaken many treatment professionals to the biological and psychological hazards involved in use of this drug.

4. Although many professionals have long scoffed at the idea—and still do—statistics clearly show that marijuana *is* a gateway drug (see Chapter 12). Consequently, parents reasoned that if they could stop their children from smoking pot, this would automatically stop use of other illegal drugs and/or of legal drugs used illegally. Furthermore, it might even have a positive impact on alcohol use, for the National High School Senior Surveys and other surveys consistently show that heavy pot-smokers tend to be heavy drinkers, whereas those who do not smoke marijuana tend not to drink heavily.

During the years 1978 and 1979, groups of parents for drug-free youth arose simultaneously and spontaneously in a number of states. Many of the groups did not know that any others existed. However, by May 1980 the shared purpose and contagious enthusiasm of parent groups throughout the nation led to the founding of an umbrella organization: the National Federation of Parents for Drug-Free Youth (NFP), which represented 350 parent groups. One year later, according to a "State of the Art Report on the Parent Movement" published by NIDA, "conservatively speaking there were 3000 parent groups." In most areas, the parent groups led in action and in positive results, while the experts looked on or, at best, joined in.

For the first years of its existence, the burgeoning movement, composed almost entirely of volunteers, was virtually unfunded. In most localities, it still is. Across the country mothers take money from their household budgets to pay for mailings, newsletters, local meetings, and the photocopying of articles.

Aside from chronic lack of funds, the groups faced—and still face—a battery of obstacles, ranging from the wall of apathy and denial among parents in general, to frequently antagonistic local TV and newspaper reporters, to numerous treatment professionals who lay the full blame on parents for their children's drug problems.

413

Marsha Manatt, the "founding mother" of the parent movement, says:

Because of the glamorization of drugs through rock music and much of the media, usage came to be regarded by young people as not only acceptable but inevitable. Consequently, the best-adjusted child from the strongest family is just as vulnerable to drug experimentation as the disturbed and neglected child. The child from the disturbed home is obviously more susceptible to chronic drug use, but unrelenting peer pressure, plus the do-drug messages created by adults for the youth market, can make any child succumb to chronic use of drugs. To try to blame parents for a mass cultural phenomenon is not only to miss the true causal key to the epidemic nature of teenage drug use, but is also to fail to mobilize the strongest instincts of decency and love that are the most effective bulwark against drug use.

The national parent movement started in two corners of the country at the same time. The year was 1976. Neither group knew that the other existed. Indeed, neither group knew that the marijuana epidemic had already pervaded junior and senior high schools across the entire country. In that year, according to the National High School Senior Survey, one out of every twelve seniors was a daily pot-user. About half the class were "sometime smokers," and they stayed stoned three or more hours every time they lit up. Perhaps the most sobering statistics were these: About *one in five* of the seniors who smoked pot at all were daily smokers, and about one in four who used marijuana at all had started their pot smoking prior to 1973 when they were in junior high.

The First Parent Group for Drug-Free Youth

The "East Coast movement" started in the Manatts' backyard in Atlanta, Georgia, at 1:00 A.M. on a hot, muggy August night.* The blaring music that had rocked through the house left deep silence in its wake. Kathy's birthday party was over, and her parents, Marsha and Ron, were crawling around in the wet grass in their pajamas, with flashlights.

Marsha had become suspicious during the party when a pale, skinny boy she'd never seen before lurched into the kitchen and asked the girl he was with, "Will he bring the stuff?" Ron had become suspicious when he had gone into the backyard during the party and heard whispers, "He's coming! Watch out!" Many of the youngsters at the party were red-eyed, stumbling. They seemed to be stoned. But these were children twelve and thirteen years old!

* At their request, the names of most of the children and several of the parents have been changed.

The parents found dozens of marijuana butts, empty packets of marijuana rolling papers, roach clips for holding marijuana butts, empty beer cans, and empty bottles of "Mad Dog 20/20" wine (20 percent alcohol).

"I felt absolutely sick," Marsha said. "And afraid. As though we were looking into an abyss, a total unknown."

Ron said, "It was as though a hawk had gotten into a dovecote. Something devastating had entered our home, undermined our family."

They realized that night that the total change that had come over twelve-year-old Kathy was probably not due to "adolescence," as they had comfortably thought. Their "sunshine child" had become increasingly hostile, irritable, lethargic. School was "a bummer." Everything else she had once loved—tennis, music, reading—was "a drag," a hassle, boring. In June, the parents had sent their daughter off to her grandmother's home in an isolated West Texas town. Kathy returned in August, her former cheerful, ebullient self. Then she had asked to have the backyard birthday party—with lots of kids. The parents now wondered whether this might have been her cry for help. She had been pot-free all summer, and she was afraid of being sucked back into the scene again. But she didn't know how to handle this—by herself.

The next morning Ron asked Kathy, "Have you been smoking marijuana?"

The child shrugged. "Well, every now and then I take a toke from the boys."

The parents made it clear that they were upset, and would "do something about the situation." But what? Even they did not know. They did, however, ask Kathy for a list of the kids who had been at her birthday party. And the child provided it, almost defiantly. She had done her part. The rest was up to them.

What happened then in that quiet, affluent tree-lined neighborhood in Atlanta, Georgia, is noteworthy for several reasons. First, what those parents went through has now been experienced by millions of parents throughout this country. Second, what those parents created was a *modus operandi*—a method of breaking down seemingly impenetrable walls and returning their kids to a drug-free existence—that lasted.

But it was not easy. And even though parents today can send to the NFP for step-by-step how-to booklets and backup material, it is still not easy.

The afternoon after the birthday party, Marsha phoned parents of the youngsters on Kathy's list. None of them were people she knew personally.

But that is one of the keys to the success of this method. *The first contacts are made with parents of your child's friends.*

Hesitantly, Marsha told the strangers at the other end of the line, "It turned into a drinking and dope-smoking party. I think we all have to do something about it."

The reactions ranged from stunned denial to open hostility, so Marsha decided to try door-to-door contact. Some of the doors were almost literally slammed in her face. One parent asked, "Why are you so uptight about marijuana? It's harmless." Another said, "It's just a 'rite of passage.' They'll grow out of it." One mother angrily informed Marsha, "I have good rapport with all those kids, and I'm going to tell them what you're doing!"

Finally, at five o'clock that afternoon, Marsha decided to knock at one more door—that of David Hardy's family. This time the response was different. Mrs. Hardy said, "If you *really* want to know what's going with the kids, come on in."

Twelve-year-old David had smoked a PCP-laced joint and had gone into convulsions. His pediatrician told mother and son that marijuana was harmful, and gave them an article by Dr. Hardin Jones from a journal, *Private Practice.* Called "What the Practicing Physician Should Know about Marijuana," it described the drug's deteriorating effects on the personalities of young users.

Mrs. Hardy had then approached the school authorities, and received a cold shoulder. ("We have no drug problems!") Meanwhile, David slid back into the drug culture. The Hardys tried keeping track of the kids their son hung out with. "As far as I can tell," Mrs. Hardy said, "all of them are involved with marijuana." She showed Marsha Manatt the list. It was almost a duplicate of Kathy's birthday party list. Some were youngsters she had known since they were in first grade. They were "nice, normal kids" from "good, happy homes."

Manatt drove to the lake where her daughter was spending the afternoon. She threw the list at Kathy and demanded, "Why did you have these people at our house?" She burst into tears, and cried all the way home on the freeway. Kathy cried too. Then she opened up, and talked. It was clear that the child was, as her mother put it, "a totally embedded part of the peer group." It was also clear that if there was hope for these children, the whole peer group would have to be turned around. Peer pressure was the strongest element in their lives. But why couldn't it be combated by *parent peer pressure?* If the parents stuck together, made rules, set down curfews, gave a clear no-drugs message to their youngsters, then Johnny need no longer say "I have to. Everyone does." Because it would now be "Everyone *doesn't.*"

The concept sounded simple enough. But could it be made to work?

Mrs. Hardy agreed to help. She and the Manatts got fifteen sets of parents to agree to come to the first meeting in the Manatts' living room. Prior to the meeting, Marsha went to local drug-abuse agencies and collected a batch of government-issued booklets. Their message was that not much was known about marijuana, but it seemed less harmful than tobacco and alcohol. Therefore, by default, pot officially came off as a benign drug. There was also Do It Now material, which warned parents about a "reefer madness" approach to educating their children about drugs.

Marsha Manatt learned that in 1973 the federal government's Department of Health, Education and Welfare had declared a moratorium on information-based drug-prevention programs—because of fears that the approach had backfired. From what the parents learned from Kathy and David, it was clear that the educational vacuum had been filled with "drugs are harmless . . . drugs are fun" messages from the commercialized drug culture.

The single piece of material that the parents felt related to what they were seeing in their own kids was the article by Dr. Hardin Jones. So Marsha made copies of it at the corner drugstore's Xerox machine. ("That," she said later, "was the beginning of the parents' boon to the photocopy industry. The copying machine was the major medium of communication in the parents' emerging educational movement concerning marijuana.")

At the meeting, defensive hostility bristled. One mother said, "I don't know why I'm here. *My* son isn't involved in any of this."

A father informed her, "I hate to disillusion you, but your son sells pot to mine in the woods behind my house. They like to get high before catching the school bus."

Another father said, "Listen. The kids know why we're here tonight. Let's not go back home with our blinders on, or they'll know we're still blind."

Assignments were given out. The parents determined to familiarize themselves with their children's world. They interviewed teachers, the school bus driver, chaperones at school dances, employees of a pinball parlor and a pizza hangout frequented by kids in the local junior high. Three days later they met again to give their reports. It was decided to ground all their youngsters for two weeks, with no telephone calls permitted. Sticking to that single rule was the supreme test of the parents' conviction and the children's recognition of the fact that their parents were serious.

During those two weeks many of the parents drove their children to school and home again. And the kids began to open up about their drug use. What shocked the parents most was the casual attitude their youngsters had about smoking dope, which they insisted was not only harmless, but good for you. "It cures nearsightedness and cleans out your lungs. That's why people with asthma smoke it."

Armed with the information in Dr. Jones's article, the parents were able to supplant such myths with scientific information. And they had subjects to illustrate their points, high-school kids labeled burnouts, or wasted—some of whom were selling pot to the junior high youngsters. The parents threatened legal action if they continued to do so. More rules came swiftly. An eleven o'clock curfew on Friday and Saturday. Group members to chaperone all school functions, from float-building parties to school dances. Places like the pinball parlor, where drug usage was common, were now off limits, as were rock concerts. All telephone callers had to identify themselves, and there was a nine o'clock curfew for phone calls. Allowances would henceforth have to be earned and would then be monitored carefully. And *no* drug use, alcohol, or cigarette smoking would be permitted.

The parents monitored school bus stops where most before-school smoking occurred. Local police were asked to increase surveillance of known points of drug exchange, such as parking lots. Since many children used empty houses as convenient meeting places for "partying," working parents were urged to call upon at-home parents for help in looking after their kids.

Some of the children, as expected, were resentful. Most, however, seemed rather stunned by the parents' all-out efforts. And when they saw that their friends were "getting it" in exactly the same way, they took it all in stride. Indeed, their overriding reaction seemed to be intense relief.

The parents then decided that if they were closing off one world for their kids, they should do their best to open other avenues. And youngsters who had once insisted it was cool to be stoned now decided that it was far more fun to act in plays, to go skating, to play tennis, to dance, to work at part-time jobs.

Within six months the number of concerned parents had increased from thirty to almost a hundred—including many whose children were not users yet. Among the parents of pot-smokers, those who waffled and made exceptions made little or no headway with their youngsters. But the parents who stuck strictly to the rules suggested by the group found that parent peer pressure turned the tide of teen peer pressure. Their youngsters became drug-free.

The kids labeled the group the Nosy Parents Association (NPA). And by the time their grade-school siblings entered junior high, the NPA had become an accepted part of life—a drug-free life.

Drugs were regarded as "yukky," "totally stupid." The youngsters were well aware of the scientific research about marijuana, which they translated into such terms as "stay away from dope if you want a good bod" or "pot's full of fungus." Consequently, they would say of a pot-smoker, "There's a fungus amongus."

And the no-dope dictum persisted. In 1982, when Kathy's younger sister, Emily, entered eighth grade, she reported to her parents: "The seniors say we're the first no-drugs freshman class, and they admire us because we have such a good time. There's no one in my class that I know of that does drugs. It's not like there's a campaign or anything anymore. It's just that we think it's gross and tacky to be stoned."

The Atlanta parents had set out to get their youngsters off drugs. They succeeded far beyond their own expectations. And their success set off reverberations throughout the entire country.

It happened like this: In visiting their local drug treatment facilities, NPA members had learned that there were no centers or resources for dealing with teenage pot-smokers who were not polydrug-users or addicts. Indeed, no one in the city, county, state, or federal government seemed to be particularly concerned about the pot epidemic among junior high and high-school children. Consequently, on March 17, 1977, Marsha Manatt wrote to Dr. Robert DuPont, director of NIDA, pointing out that the government was failing to differentiate between adult and juvenile use of marijuana. She invited DuPont to Atlanta where he talked with (not *to*) a group of teens and preteens.

It was DuPont who first saw the broader ramifications of what these parents had done. He put it this way:

> Among drug-abuse professionals and guidance counselors, parents had long been the subjects of put-downs. Here was a radical way of saying parents are not only *not* the cause of the problem—but they are a major part of the solution. I don't mind saying that it was parent power that changed my attitude about marijuana. That trip to Atlanta was what really opened my eyes as to what was going on. And what could be done about it. It was the beginning of a process.

DuPont returned to Washington and phoned Tom Adams in California. Adams, a sociologist, was director of NIDA's Pyramid Project, which had been set up by Dr. DuPont in 1975 to provide technical assistance to groups combating drug abuse.

In July 1977, Adams visited Marsha Manatt in Atlanta, and was so impressed by her ability and determination to get things done that he suggested to the Primary [drug] Prevention Conference in South Carolina that Manatt be invited to give a workshop on how to establish parent groups. This was her first encounter with drug-abuse professionals. She was surprised by their open hostility toward her, by their claim that marijuana was harmless, and by their insistence that the major problems kids have were caused by their parents and these problems led to drug abuse. Manatt countered that, from her experience, it was, in most cases, vice versa. Drugs led to problems with parents.

Manatt's experience with the professionals proved to be a forerunner of similar encounters by many parent groups throughout the country in the years that followed. Was it that the professionals felt threatened by the parents, who were achieving, without special education and without paychecks, what the professionals had been failing at for years?

PRIDE

In September 1977, Tom Adams introduced Marsha Manatt to one drug-abuse professional who differed markedly from the rest. Dr. Thomas Gleaton, professor of health education at Georgia State University, had been teaching drug education to teachers and drug-abuse counselors for a decade, and had become increasingly upset by the lack of positive impact these programs were having. He was also upset by the professionals' resistance to incorporating accurate information about marijuana health hazards into their curricula. As one effort to educate professionals about drug abuse, he had run the Southeast Drug Conference at Georgia State University every year since 1975. In 1977, when speaking to Tom Adams about the forthcoming conference, Gleaton heard, for the first time, about the Nosy Parents Association. A meeting was arranged with Marsha Manatt that lasted for five hours—after which Gleaton called Tom Adams in California to say that he was "revitalized." He felt that, for the first time, "something new and powerful was emerging in the drug prevention field."

Two important ideas came from that meeting. The next Southeast Drug Conference would, for the first time, be devoted to parents and to the new marijuana research. Also, since there was such a dearth of accurate information about marijuana, a new organization would be formed to collect and disseminate such information. This concept took shape and developed into PRIDE, Parent Resources Institute on Drug Education.

One of the most important information sources sent out by **PRIDE** and by NIDA was a ninety-seven-page booklet, suggested by Tom Adams and commissioned by Dr. DuPont, on how to set up a parent group. Written by Marsha Manatt, it was called *Parents, Peers, and Pot*; over one million copies were distributed by NIDA, free of charge.

PRIDE soon extended its activities beyond the dissemination of information about marijuana and other drugs and beyond the parent peer group concept. Within two years, the organization—existing on a very thin shoestring—had run workshops for parents and for teams of teachers and guidance counselors from 144 elementary, junior high, and high schools in Atlanta and nearby counties. They had also run annual three-day national conferences for parent-group leaders. Speakers included the foremost marijuana researchers and top government officials. These PRIDE conferences, held every year since 1978, proved to be a vital part of the foundation for the emerging parent movement. Indeed, it was at the 1980 PRIDE conference that the National Federation of Parents for Drug-Free Youth was born, at the initial suggestion and instigation of Dr. Gleaton, who dreamed up the name. "We can't have 'against' in the name," he said. "We've got to be 'for.' "

The Bartons, NIP, and NFP

Bill Barton, from Naples, Florida, was the first president of the National Federation of Parents for Drug-Free Youth, which announced its formation at a press conference in the Dirksen Senate Office Building in May 1980.

As founding members of the parent movement, Bill and his wife, Pat, appeared on *The Today Show* and *Good Morning America;* their personal story was featured in the *Ladies' Home Journal* and in a widely syndicated *Washington Post* story. "As a result," said Pat,

> we were bombarded with letters and phone calls, all of them requests for help. For years, the phone calls often started before we got out of bed in the morning; it went on all day. After the *Today Show,* the post office delivered our mail in a truck. Our postman couldn't carry it all. We rarely sat down to dinner without the phone ringing. A hurting parent somewhere in the country would say something like, "Are you the family that got your child off pot? I have the same problem. Could you tell me more about how you handled it?"
>
> We felt we'd been so fortunate with Tracy that if we could help others solve the drug problem in their home, it was something "we owed."

But for some who called or wrote, help was too late. In January 1984 Pat Barton said, "I still hear—about once a week—from some parent who has lost a child to drugs, either through accidental death, usually in a car crash, or through overdose, or drug-related suicide." Almost inevitably these youngsters began their bottomless slide into drug abuse with marijuana.

The Bartons had become involved in the youth-drug issue on a misty March night in 1978. They were at a gala street party, sitting at a candlelit table with friends, the Conners. Suddenly Ann Conner said, "Do you realize your daughter is going steady with a professional drug dealer? We know about him because he used to date *our* daughter."

The Bartons drove home, devastated. "I'm praying Tracy doesn't know how Andrew makes his living," Pat said. But when they put the question to her, fifteen-year-old Tracy went pale. Then she insisted, "Andrew never deals when I'm around. He *likes* it that I don't do drugs."

Later that night, the Bartons' sixteen-year-old son, Nick, came into their bedroom. He had been worried about his sister, and had wanted his parents to find out so he wouldn't get into trouble for "narcing" on her. "She's really going down the tubes," he said. He told them Tracy smoked from two to ten joints a day.

As a first step Bill Barton phoned Andrew and told him, "Keep away from Tracy. Otherwise, I'll take legal action." A few weeks later, washing their daughter's jeans, Pat found a note from Andrew, arranging a meeting. When she showed it to Tracy the girl screamed, "You don't need to worry. Because of you he's moving to Macon, Georgia!"

But the parents *were* worried. Tracy had been an A student. Now she was getting Bs and Cs. She'd been effervescent, abounding with interests. Now she was lethargic, sullen, always antagonistic; her favorite phrase: "Stop hassling me!"

And Nick had told them the cause: marijuana. The Bartons put Tracy under strict surveillance. Bill drove her to school. Pat picked her up. They told the school they wanted her "monitored." If she cut a class, the school office was to be notified at once, and they promised to let the Bartons know.

At home, she was grounded. No dates. No "private" telephone calls. And either Bill or Pat was in the house with her when she was not in school. Tracy veered between glowering hostility and screaming tantrums. Her parents were ruining her life! In the privacy of their own room Bill and Pat argued, wavered. Maybe everything they were doing was wrong. But they didn't know what else to do. They felt, instinctively, that the drug was bad for their daughter. So the only obvious course was to try to separate her from the drug.

They allowed Tracy to get an after-school job as a utility aid at Naples Community Hospital, a half block from their home, and told the staff about her drug problem. "She thought we were being unfair and distrustful," Pat said. "And we were. Totally distrustful. She didn't pitch fits, though. She was just sullen and resentful all the time. Or, at least, it seemed like all the time."

One day there was a call from the hospital. Tracy had OD'd. "She's okay," the doctor said. "Just tell me what the orange pills were that she took from your medicine chest." Tracy had swallowed twenty-five Ascriptin (aspirin-Maalox) tablets.

"Bill and I were desperate," Pat recalled. "We didn't know where to turn. Or what to do. We felt so horribly helpless and alone. I can't tell you how awful it was."

They took Tracy to a child psychiatrist, who supported what they were trying to do; but Tracy refused to go back to her. That summer, Tracy got a full-time job at the hospital. And Pat quit *her* job so she could be home whenever her daughter was not working. On weekends, Pat drove her to and from the beach, a few minutes from the house. "I'd keep driving down at odd moments," she said. "Tracy knew, if I saw her smoking, no more beach for the rest of the summer."

Finally, the parents felt "she was beginning to get squared away," and they allowed her to go to a movie at night with a girlfriend. Instead, she visited a friend of Andrew's, also a drug dealer. The police were watching the place, and chose that night to raid it. Tracy was turned over to the custody of her parents.

Despairing, the Bartons sent their daughter to a drug-free behavior modification center in Ft. Lauderdale. "I hated it," Tracy said later. "But in a way it was good. During the rap sessions the kids pointed out that I'd been thinking only of myself. They made me realize, for the first time, how I'd been making my parents suffer."

After three weeks she ran away—and came home. "She promised she would stay straight," Pat said. "And, for the first time, we believed her. She'd been pretty much drug-free for three months. And she could see what marijuana had done to her."

Tracy did stay off drugs. And she returned to the sunny, spirited, enthusiastic teenager she once had been.

A year later Pat Barton came across a newspaper interview with Dr. Harold Voth, then senior psychiatrist and psychoanalyst at the Menninger Foundation. Voth had said:

In my experience there is only one certain way to be cured from marijuana smoking. *The user must be totally isolated from the drug for a minimum of three months. Only then will he become aware of the profound effects the drug has had on him and at the same time become free of its addictive effects.* The inability of the user to perceive what has happened to him is one of the truly pernicious effects of marijuana. Thus the chronic heavy—and probably even moderate—user cannot take responsibility for stopping on his own. Talking rarely works. Forthright, decisive action is usually necessary. Someone who cares must intervene totally, consistently, and with unrelenting perseverance. Efforts short of all-out effort generally fail.

The Bartons' efforts *had* been all-out. And they had succeeded.

Looking back, Tracy said:

I feel my parents did the right thing—though I hated it at the time. And I hated them. Most parents just try to ground the kid for a weekend, or take the car away, or else they don't do anything. And all that is dumb. You have really got to hang in there. Pot is everywhere and a kid can be high every day all day long without the parents knowing— because it's easy to hide your high. Being soft with a kid is definitely not the way to go. Being firm and strict is the only thing that will work. And even though, openly, the kid gets very mad, maybe, in his subconscious, he's *glad* because he needs what his parents are doing for him. In the end the kid will thank you and respect you for really taking hold. I feel so much better in every way since I stopped smoking pot. Including— I feel better about myself!

While the Bartons were striving to get their daughter drug-free, they also tried to share what they had learned and to awaken the adult community of Naples as to what was going on with the kids. In April 1978, a meeting of parents was held in the Bartons' living room. "In looking back," Bill Barton said, "the main emotion we all felt was—intimidation. When you're coming from a position of ignorance, it's very easy to be intimidated by your children. We decided we'd better get informed about the drug scene in Naples, and about what drugs—marijuana in particular—can do to young users."

One of the mothers had read about the 1978 PRIDE drug conference for parents, which had just been held in Atlanta. Pat Barton put in a call to Marsha Manatt. ("That," said Pat, "was the start of my three hundred dollar telephone bills.") It was eventually decided that Manatt would come to Naples in October for a three-day Community Awareness Program. She would speak to school administrators, mental health personnel, physicians, sheriff's department youth deputies, civic and service clubs, and students. The Naples parents agreed to spend the summer laying the groundwork.

"Only *after* this is done," Manatt advised, "should you approach the media. Explain what you've been trying to do; ask for their help."

After receiving and absorbing the thin packet of information about marijuana from PRIDE, the Naples group chose their name: Naples Informed Parents (NIP). They operated on many fronts, from the high school to the business community, to the police, to senior citizens—whose Naples Civic Association provided NIP with some financial support "as a project for our grandchildren." Then, in September, NIP parents arranged a meeting with the publishers and editors-in-chief of both of the local newspapers and the general manager of the local radio and TV stations—whom they addressed as "fellow concerned citizens." The media were supportive, and have remained so.

When Manatt arrived in Naples to keynote the Drug Awareness Program, she was welcomed by all facets of the community to whom she spoke. Her visit proved to be a kickoff for a Naples "antidrug initiative," which was to have impact throughout Florida as new groups were spawned. NIP membership grew in nine months from ten to five hundred.

One important function of NIP was collecting and disseminating scientific data on marijuana, which was brought to schools, women's groups, men's clubs, PTAs', drug prevention people, doctors—and to their own children.

Among the first steps NIP had taken was the appointment of Bill Barton to ask the high school administration to "do something about the school parking lot," but Barton was told that the school didn't have the personnel.

The Bartons then went to the sheriff of Collier County, who set up a three-week surveillance of the parking lot. A detective in a van with a hidden camera took 432 pictures proving that this was an active center for the selling and smoking of marijuana. Six boys were arrested. They were suspended from school and assigned to work in the Community Betterment Program during their suspension. The drug bust and the films the police had taken awakened outspoken concern among parents, especially those whose teenagers were shown in full color on the large screen puffing joints in the parking lot and ducking behind cars when adults came by.

At Naples High, NIP asked for a new assistant principal to handle the drug problem. One was hired, and a committee of parents, teachers, *and students* was formed to make suggestions, which the school then implemented.

A new handbook was issued setting forth a new student code on conduct and discipline. This included: "No drug or alcohol use or possession on school grounds or at any school function." For a first offense a student

425

receives a ten-day suspension and referral to appropriate police authorities. The second offense results in the same, plus recommendation for expulsion.

Every teacher had to turn in an attendance report at the end of every period. If a child was absent from school, or from a class, the parent was notified at once—by a parent volunteer working from the school office. Attendance at Naples High is now 95 percent.

"Before NIP started," said Bill Barton, "we had smoking and dealing on the school grounds. One year later it had become a very rare occurrence." This relatively drug-free situation continues at Naples High.

NIP also put out a monthly newsletter, and organized an active speakers' bureau—whose roster includes both Bartons. "The main message I give to parents," said Pat,

> is *do* feel responsible—but *don't* feel guilty. You're not going to like the kid while he's going through this. And your child will probably hate you. You just have to remember that if you don't do something, you're going to be stuck with the situation, and it'll only get worse. Someone once said that the key to success is to be tenacious. If you persevere with your plan, and endure the whole mess that you go through in sitting on your kid for three months—or however much longer it takes—then you've saved your child and, often, your family. And you can go on living a normal life.

In the summer of 1980 Pat Barton was hired by the state of Florida to "network" the existing parent groups and to encourage the development of new ones. This was the first such statewide network in the country. In the summer of 1982, Pat became the parent group development chairman of NFP. By July 1984 there were "networkers" in thirty-seven states; some were hired by the states, some by the parent groups, and some were volunteers.

Bill Barton served as president of NFP from April 1980 to April 1982, volunteering an average of twenty hours a week of his time. This included extensive travel to numerous states, during which he made over 200 speeches to parent groups, civic organizations, school administrators, law enforcement agencies, and government leaders. NIP and the Bartons had, therefore, an impressive impact on the parent movement in their town, in their state, and in the nation.

Sue Rusche and Families in Action

Another key individual in the parent movement, Sue Rusche, and the local organization she formed, Families in Action, also had national impact.

In September 1977, five stores in the Druid Hills area of Atlanta, where she lived, introduced lines of drug paraphernalia. One Saturday afternoon, Rusche, her boys (age seven and eight), and "half their soccer team" entered the Doodah's Record Shop to buy a *Star Wars* record—and found a display case full of bongs that looked like *Star Wars* space guns, Catch-a-Buzz pot pipes designed to look like "frisbees," and other "druggie toys" aimed at kids.

Rusche hurried the boys out, then returned and bought a few pieces of drug paraphernalia and *High Times*—which she brought to the next PTA meeting. Parents and teachers who had previously doubted the existence of drug abuse among children were now appalled by the marketing effort of the drug paraphernalia industry to lure youngsters into illegal drug use.

Rusche recalled:

The thing that had made it so difficult back in those "dark ages" for anyone to admit that children as young as twelve had become drug users was the clear but unspoken statement that invariably followed: "You must be a bad parent." The kiddie paraphernalia helped everybody see that something else was at work. This was an important lesson; the wall of resistance came crashing down.

Rusche then moved in two directions at once. The first decision was to begin collecting as much information as was available about the whole phenomenon of drug use. The second was to unite concerned parents with community leaders who could make change happen. On November 7, 1977, people from two local communities, Druid Hills and Stone Mountain (where another headshop had opened) joined to form Families in Action. Their board of directors included political leaders, school and church officials, police and judges, and physicians. The legislators on the board drafted and introduced into the 1978 Georgia legislature the nation's first antidrug paraphernalia law. The press publicity this engendered brought calls to Sue Rusche from all over the country—people wanting copies of the law, information on how Families in Action was organized, and information on effects of drugs and the extent of use among kids.

"In self defense" says Rusche, "I wrote a manual called 'How to Form a Families in Action Group in Your Community.' " Five thousand of them have been sold at ten dollars apiece and revenues from manual sales help fund the FIA Drug Information Center. The manuals assisted other parent groups throughout the nation in organizing their own parent-community group (see Resource list).

The day that Georgia's Governor Busbee signed the paraphernalia bills into law, the industry filed suit in federal court to have the law declared unconstitutional. When Rusche went to get a copy of the lawyers' briefs, she discovered that NORML was party to the suit, and an additional category was promptly added to the Families in Action information files. This collection of information prepared Rusche to testify at the hearing on paraphernalia held by the House Select Committee on Narcotics Abuse and Control in November 1979. Out of these hearings came the Model Anti-Drug Paraphernalia Law prepared by the DEA (see Appendix). Because of her background garnered from the ever-expanding information collection, Rusche has since been invited to testify at Congressional hearings on drug smuggling, drugs in the schools, and the parent movement.

The collection that started in the Rusches' attic now numbers close to 200,000 documents filed under 750 subject categories, all relating to drug and alcohol abuse. Volunteers who had once formed Families in Action chapters within the county now make up the staff of the Families in Action Drug Information Center, which has a suite of offices in a building on the outskirts of Atlanta. "What's neat about it," says Rusche, "is that legislators, parents, teachers, and so on call us daily from all over the country for information. At the same time local fifth- and sixth-grade students are brought in by their parents to do research for drug projects assigned in schools." The Families in Action Center is listed by the U.S. Library of Congress as a national referral center for drug information.

The staff publishes a quarterly digest of information collected at the Center called *Drug Abuse Update,* which goes out to three thousand subscribers across the country. *Update* lists the source of each article it abstracts. Readers who want more information can order copies of the original article from the Center.

"One of the things I like about *Update*," says Rusche, "is that we've managed to involve the kids in selecting the material that is to be abstracted. We sort through three thousand articles each quarter and get that down to about three hundred. The kids then come in and vote for those articles they think their friends ought to know about. In this way we feel pretty sure that *Update* is alerting students as well as parents and other concerned adults about information they are looking for."

On February 6, 1984, Sue Rusche began writing the first nationally syndicated column on drug and alcohol abuse. Distributed by King Features Syndicate (under titles ranging from "Striking Back" to "The Drug Scene"), it appears once or twice a week in such major newspapers as *The Los Angeles Times, The Chicago Tribune, The Denver Post, The Atlanta Journal Constitu-*

tion, *The San Francisco Examiner,* and *The Seattle Times.* Within its first month of publication, over sixty papers contracted to carry Rusche's column on a regular basis.

Joyce Nalepka and the NFP

Like Sue Rusche, Joyce Nalepka was the mother of two small boys when she abruptly "became involved." She lives in Silver Spring, a suburb of Washington, DC, and one afternoon in 1978 a boy up the street asked her to buy his three tickets to a "Kiss" concert at the Capital Center, since he couldn't go. "Little kids love this group," he assured her. "Especially seven- to eleven-year-olds." Kevin was nine and Keith five, and they were ecstatic about the concert—until they got there.

Kevin later described the scene. "A lot of the audience were my age and younger. There were also young parents with three- and four-year-old kids. As soon as the lights went off, everybody lit up. It looked like little flames everywhere. Within twenty minutes you couldn't see the other side of the arena because of all the pot smoke. After a while, I felt like my head wasn't attached to my shoulders. And Keith said, 'Mom, my head is spinning. I feel like I'm gonna throw up.' "

Joyce remembers the scene at the concert: "It was the first time I'd ever smelled pot, or seen a bong, which they were passing around behind us. My clearest emotion was anger. About 15,000 kids were sitting there getting their minds blown away on pot!"

They left early. Nalepka said to the guard at the door, "There's a federal law and a state law that pot is illegal. You don't allow smoking at other events. During ice hockey and basketball there's a loudspeaker announcement at regular intervals, 'No smoking!' "

"This is a different audience," said the guard. "If we tried to arrest anyone, we'd start a riot."

The next day Nalepka phoned Prince George's county executive six times, but the calls were not returned, so she wrote to the governor of Maryland who contacted the county executive, who called Nalepka to tell her that since the arena was a privately-owned business, the police could not go in unless asked to. She reminded him that the arena was built on government property, and that she was only requesting him to enforce the law. She kept up the pressure. Six months later, at the Jefferson Starship rock concert at the arena, seventeen drug dealers were arrested.

Meanwhile, Joyce and her husband, Ray, took a long look at their own very typical middle-class neighborhood and were appalled to find that drugs were being dealt by older boys outside the elementary school their sons attended.

Then Nalepka learned that her congressman, Newton Steers, from Maryland's eighth district, was a sponsor of a House bill favoring decriminalization; "possession, distribution, or transfer of an ounce or less of marijuana in a private dwelling or public area" would be "subject to a civil fine of not more than $100."

Nalepka asked a number of youngsters what they thought "decriminalization" meant. The children "knew." It meant, as one ten-year-old explained, "the government says it's legal to smoke pot because it's an okay drug."

As it happened, Congressman Newton Steers was running for re-election. Nalepka had thousands of copies of his bill, H. R. 4737, printed. She stapled her memo to it: "Congressman Newton Steers is in favor of DECRIMINALIZATION OF MARIJUANA. In light of the recent DRUG PROBLEMS THAT FACE MONTGOMERY COUNTY PUBLIC SCHOOLS it is time for a change in this kind of thinking. Let us vote for people who uphold the DRUG LAWS AND AGAINST NEWTON STEERS." She and a few friends distributed these at "Meet the Candidate Nights," and in grocery stores, apartment buildings, churches, even department store ladies' rooms. "Any place anyone would stick out their hands to take one," Nalepka said.

She also set up a telephone chain concerning the congressman's decrim stand. The "distribution system" worked. "If you know a child who's been hurt by marijuana, call five people, and ask them to call five more. If you know a child who started on pot and went on to harder drugs, call ten people, and ask them to call ten more. And if you know a child who started on pot, went on to harder drugs and OD'd, call twenty-five people, and ask them to call twenty-five more."

Twenty mothers picketed Steers's headquarters with, says Nalepka, "gentle signs that read 'A drug-pusher cheers for every vote for Steers,' and 'Mr. Steers should be for Dick and Jane, not Mary Jane.' " (Mary Jane, or M. J., is marijuana.) She contacted local radio and TV stations, and a few of them covered the story of the picketing antipot moms.

One afternoon Nalepka visited Steers's campaign headquarters and showed the congressman a one-ounce jar of dried parsley, six inches high and two and a half inches in diameter. She informed him, "If this were one ounce of marijuana—which you want to decriminalize—it would make twenty to sixty joints." The congressman did not reply.

The papers had all predicted a large win for Newton Steers. But he was roundly defeated. An angry aide asked Nalepka who had funded her. She told him, "All I spent was $29.70 for printing."

Several days later, ex–Congressman Steers telephoned and said, "My friends are now telling me that I lost on the marijuana issue. I have to compliment you for doing a very effective job." Then, he added: "I was shocked when you showed me how much an ounce of marijuana really *is*." (Steers later took a strong antipot position.)

The day after Congressman Steers was defeated, Ray Nalepka told his wife, "For God's sake, get all these papers off the dining room table so we can stop eating in the kitchen." So she went to People's Drug Store to buy some file folders. Displayed at the checkout counter were E-Z Wider rolling papers, used for rolling joints. She promptly contacted the president of People's, as well as the president of Drug Fair, another chain. The result of her one-woman campaign: In November 1979 both announced their stores would no longer sell rolling papers. Subsequently, Drug Fair became the first large firm in America to mount a major (half-million-dollar) drug-abuse prevention campaign, focused around the parent movement, called Straight Talk on Drugs. Drug Fair developed a series of pamphlets on various drugs, offered free through their stores, plus an instructional pamphlet on how to set up a parent group. In 1983 People's Drug Store also mounted a major antidrug campaign with similar pamphlets in all states where their stores are located.

In November 1979, Nalepka was invited to testify at U.S. Senate hearings on drug paraphernalia. She heard the manufacturers argue that "you can't outlaw drug paraphernalia. Kids can make it out of anything." They held up cardboard toilet-paper rolls lined with tin foil (homemade bongs), and McDonald's plastic stirring spoons, which the paraphernalia people claimed were "the best cocaine spoons in town—free with every cup of coffee." That evening Nalepka made three phone calls and finally got through to McDonald's president in Illinois. She said that she was testifying the next day, and that she would like to be able to announce that McDonald's was withdrawing and redesigning their plastic spoons. The president, Ed Schmidt, was immediately sympathetic. He made the decision within an hour. Nalepka sat up until 1:00 A.M. typing out a press release, which she took to the printer at 8:30 the next morning. She arrived at the hearings with a stack of press releases announcing that McDonald's was withdrawing the spoons in their four thousand outlets nationwide, and would replace them with a flat paddle stirrer. Her release was used throughout the United States and abroad.

Prior to these drug-related activities Nalepka's only experience in working outside the home was occasionally teaching neighbors how to bake bread.

But, undaunted by her lack of professional experience, Nalepka and her Washington, DC, lawyer friend Jill Gersteinfield spent the next months speaking to PTAs and community groups, and appearing on radio and TV. Their subject: adolescent alcohol and drug abuse. They also testified on drug-related issues before the Maryland state legislature and committees of the U.S. Senate and House of Representatives. In so doing, they became acquainted with their own senator, Charles Mathias of Maryland, who was interested in the drug issue. Nalepka gave him some up-to-date material on the health hazards of marijuana—which proved to be a fortunate move. One morning in November 1979, she called the office of Senator Edward Kennedy, then chairman of the Senate Judiciary Committee, to inquire as to the status of the Criminal Code Revision, a massive document containing a variety of revisions of many sections of the federal Criminal Code. She had just learned that this revision included a small section that would decriminalize personal possession of 30 grams or less of marijuana (about 1 ounce).

She was aware that if decrim became federal law, this would put pressure on the thirty-nine states that had not yet decriminalized—especially since NORML was sponsoring lawsuits and otherwise pushing hard for decrim in many of these states. Nalepka determined to do what she could to have this segment of the bill removed from the package. She immediately phoned Mathias, also a member of the Senate Judiciary Committee, and was told he was out of town. She managed to contact the senator, who returned to Washington at once—just in time for the Judiciary Committee meeting.

The entire Criminal Code revision was voted out of committee and was therefore on its way to the Senate floor. But Mathias asked for permission to hold hearings on the scientific and medical evidence of marijuana's harmfulness, and the committee agreed that the bill could be held up until after the hearings. Mathias promptly called in David Martin, who had organized the six-day Senate hearings on marijuana in 1974 (see Chapter 1) and, within a month, Martin lined up a group of leading marijuana researchers, as well as parent group leaders and educators. Since the 1974 hearings had been criticized by the media as being "one-sided," Martin also invited four members of the advisory board of NORML to testify: Dr. Lester Grinspoon, Dr. Norman Zinberg, Dr. Thomas Ungerleider, and Dr. Dorothy Whipple.

In the weeks prior to the hearings, Nalepka and two other Maryland mothers, Pat Burch and Susan Silverman, bought a hundred 1-ounce jars of dried parsley. They visited the offices of over half the senators on the Hill, managing to see either the senator or a top aide. The great majority of those they spoke to were surprised to learn that 30 grams of marijuana (the amount scheduled to be decriminalized) equaled the amount of parsley in the six-inch-high jar. The mothers gave each of the senators or aides information on the health hazards of marijuana. And they left with each a parsley jar, plus a copy of the just-published *Reader's Digest* article, "Marijuana Alert: Brain and Sex Damage." The three mothers impressed the senators by their genuine concern. Various senators later called this the single most effective piece of lobbying they had ever seen on the Hill.

The Mathias hearings took place on January 16 and 17, 1980. The hearings made it obvious to the senators that there was no longer any meaningful controversy in the scientific community. Marijuana was a health hazard. No responsible senator could vote for a law that would be "read" as government approval of this drug.

This point had been tellingly made at the hearings by Jeff Hamilton, son of TV-producer Joe Hamilton, stepson of Carol Burnett Hamilton, and a former heavy pot-user. He told the senators:

The worst thing about decrim is the unmistakable message of "okayness" it gives to kids. Not only that it's okay to smoke grass, but also that pot must be harmless, since the government would obviously not decriminalize a harmful drug. I have searched, and honestly can find no sound reason to feel that decriminalization would have any other effect than a negative and slow deterioration of the minds of the people of this nation.

After the hearings Mathias co-sponsored an amendment to remove the decriminalization segment of Senate Bill 1722 (the Criminal Code revision) and "return to current law." The amendment was passed.

Not a single state has decriminalized marijuana since the Mathias hearings.

Five months after the hearings, the National Federation of Parents for Drug-Free Youth was officially born. Joyce Nalepka was made the executive coordinator, and, in July 1984 she became president, with a paid staff of eight full-time (usually overtime) assistants, plus volunteers. All other NFP officers and all board members are volunteers—including the two-woman legislative committee, Pat Burch and Susan Silverman, who worked on such issues as lifting the ban on paraquat spraying, the change in the Posse Comitatus law, the crime package including bail reform and forfeiture, and keeping marijuana a Schedule I drug.

"When we started," said Burch, "it was difficult to get most congressman or senators to address the drug issue. But by 1982, the climate had changed. There were over a hundred drug-related bills and most of the Congressmen sponsoring these bills were anxious for NFP's endorsement."

Congressional staffers frequently say that Burch and Silverman are one of the most effective lobbies in Congress. Their goals are simple—though difficult. As Silverman puts it: "We must do everything we can to give a clear message to the American people that the U.S. government will not tolerate the use of illegal drugs."

One reason congressional attitudes have changed toward the drug issue is that, since 1980, congressmen and women have been hearing from their antidrug constituents throughout the country. And the man who has done most to encourage people to let congressmen know their concerns on this matter is Otto Moulton.

Otto Moulton

Unlike most other NFP founding members, Moulton did not start *a* parent group; instead, he helped start about a hundred.

Since his entry into the antidrug movement, he has often responded to requests for aid and information from embryonic parent groups by flying out to answer the request in person. He has visited over thirty states, from Alaska to Arkansas, from Wyoming to the state of Washington, from Nevada to New Mexico—in most cases paying his own way—and invariably arriving with two heavy valises filled with up-to-date information on marijuana. Unlike other "traveling salesmen," he usually gives his wares away, often accompanied by a few hundred dollars to help a new parent group fund its next meeting. When Moulton hits town, he not only speaks to the parent group, but he goes into the schools and talks to classes of kids from grade school through high school. He talks to the school administrator, to teachers, to service clubs; indeed, as his wife, Connie, puts it, "to anyone who will listen." His message: "America, wake up! We're losing our children to the drug culture."

And when Moulton leaves—people have awakened! As a parent leader from Pennsylvania put it at the 1983 NFP national conference: "A tornado hit our town. Its name was Otto Moulton!"

One of many hundreds of thank-you letters Moulton received summed him up in another way. It came from an Indian reservation in the state of Washington. The writer had attended a state conference at which Moulton spoke in August 1983. She said: "You instilled a fire so desparately needed to ignite an uninformed public. Please keep pace with yourself and prevent 'burnout!' "

Moulton comes from Danvers, Massachusetts, which he calls Average-town, U.S.A. He graduated from Lynn Vocational High School and, after three years in the Coast Guard, went to work in a machine shop. At age twenty-nine, with four children under the age of five, he and Connie opened their own precision tool business in the cellar of their small home. Otto worked from 5:00 A.M. till nine at night. Hard work paid off, and by 1974, he had become sole owner of the Fairview Machine Company, the largest industry in nearby Topsfield. He kept up his sixteen-hour work days, which gave reality to the term "hard-earned money"—much of which Moulton later dispensed in his support of the emerging parent movement.

His contributions have come in other ways as well. His initial involvement started in October 1977 when he stopped at an all-night newspaper shop before going to work at 4:30 A.M. He noticed *High Times* on the shelf next to *Sesame Street.* As the pro-drug publication *Head* later reported: "Moulton was so enraged that kids could buy the head products in the local news shop where they were displayed in close proximity to *Sesame Street* coloring books and Santa Claus paraphernalia, that he organized a town meeting. . . . Two hundred parents showed up."

In Atlanta, Marsha Manatt read this item, phoned Moulton—and an important new link in the embryo parent network was forged.

Otto Moulton soon took on such organizations as NORML and Do It Now, letting government officials—among others—know exactly what mass-market marijuana misinformation these powerful groups were putting out to the public. Moulton went to Washington, met with senators and congress-men, and was told by all: "We've been hearing for years from pro-pot people. And that's *all* we hear from." He therefore organized an expert team of researchers, and created—and funded—the Committees of Correspondence, which sends members "Drug Abuse Issues," encouraging them to write their views to elected representatives and others who can influence the outcome of each issue (see Resource list).

In addition, since 1978, Moulton has sent off what he calls "Otto-bombs" to parent groups, legislators, attorneys general, pediatricians, teachers, news-paper editors, and young people throughout the country. These contain accu-rate information on marijuana, as well as news on drug legislation, exposés of pro-pot organizations, and so on. Much of the material in the Otto-bombs shows up in parent group newsletters throughout the country. It is said that Otto Moulton has done more than any government agency to distribute updated information on the health hazards of marijuana, and to awaken people to the false messages they have been receiving about this drug for so many years.

One of the regular Otto-bomb recipients is Senator Gordon Humphrey of New Hampshire. Moulton first met the senator in 1979. "I brought him all the information I had on marijuana," Moulton recalls. "He knew very little about the drug culture and the epidemic among our children. And he didn't seem very receptive." However, Moulton was in for a surprise. Humphrey turned out to be one of the most active senators in the drug-abuse area. In 1980, he asked to chair the Senate Subcommittee on Alcohol and Drug Abuse, and his committee held numerous important and influential hearings on various aspects of the subject.

In 1980, as a founding member of NFP, Moulton was elected vice president. In 1982 he became the treasurer, and in 1983 he was elected to the nine-member executive board. He was also asked to serve as chairman of NFP Materials Review Committee. He is, thus, officially, what he has been from the start—the parent movement's chief watchdog regarding inaccurate information on marijuana. "This is a very discouraging job," says Moulton.

Since 1978 I've gone into bookstores and libraries all over this country and all I find are publications with a pro-marijuana theme: books that are far more interested in the legalization or the decriminalization of the drug than they are in the health hazards. I think this one of our major problems. The confusion it puts into people's minds leads to complacency and apathy. We have got to get major publishers distributing books on the biological and psychological damage caused by marijuana. If people don't have the accurate information, how can we hope to solve the problem?

Carla Lowe, CAADA, and Californians for Drug-Free Youth

Carla Lowe, a California schoolteacher and mother of five teenagers, is also a founding member of NFP. Lowe started her antidrug activities in 1977—the year PRIDE, NIP, and Families in Action were organized in the East. But, one coast did not know what the other coast was doing.

In 1977, Lowe was president of the Del Campo High School PTA in Sacramento, California. Her group sent a questionnaire to all school parents to determine their areas of greatest concern. They learned, somewhat to their surprise, that a top concern of parents was alcohol and drug abuse among their teenagers. Consequently, the PTA ran forums on drug abuse. The most heavily attended was the session on marijuana. But the "experts" from the local drug-abuse agencies who gave the lectures told the audiences: "If you can keep your kids off the heavy stuff, there's nothing much to worry about with marijuana."

Operating on this advice, the PTA mothers diligently imparted information about alcohol, PCP, uppers, downers—the whole cornucopia of drugs. But nothing was said about marijuana. So splendid a job did they do that in 1978 they received an award as the outstanding PTA unit in the state of California. They sent a 200-page mimeographed opus to a number of PTAs throughout the state who expressed an interest in the drug issue. As a result, other PTAs took up the drug issue—but not much was mentioned about pot.

Meanwhile, Carla's fifteen-year-old son, Bill, like millions of teenagers throughout the country, had changed into a gaunt, pale, antagonistic kid. His grades were down, his truancies up. He'd been a top-ten West Coast swimmer for his age group and a good musician, but he had even lost interest in sports and music—except rock music.

In December 1979, Carla Lowe received a call from the assistant principal of Bill's school, who said with some embarrassment, "I'm sorry to have to tell you this—you've been doing such great things about the drug issue— but I have your Bill here in my office. He had a bong in his locker."

"A *bomb!*" the mother gasped. "What's Bill doing with a bomb?"

"A *bong!*" the assistant principal repeated. "Drug paraphernalia. Like a water pipe—for smoking pot."

Lowe had never heard of a bong *or* drug paraphernalia. But she found out soon enough, and through the paraphernalia issue, she learned a great deal about marijuana.

A week later, a friend, Kaye Kane, chairman of the PTA Drug Committee, read that Assemblyman Robert Hayes had introduced a bill to ban the sale of drug paraphernalia to minors. Though both mothers worked—Lowe as a teacher, Kane as a school nurse—they found time to get thousands of names on petitions favoring the bill, and they packed the hearing room with backers. There was standing room only. Lowe recalls:

We were astonished, heartsick and angered at the legislative procedure we witnessed. One of the ten members of the Criminal Justice Committee was reading the newspaper. Another was flipping paper airplanes. Others were milling about, talking to one another. When Kaye Kane testified, they were so rude and crude to her that she broke down in tears. I resolved then and there that we would get an anti-drug paraphernalia bill passed first in Sacramento [the state capital] and then in all of California. And, it would not be the watered down Hayes bill merely banning sale to minors; it would be a total ban for everyone.

Later, everywhere she turned, people told her there was not a chance of such a bill's ever passing—not in *California,* where the legislature "was running with grasshoppers" (pot smokers) and the men's restrooms in the capitol building often smelled of pot. The marijuana growers and organized drug-money equaled one thing: Go Home. Forget it. But Lowe said, "When you know you're right, you have to keep trying."

There had been one happy result of those first paraphernalia hearings. Otto Moulton attended, and this was the first linking of the East and West coasts' parent movement. "I started learning a lot about marijuana," Lowe recalls. "Not from the government, but from records of congressional hearings, from Otto, Sue Rusche, and Gerri Silverman." Lowe passed on the information to her son who eventually got off the drug. Then, along with her paraphernalia battle, she started speaking about pot in schools, at PTAs, service clubs, and churches. She quit her teaching job so she could devote full time to this. Since 1979, she has made about two trips a week traveling throughout the state and country—from cities to rural villages in "marijuana country," often speaking to four to five groups a day.

During three weeks in May 1980, she and Kaye Kane got seven thousand names and over one hundred organizations to back what became the precedent-setting first total ban of drug paraphernalia to be passed in the state of California. The ordinance was based on the DEA's Model Anti-Drug Paraphernalia Law which Lowe and Kane had brought to the Sacramento County Board of Supervisors. (See Appendix.) Because of the tremendous response of the community, the two women formed CAADA, Community Action Against Drug Abuse.

Other parents in other communities were speaking out now on the drug issue. Carol Stein, a housewife in Conejo Valley (a suburb of Los Angeles), had also formed an active parent group, and in October 1980, Lowe and Stein met with fifteen other parents at the halfway point (Fresno) and organized Californians for Drug-Free Youth, the first state network organized entirely out of parents' pocketbooks. The new coalition of parents agreed that their initial projects would be to start more "parent/community" groups and to back CAADA's efforts to sponsor legislation making the manufacture and sale of drug paraphernalia illegal throughout the state.

During the next two years, this small coalition of groups won the backing for the paraphernalia bill of one hundred fifty important statewide organizations representing, said Lowe, "every facet of life in the state except the paraphernalia merchants, the pot-growers, and the ACLU."

Lowe was on hand every day of what became a two-year fight to see the paraphernalia bill passed. Being a novice at legislation, she was unaware that the early "strange happenings" to the bill were really results of political maneuverings by the assembly leadership of Willie Brown. Early on, the bill was almost "lost through a crack" in the assembly. It was picked up by a member of the senate, Newton Russell, and the sailing looked smooth as the senate passed the bill unanimously within one month.

Back in the assembly, however, the bill was subjected to, as Lowe put it, "all manner of curious happenings: lost papers, cancelled meetings, 'yes' votes pulled from committees, etc." Lowe and Dan Kinter, a deputy district attorney, tracked these happenings and passed them on to the press.

At a major press conference in the governor's press room attended by key dignitaries, a significant finding was announced. The major campaign contribution received by Speaker Willie Brown was from California Progressive Business Association, the consortium of paraphernalia manufacturers and dealers. The news made headlines throughout the state.

Soon the tremendous coalition of support for the bill began to see results and the bill finally passed from the assembly Criminal Justice Committee (called the graveyard committee for tough anticrime bills) and was passed by the full assembly without a dissenting vote. The bill became law in January 1983. Californians for Drug-Free Youth had earned its credibility as an organization working to reduce teenage drug use through education and community action.

And Carla Lowe's five teenaged children, who attended many of the hearings, learned that people power can prevail over tremendous obstacles and political maneuverings.

Vonneva Pettigrew, PYADAA, and the Multicultural Family Network

Another founding member of NFP is Vonneva Pettigrew, a black divorced single parent who lives in Washington, DC. In 1980, she was elected to the executive committee; she also served as NFP's minority coordinator.

Prior to her emergence on the antidrug scene, Pettigrew felt that "the answer" was devoting all her time to her full-time job at the National Child Day Care Association and to the care of her three children. Then, in 1974, one of them was shot and seriously wounded by a teenage drug-user. "Why *my* child?" Pettigrew demanded of the detective. "I kept my kids drug free!" (And she had.)

"Lady," he said, "you can't go into your house and close the door. You have to get involved with what's happening to other kids, in order to protect your own."

"That," said Pettigrew, "struck home." Her first step was to organize a youth group, Talent Incorporated, to provide inner-city teenagers with "creative and wholesome alternatives" to truancy, juvenile crime, and drug and alcohol abuse. The alternatives included ballgames, fashion and talent shows, and plays put on in neighborhood parks, churches, and schools. The sole requirement to participate in the group: being and remaining drug-free.

In 1980 Pettigrew attended a national parent group conference sponsored by NIDA in Washington, DC. There, for the first time, she met representatives from parent groups all over the country. "All of them—except me—" she said, "represented the white middle class. I decided I could do the same thing in my community." She went back and reorganized Talent Incorporated as PYADAA (Parents and Youth Against Drug and Alcohol Abuse), which responded to the need for a family approach to the problem, and which now focused exclusively on the rising epidemic of drug and alcohol abuse among youth in their inner-city community. By 1983 PYADAA numbered over 250 members, all black. It runs workshops for over one thousand families of various ethnic groups in Washington, and has helped organize other parent groups in Baltimore, Maryland; Arlington, Virginia; Birmingham, Alabama; Topeka, Kansas; Houston, Texas; Oakland, California, and other communities. PYADAA is now the most active and effective parent group in Washington, DC.

Pettigrew's son, Keith, at age sixteen, became the head of PYADAA's Youth Group. He traveled to Georgia and Mississippi doing workshops on organizing youth groups.

In August 1983, he was appointed by the Secretary of Health and Human Services, Margaret Heckler, to the National Advisory Council on Drug Abuse, of the Alcohol, Drug Abuse and Mental Health Administration. Keith was the youngest advisor ever appointed to the position.

In 1983, Vonneva Pettigrew, while continuing as head of PYADAA and as a board member of NFP, began to work on a larger scale to bring more ethnic minorities into the national parent movement. She took a leave of absence from the Day Care Association to work full-time on this project in conjunction with NIDA's Pyramid Project. In July 1983, the first meeting of representatives from eight states and five ethnic groups was held in Washington, DC. Representatives included professionals and parents from American Indian, Asian-American, black, Mexican-American and Puerto Rican-American communities. They met for two days to discuss and recommend the most viable approaches for developing and sustaining the interest and involvement of ethnic families.

The meeting resulted in the formation of a Multicultural Family Network.

The initial group formed the first steering committee. They went back to their communities to inform them of the network and to identify groups and families already involved in drug abuse prevention efforts—to get their support and recommendations for a plan of action.

A follow-up meeting of the steering committee was held in Washington in January 1984. There the members discussed successful prevention strategies that had been used in the various ethnic communities, obstacles the groups had faced, their differences and commonalities, and they developed an overall purpose for the network. This included "assisting individuals, families and communities who need help in organizing groups for prevention of drug and alcohol abuse and to establish a system for the exchange of information and resources between and among these groups."

Said Pettigrew, "We discovered that we have more commonalities than differences; especially in the problems that lead to drug and alcohol abuse, such as high unemployment and lack of adequate treatment facilities—but mostly the lack of adequate health and drug information programs."

In the fall of 1983, the Multicultural Family Network held its first national conference to bring together leaders of the organized ethnic parent and community groups. Pettigrew said:

> This is the first time that we've had a national ethnic network to deal with the specific problems of drug and alcohol abuse prevention. To date, we have identified over 100 organized prevention groups throughout the country. We've touched base with all of them, to inform them of who we are, what we're doing, and why we're doing it, and to ask them to support the effort by sharing information about themselves; how they're funded, what they do, what type of activity they're involved in; how they're structured, and to give suggestions for helping similar communities to fight back.

For more information and for technical assistance to help organize an ethnic community, write Vonneva Pettigrew, Pyramid Project, 7101 Wisconsin Ave., Bethesda, Maryland 20814. Telephone: (301) 654–1194.

Judy Reidinger and the NDAF

Judy Reidinger was another founding member of NFP, and was elected to the board of directors in 1980. Her involvement with the drug-abuse issue came abruptly at 6:30 A.M. on July 31, 1978, when she opened the door of her brother-in-law's room. The shade was drawn. The bedside lamp was on. A gun lay beside him on the bloody pillow. He had shot himself in the head.

In high school, Frank Reidinger had seemed to be drug-free. "He was a super kid," his older brother, Dick, remembered. "Different people have different talents. And his was with people. Everyone loved him."

In 1977, while at the University of Tennessee, Frank lived in a house in Knoxville, left him by his mother, who had died the year before. Within a year the house had changed; it was filthy. And Frank had changed. "Looking back," Dick said,

> we realized that his symptoms of deterioration were those of a typical pothead. But at the time we thought it was just a stage. If you have no way to connect the dots on the drawing, you don't get a picture of what is happening. One of his girlfriends told me that he was heavily into pot. I tried to tell Frank that this was harmful—but I had no scientific evidence to back up my feelings. Frank assured me he wasn't smoking very much, and that it wasn't affecting him.

The following year Frank dropped out of college, taking a part-time job as a factory security guard at night. ("We later learned that he often got zonked on the job," said Dick.) He developed a tolerance for pot, added pills to get his "high," then bought what he thought was cocaine. But it was PCP. He snorted it, became violently psychotic, was in and out of mental hospitals for four months, and was finally released. Judy got him a job at her father's lumberyard in Kansas City, and traveled with him to her parents' home where he would be staying. At 6:30 A.M. she knocked on the door of his room. "It was his first day on the new job and he was supposed to be up by six," she said. "When he didn't answer, I opened the door and looked in."

Because Frank was a boy everyone had loved, there were many people at the funeral. A number of them wanted to send a check in his memory to a national drug-abuse prevention foundation. Dick told them he would let them know the name of such an organization. But, it turned out, there *was* none. So Dick and Judy Reidinger started one.

The National Drug Abuse Foundation (NDAF) was incorporated on May 12, 1979, with an impressive board of advisors and taxfree status. As their own memorial to Frank, the Reidingers worked to increase national awareness about youthful drug abuse, and to provide information resources for parents. Said Judy,

> One of our main goals was to let people know what the "marijuana portrait" is for young users; how to recognize the signals, and to realize that they are *danger* signals. The first scientific information Dick and I

ever had about the health hazards of marijuana came from a *Washington Post* "Outlook" article. We read it the day after Frank's funeral.

The Reidingers hoped to establish a national drug-abuse hotline manned twenty-four hours a day by experts who could help desparate people with nowhere to turn for answers, and who could recommend treatment centers in the caller's vicinity—centers informed about marijuana abuse as well as about other drugs. Said Judy, "We'd had a nightmare trying to find help for Frank. Therefore, we wanted to offer other people assistance in the referral area."

Another goal of the National Drug Abuse Foundation (NDAF) was to get out as much accurate information to as many people as possible on all drugs, but marijuana in particular; and to let more people know about the excellent material available from PRIDE, ACM (the American Council on Marijuana), and CICOM (Citizens for Informed Choice on Marijuana).

All of this, of course, required funding. A minimal amount had been donated by friends who attended Frank's funeral. Judy and Dick Reidinger put in a good deal of their own money. Judy gave up her budding career as composer, guitarist, and singer to devote herself full time to this effort. Dick, in his job as an economist with the World Bank, spent four months a year in India, so most of the work fell to Judy—who also kept house and parented their two preteens.

The Reidingers listed the National Drug Abuse Foundation in the Yellow Pages under Drug Abuse Programs. (Few of the Washington, DC, area hotlines or drug-abuse treatment agencies were listed at the time.) Result: Their hotline was so busy that they had to install three telephones. Requests for information, as well as desperate crisis calls, came at all hours of the day or night. "The most common call," Judy reported,

> was from mothers who said, "My kid is in real trouble from drugs. What can I do?" Obviously, we were filling a need. And just as obviously, we weren't trained to do what we were doing. Yet, just telling people of our own experiences with Frank helped others. Also, we developed packets of information, which we mailed off all over the country. We sent out thousands of packets. Each one included the marijuana portrait.

Finally, word from the foundations came in. The major contribution was from the Reader's Digest Foundation: twenty-five hundred dollars. Since specialists could not be hired for the National Drug Abuse Hotline, that idea was dropped, and Judy turned more of her energies from national to local: Fairfax County, Virginia, where she and Dick live.

She helped to organize a "pyramid" of school-connected parent groups.

"The goal," she said, "was to have a drug-abuse prevention program in every school. We worked closely with the schools, helping to set up parent groups, workshops, and programs." By 1981 there was a parent-school prevention group in most of the twenty-three high schools, and some of the junior highs and elementary schools in Fairfax County.

In addition to working with the schools, Reidinger helped introduce drug-abuse prevention programs in PTAs and other parent groups, in church groups, and youth groups, and she helped start the Metropolitan Washington Parent Network in connection with the Straight Talk on Drugs Program sponsored by Drug Fair.

In 1980, Judy Reidinger became a founding member of NFP and was elected co-chairperson of NFP's Creative Alternatives Committee. Since she could not actively work two time- and effort-intensive volunteer jobs at once, the National Drug Abuse Foundation became, in large measure, inactive at the end of 1981.

Then, on July 7, 1982, Judy Reidinger took a courageous step in a totally new direction. For the preceding thirteen years, the pro-pot organizations and the Yippies had held an "annual White House smoke-in," usually in Lafayette Park, opposite the White House. In addition to open pot-smoking and promises of "free pot," there were pro-legalization speeches and distribution of pro-pot literature, plus distribution of the Yippies' publication *Overthrow*. All of this, with the White House in the background, was shown each year on the nightly TV news on July 4. Judy Reidinger decided it was time for another scene to be shown. Consequently, on July 7 she went to the National Park Service Building and reserved Lafayette Park and the White House sidewalk ("so we wouldn't have hecklers across the street") for July 4, 1983.

Her plan: "We don't want to make it confrontative. We want to say: 'We have a message too: the importance of a healthy, drug-free environment for our kids.' " Instead of the grassy green area in front of the White House being clogged with people smoking pot, Reidinger envisioned a "family celebration" on the site, replete with speakers, music, singing, dancing, skits, balloons, young people's programs, and booths with literature on family resources and on drug abuse.

During the months that followed, Judy Reidinger, together with William Brown, president of the DC PTA, organized a coalition of more than thirty metropolitan Washington and national groups including the NFP, the United Black Fund, church groups, Lions Clubs, local PTAs, Boy Scouts, the National Recreation and Parks Association, and WACADA (the Washington

Area Council on Alcohol and Drug Abuse). They planned a six-hour Fourth of July celebration.

At 6:00 P.M., June 9, Judy was preparing dinner when there was a knock on the door. She was served a summons for a six-hundred-thousand-dollar lawsuit by the Yippies and Citizens Against Marijuana Laws (CAML), charging that Reidinger had not applied for Lafayette Park on July 7, but had "conspired with the Park Service" to predate the application—so that the Yippies could not have their annual smoke-in as usual.

After a sleepless weekend Reidinger learned of the Washington Legal Foundation, a public-service law firm, which agreed to take the case for nothing. With the foundation's help—especially that of Nick Calio—the Yippies were persuaded to dismiss the suit so that they would not be countersued for their false claim that Reidinger had "conspired with the National Park Service." The Family Day Celebration would go on as planned. Furthermore, Congressman Walter Fauntroy, chairman of the Metropolitan Congressional Caucus, introduced a joint resolution in the House of Representatives and in the Senate proclaiming July 4, 1983, National Family Celebration Day.

Meanwhile, the Yippies, Citizens Against Marijuana Laws, and others procured a marching permit. A Yippie spokesman announced: "We will be in Lafayette Park on July fourth. This will be the most memorable and interesting smoke-in since 1970."

According to the Yippies' permit they were to be finished with their march by 1:00 P.M.—the time the Family Celebration was scheduled to start. Instead, at 1:15 they sat down in Pennsylvania Avenue, adjacent to Lafayette Park, blocking the street. Traffic could not move. Then they set up a sound system and their speeches blasted through the afternoon. Mounted police, park police, and squad cars appeared, and effectively encouraged the Yippies to "start moving."

"While they were passing," said Reidinger, "we had the Grandland Singers singing and dancing away. People were clapping along and dancing. We had a full sound system with eleven mikes." Congressman Fauntroy stood on the Lafayette Park podium and not only spoke, but sang. Activities ranged from Jimmy Arnold's bluegrass and country western group to a top karate group to Kids Musical Theatre, a teenage musical group—with Shaunti, the Reidingers' daughter. Master of ceremonies was Dr. Calvin Rolark, chairman of the United Black Fund. The crowd was a decidedly multiethnic one, families and kids—most of whom bought brightly colored balloons reading *July 4th Family Day Celebration*.

There was TV, radio, and newspaper coverage of the event. A *Washington*

Post editorial keynoted the event in its headline: SMOKE-IN SMOKED OUT BY THE JULY 4TH FAMILY DAY CELEBRATION.

"What better time or place is there," said Judy Reidinger, "to stand up for what we think is important: strengthening the family, a healthy environment for our children, and the working together of many groups to build a strong future for America?"

The Four Thousand Parent Groups

The parent movement's greatest strength lies in its diversified but genuine grassroots base. As the older groups solidify, expand, and strengthen, their efforts have growing impact in their local communities. And new groups keep forming so fast that there is no way they can be counted. As Joyce Nalepka, NFP's president, puts it:

In Pennsylvania, for example, we heard in late 1981 that there were probably 6 parent groups in the state. When I traveled to Pittsburgh in November 1982, I was told that there were 112 parent groups in that one city alone. Of these groups only 8 were accounted for in our statistics. We are in touch with over 4,000 parent groups, but given the continual spawning of new ones, our guestimate is that there are more than 10,000 groups of parents for drug-free youth.

How to decide in this final chapter which of the parent groups to include? Virtually all of the countless groups I know about have a story well worth recording. I decided, however, to limit the "entries" to the first individuals and groups to emerge, since they have a historical as well as a national impact. There are also dozens more parent groups that started almost as early. They arose spontaneously in different parts of the country, usually unaware that they were, in fact, part of a new national movement.

According to Joyce Nalepka:

One reason that accounts for the momentum of the movement is that when we started out we were twelve years behind—because for all those years the pro-drug lobby had been well financed, well organized and well quoted in the press. They had convinced kids, parents, and many professionals that pot was harmless. We had a lot of catching up to do—fast.

Many, but not all, of the four thousand identified groups are affiliated with the National Federation of Parents for Drug-Free Youth. But even the affiliates retain their own identities, and they come at the problem in wide varieties of ways. The groups have an intriguing spate of names, many of them acronymic, for example: AID (*A*dults *I*nformed about *D*rug-Abuse); COPE (Concerned Organization of Parents to Educate); FACT (Family Action Council of Texas); GATE (Gain Awareness Through Education); HIP (Houston Informed Parents); IDEA (Illinois Drug Education Alliance); KIDS (Keeping Informed on Drugs in Society); LIFE (LaBell Informed Families Endeavor); LEAD (Learning Effective Alternatives to Drugs); MAD (Midlanders Against Drugs); PAC (People Are Concerned); PANDAA (Parents Association to Neutralize Drug and Alcohol Abuse); SOC (Save Our Community); YES (Youth Education and Solutions).

There are also names that carry their message directly, such as Dare to Care and Parents Who Care. Behind most of the names lie dramatic, often heartrending stories. Many of the groups have developed their own unique approaches to the local problem.

Some groups are begun by parents whose children are not involved with drugs. For example, GATE (Gain Awareness Through Education) in Jupiter, Florida, was started in 1982 by Nancy Saylor, mother of Paige, then eight, and Christopher, two. This group concentrates on grade-school presentations about marijuana health hazards and decision-making skills, which includes, as Saylor puts it: "When is tellin' tattlin'?"

One mother became involved in starting the Cedar Rapids Regional PRIDE parent group after someone tried to sell her child pills in the elementary school playground. "I would've bought you some, Mom," he told her. "But I didn't have any money."

Says Joyce Nalepka:

> The answer for the prevention of this epidemic is for parents of fourth-, fifth-, and sixth-graders to become knowledgeable and provide positive alternatives for their children at this young age, and then to keep up the prevention efforts through junior and senior high school. Prevention is a lot easier than intervention. It's fun instead of harrowing. It's also far less expensive. It is NFP's hope that by 1988 we will have a parent prevention group attached to every grade school, junior high, and high school in the United States, with a single focus: drug-free youth.

Many groups start with an opposite propulsion: tragedy or near-tragedy involving drugs. For example, the two mothers mentioned in Chapter 12, whose children committed suicide, each started a parent group. Mrs. Wilcox, Mark's mother, called her group PRIDE of Polk County. Their goal is a drug-free county.

Ann Blount, mother of Kaye (who started pot smoking at age 12½ and killed herself a year later), called her group DASP (Drug Awareness and Suppression Program of Bartow). Mrs. Blount's words echo those of many other courageous parents who become involved in the parent movement after the death or destruction of a child due to drugs. "We thought if we could just reach other parents," Mrs. Blount said, "and let them know what was going on, it might help to save someone else's son or daughter."

Some groups "specialize." For example, Parents Who Care, in California, concentrates on "turning it around by peer pressuring *not* to do drugs." The group was started by Joanne Lundgren, a former school principal and the mother of four teenagers. She was shocked by a story she read in the *San Francisco Chronicle* (June 16, 1978) headlined SENIOR PROM—NIGHT OF GLAMOR, which described in "trendy terms" seniors lining up champagne, cocaine, and bottles of pills, getting set up for the big night.

Parents Who Care started in the Lundgren living room with fifteen parents in November 1979. Eight months later they were a nonprofit corporation with 124 chapters, representing 182 schools throughout the San Francisco Bay Area. Their emphasis has been (as their booklet describes) on how to involve youth in changing the "scene" (see Resource list). At initial rap sessions between parents and kids (sometimes following pot-luck dinners) parents learned that, after entering high school, most youngsters had never been to a party where the main activity was other than getting high and getting drunk. Yet the kids seemed to agree with a boy who said, "Partying is boring. But there's nothing else to do."

The kids soon had much else to do. In the summer of 1980 Parents Who Care invited some college students to help them plan workshops for teenagers on how to give a successful party without drugs or alcohol. The workshops were so successful that the teens agreed to work with Parents Who Care to develop alternative parties for younger kids. They formed Parents Who Care student groups and the drug- and alcohol-free parties "caught on." They were not restricted to "straights," but the rule was that no one should come to the party high, or use drugs or alcohol while there. As one girl put it: "This was important in avoiding the image that the straight parties were just for prudes or nerds."

By 1983, all of the organization's funds had been spent and no additional funding for office operations could be raised. Consequently, chapters were forced to handle drug and alcohol prevention on their own, without coordination and assistance. As a result, in May 1984, the number of chapters had dwindled to four in Northern California and the focus is now school-based rather than community-based.

Said Margery Ranch, past director of Parents Who Care:

It's not glamorous to fund pencils and paper and phone bills—but parents can't keep funding these expenses from their own pockets. I still put in over ten hours of volunteer work a week, in addition to my own job. This is typical of many of us. But when we had funding we were able to staff some of the time-consuming jobs, such as answering the phone and typing, so that the group volunteers were free to go out in the community and work—as we once did—for drug and alcohol prevention among our children.

The Stumbling Blocks

From the beginning, the most serious hurdle the parent movement has had to face was lack of funding. It hampers the work of virtually all of the groups, from the national organizations on down. The concept of mothers' taking household money out of the cookie jar to pay for the mailing of a newsletter may sound romantic. But when the cookie jars are empty, the newsletter remains unmailed. It also seems to many parent-volunteers highly unjust that not only should they be doing what they have already paid tax dollars to be done by local, state, and federal drug-abuse prevention agencies (a job that often remained undone), but they are now also having to foot the bill for their own parent-group projects.

Funding was such a problem for the national organizations that, at the start, it was touch and go for all of them. And one of them "went." While the Drug Abuse Council was dispensing its "responsible use of drugs" philosophy, courtesy of two million dollars a year obtained from foundations and industry, another national organization, Citizens for Informed Choice on Marijuana (CICOM), was struggling for funding to enable it to continue its valuable operations; it finally had to close up shop because Dr. August Fink, founder of CICOM, could no longer afford to fund the organization. Fink, publisher of *Patient Care* magazine (for the primary-care physician), put over fifty thousand dollars of his personal funds into CICOM. From its inception in 1978 to its demise in 1981, the organization played an important role in aiding the development of parent groups and disseminating up-to-date information about marijuana.

Among CICOM's most notable contributions were starting numerous parent groups in five major locations, from New England to the state of Washington, and helping to organize and promote major regional drug conferences. CICOM also initiated and published *Getting Your Child Off Marijuana* by Dr. Harold Voth, and a series of booklets on how to set up a parent

449

group. Says Dr. Fink, "Although CICOM no longer exists as an organization, our publications are still available and are being used by the armed forces, as well as by numerous parent groups" (see Resource list).

During its first year, the NFP almost sank into insignificance because funding was not forthcoming. It was able to rise beyond its status—powerful idea, dedicated board members, and tremendous overdue phone bills—because of one man, Tom Marquez, chairman of the education committee of Texans' War on Drugs. NFP's president, Bill Barton, asked Marquez for his advice and help in raising money. "Parent groups nickle-and-diming it can work for a while in local communities," said Barton, "but it doesn't work for a national organization." Marquez asked how much was needed, and Barton told him: "A hundred thousand dollars."

"Okay," said Tom Marquez. "I'll give that to you. Now let's go have lunch and talk about what the parent movement is going to accomplish."

By 1983 minimal funding was forthcoming for the four national organizations concerned with drug-free youth: NFP, PRIDE, Families in Action, and American Council on Drug Education—ACDE (formerly American Council on Marijuana, which, from its genesis in 1977, was concerned with getting out accurate information, particularly about marijuana, but which did not foster the formation of parent groups). However, because the funding *was* minimal, some of the best-laid plans of these organizations have had to be "postponed."

Joyce Nalepka had this to say on the subject:

> Funding continues to be an ever-present problem, primarily because prevention is not an easy concept to sell. For example, it's far easier to raise money to support emergency treatment for drug-addicted teenagers than to support a drug-abuse prevention program for sixth-graders. But, in the main, prevention is what NFP is all about. We have many important projects and plans, such as a national crisis telephone hotline, and a national school drug prevention program for each grade, K through twelve. We have all the expertise we need for developing these programs but no funding for them.

In May 1984, Carla Lowe, northern chairperson of Californians for Drug-Free Youth, put it this way:

> In 1983, we were given a $40,000 grant from ACTION for one year to further expand the state network that we had begun in 1980—the first state network in the country. With this money we built a mailing list from 7,500 to 18,000. We put on two successful parent/professional statewide conferences. We published four newsletters. We took our prevention program to some 200 schools. We organized 6 regional training workshops.

And now, due to our involvement, we have some kind of parent/community action group for drug-free youth in every major city in the state. We need to be able to network and nourish all these new groups. But instead, we may have to close our doors because we have no more funding. The irony is that the success which has come about through our volunteer efforts has the potential to defeat us. We have come to the point where it requires a full-time administrator and basic staff to cope with the tremendous demands which are now recognized by youngsters, parents, schools and professionals and throughout the communities in our state, and which so desperately need to be met.

The school which gave us free headquarters is closing down. We need rent money. We need money for a full-time staff. We need money to pay for the publications we distribute, for newsletters, for speakers, for conferences and other educational programs. We need money to pay the phone bills.

Since the ACTION grant came to an end we have written 85 grant applications to foundations. We have proved that not only do we know what to do, but we know how to do it, and we have done it successfully for four years. Our Advisory Council includes some of the most important elected officials and highly regarded medical and other professional people in the state. Everyone agrees that youth drug abuse is one of the most horrendous problems facing our nation today. Yet, from our 85 grant proposals, we received one positive response—for $500. And our story is no different from that of countless parent groups all over the country. I believe that unless adequate funding is forthcoming the parent movement will die—of a broken heart.

The other major stumbling block which brings many local parent groups to their knees is one which, fortunately, has a simple solution. Sociologist Doug Bachtel did a study of local parent groups in Georgia and sums up: "The problem is lack of organizational skills. The group starts off wanting to conquer the [drug abuse] world. But they think they have to reinvent the wheel, and they can't seem to get their act together. Each of the group meetings turns into a recitation of drug horror stories. Because they don't know how to organize, the next meeting turns into the same thing. And, by the third meeting, all but the die-hards are turned off and don't turn up." On the other hand, Bachtel has noted that those who put their plans on paper with short-term objectives and long-term goals, and make specific, well-defined assignments, do tend to get off the ground and keep moving.

Two valuable "specific assignment ideas" were suggested by Carol Stein, southern California chairperson of Californians for Drug-Free Youth.

1. Do a baseline drug-abuse questionnaire survey of the students in your area whom you plan to reach with your program. This may well have a

galvanizing effect on your group. One year later, repeat the survey. Hopefully, you will see that your work is paying off. (The first parent group Stein organized, Conejo Families in Action, did a baseline survey in 1981 and learned, for example, that 14.7 percent of eleventh graders smoked pot "once a day or more." One year later this figure was halved to 7 percent, "and similar downward trends were seen for amphetamines and cocaine.")

2. Contact the single-state agency and inquire how the federal prevention money allocated to the state is being used. According to federal block grant regulations, 20 percent of the block grant for drug abuse is to be used for prevention. Says Stein: "Since parent groups have a proven track record concerning prevention, have a dialogue with the state agency. Find out how they can cooperate. In many states this money is dispersed through county drug and alcohol programs. The funds are basically geared to local, county and community-involved groups. The trouble is that most parent groups are not aware of the fact that this money may be available—if they write a successful grant proposal showing how they will involve the various facets of the community in their plan of action.

Fortunately, no parent group has to "reinvent the wheel" any longer. Lack of organizational skills need not be a stumbling block—since National Federation of Parents has an excellent Parents Group Starter Kit, Families in Action has "How to Start a Parent Group in Your Community," and *Patient Care* has CICOM's series of booklets on how to set up a parent group. All of these resources are excellent. They set down step-by-step organizational methods that are not theoretical, but come from hard-won trial-and-error experience. Any new parent group that follows these steps can avoid the errors, which means a giant step forward on the road to success. (See Resource list.)

The Parent Movement Goes International

Despite the multilayered problems and pitfalls that met the emerging parent movement every step of the way, the success they have achieved in a short space of time is regarded by many as phenomenal. Top state and federal officials and countless others in the drug-abuse prevention area frequently refer to the parent movement as the nation's single greatest hope for combating the drug epidemic.

The first national conference of the National Federation of Parents for

Drug-Free Youth was held in Washington, DC, October 10–13, 1982, and the caliber of the speakers who addressed the more than five hundred parent group leaders from forty-six states is indicative of the importance of this movement. Speakers included Nancy Reagan, who was honorary chairperson of the conference; Dr. Carlton Turner, director of the White House Drug Abuse Policy Office; Richard S. Schweiker, Secretary of Health and Human Services; Dr. William Mayer, administrator of the Alcohol, Drug Abuse and Mental Health Administration; Dr. William Pollin, director, National Institute on Drug Abuse; Francis Mullen, acting administrator, Drug Enforcement Administration; and Dr. C. Everett Koop, Surgeon General of the United States.

NFP's 1983 national conference in Washington, DC, was termed "even bigger and better." It was attended by over six hundred parent-group leaders from forty-seven states and seven foreign countries. One of the newest parent groups attending was composed of congressional wives from the seventy-five member Congressional Families for Drug-Free Youth—who said they were "anxious to learn and anxious to help establish new parent groups." The congressional wives served as hostesses at a reception given for NFP at the capitol, where the number of senators and congressmen and their wives who turned up was said to be unprecedented for a nongovernmental function.

By July 1984, thirty-seven states had been networked with parent groups for drug-free youth, and the parent movement was beginning to spread hope and help to nations overseas being hit by the drug epidemic among their young people.

A start along these lines had been made in April 1983 at PRIDE's Ninth Annual Conference on Youth and Drugs, attended by parent group leaders from forty-four states—and seventeen foreign countries. Jon Thomas, deputy secretary for international narcotics in the State Department, pointed out that "for many years there was a perception abroad that drug abuse was a peculiarly American phenomenon," and observed that although there was once some validity to that view, it is no longer the case. This message was clearly brought forth by the foreign participants.

Lars Kvam from Norway expressed a problem faced by many when he said,

> In our country most people think that families who have drug problems are "bad" families and parents. We are doing a lot of lobbying to convince political persons that we are "normal" persons and to convince the doctors and nurses of what it means to have someone on drugs in the family. I

think this was perhaps the first international parents' conference. I urge you to make it more international next year. Parents all over the world are the same; they can be poor or rich, but they are still caring for their children.

PRIDE did make it "more international next year." In March 1984, parents and professionals came to Atlanta, Georgia, from thirty-four different nations and all five continents to attend three days of meetings where they learned about the detrimental health effects of drugs on youth, and what parents can do to prevent their children from becoming involved in the drug culture. Parents shared their concern; they shared their experiences and efforts in their own countries—their successes and their failures. Said Dr. Gleaton: "Since, during the decade, youth drug abuse has become a massive global problem, it became clear to the delegates of the various countries that an international parents organization for drug-free youth should be formed." It was decided that Swedish Parents Against Narcotics (the oldest such parent organization in the world) and the Swedish Carnegie Institute would act as a clearinghouse for the first year, and would send an international parents for drug-free youth newsletter to parent groups and individual parents throughout the world who are interested in this movement. The next large international meeting of parents was scheduled for April 1985, at the Georgia World Congress Center in Atlanta.

Perhaps the most unique attribute of the U.S. and the international parent movement is its spirit, which becomes palpably clear at the national conferences. Kenneth Gilmore, editor-in-chief of the *Reader's Digest,* was one of the speakers at NFP's 1983 national convention. Upon his return he said: "Next year we should be sure that a couple of our editors attend—just to experience the enthusiasm and knowledge of these parents."

At NFP's first national conference the special emotions engendered in others by the parent group were expressed by Dr. William Mayer, then administrator of the Alcohol, Drug Abuse and Mental Health Administration. It is an emotion now echoed by countless others throughout the country:

You parents are the heart of it. This getting together, this talking about basic values in response to the crisis, this organizational surge that has occurred—these things will endure because they must endure if this country is to endure.

So, as one of your fellow parents, I thank you and I love you for what you are doing. I think you are the greatest reaffirmation of the basic goodness and the basic strength of this country that has happened in my lifetime, and I am proud to be associated with you.

The pioneering parents have seen firsthand some of the tragic byproducts of the powerful, relentless multibillion-dollar illegal drug conglomerate—and their flacks who turn up in various respectable guises in all strata of our society. These parents have recognized their responsibility to fight back, and their actions provide a massive blueprint for the rest of us. But the parent groups also recognize that they cannot hope to win the battle alone. It is, in its way, a kind of civil war between the drug-free and the drug proponents—perhaps the most pernicious and difficult battle our country has ever faced.

We all have the responsibility to do all that we can about the situation we have all allowed to happen. If each affected element in our society joins with the parents—schools, physicians, business and industry, law enforcement, the judiciary, legislative bodies, government agencies, public health, the military, the entertainment industry, and media—if we put blame and shame behind us, and forge ahead, we will win the battle. Because we must. What is the alternative?

Appendix

The Model Drug Paraphernalia Act

By May 1984, the Model Drug Paraphernalia Act, forbidding manufacture or sale of drug paraphernalia, had been passed in the following states: Arkansas, Arizona, California, Connecticut, District of Columbia, Delaware, Florida, Georgia, Idaho, Indiana, Kansas, Kentucky, Louisiana, Maine, Maryland, Massachusetts, Mississippi, Minnesota, Missouri, Montana, Nebraska, Nevada, New Jersey, New Hampshire, North Carolina, North Dakota, New Mexico, New York, Oklahoma, Pennsylvania, Rhode Island, South Carolina, South Dakota, Texas, Utah, Vermont, Washington, Wyoming, Virginia.

Note: Passing any law is only the first step. Police and prosecutors may need encouragement from the community to aggressively enforce the law; they have limited resources, which some may prefer to target on violent crimes. One successful step used by many communities has been to persuade the local police chief to close down a few headshops and confiscate their wares. This usually results in voluntary compliance by "secondary stores" (such as record stores and novelty shops, which only sell paraphernalia as a sideline) in dispensing with these offerings. As for the headshops *per se,* many communities have found that once the owners have been convinced that the law is constitutional and will be enforced, they voluntarily go out of business, start carrying other products—or move to another location.

For a free copy of the sixteen-page Model Drug Paraphernalia Act and supporting comments, write to Harry Myers, Assistant Chief Counsel, DEA, 1405 I Street, NW, Washington, DC 20537.

For a copy of the Model Forfeiture of Drug Profits Act, write to William M. Lenck, Forfeiture Counsel, DEA, U.S. Dept. of Justice, 1405 I St., NW, Washington, DC 20537. Also available is the four-hundred-page *Drug Agents' Guide to Forfeiture of Assets,* which contains over eight hundred citations of state and federal forfeiture cases. The first seven chapters explain all aspects of civil forfeiture law, including a comprehensive analysis of the 1978 federal law on which the model act is based. The eighth chapter discusses criminal forfeiture law. The ninth chapter probes the practical problems facing agents investigating cases involving substantial drug-related assets. The tenth chapter contains the model act, with a prefatory note and comment.

The guide is available through the Superintendent of Documents, U.S. Government Printing Office, Washington, DC 20402. At present, it sells for $9.50, which includes postage and handling. The GPO stock number is 027–004–00034–2.

The Twelve Task Forces

Officially known as Organized Crime/Drug Enforcement Task Forces, this network covers the entire nation. Following are the regions covered by the twelve task forces, together with their major city headquarters:

New England Region: Massachusetts, Maine, New Hampshire, Vermont, Connecticut, Rhode Island, western and northern districts of New York. Headquarters: Boston.

New York–New Jersey Region: southern and eastern districts of New York, New Jersey. Headquarters: New York City.

Mid-Atlantic Region: Maryland, Virginia, Washington DC, Delaware, eastern and middle districts of Pennsylvania. Headquarters: Baltimore.

Southeast Region: Georgia, North Carolina, South Carolina, Alabama, middle and eastern districts of Tennessee. Headquarters: Atlanta.

Gulf Coast Region: Texas, Louisiana, southern district of Mississippi. Headquarters: Houston.

South Central Region: Missouri, Arkansas, Oklahoma, Kansas, western district of Kentucky, western district of Tennessee, northern district of Mississippi. Headquarters: St. Louis.

North Central Region: Illinois, Indiana, Wisconsin, Iowa, Minnesota. Headquarters: Chicago.

Great Lakes Region: Michigan, Ohio, West Virginia, western district of Pennsylvania, eastern district of Kentucky. Headquarters: Detroit.

Mountain States Region: Colorado, Utah, Nebraska, Wyoming, North Dakota, South Dakota, Idaho, Montana. Headquarters: Denver.

Los Angeles–Nevada Region: Nevada and central district of California. Headquarters: Los Angeles.

Northwest Region: Washington, Oregon, Hawaii, Alaska, northern and central districts of California. Headquarters: San Francisco.

Southwest Border Region: Arizona, New Mexico, southern district of California. Headquarters: San Diego.

Single State Agencies

Alabama

Director
Div. of Mental Illness and
Substance Abuse Community Programs
State Department of Mental Health
P.O. Box 3710
200 Interstate Park
Montgomery, Alabama 36193–5001
Tel. (205) 271–9253

Alaska

Coordinator
Office of Alcoholism and Drug Abuse
Alaska Dept. of Health and Social
 Services
Pouch H-05-F
Juneau, Alaska 99811
Tel. (907) 586–6201

Arizona

Manager, Drug Abuse Section
Bureau of Community Services
Arizona Dept. of Health Services
2500 East Van Buren Street
Phoenix, Arizona 85008
Tel. (602) 255–1240/3858

Arkansas

Director
Alcohol and Drug Abuse Prevention
Department of Human Services
1515 West 7th Street, Suite 310
Little Rock, Arkansas 72202
Tel. (501) 371–2604

California

Director
Department of Alcohol and Drug
 Programs
111 Capitol Mall, Suite 450
Sacramento, California 95814
Tel. (916) 445–1940

Colorado

Director
Alcohol and Drug Abuse Division

Department of Health
4210 East 11th Avenue
Denver, Colorado 80220
Tel. (303) 320–6137, x374

Connecticut

Executive Director
Connecticut Alcohol and Drug Abuse
 Commission
999 Asylum Avenue
Hartford, Connecticut 06105
Tel. (203) 566–4145

Delaware

Chief
Bureau of Alcoholism and Drug Abuse
Department of Health and Social
 Services
1901 N. DuPont Highway
New Castle, Delaware 19720
Tel. (302) 421–6101

District of Columbia

Office of Planning and Development
1875 Connecticut Avenue, NW, Suite
 836A
Washington, D.C. 20009
Tel. (202) 673–7481

Florida

Administrator, Drug Abuse Program
Alcohol, Drug Abuse, and Mental
 Health Program Office
Dept. of Health and Rehab. Services
1317 Winewood Boulevard
Tallahassee, Florida 32301
Tel. (904) 488–0900

Georgia

Director
Alcoholism and Drug Abuse Services
Division of Mental Health
Department of Human Resources
Suite 1170–East Twin Towers
Martin Luther King Drive

Atlanta, Georgia 30334
Tel. (404) 656–7310

Hawaii

Chief
Alcohol and Drug Abuse Branch
Mental Health Division
Department of Health
P.O. Box 3378
Honolulu, Hawaii 96801
Tel. (808) 548–4280

Idaho

Supervisor, Substance Abuse Section
Division of Health
Bureau of Preventive Medicine
Department of Health and Welfare
450 West State Street, 4th Floor
STATEHOUSE Mail
Boise, Idaho 83720
Tel. (208) 334–4368

Illinois

Illinois Dangerous Drugs Commission
300 North State Street, Suite 1500
Chicago, Illinois 60610
Tel. (312) 822–9860

Indiana

Director
Department of Mental Health
Division of Addiction Services
429 N. Pennsylvania Street
Indianapolis, Indiana 46204
Tel. (317) 232–7816

Iowa

Director
Department of Substance Abuse
Insurance Exchange Building, Suite 202
505 Fifth Avenue
Des Moines, Iowa 50319
Tel. (515) 281–3641

Kansas

Commissioner, Alcohol and Drug Abuse
  Services
State Dept. of Social and Rehab. Services
Topeka State Hospital

Biddle Building, 2nd Floor
2700 West Sixth Street
Topeka, Kansas 66606
Tel. (913) 296–3925

Kentucky

Branch Manager, Substance Abuse
  Branch
Division for Community Services for
  Mental Health
275 East Main Street
Frankfort, Kentucky 40621
Tel. (502) 564–2880

Louisiana

Office of Mental Health and Substance
  Abuse
Department of Health and Human
  Resources
P.O. Box 4049
Baton Rouge, Louisiana 70821
Tel. (504) 342–2565

Maine

Director
Alcoholism and Drug Abuse Prevention
Bureau of Rehabilitation
Department of Human Services
32 Winthrop Street
Augusta, Maine 04330
Tel. (207) 289–2781

Maryland

Director, Drug Abuse Administration
Maryland Dept. of Health and Mental
  Hygiene
201 West Preston Street, 4th Floor
Baltimore, Maryland 21201
Tel. (301) 383–3959

Massachusetts

Director, Division of Drug
  Rehabilitation
Massachusetts Department of Mental
  Health
600 Washington Street, Room 620
Boston, Massachusetts 02111
Tel. (617) 727–8614

Michigan

Administrator
Office of Substance Abuse Services
3500 North Logan Street
P.O. Box No. 30035
Lansing, Michigan 48909
Tel. (517) 373–8603

Minnesota

Director
Chemical Dependency Program Div.
Department of Public Welfare
Centennial Office Building, 4th Floor
St. Paul, Minnesota 55155
Tel. (612) 296–4610

Mississippi

Director
Division of Alcohol and Drug Abuse
State Dept. of Mental Health
1100 Robert E. Lee Office Building,
12th Floor
Jackson, Mississippi 39201
Tel. (601) 359–1297

Missouri

Director, Department of Mental Health
Division of Alcohol and Drug Abuse
P.O. Box 687
2002 Missouri Boulevard
Jefferson City, Missouri 65102
Tel. (314) 751–3090

Montana

Administrator
Alcohol and Drug Abuse Division
Montana State Department of
 Institutions
1539 Eleventh Avenue
Helena, Montana 59620
Tel. (406) 449–2827

Nebraska

Director
Div. on Alcoholism and Drug Abuse
State Department of Public Institutions

P.O. Box 94728
Lincoln, Nebraska 68509
Tel. (402) 471–2851, x415

Nevada

Chief
Bureau of Alcohol and Drug Abuse
Department of Human Resources
Kinkead Building, 5th Floor
505 E. King Street
Carson City, Nevada 89710
Tel. (702) 885–4790

New Hampshire

Director
Alcohol and Drug Abuse Prevention
Health and Welfare Building
Hazen Drive
Concord, New Hampshire 03301
Tel. (603) 271–4627

New Jersey

Commissioner
Alcohol, Narcotic and Drug Abuse
New Jersey State Department of Health
CN 362
Trenton, New Jersey 08608
Tel. (609) 292–5760

New Mexico

Chief, Drug Abuse Bureau
Division of Behavioral Health Services
New Mexico Department of Health and
 Environment
P.O. Box 968
Santa Fe, New Mexico 87504–0968
Tel. (505) 984–0020, x336

New York

Director
Division of Substance Abuse Services
Executive Park South
Stuyvesant Plaza
Albany, New York 12203
Tel. (518) 457–2965

North Carolina

Deputy Director for Alcohol and Drug Abuse

Division of Mental Health, Mental Retardation and Substance Abuse Services

Department of Human Resources

325 North Salisbury Street, Room 1100

Raleigh, North Carolina 27611

Tel. (919) 733–4670

North Dakota

Director

Division of Alcoholism and Drug Abuse

Mental Health, Alcoholism and Drug Abuse Services

State Department of Human Services

Capitol Building

Bismarck, North Dakota 58505

Tel. (701) 224–2769

Ohio

Chief, Bureau of Drug Abuse

Ohio Department of Mental Health

65 S. Front Street, Suite 211

Columbus, Ohio 43215

Tel. (614) 466–9023

Oklahoma

Chief of Programs

State Department of Mental Health

P.O. Box 53277, Capitol Station

Oklahoma City, Oklahoma 73152

Tel. (405) 521–0044

Oregon

Administrator

Programs for Alcohol and Drug Problems

Mental Health Division

2575 Bittern Street, NE

Salem, Oregon 97310

Tel. (503) 378–2163

Pennsylvania

Secretary for Drug and Alcohol Programs

Room 809, Health and Welfare Building

P.O. Box 90

Harrisburg, Pennsylvania 17108

Tel. (717) 787–9857

Rhode Island

Director for Substance Abuse

Dept. of Mental Health, Retardation and Hospitals

Administration Building

Rhode Island Medical Center

Cranston, Rhode Island 02920

Tel. (401) 464–2091

South Carolina

Director

Commission on Alcohol and Drug Abuse

3700 Forest Drive, Suite 300

Columbia, South Carolina 29204

Tel. (803) 758–2521

South Dakota

Director

Division of Alcohol and Drug Abuse

Joe Foss Building, Room 119

Pierre, South Dakota 57501–2283

Tel. (605) 773–3123

Tennessee

Commissioner

Div. of Alcohol and Drug Abuse Services

Dept. of Mental Health and Mental Retardation

James K. Polk State Office Building, 4th Floor

505 Deaderick Street

Nashville, Tennessee 37219

Tel. (615) 741–1921

Texas

Director

Drug Abuse Prevention Division

Texas Department of Community Affairs

P.O. Box 13166

Austin, Texas 78711

Tel. (512) 443–4100

Utah

Director
Division of Alcoholism and Drugs
Department of Social Services
P.O. Box 2500, Room 350
Salt Lake City, Utah 84110–2500
Tel. (801) 533–6532

Vermont

Director
Alcohol and Drug Abuse Division
Waterbury Office Complex
103 South Main Street
Waterbury, Vermont 05676
Tel. (802) 241–2170

Virginia

Commissioner
Division of Substance Abuse
State Department of Mental Health and
  Mental·Retardation
P.O. Box 1797
Richmond, Virginia 23214
Tel. (804) 786–5313

Washington

Chief, Office on Drug Abuse Prevention
Bureau of Alcohol and Substance Abuse
Mail Stop OB-44W
Olympia, Washington 98504
Tel. (206) 753–5866

West Virginia

Director
Div. of Alcoholism and Drug Abuse
  Services
Office of Behavioral Health Services
State Capitol Complex
Charleston, West Virginia 25305
Tel. (304) 348–2276

Wisconsin

Director
Office of Alcohol and Other Drug Abuse
Division of Community Services
Wisconsin Department of Health and
  Social Services
P.O. Box 7851

1 West Wilson Street
Madison, Wisconsin 53707
Tel. (608) 266–3442

Wyoming

Substance Abuse State Program
  Manager
361 Hathaway Building
Cheyenne, Wyoming 82002
Tel. (307) 777–6494

American Samoa

Director, Human Services Clinic
LBJ Tropical Medical Center
Pago Pago, American Samoa 96799
Tel. (Overseas Operator and) 633–5139
  or 633–1222, x281

Guam

Administrator
Mental Health and Substance Abuse
  Agency
Government of Guam
P.O. Box 20999
Guam Main Facility
Guam 96921–0102

Northern Mariana Islands

Director
Public Health and Environmental
  Services
Commonwealth of the Northern
  Mariana Islands
Dr. Torres Hospital
Saipan, Mariana Islands 96950
Tel. (Overseas Operator and) 6110, 6112,
  6113, 6118

Puerto Rico

Secretary for Treatment
P.O. Box B-A
Rio Piedras Station
Rio Piedras, Puerto Rico 00928
Tel. (809) 763–7575, x212, 213
  (809) 763–8957

Trust Territory

Director, Office of Health Services
Trust Territory of the Pacific Islands
Saipan, Mariana Islands 96950

MARIJUANA ALERT

Tel. (Overseas Operator) 670–9355,
  9422, 9370

Virgin Islands

Director
Div. of Mental Health, Alcoholism
  and Drug Dependency Services

Department of Health
Government of the Virgin Islands
P.O. Box 7309
St. Thomas, Virgin Islands 08001
Tel. (809) 773–1992
    (809) 774–4888
    (809) 774–4701

Resource List

Organizations, Publications, and Films

The following offer excellent, accurate, and up-to-date information about marijuana and other drugs.

Addiction Research Foundation. Established in 1949, the ARF is an agency of the Province of Ontario that operates specialized research, educational, clinical, and community service development programs throughout the province. In addition, the foundation has been designated a Collaborating Center for Research and Training on Drug Dependence by the World Health Organization. This is the largest organization of this dimension in Canada and has been known internationally for two decades as a leading research institute in the field of alcohol and drug dependency problems. Two of ARF's important publications are listed below. For these and for additional information on marijuana and other drugs, contact Marketing Services, Dept. MH, Addiction Research Foundation, 33 Russell St., Toronto, Ontario M5S 2S1.

The ARF's monthly publication, *The Journal,* a sixteen-page newspaper for professionals in drug abuse and related areas, goes to some twenty-six thousand subscribers in many countries. It is the only publication of its kind with a network of correspondents around the world, and it brings readers the most up-to-date information on cannabis and other drugs, as well as related information in this area of interest to readers in law enforcement, education, government policy planning, research, and so on. Subscription: $24.00 a year in United States and elsewhere; $18.00 in Canada.

"Marijuana: Answers for Young People and Parents." This 16-page booklet, published in 1984, was prepared by a team of ARF staff scientists and information specialists. It is available free to residents of Ontario. For others, $1.00 prepaid.

American Council on Drug Education. Founded (as American Council on Marijuana) in 1977 to educate the public about the health hazards associated with the use of marijuana in particular, and also the use of other psychoactive substances. Booklets on specific health hazards of marijuana include:

- "Marijuana and Alcohol," by Dr. George K. Russell, $2.50.
- "The Marijuana Controversy," by Dr. Carlton Turner, $2.00.
- "Marijuana and the Brain," by Dr. Robert G. Heath, $1.50.
- "The Marijuana Epidemic: A Physician's Guide" (literature, speeches and slides). Designed for physicians to use in educating community groups about the health hazards of marijuana. Contains background materials for the physician, speeches for youth and adult audiences, frequently asked questions and answers, slides to use with the speeches, and resource information, $15.00.
- "Marijuana: The National Impact on Education," a summary of a national conference of leading education organizations that considered the issue, $2.50.
- "Marijuana and Reproduction," by Dr. Carol Grace Smith, $2.50.
- "Marijuana, Smoking and Its Effects on the Lungs," by Dr. Donald Tashkin and Dr. Sidney Cohen, $2.50.
- "Marijuana Today, A Compilation of Medical Findings for the Layman," by Dr. George K. Russell, $3.00.
- "A Pediatrician's View of Marijuana," by Dr. Ingrid Lantner and Rose Barth, $2.50.
- "Therapeutic Potential of Marijuana's Components," by Dr. Sidney Cohen and Therese Andrysiak, $2.50.
- "Treating the Marijuana-Dependent Person," by Dr. Robin de Silva and Robert L. DuPont, $2.95.
- "Urine Testing for Marijuana Use," by Margaret Blasinsky and George K. Russell, $2.50.

Films and Audio Visuals

Available from American Council on Drug Education: *Danger Ahead: Marijuana on the Road.* This twenty-two-minute, 16-mm. color film was produced in 1981 by ACDE and the National Association of Independent Insurers. Narrated by Jason Robards, Jr., it depicts the hazards of driving under the influence of marijuana, and marijuana and alcohol combined, and offers personal experiences of teenage and young adult users, plus commentary by medical experts. Film comes with discussion guide. Purchase: $225.00; rent: $25.00. Address: 6193 Executive Blvd., Rockville, Maryland 20852.

Wasted. A thirty-minute, 16-mm. color film for ages nine to fourteen. Animated characters and documented real-life vignettes featuring children are used to convey information on the health hazards of marijuana. The film is intended for children who are experimenting, undecided and uninformed about marijuana. Contact ACDE for further information.

The following films are available from PRIDE.
Breaking Free. For junior high and high school. The film's focus is on marijuana. "For two decades now," said Dr. Thomas Gleaton, "the merchandising of drugs to our children has cocooned them into a drug-using peer culture. This upbeat, twenty-

seven-minute color film shows our young people breaking free from harmful drugs and turning toward a variety of alternatives to drug use." 16-mm. film for purchase only, $195; ¾-inch video and ½-inch video, VHS rental: $30.00, purchase, $165; sixteen-page leader's guide accompanies film and video cassettes.

How Do You Tell? This 13-minute 16-mm. color film uses a combination of live footage and animation to deal directly with peer pressure and the ability to say no! to smoking, drugs, and alcohol. Besides heightening the awareness of the dangers of drug and alcohol use, it shows that there are always choices available. Encourages young people between the ages of seven and twelve to connect with the idea "If it isn't healthy, don't do it." Film accompanied by a leader's guide. Purchase $295.00; purchase of video, $265.00; rental of film, $50.00.

PRIDE sound/slide presentation for parents: *Marijuana: What Impact Is It Having on Our Youth?* This slide show, in color, includes an educational overview of the marijuana plant, statistics, trends, latest scientific data of effects on males and females, drug paraphernalia, and resources, plus key recommendations to counteract the drug problem. Purchase, $100.00; rental, $30.00.

Epidemic I: Kids, Drugs and Alcohol (DuPont Columbia Award winner). This twenty-seven-minute, 16-mm. color film explores the reasons behind drug and alcohol use in our society, with sharp focus on the influence of the media, music, and peers on our attitudes. For young people and adults. Film purchase, $495.00; video purchase, $450.00.

Epidemic II: America Fights Back. This new fifty-one-minute, 16-mm. color film (the TV version) demonstrates solutions to the drug and alcohol abuse problem in communities, the workplace, and the military. Case histories serve as a road map to positive approaches implemented by parents, children, teachers, politicians, business leaders, and helping services. Film purchase $750.00; video purchase is $675.00. Two excerpts are also available:

"Community Action Segment" (16-mm. color, thirty-two minutes). This excerpt suggests that the solution to the epidemic of drug and alcohol abuse depends upon adults and young people who are willing to take charge of their own lives. Profiled are four American communities successfully fighting drug and alcohol abuse: Naples, Florida; Springfield, Massachusetts; Tampa, Florida, and a West Dallas community. Film purchase $550.00, video purchase $495.00.

"Business and Industry Segment" (16-mm. color, twenty-three minutes). This excerpt shows the positive effects employee assistance programs have on drug and alcohol abuse in the workplace. Through an EAP program, business and industry can increase productivity, lower accident rates, and decrease absenteeism, health insurance claims, and sick benefits. The excerpt leads the way in helping to confront and combat the epidemic of substance abuse in all levels of business and industry. Film purchase $495.00; video purchase $445.00.

PRIDE audio/visual materials also include

- Dr. Donald Ian Macdonald: "Marijuana & Addiction."
- Dr. Lee Croft: "Drug Use in Business and Industry."
- Dr. Robert Heath: "Effects of Drugs on Brain Pleasure Centers."
- Dr. Carol Smith: "Impact of Marijuana on Female Primates."
- Dr. Ingrid Lantner: "Clinical Observations Data on Marijuana Use Among Youth."
- Dr. Harold Voth: "Drug Abuse and the Military."
- Pat Burch, Legislation Committee, National Federation of Parents: "Who to Write/What You Can Do."
- Dr. Lee Croft: "Use of EMIT Test in Counseling."
- Dan MacDougald, Jr.: "Use of EMIT Test for Crime Abatement."
- Bill Rudolph, principal, Northside High School: "How Schools/Parents/Administration/Community Can Work Together."
- Dr. Richard Hawley: "Marijuana and Intellectual Performance."
- Dr. Marietta Issidorides: "Biological Risks of Cannabis: Results of a Greek Study."
- Dr. Susan Dalterio: "Sexuality and Reproduction."
- Dr. John Johns, former deputy assistant secretary of defense: "Drug Abuse Prevention in the Military."
- Peter Bensinger: "Industry and Productivity."
    All available in both audio and video—Audio $5.00, Video $50.00

Publications

Arrive Alive: How to Keep Drunk and Pot High Drivers off the Highway, by Peggy Mann. "*Arrive Alive* is full of preventative actions—which work—derived from many authoritative sources, presented in an easy-to-follow manner. The need for these pilot project ideas becomes grimly apparent in Section One of this book which contains the latest facts and figures concerning the devastating effects of drugs and alcohol on the drivers of motor vehicles. A wonderful and imperative work which will benefit an untold number of Americans" (Robinson Risner, executive director, Texans' War on Drugs). $7.95 plus $1.50 postage and handling. Woodmere Press, Box 1590 Cathedral Station, New York, New York 10025.

Californians for Drug-Free Youth: Each of the following costs $1.00 for 10 copies, prepaid. "Parents' Pledge: Guidelines for Social Activities." A pamphlet with social guidelines for teenagers' social activities. For example, parents pledge to have drug and alcohol-free parties for their youngsters, set reasonable curfew times, etc. This pledge often becomes the basis of a neighborhood support group of parents whose youngsters are on the same soccer team, church group or school group. "Pledge for the Privilege of Driving." Information regarding driver-impairing effects of alcohol and marijuana and a contract to be signed by parents and teenager pledging not to drive after having used alcohol, marijuana or other drugs. P.O. Box 60962, Sacramento, California 95860.

Committees of Correspondence. Members of this national organization receive regular Drug Abuse Issues, which clearly set forth the facts, and what you can do—

including whom to write to for greatest effectiveness. Each separate drug abuse issue is written by an expert in that particular area. Typical subjects are "Nipping Marijuana in the Bud" (about paraquat), "How to Control Drunk/Drugged Driving," and "Why Do So Many Pediatricians and Family Doctors Know So Little about the Health Hazards of Marijuana?" The subscriber receives four Drug Abuse Issues a year for $10.00, plus much additional information. Committees of Correspondence, P.O. Box 2321, Topsfield, Massachusetts 01983.

Drug Abuse Update: A quarterly twelve-page publication that abstracts the latest information collected at the Families in Action National Drug Information Center in Atlanta, Georgia (which is listed by the U.S. Library of Congress as a national resource for drug information). The short articles in *Update* are abstracts of articles published in medical and academic journals, and in newspapers throughout the country. They are organized under such subject headings as Drug Use and Effects, Drugs and Crime, Drugs and Education, Drugs and Parent Groups, Drugs and Kids, Drugs and Death. Subscription: "10.00 per year. Back issues, $3.00 each. Also available, an annual index: $5.00. Suite 300, 3845 N. Druid Hills Road, Decatur, Georgia 30333.

"Helping Your Child Resist the Marijuana Culture." A twenty-six-page booklet that summarizes effects of marijuana and offers advice to parents on what they can do to combat it. Sections on how to protect your child from the drug culture, drug use in schools, and step-by-step directions for organizing parent peer groups. $2.50. Published by CICOM (Citizens for Informed Choices on Marijuana), c/o Logical Communications, 16 Thorndale Circle, Darien, Connecticut 06820.

How to Form a Families in Action Group in Your Community. A 164-page manual by Sue Rusche that tells how to organize a parent/community group to prevent drug and alcohol abuse among teenagers. It teaches parents how to bring the community's responsible adults together to identify and solve local problems in adolescent drug and alcohol abuse. $10.00. Reduced rates for bulk orders. Families in Action, Suite 300, 3845 N. Druid Hills Road, Decatur, Georgia 30333.

How Much Do You Really Know About Marijuana? Six-panel Q and A pamphlet capsulizing important health hazard material, plus scientific references. $1.00, or 100 copies for $10.00, prepaid. Woodmere Press, Box 1590, Cathedral Station, New York, N.Y. 10025.

"How to Get Your Child Off Marijuana," by Harold Voth, M.D. A twenty-four-page booklet giving step-by-step process for identifying the problem and coping with it successfully. Psychiatrist Voth has dealt with numerous marijuana-abusing youngsters and adults for over a decade. Logical Communications, 1980. $3.00. 16 Thorndale Circle, Darien, Connecticut 06820.

Listen. A youth-slanted, full-color monthly magazine that emphasizes education for the prevention of drug problems. Frequently specializes in current material on marijuana, and points the reader to positive alternatives. Special issue: February 1984, "Putting Families Back Together" (dealing with drug problems in the home). Single copy: $1.00. Write for full subscription information. (See address for Narcotics Education, Inc., below.)

Marijuana: Deceptive Weed, third edition. Vol. I, *The Escape of the Genie,* historical and social aspects, 400 pp. Vol. II, *A Decade of Research. Scientific Aspects: Botany, Chemistry, Toxicology, Pharmacology, Medical Applications and Psychiatric Aspects,* 600 pp. Total of three thousand references in both volumes. By G. G. Nahas, M.D., Ph.D., in cooperation with H. C. Frick, II, M.D.; and N. Bejerot, M.D.; Vol. II in cooperation with M. Paris, Ph.D.; David Harvey, Ph.D.; and Henry Brill, M.D., 1984. Vol. I, $25; Vol. II, 49.50, Raven Press, 1140 Avenue of the Americas, N.Y., New York 10036.

Narcotics Education, Inc. Producers and distributors of educational audiovisual and printed materials on drug problems, including marijuana. Six "Q and A" booklets on marijuana, PCP, and "Parents Guide to Drug Abuse," $2.00. (Includes: "Is Marijuana Really All That Bad?" by Gabriel G. Nahas, M.D., Ph.D.; "Marijuana, Sex and the Unborn Child," by Hardin Jones, M.D.; "Our Most Dangerous Drug," by Harvey Powelson, M.D.; "What Marijuana Really Does," by Hardin Jones, M.D.)
Also available: *Potluck,* a sixty-four-page paperback with the real story about pot in the personal experiences of those who have found out the hard way. $1.00.
Narcotics Education, Inc., 6830 Laurel St., NW, Washington, DC 20012.

National Federation of Parents for Drug-Free Youth (NFP). Both individual and group membership includes "How to Start a Parent Group in Your Community"; quarterly newsletter; regular legislative update from NFP's Legislative Committee; also, educational brochures including "What Parents Must Learn about Marijuana," and, for teens, "Straight Pitch about Marijuana" (also available in Spanish). (Single copies of both brochures free with membership; bulk orders, $8.00 per hundred.)

Also available: Education kit and public speaking manual, which includes sample speeches ready for delivery on kids and drugs; $5.00; and Parent/Community Task Force Manual, which gives alternative activities to drug use; $5.00.
"Press Media Guidelines," for parents working with local media, $4.00.

NFP's Resource List includes recommended films, tapes, books, educational pamphlets on the spectrum of drug abuse including individual drugs (and alcohol) and the youth-drug scene, and further information on how to form parent groups.
Membership for new groups ($25.00); this provides eligibility for tax-exempt status under NFP "umbrella." Membership for individuals: $10.00. All new members will be sent a list of parent groups nearest them.
NFP, 1820 Franwall Avenue, Silver Spring, Maryland 20902. Toll-free number: 1–800–554–**KIDS.**

National Institute on Drug Abuse: Most of the NIDA publications mentioned in the References which follow this section are available from the U.S. Government Printing Office, Superintendent of Documents.

The following three NIDA publications specifically on marijuana and of special interest to parents and youngsters are available directly from NIDA. Single copies are free. Write P.O. Box 416, Kensington, Maryland 20795:

Parents, Peers and Pot II: Parents in Action by Marsha Manatt: 160-page paperback; describes programs and activities for drug-free youth conducted by parent groups around the country.

"For Kids Only": 12-page booklet for youngsters 8 to 14 in a Q and A format; explains marijuana and some of its detrimental physical and psychological effects.

"For Parents Only; What You Need to Know about Marijuana:" This booklet was designed to accompany a NIDA-produced 30-minute, 16-mm film of the same name available on free loan to parent groups and adult community organizations. Specify needed date. Contact Modern Talking Picture Service, 5000 Park St. North, St. Petersburg, Florida 33709. With film comes discussion guidebook and 25 free copies of "For Parents Only" booklet.

Parents Who Care. An organization of parents who have included the youth of the San Francisco Bay area as a part of the solution to the problem. The young people's "branch" includes active youth involvement in role modeling; speaking out on the issue to adults, their peers, and younger children; and providing drug- and alcohol-free alternative activities, such as parties, dances, new games and programs, and sports activities. For their pamphlets, "How to Start a Parent Group," ($5.00) and "Involving Youth in Changing the Scene," ($5.00) write to Parents Who Care, Inc., 650 Castro Street, Mountain View, California 94040.

Phoenix House. The nation's largest residential drug treatment facility offers free information on drugs for young people and for parents, plus advice on school programs. 164 West 74th Street, New York, New York 10023.

PRIDE (Parent Resource Institute on Drug Education). A resource, information, conference, and training organization for parents, teachers, youth, and others concerned about adolescent drug abuse. PRIDE, started in 1977, was the first resource center in the country to focus on the education and mobilization of parents for the prevention of adolescent drug abuse, with emphasis on marijuana. PRIDE operates a toll-free drug information line: (800) 241–9746. The organization maintains a library of films, slide shows, tapes, conference proceedings, and printed materials. In addition, it produces a quarterly national newsletter. Address: PRIDE, 100 Edgewood Avenue, Suite 1261, Atlanta, Georgia 30303.

Materials available from PRIDE:

PRIDE packet of information on drugs: $12.00; PRIDE newsletter: $8.00 per year; PRIDE Community/School Plan: $3.00; "Be Fantastic:" teaching tool with quiz, grades 4–6, set of twenty-five: $7.95; PRIDE Southeast Drug Conference Proceedings, 1979: $2.00; 1980 and 1981 in one volume: $10.00; 1982: $12.00; *Parents, Peers and Pot,* by Marsha Manatt: $3.00; and *Parents, Peers and Pot II: Parents in Action,* by Marsha Manatt: $3.00; *Drug Abuse in the Modern World,* by Gabriel G. Nahas, M.D.: $10.50; *Marijuana, Time for a Closer Look,* by Curtis Janeczek: $5.95; Teacher's Guide: $3.00; *Sensual Drugs* by H. and H. Jones: $9.95; "Marijuana: The Myth of Harmlessness Goes Up in Smoke," by Peggy Mann: $1.00, Teacher's Guide, $.25; "The Family Connection: A Guidebook for Family Decision-Making," by parents from four Atlanta high schools, including Northside High—a practical guide about the complexities, hazards, responsibilities, and pleasures of adolescent and parental relationships, $3.00; *Pot: What It Is, What It Does,* by Ann Tobias, for grades 3–6: $2.95.

Stay Real, a 26-page booklet addressed to teenagers and their parents and designed to promote discussion between them. Published by the Department of National Health and Welfare, Government of Canada. Free to Canadians. Americans may write Lavada Pinder, Director, Program Resources, Health Promotion Directorate, Jeanne Mance Bldg., Tunneys Pasture, Ottawa, Ontario K 1A012.

STRAIGHT, Inc. A drug-rehabilitation program for adolescents with branches in St. Petersburg and Sarasota, Florida; Atlanta, Georgia; Cincinnati, Ohio; and Fairfax County, Virginia. The program shares its knowledge of adolescent marijuana and other drug use in the book *Gone Way Down* by STRAIGHT's former director Miller Newton. Also available in a forty-five-minute videotape, with Newton and kids and parents discussing their experiences with drug use. Both book and tape present the four stages of progressive involvement with marijuana and other drugs, and the progressive deterioration of behavior, social relations, achievement, feelings, self-worth, and health. Book, $3.95; videotape, $300.00. STRAIGHT, P.O. Box 1577, Pinellas Park, Florida 33565.

References

All statements quoted in this book not otherwise identified below were obtained by the author in personal interviews with the individuals concerned.

CHAPTER 1: THE BRIEFING

(3, 4) 1. "Remarks of the President Regarding the Drug Abuse Program: The Rose Garden, 11.16 A.M. E.D.T.," June 24, 1982, Office of the Press Secretary.

(5) 2. C. W. Waller, J. J. Johnson, J. Buelke, and C. E. Turner, *Marijuana: An Annotated Bibliography*, vol. I (New York: Macmillan, 1976), 560 pp. Summaries of 3,045 papers from international scientific journals published from 1964 through 1974.

(5) C. W. Waller, R. S. Nair, A. F. McAllister, B. Urbanek, and C. E. Turner, *Marijuana: An Annotated Bibliography*, vol. II (New York: Macmillan, 1982), 620 pp. Summaries of 2,669 papers published in international scientific journals from 1974 to 1980.

(5) 3. CODAP (Client-Oriented Data Acquisitions Process; formerly DAWN, Drug Abuse Warning Network) collected the data on admissions to federally funded drug treatment facilities from 1975 through 1981. National Institute on Drug Abuse Statistical Series: *Annual Data*. Series E. *Reports*. 1976–1981.

(7) 4. Statement by C. Everett Koop, M.D., Surgeon General of the U.S. Public Health Service, U.S. Department of Health and Human Services. *HHS News*, August 12, 1982.

(8) 5. National Roper Poll, 1980. *Reports*, issue 80–3. Field work done in February 1980; report issued April 1980.

(8) 6. Gallup Poll, 1978. "Tenth Annual Survey of the Public's Attitude Toward the Public Schools." Published in *Phi Delta Kappan*, September 1978.

(10, 11) 7. Dr. Robert DuPont, "Global Silence Reigns on Cannabis," *The Journal* of the Addiction Research Foundation, World Health Organization Collaborating Centre for Research and Training on Drug Dependence Problems (Toronto, Ontario, Canada, January 1978), p. 7.

(13) 8. Dr. William Pollin, "NIDA Concern: Misleading Media Reports," *PRIDE Newsletter*, vol. 5, no. 2 (June 1983), p. 2.

(13) 9. *524-page volume of testimony on the U.S. Senate hearings on the Marijuana-Hashish epidemic.* Hearings before the Subcommittee to Investigate the Administration of the Internal Security Act and Other Internal Security Laws, Committee on the Judiciary, U.S. Senate. 93rd cong., 2nd sess., May 9, 16, 17, 20, 21, and June 13, 1974.

CHAPTER 2: THE SITUATION

(17–19) 1. J. D. Miller, I. H. Cisin, H. Gardner-Keaton, A. V. Harrell, P. W. Wirtz, H. I. Abelson, and P. M. Fishburne, *National Survey on Drug Abuse: Main Findings, 1982.* National Institute on Drug Abuse, DHHS pub. no. (ADM) 83–1263 (Washington, DC: Supt. of Docs., U.S. Govt. Printing Off., 1983), 160 pp. (Note: This survey is generally called the National Household Survey.)

(19) 2. L. D. Johnston, J. G. Bachman, and P. M. O'Malley, *Student Drug Use, Attitudes and Beliefs, National Trends, 1975–1982* (Based on the National High School Senior Survey). National Institute on Drug Abuse, DHHS pub. no. (ADM) 83–1260 (Washington, DC, Supt. of Docs., U.S. Govt. Printing Off., 1983), 139 pp.

(20) 3. Weekly Reader Periodicals of Xerox Education Publications in cooperation with the Drug Abuse Policy Office, Office of Policy Development, et al., "A Study of Children's Attitudes and Perceptions about Drugs and Alcohol," (Middletown, CT: Weekly Reader Publications, 1983), 19 pp.

(20, 21) 4. "The Critical Need for Volunteers: A Survey of the Nation's Mayors," conducted by the Elks (BPOE), Chicago, 1983.

(22) 5. Keith Stroup's statement reported by Brenda Bell, "Cat Out of Baggie—NORML Wants Legal Pot," *Atlanta Journal,* December 29, 1978.

(22) 6. NORML's official 1979 policy was published that year in the NORML Official Policy booklet.

(22) 7. Increase in California's DWI . . . in "A First Report of the Impact of California's New Marijuana Laws," 5B95, Health and Welfare Agency, State Office of Narcotics and Drug Abuse, January 1977, pp. 7–8.

(23) 8. Norman Darwick's statement made at Washington Journalism Center, Annual Roundtable Conference for Journalists, January 27, 1983.

(23) 9. Dr. Robert Dupont, "Marijuana Decriminalization: A Personal Reassessment." Speech given at the Second Annual Conference on Marijuana, sponsored by the American Council on Marijuana, June 28–29, 1979.

(23) 10. National Roper Poll, 1981, "How important to society do you feel it is that laws related to the use of marijuana be strictly enforced?" Roper *Reports,* March 1981.

(24) 11. NORML's 1982 conference, reported in *The Leaflet* (NORML's publication), December 1982.

(24) 12. NORML's seminars for lawyers reported on by Brenda Bell, "Lawyers Study Tricky Pot Problems," *Atlanta Journal-Constitution,* December 3, 1978.

(25, 26) 13. Nancy Gray, "Chemical Use/Abuse: Its Effect on the Female Reproductive System and Pregnancy," DIN 211 (Phoenix, AZ: Do It Now Foundation, Institute for Chemical Survival, April 1976; 2nd rev. ed., April 1979).

(26, 27) 14. Vic Pawlak, "Drug Abuse: A Realistic Primer for Parents, or Things You Should Know About Drugs After Reading the Scare Pamphlets," DIN 204 (Phoenix, AZ: Do It Now Foundation, undated. (A new updated edition by Dario McDarby was published in 1980.)

(26) 15. "Drug I.Q. Test," DIN 113 (Phoenix, AZ: Do It Now Foundation, National Media Center, 1974).

(26, 27) 16. "Drugs: A Primer for Young People," 2nd rev. ed., DIN 212 (Phoenix, AZ: Do It Now Foundation, May 1976), p. 18.

(27) 17. Vic Pawlak, "Conscientious Guide to Drug Abuse," 6th rev. ed. (Phoenix, AZ: Do It Now Foundation, originally printed in 1974).

(28, 30) 18. Foundations contributing to DAC disclosed in Drug Abuse Council IRS tax returns, The Foundation Center, New York, 1971, 1974–78.

(29) 19. Sue Rusche, "Drug Education—or Drug Information," in *Drug Abuse in the Modern World,* (New York: Pergamon Press, 1981), p. 205.

(29, 30) 20. Wald and Hutt's 1972 report quoted in Drug Abuse Council, *The Facts about "Drug Abuse,"* (New York: Macmillan/Free Press, 1980), Foreword, p. iv.

(29) 21. In the 1960s less than 5 percent of the population had any experience with any illegal drug, according to Ira Cissin, Judith D. Miller, and Adele V. Harrell, "Highlights from the National Survey on Drug Abuse" (Rockville, MD: NIDA, 1978), p. 17.

22. Quotes from *The Facts about "Drug Abuse"*—See note 20 above, pp. 6, 17, 189, 191–96.

CHAPTER 3: CRISIS IN THE WORKPLACE

(35) 1. Dr. Pursch interviewed for "NBC White Paper: Pleasure Drugs—The Great American High," hosted by Edwin Newman. Originally aired April 20, 1982.

(35) 2. Comp Care survey results in Comprehensive Care Corporation, "Alcohol and Drug Abuse: The Medical Complications." July 15, 1983, 30 pp.

(35) 3. D. T. Friendly, "Drugs on the Job: The Quiet Problem," *Newsweek,* September 15, 1980, pp. 83–84.

(36) 4. Dr. William Mayer, then administrator of the Alcohol, Drug Abuse, and Mental Health Administration, Department of Health and Human Services, Statement before the Senate Subcommittee on Alcoholism and Drug Abuse and the Subcommittee on Employment and Productivity, Committee on Labor and Human Resources, U.S. Senate, July 14, 1982, p. 3.

(36) 5. For the follow-up survey on daily pot-smokers, see L. D. Johnston, "The Daily Marijuana User," paper delivered at the first annual meeting of the National Alcohol and Drug Coalition, Washington, DC, September 18, 1980. Unpublished paper available from the author, Box 1248, Univ. of Michigan, Ann Arbor, MI 48106.

(36) 6. *The Conference Board report* published as "Industry Roles in Health Care," chapter 8 of *Alcohol and Drug Abuse.* (New York: The Conference Board, 1974).

(37) 7. CONSAD Research Corporation, "Drug Use in Industry," NIDA Division of Research Contract, number HSM-4273-210-NDA. DHHS pub. no. (ADM) 81–

811 (Washington, DC: U.S. Govt. Printing Off., 1979), stock number 017–024–00852–4, p. 38.

(37) 8. Lee Croft, "Industrial Drug Use: Impact on Productivity," *PRIDE National Drug Conference Highlights* (Atlanta, GA: PRIDE, Georgia State University, 1982), p. 105.

(37) 9. Benno Isaacs noted the small-town drug use in *Family Economist,* August 31, 1981. (Washington, DC: Health Insurance Association of America and the American Council of Life Insurance), p. 1.

(38) 10. D. Lindorff, "Fair Weather Bright Market Surge," *Forbes,* March 17, 1980, p. 166.

(39) 11. Doyle quoted by S. Trausch in "Drugs Move to the Workplace," *Los Angeles Times,* September 10, 1980.

(40) 12. Mark Lipman, *Stealing: How America's Employees Are Stealing Their Companies Blind,* (New York: Harper's Magazine Press, 1975), pp. 152–54, 160.

(41) 13. The benefit and cost of the General Motors Substance Abuse Programs (13-plant survey) was the subject of "A Review of Available Data," Report to the GM Health Services Section, July 31, 1979, prepared by A. Foote and J. C. Erfort, Research Consultants, Substance Abuse Recovery Program.

14. Lee Croft—see note 8 above.

(44) 15. Alvin M. Cruze, et al., *Economic Costs to Society of Alcohol and Drug Abuse and Mental Illness,* Final Report no. RTI 1925/00–14F (Research Triangle Park, NC: Research Triangle Institute, October 1981).

16. For Dr. Mayer's testimony, see note 4 above.

(45) 17. "Marijuana Smoking in Medical Schools," *Journal of the American Medical Association,* vol. 216, no. 11 (June 14, 1971), p. 1708.

(46) 18. H. Eisenberg, "Why Some of Your Colleagues Are Going to Pot," *Medical Economics,* January 17, 1972.

(46) 19. John Brecher, "Drugs on the Job," *Newsweek,* August 22, 1983, pp. 55–60.

(46) 20. Information on nuclear power plants from the *Philadelphia Sunday Bulletin,* July 27, 1980.

CHAPTER 4: CRISIS IN THE ARMED FORCES

(49) 1. Congressman English's report in "Drug Abuse in the Military—1981," Hearings Before the Select Committee on Narcotics Abuse and Control, U.S. House of Representatives, 97th cong., 1st sess., September 17, 1981. SCNAC-97-1-5, p. 3.

(50) 2. Congressman English, "Drug Abuse in the Military," Hearings Before the Select Committee on Narcotics Abuse and Control, U.S. House of Representatives, 95th cong., 2nd sess., April 27, May 24, June 2, 6, and 16, and July 27, 1978. SCNAC-95-2-7, pp. 8–10.

3. For Congressman Addabbo's statement, see note 1 above, p. 5.

(51) 4. General Fitt's statement and information on the decriminalization of marijuana in "Drug Abuse in the Armed Forces of the United States, A Report of the Select Committee on Narcotics Abuse and Control," U.S. House of Representatives, 95th cong., 2nd sess., 1978. SCNAC-95-2-14, pp. 8–9.

(51) 5. Dr. John Johns quoted in "Drug and Alcohol Abuse in the Armed Services," Joint Hearings before the Subcommittee on Manpower and Personnel and the

Subcommittee on Preparedness of the Committee on Armed Services, U.S. Senate, 97th cong., 1st sess., May 18, 1982. 96-5620, p. 15.

(51) 6. Dr. Johns' statement on honorable discharge in "Drug Abuse in the Armed Forces of the United States: Oversight Update," 96th cong., November 7, 1979. SCNAC-96-1-18, p. 39.

(52, 7. Questionnaire administered at thirteen U.S. military installations in Germany
53, (Illesheim, Bamberg, Nuremburg, Eschborn, Babhousen, Aschaffenburg, Wuerz-
58) burg, Schweinfurt, Bad Kreuznach, Mainz, Budingen, Hanau, and McNair), November 14-17, 1978.

(53) 8. Blanchard's statements after the Stuttgart hearings in "Drug Abuse in the Armed Forces in the Federal Republic of Germany and West Berlin," Hearings Before the Select Committee on Narcotics Abuse and Control, House of Representatives, 95th cong., November 20 and 22, 1978. SCNAC-95-2-26. p. 235.

(54- 9. Agreement on eight major observations in "Drug Abuse Among U.S. Armed
58) Forces in the Federal Republic of Germany and West Berlin," Report of the Select Committee on Narcotics Abuse and Control, U.S. House of Representatives, 95th cong., 2nd sess., 1979. SCNAC-95-2-2-27, p. 22.

(60) 10. Marvin R. Burt and Mark M. Biegel, with the assistance of Y. Carnes and C. Farley, "Highlights from the Worldwide Survey of Nonmedical Drug Use and Alcohol Use Among Military Personnel." Published under Department of Defense contract no. MDA903-79-C-0667 (Bethesda, MD: November 14, 1980). Text references from these pages in the report (the following order): 6,3,7,20,18.

(62) 11. Dr. Johns' statement comparing the two surveys in "Drug Abuse in the Armed Forces of the United States: Oversight Update," A Report of the Select Committee on Narcotics Abuse and Control, U.S. House of Representatives. 96th cong., 2nd sess. 1980. (SCNAC-96-2-9, p. 29.

The Select Committee's conclusions in the Oversight Update—see note 11 above, p. 1.

(63) 12. "Task Force on Drugs in the Military. Results: Personal Drug Use Survey Study Mission to Italy and the Federal Republic of Germany, June 26–July 7, 1981." Report submitted to the Select Committee on Narcotics Abuse and Control, U.S. House of Representatives, September 10, 1981. Text references are from these pages in the report (in the following order): 9, 10, 15, 17, 29, 30, 60, 45–47.

(65) 13. General Louisell quoted by Milan Korsok in "DOD Directive—Deter and Detect," The U.S. Journal of Drug Abuse and Alcohol Dependence, September 1980, p. 8.

(65) 14. Results of crash on Nimitz in "A Report to the Committee on Appropriations, U.S. House of Representatives on Drug and Alcohol Abuse by Military Personnel," Surveys and investigation staff, February 1982, p. 14.

CHAPTER 5: CRISIS IN SCHOOLS AND COLLEGES

(67) 1. L. D. Johnston, J. G. Bachman, and P. M. O'Malley, Student Drug Use in America, 1975–81; National Institute on Drug Abuse, DHHS pub. no. (ADM) 82-1221 (Washington, DC: Supt. of Docs., U.S. Govt. Printing Off., 1981), 433 pp.

(67) 2. Dr. Pollin's statement in PRIDE Newsletter, June 1983, p. 2.

(68)   3. Dr. Carlton Turner, testimony before the House of Representatives, Select Committee on Narcotics Abuse and Control, U.S. House of Representatives, November 19, 1981, p. 4.

(68)   4. "Survey of Drug Use Among Adolescents: General Report," Maryland Department of Health and Mental Hygiene, March 23, 1979, 124 pp.

(68, 69)   5. For national household surveys see Chapter 2, note 1. Also see P. M. Fishburne, H. I. Abelson, and I. Cisin, *National Survey on Drug Abuse: Main Findings: 1979*, National Institute on Drug Abuse, DHHS pub. no. (ADM) 80–976, (Washington, DC: Supt. of Docs., U.S. Govt. Printing Off., 1980), pp. 32, 35, 36, 45, 49, 53.

(70)   6. The "new teenage cocaine vogue" is reported by M. S. Gold in *800-Cocaine* (New York: Bantam Books, 1984).

(70)   7. For material on the federal government's reporting network, see note 3 above, page 5.

(70)   7a. Statistics showing that "no section of our nation is immune" from Adele V. Harrell and Ira H. Cisin, *Drug Use in Rural America,* DHHS pub. no (ADM) 81-1050 (Washington, DC: U.S. Gov. Print. Off., 1981), p. iii.

(72)   8. *Weekly Reader Survey:* See chapter 2, note 3.

(72)   9. Statistics on Maine survey in "An Evaluation of the Decriminalization of Marijuana in Maine—1978," State of Maine Dept. of Human Services, Office of Alcoholism and Drug Abuse Prevention, Augusta, January 5, 1979, p. 2.

(74) 10. "Drug Use Among College Students in New York State," a survey conducted by New York State Division of Substance Abuse Services, Albany, NY, March 1981.

(75) 11. A. Weil and W. Rosen, *Chocolate to Morphine,* (Boston: Houghton Mifflin, 1983), p. 228.

(76) 12. "Drugs in Our Schools," a report by the Select Committee on Crime, 93rd cong., 1st sess., House of Representatives, June 29, 1973. No. 93-357.

      13. For 1972 and 1982 national surveys, see chapter 2, note 1.

(79) 14. "Drug Use and Abuse in the Memphis-Shelby County School System," Hearings before the Select Committee on Narcotics Abuse and Control, U.S. House of Representatives, January 17–18, 1980. 184 pp.

(82) 15. *McGrassey's Reader,* Million Dollar Enterprises, California.

(83) 15a. *The Whole Drug Manufacturers' Catalogue* (Manhattan Beach, CA: Prophet Press, 1977).

(85) 16. "A Nation at Risk," report to the nation and the secretary of education, U.S. Dept. of Education, by the National Commission on Excellence in Education, April 1983, 65 pp. Including a two-page list of seventeen public events, commission meetings, hearings, panel discussions, and symposiums that the commission members attended over the course of eighteen months (October 9, 1981 through April 26, 1983). Also, over five pages listing commissioned papers, their authors and subjects, plus twelve pages listing the names of speakers at hearing testimonies on education.

(86) 17. Joseph H. Spitzner, "Drug Use in Ohio: The Incidence and Prevalence of Drug Use Among the Secondary School Population," A Projection to the State Population from Research Done in Five Ohio School Systems, during 1982, by TEAM

associates, Office of Education and Training, Ohio Dept. of Mental Health, Westerville, Ohio.

(87) 18. J. Goodlad, *A Place Called School: Prospects for the Future,* (New York: McGraw-Hill, 1984), pp. 310–11.

(87) 19. L. D. Johnston, J. G. Bachman, and P. M. O'Malley, *Student Drug Use, Attitudes and Beliefs: National Trends 1975–1982,* National Inst. on Drug Abuse (Washington, DC, U.S. Gov. Print. Off., 1982).

(88, 20. Health hazard articles: Peggy Mann, "The Case Against Marijuana," *Washington*
89) *Post,* "Outlook" section, July 30, 1978. Peggy Mann, "The Case Against Marijuana: New Medical Findings," *Family Circle,* February 20, 1979.

Susan Bromwell, "How I Got My Daughter to Stop Smoking Pot," *Good Housekeeping,* March 1979.

Peggy Mann, "Marijuana and Driving: The Sobering Truth," *Reader's Digest,* May 1979.

Merrill Rogers Skrocki, "Marijuana: The Disturbing New Facts," *McCalls,* June 1979.

Peggy Mann, "Do You Know Where Your Children Are and What They're Doing?" Special Report on children and drugs, *Ladies' Home Journal,* October 1979.

Peggy Mann, "Marijuana Alert: Brain and Sex Damage," Walter X. Lehmann, "Enemy of Youth," *Reader's Digest,* December 1979.

David Zimmerman, "Marijuana: Separating Facts from Myths," *Woman's Day,* April 22, 1980.

Peggy Mann, "Marijuana: The Myth of Harmlessness Goes Up in Smoke," *Saturday Evening Post,* August/September 1980.

Peggy Mann, "Marijuana Alert II: More of the Grim Story," *Reader's Digest,* November 1980.

Jason Baron and Peggy Mann, "Kids and Drugs," *Family Circle,* April 7, 1981.

Peggy Mann, "Marijuana: The Myth of Harmlessness," six-part series, King Features Syndicate, May 1981.

Peggy Mann, "Marijuana Alert III: The Devastation of Personality," *Reader's Digest,* December 1981.

Peggy Mann, "Death on the 'High'-Ways: Driving on Drink and Pot," *Saturday Evening Post,* September and October 1981. Reprinted in *Families,* January 1982.

CHAPTER 6: WHAT *Is* Marijuana?

(93) 1. The information on varieties of cannabis throughout the world is from Carlton E. Turner, *The Marijuana Controversy: Definition Research Perspective and Therapeutic Claims,* (The American Council for Drug Education, 1981), pp. 5–8.

(93) 2. *The Single Convention on Narcotic Drugs,* U.N. Publications, E. 77, XI. 3. Legal Treaty Division, 1961.

(94) 3. Chemicals produced when cannabis is smoked: Carlton E. Turner, "Chemistry and Metabolism of Marijuana," in *Marijuana Research Findings,* 1980, R. C.

Peterson, ed., National Institute on Drug Abuse, monograph 31, DHHS publ. no. (ADM) 80-100, (Washington, DC: U.S. Govt. Printing Off., 1980), p. 87.

(95) 4. The known metabolites of delta-9-THC—see note 1 above, p. 11.

(96) 5. The cancer-inducing chemicals in cannabis are discussed by D. Hoffman, K. D. Brunnemann, G. B. Gori, and E. L. Wynder, "On the Carcinogenicity of Marijuana Smoke," in *Recent Advances in Phytochemistry*, vol. 9, V. C. Runeckles, ed., (New York: Plenum, 1975), pp. 63–81.

6. Concerning eleven different THCs—see note 1 above, pp. 11 and 20.

(96) 7. Concerning one percent THC can induce a "high," and determination of THC potency—see note 1 above, p. 8 and footnote.

(97) 8. Dr. Turner's discussion of chemical complexity of cannabis in *Health Consequences of Marijuana Use*, Hearings Before the Subcommittee on Criminal Justice, Committee on the Judiciary, U.S. Senate, 96th cong., 2nd sess., January 16–17, 1980. Serial no. 96-54, pp. 103–104.

(98) 9. Charles A. Dackis, A. L. C. Pottash, William Annito, and Mark S. Gold: "The Resistance of Urinary Marijuana Levels After Supervised Abstinence," *American Journal of Psychiatry*, vol. 139, no. 9 (September 1982), pp. 1196–98.

(99) 10. Concerning average THC potency of .5 percent in early 1970s—see note 8 above, p. 106.

(100) 11. Concerning the impossibility of standardizing marijuana—see note 1 above, p. 12.

(102) 12. Concerning short-term research protocol—see note 1 above, p. 13.

(103) 13. Dr. Turner's statement, "I have never read a scientific publication which exonerates cannabis from [causing] some health effects"—see note 8 above, p. 107.

CHAPTER 7: EFFECTS ON THE LUNGS AND THE HEART

(104) 1. For the comparison between tobacco and marijuana cigarettes, see D. Hoffman, et al.—chapter 6, note 5.

(104) 2. R. C. Petersen, "Importance of Inhalation Patterns in Determining Effects of Marijuana Use," *The Lancet*, March 30, 1979, pp. 727–28.

(107) 3. Forest S. Tennant, Jr., "Clinical Toxicology of Marijuana Use," *Cannabis and Health Hazards*, K. O. Fehr and H. Kalant, eds. (Toronto: Addiction Research Foundation, 1983), pp. 69–85.

(108) 4. *Smoking and Health: A Report of the Surgeon General*, U.S. Dept. of Health, Education and Welfare, stock no. 017–000–00218–0. (Washington, DC: U.S. Govt. Printing Off., 1979).

(109) 5. C. Leuchtenberger, R. Leuchtenberger, and A. Schneider, "Effects of Marijuana and Tobacco Smoke on Human Lung Physiology," *Nature*, vol. 241 (1975), pp. 137–39.

(109) 6. C. Leuchtenberger and R. Leuchtenberger, "Cytological and Cytochemical Studies of the Effects of Fresh Marijuana Smoke on Growth and DNA Metabolism of Animal and Human Lung Cultures," *The Pharmacology of Marijuana*, M. C. Braude and S. Szara, eds. (New York: Raven Press, 1976), pp. 595–612.

REFERENCES

(*109*) 7. C. Leuchtenberger, R. Leuchtenberger, J. Zbinden, and E. Schleh, "Cytological and Cytochemical Effects of Whole Smoke and of the Gas Vapor Phase from Marijuana Cigarettes on Growth and DNA Metabolism of Cultured Mammalian Cells," *Marijuana, Chemistry, Biochemistry, and Cellular Effects,* G. G. Nahas, and W. D. M. Paton, eds. (New York: Springer-Verlag, 1976), pp. 243–56.

(*110*) 8. H. Rosenkrantz, "The Immune Response and Marijuana." See note 7, pp. 441–56.

(*111*) 9. H. Rosenkrantz, R. W. Fleischman, and J. R. Baker, "Pulmonary Pathology in Rats Exposed to Marijuana Smoke for One Year," *Toxicology Applied Pharmacology,* vol. 45, no. 1 (1978), p. 288.

(*112*) 10. The effects of tobacco and pot smoke are compared in H. Rosenkrantz and R. W. Fleischman, "Effects of Cannabis on Lungs," in *Marijuana: Biological Effects,* G. G. Nahas and W. D. M. Paton, eds. (New York: Pergamon Press, N.Y. 1979), pp. 279–99.

(*112*) 11. For Rosenkrantz study on pot's effects on immune system, see note 7, pp. 441–56.

(*113*) 12. G. L. Huber, V. E. Pockay, W. Pereira, J. W. Shea, W. C. Hinds, M. W. First, and G. C. Sornberger, "Marijuana, Tetrahydrocannabinol and Pulmonary Antibacterial Defenses," *Chest,* vol. 77 (1980), pp. 403–10.

(*113*) 13. P. Bernfeld, F. Homburger, E. Soto, and K. J. Pai, "Cigarette Smoke Inhalation Studies in Inbred Syrian Golden Hamsters," *Journal of the National Cancer Institute,* vol. 63 (September 1979), pp. 675–89.

(*113*) 14. P. E. Roy, F. Magnan-Lapointe, N. D. Huy, and M. Boutet, "Chronic Inhalation of Marijuana and Tobacco in Dogs' Pulmonary Pathology," *Research Communication Chemical Pathology and Pharmacology,* vol. 14 (1976), pp. 305–417.

(*114*) 15. D. P. Tashkin, B. J. Shapiro, Y. E. Lee, and C. E. Harper, "Subacute Effects of Heavy Marijuana Smoking on Pulmonary Functions in Healthy Men," *New England Journal of Medicine,* vol. 294 (1976), pp. 125–29.

(*115*) 16. D. P. Tashkin, B. M. Calvarese, M. S. Simmons, and B. J. Shapiro, "Respiratory Status of Seventy-four Habitual Marijuana Smokers," *Chest,* vol. 78 (1980), pp. 699–706.

(*116*) 17. For Tennant questionnaire survey of 492 hash-smoking soldiers, see note 3, p. 70.

(*117*) 18. Tennant's "hash records" on over a thousand soldiers are discussed in F. S. Tennant, M. Preble, T. J. Prendergast, and P. Ventry, "Medical Manifestations Associated with Hashish," *Journal of the American Medical Association,* vol. 216 (1971), pp. 1965–69.

(*118,* 19. For Tennant's study and lung biopsies of hash-smoking soldiers, see F. S. Tennant,
119)   R. L. Guerry, and R. L. Henderson, "Histopathologic and Clinical Abnormalities of the Respiratory System in Chronic Hashish Smokers," *Substance and Alcohol Actions/Misuse,* vol. 1 (1980), pp. 93–100.

(*122*) 20. *Report on Marijuana of the Indian Hemp Commission, 1893–1894* (Silver Spring, MD: Thomas Jefferson Press, 1969)

(*122*) 21. G.S. Chopra, "Studies on Psycho-clinical Aspects of Long-term Marijuana Use in 124 Cases," *International Journal of Addiction,* vol. 8 (1973), pp. 1015–26.

481

(*122*) 22. V. Rubin and L. Comitas, *Ganja in Jamaica: A Medical Anthropological Study of Chronic Marijuana Use* (The Hague: Mouton, 1975), pp. 88–102.

(*122*) 23. G. G. Nahas, "Ganja in Jamaica, a Critique," *Bulletin of Narcotics,* vol. 86 (1984).

(*123*) 24. J. A. S. Hall, testimony in *Marijuana/Hashish Epidemic Senate Hearings,* see chapter 1, note 9, pp. 147–54.

(*123*) 25. The Institute of Medicine's recommendations for essential research are included in *Marijuana and Health,* Report of a Study by a Committee of the Institute of Medicine, Division of Health Sciences Policy (Washington, DC: National Academy Press, 1982), p. 66.

(*124*) 26. R. I. Macdonald, *Drugs, Drinking and Adolescence* (Chicago: Yearbook Medical Publishers, 1983).

(*127*) 27. A. Sulkowski, L. Vachon, and E. S. Rich, Jr., "Propranolol Effects on Acute Marijuana Intoxication in Man," *Psychopharmacology,* vol. 52 (1977), pp. 47–53.

(*126*) 28. W. S. Aronow and J. Cassidy, "Effect of Marijuana and Placebo Marijuana on Angina Pectoris," *New England Journal of Medicine,* vol. 291 (July 11, 1971), pp. 66–67.

(*127*) 29. G. L. Huber and V. K. Mahajan, "An Overview, Marijuana's Effects on the Cardiopulmonary System" (part 2 of a two-part article), *Primary Cardiology,* July/August 1978.

(*129*) 30. W. S. Aronow and J. Cassidy, "Effect of Smoking Marijuana and of a High Potency Nicotine Cigarette on Angina Pectoris," *Clinical Pharmacology and Therapeutics,* vol. 17 (May 1975), pp. 549–55.

CHAPTER 8: EFFECTS ON SEX AND REPRODUCTION: FEMALE

(*131*) 1. Joan E. Bauman reported the findings of her study with Dr. Kolodny in "Marijuana and the Female Reproduction System," in *Health Consequences of Marijuana Use,* Senate Hearings, see chapter 6, note 8, pp. 83–88.

(*132*) 2. Josel Szepsenwol, "Long Term Effects of THC in Mice," in *Marijuana: Biological Effects,* G. G. Nahas and W. D. M. Paton, eds. (New York: Pergamon Press, 1979), pp. 359–69.

(*132*) 3. Carlton Turner—see *Health Consequences of Marijuana Use,* chapter 6, note 8, p. 103.

4. Animal studies of radioactively tagged THC found in suckling babies include the following:

(*132*) L. A. Borgen and W. M. Davis, "Effects of Chronic Delta-9-THC on Pregnancy in the Rat," *Pharmacologist,* vol. 12 (1970), p. 259.

(*132*) H. A. Klausner and J. V. Dingell, "Metabolism and Excretion of Delta-9-THC in the Rat," *Life Science,* vol. 10 (1971), pp. 49–59.

(*132*) A. Jukabovic, T. Hattori and P. L. McGeer, "Radioactivity in Suckled Rats after Giving 14C-THC to the Mother," *European Journal of Pharmacology,* vol. 22 (1973), pp. 221–23.

(*133*) 5. Dr. Smith reported on THC's disruption of the menstrual cycle in C. S. Smith, and R. H. Asch, "Acute Short-Term and Chronic Drug Effects on Female Reproductive Function," in NIDA research monograph, "Marijuana Effects on the Endocrine and Reproductive System" (Washington DC: U.S. Gov. Print. Ofc., 1983).

(134) 6. C. S. Smith, R. G. Almirez, and J. Berenberg, "Tolerance Develops to the Disruptive Effects of Delta-9-THC on Primate Menstrual Cycle," *Science,* vol. 219 (March 25, 1983), pp. 1453–55.

(135) 7. E. N. Sassenrath, E. N. Chapman, and G. P. Goo, "Reproduction in Rhesus Monkeys Chronically Exposed to Delta-9-THC," *Advances in the Biosciences,* vol. 22–23 (1979), pp. 501–22.

(135)   Also, E. N. Sassenrath, C. A. Banovitz, and L. F. Chapman, "Tolerance and Reproductive Deficit in Primates Chronically Drugged with Delta-9-THC," *The Pharmacologist,* vol. 21, no. 3 (1979).

(140) 8. M. S. Golub, E. N. Sassenrath, L. F. Chapman, "An Analysis of Altered Attention in Monkeys Exposed to Delta-9-THC During Development," *Neurobehavioral Toxicology and Teratology,* vol. 4 (1982), pp. 469–72.

(140) 9. C. Barnes and P. A. Fried, "Tolerance to Delta-9-THC in Adult Rats with Differential Delta-9-THC Exposure when Immature or During Early Adulthood," *Psychopharmacologia* (Berlin), vol. 34 (1974), pp. 181–90.

(142) 10. P. A. Fried, "Marijuana Use by Pregnant Women and Effects on Offspring: An Update," *Neurobehavioral Toxicology and Teratology,* vol. 4 (1982), pp. 451–54.

(142) 11. S. Greenland, K. J. Staisch, N. Brown, and S. Gross, "The Effects of Marijuana Use During Pregnancy, A Preliminary Epidemiologic Study," *American Journal of Obstetrics and Gynecology,* vol. 143 (June 15, 1982), pp. 408–13.

(144) 12. The Boston City Hospital study was reported in R. Hingson, J. Alpert, N. Day, E. Dooling, H. Kayne, S. Morelock, E. Oppenheimer, and B. Zuckerman, "Effects of Maternal Drinking and Marijuana Use on Fetal Growth and Development," *Pediatrics,* vol. 70 (October 1982), pp. 539–46.

(147) 13. The hamster fetus–THC study was reported in J. Idanpaan-Heikkila, G. E. Fritchie, L. F. Englert, B. T. Ho, and D. M. McIssac, "Placental Transfer of Tritiated-1-Delta-9-THC," *New England Journal of Medicine,* vol. 281 (1969), p. 330.

(148) 14. The many animal studies showing that THC easily passes through the placenta include these two: H. B. Pace, W. M. Davis and L. A. Borgen, "Teratogenesis and Marijuana," *Annals of the New York Academy of Science,* vol. 191 (1971), pp. 123–31.

(148)   R. D. Harbison and P. B. Mantilla-Plata, "Prenatal Toxicity, Maternal Distribution and Placental Transfer of THC," *Pharmacology and Experimental Therapeutics,* vol. 180 (1972), pp. 446–53.

(148) 15. N. H. Huang, M. Younes, N. F. Besch, and P. K. Besch, "*In vitro* Studies of Delta-9-THC Metabolism in Human Term Placental Microsomes," *Federation Proceedings,* vol. 40, no. 252 (1981), p. 279.

(150) 16. O. Shinohara, R. T. Henrich, and A. Morishima, "The Effects of Chronic Administration of Delta-9-THC on Early Embryogenesis of the Mouse," *Biology of Reproduction,* vol. 29 (1983), pp. 663–70.

(151) 17. H. Rosenkrantz, "Effects of Cannabis on Fetal Development of Rodents," in

Marijuana: Biological Effects," G. G. Nahas and W. D. M. Paton, eds. (New York: Pergamon Press, 1979), pp. 479–99.

Also, R. W. Fleischman, J. R. Baker, and H. Rosenkrantz, "Effects of Marijuana on Reproduction and Gonads," NIDA Report no. MRI-DA 07–79–26, June 8, 1979, pp. 1–66.

(*153*) 18. The "disappearing litters" were in Rosenkrantz's "Effects of Cannabis on Fetal Development of Rodents"—see note 17.

(*153*) 19. V. Lynch, "Marijuana-Induced Birth Defects," presentation to the Federation of American Societies for Experimental Biology, Columbus, Ohio, October 10, 1977, p. 161-a.

(*154*) 20. P. A. Fried, and A. T. Charlebois, "Cannabis Administered During Pregnancy: First- and Second-Generation Effects in Rats," *Physiological Psychology,* vol. 7, no. 3 (1979), pp. 307–10.

(*154*) 21. P. A. Fried and A. T. Charlebois, "Effects upon Rat Offspring Following Cannabis Inhalation Before and/or After Mating," *Canadian Journal of Psychology,* vol. 33, no. 3 (1979).

(*155*) 22. Institute of Medicine, *Marijuana and Health* (Washington, DC: National Academy Press, 1982).

(*155*) 23. The quote from the pot-smoker about her gynecologist was reported by Robin Traywick in "They're Professionals, Over 30, Pot Smokers," *Richmond Times-Dispatch,* July 20, 1980.

(*156*) 24. John B. MacDonald, "Cannabis, Health and the Law" (Toronto, Canada: Addiction Research Foundation, 1981), pp. 7–8.

CHAPTER 9: EFFECTS ON SEX AND REPRODUCTION: MALE

(*157*) 1. R. C. Kolodny, W. H. Masters, A. B. Kolodny, and G. Toro, "Depression of Plasma Testosterone Levels after Chronic Intensive Marijuana Use," *New England Journal of Medicine,* vol. 290, pp. 872–74.

(*158*) 2. G. S. Chopra, "Man and Marijuana," *International Journal of Addiction,* vol. 4 (1969), p. 215.

(*158*) 3. W. C. Hembree, P. Zeidenberg, G. G. Nahas, "Marijuana's Effects on Human Gonadal Functions," in *Marijuana: Chemistry, Biochemistry and Cellular Effects*—see chapter 7, note 7, pp. 521–23.

(*159*) 4. For Hembree's comments on the reversibility factor see *Health Consequences of Marijuana Use,* chapter 6, note 8, p. 99.

(*159*) 5. L. E. Perez, C. G. Smith, and R. H. Asch, "Delta-9-Tetrahydrocannabinol Inhibits Fructose Utilization and Motility in Human, Rhesus Monkey, and Rabbit Sperm in Vitro," *Fertility and Sterility,* vol. 35 (1981), p. 703.

(*159*) 6. Asch's studies on THC and the neurotransmitters were reported in R. Steger, A. Y. Silverman, R. M. Siler-Khodr, and R. H. Asch, "The Effects of Delta-9-THC on the Positive and Negative Feedback Control of Luteinizing Hormone Release," *Life Sciences,* vol. 27, p. 1911.

See also R. H. Asch and C. G. Smith, "Effects of Marijuana on Reproduction," *Contemporary OB-GYN,* vol. 22 (October 1983), pp. 217–36.

R. H. Asch, C. G. Smith, T. M. Siler-Khodr and C. J. Paverstein, "Effects of Delta-9-Tetrahydrocannabinol During the Follicular Phase of the Rhesus Monkey," *Journal of Clinical Endocrinology and Metabolism,* vol. 52 (1981), p. 50.

(*160*) 7. For an example of medical-journal case-history reports on pubertal arrest in heavy pot-smoking teenage boys, see K. C. Copeland, L. E. Underwood, and J. J. Van Wyk, "Marijuana Smoking and Pubertal Arrest," *The Journal of Pediatrics,* June 1980, pp. 1079–80.

(*160*) 8. C. G. Smith, N. F. Besch, and R. H. Asch, "Effects of Marijuana on the Reproductive System," *Advances in Sex Hormone Research,* J. A. Thomas and R. Singhal, eds., *Urban and Schwarzenberg* (Baltimore-Munich), vol. 4 (1980), pp. 273–94.

(*161*) 9. S. Dalterio and A. Bartke, "Fetal Testosterone in Mice: Effect of Gestational Age and Cannabinoid Exposure," *Journal of Endocrinology Ltd.* (Great Britain), vol. 91 (1981), pp. 509–14.

(*161*) 10. "Delta-9-THC and Cannabinol Effects on the Testis," S. Dalterio, A. Bartke, C. Roberson, D. Watson, and S. Burstein, "Direct and Pituitary Mediated Effects of THC"; *Pharmacology, Biochemistry and Behavior,* vol. 8 (1978), pp. 673–78.

(*161*) 11. J. L. Harclerode, H. Sawyer, V. Berger, R. Mooney, and R. Smith, "Sex Hormone Levels in Rats Injected with Delta-9-THC and Phencyclidine Hydrochloride," Cannabinoid '82 meetings in Louisville, Kentucky, August 1982.

(*162*) 12. A. M. Zimmerman, W. R. Bruce, and S. Zimmerman, "Effects of Cannabinoids on Sperm Morphology," *Pharmacologist,* vol. 18 (1979), p. 143.

(*162*) 13. Dalterio's study of mice exposed to THC and CBN only through their mother's exposure during pregnancy and nursing was reported in S. Dalterio, "Perinatal or Adult Exposure to Cannabinoids Alters Male Reproductive Functions in Mice," *Pharmacology, Biochemistry and Behavior,* vol. 12 (1980), pp. 143–53.

(*162*) 14. S. Dalterio, F. Badr, A. Bartke, and D. Mayfield, "Cannabinoids in Male Mice: Effects on Fertility and Spermatogenesis," *Science,* vol. 216 (April 16, 1982), pp. 315–16.

(*165*) 15. Dalterio's testimony is in *Health Consequences of Marijuana Use,* see chapter 6, note 8, pp. 95–96.

(*167*) 16. C. N. Stefanis and M. R. Issidorides, "Cellular Effects of Chronic Cannabis Use in Man" in *Marijuana: Chemistry, Biochemistry and Cellular Effects*—see chapter 7, note 7, pp. 533–50.

CHAPTER 10: EFFECTS ON THE BRAIN

(*171*) 1. For Dr. Robert G. Heath's early work on marijuana and brain sites in man, see R. G. Heath, "Marijuana: Effects on Deep and Surface Electroencephalograms of Man," *The Archives of General Psychiatry,* vol. 26 (1972), pp. 577–84.

(*172*) 2. R. G. Heath, "Marijuana: Effects on Deep and Surface Electroencephalograms of Rhesus Monkeys," *Neuropharmacology,* vol. 12 (1973), pp. 1–14.

(*173*) 3. Among the reports of Heath's landmark brain-cell studies on rhesus monkeys exposed to pot smoke are the following: R. G. Heath, A. T. Fitzjarrell, C. J. Fontana, and R. E. Garey, "Cannabis Sativa: Effects on Brain Function and Ultra-Structure in Rhesus Monkeys," *Biological Psychiatry,* vol. 15, no. 5 (1980), pp. 657–90.

(174)   R. G. Heath, "Marijuana and Delta-9-THC: Acute and Chronic Effects on Brain Function in Monkeys," in *Pharmacology of Marijuana*, M. C. Braude and S. Szara, eds. (New York: Raven Press, 1976), pp. 345–56.

(174)   R. G. Heath, A. T. Fitzjarrell, R. E. Garey, and W. A. Myers, "Chronic Marijuana Smoking: Its Effects on Function and Structure of the Primate Brain," in *Marijuana: Biological Effects*—see chapter 7, note 10, pp. 713–30.

(181) 4. T. Hattori, A. Jakubovic, and P. L. McGeer, "Reduction in Number of Nuclear Membrane-Attached Ribosomes in Infant Rat Brain Following Delta-9-THC Administration," *Experimental Neurology*, vol. 36, no. 1 (July 1972), pp. 207–11.

(182) 5. P. L. McGeer and A. Jakubovic, "Ultrastructural and Biochemical Changes in CNS Induced by Marijuana," in *Marijuana: Biological Effects*—see Chapter 7, note 10, pp. 519–29.

(182) 6. THC's acetylcholine-suppressant effects were noted by E. F. Domino, A. C. Donelson, and T. Tuttle in "Effects of Delta-9-THC on Regional Brain Acetylcholine," in *Cholinergic Mechanisms and Psychopharmacology*, D. J. Jenden, ed. (New York: Plenum Press, 1978), pp. 673–78.

See also E. F. Domino, "Cannabinoids and the Cholinergic System," *Journal of Clinical Pharmacology*, vol 21 (suppl.) (1981), p. 2495ff.

(183) 7. Heath's comments on reason for mild withdrawal symptoms, in *Health Consequences of Marijuana Use*—see chapter 6, note 8, pp. 255–56.

(184) 8. A. M. G. Campbell, M. Evans, J. L. G. Thompson, and M. J. Williams, "Cerebral Atrophy in Young Cannabis Smokers," *Lancet*, 1971, pp. 1219–24.

(185) 9. J. P. McGahan, A. B. Dublin, and E. Sassenrath, "Computed Tomography of the Brains of Rhesus Monkeys after Long-Term Delta-9-THC Treatment," paper presented at the 67th Scientific Assembly and Annual Meeting of the Radiological Society of North America, Chicago, 1981.

(186) 10. Gilkeson's EEG studies on teenage pot smokers described in *Health Consequences of Marijuana Use*—see chapter 6, note 8, pp. 258–73.

(190) 11. Concerning Gilkeson's statements on marijuana's inhibition of essential calcium uptake and the destruction of the synaptosomal membrane which supports Heath's findings of increased synaptic clefts, see R. A. Harris and J. A. Stokes, "Cannabinoids Inhibit Calcium Uptake by Brain Synaptosomes," *Neuroscience*, vol. 2, no. 4 (April 1982), pp. 443–47.

CHAPTER 11: THE IMMUNE SYSTEM AND OTHER CELLULAR EFFECTS

(193) 1. Issidorides and Stefanis, "Cellular Effects of Cannabis Use in Man," in *Marijuana: Chemistry, Biochemistry and Cellular Effects*—see chapter 7, note 7, pp. 533–50.

M. R. Issidorides, "Observations in Chronic Hashish Users: Nuclear Aberrations in Blood and Sperm and Abnormal Acrosomes in Spermatozoa," in *Marijuana: Biological Effects*—see chapter 7, note 10, pp. 377–88.

(193) 2. M. Bessis, *Living Blood Cells and Their Ultrastructure* (Berlin: Springer-Verlag, 1973).

(194) 3. The finding on pot-smoking males with enlarged breasts was reported by J. Harmon and M. A. Aliapoulios in "Gynecomastia in Marijuana Users," *New England Journal of Medicine*, vol. 287 (1972), p. 936.

(194) 4. Summation of Issidorides' arginine hypothesis in: "Report of an Addiction Research Foundation/World Health Organization Scientific Meeting on Adverse Health and Behavioral Consequences of Cannabis Use," Toronto, Ontario, Canada, March 20–April 3, 1981.

(194) 5. Published paper on Issidorides' arginine hypothesis in: M. R. Issidorides, "Interaction of Cannabis with Arginine Metabolism: A New Hypothesis of Action," in *Adverse Health and Behavioral Consequences of Cannabis Use,* K. O. Fehr and H. Kalant, eds. (Toronto: Addiction Research Foundation, 1983).

(195) 6. M. Issidorides, "Cellular Effects of Cannabis Supporting Interference of the Drug with Arginine Utilization and/or Metabolism: A New Hypothesis on Mechanism of Action," *The Cannabinoids: Chemical, Pharmacologic and Therapeutic Aspects,* S. Agurell, W. L. Dewey, and R. E. Willette, eds. (New York: Academic Press, 1984), pp. 669–706.

(197) 7. G. G. Nahas, N. Suciu-Foca, J. R. Armand, and A. Morishima, "Inhibition of Cell-Mediated Immunity in Marijuana Smokers," *Science,* vol. 183 (1974), pp. 419–20.

G. G. Nahas, B. DeSoize, J. Hsu, and A. Miroshima, "Effects of Delta-9-THC on Nucleic Acid Synthesis and Proteins in Cultured Lymphocytes," in *Marijuana and Membranes: Quantitation, Metabolism, Cellular Responses, Reproduction and Brain.* G. G. Nahas and W. D. M. Paton, eds. (New York, Pergamon Press, 1979), pp. 299–312.

(200) 8. B. H. Petersen, J. Graham, L. Lemberger, and B. Dalton, "Studies of the Immune Response in Chronic Marijuana Smokers," *Pharmacologist,* vol. 16, pp. 259.

(200) 9. P. S. Morahan, P. C. Klykken, S. H. Smith, L. S. Harris, and A. E. Munson, "Effects of Cannabinoids on Host Resistance to Listeria Monocytogenes and Herpes Simplex Virus," *Infection and Immunity,* vol. 23, no. 3 (March 1979), pp. 670–74.

(200) 10. O. Baczumsky and A. Zimmerman, "Effects of Delta 9 Tetrahydrocannibol, Cannabinol and Cannabidiol on the Immune System in Mice," *Pharmacology,* vol. 26 (1983), pp. 1–19.

(202) 11. R. T. Henrich, T. Nogawa, and A. Morishima, "Segregational Errors of Chromosomes Induced by Delta-9-THC in Normal Human Lymphocytes," *Environment Mutagenesis,* vol. II, no. 2 (1980), pp. 139–47.

(202) 12. A. Morishima, M. Milstein, R. Henrich, and G. G. Nahas, "Effects of Marijuana Smoking, Cannabinoids and Olivetol on Replication of Human Lymphocytes, Formation of Micronuclei," in *Pharmacology of Marijuana,* vol 2, M. C. Braude and S. Szara, eds. (New York: Raven Press, 1976), pp. 711–22. (Note: Olivetol is part of the chemical structure of THC.)

A. Morishima, R. T. Heinrich, J. Jayaraman, and G. G. Nahas, "Hypoploid Metaphastes in Cultural Lymphocytes of Marijuana Smokers," in *Marijuana: Biological Effects*—see chapter 7, note 10, pp. 271–76.

(204) 13. M. A. Stenchever, T. J. Kunysz, and M. A. Allen, "Chromosome Breakage in Users of Marijuana," *American Journal of Obstetrics and Gynecology,* vol. 118 (1974), pp. 106–13.

(205) 14. For Stenchever's testimony at U.S. Senate Hearings, see chapter 2, note 9, pp. 84–92.

(206) 15. A. M. Zimmerman, W. R. Bruce, and S. Zimmerman, "Effects of Cannabinoids on Sperm Morphology," *Pharmacology,* vol. 18 (1979), pp. 143–48.

A. M. Zimmerman and A. Y. Raj, "Influence on Cannabinoids on Somatic Cells *in Vivo,*" *Pharmacology,* vol. 21, (1980), pp. 277–287.

A. M. Zimmerman, S. G. Zimmerman, and A. Yesoda Raj, "Effects of Cannabinoids on Spermatogenesis in Mice," in *Marijuana: Biological Effects*—see chapter 7, note 10, pp. 407–18.

(207) 16. Szepsenwol's first study on cannabinoid carcinogenicity was reported in J. Szepsenwol, J. Fletcher, G. E. Murison, and E. Casales, "Long-term Effects of Delta-9-THC in Mice," in *Marijuana: Biological Effects*—see chapter 7, note 10, pp. 359–70.

(209) 17. G. G. Nahas, A. Morishima, and B. DeSoize, "Effects of Cannabinoid on Macromolecular Synthesis and Replication of Cultural Lymphocytes," *Federation Proceedings,* vol. 36 (April 1977), pp. 714–52.

(209) 18. A. Jakubovic and P. L. McGeer, "Inhibition of Rat Brain Protein and Nucleic Acid Synthesis by Cannabinoids *in Vitro,*" *Canadian Journal of Biochemistry,* vol. 50 (1972), p. 654.

(210) 19. A. Jakubovic and P. L. McGeer, "Intracellular Contribution of Delta-8-THC in Rat Organs after i.v. Administration," *Research Communications Chemical Pathology and Pharmacology,* vol. 9 (1974), p. 197.

(210) A. Jakubovic and P. L. McGeer, "*In vitro* Inhibition of Protein and Nucleic Acid Synthesis in Rat Testicular Tissue by Cannabis," in *Marijuana: Biological Effects*—see chapter 7, note 10, pp. 223–64.

(210) A. Jakubovic and P. L. McGeer, "Biochemical Changes in Rat Testicular Cells *in vitro* Produced by Cannabinoids and Alcohol, Metabolism and Incorporation of Labeled Glucose, Amino Acids and Nucleic Acid Precursors." *Toxicology and Applied Pharmacology,* vol. 41, no. 3 (1977), pp. 473–86.

(210) 20. For Paton's statement to the U.S. Senate Committee see chapter 1, note 9, pp. 70–79.

CHAPTER 12: PSYCHOLOGICAL EFFECTS

(212) 1. R. E. Hart, *Bitter Grass: The Cruel Truth About Marijuana* (Shawnee Mission, Kansas: Psychoneurologia Press, 1979).

(214) 2. For CODAP references, published by NIDA, see chapter 1, note 3, 1981, series E, no. 25.

(217) 3. H. Kolansky and W. T. Moore, "Effects of Marijuana on Adolescents and Young Adults," *Journal of the American Medical Association,* vol. 216 (1971), pp. 486–92.

(217) 4. D. A. Milman, "The Psychological Effects of Cannabis in Adolescence," in *Marijuana and Youth,* National Institute on Drug Abuse, DHHS pub. no. (ADM) 82–1186, 1982, p. 31.

(217) 5. J. E. Meeks, "Some Clinical Comments on Chronic Marijuana Use in Adolescent Patients," in *Marijuana and Youth*—see note 4, p. 38.

(222) 6. S. Cohen, "Cannabis: Impact on Maturation," *Vista Hill Drug Abuse and Alcoholism Newsletter,* Vista Hill Foundation, San Diego, CA, vol. 9 (December 1980), pp. 1–4.

(222) 7. A. Sulkowski, "Marijuana High: A Model of Senile Dementia?" *Perspectives in Biology and Medicine,* vol. 23, no. 1, (Winter, 1980), pp. 209–14.

(224) 8. S. G. Williams and J. Baron, "Effects of Short-Term Intensive Hospital Therapy on Youthful Drug Abusers: I. Preliminary MMPI data," *Psychological Reports,* vol. 50 (1982), pp. 79–82.

(225) 9. Rosenthal and interference with the maturation process is in: *Health Consequences of Marijuana Use*—see chapter 6, note 8, pp. 143–44.

(226) 10. M. Newton, *Gone Way Down: Teenage Drug Use Is a Disease* (Tampa, FL: American Studies Press, 1981).

(227) 11. Dr. Gold's study on marijuanaholics has not yet been written up for publication since, directly after concluding the study, Dr. Gold created and became deeply involved in the 800-COCAINE hotline and its research.

(232) 12. D. Milman, "Psychological Effects of Cannabis in Adolescence"—see note 4.

(233) 13. J. Carranza, "Marijuana Induced Psychosis," in *Drug Abuse in the Modern World,* G. G. Nahas and H. C. Frick II, eds. (New York: Pergamon Press, 1981), pp. 57–61.

(234) 14. M. A. el Yousef, D. Janowsky, J. M. Davis, and J. Rosenblatt, "Induction of Severe Depression by Physostigmine in Marijuana Intoxicated Individuals," *British Journal of Addiction,* vol. 68 (1973), pp. 321–25.

(235) 15. For the National High School Senior Survey findings, see L. D. Johnston, J. G. Bachman, and P. M. O'Malley, *Highlights from Student Drug Use in America, 1975–1980,* National Institute on Drug Abuse, DHHS pub. no. (ADM) 81–1066 (Washington, DC: Supt. of Docs. U.S. Govt. Printing Ofc., 1980).

(235) 16. D. Kandel, "Stages in Adolescent Involvement in Drug Use," *Science,* vol. 190 (November 28, 1975), pp. 912–14.

Also in D. Kandel, "Developmental States in Adolescent Drug Involvement in Theories of Drug Abuse," D. Lettieri, N. Sayers, and H. Pearson, eds., NIDA Research Monograph 30, 1980.

Concerning D. Kandel's 1980–81 follow-up study, see K. Yamaguchi and D. Kandel, "Patterns of Drug Use from Adolescence to Young Adulthood: II Sequences of Progression," *American Journal of Public Health,* vol. 74 (July 1984).

(236) 17. R. R. Clayton and H. L. Voss, "Smoking and Health, Marijuana and Use of Other Illicit Drugs: Causal Relationships," presented to the National Advisory Council on Drug Abuse on January 20, 1982.

R. Clayton and H. L. Voss, "Marijuana and Cocaine: the Causal Nexus," presented to the National Association of Drug Abuse Problems on March 30, 1982.

For the National High School Senior Survey results, see note 15.

(238) 18. A. I. Malcolm, *The Pursuit of Intoxication: An Historical and Scientific Source Book on the Use of Psychoactive Drugs* (New York: Simon and Schuster, 1972).

A. I. Malcolm, "The Alienating Influence of Marihuana," Proceedings of the Eastern Psychiatric Research Association, 15th Annual Meeting, New York, November 7, 1970.

(238) 18. W. Pollin, "Health and Educational Effects of Marijuana on Youth," Subcommittee on Alcoholism and Drug Abuse of the Committee on Labor and Human Resources, U.S. Senate, October 21, 1981.

(239) 19. *Healthy People: The Surgeon General's Report on Health Promotion and Disease Prevention,* Dept. of Health, Education and Welfare, DHEW. (PHS) Pub. No. 79-55071, stock no. 017–001–00416–2. (Washington, DC: Supt. of Docs., U.S. Gov. Print. ofc, 1979), p. 43.

(243) 20. H. Hendin, A. Pollinger, R. Ulman, and A. C. Carr, "Adolescent Marijuana Abusers and Their Families," NIDA Research Monograph 40, September 1981.

(244) 21. E. Good, "Drug Use and Sexual Activity on a College Campus," *American Journal of Psychiatry,* vol. 128 (1972), pp. 1272–76.

(244) 22. S. L. Jessor and R. Jessor, "Transition from Virginity to Non-Virginity among Young: A Social-Psychological Study over Time," *Developmental Psychology,* vol. 11 (1975), pp. 475–84.

(247) 23. *Drug Abuse: A Guide for the Primary Care Physician* (Chicago, IL: American Medical Association, 1981).

CHAPTER 13: MARIJUANA AS MEDICINE?

(248) 1. For details on the FDA vote on THC capsules, see "Minutes for Meeting of the Division of Oncology and Radiopharmaceutical Drug Products, Food and Drug Administration," June 1980. (Minutes are available from FDA. Moertel's letter referred to in minutes.)

(248) 2. S. Frytak and C. G. Moertel, "Management of Nausea and Vomiting in the Cancer Patient," *Journal of the American Medical Association,* vol. 245 (1981), pp. 393–96.

(249) 3. "Many Cancer Patients Receiving THC as Anti-Emetic," *Journal of American Medical Association,* vol. 245 (April 17, 1981), pp. 1515–18.

(249) 4. The study comparing THC, a placebo, and Compazine, was reported by S. Frytak, C. G. Moertel, J. R. O'Fallon, et al., in "Delta-9-THC as an Antiemetic for Patients Receiving Cancer Chemotherapy," *Annals of Internal Medicine,* vol. 91, no. 6 (December 1979), pp. 825–30.

(249) 5. Council on Scientific Affairs of the American Medical Association, "Marijuana: Its Health Hazards and Therapeutic Potential," *Journal of the American Medical Association,* vol. 246, no. 16 (October 16, 1981), p. 1826.

(250) 6. Positive THC results for patients who had not responded to standard antiemetic therapy were reported by L. E. Orr, J. F. McKernan, B. Bloome, et al. in "Antiemetic Effect of THC," *Archives of Internal Medicine,* vol. 140 (1980), pp. 1431–33.

(250) 7. S. Rusche, "Better Antiemetics on the Horizon," *U.S. Journal on Drug and Alcohol Dependence,* April 1982, pp. 10–11.

(250) 8. Charles Seabrooke, "Pot, THC Are Effective Anti-Nausea Agents, Ga. Study Finds," *Atlanta Journal-Constitution,* February 5, 1983, p. 3-B. (Report given by oncologist Dr. Nixon of Emory University Medical School.)

(251) 9. S. Kagen, letter to *New England Journal of Medicine,* vol. 304, no. 8 (February 19, 1981).

See also S. L. Kagen, V. P. Kurup, P. G. Sohnle, and J. N. Fink, "Marijuana Smoking and Fungal Sensitization," *Journal of Allergy and Clinical Immunology,* vol. 71, no. 4 (April 1983), pp. 389–93.

254) 10. S. Cohen and R. C. Stillman, eds., *Therapeutic Potential of Marijuana* (New York: Plenum Medical Book Co., 1976).

255) 11. The National Eye Institute's report on glaucoma was reported in "From the NIH—Research Findings of Potential Value to the Practitioner," *Journal of the American Medical Association,* vol. 242, no. 18, (November 1979). Note: The National Eye Institute is part of the National Institutes of Health (NIH).

257) 12. "Wheel Interview: NORML Chairman Keith Stroup Talks on Pot Issues," *Emory Wheel,* February 6, 1979, pp. 18–19. (See chapter 2 for more on NORML.)

258) 13. "The Convention of Psychotropic Substances," United Nations, 1971. (See 21 *U.S.C.* 8 11 (d) (2) (A).)

259) 14. NORML's Administration Petition to Reschedule Cannabis, NORML *v.* Ingersoll, 497 F. 2d 654 (DC CIR. 1974).

NORML *v.* DEA, 559 F 2d 735 (DC CIR. 1977).

NORML *v.* DEA and DHEW, 79–1660 (DC CIR. October 16, 1980 and June 4, 1982). (D.C. CIR means Circuit Court of Appeals, District of Columbia. DHEW is the Dept. of Health, Education and Welfare, now known as Health and Human Services. The third reference is an unreported decision, available only through the clerk of the Federal Court of Appeals for the District of Columbia.)

260) 15. For figures on the demand for NIDA joints for therapeutic programs and on NIDA's overstock of cannabis see R. B. Hawks, "Information on Marijuana Cigarettes Supplies," unpublished memorandum: Department of Health and Human Services, October 13, 1981.

262) 16. "Bill Would Permit Medical Use of Marijuana," *New York Times,* August 15, 1983, p. A-11.

CHAPTER 14: MARIJUANA AND DRIVING

265) 1. *National Survey on Drug Abuse*—see chapter 2, note 1.

265) 2. Statistics from the surveys reported by NIDA can be found in *Marijuana and Health: Eighth Annual Report to Congress from the Secretary of Health, Education and Welfare,* 1980.

266) 3. "NORML Policy Brochure" (Washington, DC: revised annually), p. 3.

266) 4. Statistics on highway deaths between 1961 and 1971 from *Motor Vehicle Safety: 1980,* Dept. of Traffic and Highway Safety, November 1982.

268) 5. J. Davis, "Marijuana and Driving Performance," American Society of Clinical Pathologists, 1970.

See also J. Davis, *Journal of Drug Issues,* vol. 1, no. 1 (January 1971), pp. 18–26.

270) 6. The motorcycle-magazine ad for "smoking doobie" was in *Iron Horse,* August 1979.

270) 7. *Marijuana and Health*—see note 2.

270) 8. For studies on hallucinogenic flashbacks caused by marijuana, see M. H. Keeler, "Marijuana-Induced Hallucinations," *Diseases of the Nervous System,* vol. 29, no. 9 (1968), pp. 314–15.

See also M. D. Stanton, J. Mintz, and R. M. Franklin, "Drug Flashbacks

II: Some Additional Findings," *International Journal of the Addictions,* vol. 11, (1976), pp. 53–69.

(271) 9. The tracking performance example was reported by J. Davis—see note 5.

(271) 10. The following are some of the studies Moskowitz has conducted on various facets of marijuana-impaired driving:

H. Moskowitz, S. Sharma, and W. McGlothlin, "Effect of Marihuana upon Peripheral Vision as a Function of the Information Processing Demands in Central Vision," *Perceptual Motor Skills,* vol. 35 (1972), pp. 875–82.

S. Sharma and H. Moskowitz, "Effect of Marihuana on the Visual Autokinetic Phenomenon," *Perceptual Motor Skills,* vol. 35 (1972), pp. 891–94.

S. Sharma and H. Moskowitz, "Marihuana Dose Study of Vigilance Performance," *Proceedings,* 81st annual conference of the American Psychological Association, 1973, pp. 1035–36.

H. Moskowitz, R. Shea, and M. Burns, "Effect of Marihuana on the Psychological Refractory Period," *Perceptual Motor Skills,* vol. 38 (1974), pp. 959–62.

S. Sharma and H. Moskowitz, "Effects of Two Levels of Attention Demand on Vigilance Performance under Marihuana," *Perceptual Motor Skills,* vol. 38 (1974), pp. 967–70.

H. Moskowitz, "Marihuana and Driving," *Accident Analysis and Prevention,* vol. 8, no. 1, (1976), pp. 21–26.

H. Moskowitz, W. McGlothlin, and S. Hulbert, "Marijuana Effects on Simulated Driving Performance," *Accident Analysis and Prevention,* vol. 8 (1976), pp. 45–50.

H. Moskowitz, S. Sharma, and K. Ziedman, "Duration of Skills Performance Impairment under Marijuana," Proceedings of the American Association for Automotive Medicine, October 1–3, 1981, San Francisco, pp. 87–96.

(273) 11. H. Klonoff, "Effects of Marijuana on Driving in a Restricted Area and on City Streets: Driving Performance and Physiological Changes," in *Marijuana: Effects on Human Behavior,* L. L. Miller, ed. (New York: Academic Press, 1974), pp. 359–97.

D. Johnston, J. G. Bachman, and P. M. O'Malley, *Monitoring the Future: Questionnaire Responses from the Nation's High School Seniors,* (Ann Arbor, MI: Institute for Social Research, 1984).

M. Burns and H. Moskowitz, "Alcohol, Marijuana and Skills Performance," *Alcohol, Drugs and Traffic Safety,* vol. 3, L. Goldberg, ed. (Stockholm; Almquist & Wiksell International, 1981), pp. 954–68.

A. Smiley, H. Moskowitz, and K. Ziedman, "Driving Simulator Studies of Marijuana Alone and in Combination with Alcohol," *Proceedings* of the 25th Conference of the American Association for Automotive Medicine, 1981, Morton Grove, Illinois, pp. 107–16.

L. Sutton, "The Effects of Alcohol, Marijuana and Their Combination on Driving Ability," *Journal of Studies on Alcohol,* vol. 44, no. 3 (May 1983), pp. 438–45.

(279) 12. V. Reeve, et al., "Marijuana and Alcohol Driver Performance Study—Phase II," California Office of Traffic Safety Grant no. 087902, 1984.

(281) 13. V. Reeve, W. Robertson, J. Grant, J. Soares, E. Zimmermann, H. Gillespie, and L. Hollister, "Hemolyzed Blood and Serum Levels of Delta-9-THC. Effects on the Performance of Roadside Sobriety Tests," *American Academy Journal of Forensic Sciences,* vol. 28, no. 4 (October 1983), pp. 963–71.

(285) 14. V. Reeve, "Incidence of Marijuana in a California Impaired Driver Population," Sacramento, California, Department of Justice, Division of Law Enforcement, Investigative Services Branch, 1979.

(285) 15. Concerning RIA method of detecting cannabinoids in blood, see E. P. Yeager, U. Goebelsmann, J. Soares, J. D. Grant, and S. Gross, "Delta-9-Tetrahydrocannabinol by GLC-MS Validated Radioimmunoassays of Hemolyzed Blood or Serum," *Journal of Behavioral Toxicology,* vol. 5 (March/April 1981), pp. 81–84.

(287) 16. J. Pirl, V. M. Papa, and J. J. Spikes, "The Detection of Delta-9-THC in Postmortem Blood Samples," *Journal of Analytical Toxicology,* vol. 3 (1979), pp. 129–32.

V. M. Papa, J. J. Spikes, and J. N. Pirl, "Quantitation of Delta-9-THC in Postmortem Blood Samples from Traffic, Homicide, Suicide and Other Forensic Cases," *Proceedings* of the Italian Society of Mass Spectrometry in Biochemistry and Medicine, July 1980.

(287) 17. For the Ontario study, see R. Warren, H. Simpson, D. M. Lucas, C. Cimbura, and R. C. Bennett, *Drug Involvement in Traffic Fatalities in the Province of Ontario,* Traffic Injury Research Foundation, Centre of Forensic Sciences, Deputy Chief Coroner, Province of Ontario, presented at American Association of Automotive Medicine 24th Conference, Rochester, New York, October 1980.

(287) 18. The Washington study was reported by A. J. Crancer and D. L. Quiring in "Driving Records of Persons Arrested for Illegal Drug Use" report no. 011 (Washington: Dept. of Motor Vehicles, 1968).

(288) 19. R. S. Sterling-Smith, "Alcohol, Marihuana and Other Drug Patterns among Operators Involved in Fatal Motor Vehicle Accidents," in *Alcohol, Drugs and Traffic Safety,* S. Israelstam and S. Lambert, eds. (Toronto: Addictive Research Foundation of Ontario, 1975), pp. 93–105.

(288) 20. M. Burns, *Marijuana Effects on Driving: A Survey of the Perceptions, Attitudes and Practices of High School Students* (Los Angeles: Southern California Research Institute, 1981).

(289) 21. For more information on Minnesota's "pot course," see B. Bomier, "Drug Overview and Encounter" (Anoka, MN: Minnesota Behavioral Institute, 1980). (Minnesota's "open baggie law" M.S. 152.15.)

See also "An Evaluation of Minnesota's Drug Education Program for Minimal Possession Violators," University of Minnesota, 1978.

(291) 22. The Canadian Medical Association resolution was published in "CMA Calls for Blood Samples," *Council on Drug Abuse Newsletter,* Toronto, Canada, December 1982, p. 6.

CHAPTER 16: FEDERAL STRATEGY

(299) 1. "Federal Strategy for Prevention of Drug Abuse and Drug Trafficking 1982," prepared for the president pursuant to the Drug Abuse Office and Treatment

Act of 1972. Participating departments and independent agencies: Department of Agriculture, Department of Defense, Department of Education, Department of Health and Human Services, Department of Justice, Department of Labor, Department of State, Department of Transportation, Department of the Treasury, ACTION, U.S. International Communication Agency, Veterans' Administration, Drug Abuse Policy Office, Office of Policy Development, the White House. August 20, 1982 (Washington, DC: U.S. Gov. Printing Ofc.).

(301) 2. Rinkevich quoted by H. McConnell in "Traffickers Being Worn Down as Florida Closes Drug Pipeline," *The Journal* of the Addiction Research Foundation, Ontario, Canada, vol. II, no. 10 (October 1, 1982), pp. 1–2.

Also concerning the results of South Florida Task Force, see President Reagan's Campaign against Drug Abuse, The White House, Office of the Press Secretary, October 5, 1982, pp. 3–4.

(302) 3. Creation of the Twelve Task Forces Program announced by Attorney General William French Smith at a speech at the U.S. Justice Department, October 14, 1982.

(303) 4. Remarks by William H. Webster, Director, Federal Bureau of Investigation before the National Federation of Parents for Drug-Free Youth National Conference, Washington, D.C., September 26, 1983, pp. 10–12.

(304) 5. Announcement of the Creation of NNBIS by Vice President Bush, National Press Club, Washington, D.C., June 17, 1983.

(304) 6. Larry L. Ortin, Special Agent in Charge of EPIC, "Epic," *Drug Enforcement,* Fall, 1983, pp. 22–26.

(305) 7. Judith Friedman, speech given at the National Conference of U.S. Marshalls, Asheville, North Carolina, September 13, 1983.

(306) 8. Concerning DEA/FBI Cooperation: Remarks by William H. Webster, Director of FBI, before the society of former special agents, Washington, D.C., March 24, 1983, pp. 11–12.

(307) 9. Concerning IRS cooperation, see Public Law 97-248 signed by the President on September 3, 1982.

(308) 10. Francis Mullen, Jr., director of DEA, address to initial meeting of the President's Commission on Crime, December 13, 1983.

(308) 11. The Amendments to the Posse Comitatis statute Public law 97-86, 12/1 (1981). 18 U.S.C., Sec. 1385.

Also, see Steven Zimmerman, "Posse Comitatus," *Drug Enforcement,* Summer, 1982, p. 17.

(309) 12. Concerning civil forfeiture see Harry C. Myers and Joseph P. Brozostonski, "Dealers, Dollars and Drugs," *Drug Enforcement,* Summer, 1982.

Also: Model Forfeiture of Drug Profits Act, drafted by DEA, January 1981.

Also: The Controlled Substances Act, Public Law 91-513 (10/27/80). 21 U.S.C., Sec. 881.

(313) 13. Eradication/suppression program final report, prepared by DEA Cannabis Investigations Section, December 1982.

(314) 14. For more on the Mexican paraquat spraying program, see "Cannabis Eradication in Foreign Western Hemisphere Nations," Draft Programmatic Environmental Impact Statement of the Effects in the United States, U.S. Department of State, contract no. 2071-010065 (McLean, VI: MITRE Corporation), p. E-3.

(*315*) 15. "Methods for the Eradication of Illicit Narcotic Crops," Report of a Study Group, July 25–27, 1979, United Nations Narcotics Laboratory (a typewritten seventeen-page report).

Also see "Fact Sheet: Paraquat," U.S. Department of Justice, DEA, August 1983, p. 3.

(*316*) 16. C. Turner, M. Elsohly, F. Ping Cheng, and L. Torres, *Journal of American Medical Association,* vol. 240, no. 17 (1978), p. 8157.

Also see C. E. Turner, F. Ping Cheng, L. M. Torres, and M. A. Elsohly, "Detection and Analysis of Paraquat in Confiscated Marijuana Samples," *Bulletin on Narcotics,* vol. XXX, no. 4 (October–December 1978), pp. 47–56.

(*316*) 17. Results of the CDC study of street samples and Dr. Hawks' NIDA study were reported by William H. Foege, M.D., Director of Centers for Disease Control of U.S. Public Health Service, testimony before Committee on Judiciary, Subcommittee on Crime, U.S. House of Representatives, October 5, 1983, pp. 5–7.

(*317*) 18. For the 1978 HEW report on the possibility of lung damage in "the worst possible scenario," see "Final Report on Paraquat Hazards," *NIDA Capsules,* C78–15, August 1978.

(*318*) 19. For the EIS on health impacts in United States from spraying paraquat in foreign countries, see note 14, pp. 20–21.

(*319*) 20. For the Public Health Service statement, see note 17, p. 1.

(*320*) 21. Lawsuits over aerial paraquat:

National Organization for the Reform of Marijuana Laws (NORML) *vs.* The United States Drug Enforcement Administration, *et al.,* U.S. District Court for the District of Columbia, civil action no. 83-2595. North Georgia Citizens Opposed to Paraquat Spraying *vs.* Ronald Reagan, Northern District of Georgia, civil action no. 383-1710-A, August 1983.

Jack Watts *vs.* Drug Enforcement Administration, Eastern District of Kentucky, civil action no. 83–250, August 1983.

(*321*) 22. Jerome A. Miles, deputy chief of the National Forest Service, U.S. Department of Agriculture, Statement before the Subcommittee on Crime of the Committee on the Judiciary, U.S. House of Representatives, November 17, 1983.

(*322*) 23. Ernest V. Andersen, U.S. Forest Service, affidavit given in U.S. District Court for the District of Columbia, September 7, 1983.

(*323*) 24. Sierra Club, *et al. vs.* Francis M. Mullen, Jr. [DEA Administrator] *et al.,* Consol. civil nos. 83-2592.

(*323*) 25. For additional information on paraquat spraying of cannabis, see "The Use of Paraquat to Eradicate Illicit Marijuana Crops and the Health Implications of Paraquat-Contaminated Marijuana on the U.S. Market," a report of the House Select Committee on Narcotics Abuse and Control, U.S. Gov. Printing Ofc., 1980.

CHAPTER 17: MARIJUANA DETECTION TESTS

(*334*) 1. Concerning the GC/MS, developed in early 1970s, see S. Agurell et al., "THC in Blood," *Journal of Pharmaceutical Pharmacology,* vol. 25 (1973).

(*335*) 2. The most recent GC/MS developments are described in R. Foltz, K. McGinnis, and D. Chinn, "Quantitative Measurement of Delta-9-Tetrahydrocannabinol and Two Major Metabolites in Physiological Specimens Using Capillary Column

Gas Chromotography/Negative Ion Chemical Ionization Mass Spectrometry," *Biomedical Mass Spectrometry,* Center for Human Toxicology, vol. 10 (June 1983).

See also R. Detrick and R. Foltz, "Quantitation of Delta 9-Tetrahydrocannabinol in Body Fluids by Gas Chromatography/Chemical Ionization Mass Spectrometry," in R. Willette, ed. *Cannabinoid Assays in Humans,* NIDA Research Monograph no. 7, 1976, pp. 88–95.

See also J. Teale, L. King, E. Forman, et al., "Radioimmunoassay of Cannabinoids in Blood and Urine," *Lancet,* September 7, 1974.

See also A. Chase, P. Kelley, A. Taunton-Rigby, et al., "Quantitation of Cannabinoids in Biological Fluids by Radioimmunoassay," *Cannabinoid Assays in Humans,* pp. 1–9.

See also C. Cook, M. Hawes, E. Amerson, et al., "Radioimmunoassay of Delta-9-Tetrahydrocannabinol," *Cannabinoid Assays in Humans,* pp. 15–27.

(335) 3. Concerning the basic principle on which the Agglutex THC is based, see R. Ross, et al., "Preliminary Evaluation of a Latex Agglutination-Inhibition Tube Test for Morphine," *Clinical Chemistry,* vol. 21, no. 1 (1975), pp. 139–43.

(336) 4. "EMIT d.a.u. TM, "Cannabinol Urine Assay, For Use in Semi-Quantitative Enzyme Immunoassay of Cannabinoids in Human Urine," Palo Alto, California, Syva Company, June 1982.

See also R. Bastiani, R. Phillips, R. Schneider, et al., "Homogeneous Immunochemical Drug Assays," *American Journal of Medical Technology,* vol. 39 (1973), pp. 211–16.

See also K. E. Rubenstein, "Homogeneous Enzyme Immunoassay Today," *Scandinavian Journal of Immunology,* vol. 8, Suppl. 7 (1978), pp. 57–62.

See also R. Bastiani, "The EMIT System: A Commercially Successful Innovation," *Antibiotics and Chemotherapy,* vol. 26 (1979), pp. 89–97.

(337) 5. J. D. Grant, S. J. Gross, P. Lomax, and S. L. R. Wong, "Antibody Detection of Marijuana," *Nature-New Biology,* vol. 236 (1972), p. 216.

(337) 6. Information on the saliva test in J. R. Soares, J. D. Grant, and S. J. Gross, "Significant Developments in Radioimmune Methods Applied to Delta-9-Tetrahydrocannabinol and Its 9-Substitutes Metabolites," *The Analysis of Cannabinoids in Biological Fluids,* NIDA Research Monograph Series no. 42, 1982, p. 44.

(338) 7. Concerning a sum-up of all current methodologies for cannabinoid analysis and related papers, see "The Analysis of Cannabinoids in Biological Fluids," R. Hawks, ed. (Washington, DC: U.S. Govt. Printing Ofc., 1982), p. 141, no. S/N 017-024-01151-J.

See also L. E. Hollister, S. L. Kanter, F. Moore, et al., "Marijuana Metabolites in Urine of Man," *Clinical Pharmacology and Therapeutics,* vol. 13 (1972), pp. 849–55.

See also M. E. Wall, T. M. Harvey, J. T. Bursey, et al., "Analytical Methods for the Determination of Cannabinoids in Biological Material," in *Cannabinoid Assays in Humans,* note 2, pp. 107–17.

(339) 8. M. Peres-Reyes, "Passive Inhalation of Marijuana Smoke and Urinary Excretion of Cannabinoids," *Clinical Pharmacology and Therapeutics,* vol. 34 (1983), pp. 36–41.

340) 9. S. Cohen, "Marijuana Use Detection: The State of the Art," *Drug Abuse and Alcoholism Newsletter,* Vista Hill Foundation, vol. XII, no. 9 (May 1983).

340) 10. R. Willette, "Cannabinoids," *Clinical Chemistry News,* vol. 8 (December 1983).

341) 11. R. Wynstra, "Urinalysis Screening for Marijuana Use: Legal and Ethical Considerations," in *Urine Testing for Marijuana Use: Implications for a Variety of Settings,* M. Blasinsky and G. Russell, eds. (Rockville, MD: The American Council on Drug Education, 1982), pp. 19–24.

CHAPTER 18: SCHOOLS: SUCCESSFUL PROGRAMS

353) 1. Presentment of the Sixth Essex County Grand Jury, 1978 Term, Concerning Drug Abuse Among School-age Children in the County of Essex, State of New Jersey; Superior Court of New Jersey Law Division, County of Essex Prosecutor's Office, New Courts Building, (Newark, New Jersey, published March 8, 1979), p. 58.

360) 2. Part of the North Side High story was reported by Harvey McConnell in "High School Ousts Drugs, Scores Academically," *The Journal* of the Addiction Research Foundation, Ontario, September 1, 1982, p. 7.

365) 3. F. Burford, W. Cebrynsky, G. W. Peck, and Norman Panzica, "The Marijuana Issue: A Headmaster's Perspective," report published by Ontario Secondary School Headmaster's Council in February 1980.

    See also Fred Burford and Tom Tittel, *Positive Peer Culture at Downsview Secondary School,* published by the Board of Education, Downsview, Ontario, M3K 1W3, March 1981.

366) 4. *Stay Real: Straight Talk about Marijuana and Hashish for Young People,* published by the Canadian Minister of National Health and Welfare, catalog no. H39–64/1983E, ISBN 0-662-12479-0, p. 24.

CHAPTER 19: THE ARMED FORCES

367) 1. For the 1980 Burt and Biegel survey, see chapter 4, note 10.

367) 2. R. M. Bray, L. L. Guess, R. E. Mason, R. L. Hubbard, D. G. Smith, M. E. Marsden, and J. V. Rachal, "Highlights: 1982 Worldwide Survey of Alcohol and Nonmedical Drug Use Among Military Personnel," Research Triangle Institute, July 1983, p. 45, RTI/2317/01/01F.

369) 3. Booz, Allen, and Hamilton, Inc., "Urinalysis Test Results Analysis" for the Human Resources Management and Personal Affairs Department (N-6), Naval Military Personnel Command, Washington, D.C., Arlington, Virginia, April 21, 1981. EG-15 on contract N00600-79-D-0845.

369) 4. U.S. *vs.* Ruiz, 48 C.M.R. 797 (1974). (C.M.R. is the Court of Military Review.)

370)   U.S. *vs.* Armstrong, 9 M.J., 374 C.M.R. (1980). (M.J. is *Military Justice,* a publication.)

371)   Murray *vs.* Haldeman, 16 M.J. 74 (1983). (In the Murray case, the court determined that the concept of compulsory urinalysis did not violate the constitutional or statutory protections against self-incrimination or unreasonable searches and seizures.)

(372) 5. For information on the army's program, see "The Army Alcohol and Drug Abuse Prevention and Control Program," Statement by Brigadier General John H. Mitchell, Director of Human Resources Development, Office of the Deputy Chief of Staff for Personnel, U.S. Army, before the Committee on Appropriations, U.S. House of Representatives, 97th Cong., and before the Committee on Preparedness, Committee on Armed Services, U.S. Senate, May 18, 1982.

(375) 6. For information on the U.S. Air Force program on drug-abuse prevention, see Maj. Gen. William R. Usher, Director of Personnel Plans, U.S. Air Force, Statement on Drug and Alcohol Abuse to the Joint Hearing of Subcommittees on Manpower and Personnel and on Preparedness, U.S. Senate Armed Services Committee, May 18, 1982.

(376) 7. For testimony on the USS *Nimitz* crash, see "Drug Abuse in the Military—1981," see chapter 4, note 1.

   See also "A Report to the Committee . . ."—chapter 4, note 14, pp. 15–16.

(376) 8. For a report on Admiral Hayward's navy-wide message, see Hilary DeVries, "Business and the Military Face Up to Drug Challenge," *Christian Science Monitor,* May 5, 1982, p. 13.

   See also "Facing Reality on Drugs" (editorial), *Boston Herald American,* December 26, 1981.

(380) 9. Rear Adm. Paul J. Mulloy, U.S. Navy, Director, Human Resources Management Division, Office of the Chief of Naval Operations, statement before the Subcommittees on Defense Manpower and Personnel and Defense Preparedness, U.S. Senate, 98th Cong., October 4, 1983.

10. For information on the Marine Corps' War on Drugs, see Brig. Gen. Anthony Lukeman, Director, Manpower Plans and Policy Division, U.S. Marine Corps, statement at Hearings on "Drug and Alcohol Abuse in the Armed Services," Joint Hearing before the Subcommittee on Manpower and Personnel and the Subcommittee on Preparedness of the Committee on Armed Services, U.S. Senate, 97th Cong., May 18, 1982, pp. 25–30.

CHAPTER 20: THE WORKPLACE: SUCCESSFUL PROGRAMS

(386) 1. William Meyer, M.D., administrator, Alcohol, Drug Abuse and Mental Health Administration, U.S. Public Health Service, Department of Health and Human Services, before the Subcommittee on Alcoholism and Drug Abuse and the Subcommittee on Employment and Productivity, Committee on Labor and Human Resources, U.S. Senate, July 14, 1982.

(387) 2. Firestone's 18/15 figures have emerged after a compilation of Firestone's EAP figures over twelve years.

(388) 3. The National Supply Company story was reported by S. Rusche, ed., "Drugs and Industry," *Drug Abuse Update,* a periodical, Families in Action Drug Information Center, June 1982.

(388) 4. For the report on Compugraphic Corp. of Wilmington, MA, see "Drugs on the Job: The Quiet Problem," *Newsweek,* Sept. 15, 1980.

(391) 5. Virginia Electric Power Company information supplied by Peter Bensinger.

(391) 6. For more on health promotion programs, see J. R. Vicary and H. Resnik, "Preventing Drug Abuse in the Workplace," Drug Abuse Prevention monograph series, (Rockville, MD: National Institute on Drug Abuse, 1980), pp. 26–38.

(392) 7. "The Supervisor's Handbook on Substance Abuse," published by Health Communications, Inc., 2119-A Hollywood Boulevard, Hollywood, FL; 1977; p. 16.

(396) 8. "The Impact and Cost Benefit of the General Motors Substance Abuse Program: A Review of Available Data," report to the General Health Services Section, prepared by A. Foote and J. C. Erfort, Research Consultants, Substance Abuse Recovery Program, July 31, 1979.

See also, R. G. Wiencek, "Marijuana in the Work Place," in *Drug Abuse in the Modern World: A Perspective for the Eighties* (New York: Pergamon Press, 1981), pp. 121–126.

Also of interest is an unpublished paper by Daniel Lanier, Jr., associate director of GM's EAP, "Marijuana Usage in the World of Work," 1983, 12 pages.

CHAPTER 21: THE TEXANS' WAR ON DRUGS

(403– 404) 1. TWOD-proposed bills passed: HB733/SB395—Sale to minors; HB730/SB 393— Drug trafficking bill; "Head shop" bill; HB729/SB397—HB731/SB394; HB732/ SB396—Professional license revocation bill. The Triplicate Prescription bill is not contained in a single section. It is found mostly in Section 3.08 and 3.09 of Article 4476-15 of *Vernon's Texas Civil Statute.*

(404) 2. "TWOD Is the Action Arm of the Texans' War on Drugs Committee," published by TWOD, 7800 Shoal Creek Blvd., Suite 381-W, Austin, TX 78757.

See also "History of Texans' War on Drugs," published by TWOD, from the same address. Updated in 1984.

(402) 3. For more information on PTA involvement in the War on Drugs, write Texas Congress of Parents and Teachers, 408 West 11th, Austin, TX 78701.

(405) 4. For information on materials from the Texas Medical Association Auxiliary, write TMAA, 1801 North Lamar Blvd., Austin, TX 78701. Materials include:

(407) 5. For more information on the Lions Club programs and for a copy of the slide show, write Lions Club International, 300 22nd Street, Oakbrook, IL 60570. Slides and script cost ten dollars.

- "The Dirty Dozen: Things You Need to Know about Marijuana." Available in Spanish or English, six dollars per hundred.

- "Fonzie and Friends Puppet Show." Script available free.

- Summary of TWOD suggestions to the Textbook Committee, State Board of Education, regarding health chapters dealing with drugs and alcohol, June 1982. "Court Watchers' Manual," 38 pp.

(407) 6. B. D. Martin, Narcotics Service, Texas Dept. of Public Safety, and past president of Texas Narcotics Officers' Association, "Report to TWOD Committee on Change in Public Attitude Toward Users and Traffickers of Narcotics: A Result of TWOD Activities," April 4, 1983.

(409) 7. For TWOD accomplishments, see Texans' War on Drugs, Status Report, March 28, 1984.

(410) 8. For information on DREAM, Inc. (Drug Research and Education Association in Mississippi), see "Open Your Eyes: DREAM," available from DREAM, Suite B, 1991 Lakeland Drive, Jackson, MS 39216.

CHAPTER 22: PARENTS FOR DRUG-FREE YOUTH

The author has covered the parent movement since 1978. She was present at almost all of the national conferences of PRIDE and the National Federation of Parents for Drug-Free Youth (NFP); at the January 1980 meeting after the Senate Mathias hearings when the idea for a national organization was first discussed; at the April 1980 PRIDE National Conference when the National Organization for Drug-Free Youth was created; at the May 1980 Press Conference in the U.S. Senate building where the existence of the NFP was officially announced. At these and other meetings, she interviewed parent group leaders from all over the country.

Her article "The Parent War Against Pot" appeared in the January 6, 1980, "Outlook" section of the *Washington Post.* It was widely syndicated in other major newspapers and was the first article to bring information about the emerging parent movement to the American public. Her subsequent articles on the subject included "How Parents are Fighting to Keep Children Off Drugs: The Battle Against Pot," *Ladies' Home Journal,* October 1980, and "Parents Against Pot," *Reader's Digest,* June 1983. Consequently, aside from the surveys and reports noted in the references for this chapter, virtually all the material is drawn from extensive interviews with those parent group leaders mentioned here. As for the many interviews she has done with other parent group leaders throughout the country, unfortunately, their stories—most of them equally dramatic and newsworthy—could not be included due to lack of space.

(411) 1. "Operation Wake-Up," Anderson Township Survey of Drug and Alcohol Use among High School Students, September 1981.

(413) 2. "State of the Art Report on the Parent Movement," Rayburn-Hess Associates, prepared for National Institute on Drug Abuse, 1981.

(416) 3. H. T. Jones, "What the Practicing Physician Should Know about Marijuana," *Private Practice,* January 1976, pp. 25–40.

(421) 4. M. Manatt, *Parents, Peers, and Pot* (Rockville, MD: National Institute on Drug Abuse, 1980), 98 pp. (Available from PRIDE; see Resources.)

(431) 5. Drug Paraphernalia and Youth," Subcommittee on Criminal Justice of the Committee on the Judiciary, U.S. Senate, 96th Cong., 2nd Sess. November 16, 1979. Serial 96-68.

(432) 6. For the testimony given at the Mathias hearings, see *Health Consequences of Marijuana Use,* chapter 6, note 8, p. 477.

(454) 7. W. B. Meyer, then administrator, ADAMHA, Address to First National Conference of National Federation of Parents for Drug-Free Youth (NFP) (Silver Spring, MD: NFP), pp. 4–5.

Acknowledgments

(Note: In the acknowledgments and throughout the book I have made no distinction between M.D.s and Ph.D.s; all are referred to as Dr.)

Chapter 1: The Briefing. Read in its entirety by Dr. Carlton Turner, special assistant to the president for Drug Abuse Policy. (Note: Dr. Turner also checked all subsequent sections in which he is quoted in this book.) Also, sections were checked by Dr. Robert DuPont, founding director, National Institute on Drug Abuse. (Note: Dr. DuPont checked all subsequent sections in which he is quoted throughout the book.) Sections were also checked by Colin Seidor, producer of *Epidemic;* and by David Martin, senior analyst on the Senate Subcommittee on Internal Security (who organized the 1974 Senate marijuana health hazard hearings).

Chapter 2: The Situation. This and all other sections in the book concerning the National Drug Abuse (Household) Survey were checked by researchers Dr. Judith Miller, project director, and Dr. Ira Cisin of George Washington University. All sections in this chapter and throughout the book concerning the National High School Senior Survey were checked by Dr. Lloyd Johnston, Dr. Jerald Bachman, or Dr. Patrick O'Malley, researchers at the University of Michigan's Institute for Social Research. Sections in this chapter were also checked by Major H. D. Watson, then head of the Oregon State Police Narcotics Division; Dr. William Pollin, director, National Institute on Drug Abuse; Peter Bensinger, former administrator, Drug Enforcement Administration. (Note: Pollin and Bensinger also checked for accuracy all subsequent sections in which they are quoted in this book.)

Chapter 3: Crisis in the Workplace. Their sections were checked for accuracy by David Langness, senior writer, Comprehensive Care Corp.; Dr. William

Mayer, former administrator, Alcohol, Drug Abuse and Mental Health Administration; Dr. Lee Croft, director, Croft Consultants; Inspector Dennis Ryan, commanding officer of the New York police narcotics division; Otto Jones, director of Human Affairs, Inc.; David R. Dearborn, assistant vice president of Pinkerton; Ira Lipman, director of Guardsmark, Inc.; William H. Taft, president of the Manufacturers Association of Southern Connecticut; Ed Johnson, manager, Firestone Tire and Rubber EAPs; Dr. Alvin Cruze, Research Triangle Institute; Dr. Robert Wiencek, GM's director, Occupation Safety and Health; Daniel Lanier, Jr., associate director, GM's Alcoholism and Drug Abuse Programs, and Jim Burnett, chairman, National Transportation Safety Board.

Chapter 4: Crisis in the Armed Forces. This entire chapter was read for accuracy by Dr. James E. McDonald, special assistant to Congressman Glenn English; Robert Stein, Director, Education and Employee Assistance Programs, Office of the Asst. Secretary of Defense for Health Affairs, and by Dr. John Johns, deputy assistant secretary of defense for health promotion.

Chapter 5: Crisis in the Schools. The following read sections for accuracy: Lynn Ansara, communications director, New York State Division of Substance Abuse Services; Dr. Eugene Farrell, deputy director, Maryland Drug Abuse Administration; Dr. Ingrid Lantner; Cpl. Ed Moses, drug information officer of the state of Missouri; Dr. Scott Thomson, executive director, National Association of Secondary School Principals; and Sue Rusche, director, Families in Action.

Chapter 6: What Is Marijuana? The entire chapter was read for accuracy by Dr. Carlton Turner and Dr. Coy Waller, both former directors, NIDA Marijuana Project, University of Mississippi, and by Dr. Harris Rosenkrantz, director of biochemical pharmacology of the EG&G Mason Research Institute, Worcester, Massachusetts.

Chapter 7: Effects on the Lungs and the Heart. The entire chapter was read for accuracy by Dr. Donald P. Tashkin, director of the Pulmonary Function Laboratory at UCLA Hospital, and by Dr. Harris Rosenkrantz. Their sections were read by Dietrich Hoffman, American Health Foundation, Valhalla, New York; Dr. Forest S. Tennant, Jr., director, Community Health Projects, Inc. West Covina, Calif.; Dr. Stephen Szara, chief of the biomedical branch, NIDA; Dr. Cecile Leuchtenberger, former head of the department of cytochemistry at the Swiss Institute for Experimental Cancer Research, Lausanne; Dr. Freddy Homburger, director, Bio-Research Institute, Inc.; Dr. Donald Ian

Macdonald, president, Florida Pediatric Society; Dr. Ingrid Lantner; Dr. Gary Huber, professor of medicine, Medical College, University of Kentucky; Dr. Vijay Mahajan, chief of pulmonary medicine, St. Vincent's Hospital, Toledo, Ohio; and Dr. Wilbert S. Aranow, professor of medicine and director of cardiovascular research, Creighton University School of Medicine, Omaha, Nebraska.

Chapter 8: Effects on Sex and Reproduction: Female. This entire chapter was read for accuracy by Dr. Carol Grace Smith of the School of Medicine of the Uniformed Services of the University of the Health Sciences, Bethesda, Maryland; and by Dr. Harris Rosenkrantz. Sections were read for accuracy by Dr. Joan Bauman of the Biology Research Foundation; Dr. Josel Szepsenwol of the department of biological sciences, Florida International University; Dr. Alexander Jakubovic of the University of Vancouver, Canada; Dr. William Bates, University of Mississippi Medical Center in Jackson; Dr. Ethel Sassenrath and Dr. Gail Goo, University of California Medical School at Davis; Dr. Peter Fried, Carlton University, Ottawa, Canada; Dr. Stanley Gross, UCLA Medical School, Los Angeles; Dr. Ralph Hingson, Boston City Hospital; Dr. Paige Besch, Reproductive Research Laboratory, Baylor College of Medicine, Houston; Dr. Akira Morishima, director of the division of pediatric endocrinology, Columbia University College of Physicians and Surgeons; Dr. Vincent de Paul Lynch, professor of pharmacology and toxicology, St. John's University, Jamaica, New York; and Dr. Ingrid Lantner. (Note: Pediatrician Lantner also checked for accuracy other sections in this book concerning her clinical observations.)

Chapter 9: Effects on Sex and Reproduction: Male. This chapter was read in its entirety by Dr. Carol Smith, Dr. Harris Rosenkrantz, and by Dr. Susan Dalterio, University of Texas Health Science Center at San Antonio. Sections were read by Dr. Ricardo Asch, director, department of clinical research in the department of obstetrics and gynecology at University of Texas Health Science Center; Dr. Wylie Hembree, Columbia University College of Physicians and Surgeons. Dr. Arthur Zimmerman, University of Toronto, Canada; Dr. Peter Fried, Carlton University, Ottawa, Canada; Dr. Marietta Issidorides, University of Athens, Greece; and Dr. William Pollin, director, NIDA.

Chapter 10: Effects on the Brain. This chapter was read in its entirety by Dr. Robert Heath, former director of the department of psychiatry and neurology at Tulane Medical School (retired), by Dr. Heath's associate, Dr. Austin

Fitzjarrell; and by Dr. Harris Rosenkrantz. Sections were read by Dr. Alexander Jakubovic; Dr. John P. McGahan, University of California School of Medicine, and Dr. Robert C. Gilkeson, director, Center for Psychoneurologic Research, Los Angeles.

Chapter 11: The Immune System and Other Cellular Effects. This chapter was read in its entirety by Dr. Harris Rosenkrantz and by Dr. Gabriel Nahas, Columbia University College of Physicians and Surgeons. Sections were read by Dr. Marietta Issidorides, professor, Department of Biology, Athens Medical School, Athens, Greece; Dr. Al Munson, Medical College of Virginia; Dr. Arthur Zimmerman; Dr. Robert McDonough of the Georgia Mental Health Institute; Dr. Akira Morishima; Dr. Morton Stenchever, chairman, department of obstetrics and gynecology, University of Washington, Seattle; Arthur Zimmerman, University of Toronto; Dr. Josel Szepsenwol, Florida International University; Sir William Paton, chairman, department of pharmacology, Oxford University, England.

Chapter 12: Psychological Effects. This chapter was read in its entirety by three noted psychiatrists who specialize in problems of drug abuse: Dr. Mark Gold, director of research, Fair Oaks Hospital, Summit, New Jersey; Dr. Lawrence Kirstein, clinical director, Regent Hospital, New York City; and Dr. Robert DuPont, former director of the drug dependence section of the World Psychiatric Association. Sections were read by Dr. Robert Gilkeson, director, Center for Psychoneurologic Research, Los Angeles; Dr. Mitchell Rosenthal, director, Phoenix House, New York City; Joyce Nalepka, president, National Federation of Parents for Drug-Free Youth; Dr. Doris H. Milman, professor of pediatrics, State University of New York; Dr. Dean Parmalee, former director of adolescent in-patient services, Charles River Hospital (a Boston University School of Medicine teaching hospital); Dr. Harold Voth; Dr. Sidney Cohen, professor of clinical psychology, UCLA Medical School, Los Angeles; Dr. Adam Sulkowski, Boston School of Medicine and Bedford (Mass.) Veterans Administration Medical Center; Dr. Stephen Williams, Houston, Texas; Dr. Jason Baron, medical director, Deer Park Hospital, Deer Park, Texas; Dr. Miller Newton, former program director, STRAIGHT (an adolescent drug treatment program); Dr. David Janowsky, University of California at San Diego; Dr. José Carranza, Baylor College of Medicine, Houston, Texas; Dr. Denise Kandel, Columbia University and New York State Psychiatric Institute; Dr. Richard Clayton, professor of sociology, University of Kentucky, Lexington; and Dr. Andrew Malcolm, University of Toronto, Canada.

Chapter 13: Marijuana as Medicine? This chapter was read in its entirety by Dr. Coy Waller, founding director, NIDA's Marijuana Research Project, University of Mississippi at Oxford, and by Sue Rusche, who covered the National Conference on the Therapeutic Applications of the Cannabinoids for the *U.S. Journal on Drug and Alcohol Dependence* and for her column on drug and alcohol abuse, syndicated nationally by King Features. Sections were read by oncologists Dr. Charles Moertel, director of Mayo Clinic's Comprehensive Cancer Institute; and Dr. George Hyman, Columbia College of Physicians and Surgeons. Sections were also read by Dr. Steven L. Kagen, clinical professor, allergy and immunology, Medical College of Wisconsin; Dr. Edward G. Tocus, chief, drug abuse staff, Food and Drug Administration; Dr. Sidney Cohen, Neuropsychiatric Institute, UCLA; Dr. Eugene McCormick of Wellington, Kansas; and Fred Degnan, attorney, Food and Drug Administration.

Chapter 14: Marijuana and Driving. This chapter was read in its entirety by Victor Reeve, state of California Department of Justice, Investigative Services Branch. Sections were read by Dr. Herbert Moskowitz, Southern California Research Institute, Cpl. Ed Moses, Missouri State Highway Patrol; Dr. Joseph Davis, chief medical examiner, Dade County, Florida; Bruce Bomier, executive director, Minnesota Institute; Dr. Harry Klonoff, professor of psychiatry, University of Vancouver, Canada; Dr. Lawrence Sutton, executive director, Pittsburgh Institute for Driver Research and Substance Abuse; Dr. John Spikes, director of toxicology, Department of Public Health, Chicago, Illinois; and Dr. Robert Sterling-Smith, former director, Boston University Traffic Accident Research Team.

Chapter 16: The Federal Strategy. I am grateful to Dr. Carlton Turner, special assistant to the president for Drug Abuse Policy, and his public affairs representative, Pat McKelvey, for reading this chapter in its entirety. I am also grateful to the following for reading sections of the chapter pertaining to their specific areas: Meredith Armstrong, communications officer, South Florida Task Force; Roger Yang, public affairs, FBI; Judith Friedman, administrator, Law Enforcement Coordinating Committees; Robert Feldkamp, director, public affairs, Drug Enforcement Administration and Ted Swift, public affairs, DEA; Harry Myers, assistant chief counsel, DEA; William M. Lenck, DEA Forfeiture Counsel; James A. Miles, deputy chief, Forest Service, U.S. Department of Agriculture; James T. Draude, attorney, Land and Natural Resources Division, U.S. Department of Justice; Dr. Coy Waller; Bob Alden, public affairs, Centers for Disease Control; Angie Hammock, director, ACTION Drug Prevention Program; Brian Vogt, special assistant to the director, ACTION; David Gurr, policy development analyst, ACTION; Albert P. Catalbo, McNeil Pharmaceutical's director of professional pharmacy relations; Joe Bond, special assistant to the deputy assistant U.S. attorney general; Rayburn Hess, U.S. State Department; Mildred Lehman, associate administrator for communications and public affairs, Department of Health and Human Services; James Helsing, public affairs, Alcohol, Drug Abuse and Mental Health Administration.

Chapter 17: Marijuana Detection Tests. My gratitude to Dr. Richard Hawks, NIDA's specialist in marijuana detection tests; Dr. Robert E. Willette, director of Duo Research; Dr. Joseph Balkon, Professor of Pharmacology and Toxicology, St. John's University, Jamaica, New York; and Major R. Dennis Smith, deputy for identification, Department of Defense, for reviewing the technical aspects of this chapter. My gratitude also to the following for reading their specific sections of the chapter: Larry Horton Roche, Diagnostics; Joel Asch, SYVA; Dr. James Soares, Immunalysis Corporation, Glendale, California; Nancy Winstra, Chief Counsel, Michael Reese Hospital; Dan MacDougald, Jr., director, Albany (Georgia), Advisory Council for Probation; Dr. Herbert Kleber, professor of psychiatry, Yale Medical School, and Dr. Donald Ian MacDonald.

Chapter 18: Schools: Successful Programs. Sections of this chapter were read for accuracy by Richard Roberts, former assistant prosecutor of Essex County (New Jersey) Bureau of Narcotics; Gerri Silverman, Millburn/Short Hills PTA Drug Awareness chairperson; Bill Rudolph, principal, Northside High, Atlanta, Georgia; Billy Coletti, originator, STAMP; and Fred Burford, president, Ontario (Canada) Council on Drug Abuse and chairman, Headmasters Council's Marijuana Committee of Ontario.

Chapter 19: The Armed Forces. My gratitude to Dr. John Johns, who read this chapter in its entirety. I am also grateful to the following, who read specific sections of the chapter: Maj. R. Dennis Smith, DOD's urine testing specialist; Col. Patrick O'Meara, chief of the army's Drug and Alcohol Abuse Policy Office; Lt. Col. Jack Killeen, chief, Drug and Alcohol Abuse Center, U.S. Air Control; Rear Adm. Paul J. Mulloy, director of the navy's Human Resources Management Division; Lt. Comdr. Larry Ledford, navy Substance Abuse Office; Lt. Col. Marguerite Campbell, chief of the marines' Drug and Alcohol Section; and Dr. Harold Voth, rear admiral, Medical Corps, U.S. Naval Reserve.

Chapter 20: The Workplace: Successful Programs. Ed Johnson; David R. Dearborn; Ira Lipman; C. Gregory Thomas, general manager, Wood Products manufacturing plant; Peter Bensinger, director, Bensinger/DuPont; Dr. Robert Wiencek; Daniel Lanier, Jr.; and Perry Izenson, director, Pot Smokers Anonymous, New York City.

Chapter 21: The Texans' War on Drugs. My gratitude to Jo White, Texans' War on Drugs administrative assistant, who read this chapter in its entirety. Also to those who read sections of the chapter: Tom Marquez, director, TWOD Education Subcommittee; Robinson Risner, former executive director, TWOD; Amy Wilson, executive director Texas Medical Association auxiliary; John F. Stewart, manager, Lions Club International, activities and program development division, and Beverly Baron, region B coordinator of TWOD.

Chapter 22: The Parent Movement for Drug-Free Youth. My appreciation to Joyce Nalepka, president, National Federation of Parents for Drug-Free Youth for reading the entire chapter; also to all the parent group leaders who read their sections for accuracy: Marsha Manatt, Thomas Gleaton, Bill and Pat Barton, Sue Rusche, Pat Burch, Susan Silverman, Otto Moulton, Carla Lowe, Carol Stein, Vonneva Pettigrew, Judy Reidinger and Jo Ann Lundgren.

Index

AAA (*see* American Automobile Association)
ABC News, 71
Abnormalities, birth, 156, 159, 161, 170
  (*See also* Generational Carryover)
Absenteeism in industry, 393, 396
Abuscreen (*see* Roche)
Accidents on the job, 41–42, 44, 396–397
ACDE (*see* American Council for Drug Education)
Acetylcholine, 182–183, 234
ACLU (*see* American Civil Liberties Union)
ACM (*see* American Council on Marijuana)
ACS (*see* American Cancer Society)
ACT (*see* Alliance for Cannabis Therapeutics)
ACTION, 325–326, 450, 451
ADAMHA (*see* Alcohol, Drug Abuse, and Mental Health Administration)
Adams, Tom, 419–421
ADAPCPs (*see* Alcohol and Drug Abuse Prevention and Control Program)
Addabbo, Joseph, 50
Addiction, psychological, 228–229, 231, 242, 247, 395
Addiction Research Foundation (ARF—Ontario), 156, 194
"Adolescent Marijuana Abusers and Their Families" (Hendin, Pollinger, Ulman, and Carr), 243–245
Agents, undercover, 298
  in ports (Navy), 379
  in schools, 353–354, 425
  in workplace, 40, 388–389, 392
  (*See also* FBI)
Air encephalography, 184–185
Air Force (*see* Armed forces)
Airflow resistance, 115–116, 123, 263
Air-traffic controllers, 45
Albany, Georgia, and urine tests, 343–347
Alcohol, 19, 20, 24, 27, 28, 30, 32, 35, 36, 39, 40, 42, 59, 64, 74, 95, 97, 209–210, 219, 221, 231, 235, 236, 240, 330–331, 346, 374, 395, 413
  alcoholism among physicians, 229

plus cannabis, 59, 69–70, 76, 145–147, 276
  and driving, 268, 276–284, 285–289, 293
  and driving, 265–266, 267, 269, 270, 271–275, 277, 281, 287, 292
  fetal alcohol syndrome, 144–146, 170
  national alcohol-awareness program, 75–76
Alcohol, Drug Abuse, and Mental Health Administration (ADAMHA), 36, 44, 347, 386, 440, 453, 454
Alcohol and Drug Abuse Prevention and Control Program (ADAPCP—Army), 373–374
Alcott, Hugh, 268
Alienation, 220, 232, 395
Allen, Woody, 85
Alliance for Cannabis Therapeutics (ACT), 258, 262
Alzheimer's disease, 222–223
AMA (*see* American Medical Association)
AMA Journal (*see* *Journal of the American Medical Association*)
American Automobile Association (AAA), 291
  Foundation for Traffic Safety, 288
American Cancer Society (ACS) cancer-prevention study, 123–124
American Civil Liberties Union (ACLU), 438
American Council for Drug Education (ACDE), 31, 325, 450
American Council on Marijuana (ACM), 443, 450
American Health Foundation, 105
American Journal of Obstetrics and Gynecology, 204
American Journal of Psychiatry, 213
American Medical Association (AMA):
  Council on Scientific Affairs, on THC toxicity, 249–250
  on effects of marijuana, 247
  (*See also* *Journal of the American Medical Association*)
American Society of Contemporary Ophthalmology, 253
American workmanship, decline of, 42–43
Amino acids, 194

INDEX

INDEX

Psychological symptoms and effects (*cont.*):
  scope of the problem, 213–216
  self-esteem, loss of, 220, 224, 228, 242–243, 395
  senility symptoms, 176, 177, 178, 185, 222–225
  siblings as controls, 243–245
  social and family dysfunction, 229
  suggestibility, 238
  suicidal ideation and suicide, 218, 220, 228, 232, 239–243
  time perception, 223, 247
    (*See also* Driving)
  treatment, non-compliance with, 234–235
Psychology Today, 254–255
Psychotic thinking, 229–230, 232
Psychotropic Convention Treaty of 1971, 258–259
PTA:
  California, 436–438
  District of Columbia, 444
  Florida, 425
  Georgia, 427
  Maryland, 432
  New Jersey, 356, 358
  Texas, 402, 405–406, 409
  Virginia, 444
PTA Drug Awareness, 107
Puberty and development, 131–132, 135
Public concern with drug abuse, 8–10, 20, 71
  (*See also* Drug Abuse Council; Parent movement)
Public Health Service (PHS):
  and eradication of cannabis, 319
  and health consequences of marijuana, 7–8
Public Law 97–86, 308–309
Public officials, corruption of, 303
Public service announcements (PSAs), 324–325
"Puff, the Dangerous Driver," 274–275
Pulmonary Function Laboratory, UCLA Hospital, 114–116
Pulmonary tree, 109, 114
Pursch, Joseph, 35, 42
PYADAA (*see* Parents and Youth Against Drug and Alcohol Abuse)
Pyramid Project (NIDA), 419, 421, 440

Radioimmunoassay (RIA), 285, 335–336, 337, 370
Ranch, Margery, 449
Randall, Robert, 254, 258, 262–263
Rastafarian cultists, 123
Reader's Digest, 9, 88, 360, 433, 454
Reader's Digest Foundation, 443
Reagan, Nancy, 326, 328, 329, 331–332, 453
Reagan, Ronald; Reagan administration, 3–4, 266, 328, 347
  and block grants for prevention, 331
  policy document, 299–300
  (*See also* Federal strategy)
Reeve, Victor, 279–284, 285–287
Regional task forces, 302–303
Reid, Jim, 79–80
Reidinger, Dick, 442, 443
Reidinger, Frank, 441–443
Reidinger, Judy, 441–446
Reidinger, Rickie, 443
Reidinger, Shaunti, 445

Remedial measures:
  overview, 297–298
  (*See also* Armed forces; Detection; Federal strategy; Parent movement; Schools; Texans' War on Drugs; Workplace)
Remove Intoxicated Drivers (RID), 266
Renal tubular necrosis, 137
Report on Marijuana of the Indian Hemp Commission, 1893–1894, 122
Reproductive Research Laboratory, Baylor College of Medicine, 148
Reproductive system, female, 25–26, 97, 102, 103, 130–156, 170, 180
  birth impairments and defects, 135–156, 165–166, 170
  birth loss, 136–138, 148–149, 151–154
  and the brain, 130–131
  gonadotropins, 131–132, 134
  infertility and pregnancy, 133–140, 154–155
  labor difficulties, 243–244
  maternal illnesses, 146–147
  menstrual cycles, defective, 131, 133–135, 136, 194, 195
  and mother's milk, 132–133
  ovaries, accumulation in, 150–155, 357
  placenta, 137, 138, 139, 143, 144, 147–148, 156
  prolactin, 132, 194
  puberty and development, 131–132, 135
  resorption of embryo, 136, 153
  and testosterone, 131, 357
Reproductive system, male, 97, 102, 103, 157–170, 180
  and birth defects, 165–166
  and the brain, 130–131
  chromosomal abnormalities, 163–165, 194, 195, 196, 202–211, 212
  erection and orgasm, 157–158
  gonadotropins, 159, 160
  infertility, 163
  long-term users, 166–170
  penis, development of, 160
  potency and interest, lack of, 157–158, 162–163, 165, 166
  sexual organs, abnormalities of, 160, 162
  sperm count, motility, and changes, 158–162, 163, 166–170, 194–195, 246
  sperm production, 150
  testosterone, 131, 160–162, 166, 357
RER (*see* Rough endoplasmic reticulum)
Research (*see* Studies)
Research Designs, Inc., 340
Research Institute of Pharmaceutical Scientists (RIPS), 99–100, 101–103
Research Triangle Institute, 36, 44, 101, 367
Resorption, fetal, 136, 153
Response Analysis Corporation (Princeton, N.J.), 17
Resuscitation of neonates, 143, 144
Reversion, risk of, 231
RIA (*see* Radioimmunoassay)
Ribosomes, 182, 208
Richmond, Julius B., 108
Ricks, Bob A., 312
RID (*see* Remove Intoxicated Drivers)

INDEX

INDEX